OXFORD STUDIES IN AFRICAN AFFAIRS

*General Editors*

JOHN D. HARGREAVES *and* GEORGE SHEPPERSON

# PAN-AFRICANISM
# AND NATIONALISM
# IN WEST AFRICA
# 1900–1945

# PAN-AFRICANISM AND NATIONALISM IN WEST AFRICA

## 1900—1945

### A STUDY IN IDEOLOGY AND SOCIAL CLASSES

BY

J. AYODELE LANGLEY

OXFORD
AT THE CLARENDON PRESS
1973

*Oxford University Press, Ely House, London W.1*

GLASGOW NEW YORK TORONTO MELBOURNE WELLINGTON
CAPE TOWN IBADAN NAIROBI DAR ES SALAAM LUSAKA ADDIS ABABA
DELHI BOMBAY CALCUTTA MADRAS KARACHI LAHORE DACCA
KUALA LUMPUR SINGAPORE HONG KONG TOKYO

75 - 155448

*Printed in Great Britain by*
*Richard Clay (The Chaucer Press), Ltd.,*
*Bungay, Suffolk*

TO MY PARENTS

# ACKNOWLEDGEMENTS

I SHOULD like to thank the many people, including friends and fellow-researchers, who have helped in various ways in the writing of this book. In particular, I wish to express my gratitude to the Scholarships Advisory Committee and the Ministry of Education (Gambia) for generously providing me with a travel grant without which it would have been impossible to reach various archives and libraries in West Africa. I also wish to express my gratitude to the Revd. J. P. Ross, Senior Administrative Officer of the Faculty of Social Sciences, University of Edinburgh, and to the Faculty for the generous assistance in the preparation of this book. I am also grateful to Professor H. J. Hanham, now at Harvard, for his assistance and advice throughout my research, particularly at critical moments when it seemed impossible to have access to certain types of material or to travel grants. Professor G. A. Shepperson's counsel and deep knowledge of the history of Pan-Africanism has been invaluable, and his approach to the subject is evident in parts of this book. My special thanks are due to my teacher and colleague Christopher H. Fyfe, Reader in African History, for some forthright criticisms and very useful leads—and for our periodic disagreements. Christopher Fyfe gave generously of his time, and his knowledge of West African history prevented many a stumble and opened up many lines of inquiry. I should also like to thank a former teacher, Dr. Florence K. Mahoney (Gambia), for directing my attention to correspondence in the Gambia Co-operative Department relating to E. F. Small; to Professor John Erickson of the Department of Politics (Edinburgh); to Mrs. Amy Jacques Garvey (Kingston, Jamaica); to Mr. F. U. Allen, head of the Gambia Records Office for his courtesy and kindness; to my friends Messrs. T. Ayodele George, M. K. B. Faal, and W. Sidor Jnr.; to 'Pa' J. W. Kuye (an old Pan-Africanist in the tradition of Blyden and Casely Hayford) and Shonu O'Brien Coker for their help with newspapers and documents; and to my father, who on various occasions assisted me with inquiries and with copies of newspapers and documents of historical interest. My thanks also to T. Ras Makonnen for stimulating conversations in Nairobi and for reminiscences which did much to capture the personalities and the ideological flavour of Pan-Africanism in the 1930s and 1940s. I am also grateful to the anonymous reader to whom the original manuscript was sent by the publishers. Without his advice and criticism there would have been far more errors and infelicities in this book. I should like to acknowledge permission from the editors of *Africa*, *Journal of Modern African Studies*, and *Phylon* to reproduce material already published in their journals.

I am also indebted to the following scholars whose writings have directly or indirectly influenced my thinking on the subject of nationalism and pan-movements: Professors George Shepperson, E. Essien-Udom, and Ali A. Mazrui; Professor Masao Maruyama's *Thought And Behaviour in Modern Japanese Politics*; and Professor John Erickson's *Pan-Slavism*. Needless to say, the above-mentioned scholars are in no way responsible for my interpretations. Finally, my warm thanks are due to Miss Campbell of the Celtic Department and to Miss Grace Hunter of the Centre of African Studies who have typed and retyped draft after draft of what I am finally offering to the reading public. As I have indicated in the Introduction, although one may, in the absence of concrete evidence, assemble any number of incidents and ideas and call it Pan-Africanism (as some have tended to do), this method of proceeding tends to obscure the dynamics and complexity of the movement. Pan-Africanism is not a movement that should be boxed and frozen into epochs and categories. I therefore make no apology for the different way in which I have treated the subject, as there are no ways of dealing with history *intrinsically* superior to others.[1]

[1] Elton, G. R., *The Practice of History* (Fontana Books, London, 1969), p. 28.

# ERRATA

Page 248, last line, footnote 23, *delete* p. 1920.
Page 305, line 16, *for* was released in late 1927—*read*—was released later in 1927.

# CONTENTS

# INTRODUCTION

## 1

THIS book does not pretend to be an exhaustive history of the Pan-African movement. Many indeed are the books and articles on Pan-Africanism, most of them repetitions of ancient orthodoxies. It is merely a contribution to the growing literature on the subject, and an attempt to explore the origins, evolution, ideas, and orientations of this complex movement in its West African aspects and the historical and social conditions which both united it with, and distinguished it from, the New-World Pan-Africanism of Marcus Garvey and W. E. B. Du Bois. It is an attempt to reinterpret a complex and many-sided phenomenon whose history has been misunderstood largely because of inadequate documentation and undue dependence on the accounts of contemporary participants. West Africa has been chosen as the focus of this study not from any narrow-minded pre-occupation but for the following reasons: first, within the triangle of transatlantic influences, West Africa was at once the recipient, critic, and disseminator of Pan-Negro ideas; secondly, West Africa was, with the exception of South Africa, the only region in colonial Africa where a nationalist intelligentsia of lawyers, merchants, journalists, doctors, and clergymen successfully sought to share political power with the colonial ruler, and took upon itself the duty of disseminating political ideas and values; thirdly, it was in this area, perhaps more than any other part of Africa, that Pan-Negro ideas and organizations were first started by an intelligentsia which was in touch with the Pan-Africanism of New-World Afro-Americans, and indeed accepted the major premises of the world-wide move-ment, but differed in its interpretation of its political goals; finally, focus on West Africa also makes it possible to deal with a neglected or relatively unknown feature in the history of Pan-Africanism—the contribution of French-speaking Africans to *political* Pan-Africanism during the inter-war period. The vast amount of literature on the history of Pan-Africanism has either merely relied on the accounts of Padmore and Du Bois (which do not deal with this aspect in depth) or concentrated on the evolution of the literary doctrine of *Négritude* developed by French West Indians and West Africans, notably by Aimé Césaire and President Léopold Sedar Senghor.

We have already remarked that this work is mainly a work of re-interpretation on the basis of new material on the subject; accordingly, most of the interpretations advanced will be found to differ somewhat from the standard interpretations. In some cases, however, the area of disagreement is very small and the author has made use of Padmore's major work *Pan-Africanism or Communism?* which, in spite of a few prejudices and omissions, is still indispensable in any study of Pan-Africanism. Recent scholarly contributions to the history of Pan-Africanism are Imanuel Geiss's *Panafrikanismus— Zur Geschichte der Dekolonisation*[1] and James Spiegler's 'Aspects of Nationalist Thought among French-speaking West Africans 1921–1939'.[2] In the majority of cases in this study, however, entirely new material from a wide range of sources has been used. Chapter I, which is also a background chapter, attempts briefly to trace the origins of Pan-Negro sentiments in the New World from the Abolition era to the end of the nineteenth century, and the impact and reception of these ideas in West Africa during the same period. It is also an appraisal of what the author would prefer to call the Sheppersonian thesis of Afro-American influences on African political thought; the views of West African nationalist writers and publicists are considered in this context as a method of assessing the significance and extent of these influences. Chapters II to VI deal in great detail with the Pan-African movements of the 1920s and their West African counterpart, the National Congress of British West Africa. The main purpose of these chapters is to assess the impact of the Pan-African movements of this period on West African nationalism and to illustrate how historical and economic factors influenced the attitude of the intelligentsia towards New-World Pan-Africanism. It is also a study in ideology and the socio-economic and cultural factors which condition it—in this case, the unique complex of factors that accounted for the intelligentsia's attitude to Garveyism. Chapter VII examines an entirely new aspect of the movement on the French-speaking side: it seeks to show that there was *rapport* between the

---

[1] Frankfurt A/M, 1968.
[2] Oxford University D. Phil. thesis, 1967.

French Africans and Garvey's Universal Negro Improvement Association and African Communities League; that the leadership was Left-oriented but non-aligned in that it persistently maintained a Pan-Negro policy, and that its Pan-Negroism was closer to Garveyism but differed from it in its view of the political relations of French Negroes with the colonial power—France. Although most of the action described in chapter VII took place in Paris instead of Dakar or Porto Novo or Bamako, there are good reasons for including it in this book. First, by definition, the type of agitational and ideological politics described in chapter VII could not possibly have been allowed in the French colonies. It is only natural that the focus of activity, whether literary or political, should have been Paris, 'the metropolitan axis of reference'. Secondly, omission of the politics and ideas of Francophone West Africans would considerably distort and limit this study, as well as perpetuate the old academic prejudice against treating Anglophone and Francophone colonial experience within the same context. I am aware that Dr. James Spiegler has dealt with the subject examined in chapter VII in a much wider context, but as neither of us was aware of each other's researches, and since we have treated a similar subject from different contexts, I have decided to retain chapter VII in its original form.[3] The resulting picture is one of a complex movement (not the succession of Du Boisian congresses generally listed by historians) acquiring varying connotations in different parts of the African Diaspora[4] but retaining a basic unity on the 'question of the color-line', political autonomy for Negro peoples, and racial self-assertion. There was not one single Pan-African movement but several, at least up to the close of the 1920s.

If, after 1918, economic and educational development in West Africa was partially retarded, the effects of the Great War on the nature of anti-colonial politics between the two world wars was the reverse. In the inter-war period economic and political development proceeded at an uneven pace; in the late 1920s and in the 1930s there was stagnation due to the world economic crisis, and it was during this period that West African nationalism became more explicit in its criticisms, especially against unemployment and economic

[3] A shorter version appeared as 'Pan-Africanism in Paris, 1924–1936' in *Journal of Modern African Studies*, vii, no. 1 (1969), 69–94.
[4] A similar observation was made by John Erickson in *Pan-Slavism* (Historical Association pamphlet, no. 55, 1964), p. 3.

4    INTRODUCTION

exploitation. Nationalism and Pan-Negro thinking in West Africa did not begin in or just after 1914 as some writers have wrongly supposed,[5] but the period 1918–39 is important not only because it concerns a variety of anti-colonial politics which has received little attention from scholars,[6] but because it is a most vital period in the history of the growth of nationalism in West Africa, in the sense that it illustrates several facets of present-day African nationalism: for example, African attitudes to European civilization and racism, problems of Pan-African unity, and African attitudes to international organizations, in this case the League of Nations. This period also deserves study because it illustrates West African attitudes to Pan-Negro movements like the Pan-African movement of W. E. B. Du Bois and Marcus Garvey's U.N.I.A. Finally, the inter-war period also forms an important prelude to the more articulate and decisive phase of both the nationalist and the Pan-African movements after 1945. As one writer correctly argued in 1951, 'Those thirty years [i.e. the period roughly from 1918 to 1945] formed the present day leaders of nationalism and their political memories, and in this work of political construction the intelligentsia of the colonies were vitally concerned.'[7]

It is fashionable nowadays to speak as if Pan-Africanism is an entirely new and exotic phenomenon that began in 1900, or to speak as if the Du Boisian congresses constituted its sum total. But as a leading authority on the subject has rightly cautioned, it is misleading to concentrate exclusively on the role of Du Bois and his congresses, important as these were in the development of the Pan-African idea: 'His role, of course, in the emergence of Pan-Africanism was profound: but the scholarly study of the phenomenon, in all its multifarious complexities, will suffer if too much emphasis is placed on his role and his writings. We still need to know more about the pre-1919

[5] W. D. Edmonds, for example, talks about 'the relative novelty of this phenomenon in West Africa', and 'the relative underdevelopment of the nationalist movement up to 1939', and of British West Africa as 'perhaps the last part of the Colonial Empire to awake to politico-nationalist consciousness', 'The Newspaper Press in British West Africa, 1918–1939' (M.A. thesis, University of Bristol, 1951–2), p. 74. F. Znaniecki in a recent study, *Modern Nationalities* (Urbana, Ill., 1952), also errs when he states that West African nationalism began in the 1950s. But see the remarks by E. A. Ayandele in 'An Assessment of James Johnson and His Place in Nigerian History, 1874–1917', part I, *Journal of the Historical Society of Nigeria*, ii, no. 4 (1964), 488–9.
[6] See Ballard, John, 'The Porto Novo Incidents of 1923: Politics in the Colonial Era', *Odu*, ii, no. 1 (1965), 52.　　　[7] Edmonds, op. cit., p. 164.

forces and personalities.'[8] It is hoped that this study will go some way in illustrating this complexity both in its transatlantic and in its West African aspects. Hitherto the development of Pan-Africanism has been seen largely as the history of congresses led by New-World Negroes: it is the author's view, however, that this interpretation is inadequate and needs radical revision. In order to do this the subject has been examined both from a general and from a particular or individual point of view. Chronology has been adhered to as strictly as possible but to make it a rigid practice would not only distort historical judgement but would hamper the formulation of meaningful generalizations about the subject under review. Historical writing on the subject of Pan-Africanism is a good example of this rigid periodization of history; not only is the historian's difficulty increased by the tyranny of dates and labels (a tyranny usually created by the accounts given by the participants themselves), he is also tempted to accept uncritically the version of the participants, versions which are usually partisan in nature and tend to create a kind of mythology about these movements. This study, therefore, is not strictly confined to the period 1900–45, nor is it confined solely to West Africa; the period before 1900 is briefly reviewed as well as the immediate post-1945 period in order to put the West African aspects of the Pan-African movements in historical perspective.

No single approach to the study of the development of Pan-Africanism can be expected to be faultless; but in case objections are raised on the grounds of a departure from orthodoxy, a little advice from a distinguished historian and philosopher of history might put us on our guard against accepting orthodoxy for the sake of orthodoxy. According to Croce

'Historical Epochs' bounded chronologically and countersigned with a concept or a general representation, with the figure of some personage or other symbol, are divisions of use to the memory, legitimate to this end and even indispensable. . . . When, however, their origin and purpose is forgotten, when they stiffen into concepts or philosophical categories, they no longer serve to make the memory of history easier, but rather to compress it, deform and mutilate it, and so, indeed, to make its truth forgotten . . . from forgetfulness of the practical origin and empirical use of divisions by chronological periods arise inextricable controversies about the character of this epoch or that. . . . A vain attempt is made to arrive at elaborate definitions which will embrace all the facts contained in these

[8] Shepperson, G. A., 'The African Abroad or the African Diaspora'; paper read at the International African History Conference, Tanzania, 1965, p. 10.

chronological partitions, whereas the real problem, in these cases, is to define the universal forms and modes of the spirit which the titles indicate. These cannot be confined within chronological limits, but by their nature are extra-temporal. The definitions obtained should then be used in order to understand certain aspects of the facts gathered into the framework of the relative chronological epoch, which aspects are the objects upon which the real interest of the historian is directed. . . . We have wished only to put historians on their guard against the confusion of chronological periods with real periods, and against false judgments and false problems, as tiresome as they are insoluble, derived from this confusion. . . .[9]

In our study of the evolution of the Pan-African idea in the history of West African nationalist politics, the approach is in general of an ordering and schematizing nature. Mannheim has suggested three possible approaches to the study of ideologies: (1) they may be presented in a manner which detaches them from 'the historical moments and the concrete social situations to which they refer', in which case we aim at categorizing the ideologies principally as an attempt to discover some purely theoretical principle for differentiating between them. This approach Mannheim calls 'surface typology' since it attempts 'to present the manifoldness of life upon an artificially uniform level'.[10] Another variant of this approach is that of the 'philosophical systematizer', but this tends to lay undue stress on theoretical principles which may be useful but not decisive.[11] (2) We could also adopt a strictly historical approach. This method, however, while putting theories in the immediate historical context in which they developed, goes to the other extreme of 'clinging too closely to the historical'. The historian may accordingly be interested in the unique complex of causes that account for these political ideas, and to arrive at these he takes into account all the antecedents in the history of ideas and connects the ideas with the unique personalities of creative individuals. He may, however, become so involved in the historical uniqueness of the events he is examining that he may fail to give any general conclusions about the historical and social pro-

[9] Croce, Benedetto, *History As The Story of Liberty* (London, 1941), pp. 301–5. See also Elton, op. cit., pp. 28–30.

[10] Mannheim, Karl, *Ideology And Utopia* (tr. Louis Wirth and Edward Shils, London, 1936), p. 155.

[11] ibid., p. 156; this approach is referred to by Pocock as the 'tradition of intellectualizing', Pocock, J. G. A., 'The History of Political Thought: A Methodological Enquiry' in *Philosophy, Politics and Society*, ed. Peter Laslett and W. G. Runciman, 2nd Ser. (Oxford, 1962), pp. 185 ff.

cess. If, then, the first approach errs on the side of being too abstract, the strictly historical approach errs on the side of being too specifically concrete—too 'bound up with the immediacies of history'. (3) Between these two extremes lies a third approach which seeks to avoid abstract schematization on the one hand and historical immediacy on the other. According to Mannheim, it is in this group that 'every clear-sighted political person lives and thinks, even though he may not always be aware of it'. This intermediate approach seeks to understand ideologies and their mutations in close relation to the 'structural situations' and groups out of which they arose and whose opinions and interests they express. In this case, it is 'the inner connections between thought and social existence' which must be reconstructed around a narrative theme on which to organize the piece of history under study. In general, this is the approach that has been attempted in this study of the thought and politics of the Pan-African movement in West Africa. It is hoped that this method will throw some light on the evolution and reception of the Pan-African idea in Africa, and provide a useful background to our understanding of the unity *and* diversity of the politics of black liberation today.

It must be emphasized at the outset, however, that Pan-Africanism is neither an exotic movement nor an entirely new phenomenon fundamentally different from other pan-movements. Like all pan-movements it has no single intellectual pedigree and is difficult to define comprehensively for the simple reason that it has assumed different meanings and orientations at various stages in its evolution. This is not to say that Pan-Slavism and Pan-Africanism, for example, are identical, but the parallels are instructive. Both movements, like other pan-movements, are characterized by their eclecticism and by a sense of inferiority or relative deprivation, both emphasize the importance of solidarity, whether racial, religious, or linguistic: the Pan-African preoccupation with race and geography parallels the Pan-Slav preoccupation with religion and the unity of Slavonic peoples, and the effect of the counter-reformation on the development of nationalities in Europe could also be compared to the impact of the European colonization of Africa on the growth of African political and racial consciousness. Like the Pan-Slav movements, Pan-African politics during the colonial era has been directly concerned with constitutional issues. Nearly all pan-movements, from Pan-Turanism to the Japanese concept of an East Asia Co-Prosperity Sphere of the 1940s, have been concerned with religious, racial, territorial, or economic unification, and their programmes have often implied a challenge to a powerfully entrenched *status quo*. That section of mankind generally referred to as the Third World is no exception. Indeed Yambo Ouloguem has given it a politico-racial designation, 'la négraille'.[12]

To compensate for their military and political impotence and to reaffirm their cultural values, these movements tend to ascribe a spiritual world-role to themselves. From E. W. Blyden's 'African Personality' to Dostoyevsky's idealization of Slavic man, the 'Russian soul', and the 'Russian idea', the phenomenon is the same. Where Blyden writes of Africa as the 'spiritual conservatory of the world', Dostoyevsky writes of the Russian 'belief in our individuality, in the sacredness of our destiny' and in Russia's 'exclusive orthodox mission to mankind'.[13] This attitude, which the Polish historian Handelsmann called 'moral imperialism', has in the case of most pan-movements been usually accompanied by a primitivistic ideal-ization of the past which, paradoxically, tends to act as a programme of reform—of reform through reversion;[14] there is a recurrence of this idea in S. R. B. Attoh-Ahuma's philosophy of 'intelligent retrogression' in his *The Gold Coast Nation and National Con-sciousness* (1911), in the works of Blyden, and in the literature of *Négritude*. In all these cases, these utopias were designed to create a sense of worth, dignity, and unity among people whose leaders have decided to reassert and rediscover themselves after the dehumanizing experience of alien rule.[15]

---

[12] Ouloguem, Yambo, *Le Devoir de violence* (Paris, 1968).

[13] See Dostoyevsky, F. M., *Letters and Reminiscences* (letters to A. N. Maikov), tr. S. S. Koteliansky and J. Middleton-Murry (London, 1923), p. 95; Dostoyevsky, F. M., *The Diary of a Writer*, 2 vols., tr. Boris Brasol (London, 1949), ii. 202–5, 293–7, 358–60; in particular see 'The Utopian Conception of History' at pp. 360–5, 579–82, 626–37, 897–902. Also Utechin, S. V., *Russian Political Thought* (London, 1963), chapter V.

[14] See Whitney, Lois, *Primitivism and the Idea of Progress* (Baltimore, Md., 1934).

[15] This latter aspect of the colonial situation, the psychodynamic, has been dealt with by a number of commentators, poets, and revolutionaries from René Maunier and Manoni to Aimé Césaire and Léon Damas, but notably by Frantz Fanon.

2

WHEREVER contact between Europeans and non-Europeans has occurred, it has usually been conceptualized as a 'contact of races' or of social types, between 'civilized' and 'uncivilized' groups,[16] the racial factor in this relationship varying with the degree of contact. From the age of Vasco da Gama to the scramble for Africa, this contact has involved a constant struggle for economic and political mastery throughout the world. European technology and military power from the fifteenth century onwards, therefore, meant the political and economic supremacy of Europe over a wider world of non-Europeans.

In the nineteenth century, largely as a result of economic and technological factors, and a corresponding change in attitudes to non-European peoples,[17] greater and permanent contact was established with a wider world, culminating in a crisis of race relations; so that by the turn of the century it was no longer a Colonial Question or a question of power imperialism but, as Du Bois rightly discerned it, 'the problem of the color-line—the relation of the darker to the lighter races of men in Asia and Africa, in America, and the islands of the sea'. Hence it came about that, as a result of this crisis, certain European writers and propagandists began to interpret the self-assertion or reaction of colonized and minority groups in terms of 'the Yellow Peril', 'the Black Peril', or, as writers like Madison Grant and Lothrop Stoddard would have it, the 'rising tide of color against white world supremacy'. By the turn of the century, then, pan-coloured or race thinking had become the ideology of the colonized peoples; or more precisely, the utopian programmes of non-European pan-movements had become the symbols of resistance to or protest against the injustices of European rule and the racist ideology that justified it.

It might be useful at this point to recall Karl Mannheim's functional differentiation between ideologies and utopias as they relate to social movements. Ideologies are defined by Mannheim as 'the situationally transcendent ideas which never succeed *de facto* in the realisation of their projected contents'. Utopias, too, transcend the

[16] Maunier, René, *The Sociology of Colonies: An Introduction to the Study of Race Contact*, ed. and tr. E. O. Lörimer (London, 1949), i, pp. xi–xii.
[17] See Curtin, P., *The Image of Africa: British Ideas and Action, 1780–1850* (London, 1965).

social situation, but are not ideologies: they are 'those orientations
transcending reality . . . which, when they pass over into conduct,
tend to shatter, either partially or wholly, the order of things prevailing at the time'.[18] Mannheim gives as examples of the utopian
mentality chiliastic utopias which are universalistic in outlook and
attribute a millennial and messianic world-role to a particular social
group or class, the utopia of liberal humanitarianism with its
emphasis on the 'idea' as a regulative device in the mundane affairs
of a projected future,[19] the Conservative counter-utopianism, and
the Socialist–Communist Utopia. Some of these ideologies tend not
only to unite oppressed groups and minority groups across national
boundaries but also, because of the political ineffectiveness of the
oppressed, to internationalize local disabilities.[20] Hence a political
system legitimized by race, power, and the values and interests of
the dominant group is opposed by a counter-system or ideology—
the utopian nationalism of the oppressed, a phenomenon which is
usually seen as anti-white by the dominant group.[21] This ideology of
the oppressed takes the form of race pride; in their defensive posture,
race becomes the measure of all things. Race pride finds expression
in several forms: racial achievements are magnified to compensate
for the memory of collective humiliation, an 'ideology of saviours'
(that is, glorification of the individually great of the race) is developed,
and a new interest is taken in the history and culture of the racial
group:

The psychological states of depression, sense of inferiority and humility
give way to those of a feeling of personal worth and pride. . . . The race

[18] Mannheim, op. cit., pp. 173–6.
[19] ibid., pp. 199–206.
[20] See Myrdal, Gunnar, *An American Dilemma* (New York, 1964), ii. 810–12.
The history of Negro nationalism in America, from the Abolition era to the
Garvey movement and the current Black Power movement, gives ample proof of
this tendency. Not only has the theme of Negro identification with Africa appeared in recent Black Power literature, Stokely Carmichael has even drawn
parallels between colonialism in Africa and what he calls the 'internal imperialism'
and 'institutional racism' of America; for details, see Carmichael, Stokely, and
Hamilton, Charles V., *Black Power: The Politics of Liberation in America* (New
York, 1967), pp. vii–32, 38–9, 45. A useful contribution here is Edmondson,
Locksley, 'The Internationalization of Black Power: Historical and Contemporary Perspectives', *Mawazo*, i (Dec. 1968), 16–30, and 'The Challenge of Race:
From Entrenched White Power to Rising Black Power', *International Journal*
(Canada), xxiv, no. 4 (Autumn 1969), 693–716.
[21] Philipps, J. E. T., 'Pan-Africa and Anti-White', *Journal of the Royal African
Society*, xxi (1921–2), 129–35; Park, R. E., *Race and Culture* (Glencoe, Ill., 1950),
pp. 81–116.

conscious of the low status group are aware of past and present exploitation. They recall with bitterness the limitation of their freedom and their
debasement. Grievances are formulated, becoming a part of their ideology.
. . . The race conscious easily believe in a portentous destiny for their
race. . . . For the race conscious among the races of low status to believe
in a better future is essential. Race consciousness otherwise would atrophy
and die. Hope is essential to its vitality. And to be able to believe that
while they suffer and 'envision the stars' they are at the same time per-
forming a mission that satisfies the human need for the feelings of worth
and superiority.[22]

The race-conscious Afro-American, for example, would generally
sympathize with the nationalism of the Africans, with anti-imperialist protests in the Caribbean, and with Asian nationalism. Like
Du Bois, he senses a spiritual unity and is aware of a common
cause of coloured peoples against the white peoples of Western
Europe and the United States.

The race idea is an attempt to integrate a community spiritually
and politically. It is neither true nor false; it is not a body of knowledge organized in systematic form, but a political idea in the
technical sense of the word. It does not purport to describe social
reality as it is but is designated to set up symbols whether in the form
of language units or more elaborate dogmas which serve to portray
the group as a unit. As Voegelin has rightly argued,

A symbolic idea like the race idea is not a theory in the strict sense of the
word. And it is beside the mark to criticize a symbol, or a set of dogmas,
because they are not empirically verifiable. While such criticism is correct,
it is without meaning, because it is not the function of an idea to describe
social reality, but to assist in its constitution . . . the ethical or meta-
physical value of an idea does not depend upon its correctness as a picture
of social reality. A political idea is not an instrument of cognition. But
this does not mean that it has no relation to reality, or that any product
of a fertile imagination can serve as a political symbol. . . . The symbol is
based on an element of reality, but it does not describe reality. It uses the
datum in order to represent by means of that single, comparatively simple
element a diffuse field of reality as a unit.

Voegelin goes on to state that a scientific analysis ought to avoid
heated arguments about the merits of such symbols and to describe

[22] Brown, W. O., 'The Nature of Race Consciousness', in *When Peoples Meet:
A Study in Race and Culture Contacts*, ed. Alain Locke and Bernhard J. Stern (New
York, 1949), pp. 523–5.

realistically their growth and function.[23] They are mistaken, therefore, who dismiss ideology as mere 'froth on the beer of local
politics'—after all, as the connoisseurs say, it is the froth that
determines the quality of the beer.[24] This observation must constantly be borne in mind in the study of the history of Pan-Africanism as a utopian thought-style. A distinction must be made, however,
between Pan-Negro sentiments, which are generally a movement of
ideas and emotions and have not taken organizational or associa-
tional form,[25] and Pan-African sentiments which became institutionalized in international and regional organizations.

Pan-Africanism is at the same time a protest, a refusal, and a
demand. It is a utopia born of centuries of contact with Europe, the
most decisive phase of this contact, as far as racial attitudes were
concerned, being the African slave trade which dispersed large
numbers of African peoples throughout the New World. This
historic episode in the history of race relations might be conceptualized either as the African Diaspora (in the Sheppersonian sense)[26]
or as 'The Pan-African Aggregate' as defined by Bronislaw Malinowski in the cultural anthropological sense.[27] We are concerned here,
however, not with the social anthropological but with the political
aspects of the Pan-African Aggregate and attempts to make it an
international protest and race movement.[28] There was little political
contact between Africans and New-World Negroes at least up to the
end of the nineteenth century, although Afro-American interest in

[23] Voegelin, Eric, 'The Growth of the Race Idea', *Review of Politics*, xi (July
1940), 283–317.
[24] For a convincing dismissal of the 'end of ideology' school, see Patridge,
P. H., 'Politics, Philosophy, Ideology', *Political Studies*, ix (1963), 217–35.
[25] Drake, St. Clair, 'Value Systems, Social Structure and Race Relations in
the British Isles' (University of Chicago Ph. D. thesis, 1954), p. 18; Legum, Colin,
*Pan-Africanism: A Short Political Guide* (New York, 1965), pp. 14–15.
[26] Professor Shepperson has argued the thesis of the African Diaspora and its
significance for the development of Pan-Africanism and African political thought
in several important articles: 'Notes on Negro American Influences on the Emergence of African Nationalism', *Journal of African History*, i, no. 2 (1960), 299–
312; 'Abolitionism and African Political Thought', *Transition*, iii, no. 12 (1964),
22–6; 'The African Diaspora—or The African Abroad', *African Forum*, ii, no. 1
(1966), 76–91; 'Pan-Africanism and "Pan-Africanism": Some Historical Notes',
*Phylon*, xxiii, no. 4 (1962), 346–58; also Shepperson, George, and Price, Thomas,
*Independent African: John Chilembwe and the Origins, Setting and Significance of
the Nyasaland Native Rising of 1915* (Edinburgh, 1958).
[27] See Malinowski, Bronislaw, 'The Pan-African Problem of Culture Contact',
*American Journal of Sociology*, xlviii, no. 6 (1943), 649–66.
[28] Drake, op. cit., p. 19.

Africa found expression in Pan-Negro literature, Christian missions, and colonization schemes throughout the nineteenth century, and even into the twentieth century; but as a political idea New World Pan-Africanism remained an undefined movement lacking in clear-cut aims.[29] Nevertheless, as Maunier has observed, it remained a pro-Negro movement and overflowed continental boundaries.[30] It was only after the historic Manchester Congress that the new-style Pan-Africanists expressed in positive terms the determination of black people to organize and unite against the 'oppressors' and to make radical Pan-Africanism the ideology of the new liberation movements throughout colonial Africa.

The subject of this study, as we have already explained, has been approached not only from the point of view of political history but also from the point of view of socio-economic analysis and the history of political thought. I have endeavoured, as far as the scope of the study permits, to draw attention to minor but interesting or neglected figures in the history of Pan-Africanism.[31] I have also attempted to see the Pan-African movement in the period under review in its widest context, although my main concern is with its West African aspects and the West African participants and ideologues. Wherever space allows, I have allowed the theoreticians, pamphleteers, prophets, and ideologists to speak for themselves, although I have tried to avoid the error of taking their utterances at face value. Yet no account of any movement is complete that does not take account of the ideas, emotions, and even fantasies of its leaders—in short, the *idées forces* in the evolution of the Pan-African idea.

The careful reader will no doubt notice that because of the complex nature of this study I have been unable to carry out fully my intention to combine a discussion of political ideas with the political movements discussed in this book.[32] My forthcoming biography of Kobina Sekyi of Ghana together with an annotated edition of his political

[29] Snyder, Louis L., *Race: A History of Modern Ethnic Theories* (New York, 1939), chapter 18, 'Pan-Africanism: "Africa For the Africans" ', p. 280.

[30] Maunier, op. cit., chapter xxxviii, 'Black Autonomism', pp. 410–11.

[31] See Shepperson, G. A., 'External Factors in the Development of African Nationalism, with Particular Reference to British Central Africa', *Phylon*, xxii, no. 3 (1961), 224–5.

[32] For a stimulating and useful discussion of the methodological problems involved in combining intellectual history with historical explanation, see Skinner, Quentin, 'The Limits of Historical Explanations', *Philosophy*, xli, no. 157 (July 1966), 199–215, especially 214–15.

and legal writings, will, I hope, add to our understanding of the political ideas of West African nationalism, as well as throw more light on some of the issues dealt with in this book. The movements and ideas discussed here can be seen as dramatic responses to over sixty years of European domination. The concerted articulation of political demands and the popularization of a philosophy of unity by the nationalist intelligentsia and the unprecedented preoccupation with self-definition was quite clearly a phenomenon the colonial bureaucrats and ideologues of trusteeship had not foreseen before the outbreak of World War I. It is as if they had failed to understand that the war had not only revolutionized European society itself but had brought to the surface all those emotional, economic, and cultural forces generated by the colonial system. It is therefore not surprising that the immediate reaction of the colonial authorities was to label these essentially reformist movements 'subversive' and then proceed to concede limited reforms while pretending to do so as a matter of grace. The revolution of the twentieth century was finding echoes in colonial Africa giving rise to racial ideologies, reformism, trade unionism, and criticism of the values of European civilization itself.

# PART ONE

. . . Experience shows that the *framing of a future, in some indeterminate time*, may, when it is done in a certain way, be very effective, and have very few inconveniences. This happens when the anticipations of the future take the form of myths, which enclose with them all the strongest inclinations of a people, of a party or of a class, inclinations . . . which give an aspect of complete reality to the hopes of immediate action. . . . It must be admitted that the real developments of the Revolution did not in any way resemble the enchanting pictures which created the enthusiasm of its first adepts; but without those pictures would the Revolution have been successful?

GEORGES SOREL: *Reflections on Violence*

. . . each idea not yet realised curiously resembles a utopia; one would never do anything if one thought that nothing is possible except that which exists already.

SIMONE DE BEAUVOIR: *Les Mandarins*

CHAPTER I

# New-World Origins of Pan-Negro Sentiment

THE nineteenth century not only witnessed a major crisis in race relations: anti-Negro propaganda intensified, and the political, social, and economic subjugation of the Negro increased throughout the world. Racialist thinkers, amateurs, and propagandists in the service of imperialism took refuge in pseudo-science in elaborate attempts to 'prove' the Negro's alleged inferiority. The voices of the humanitarians, abolitionists, and the few white friends of the Negro were virtually drowned by the pretentious outpourings of the 'anthropologists'.[1] Even after emancipation New-World Negroes still suffered from the stigma of inferiority—slavery was legally abolished but the spirit remained the same; and the European colonization of Africa further served to encourage the perpetuation of this myth.[2] In this chapter we shall briefly examine the responses of some of the leaders of the New-World Negroes and their attitudes to Africa; we shall also examine the views of the leaders of African thought on the West African end of the African Diaspora. In short, we shall restate and amplify what I have already described as the Sheppersonian thesis of Negro American influences on African nationalism.

We have already mentioned that the African Diaspora was the direct result of the African slave trade which scattered peoples of Negro descent throughout the New World, particularly in the United States, Brazil, and the West Indies. From about 1500 to 1900, there-

[1] Race theory in the history of European ideas can be traced into the eighteenth century; see Barzun, Jacques, *Race: A Study in Superstition* (rev. ed., New York, 1965), and Curtin, P., *The Image of Africa*; also Detweiler, Frederick G., 'The Rise of Modern Race Antagonisms', *American Journal of Sociology* (1932), pp. 738–47; Hawkins, Frank H., 'Race As A Factor in Political Theory' in Merriam, Charles E., and Barnes, Harry Elmer, *A History of Political Theories, Recent Times* (New York, 1924), pp. 508–48.

[2] Lynch, Hollis R., *Edward Wilmot Blyden 1832–1912. Pan-Negro Patriot* (London, 1967), pp. 1–3.

fore, Pan-Africanism remained merely an 'informal organization of memories' among articulate members of the Black Diaspora. Black Americans came to use the word 'African' to describe their churches and other organizations, and Negroes in Brazil and the West Indies retained in varying degrees of intensity aspects of their African cultural past. This consciousness of aspects of their African past (depending on the degree of acculturation) generally led New-World Negroes either to affirm positively their 'Africanity' or to reject it entirely as a stigma that prevented their assimilation into a predominantly white society.[3]

## 1. *Ideological Origins in America*

FROM the early nineteenth century to the end of World War II three major themes have dominated Afro-American attitudes towards Africa—African colonization schemes, missionary activity, and racial Pan-Africanism.[4] We shall consider these themes in two parts: from the beginning of the nineteenth century to 1862, and from the late nineteenth century to 1914.

Toussaint L'Ouverture's successful revolution in Haiti (1804) perhaps provided the first base for pan-Negro consciousness. The fact that former black slaves had successfully seized power from their European masters and had indicated their desire to govern themselves meant that they could now at least negatively counter the

[3] There has been much academic controversy over the years as to the nature and significance of African cultural survivals in the New World, particularly the U.S.A. The controversy, whose political implications must not be underestimated, was sparked off by Herskovits, Melville, *The Myth of the Negro Past* (Boston, Mass., 1958), which sought to show the extensive persistence of these survivals. Generally, however, it is agreed that, with the exception of Brazil, African cultural survivals in America and the West Indies are relatively insignificant. But the controversy has produced much heat: see Frazier, E. Franklin, *The Negro in the United States* (New York, 1957), pp. 3–21; Freyre, Gilberto, *The Masters and the Slaves*, tr. Samuel Putnam, 2nd. rev. English ed. (London, 1963); Patterson, Orlando, *The Sociology of Slavery* (London, 1967); Maquet, Jacques, ' "Africanity" and "Americanity" ?', *Présence Africaine*, xxxi, no. 59 (1966), 7–15, and the provocative article by Glicksberg, Charles, 'Negro Americans and the African Dream' in *Phylon* (1947), pp. 323–30. Recently, however, the controversy has been revived under the new orthodoxy of 'linguistic Pan-Africanism' or 'black English', which seeks to 'explain' aspects of black American speech and behaviour patterns in terms of African linguistic and cultural patterns, see Dalby, D., 'Americanisms that may once have been Africanisms', *The Times* (London, 19 July 1969), p. 9.

[4] Drake, St. Clair, 'Negro Americans and "the African Interest" ', in *The American Negro Reference Book*, ed. John P. Davis (New Jersey, 1966), p. 667.

charge of Negro inferiority and incapacity for self-rule. Even though Haiti failed as an attempt at Negro self-government, Afro-Americans continued to show interest in, and even emigrate to, the newly established colony of Sierra Leone. In America itself the Afro-Americans suffered various disabilities, especially in parts of the South where the institution of slavery still existed; his struggle for political freedom, therefore, was paralleled by his interest in colonization schemes, although there was a tendency before 1850 to see the efforts of the American Colonization Society (founded in 1817) as a device of slaveholders to rid America of troublesome Negro freemen.[5]

From the early decades of the nineteenth century onwards, however, a vocal minority among the Afro-Americans came to the conclusion that the political, social, and economic condition of the black man in America was so hopeless that the only solution to his plight lay in emigration to Haiti, Liberia, or Sierra Leone. The passage of the Fugitive Slave Law of 1850 had endangered the very physical security of the Negro. Among this minority of Pan-African nationalists with visions of a regenerated African continent were Paul Cuffee, Lott Carey, Daniel Coker, and John Russwurm. Cuffee in 1811 formed the Friendly Society of Sierra Leone to resettle selected Afro-Americans there and to promote education in Sierra Leone. In 1815 he again resettled over thirty black families in Sierra Leone and co-operated with the American Colonization Society although he had some reservations about the schemes of the latter body.[6] Cuffee died shortly after his 1815 trip to Sierra Leone; and Daniel Coker, ex-slave and founder member of the breakaway African Methodist Episcopal Church, sought the support of the Colonization Society in an attempt to emigrate to West Africa. Coker settled eighty-eight emigrants at Cape Mesurado in Liberia while he himself settled in Sierra Leone. Lott Carey, another ex-slave, went to Liberia as missionary, builder, doctor, and above all as mediator between the colonists and the indigenous peoples. He died in November 1828. John Russwurm, born in Jamaica and one of the first Negro graduates from an American college, founded and edited the first Afro-American newspaper, *Freedom's Journal* in 1827. He at first opposed the Colonization Society but later (1829) supported its scheme and

[5] Lynch, Hollis R., 'Pan-Negro Nationalism in the New World before 1862', *Boston University Papers on Africa, vol. II, African History*, ed. Jeffrey Butler (Boston, 1966), pp. 150–3.

[6] ibid., pp. 154–5.

went to Liberia in 1830, founding the *Liberia Herald* the same year. He held various important posts in the Liberian government between 1836 and 1851.

West Indians and Afro-Americans continued to take interest in emigrating to Liberia when the latter country became independent in 1847. Barbados, for example, had a Fatherland Union Society and a Colonization Society 'for assisting in the suppression of the Slave Trade, and the introduction of civilization into Africa', and welcomed Liberia's attainment of independence as proof of the Negro's capacity for self-government. Within the next thirty years another West Indian, Edward Blyden, was to become the best-known defender of the new republic and the most original exponent of Pan-Negro ideas.

Meanwhile in America Martin Delany, a Negro doctor trained at Harvard and an abolitionist, was preparing a colonization scheme with the object of creating a black empire in the Caribbean or in South and Central America. Impatient with the white abolitionists and with the slow progress the Negro was making in the matter of civil rights, Delany urged Afro-American colonization of South America where a black state would hasten the end of slavery in America and establish an economic base for New-World Negroes. Delany stated these views in 1852 in an important treatise entitled 'The Condition, Elevation and Destiny of the Colored People of the United States, Politically Considered'. In it he also criticized Liberia's dependence on the American Colonization Society which, he suspected, was an agent of slave interests—a view which Blyden rejected. Delany later widened his scheme from mere emigration to the establishment of a Negro nation in East Africa as a means of winning respect for the Negro race. Like the early Zionists, the location of his projected Negro homeland did not matter as long as the oppressed Afro-Americans could find a place where they could establish themselves as a self-respecting nation. It was only later in his *Official Report of the Niger Valley Exploring Party* that he spoke of Africa as 'our fatherland' and stated that 'our policy must be *Africa for the African race, and black men to rule them*'; black men he defined as 'men of African descent who claim an identity with the race'.[7]

Delany and his emigrationist friends, however, constituted a

[7] Brotz, Howard, ed., *Negro Social and Political Thought, 1850–1920* (New York, 1966), pp. 2–3; also Kirk-Greene, A. H. M., 'America in the Niger Valley: A Colonization Centenary', *Phylon*, no. 3 (1962), 225–39.

minority among the abolitionists, the majority of whom, led by Frederick Douglass, were against any form of Negro emigration. Whereas Delany, supported by Henry Highland Garnet, now turned to West Africa as the 'geographical centre for their pan-Negro programme'[8] and as an area where cotton could be grown to undersell American slave-grown cotton and thus hasten the collapse of slavery, Douglass and his assimilationist Negro spokesmen argued that the Afro-American was destined to solve his problems in America and that slavery could only be defeated by Americans in America. In an attack on the African Civilization Society of Garnet and Delany he argued:

The African Civilization Society says to us, go to Africa, raise cotton, civilize the natives, become planters, merchants, compete with the slave States in the Liverpool cotton market, and thus break down American slavery. To which we simply and briefly reply, 'we prefer to remain in America'. . . . No one idea has given rise to more oppression and persecution toward the colored people of this country, than that which makes Africa, not America, their home. It is that wolfish idea that elbows us off the side walk, and denies us the rights of citizenship . . . we instinctively shrink from any movement which involves a substitution of a doubtful and indirect issue, for one which is direct and certain. . . . The African Civilization Society proposes to plant its guns too far from the battlements of slavery for us. Its doctrines and measures are those of doubt and retreat . . . the means for accomplishing our object are quite as promising here as there, and more especially since we are here already, with constitutions and habits suited to the country and its climate, and to its better institutions.[9]

The debate between the pan-Negroists and the assimilationists continued throughout the nineteenth century and into the early decades of the twentieth, culminating in the Garvey movement of the 1920s. It is still continuing.

The Revd. Alexander Crummell was perhaps the last major Afro-American leader with African interests during the period under review, and is of interest for his theological politics and providential theory of African liberation. Crummell went to Liberia from America in 1853 after graduating from Queens' College, Cambridge, and was associated with Blyden in various reform and race activities in Liberia. In his *The Relation and Duties of the Free Colored Men*

[8] Lynch, H. R., 'Pan-Negro Nationalism in the New World, before 1862', p. 168.
[9] Brotz, op. cit., pp. 263–5.

*in America to Africa,* published in 1861, he supported the emigrationists and stressed the leadership of Afro-Americans in the civilization and Christianization of Africa. He also urged greater Negro
participation in African education and commerce and the resulting
benefit to both Afro-Americans and Africans. Just as James Holly
saw the Haitian revolution as a demonstration of the capacity of the
Negro for self-government and civilized existence,[10] so did Crummell
see the establishment of Liberia as a providential act for the re-
habilitation and progress of the Negro by New-World Negroes:
'without doubt God designs great things for Africa and . . . black
men themselves are without doubt to be the chief instruments', and
like most Pan-African visionaries saw the rise of the black republic
as the dawn of a new history and civilization to succeed a declining
Anglo-Saxon civilization.[11] As early as 1853, taking Psalm 68 : 13 as
his text ('Ethiopia shall soon stretch out her hands unto God'), he
preached not only the 'mental and spiritual regeneration' of West
Indian Negroes but sought to connect this idea with 'another
important purpose'—the sending abroad of 'healthful influences and
a saving power—even to the benighted father-land, whence the
ancestors of the sable dwellers upon these islands were first brought;
and thus help to raise up the great African family, in its several
sections, to civilization and enlightenment . . .'.[12] Turning to 'the
history of the Cushites, in its African section', Crummell noted that
the African Diaspora or dispersion had been brought about primarily
by two factors—the European age of reconnaissance and the slave
trade, through which Europe established contact with Africa and the
New World. As a result of this contact, 'the Negro race is to be found
in every quarter of the globe. Stolen from their homes, and reduced
to abject vassalage, they are gathered together by thousands and tens
of thousands, and even millions, in lands separated, by thousands of
miles, from the primitive seat of their ancestors, and the rude
hamlets of their sires.' It was therefore with respect to the Negro race,
'as thus scattered through the world, as well as dwelling in their

[10] Holly, James T., *A Vindication of the Capacity of the Negro Race for Self-
Government, and Civilized Progress, as Demonstrated by Historical Events of the
Haitian Revolution; and the Subsequent Act of the People since their National
Independence* (New Haven, Conn., 1857), reprinted in Brotz, op. cit., pp. 140–70.
[11] Crummell, Alexander, quoted in Lynch, H. R., 'Pan-Negro Nationalism in
the New World before 1862', pp. 175, 177.
[12] Crummell, Alexander, *Hope for Africa—A Sermon on Behalf of the Ladies'
Negro Education Society* (London, 1853), p. 1.

homes in Africa' that he was going to apply the well-known Ethiopian text.[13] He noted that although slavery had been officially abolished in the British Empire, there were still a few signs of it in Brazil, the United States, and in Cuba, but its end was inevitable 'for the commerce of the world is against slavery: the free trade principle of the age is against it: science in her various developments is against it: the literature of the day is just being brought to bear, in a most marvellous manner, against it, and the free sentiments of the world are against it. . . .' Crummell then dwelt on the familiar theme of Africans who had 'achieved fame and celebrity' like Anton William Amo, Ignatius Sancho, Job Ben Solomon, and, above all, Toussaint L'Ouverture of Haiti, the only successful black revolutionary. He took up the cudgels in defence of Haiti against a prejudiced Thomas Carlyle who called the republic 'a tropical dog-kennel and a pestiferous jungle', and asserted that far from being a failure Haiti was an evidence of the progress of the black race and that unlike the South American Republics it had not been 'rent asunder by repeated revolutions' but had had only one revolution—that of Toussaint L'Ouverture. As for the strictures of Carlyle, he said that one simply had to endure his 'brutum fulmen' and quietly smile at 'the *frantic* heat, the blind hysterics of *that* Celt'.[14] Finally, Crummell lauded Sierra Leone as 'the cradle of missions, the mother of churches, the parent of colonies' and stated that the movement in the West Indies to send skilled colonists to the West African coast contained 'the germs of a new African nationality of a civilized and Christian type'.[15]

## 2. *Racism, Colonialism, and Pan-Africanism*

I F before 1862 New-World Pan-Negro nationalists neither succeeded in initiating a large-scale African colonization movement nor established significant and permanent contact with Africa,[16] the post-reconstruction period, together with the economic and racial difficulties of Southern Negroes, created a situation in which internal migration or colonization seemed the only alternatives to a large number of Afro-Americans. The period roughly from 1878 to 1914—

[13] ibid., p. 5.
[14] ibid., p. 10.
[15] ibid., p. 14.
[16] Lynch, H. R., 'Pan-Negro Nationalism in the New World before 1862', p. 178.

from the Kansas Exodus of 1879 to utopian attempts to found an all-Negro community in Oklahoma Territory in the 1890s and the Chief Sam 'African Movement' of 1914–15—can perhaps be said to mark the zenith of the emigrationist ideology and of Afro-American identification with Africa.[17] There were indeed leaders who opposed emigration to Africa: in fact, the majority of Afro-American leaders opposed the idea and opted for the integrationist philosophy. A very articulate minority, led by Bishop Henry McNeal Turner of the American Methodist Episcopal Church, consistently and actively propagated the emigrationist ideology, while somewhere in the middle was another group sympathetic to the establishment of a 'Christian Negro Nationality' in Africa through commerce and limited voluntary emigration. This last group was led by Bishop Arnett and T. McCants Stewart. The most consistent, articulate, and pro-African among the emigrationists, however, was the controversial Bishop Turner, whose Pan-Negroism and support for Ethiopianism took him to South and West Africa.[18]

Henry McNeal Turner was born in South Carolina and was largely self-taught. He was appointed the first Afro-American chaplain during the Civil War, after which he entered politics in Georgia. In 1868 when the black members of that legislature were expelled by the whites, Turner turned to the Church, becoming a bishop in the American Methodist Episcopal Church in 1880. In 1874 he and Bishop Jabez P. Campbell of the A.M.E. Church espoused the emigration idea and became officials of the American Colonization Society. Turner's view was that there was no future for the black man in America; like James Holly and Alexander Crummell, his emigrationist theory was blended with that of 'Providential design'. He argued that God had brought the black man to America to be Christianized and civilized so that he could return to Africa and develop the continent. Indeed, so deep-seated was his hatred of Anglo-

[17] In its efforts to alleviate the economic hardships of the Negro, The Kansas African Emigration Association in 1887 proposed the establishment of a 'United States of Africa . . . for the elevation of the African and for the perpetuity of our race, which is here losing its identity by intermixture'. Quoted in Meier, August, *Negro Thought in America, 1880–1915* (Ann Arbor, Mich., 1963), pp. 65, 67.

[18] The 'Back-to-Africa' movements from 1890 to 1910, in which Bishop Turner figures, are being studied by E. S. Redkey of Yale University. See his article 'Bishop Turner's African Dream', *Journal of American History* (formerly *Mississippi Valley Historical Review*), liv, no. 2 (Sept. 1967), 271–90. For a more detailed study, see Redkey's recent *Black Exodus: Black Nationalist and Back-to-Africa Movements, 1890–1910* (New Haven, Conn., and London, 1969).

Saxon America that he wished it 'nothing but ill and endless misfortune' and to see it 'go down to ruin and its memory blotted from the pages of history'.[19] And as late as 1901 he wrote in his journal *Voice of the People*:

> The Negro race has as much chance in the United States . . . of being a man . . . as a frog has in a snake den. . . . Emigrate and gradually return to the land of our ancestors. . . . The Negro was brought here in the providence of God to learn obedience, to work, to sing, to pray, to preach, acquire education, deal with mathematical abstractions and imbibe the principles of civilization as a whole, and then to return to Africa, the land of his fathers, and bring her his millions. . . .[20]

Bishop Turner was not only concerned with Pan-Negro nationalism and African colonization; he took a deep and passionate interest in its ecclesiastical counterpart, Ethiopianism. He encouraged the establishment of A.M.E. churches both in Sierra Leone and Liberia; these were to be staffed by Negro pastors. He was also in direct touch with the leaders of the Ethiopian movement in South Africa in the 1890s, his *Voice of Missions* reaching many parts of the continent. Much of the Ethiopian agitation in South Africa was inspired by Afro-American missions, notably Turner's A.M.E. Church; in fact, Turner visited South Africa in March 1898, where he made several public speeches, consecrated African bishops, and denounced slavery and racism.[21]

In contrast to Bishop Turner, T. Thomas Fortune, editor of the *New York Age* and *New York World* as well as one of the most articulate anti-emigrationists and advocates of Afro-American participation in politics, argued that the black man, especially the Southern Negro, was in the United States to stay and that it was the duty of white America to educate him to exercise his rights as a citizen:

> The talk about the black people being brought to this country to prepare themselves to evangelize Africa is so much religious nonsense boiled down

---

[19] Bishop Henry McNeal Turner, quoted in Meier, op. cit., p. 66.

[20] ibid., quoted in Drake, St. Clair, 'Negro Americans and "The African Interest" ', p. 674.

[21] For details of Turner's activities in South Africa and his relations with the leaders of the Ethiopian movement there, see Burnet, Amos, 'Ethiopianism', *Church Missionary Review* (1922), pp. 29–34; Leenhardt, M., *Le Mouvement éthiopien au sud de l'Afrique de 1896 à 1899* (Cahors, 1902), pp. 28–64, and D. Thwaite's hysterical *The Seething African Pot: A Study of Black Nationalism, 1882–1935* (London, 1936), pp. 25–57.

to a sycophantic platitude. The Lord, who is eminently just, had no hand in their forcible coming here. . . . Africa will have to be evangelized *from within*, not *from without*. The Colonization society has spent mints of money and tons of human blood in the selfish attempt to plant an Anglo-African colony on the West Coast of Africa. The money has been thrown away and the human lives have been sacrificed in vain. The black people of this country are Americans, not Africans; and any wholesale expatriation of them is altogether out of the question.[22]

Turner and Fortune were to express divergent views again, this time at a conference on Africa sponsored by the Gammon Theological Seminary in Atlanta in 1895 which was attended by Alexander Crummell who spoke on the need for indigenous missions in Africa and by the Revd. Orishatukė Faduma from Sierra Leone, who will be considered later. At that conference, Turner restated his emigrationist philosophy more vigorously, the only concession he made being that not all Negroes, but two or three million should return to Africa:

*There is no manhood future in the United States for the Negro.* He may eke out an existence for generations to come, but he can never be a *man*. . . . Upon this point I know thousands who make pretentions to scholarship, white and colored, will differ and may charge me with folly, while I in turn pity their ignorance of history and political and civil sociology . . . the argument that it would be impossible to transport the colored people of the United States back to Africa is an advertisement of folly. . . .[23]

Fortune, on the other hand, reiterated his assimilationist theory in a paper on 'The Nationalization of Africa'. He did not talk of African nations or of African nationalism: by 'nationalization' he meant the colonization and partition of Africa by Europe and the inevitable transference to Africa of European concepts of statehood. He predicted that by 1979 the whole of Africa would, through European colonization, be Europeanized 'physically and mentally and morally', and that 'the demoralizing heterogeneousness which now prevails over the whole continent will give place to a pervading homogeneity in language, in religion, and in government'. Having said this he went on to state his 'iron law' of the eventual assimilation or

[22] Fortune, T. Thomas, 'Solution of the Political Problem', quoted in Brotz, op. cit., p. 349.
[23] Turner, Bishop H. M., 'The American Negro and the Fatherland', in *Africa and the American Negro: Congress on Africa*, ed. J. W. E. Bowen (Atlanta, Ga., 1896), pp. 195–8.

'nationalization' of the European minority in Africa, observing that just as the Negro was being assimilated into American society and culture in spite of the resistance of the whites and a few Negroes, 'The rigid laws and rules and regulations already adopted by the English, the Germans and the French and the Belgians in Africa to keep the natives in their place will prove as ineffectual to their purpose as such laws and rules and regulations now prove in the United States. . . .'[24]

Fortune, however, does not seem to have been unaware of a wider unity of Negro peoples, for he later claimed that the idea of the Pan-African Conference of 1900 was his.[25] That first of Pan-African conclaves was convened in London at Westminster Town Hall by a Trinidad barrister practising in London, Henry Sylvester Williams. Williams, about whom little is known so far, is believed to have introduced the concept of Pan-Africanism. He was assisted by Bishop Alexander Walters of the American Methodist Episcopal Zion Church,[26] who was also the president of the National Afro-American Council. According to current newspaper reports, the conference was organized by a committee of the African Association in London to discuss the Native Races Question. The African Association, formed by students in London during Queen Victoria's Diamond Jubilee, also included members from the West Indies, West Africa, South Africa, and white supporters like Mrs. Cobden-Unwin (daughter of the Free Trade champion Richard Cobden), Mrs. Colenso and Dr. Colenso, and Bishop Creighton of London. Its constitution aimed:

To encourage a feeling of unity, to facilitate friendly intercourse among Africans in general; to promote and protect the interest of all subjects claiming African descent, wholly or in part, in British Colonies and other places, especially in Africa, by circulating accurate information on all subjects affecting their rights and privileges as subjects of the British Empire, and by direct appeals to the Imperial and local Governments.[27]

[24] Fortune, T. Thomas, 'The Nationalization of Africa', in Bowen, op. cit., pp. 199–204.
[25] Rudwick, Eliot M., *W. E. B. Du Bois: A Study in Minority Group Leadership* (Philadelphia, Pa., 1960), p. 209.
[26] Bishop Walters later described the 1900 Pan-African Conference in his *My Life and Work* (New York, 1917), pp. 253–64.
[27] See *The Times* (24 July 1900), p. 7: 'Pan-African Conference'; *The Gold Coast Leader* (31 Aug. 1912), p. 5; *The Lagos Standard* (17 Oct. 1900): 'The Pan-African Conference'.

The conference, which was also attended by Du Bois, lasted from 23 to 25 July, with Bishop Walters in the chair. Walters remarked on the uniqueness of this Pan-African conclave and spoke of the black man's struggle for social and political rights in America, suggesting that a bureau should be created in London to act as a pressure group in influencing all legislation affecting non-European races. A delegate from Kansas (U.S.A.) spoke on the preservation of race individuality, while Mr. Benito Sylvian (an officer in the Haitian navy and aide-de-camp to the Emperor Menelik) read a paper on 'The Necessary Concord to be Established between Native Races and European Colonists', commenting on the regressive colonial policy adopted towards the close of the nineteenth century and on the 'most frightful deeds of colonizing companies'. Black men, he said, had everywhere proved themselves worthy of liberty and the question of the day was going to be whether Europe was prepared to come to an understanding with the black man, for 'No human power could stop the African natives in their social and political development'. The Bishop of London urged restraint and spoke on human brotherhood and the inevitable contacts between races and its resulting problems.

On 25 and 26 July the conference discussed 'The progress of our people in the light of current history' and the South African war. Pro-African speeches were made by F. S. R. Johnston, a former Attorney-General of Liberia, Mr. Meyer and Dr. R. Akiwande Savage, delegates from the Afro-West Indian Literary Society of Edinburgh, and D. Tobias who in a discussion on 'Africa, the sphinx of history' claimed that civilization began with the black man. G. W. Christian (Dominica), whose speech was widely quoted in the British West African press, spoke on the South African question and on Rhodesia, urging greater attention to the welfare and liberty of the African in South Africa after the settlement of the war. And Sylvester Williams, who had visited South Africa, condemned racial segregation and recommended a protest movement against it. Then the conference, aided by Du Bois, drew up an address to the world which they sent to various governments and to Queen Victoria. The address condemned the exploitation of subject peoples and admonished: 'Let not the cloak of Christian missionary enterprise be allowed in the future, as so often in the past, to hide the ruthless economic exploitation and political downfall of less developed nations whose chief fault has been reliance on the plighted troth of

NEW-WORLD ORIGINS OF PAN-NEGRO SENTIMENT 29

the Christian Church.' It was also at that conference that Du Bois made his prophetic remark to the effect that 'The problem of the twentieth century is the problem of the color line'.[28]

The Pan-African Association, formed after the 1900 Conference, started a paper called *The Panafrican* in 1901, edited by H. Sylvester Williams, of which probably only one issue appeared. According to Dr. Geiss, some of the members attempted to dissolve the Association after the Conference but it was revived by Bishop Walters and Sylvester Williams. In less than a year the Association, together with its ambitious programme, passed into oblivion.[29] But contemporaries, particularly the budding nationalists in West Africa, gave wide coverage to the 1900 Conference and were optimistic about its potentialities. The *Lagos Standard*, for example, observed:

The last year of the present century will long be memorable to all people of African descent for an event in the history of race movements, which for its importance and probable results, so far as its aims and objects are concerned, is perhaps without parallel. The unprecedented spectacle of a Conference of members of the Negro race gathered together in the world's Metropolis, discussing their wrongs and pleading for justice for the race, is sufficiently striking to attract public attention in an unusual degree. . . .

The *Lagos Standard* also endorsed G. W. Christian's speech calling for greater autonomy in the colonies.[30] In the Gold Coast, the *Gold Coast Aborigines* lamented: 'The feverish rush for plunder and division of Africa is about to be, if not already, consummated on this eventful eve of the Twentieth Century. The saying "Rule Africa for the African" is but the reverse of "Rule Africa for self" on the sheer principle of aggrandizement. If only the blackman would be more alive to his interest and make a couple of strides towards the goal of advancement things would be different.'[31] The editorial viewed

[28] The proceedings of the 1900 Conference can be found in *The Times* (24 July 1900), p. 7, (25 July 1900), p. 15, (26 July 1900), p. 11; *The Anti-Slavery Reporter* (Aug.–Oct. 1900), pp. 139–41; *Bulletin du Comité de l'Afrique Française* (1900), pp. 283–4: 'Le Panafricanisme'; and *South Africa*, xlvii, no. 602 (28 July 1900), 197: 'Pan-African Conference'. I owe the last reference to Mr. Neil Parsons, Edinburgh University. For the 'Address to the Nations of the World', see Walters, op. cit., pp. 257–60.

[29] Geiss, Imanuel, 'The Development of Panafricanism in the Twentieth Century', p. 6, paper read at a seminar in the Centre of African Studies, Edinburgh University, June 1966. A copy of the *Pan-African* can be found in the British Museum International Newspaper Library at Colindale.

[30] *The Lagos Standard* (17 Oct. 1900): 'The Pan-African Conference'.

[31] The *Gold Coast Aborigines* (31 Aug. 1900), p. 3.

the Pan-African conference in the context of a colonial policy which was becoming more reactionary, and in the context of the anti-foreign Boxer Rebellion in China, and added prophetically and in anticipation of modern Pan-Africanists:

The insolent whites thought that China was dead, but they now find her very much alive. The same will be found true with the blacks. They are not going to die out. We predict that Africa will always remain what it has always been—the black man's continent. There may be fringes of population of whites here and there, but the main bulk of the people will be black. We talk of Boer and Briton in South Africa, as if that were a statement of the whole matter. What if, at some distant date in the future, South Africa should belong neither to Boer nor Briton, but to the Negro—his by right, by superior numbers, and superior power? We may smile at the idea, but it may easily become a tremendous reality. . . .

The old slavery is dead, but a more subtle if not more cruel slavery may take its place. The demand of the capitalist everywhere is for cheap and docile labour. . . . Hence the China crisis, hence the danger to the blacks of Africa. We have little to be thankful for to men like Rhodes. But we may thank him for exposing his designs and so warning the Negro race of the evils in store for them if he and his like are to bear sway. . . .

Now the Negro must be protected against this insidious conspiracy. But that protection must largely depend on himself. We can help him; but he must in the main work out his own salvation, as all men have had to do since history began.[32]

The *Gold Coast Chronicle* too was affected by the new spirit. It vehemently defended the right of the press to 'vindicate the cause of the oppressed' and to 'point out and express freely our opinion on the conduct of the Government when it is associated with evils and grievances detrimental to public interests', and roundly declared: '. . . WE ARE NO LONGER CHILDREN. The absurdity of the idea that we shall be afraid in the least to point out to the Government what would contribute to the public weal needs no comment.'[33] This growing African consciousness of a wider racial unity was, as we have noted, influenced both by indigenous factors and by outside influences, so that even before 1919 a few Africans were directing their attention to the question of race development and solidarity. For example, P. Isaka Seme, an American-educated

---

[32] The *Gold Coast Aborigines* (31 Aug. 1900), part of the editorial was a reprint from *Reynolds' Newspaper* (29 July 1900).

[33] The *Gold Coast Chronicle* (18 Aug. 1900), p. 3. The Gold Coast delegate to the 1900 Pan-African Conference was A. F. Ribero, a barrister. Bishop James Johnson ('Holy Johnson') of Nigeria also attended the Conference.

South African and one of the founders of the South African National Congress, wrote on 'The Regeneration of Africa',[34] while Bandele Omoyini, a Nigerian student at Edinburgh University, thought it proper to write a book entitled *Defence of the Ethiopian Movement* in 1908, and S. R. B. Attoh-Ahuma and Casely Hayford of the Gold Coast and Edward Blyden of Liberia wrote several important works on the subject of cultural and Pan-Negro nationalism.

More encouragement was given to this Pan-Negro consciousness by the two inter-racial gatherings of 1911 and 1912—the Universal Races Congress and Booker T. Washington's small-scale pan-African conference of 1912. The first congress, held in London, was an international seminar on race relations 'to discuss in the light of science and the modern conscience the general relations subsisting between the peoples of the West and those of the East, between so-called white and so-called coloured peoples, with a view to encouraging between them a fuller understanding, the most friendly feelings, and a heartier co-operation';[35] but for a few articulate Africans it was regarded as a major gathering which had at last established the equality of races.[36] Mojola Agbebi, director of the Niger Delta Mission, who spoke at the congress, rejected the current view that the African was a child and observed that the object of the congress was to foster mutual respect and knowledge between Eastern and Western peoples and that 'The triumph of the principles for which the Congress stands will . . . go a long way towards the solution of the African problem.' G. K. Gokhale, president of the Indian National Congress, also referred to 'the monstrous indignities and ill-treatment' meted out to Indians in South Africa. For most

[34] Shepperson, G., 'Notes on Negro American Influences on the Emergence of African Nationalism', p. 304 n. 36; also Cameron, N. E., *The Evolution of the Negro* (Georgetown, Demerara, 1929), i. 190–6.
[35] See Spiller, Gustav, *Inter-Racial Problems* (London, 1911), p. v.
[36] See, e.g., J. E. Casely Hayford's 'An Open Letter to Dr. G. Spiller, Organizer of the First Universal Races Congress' in the *African Times and Orient Review* (Aug. 1913), p. 67. The pan-coloured *African Times and Orient Review* was edited by a somewhat neglected figure in the history of Pan-Negro nationalism, the part-Sudanese, part-Egyptian Dusé Mohammed Ali (1867–1945) who was associated at different times with Pan-Negro and African nationalist groups and finally chaired a meeting in Nigeria at which Zik's National Council of Nigeria and the Cameroons was founded. The *Gold Coast Leader* (13 Aug. 1912) saw Dusé Mohamed Ali's paper as the continuation of the efforts of Henry Sylvester Williams and the Pan-African Association he founded in 1900, while a modern student of Pan-Africanism (Geiss, op. cit., p. 7) has described his journal as 'a journalistic forerunner of the Bandung movement'.

European liberals, however, the congress was regarded as a major step towards understanding with Asia, particularly Japan, and Germany whose relations with Britain had deteriorated to a point where conflict between the two was generally regarded as inevitable.[37]

The London Inter-Racial Congress was followed by Booker T. Washington's International Conference on the Negro at Tuskegee on 17–19 April 1912. Over a hundred delegates attended, the majority representing various Negro American missionary bodies, with less than a dozen African delegates. Missionary work and the role of Negro educational institutions featured prominently in the discussions, as well as a growing awareness of Pan-African thinking. Blyden was already dead; the Revd. Mark C. Hayford gave a lengthy and interesting address as well as a letter from his brother J. E. Casely Hayford of the Gold Coast.

The 1912 Tuskegee Conference on Africa discussed the methods of missionary activity in Africa: how were they to teach the French Africans and could they teach skills to the African in South Africa without antagonizing the whites? At the end of the conference both white and black missionaries thrashed out the question and agreed to invite Washington to visit South Africa to seek a working basis whereby Negro American missionaries could play their part in the development of the country.[38] Perhaps this question became more urgent because of the presence of Pan-African oriented Negro missions at the conference led by Bishop H. M. Turner whom a press release described as one of the 'stormy Negro orators . . . the well-known apostle of the Back-to-Africa movement which is the lost cause of the Negro race . . .'.[39] Obviously the good bishop was not satisfied with a programme for the redemption of Africa that lacked the flavour of a radical Pan-Negroism. It was precisely this 'subversion' that the Hampton–Tuskegee approach to Africa was determined to avoid. In fact, the conference showed Booker Washington not as the Negro isolationist leader which his rivalry with Du Bois led observers to think he was, but as one whose approach to racial solidarity was based on political realism and a preference for tech-

[37] Avebury, The Rt. Hon. Lord, 'Inter-Racial Problems', *Fortnightly Review*, N.S. xc (July–Dec. 1911), 581–9.

[38] Park, Robert M. (ex-secretary of the Congo Reform Association in America), 'Tuskegee International Conference on the Negro', *Journal of Race Development*, iii (July 1912–Apr. 1913), 118–19.

[39] See Drake, St. Clair, 'Negro Americans and "The African Interest" ', p. 684 n. 45.

nical and educational development of Africa.[40] For example, at the
conference a scheme was worked out for promoting trade between
black America and West Africa, and the Africa Union Company
was formed for this purpose but the Great War supervened and the
idea was abandoned.[41] It has been argued that Casely Hayford
changed his views about the unsuitability of black Americans for
political leadership in Africa because of his agreement with the ideas
of Washington's Tuskegee Conference.[42] He agreed with Washington
precisely because of the apolitical nature of the Hampton–Tuskegee
approach to the 'regeneration' of Africa—an arrangement which
would leave nationalist agitation in the hands of the West African
bourgeois nationalists while enabling them to enjoy the benefits of
Pan-Negro transatlantic commerce and educational co-operation.
It is more likely that his strictures in *Ethiopia Unbound* were directed
against the political messianism and crusading spirit of New World
Pan-Negroists who had exalted notions about civilizing and leading
a 'benighted' Africa. Those groups were potentially subversive and
did not fit in with the views and interests of constitutional nationalists and conservative Pan-Africanists of West Africa. It is therefore
not surprising to find Casely Hayford praising the efforts of the
Tuskegee Conference on the one hand and on the other hand
reminding the conference that there existed such a thing as an
'African Nationality'.[43] As we shall show in subsequent chapters, the
attitude of the West African nationalist leadership to the Pan-
African movements of the 1920s was deeply influenced by this
dualism.

[40] Harlan, Louis R., 'Booker T. Washington and the White Man's Burden',
*American Historical Review*, lxxi, no. 2 (Jan. 1966), 441–67.
[41] It seems to have been revived in 1923, with Dusé Mohamed Ali as its president, under the title of the *American African Oriental Trading Company*; see Dusé
Mohamed Ali to Dr. R. R. Moton, Principal, Tuskegee Institute, 19 Feb. 1923,
and interview with Dusé Mohamed Ali published in the *St. Louis Clarion* (19
Oct. 1923). I owe this information to Professor G. A. Shepperson.
[42] Shepperson, G., 'Notes on Negro American Influences on the Emergence of
African Nationalism', p. 311 n. 87.
[43] See Park, Robert M., 'Tuskegee International Conference on the Negro',
pp. 117–18.

## 3. African Responses

AFRICAN political thinking and ecclesiastical and cultural nationalism drew inspiration from several sources, some of them, as in the
case of the Ethiopian movement, indigenous. Exactly what the
extent of these influences was is problematical,[44] although there is
general agreement as to their significance in the evolution of Pan-
African and nationalist thought and politics. New-World Pan-Negro
literature and Abolitionist literature were utilized by race-conscious
African writers during the early part of the nineteenth century, but
as that century drew to a close specifically African contributions
beginning with the cultural nationalism of Edward Blyden began to
emerge, particularly in the writings and journalistic efforts of West
African nationalists.[45] What were these influences and what was the
African response?

The origins of the concept of self-government for Negro peoples
can be traced to the emancipationist categories of thought in
Abolitionist literature during the campaign for the abolition of
slavery and in the establishment of Sierra Leone and Liberia. So
closely connected were these three major events with the beginnings
of Negro self-assertion that a writer has argued that '. . . it is no
exaggeration to say that much of the work of the emerging African
political thinkers of the Abolitionist Epoch centres on the issue of
racialism'.[46] Dr. James Africanus Beale Horton of Sierra Leone,
for example, utilized anti-slavery literature in his *West African
Countries and Peoples: A Vindication of the African Race* (1868) and
in his *Political Economy of British Western Africa. . . . The African
view of the Negro's place in nature* (1965).[47] Many of the writings of
Africans and New-World Negroes on Pan-Negroism owed their
inspiration to Abolitionist literature, notably the Abbé Henri
Grégoire's pro-African *An enquiry concerning the intellectual and*

[44] Shepperson, G., 'Notes on Negro American Influences on the Emergence of
African Nationalism', p. 312.
[45] See July, Robert W., 'Nineteenth Century Négritude: Edward W. Blyden',
*Journal of African History*, v, no. 1 (1964), 73–86; id., *The Origins of Modern
African Thought* (London, 1968), *passim*; Ellis, George W., 'Liberia in the Political
Psychology of West Africa', *Journal of the Royal African Society*, xii (1912–13),
55–6.
[46] Shepperson, G., 'Abolitionism and African Political Thought', p. 23.
[47] For details, see July, Robert W., *The Origins of Modern African Thought*,
pp. 112–29; id., 'Africanus Horton and the Idea of Independence in West Africa',
*Sierra Leone Studies*, N.S. xviii (Jan. 1966), 2–17.

*moral faculties and literature of negroes: followed with an account of the life and work of fifteen negroes and mulattoes, distinguished in science, literature and the arts* (1810) and Wilson Armistead's *A Tribute for the Negro: being a vindication of the moral, intellectual, and religious capabilities of the coloured portion of Mankind; with particular reference to the African race* (1848). In particular, Abolitionist literature on the 'noble savage' and sometimes idyllic reference to the 'Negro Heritage' indirectly influenced the political thinking and attitudes of West Africans such as the William James Davies of Sierra Leone who changed his name to Orishatukė Faduma and later expressed ideas similar to those of Blyden; D. B. Vincent of Nigeria who became Mojola Agbebi; and the Ghanaian S. R. B. Solomon who became Attoh-Ahuma. Emancipationist literature may also have stimulated the Pan-Africanism of one of West Africa's leading nationalist thinkers, J. E. Casely Hayford.[48]

More direct contact between Afro-Americans and Africans between the end of the nineteenth century and the post-1918 period led to a greater 'commerce of ideas'. For example, future South African nationalist leaders like John L. Dube, Sol Plaatje, P. Isaka Şeme, and D. D. T. Jabavu were educated in Negro American colleges; so was John Chilembwe, leader of the 1915 Nyasaland uprising; and Pan-Negroists like John Edward Bruce were able to establish contact with leading West African nationalists and intellectuals such as Casely Hayford, J. E. K. Aggrey, Mojola Agbebi, and W. E. G. Sekyi.[49] On the political level Afro-American Pan-Negroists prepared the ground for the future Pan-African gatherings both in their propaganda for post-war reconstruction in Africa and America and in their writings on the desirability of world-wide Negro unity. James Weldon Johnson and W. E. B. Du Bois, officials of the National Association for the Advancement of Coloured People, drew attention to the significance of the Great War for Negro self-determination and reconstruction both in America and in Africa. Another Afro-American scholar Benjamin Brawley, whose *Africa and the War* (1918) was widely commented on in French and English journals concerned with African questions, asserted that 'The great

---

[48] Shepperson, G., 'Abolitionism and African Political Thought', pp. 24–5; for discussion of the ideas of S. R. B. Attoh Ahuma and Casely Hayford, see July, *The Origins of Modern African Thought*, pp. 341–4, 433–57. Some of the ideas of the Revd. Orishatukė Faduma are discussed in chapters II to IV.

[49] Shepperson, G., 'Notes on Negro American Influences on the Emergence of African Nationalism', pp. 309–10.

war of our day is to determine the future of the Negro in the World. Alsace-Lorraine, Belgium, the Balkans, and even Russia all become second in importance.'[50] Similarly Lewis Garnett Jordan, Foreign Missionary Secretary of the Negro American National Baptist Convention, wrote in 1918: 'With 600,000 Africans fighting in the trenches with the allies and an equal number in arms in various parts of Africa under governments who have taken over the continent, it can never be hoped to again make the African a docile creature, to be dumb and driven like a brute, which his oppressors have been 100 years or more in the making.'[51] Finally, radical Pan-Africanists such as Hubert Harrison, founder of the Liberty League of Negro Americans, journalist, and one of Marcus Garvey's staunchest supporters, helped to usher in the post-1918 Pan-African movement in their polemics and ideological treatises on the subject. Harrison, for example, published in 1920 a tract entitled *When Africa Awakes: the 'inside story' of the stirrings and strivings of the new Negro in the western world*,[52] in which he criticized Du Bois and the American Socialist Party, and preached the 'race first' philosophy for Afro-Americans. He welcomed Europe's 'fratricidal strife' as an opportunity for the non-white races to achieve political freedom:

We look for a free India and an independent Egypt; *for nationalities in Africa flying their own flags and dictating their own internal and foreign policies*. This is what we understand by 'making the world safe for democracy'. Anything less than this will fail to establish 'peace on earth and good will toward men'. For the majority of races cannot be eternally coerced into accepting the sovereignty of the white race. . . . So, gentlemen, when you read of the Mullah, of Said Zagloul Pasha and of Marcus Garvey or Casely Hayford; when you hear of Egyptian and Indian nationalist uprisings, of Black Star Lines and West Indian 'seditions'— kindly remember (because *we* know) that these fruits spring from the seeds of your own sowing.[53]

Another Afro-American also published a Pan-African tract, *A Plea for Unity Among American Negroes and the Negroes of the World*

[50] Quoted in Shepperson, G., op cit., p. 308.
[51] Jordan, Lewis Garnett, *Pebbles from an African Beach* (Philadelphia, Pa., 1918), quoted in Shepperson, 'Notes on Negro American Influences', p. 308; cf. Davis, S. C., *Reservoirs of Men: A History of the Black Troops of French West Africa* (Chambéry, 1934), pp. 165, 191.
[52] Porro Press, New York, 1920. Was it called 'Porro' press because of the conspiratorial nature of 'porro', a Mende secret society?
[53] ibid., pp. 97–8.

(1918). Barrett called for Afro-American unity under a National Negro Political Party but linked this to a wider unity of non-European peoples:

For while the problems—economic, social, educational and political—of Negroes outside America may differ locally and otherwise from those of the American Negro, still, in the main, their problems are not much different from ours, hence, the necessity of a world wide Negro organization. . . . After all, the problem which will confront us in the future and indeed all of the world's darker races, will be the problem of colored men— Negroes, Japanese, and East Indians—receiving a 'square deal' in a world dominated financially and generally by a white minority.[54]

In West Africa itself there was a corresponding ferment of political and cultural ideas. The best-known exponents of these ideas were Edward Blyden and his disciple J. E. Casely Hayford whose writing did much to lay the foundations of the theory of *Négritude* and the philosophy of African unity. Blyden's ideas have been ably dealt with in detail and need not detain us;[55] we are mainly concerned here with their point of departure from New-World Pan-Negro thinking. Blyden, as Dr. Lynch has shown, was more African-oriented culturally, more universal in his treatment of Negro questions, and at the same time more specifically concerned with the idea of a West African community of culture. While Afro-Americans vaguely theorized about a Pan-African utopia, Blyden in his activities and in his writings sought to establish the Pan-West African idea in practice. Dr. Lynch has argued persuasively that the idea of West African political integration, dating from Casely Hayford's National Congress of British West Africa to attempts at unification by French- and English-speaking political leaders in the early 1960s, is not a twentieth-century phenomenon but has its origins in the social and political thought of Edward Blyden. His qualified encouragement of Liberian expansion and his championing of Islam and Arabic and of Negro history and culture were all calculated to foster ethno-

[54] Barrett, Samuel, *A Plea for Unity Among American Negroes and the Negroes of the World* (3rd ed., Cedar Falls, Iowa, 1926), p. 3. The first edition was in 1918, sixth edition in 1946; see Drake, St. Clair, 'Negro Americans and "The African Interest" ', p. 696.

[55] In particular by Lynch, Hollis R., *Edward Wilmot Blyden 1832–1912. Pan-Negro Patriot*; Holden, Edith, *Blyden of Liberia: An Account of the Life and Labors of Edward Wilmot Blyden, As Recorded in Letters and in Print* (New York, 1966); July, Robert W., 'Nineteenth Century Negritude: Edward W. Blyden'; id., *The Origins of Modern African Thought*, pp. 208–23.

centricism in West Africa and the idea of a West African community transcending tribal, religious, and possibly territorial divisions created by the colonizing powers.[56] Similarly Blyden's interest in the creation of a West African university, his support for a united West African Church, and his encouragements of the local élites to use their wealth for 'constructive purposes'—all these were designed to encourage self-knowledge, a spirit of unity, and self-respect. As far as is known, he was the first African thinker to preach the philosophy of an 'African Personality'.[57] Blyden failed as a practical leader, and the majority of his contemporaries disagreed with some of his more controversial views and with his political quietism, but his ideas profoundly influenced the liberal nationalism and Pan-African outlook of two of his disciples, J. E. Casely Hayford and the Revd. Orishatukė Faduma, and the majority of the leaders of the Congress movement of the 1920s. In a very real sense, therefore, Edward Blyden was the 'ideological father of the idea of West African unity'.[58]

Of Casely Hayford it can be said that the central theme of his political philosophy was unity—unity among the Gold Coast people, unity in West Africa, and unity of the coloured races. Like Blyden he saw himself as a prophet and race leader and like Blyden the concept of a United West Africa was the key-stone of his race and political thinking. Unlike Blyden, however, he was more positively committed to political action for the realization of his goals. Only a year after Blyden's death Casely Hayford was criticizing the slavish imitation of European civilization and preaching West African nationalism and unity:

You cannot think great thoughts in Africa by adopting wholesale the hurry and the bustle and the way of life of the European. Nature did not intend it. Those who attempt it end in trouble. Nay, worse. It means death. For even the dual man cannot serve God and Mammon. And no worse burden could be imposed by civilization on African nationality than the burden of the double life. . . . Nonconformity is a great thing. . . . We want badly in West Africa the spirit of honest protest. We want personalities who will dare to lead the people back to real life . . . to aim at truth in the life of the people is the basis of national consciousness. . . . We should like to feel that one tocsin call can arouse West Africa into national consciousness. What is it that bridges creeds and dogmas, tribes

[56] Lynch, Hollis. R., 'Edward W. Blyden: Pioneer West African Nationalist'.
[57] For details, see Lynch, Hollis R., *Edward Blyden*, chapter 10: 'Towards a West African Community', pp. 170–247.
[58] ibid., pp. 248–52.

and prejudices, as broad culture? . . . I bid you shake hands across the waters over your common need, your common trouble, your common anxiety. . . . And United West Africa rises chastened and stimulated by the thought that in union is her strength, her weakness in discord.[59]

He indicted the undemocratic nature of colonial rule and the perversion of traditional institutions for the purpose of imperial rule. Like the leaders of most pan-movements he attributed a spiritual world-role to his race and saw West Africa as the vanguard of a Pan-African movement; but as we have stated, his race-consciousness was tempered by political moderation and by a recognition of the benefits of British rule. On the one hand he embraced the Pan-Africanism of New-World Negroes but on the other he emphasized the difference between the race-consciousness of Booker T. Washington and Du Bois and that of Edward Blyden, which he preferred.[60] As early as 1911 he held the view that Afro-Americans, as a result of their assimilation into American culture, were disqualified from assuming the role of political mentors to an awakened Africa:

The voice that was aforetime crying solitarily in the wilderness has suddenly become the voice of a nation and of a people, calling upon their kindred across the Atlantic to come back to their way of thinking. We notice with a pang the strivings after the wind in which our brethren in America are engaged, and we ask them to-day to return to first principles and to original and racial conceptions—to those cooling streams by the fountains of Africa which would refresh their souls.

To leave no possible doubt as to my meaning, Afro-Americans must bring themselves into touch with some of the general traditions and institutions of their ancestors, and, though sojourning in a strange land, endeavour to conserve the characteristics of the race. Thus, and only thus, like Israel of old, will they be able, metaphorically, to walk out of Egypt in the near future with a great and a real spoil.[61]

In Casely Hayford's view, this was a 'new conception of nationalisms', different from the one put forward by the Afro-American school of thought. Even the new African historiography started in America and the new interest in African culture was anticipated by Casely Hayford when he suggested the study of African institutions and traditions by Afro-Americans, for the Afro-American, he said, 'has

[59] Hayford, J. E. Casely, *The Truth About the West African Land Question* London, 1913), pp. 101–3.
[60] id., *Ethiopia Unbound: Studies in Race Emancipation* (London, 1911), pp. 163–4.
[61] ibid., p. 166.

lost absolute touch with the past of his race, and is helplessly groping in the dark for affinities that are not natural'. 'Looking at the matter closely,' he concluded, 'it is not so much Afro-Americans that we want as Africans or Ethiopians. . . .'[62] Indeed, Casely Hayford went so far as to suggest that the Pan-African initiative must come from 'cultured West Africans'.[63]

Before the outbreak of the Great War, then, Pan-Negro thinking had evolved from its origins in the New World to a point where it began to assume a distinctively African orientation in Africa. It is this African aspect in the evolution of the Pan-African idea that we shall examine in detail from chapter II onwards.

[62] Hayford, *Ethiopia Unbound*, p. 173. As we shall show in chapter II, similar views were expressed by the West African nationalist intelligentsia in relation to the Garvey movement, especially by W. E. G. Sekyi in *The Parting of the Ways*.

[63] ibid., pp. 174–82, 196–7; see also July, *The Origins of Modern African Thought*, pp. 448–50.

# The 'African Movement' and the Pan-African Movement: 1914–1927

THE death of Edward W. Blyden in 1912 can be taken as a convenient, though arbitrary, date to mark off the Pan-Negroism of the nineteenth and early twentieth centuries from the post-1918 Pan-African movements of W. F. B. Du Bois and Marcus Garvey. Much has been written about the Pan-African movements of Garvey and Du Bois; much of this, however, is either too brief or too general. In this chapter we shall attempt a more detailed account of the Garvey and Du Bois movements in the wider Pan-African context, as well as an assessment of the influence of Garveyism on African, particularly West African, nationalism.[1] But before dealing with these well-known movements, we shall briefly consider a little-known predecessor of the Garvey movement,[2] led not by an Afro-American or a West Indian, but by a West African—Chief Alfred Sam of the Gold Coast. This was the Back-to-Africa or 'African Movement' of 1914–16.

## 1. An Early Attempt at Black Zionism

THE majority of Chief Sam's recruits for the African movement came from Oklahoma, U.S.A. The historical, socio-economic, and political

[1] Material on the Garvey movement and its impact on African nationalism is hard to come by, and, as Professor George Shepperson has rightly argued, the effects of the Garvey movement in Africa are indeed difficult to trace. Nevertheless an attempt at an assessment will be made in this chapter. See Shepperson, G., 'Pan-Africanism and "Pan-Africanism": Some Historical Notes', p. 356.

[2] See the list of research possibilities in the field of Pan-African historical studies in Isaacs, Harold R., 'The American Negro and Africa: Some Notes', *Phylon*, xx, no. 3 (1959), 223–4. A recent work on the subject of Chief Sam's Back-to-Africa Movement is the one by Bittle, W. E. and Geis, Gilbert, *The Longest Way Home: Chief Alfred Sam's Back-to-Africa Movement* (Detroit, 1964). This work is informative on the American side of the movement but relies heavily on newspaper material and does not relate the movement to the incipient nationalism in parts of West Africa.

reasons which caused the Negro community of Oklahoma to respond to Sam's resettlement scheme and to regard him as a black Moses sent by God to deliver the Negro from his New World bondage to an African Canaan have already been ably analysed in the study by William Bittle and Gilbert Geis.[3] Sociologically, argue the authors, the African movement illustrated 'the desperate hopes of an utterly desperate group of people'.[4] The movement, they continue,

provides the germ of an explanation for the social unrest of an historically inarticulate group of people, a group which could not easily verbalize this discontent in florid protests .... The story of Sam's movement is the story of a group of people who probably knew that they could make no perceptible dent in the world about them, and who, therefore, remained passive and silent with reference to that world. ... The same movement illustrates an ultimate stage of passivity: not utter resignation, but the final and extreme, the most vigorous and only feasible protest— the emigration to a distant, fictionalized homeland, the rejection of an American residency.[5]

Chief Sam, who claimed his grandfather was chief of Obosse and Appasu in West Akim, was born at Appasu, Gold Coast, and attended the German Mission Seminary at Kibi. Before 1911 he had already been engaged in the export of rubber and other African goods to America and in some import business. On 15 July 1911 he formed the Akim Trading Company, chartered under the laws of New York, with headquarters in Brooklyn and with capital of over $600,000. The company seems to have been successful, with Sam and its Afro-American directors calling it 'the first Negro Corporation ever conceived amongst the race'.[6] In 1913, however, the company was reorganized, apparently without Chief Sam, by Edward G. Pettis, who became its President. It dealt mostly in the cocoa trade between New York and West Africa.[7] Sam then decided to form his own company in February 1913—the Akim Trading Company Ltd. incorporated under the laws of South Dakota. According to an American correspondent, disillusionment among Negroes of the South as a result of lynching, disfranchisement, peonage, and segregation, emigration, preferably to Liberia, was the only hope for them. An advertisement by Sam's Akim Trading Company led two leading Negroes in Oklahoma—Dr. P. J. Dorman and Professor J. P.

---

[3] Bittle and Geis, op. cit., pp. 5–67.          [4] ibid., p. 2.
[5] ibid., p. 14.                                          [6] ibid., p. 71.
[7] *Gold Coast Leader* (27 Dec. 1913), enclosed in C.O. 96/540/2558.

Liddell—to write first to Liberia and then to Chief Sam on the possibility of resettlement. Their letter, we are told, was received by Sam who discussed it with several chiefs who in turn were willing to receive the American Negroes. Accordingly, Dr. Dorman and Professor Liddell spread the idea through the Negro communities of Oklahoma.[8]

In February 1913 Sam purchased a vessel of 3,000 tons from the Munson Steam Ship Company, and in May was invited to Oklahoma, where he outlined his scheme and the programme of his company in various meetings, and sold shares. Among other things, Sam claimed that he owned land in the Gold Coast which the would-be settlers could use, though he was careful to explain that land was held in common. The object of Sam's Akim Trading Company was

to open up trade between West Africa on the one hand, and Europe and America on the other hand; to develop Africa industrially for Africa and the world; encourage the emigration of the best Negro farmers and mechanics from the United States to different sections in West Africa, so that the knowledge of practical and modern agriculture may be quickened by contact with natives; develop mining and banking in West Africa; build and purchase ships and boats for transportation and dredging; establish schools and colleges along modern lines, and undertake all interests that relate to economic independence.

This commercial venture was also described as an 'African movement': 'The movement is African, not in a selfish sense. All business interests in this movement are initiated by men and women of African blood to demonstrate their capacity to take an active part in the economic, moral and spiritual development of their people and for themselves and the world. Beginning with self-development, it aims at the development of all.' The company's capital was limited to £200,000 and shares limited to 40,000 at £5 a share. It was also proposed, significantly enough, to name the new steamship line the Ethiopian Steamship Line, reminiscent of Garvey's later Black Star Line.

From the beginning, however, Sam's scheme was regarded with suspicion and even hostility, notably by the conservative Negro press and the Colonial Office. Most critics were inclined to regard Sam as a fake and confidence trickster. In reality, however, most of the black Americans of Oklahoma took the movement seriously, regarding it as an opportunity for their salvation. In Boggs, Oklahoma, Sam

[8] *African Mail* (29 May 1914), p. 351: 'The Gold Coast and American Negroes'.

persuaded black Americans to buy shares in his company, 'with a view to inducing negroes to emigrate to the Gold Coast Colony'.[9] His agents had shown the British Consul-General at New York copies of leases showing that he, as chief of Barbianita Villa, owned land known as Subenabrabo, three miles by five miles, in the Gold Coast, together with other leases aggregating 180 square miles, and that these had been duly sworn in 1910, before the Acting District Commissioner. Sir C. Spring-Rice, the British Ambassador to Washington, 'strongly discouraged' the party of 500 black Americans who were about to sail to the Gold Coast with Chief Sam,[10] and desired to know whether Sam's leases were genuine, to which the Governor of the Gold Coast replied that they were not registered in the Gold Coast.[11] After dispatching the telegram to Sir Hugh Clifford of the Gold Coast, Sir George Fiddes was still of the opinion that the Colonial Office must take 'a stronger line' in the matter of Sam's African movement, and proposed that the Foreign Office should discuss the matter with the American ambassador and should tell him 'that we are morally certain that the whole thing is a fraud . . . and ask him . . . to do all in his power to stop the movement . . .'.[12]

Meanwhile in America, Chief Sam had shown the Consul-General at New York a copy of two leases between him and Kwaka Duro, chief of Okumering in the district of Akim, and William Harkiah Ocquiati of Winneba, for 99 years of property called Abboufurawah, $2\frac{1}{2}$ miles by 2 miles, and of land known as Subenabrabo, 3 miles by 5 miles.[13] On 19 February Sir H. J. Read argued that even if Sam's leases were genuine, the Colonial Office was of the opinion that there was a 'strong probability' that the 'back to Africa' movement was a swindle, that Chief Sam was 'a most undesirable character'; that the West African climate was 'unsuitable', that 'the inducements which have been held out are unfounded', and that Sam's scheme as a whole was fraudulent.[14] The Foreign Office, acting on the advice of the Colonial Office, dispatched a telegram to the American Ambassador in London, Walter Hines Page, explaining

[9] C.O. 96/552/6642.
[10] ibid., C.O. 6169, 17 Feb. 1914; also Sir W. Langley to the Under-Secretary of State, Colonial Office, C.O. 96/552/7116, 17 Feb. 1914.
[11] ibid., C.O. 6930, 25 Mar. 1914.
[12] ibid., minute by Sir George Fiddes to dispatch no. 6169, 17 Feb. 1914.
[13] ibid., decode telegram from Sir C. Spring-Rice, Washington, 16 Feb. 1914; African Mail (5 June 1914), p. 360: 'A "Modern Moses"'.
[14] Minute to F.O. 6169 by Sir H. J. Read, 19 Feb. 1914, C.O. 96/552.

to them that the British Government was strongly of the opinion that

> . . . the immigration of these negroes into that Colony should not be encouraged for the reason that the land is almost entirely held communally by the native chiefs and communities, so that a negro from the United States could only obtain land by adoption into a native community . . . or by lease, which could involve lengthy formalities and uncertain results. In addition to these objections, His Majesty's Government consider that the climate and conditions of the Colony are entirely unsuited to natives of the North American continent . . . his [i.e. Chief Sam's] transactions are not genuine, nor the Company for which he acts reliable. . . .[15]

A few days earlier, the telegram from Sir Hugh Clifford concerning Sam's leases had already been forwarded to Washington and to the Post-Master General and the Governor of Oklahoma, but the United States Government decided that it had no power, short of apprehending Chief Sam for fraudulent use of mails, to prevent the Negro Americans from emigrating.[16]

Seeing that Sam's African Movement party was determined to sail to West Africa, the Colonial Office was at first hesitant in passing an immigration ordinance in the Gold Coast to guard against the possibility of Sam's party being stranded; but on the recommendation of Sir George Fiddes and with the approval of the Foreign Office, the Governor of the Gold Coast was instructed to pass the ordinance requiring immigrants to deposit £25 as security for their repatriation. It was made clear, however, that the ordinance was not meant to apply to all immigrants, but was 'directed *ad hoc*', i.e. against the African Movement.[17] It is interesting to note, however, that the immigration ordinance was quickly passed in the Gold Coast legislative council, Standing Orders being suspended so that it could be passed in all its stages at one sitting. Also interesting is the fact that Mr. Hutton Mills, a merchant and unofficial member (who

[15] ibid., C.O. 6642. Sir W. Langley, Under-Secretary of State for Foreign Affairs, to U.S. Ambassador and to H.M. Ambassador at Washington, 21 Feb. 1914.

[16] ibid., minute to C.O. 7423 by J. A. Calder, 2. Mar. 1914; ibid., decipher of telegram from Sir C. Spring-Rice, Washington, 26 Feb. 1914; ibid., C.O. 11364, 23 Mar. 1914, Walter Hines Page, American Ambassador, London, to the Rt. Hon. Sir Edward Grey.

[17] ibid., minute to C.O. 9069 by J. A. Calder, 13 Mar. 1914; ibid., minute by Sir G. Fiddes, 12 Mar. 1914; ibid., Sir W. Langley to Under-Secretary of State, Colonial Office, 11 Mar. 1914; ibid., Sir H. J. Read to the Under-Secretary of State, Foreign Office, 16 Mar. 1914; ibid., draft telegram to Governor of the Gold Coast, 14 Mar. 1914.

five years later was to become one of the leaders of the National Congress of British West Africa), 'heartily supported the Bill, the latter [i.e. Mr. Hutton Mills] describing "Chief Sam's" enterprise as a "venturesome and foolhardy move" '. Also, the *Gold Coast Leader*, which only a few months later was to support the African Movement and put a highly nationalistic interpretation on it, condemned the 'Back to Africa' movement in its issue of 31 January, declaring:

We have heard before of Mr. Alfred C. Sam and we would advise coloured folks in America not to take him and his scheme of 'Back to Africa' seriously. We would welcome our coloured American brethren as traders, agriculturists, and mechanics, but they must know clearly the conditions they are coming to meet. Our climate is as bad for coloured Americans as it is for White men, and our *Anopheles* and *Stegomyiae* may play as much havoc with the constitution and system of American Negroes as they do with Europeans and other White races. This our coloured American brethren must clearly understand.[18]

E. D. Morel's *African Mail*, with its usual concern for the land question in Africa, supported the immigration bill on the ground that it would prevent Gold Coast chiefs from speculating in land entrusted to them.[19] Perhaps the most significant criticism of Sam's African Movement, from the point of view of this study, came from one of the leading Pan-Negroists of the time—Dusé Mohammed Ali, half-Sudanese, half-Egyptian editor of the pan-coloured *African Times and Orient Review* based in London. His journal had a fairly wide circulation, and was well informed on African commerce and on abuses arising from the administration of the colonies, and its criticism of Chief Sam was bound to provide ammunition for Sam's other critics. New York papers quoted him as saying: 'The name of Albert Sam as a chief is unknown to me. All the lands in that British Colony are tribal lands, which can neither be sold nor given away by the chiefs, . . . I'm sure that even if the British Government allowed them to have their own towns, it would not permit them to set up a form of government. It would be disastrous if these people were induced to go to Africa and find themselves stranded.'[20] If Dusé was

[18] Quoted in *African Mail*, 5 June 1914, p. 360: 'A "Modern Moses"'.
[19] ibid., p. 360.
[20] Dusé Mohammed Ali quoted in Bittle and Geis, op. cit., pp. 101–2. There is some evidence that Dusé later contributed to Garvey's *Negro World*; see his article on imperialism in *Negro World* (3 June 1922). I owe this information to Garvey's widow, Mrs. Amy Jacques Garvey. Mrs. Garvey also informed the author that Dusé at one time 'worked with the U.N.I.A. as an *African Consultant*'.

hostile to this commercial aspect of Pan-Africanism, perhaps fate
or chance decreed that one of his 'office boys', a young Jamaican
who between 1912 and 1914 had come into contact with his anti-
imperialist and pan-coloured views, would draw more ambitious,
albeit equally unrealistic, conclusions from Chief Sam's African
Movement. That early disciple was Marcus Garvey who six years
later was to present the world with the spectacle of a Black Moses
and a Black Napoleon.[21] His Black Star Line was to attempt the
same venture as Chief Sam's Ethiopian Steamship Line, just as his
Universal Negro Improvement Association is reminiscent of Sam's
African Movement. What Sam initiated at the beginning of the
Great War Garvey enlarged and publicized with greater effect at the
end of that war.

In spite of Chief Sam's publicity campaign in Oklahoma, for which
the movement's newspaper *African Pioneer* was created, there were
a few Negroes who were uncertain as to the soundness of the scheme
and made inquiries at the Colonial Office. One such was J. M. Standifer
of Chandler, Oklahoma, who wrote in January 1913: 'There is in
this country a man by the name of Alfred C. Sam, claiming he is
the chief of the Akin Tribe in or near the Goald Coast District he
say he will give each Negro 60 acres of land free of charge exemticd
fram tax he says it is under the British government now what I want
to know is there any truth in what he say?' Standifer wanted advice
as he had a family of eight and a job, and did not want 'to get fooled';
he wanted to know 'whether there is any place there for the Negro in
America'.[22] The Colonial Office replied that Chief Sam did not
represent the Gold Coast Government and had no authority from
them; that no land was available for immigrants and that the West
African climate on the whole was unsuitable for Afro-Americans.[23]
A Ben Willis of Beardkin in Okfuskee Co., Oklahoma, also addressed
a similar query to the Colonial Office,[24] and towards the end of 1913,
a Dr. James G. Guess, an Afro-American from Clarksville, Oklahoma, also wrote to Sir Edward Grey about Sam's scheme.[25]

By April 1914 it appears that Chief Sam 'in view of official
opposition to his original proposals' had modified his original plan

[21] Bittle and Geis, op. cit., p. 102; Padmore, George, *Pan-Africanism or Communism?* (London, 1956), p. 88.
[22] J. M. Standifer to Colonial Office, 9 Jan. 1913, C.O. 96/554/4706.
[23] ibid.
[24] ibid., dispatch no. 10904, 3 Oct. 1914.
[25] C.O. 96/540/43, 20 Dec. 1913.

of resettling 500 Negro Americans on the Gold Coast, and had settled for 50 to 60 colonists. He had also mustered enough capital (64 sixty-fourth shares) to purchase a Cuban vessel named the *Curityba* (German built) from a Cuban shipping company, the *Compania Maritima Cubana* on 4 February 1914, for $69,000, and had applied for permission to fly the British flag. The ship was equipped primarily for trading purposes, and the Negroes on board were relatively well-to-do and willing to pay the £25 per head deposit. His British nationality and his right to register the *Curityba* as a British ship were beyond doubt, and in spite of the British Ambassador's efforts in Washington, the U.S. Government was unable to take any action against the colonization movement unless it was proved conclusively that the representations made by Sam to induce Afro-Americans to emigrate to the Gold Coast were fraudulent. As it turned out, Sam had greatly impressed Mr. J. B. Keating, the British Vice-Consul in Portland, Maine. According to Keating, Sam had agreed, in view of British opposition, to confine his movement for the time being to freighting purposes and to use the ship for cargo; Negro stockholders had first approached him and broached the scheme, and evidently were confident that he would not mislead them. There was even among the colonists a Negro (M. A. Sorrell) who was formerly a judge in one of the state courts and was now the General Secretary of the Akim Trading Company. On the whole, said Keating, although he did not know much about Sam's activities in the South, he remarked that 'throughout this man has inspired me with the opinion that he is earnest, truthful and law-abiding'.[26] Eventually, Sir Edward Grey, after consultation with the Secretary of State for the Colonies, decided that there was no alternative but to allow Sam to proceed with his modified colonization scheme, even though the scheme was 'extremely inadvisable and possibly disastrous to those concerned'.[27]

On 3 July 1914 the *Curityba*, renamed the *Liberia*, left for Saltpond, Gold Coast, via Norfolk (Virginia) and Galveston with about 60 'delegates'. On 20 August it was cleared for Saltpond at Galveston and proceeded via Pensacola and Barbados.[28] The 'delegates' were

[26] C.O. 96/540/43, enclosure to dispatch no. 14537, J. B. Keating, Vice-Consul, Portland, Maine, to the Rt. Hon. Sir Cecil Spring-Rice, British Ambassador, Washington, 19 Mar. 1914.
[27] C.O. 96/552/16336, Sir Eyre A. Crowe to the Secretary to the Board of Trade, 2 May 1914.
[28] ibid., dispatch no. 32800, 29 Aug. 1914.

'carefully selected, but rather old'; 38 of them came from Oklahoma, and only Chief Sam and the Revd. Orishatukė Faduma were British subjects. Thirty-five of the colonists gave their occupation as farmers, 2 as cooks, 1 as a mechanic, and 1 as a lumberman; 31 were males, 10 of whom were married and were accompanied by their wives. The report of the Acting Consul at Galveston stated: 'It is reliably stated that a majority of the delegates were occupiers of land and farmers in the State of Oklahoma and made a considerable sacrifice financially in disposing of their property in order to purchase stock in the s/s "LIBERIA" and to accompany her on her voyage to Africa. The appearance of most of them indicated that they were fairly well to do for coloured people.'[29] The ship's cargo was mainly lumber, cement, lime, flour, agricultural implements, and household goods valued at about $15,000.[30]

When it was learnt that the *Liberia* was actually sailing for the Gold Coast, the *Gold Coast Leader* modified its criticism of the African Movement, and condemned the Government's immigration bill as 'harsh and injurious to the interest of the colony, especially to the cause of progress of natives'; the Government's assumption that the Negro American colonists were undesirables, it said, was 'unjustified and uncalled for'. A group of Afro-Americans who, in spite of discouragements, were determined to settle on the Gold Coast, 'must, on the face of it, be an industrious body of people, eager to return to the home of their ancestors', and any government which legislated against them was also acting against the interest of the people of the Gold Coast. The *Leader*'s editorial went on to say that the development of the Gold Coast required skilled people, and Afro-American skilled workmen would help to raise the standard of local workmen:

We believe we are correct in saying that the progress of natives in the colony of Lagos has been materially assisted by the immigration of South American Negroes into the country. This immigration was encouraged by the Lagos Government, and there is not the least doubt that the repatri-ates, as we believe the immigrants are called in Lagos, have contributed very largely to the progress of skilled labour in our sister colony. It is one thing to condemn the business tactics of Chief Sam, and quite another thing to put difficulties in the way of American Negroes coming to this country to settle. The Government appear to us to have confused both

[29] ibid., dispatch no. 47479, 21 Aug. 1914, S. W. Barnes, Acting Consul, to Colville Barclay, British Chargé d'Affaires, British Embassy, Washington, D.C.
[30] ibid.

issues, and have allowed themselves to be driven into an action in the matter which thoughtful natives must condemn. . . . After all [he concluded], this country is ours. . . . It is putting a strain on our endurance for the Government to place, as they have done, difficulties in the way of American Negroes, our own kith and kin, seeking a livelihood in our country. . . . The Regulation of Immigrants Ordinance [No. 4 of 1914] is, in our opinion, a class legislation, specially directed against Black men, and our chiefs and people should see to it that that particular legislation is expunged from the Statute Book of the colony.[31]

The African Movement, however, had an able ideologist and prophet in the Revd. Orishatukė Faduma, a Sierra Leonean, formerly known as James Davies, who had studied at London University in the 1880s and at Yale, had taught for seventeen years in Negro schools in America, and was now a member of Chief Sam's party. He was brought up in Freetown by the Revd. J. C. May, and had been influenced by the ideas of Blyden and the Revd. James Johnson. In fact, most of his ideas on religious, social, and political questions closely corresponded to those of Blyden and James Johnson.[32] Between September and December 1914, while the *Liberia* was still at sea, he contributed six articles to E. D. Morel's *African Mail*, outlining the history and philosophy of the African Movement. He argued that Chief Sam had been misunderstood and that the American colonists were not undesirables. He also argued the thesis that the African Movement was not a new movement but had historical antecedents: 'There was always a feeling among Negroes in the New World to return to Africa, their mother land. In the early days of emancipation, and before emancipation, philanthropists encouraged

[31] *Gold Coast Leader*, quoted in *African Mail* (5 June 1914), p. 363: 'American Negroes and the Gold Coast'.

[32] See, e.g., his 'Christianity and Islam in Africa', *African Mail* (22 May 1914), pp. 243–5; for his paper on Christianity in Africa at the Atlanta Congress on Africa held at the Gammon Theological Seminary, Atlanta, in 1896, see Bowen, J. W. E., ed., *Africa and the American Negro*, pp. 125–36; 'Lessons and Needs of the Hour—State and Church as Trustees', *Sierra Leone Weekly News* (2 Nov. 1918), p. 4; 'African Negro Education—Race Mission and Limitation', ibid. (9 Nov. 1918); 'African Negro Education—Eclectic Education for Negro', ibid. (31 Aug. 1918), p. 6; 'Depreciation of Native Talent and Lack of Mental Scope', ibid. (24 Aug. 1918), pp. 6 and 8; 'Popular Education and the State', ibid. (17 Aug. 1918), p. 4; 'Drawbacks and Successes of Missionary Work in Africa', ibid. (20 Apr.–9 May 1918). 'Africa's Claims and Needs', *Southern Workman*, liv (May 1925), 221–5. The above is merely a short list of Faduma's extensive writings on religious and social questions in relation to Africa and the Africans; his theory of nationalism and his role in the Sierra Leone branch of the National Congress of British West Africa are dealt with in chapter III. A fuller account of his life and thought would require a short biography.

the idea. . . . Nova Scotians and Maroons from British Guiana, Jamaica, Trinidad, and other West India islands, as well as Brazil in South America, have found their way to Sierra Leone and Lagos in West Africa . . .', and Paul Cuffee had also pioneered a Negro colonization movement. Therefore it was natural, he said, that the Negro who was deprived of all his rights in America should seek to return to his original country. 'The African Movement,' he continued, 'is not a spasmodic movement. It is not the result of the teaching of fanatics, nor of men whose imagination runs amok at glowing descriptions of the land of their ancestors.' On the contrary, its members were realists as well as men motivated by ideas of freedom in which they believed.[33] For Faduma, the three leading ideas of the African Movement were Negro nationalism (which he called 'Race patriotism and Individuality'),[34] Afro-American missionary enterprise in Africa, and Afro-American participation in and leadership of the industrialization of Africa by Negro technical expertise.[35]

The sailing of the *Liberia* coincided with the outbreak of war, and she was seized as a prize vessel by a British warship off the Cape Verde Islands and escorted to Freetown, Sierra Leone, where the matter was brought before an admiralty court, a proceeding which severely affected the morale and financial resources of the colonization movement. On the way to Freetown, Sam's party passed through Bathurst, Gambia; at Bathurst, on 22 December 1914, they held a meeting, explaining the objects of the African Movement and urging the necessity of mental emancipation of the African. As Faduma said on that occasion, 'If a man is a *free* man, he must be emancipated in *thought*. He must think like a *free* man, even if he is compelled by *force majeure* to forego his rights as a free man.'[36] That almost amounted to the 'cogito' of Pan-Negro nationalism.

At Freetown, Sierra Leone, where the *Liberia* had been detained

[33] Faduma, Orishatukė, 'What the African Movement Stands for', *African Mail* (25 Sept. 1914), p. 521.

[34] 'The African movement believes that every man in a race has a soul, a divinity that is never satisfied until it finds its true self; that it profits a man nothing if he gains the whole world and loses his own soul—his higher and better self. . . . If the Negro in the United States cannot find himself as a distinct and respectable species side by side with the Anglo-Saxon, the feeling is growing that he should go anywhere to find himself. . . . They are striking his race individuality. . . . The present outburst is an outburst of the Negro soul. There is no fake or fraud in it. The heart of the movement is right. . . .' Faduma, Orishatukė, 'What the African Movement Stands For', pp. 521–2.

[35] ibid. (2 Oct. 1914), pp. 2–3.

[36] Faduma, quoted in the *Sierra Leone Weekly News* (9 Jan. 1915), p. 11.

by the naval authorities, Sam's party was invited to various social gatherings, the most important of which was the one arranged by members of the local Anti-Slavery and Aborigines Protection Society, at Victoria Park on 23 December 1914. The gathering was largely attended by leading members of the Freetown community, and the Welcome Address was made by no less a person than Bishop James Johnson. Bishop Johnson first dwelt on the hardships of the black man in America from slavery to emancipation, then welcomed the Afro-American delegates in the name of both African and Afro-American: 'As we had together been Brethren through a common slave condition, so we are to-day Brethren through a common Emancipation.' He also thought that the Afro-Americans would help missionaries and other workers in the 'up-building of our desolated Aboriginal Homeland, the repeopling of it, the regenerating of West Africa religiously, intellectually, morally, socially, and otherwise'. And in characteristic fashion he added: 'Whilst we rejoice over and are thankful for what European or White evangelization has done for us, we are persuaded that the main burden of the work rests upon Africans, Africa's children, especially us the exiled ones, who have learnt in exile many practical, and helpful lessons that the old Homeland has long been waiting for.'[37] The Bishop then dwelt at length on the intellectual and technological progress made by the black men in America: 'in spite of the prejudice of the white man that has persistently dogged your steps . . . you have truly and in large and very impressive measure indicated our Race against wicked and foolish prejudice that has stood so long against us, against the doctrine of the innate incapacity of the Negro which that prejudice, for its own interest, has so long and so perseveringly preached.' He also welcomed the African Movement idea and its commercial aspects, especially

the Ethiopian Steamship Line which has been inaugurated and which is one of the schemes that are intended to interpret it to the world. We see in it, God blessing it, great possibilities for West Africa and our Race. It is evidently calculated to promote for us a large measure of commercial and other independence. With steamships of our own, traversing the ocean to and fro between West Africa, America and England, in the

[37] *Sierra Leone Weekly News* (23 Jan. 1915), pp. 6–7. For the nationalism of Bishop James Johnson, see the excellent study by Ayandele, E. A., *The Missionary Impact on Modern Nigeria: 1842–1914* (London, 1966); id., 'An Assessment of James Johnson and His Place in Nigerian History, 1874–1917, Part 1, 1874–1890'; also Ayandele's *Holy Johnson* (London, 1970).

interest of commerce, we shall in respect of carrying power, be in a great measure commercially independent.[38]

Industry would also benefit from this steamship company, and above all, it would 'greatly facilitate the gradual return of many of our exiled brethren in America, with all the enlightenment they have acquired, to the great Fatherland . . .'. Finally, after referring to Chief Sam as the Black Moses of the African Movement, 'the Moses whom He has raised up to help to bring back African Israel to their own home from the foreign land which had been to them a land of bondage', he praised the self-sacrifice of the Afro-American colonists and expressed great interest in the colonization movement.

The Freetown press, which was already in 1915 exchanging ideas with the Gold Coast press on the possibility of launching a Pan-West African movement for political and other reforms,[39] was also optimistic about the African Movement. Of Afro-American emigration to Africa it stated: 'They had stretched their hands across the Atlantic from America to us in Africa, from one side of the Atlantic to the other. If we give them a grip . . . and let the Blacks in America unite with those in West Africa as one people, this would evoke a force which nothing can resist. *L'union fait la force*. . . . Excessive regard to the white man's thought of us will never enable us to work out our own freedom and salvation.'[40] But the nearer the *Liberia* came to the Gold Coast, the more eloquent and nationalistic the editorials of the *Gold Coast Leader* became. By late January 1915 the *Liberia* had arrived at Saltpond, where the colonists were welcomed and meetings held, though Chief Sam's frenzied activities began to indicate that plans for the resettlement of the Afro-Americans were far from sound.[41] The *Leader*, however, was more interested in the new Zionism than in its legal and technical difficulties. Whatever the colonial administration may have said about the African Movement,

[38] *Sierra Leone Weekly News* (23 Jan. 1915), pp. 6–7.
[39] See, e.g., *Sierra Leone Weekly News* (13 Mar. 1915), pp. 8–9. The idea of a Pan-West African movement was first discussed in the editorials of the *Gold Coast Leader*. On 30 Jan. 1915 an editorial of the *Gold Coast Leader* published for the first time, material dealing with the proposed West African Conference (*Gold Coast Leader* (30 Jan. 1915), pp. 4–5). The time had come, it said, for leading West African publicists to plan an early conference 'for the purpose of discussing and focusing public attention upon matters of common political interest to West Africa'. A small group of 'leading thinkers' were to meet and discuss common problems and then go back and 'educate the masses'.
[40] *Sierra Leone Weekly News* (16 Jan. 1915), p. 4.
[41] For details, see Bittle, W. E., and Geis, G., op. cit., *passim*.

said its editorial, men like Faduma, Judge Sorrell, and Dr. Dorman could hardly be regarded as adventurers in quest of fortune. These men, it continued, were 'animated by a higher motive. Their purpose is to help to link Afro-Americans and West Africans by such bonds of common interest as eventually to make the latter participators in the rich experience gained by their brethren amid so much struggle and strife.' These 'bonds of common interest', however, were rather vaguely defined, and gave the impression of a curious combination of pan-Negro idealism and transatlantic commercial enterprise. Whatever these 'bonds' might be, the *Leader* was of the opinion that

... any harsh steps taken against the pioneers of this important movement will be sure to meet the resentment of enlightened West African opinion. We ask those in authority to regard the movement as actuated by the highest impulses that can move humanity, and no matter what flaws there might be in details, to respect the wishes of a people who are yearning to receive back their exiles long lost to home and peace. ... Nor is there any harm in recording the fact that this African movement is not a new-fangled notion that has been sprung upon the attention of West Africa. Those acquainted with West African history do know that this is a purposeful idea which has been realised by years of preparation. Our dreamers dreamt dreams. They foresaw a day when the Afro-American, laden with the good things stored from the land of his exile, would seek to place them upon the lap of Africa. ... Advanced people may watch the scene with amusement. They may discredit it. They may even discourage it. But we are persuaded that no amount of ridicule or persecution is going to turn this African movement back. ... For it goes without saying that movements of this sort are rare in the history of humanity, and that this one may be the beginning of great things for West Africa.[42]

At the end of January the *Leader* again claimed that the whole of British West Africa was unanimous on the idea of the African Movement and that Africans in the four colonies would not tolerate official opposition to 'this patriotic movement' whose aim was to facilitate 'the return of suitable groups of our American compatriots'.[43] Strangely enough, the Lagos press was either indifferent to the African Movement or hostile to it. Only Sierra Leone and the Gold Coast took the movement seriously and defended it from the point of view of Negro race-consciousness,[44] just as these were the

[42] *Gold Coast Leader* (23 Jan. 1915), pp. 4–5.
[43] ibid. (30 Jan. 1914), pp. 4–5.
[44] For Nigerian criticism of Sam's African Movement and of Faduma's defence of the movement, see *Times of Nigeria* (23 Feb. 1915), p. 3, and (2–16 Mar. 1915), p. 3.

only British West African colonies which were later to spearhead and sustain the National Congress of British West Africa.

But by May 1915 the much-discussed African Movement had begun to founder on the rocks of official restrictions, legal proceedings (as a result of the reseizure of the *Liberia*), and poor planning on Sam's part. There was a shortage of food, a few deaths occurred among the colonists, Sam's credentials were uncertain, and the colonists were desperate. Judge Sorrell, who always kept a level head and seems to have been more concerned with sound business organization than Sam, then wrote to the Gold Coast Aborigines Rights Protection Society concerning the seizure of the *Liberia* and the court proceedings. In the course of the letter he added:

I think you will agree with me that, not only is the pursuit of liberty and industrial development of the Black man in the United States of America at stake upon the success of the S.S. Liberia, but the whole West Coast of Africa and its future development. Therefore, it behoves the Black man to consider well this opportunity for his commercial and industrial success, if he ever hopes to be recognised in the commercial industries of the world. . . . The darkest hour is just before day. I can see daylight dawning for the Blackman.

Sorrell added, however, that it was vital that the *Liberia* be released, as the cargo on board was valuable for trading on the West Coast, especially as the war had disrupted trade. He also added that Chief Sam had instructed him to come to the Cape Coast to assess whether conditions were favourable for settlement and commerce, but he thought that the important thing to be done was first to free the ship and then put the Akim Trading Company on a sound basis.[45]

The African Movement, however, did not get off the ground; Chief Sam's colonization party did land at Saltpond where they were given a fraternal welcome, but inadequate arrangements and other hardships compelled them to call it off. A petition from the Afro-American colonists to the Gold Coast A.R.P.S. makes this quite clear:

We the undersigned accredited delegates of American immigrants to the Gold Coast for ourselves and on behalf of all concerned now in Gold Coast West Africa and United States of America do hereby humbly petition through you for the information of the Amanhin and Ahinfu and we

[45] G.C.A.R.P.S. files: 'American Negro Immigrants'. File no. 92, 179/65, Judge M. A. Sorrell to W. S. Johnson, Secretary, G.C.A.R.P.S. (undated), Cape Coast Archives, Ghana.

sincerely hope in confidence, that you neither will ignor [sic] nor put aside this petition until you have awaken your sympathy to come to our rescue.

Since our arrival from America we have gratefully observed with deep appreciation the interest your kindness shown us as well as others with whom we have had occasion to meet, which kindness assures us of your wishes towards our movement. . . .

We therefore feel our responsibility as delegates to lay before you our present circumstances, and we do earnestly hope you will endeavour to releave [sic] us from our present suffering state.

On the 13th of January we landed at Saltpond en route, for Akim our supposed destination, we continued our journey but sad to say we returned with sad and grievous disappointment. Since we returned from interior we have been closely confined on board the Liberia, suffering from want of food and water and from strenuous exertion . . . all through mis-management of our leader Chief A. C. Sam.[46]

It is not known whether the G.C.A.R.P.S. gave any assistance to the stranded colonists; it seems that they had lost sight of Chief Sam and were being looked after by Omanhin Amonu V and his people. They urged the G.C.A.R.P.S. to 'entertain this movement as national affairs for development of this country and our race in general', to assign tracts of land to them and future Afro-American immigrants to the Gold Coast, to write a letter of recommendation stating that they supported and sympathized with the colonization movement, and to help in paying the debts incurred during the detention of the Liberia, so that the ship would be able to sail for the U.S.A.[47]

By September 1915, amid great disappointment, the African Movement collapsed, and with it the hope of a twentieth-century return of the transatlantic exiles. Most of the colonists returned to America in the R.M.S. Abosso, and the Gold Coast Leader advised sympathizers to take the failure of the scheme with the 'philosophical calm' with which Faduma had taken it, and to remember that even English emigration to America encountered similar difficulties to that of the African Movement. Faduma himself returned to Freetown, Sierra Leone, where in September 1915 he was offered, and accepted, the post of principal of the Collegiate School of the United Methodist Church. His reflections on the failure of the African Movement appeared in two articles in the Sierra Leone Weekly News, but it was still Faduma the ideologue and prophet. He began by comparing the African Movement to those of Columbus, Balboa, Magellan,

[46] G.C.A.R.P.S. files (25 May 1915), Petition of Negro Immigrants to G.C.A.R.P.S., Cape Coast.
[47] ibid.

Sir Walter Raleigh, the Pilgrim Fathers, and other pioneers, concluding:

There are no difficulties which the American or African Negro will meet in pioneering which white peoples have not met in a more terrible form. Now is the time for us to prove our manhood. Let the African and Negro scattered over the world begin to read history and its philosophy with a purpose. In this tedious and often perilous task of developing Africa by Africans, 'He that loseth his life shall find it. He that seeketh to save his life shall lose it.' . . . It is certainly better for American Negroes to die of African fever in the efforts to contribute to Africa's development, than to be riddled by the bullets of the White mob who control the local governments of the United States. . . . It is better to live even among pagans, where the majority respect their laws and life is secure, than to live in a country where only the minority are law keepers as in the Southern States.[48]

Failure, he said, was not in itself a crime: it was the inability to aim at high ideals, not failure to accomplish them, that was a crime.[49] Taking his usual intellectual approach to politics, he argued that it was ideas that motivated human action. Moses, for example, was dominated by a great idea—the emancipation of Israel; in the same way Abraham set out for a land he had never seen. No doubt, he said, in a materialistic age, such men would be labelled idiots, visionaries, or idealists and considered failures even before they could begin. But, he argued, such leaders cannot be said to have failed to the extent that their ideas were carried out in stages by their successors:

Most of the ideas of the world's thinkers are carried out in the same way. In many cases they are mere projectors and injectors of ideas to be worked out by future generations. A John Sarbah of the Gold Coast, a Blyden of Liberia, a Lardner of Sierra Leone, a Frederick Douglass of the United States, a Toussaint L'Ouverture of Haiti are among the projectors and injectors of ideas who are followed up by a large number of workers struggling to perfect their systems. Men may die but ideas and movements do not. 'Crush the movement, nip it in the bud,' we hear from high authority. How can you successfully crush the idea of human progress and emancipation? Is not liberty, is not the emancipation of the soul an instinctive and natural idea? You may retard its progress, but you cannot annihilate the idea.[50]

[48] *Sierra Leone Weekly News* (11 Sept. 1915), pp. 7–8: Faduma, O., 'The African Movement: The Perils of Pioneering—A Parallel'.

[49] ibid. (2 Oct. 1915), pp. 7–8. 'The African Movement: Its Idea and Methods.'

[50] ibid., p. 8; for the wider significance of Faduma's allusions in this quotation see Shepperson, G., 'Abolitionism and African Political Thought'.

Turning to the actual administration of the African Movement, Faduma thought that the death toll and sickness among the immigrants could have been avoided had (1) fewer delegates, about twelve or eighteen, and no women, been allowed to inspect the country and then return and report to a special committee in America, (2) provision been made for their accommodation and welfare in the Colony, and introduction to local leaders made, (3) the co-operation of the G.C.A.R.P.S. been sought to sound the opinion of the people as to the distribution of immigrants, and to explain the aims of the movement both to the people and to the Governor of the Colony. (4) The Akim Trading Company should have been thoroughly organized, with two or three managers instead of one, plus other officers as required by modern business methods. Also a quarterly examination of the company's finances should have been made by an executive committee, followed by a full written and published report on the expenditure and receipts of the company. More problems were created for the movement, he said, when more immigrants than planned were allowed on the first and only trip. That was not Chief Sam's fault, for 'so anxious were the people to get away from political and social thraldom that they overcame their leader by their piteous importunities and changed his mind'.[51] It was the desperation of a minority group, desperation born of social, political, racial, and economic disabilities, that in the last analysis gave credibility, at least initially, to Chief Sam's utopia—a twentieth-century Black Zionism. It was these same factors, brought into sharper relief by post-war dislocations, that only five years later the histrionic Marcus Garvey was to exploit so brilliantly and so successfully to launch one of the most talked-about, most far-reaching, and most criticized pan-movements—the Universal Negro Improvement Association and African Communities League.

## 2. Du Bois and Garvey: Two Schools of Pan-Africa

THE failure of Chief Sam's African Movement in 1915 was by no means the last attempt by Negroes, Afro-Americans, and Africans to protest against white political and economic dominance through the unification of race effort. The same American conditions which so powerfully led to the Chief Sam African Movement before the

[51] *Sierra Leone Weekly News* (2 Oct. 1915), p. 8; Faduma. O., 'The African Movement: Its Idea and Methods'.

outbreak of the Great War, had by the end of that war created a crisis in the Afro-American leadership. Booker Washington's death in 1915, together with the social and economic problems created by black emigration from the South to the northern cities, the disillusionment and other changes resulting from the war, meant that the black American leadership, like American politics, would not be national but multiple.[52] The rivalry between Du Bois and Garvey, both in the American and the Pan-African context, perhaps marked the most important dramatization of fundamental differences of opinion in Afro-American political and social thought since the Abolition era. Was the black American going to solve his problem in America and through the American political system or must he abandon the struggle and turn to his 'motherland of the spirit'— Africa?[53] Before we describe and assess the two Pan-African schools, however, we must first briefly consider the apparently inconsistent views of W. E. B. Du Bois on the subject of Pan-Africa, bearing in mind that our purpose is not to evaluate Du Bois and Garvey in the context of Afro-American leadership in America but by analysing their leadership of the Pan-African movements, their conception of the Pan-African idea, and African, particularly West African, reactions to them, to arrive at an assessment of their impact on African nationalism and Pan-African thinking.

Du Bois's Pan-Negroism and race ideology can be traced as far back as the 1890s, after his return from post-graduate studies in Germany where it is possible he may have been exposed to current race-theories and Pan-German strands of thought. Even in the 1890s he had eulogized Africa as the 'greater fatherland' of the black race, and by the turn of the century had even toyed with the idea of organizing a small group of Negroes to develop Africa. He had also been in correspondence with the Belgian Consul-General in the United States regarding the possibility of a 'development program' for the Congo directed by Afro-Americans, Congolese, and West Indians. In 1907 he also told the German Consul-General that black Americans would welcome economic opportunities in German West

---

[52] Broderick, Francis L., *W. E. B. Du Bois: Negro Leader in a Time of Crisis* (Stanford, Cal., 1959), pp. 106–22. Rudwick, Elliott M., *W. E. B. Du Bois: A Study in Minority Group Leadership*, chapter 8, pp. 300 ff.

[53] For a fuller discussion of this point, see Glicksberg, Charles I., 'Negro Americans and the African Dream', pp. 323–30. There is a more detailed and contemporary discussion in Essien-Udom, E. U., *Black Nationalism. The Search for Identity in America* (Chicago, Ill., 1962), chapters 1–2, pp. 321–39.

Africa.[54] Moreover, as an indication of his new race outlook, the Niagara Movement, which he launched in opposition to Booker T. Washington's leadership, had a Pan-African department which, we are told, 'corresponded with African intellectuals'.[55]

In 1915 Du Bois stated that the Pan-African Movement should forge an alliance between white and black labour, yet he also spoke of a new world-wide unity based on race. Two years later he was recommending the formation of a 'great free central African state' (which was to be the result of the amalgamation of German East Africa and the Belgian Congo) as a possible solution to the race war. By 1918 he had enlarged this Pan-African state to include Uganda, French Equatorial Africa, German South-West Africa, and Angola and Mozambique, yet he was not clear as to how this black state was to be organized and administered, nor did he make it clear whether black Americans were to be sent there as colonists or whether they should accept the integrationist philosophy and become Americans first. It is more likely, however, that he envisaged the creation of this state as a symbol of the new race-consciousness, both in America and in the colonies.[56] The Du Boisian myth of Pan-Africa had a racist ideology,[57] yet sought the co-operation of white technology and missionaries and the approval of the colonial powers who, in his definition, were the exploiters of coloured folk. It saw its Pan-African State as a socialized 'industrial democracy' run by black American intellectuals, yet it welcomed white capital and took for granted the unanimous adherence of the latter to his ideas. Whatever the precise nature of his utopia, it would still be led by the élite, both American and African ('the thinking classes of the future Negro world'), unlike Garvey's broad-based but equally nebulous 'republic of four hundred million men' which Maunier aptly called 'a Liberia of infinite proportions. . . . A strange dream very American . . . in its vastness'.[58]

To this champion of the non-white races, the relations between whites and non-whites were generally seen from the 'spiritual pro-

[54] Rudwick, op. cit., p. 210.

[55] ibid., p. 210.

[56] ibid., pp. 210–11.

[57] For the sake of clarity I have used the words 'myth', 'ideology', and 'utopia' here in the 'strong' or revolutionary sense in which they are used by Georges Sorel and Karl Mannheim respectively. For a helpful discussion of the different senses of these concepts, see Halpern, Ben, '"Myth" and Ideology" in Modern Usage', *History and Theory*, i (1960–1), 129–49.

[58] Maunier, René, *The Sociology of Colonies*, i. 414.

vincialism' of race, or as he himself put it in the oft-quoted passage: 'The problem of the twentieth century is the problem of the color line—the relation of the darker to the lighter races of men in Asia and Africa, in America and the islands of the sea.'[59]

In this new dialectic of race, the Negro question in America and colonialism would achieve a synthesis and would be internationalized in his private utopia of Pan-Africa as a dramatic illustration of that 'double consciousness' he so vividly described in *Souls of Black Folk*. As Harold Isaacs has stated in an illuminating article:

This singular personification, i.e. of Africa, was not an accident nor was it a literary convenience, for Pan-Africa was the other shape of Du Bois' dream, and while he dreamed it for Africa's fulfilment, what he really saw in it was his own.

Du Bois was a romantic racist, but through all the ups and downs and twists and turns of his thinking through the years, he never got romantic enough to choose the ultimate option of urging Negroes to migrate *en masse* to Africa. . . . Du Bois had the imagination and intelligence to see, long before anyone else, that the meaningful slogan for beleagured American Negroes as far as Africa was concerned was not *Back to Africa*, but *Africa for the Africans*, and this is what he tried to promote with his Pan-African movement. . . .

Du Bois, who had long ago chosen the path of retreat into himself, had never felt the need to retreat to Africa. . . . No, Du Bois wanted to bend Africa otherwise to his designs. He had come strongly to believe . . . that the rise of the black man in America was linked with the rise of the non-white all over the world. . . . He thought that as far as the black men were concerned, the American Negro, rising steadily in education and attainment despite all obstacles, had to take the lead. . . . He tried to bring Africans on to the world scene and to make their voices heard for the first time, in the councils of power.[60]

Even in the field of scholarship, especially in history, his views on black American and African history were heavily influenced by the geopolitics of race: 'He was *for* Negroes in history, as so many others

[59] Du Bois, W. E. B., *The Souls of Black Folk* (London, 1905), p. 13. Franck L. Schoell, comparing the 'lack of world horizon' of Booker Washington's *Rise of the American Negro* (1899) and Du Bois's *The Souls of Black Folk*, wrote: 'Dans les deux plus récents livres de Du Bois, *Le Nègre* (1915) et *Darkwater* (1920), les destinées du Nègre d'Amérique sont définitivement traitées en fonction des destinées de la race africaine tout entière. Du Bois a eu la magistrale conception de l'intégration de son tout petit monde noir d'Amérique dans l'ensemble du grand, du titanesque monde noir africain qui déborde autant sur l'Asie, d'un côté, qu'il se prolonge dans le Nouveau Monde, de l'autre.' *La Question des Noirs aux États-Unis* (Paris, 1923), pp. 229–30.

[60] Isaacs, Harold R., 'Du Bois and Africa', *Race*, i, no. 2 (Nov. 1960), 17–18.

were *against* them. Du Bois knew that a people must believe in themselves, for, as he said, no people who did not had "written its name in history".[61]

By 1915, partly through his own curiosity and partly through the influence of the anthropologist Franz Boas, Du Bois had written his first work of history dealing with aspects of African history and culture, at a time when Teutonism was rampant and when only a few Afro-American scholars like Carter Woodson, Arthur Schomburg, and John Edward Bruce took active interest in African history and civilization. Again, it was the Pan-African outlook that influenced Du Bois's historiography: 'The time has not yet come,' he wrote in 1915, 'for a complete history of the Negro peoples. Archaeological research in Africa has just begun, and many sources of information in Arabian, Portuguese, and other tongues are not fully at our command; and, too, it must frankly be confessed, racial prejudice against darker peoples is still too strong in so-called civilized centers for judicial appraisement of the peoples of Africa. . . .'[62] In the same book he observed that although Negroes throughout the world were becoming aware of their problems, 'There is as yet no great single centralizing of thought or unification of opinion, but there are centers which are growing larger and larger and touching edges. The most significant centers of this new thinking are, perhaps naturally, outside Africa and in America: in the United States and in the West Indies; this is followed by South Africa and West Africa —and then, more vaguely, by South America, with faint beginnings in East Central Africa, Nigeria and the Sudan.'[63] And in the very last paragraphs of the book he concluded:

The Pan-African movement when it comes will not, however, be merely a narrow racial propaganda. Already the more farseeing Negroes sense the coming unities: a unity of the working classes everywhere, a unity of the colored races, a new unity of men. . . . In a conscious sense of unity among coloured races there is to-day only a growing interest. There is slowly arising not only a curiously strong brotherhood of Negro blood throughout the world, but the common cause of the darker races against the intolerable assumptions and insults of Europeans has already found expression. Most men in this world are colored. A belief in humanity means a belief in colored men. . . .[64]

[61] Wesley, Charles H., 'W. E. B. Du Bois—The Historian', *Journal of Negro History*, l, no. 3 (July 1965), 161.
[62] Du Bois, W. E. B., Preface, *The Negro* (London, 1916).
[63] ibid., p. 241.                                         [64] ibid., pp. 241–2.

It is clear that by 1915 Du Bois's conception of the Pan-African movement was vague and somewhat prophetic in tendency, nor is there any indication that his new ideology was shared by other black American leaders, or that he was in touch with the thinking of West Africans like J. E. Casely Hayford who had inherited the Pan-Negro nationalism of Edward Blyden. Even in 1919 when he had with some difficulty succeeded in getting the N.A.A.C.P. to approve and help finance his Pan-African crusade, his ideas on Pan-Africanism do not seem to have gone beyond that of a 'great single centralizing of thought or unification of opinion' in a kind of Niagara International. Accordingly, when Du Bois arrived in Paris in February 1919, the arrangements for a Pan-African conclave were very much *ad hoc*; it was only through the good offices of M. Blaise Diagne, Senegalese deputy and Commissioner General during the war in charge of the recruitment of black troops, that the congress was allowed to meet in Paris. In fact, Du Bois was fully aware of the difficulties and possible frustrations of his Pan-African crusade.[65] Whether the American and French Governments approved of it is uncertain; what is certain is that a congress of Negro intellectuals 'guided' by Messrs. Diagne and Du Bois was less likely to embarrass the Americans, who had preached so much about democracy and self-determination, or irritate the French who had so proudly proclaimed equality and fraternity, minus liberty, in their colonies.

The Pan-African Congress met on 19, 20, and 21 February in Paris in one of the rooms of the Grand Hotel at the Boulevard des Capucines. The Executive Committee consisted of Blaise Diagne (chairman), Du Bois (secretary), Mrs. Ida Gibbs Hunt (assistant secretary), and Mr. E. F. Fredericks, a lawyer from Trinidad. The Congress also maintained an office at the Hotel de Maulte at 63, Rue Richelieu. Fifty-seven delegates, including Africans abroad, represented fifteen countries: the United States (16 delegates), French colonies (13), Haiti (7), France (7), Liberia (3, including the future President C. D. B. King), Spanish colonies (2), and the Portuguese colonies, San Domingo, England, British Africa, French Africa, Algeria, Egypt, Belgian Congo, and Abyssinia one delegate

[65] In a report on his trip to France, Du Bois wrote: '. . . The difficulties of this undertaking have been and still are enormous. It is quite possible that I can accomplish nothing worth while . . . nevertheless the attempt was in my opinion worth while. . . .' Special File: '"Pan Africa", 1919', Fisk University Library. I owe this information to Dr. Kenneth King who worked on the Du Bois papers at Fisk University.

each. France was represented by the Chairman of the Committee of Foreign Affairs of the French Chamber, M. Franklin Bouillon; Belgium by M. Van Overgergh of the Belgian Peace Commission; Portugal by M. Freire d'Andrade, former Minister of Foreign Affairs; the United States was represented by William English Walling and Charles E. Russell.

M. Delafosse, historian, ethnologist, and authority on African questions, wrote a long and sympathetic article on the Pan-African Congress in the *Bulletin du Comité de l'Afrique Française*.[66] In that article he declared that of all the races whose fate was being decided at the Peace Conference then sitting at Paris, the Negro race had more reason to be anxious. It should surprise no one, he said, that representatives of that race had seen fit to exploit that opportunity by internationalizing their problems through such a gathering. Geographical unity based on race was not sought, nor was independence or statehood their aim. Their main purpose was to bring attention to elementary rights to be guaranteed by the colonizing power.[67] Unlike most of the hostile white critics of the Pan-African Congress, M. Delafosse rightly conceded to them the right to call themselves a Pan-African gathering.[68] He added that the absence from such a conclave of the Bambara, the Bobo, or the Banziri was due not so much to their hostility to such union as to their ignorance of its existence. Although Pan-African in a racial sense, politically, most of the issues discussed would be local ones affecting the different groups and experiences were bound to be different.[69]

Various speeches were made at this Congress, some of them reformist and mildly critical of colonial rule. Blaise Diagne eulogized

[66] On the whole, the French press gave wider and more sympathetic coverage to the 1919 Pan-African Congress than either the American or the British press. *The Times* coverage on 24 Feb. 1919, p. 9, entitled 'Rights of Coloured Races: Protection of League Demanded' was laconic and non-committal. Its version of the Congress resolutions differed slightly from that given in *Dépêche Coloniale* (25 Feb. 1913), see the comments by Delafosse in footnotes 1–5, p. 55 'Le Congrès panafricain', *Bulletin du Comité de l'Afrique Française*, xi, no. 3 (1919–20).

[67] Delafosse, op. cit., p. 53.

[68] ibid., pp. 53–4.

[69] M. Delafosse's views on the Pan-African Congress seem to have been accepted by most Paris newspapers and even some government publications like the *Dépêche Coloniale* (7 and 11 Mar. 1919: 'Les Vouex du congrès panafricain') and *Le Mouvement Geographique—Journal populaire des sciences geographiques*, deuxième année, no. 22 (1 June 1919), 255–7: 'Le Congrès panafricain'. The latter article dwelt almost exclusively on the land issue and reproduced Delafosse's views on the land question almost verbatim.

French rule: even the atrocities of Portuguese and Belgian rule were glossed over, although Afro-American speakers gave the impression of dissatisfaction with their progress in America. Among other things, the Congress petitioned the Peace Conference to administer the ex-German territories in Africa as a *condominium* on behalf of the indigenous peoples. The Congress also resolved:

(A) That the allied and associated governments establish an international code of laws for the protection of the natives of Africa and that a permanent secretariat in the League of Nations should be established to see to the application of these laws.

(B) The Negroes of the world demand that henceforth the natives of Africa and the peoples of African origin should be governed in accordance with the following principles: [70]

1. *The Land.*—The soil and its natural resources shall be reserved and held in trust for the natives; and that they shall have effective ownership of such land as they can profitably develop. [71]

2. *Capital.*—The system of concessions shall be so regulated as to prevent the exploitation of the natives and the exhaustion of the natural wealth of the country. These concessions should always be temporary and subject to State control. Note should be taken of the growing needs of the natives and part of the profits should be used for work relating to the moral and material development of the natives. [72]

3. *Labour.*—Slavery and corporal punishment shall be abolished, and forced labour, except in punishment of crime, and conditions of labour shall be prescribed and regulated by the State.

4. *Education.*—It shall be the right of every native child to learn to read and write his own language, and the language of the trustee nation, at public expense, and to be given technical instruction in some branch of industry. The State shall also educate as large a number of natives as possible in higher technical instruction in some branch of industry. The State shall also educate as large a number of natives as possible in higher technical and cultural training and maintain a corps of native teachers. . . . [73]

[70] The text quoted by Delafosse differs from those quoted in *The Times*, art. cit., and in Legum, Colin, *Pan Africanism: A Short Political Guide*, Appendix I, p. 151, para. (c). The text, as given by the Congress to the French press and reproduced by M. Delafosse, reads: 'B. Les Noirs du monde demandent que, dorénavant, les indigènes d'Afrique et les peuples d'origine africaine soient gouvernés selon les principes suivants *partout où ceux-ci ne sont pas déjà appliqués.*' My emphasis.

[71] Again, the text in *The Times*, art. cit., simply reads: '. . . shall have effective ownership of the lands they cultivate'.

[72] Colin Legum's emphasis here differs slightly from the French version.

[73] There are minor discrepancies here, perhaps due to translation, between the texts in Legum, Padmore, Delafosse, and *The Times*. Delafosse, op. cit., p. 55 n. 3, is particularly critical of *The Times* text, whereas Legum maintains Padmore's

*5. Health.*—It ought to be understood that existence in the tropics requires special safeguards as well as a scientific system of public hygiene. The State ought to take responsibility for medical treatment and health conditions, without prejudice to missionary and private initiative. A service of medical assistance, provided with doctors and hospitals, shall be established by the State.[74]

*6. The State.*—The natives of Africa must have the right to participate in the Government as fast as their development permits, in conformity with the principle that the Government exists for the natives, and not the natives for the Government. They shall at once be allowed to participate in local and tribal government, according to their ancient usage, and this participation shall gradually extend, as education and experience proceed, to the higher offices of state; to the end that, in time, Africa is ruled by consent of the Africans . . . whenever it is proved that African natives are not receiving just treatment at the hands of any State or that any State deliberately excludes its civilized citizens or subjects of Negro descent from its body politic and culture, it shall be the duty of the League of Nations to bring the matter to the notice of the civilized world.

With the passing of these resolutions the Negro and colonial question became internationalized in the new era of open diplomacy. Of particular interest is the fact that on questions like labour, civil, and human rights the Congress anticipated future developments in the duties of international organizations by charging the League of Nations and its Labour Bureau with such responsibilities. It is interesting to note that neither the French, nor the British, nor the American press included the second part of resolution 6 in their press coverage of this Congress.

It is unlikely, in spite of Du Bois's claim, that the Congress made any contribution to the evolution of the Mandates System,[75] and it is more unlikely that its arguments for racial equality convinced anyone in Europe,[76] although it is possible that it succeeded in persuading the League to protect the rights of coloured labour. In the end, its optimism proved its ineffectiveness. The men who were settling the affairs of Europe at Paris were talking *realpolitik* and Africa was merely one of their bargaining counters. They might

---

version of the text throughout. Cf. Padmore, G., *Pan-Africanism or Communism?*, pp. 124–5. But see *History of the Pan-African Congress*, ed. G. Padmore (London, 1963), p. 16.

[74] Neither Padmore nor Legum includes this section of the resolution.

[75] See Louis, Wm. Roger, 'The United States and the African Peace Settlement of 1919: The Pilgrimage of George Louis Beer', *Journal of African History*, iv, no. 3 (1963), 413–33.

[76] Even a powerful Japan was denied racial equality after the war.

make a moral gesture here and there, perhaps, but it was unrealistic to ask them to take a Pan-African manifesto seriously. The Congress itself, although financed by the N.A.A.C.P., did not have the enthusiastic support of the vast majority of Afro-Americans. There were even critics of Du Bois in the N.A.A.C.P. who counselled 'Americanism' first rather than Pan-Africanism. To most Afro-Americans Du Bois's Congress was merely a distant manifestation organized by leading Negro intellectuals. Africans in Africa, however, though slightly critical, were far more optimistic and more determined to assert themselves in the post-war world. Of the 1919 Pan-African Congress an editorial of the *Sierra Leone Weekly News* commented:

Congresses are good, but their establishment is after all a small matter—comparatively. The Pan-African Congress is a Congress of living Wills; but for years to come it shall have, opposed to its interests living Wills as formidable as Hell. . . . And has it occurred to the Negro leaders of the twentieth century that immediately after peace has come to its own in Europe and the world is delivered from the present unrest, the war to follow will be the war for the emancipation of the Negro race from European philosophizings about the Negro, and from the determination to poison Negro consciousness at the source?[77]

The radical *Gold Coast Leader* observed that the Pan-African Congress had done two things: it had brought representatives of fifteen African communities, including West Africa, onto a common platform, and had presented a 'united front' on race questions. Secondly, it had 'raised certain specific issues which the Peace Conference cannot possibly ignore and to which attention must be given if all the talk about making the world safe for Democracy is not mere vapour'. The *Leader* found minor points to criticize in the Pan-African manifesto, but was in general agreement:

There are minor propositions that may be criticized and the points of view implied corrected. But we must remember that the Congress was proceeding by such knowledge and information it possessed; and it stands to reason, for instance, that if West Africa had not been debating instead of taking prompt action, British West African representatives to the Congress might have usefully compared notes to the lasting benefit of entire West Africa. . . .
    The lesson is obvious. World interests and world policies have so contracted that there is no standing still. . . . We must be up and doing, or else go under. In plain words, if we don't think and act and make

[77] *Sierra Leone Weekly News* (12 June 1919), p. 7.

representations, others will do all three for us. . . . . *West Africans will do well to remember that to most of our Afro-American and West Indian friends we are still in the back woods of civilisation—unlettered, untutored, very much requiring articulation through our brethren on the other side of the Atlantic. They know no better. They have no means of judging. It is for us to enlighten them, to make them realise that nationhood has dawned in the West African horizon,* and that we mean to take our free, independent place in the great Imperial Chain.*[78]*

The *Leader* concluded by predicting that the next Pan-African Congress (1921) would be a far more representative gathering, that by then the Congress movement in West Africa would have been fully launched, and that West Africa would be able to be 'officially represented' at the 1921 Congress. Meanwhile it was advising its readers, as the *Crisis* had advised its readers, to 'brush up their French, for British and French interests in West Africa stand or fall together now and in the future'.[79]

At the same time on the other side of the Atlantic another brand of Pan-Africanism, more flamboyant and messianistic, and appealing directly to the black working class, was challenging Du Bois's right to speak for the new Pan-African movement. This was the Universal Negro Improvement Association and African Communities League led by the Jamaican Marcus Garvey. Garvey founded the U.N.I.A. as early as 1914 in Jamaica, after which he went to the United States where he considerably expanded its membership between 1917 and 1925,[80] and even established branches of the movement in South America, the West Indies, and in Africa. His petty-bourgeois nationalism was based on race and economic self-help through collective race effort. To this end he encouraged the establishment of Afro-American stores and co-operatives and launched the short-lived Black Star Steamship Company. Although a late-comer to Afro-American politics in America, Garvey by 1920 posed a serious challenge to the leadership of the Negro élite, for post-war conditions were such that the black masses readily re-

[78] *Gold Coast Leader* (12 July 1919), p. 3. My emphasis; the reference to 'nationhood' is to the new Pan-West African movement which is dealt with in chapters III to VI.

[79] ibid., cf. Rudwick, op. cit., p. 215.

[80] For details of the Garvey movement, see Garvey, Marcus, *Philosophy and Opinions of Marcus Garvey or Africa for the Africans,* edited and compiled by Amy Jacques-Garvey, 2 vols. (New York, 1923, 1925); Garvey, Amy Jacques-, *Garvey and Garveyism* (Kingston, Jamaica, 1963); Cronon, E. D., *Black Moses* (Madison, Wis., 1955).

sponded to the oratory, flamboyance, pomp, and spectacle and, above all, the appeal to race pride and the fiction of an African homeland of this black messiah. Garvey preached the liberation of Africa and linked it with the struggle of the blacks in America, arguing that the condition for a strong and united Pan-Negro movement lay in the economic strength and self-sufficiency of the black man in America. But from the outset he regarded Du Bois with contempt and suspicion, and his paper *Negro World* constantly heaped abuse on mulattoes and the N.A.A.C.P.[81] Curiously enough Du Bois's reaction was not immediate. Though critical of Garvey's economics, his flamboyance, lack of diplomatic tact in his rabid anti-imperialism and his dealings with the Liberian government where he hoped to settle black Americans, and of his intemperate attacks on American mulattoes, Du Bois was still impressed by Garvey's honesty and leadership; he was particularly interested in Garvey's idea of a self-sufficient black economy which might benefit blacks outside America and in the new self-respect Garvey had instilled into his black followers. Indeed, Du Bois himself had at one time advocated the self-sufficient black economy, very similar to present day Black Power economics.

What then were the ideological differences between Garvey's and Du Bois's concepts of Pan-Africa? The public controversy between the two men and their rival organizations certainly make it appear that their differences were fundamental.[82] It is true that their styles and concept of leadership differed, and we may even grant with Padmore that the Pan-Africanism of Garvey favoured capitalism while that of Du Bois was committed to socialism. It seems, however, that Padmore (aided by revisionist hindsight) exaggerates the differences when he asserts:

Common ground between them, there was none. Their concepts of political philosophies and economic systems were diametrically opposed. Dr. Du Bois was not only firmly against transporting American Negroes back to Africa, but was a staunch advocate of complete self-government for Africans in Africa organized on the basis of socialism and co-operative economy which would leave no room for millionaires, black or white. National self-determination, individual liberty, and democratic socialism constituted the essential elements of Pan-Africanism as expounded by Dr. Du Bois.[83]

[81] See, e.g., Sheppard, Wheeler, 'Mistakes of Dr. W. E. B. Du Bois . . .', pts. 1 and 2, *Negro World* pamphlet (1921–2).
[82] Rudwick, op. cit., pp. 216–21.        [83] Padmore, op. cit., p. 106.

First it must be remembered that on Pan-Negro nationalism and the segregated economy as well as on the future liberation of Africa by Negro Americans the two men were agreed. Secondly Du Bois's hatred of Anglo-Saxon Imperialism was merely a little less intense than Garvey's, and although a socialist he would have welcomed Anglo-Saxon capital, especially in the colonies. Thirdly, although it is true that Du Bois rejected Afro-American emigration to Africa, it is incorrect to suggest that Garvey advocated it. Garvey's extremism may suggest such a policy but in reality in his confused way he was advocating the same policy as Du Bois. What Garvey preached was 'Africa for Africans abroad and at home' and it is arguable that his projected African Republic was merely a utopia, a political myth, to galvanize mass support among lower-class black Americans to combat the integrationist ideology.[84] Finally, Padmore seems to be reading a later and more radical concept of Pan-Africanism into the concept Du Bois had of it in the 1920s, forgetting that in the 1920s Du Bois was very much an undecided socialist still looking for 'the right program of socialism' and generally limiting his appeal to the black 'aristocracy' of 'brains and character'.[85] It is significant that almost fifty years later, with the emergence of Black Power ideology in Afro-American and Caribbean politics, the Garvey–Du Bois dispute should be revived, embodying the old rivalry between black American and West Indian activists—a rivalry that seems to have little relevance to the actual political struggle.[86] It will be interesting to see how far the ideology and radicalism of Black Studies in the United States will affect Afro-American historiography. Already there are signs of a reassessment of Du Bois and Garvey both within a Third World and Afro-American context.

In 1921 Garvey held his second Negro Convention at Liberty Hall in New York amid great pomp, parades, and oratory principally to demonstrate his support and to challenge Du Bois's moderate brand of Pan-Africanism.[87] After a savage attack on Du Bois's leadership, he repeated his extreme racialist philosophy by arguing that unlike Du Bois's movement the U.N.I.A. sought neither integration nor social equality but 'race purity' and 'dignity'. After the congress telegrams were sent 'on behalf of the 400,000,000

---

[84] See Essien-Udom, op. cit., pp. 37 n. 43, 57–9, 61.
[85] Rudwick, op. cit., pp. 251–2.
[86] See Cruse, Harold, *The Crisis of the Negro Intellectual* (London, 1969).
[87] For details, see Cronon, op. cit., *passim*; Rudwick, op. cit., pp. 118–21.

Negroes of the world' to President Warren Gamaliel Harding of the U.S.A., to Charles Evans Hughes U.S. Secretary of State, Eamon de Valera, King George V, and Mahatma Gandhi, assuring Gandhi of Negro support 'for the rapid emancipation of India from slavery and foreign oppression'.[88]

1919–20 had witnessed serious race riots in the United States, constitutional agitation in India, and economic and political unrest in several British African colonies, in South Africa, and the Belgian Congo. The 'rising tide of colour' took various forms in different parts but on the whole it was believed that this new race-consciousness was a direct result of the Great War and that it was stimulated by Negro American self-assertion. It was under these circumstances that the first session of the 1921 Pan-African Congress met in London on 27–29 August. Again, the Congress was financed by Afro-Americans and largely organized by Du Bois in spite of the reluctant support of the N.A.A.C.P. After some rather unfruitful meetings with the Aborigines Protection Society and with sympathetic Labour Party intellectuals in London, the 113 delegates to the Congress met at Central Hall, Westminster, on Saturday afternoon the 27th. At this session in particular, the most widely discussed topics were segregation, the colour-bar, and the West African land question: 'There was the general aspect—West Africans were involved here in common with Negroes the world over in what they deem a widespread grievance—the colour bar.'[89] Apart from the fact that the African delegation was larger than that of 1919, principally because of the Africans resident in London, an interesting feature of this session was its lack of any programme or list of speakers: '. . . and the speakers called upon, either on the eve of the opening session or as they sat in the hall, to express their views on the problems of their race were mostly unprepared with their remarks. No papers were read, and the result was all the more interesting. Called upon at a moment's notice . . . the speakers spoke with all sincerity and few notes of bitterness.'[90] The meeting was opened in the absence of Blaise Diagne by Dr. John Alcindor, a West Indian doctor practising in London who was also Chairman of the African Progress Union in London. Dr. Alcindor urged restraint and circumspection

---

[88] 'Le Deuxième Congrès panafricain', *Congo* (June–Dec. 1921), pp. 568–70.
[89] 'West Africa and the Pan African Congress', Supplement to the *African World* (30 Oct. 1921), p. xi.
[90] *West Africa* (3 Sept. 1921), p. 988.

in all discussions so as not to give observers the impression that governments were the enemies of the African races. 'Governments,' he continued, 'were not the enemies of the African races. They themselves were their own enemies just because they lacked character, they lacked education, they lacked cohesion. That was the trouble. . . . The public conscience was awakening to the fact that it was not well with Africa and the Africans. It was their duty to speed up that awakening and galvanize it into activity by means of wise propaganda.'[91]

Du Bois, 'clear of speech and persuasive and courtly of manner', spoke next, briefly outlining the history of the Congress from 1900. The 1900 Congress had met, he said, in spite of the inability of governments to see why coloured people from different backgrounds should meet on one platform to discuss race problems, in order to make it known that their collective grievances constituted a world problem. Partly as a counter to Garvey's challenge and partly as an explanation to white American liberals and conservative Afro-Americans who were critical of his Pan-African venture, Du Bois admitted that it was 'somewhat peculiar' and 'rather funny' that about a dozen black intellectuals should in 1919 have formed a Pan-African group

representing folk who were not by any means fully conscious they were being represented, since the delegates were delegates of a very small part of the organised and non-organised part of the Negro world and people might say very easily that they might call it a Pan-African Congress if they wished but it was a matter of words. What did they mean when they called it 'Pan-African'. What they meant was that in the history of the world there were groups and developing groups of negroes. For a very long time the negroes of the British Dominions had been going on with their own problems. They were British subjects and their problems were problems of the British Empire. In exactly the same way in the United States perfectly good and sincere people had said they had problems of their own to look after. They were American citizens; their problems were the problems of America and the place to settle them was in America. And then in a more impressive way the people of negro descent of France and her Dominions said . . . they were citizens of France represented in the Chamber of Deputies . . . recognised under the law as absolutely equal, not only recognised but treated as equals. While, of course, there were problems under the French Government and her colonies, nevertheless they were problems of Frenchmen, not even problems of Africans,

[91] 'West Africa and the Pan-African Congress', Supplement to the *African World* (30 Oct. 1921), p. xi.

and to be settled in France. But there was a certain common denominator to all that. Throughout the world there had been opposition, a disposition not to treat civilised negroes as civilised, a disposition to consider that negro races existed in the world chiefly for the benefit of white races, a disposition to draw colour lines and race lines. All these things together, apart from the problems in the particular countries constituted a world problem. . . . They had begun to see more or less dimly there was in the world an international problem and they had got to talk about it.[92]

Du Bois, however, was realistic about what such international gatherings could achieve; for the time being, his aim was to get delegates to meet each other and discuss the problems of their particular countries in the light of a more general but in many ways related problem. Meanwhile, an attempt would be made at the second session in Brussels to make the Pan-African movement 'into an international and permanent organisation'.

Several speakers followed Du Bois at the London session. Mr. Peter Thomas, a Lagos merchant, spoke on the evils of segregation in ships and on land. Segregation, he said, was a system which was usually justified in West Africa on the ground that it was a method of preventing malaria. Mosquitoes, however, were no respecters of persons; the cause of malaria was not the African but the mosquito, 'Let them turn their attention to the mosquito and not to the African. Eliminate the mosquito and not the man.'[93] Dr. Ojo Olaribigbe, later to be connected with the Gambia branch of the National Congress of British West Africa, also made a sharp attack on the policy of segregation, asserting that the morality of the white man in Africa was worse than the bite of the mosquito. Dr. John Alcindor, like most of the Afro-Americans who later spoke on the subject, argued that apart from its medical aspects segregation in general equals discrimination, equals inferiority of the segregated, and was therefore undemocratic. Saturday's meeting ended in the evening when Miss Jessie Faussett, literary editor of the *Crisis*, spoke about African women, mentioning the educational work of Mrs. Casely Hayford and Miss Kathleen Easmon of Sierra Leone.

The second day of the London session opened on Monday morning, 29 August. Most of the delegates having met each other and exchanged views, the attendance was larger and included Mrs. Coleridge-Taylor, the Afro-American singer Roland Hayes, Mr.

[92] ibid., pp. xi–xii.
[93] ibid., p. xii; also *West Africa* (3 Sept. 1921), p. 992.

Barbour James, S. H. Baptist, Ayodele Williams, and F. W. Dove. Du Bois was in the chair and the subject was 'the great question of the ownership of land, particularly in Africa'. The Revd. W. B. Marke of Sierra Leone mixed praise of British justice with criticism of land policy in West Africa, especially on Chief Oluwa's case, concluding with a warning to the whole Congress, to the effect that 'If they did not respect themselves none would respect them. God helped those who helped themselves.'[94] The next speaker was Mr. L. B. Agusto of Lagos who 'made one of the most original speeches of the Congress, though certain ideas of his were dissented from'. Agusto's speech was uncompromising and brutally realistic. The black man, he argued, was not humiliated, exploited, and discriminated against merely because of his colour; these things were done to black men, he said, 'because of the belief that as a race they were unable to hold their own in the civilised world'. Like most young Asian and African nationalists who had drawn inspiration from Japan's power and spectacular combination of tradition and modernity, Agusto told his audience that it was only when the black man could effectively defend himself against Europeans, like the Japanese, that he would be respected as an equal. But Agusto was also a Moslem and was therefore unable to advocate passive obedience or even non-violence: 'As a Moslem he believed in the teaching of the Koran. He took the middle course between those who advocated constitutional fighting and brute force.'[95] Their wrongs, he continued, could never be righted by constitutional means—English men left him in no doubt about that:

. . . their ill treatment did not rest at all on racial grounds. It rested primarily on their political inferiority and when he said 'political' he was not talking about constitutional inferiority but militaristic and nothing more. There was no use discussing their grievances—they were too well known. They must be independent. They had their own national pride. . . . They should do something to be articulate not in theory but in practice. . . . If they did not start they could never end. . . . With regard to cohesion, there he believed the real wrong rested. When they had it, they would have achieved their salvation. . . . What he wanted the Congress to do

[94] Supplement to *African World*, op. cit., p. xiii.
[95] ibid. It is also interesting to note that Agusto, the first Moslem lawyer in Nigeria, was very influential in the history and politics of the Moslem community in Lagos, especially the Ahmadiyya Movement, which most of the progressive young Lagos Moslems joined just after 1916. See Fisher, Humphrey J., 'The Ahmadiyya Movement in Nigeria', *St. Anthony's Papers*, No. 10, *African Affairs*, *No. 1*, ed. Kenneth Kirkwood (London, 1961), pp. 62–4, 73–4.

was to suggest practical methods so as to bring about their own emancipation.[96]

Agusto's solution, though falling into the category of the usual Pan-Negro utopianism was nevertheless more realistic and perhaps more practical than the resolutions of a grand Congress. He suggested a 'help Liberia' scheme to be based on the financial contribution of Negroes. This, he argued, would help to make Liberia 'a second Japan' and silence the critics who had put about the idea that Haiti, Abyssinia, and Liberia were incapable of conducting themselves as modern states.

Councillor J. R. Archer, ex-Mayor of Battersea, took the chair at the afternoon session, stating that he hoped the British government would heed the growing political demands of the colonial peoples. He introduced Mr. Saklatvala who was then the prospective Labour candidate for Parliament for the Borough of Battersea.[97] Saklatvala gave the delegates the greetings of the Indian people, stating that India was very proud to be a part of the coloured world, and that coloured people ought to be proud of themselves. Mr. Marryshaw of Grenada, West Indies, said that although all the races in the West Indies were equal before the law and there was equality of opportunity, they were still governed by an archaic Crown Colony system, and his mission in London was 'the culmination of the agitation of the West Indian people for representative government'. He added that the standard of the population of Grenada was low, coloured men with wives and children working for $\frac{1}{2}d$. a day, which was an impossible situation for which British capitalism must take a large share of the blame.[98] Much of the discussion during the afternoon session centred on West Indian questions.

In the evening speeches were given by W. F. Hutchison (Gold Coast), John Eldred Taylor, and the Revd. E. G. Granville Sutton (formerly of Sierra Leone). Hutchison gave a long and interesting paper on the subject of Africa and Europe in the Blyden manner,

[96] Supplement to *African World*, op. cit., p. xiv.
[97] Saklatvala Shapurji was in fact elected to Parliament, though not in 1921, see *The Times* (21 Jan. 1929), p. 7, col. 5. He was also connected with the League Against Imperialism in the late 1920s. Padmore describes him as 'a brilliant left-wing Labour Party M.P. . . . a dynamic personality, who denounced British imperialism both in Parliament and from public platforms up and down Britain . . . The most independent-minded Communist ever. A Titoist before Tito!' Padmore, op. cit., p. 328.
[98] *The Times* (30 Aug. 1921), p. 10: 'A Pan-African Manifesto: "No Eternally Inferior Races" '.

digressing sometimes to deal with West African themes. He was also very anxious to emphasize the fact that the concept 'Africa' was a vague one and that there were in fact many Africas from different points of view.[99] Eldred Taylor criticized Lloyd George's handling of the South African delegation but praised the Gold Coast and West African administrations for giving opportunities and responsible posts to properly qualified Africans. Towards the end of the evening session Miss Alice Werner of the School of Oriental Studies, London, asked if indirect rule was a good policy. Mr. Peter Thomas the Lagos merchant 'emphatically dissented':

He pointed out that even in that country [England] revolutions had from time to time changed the form of Government. They in Africa had assimilated the ideas of the Colonising Powers. In a Northern Nigerian Emirate what Native dare rise against any oppressor? The people who had been taught to look at things from a Western point of view, were not satisfied with conditions as they had existed thirty or forty years ago. Native laws and native customs were hidebound for all time.[1]

The London session of the 1921 Pan-African Congress was perhaps the most radical of all the Congresses. Most of the speakers openly criticized aspects of colonial policy and of life in America, and the resolutions passed at the end of the session were soberly presented but remarkably outspoken in their condemnation of imperialism and racism. These resolutions became known as the *Declaration To The World* or the *London Manifesto*.[2] The Declaration stated, among other things:

The Suppressed Races through their thinking leaders are demanding:
1. The recognition of civilised men as civilised despite their race and colour.
2. Local self-government for backward groups, deliberately rising as experience and knowledge grow to complete self-government under the limitations of a self-governed world.
3. Education in self-knowledge, in scientific truth and in industrial technique, undivorced from the art of beauty.
4. Freedom in their own religion and customs and with the right to be non-conformist and different.
5. Co-operation with the rest of the world in government, industry and art on the basis of Justice, Freedom and Peace.

[99] *African World* Supplement, op. cit., p. xiv.
[1] ibid., p. xv.
[2] For the full text, see Appendix I.

6. The ancient common ownership of the Land and its natural fruits and defence against the unrestrained greed of invested capital.[3]

7. The establishment under the League of Nations of an international institution for the study of Negro problems.

8. The establishment of an international section of the Labour Bureau of the League of Nations, charged with the protection of native labour.

The *Declaration* continued:

The world must face two eventualities; either the complete assimilation of Africa with two or three of the great world states, with political, civil and social power and privileges absolutely equal for its black and white citizens, or the rise of a great black African State, founded in Peace and Good Will, based on popular education, natural art and industry and freedom of trade, autonomous and sovereign in its internal policy, but from its beginning a part of a great society of peoples in which it takes its place with others as co-rulers of the world.

In some such words and thoughts as these we seek to express our will and ideal and the end of our untiring effort. . . . The absolute equality of races, physical, political and social, is the founding stone of World Peace and human advancement. No one denies great differences of gift, capacity and attainment among individuals of all races, but the voice of Science, Religion and practical Politics is one in denying the God-appointed existence of super-races or of races naturally and inevitably inferior. . . .

The insidious and dishonourable propaganda which for selfish ends so distorts and denies facts as to represent the advancement and development of certain races as impossible and undesirable should be met with widespread dissemination of the truth. . . .

The beginning of Wisdom in interracial contact is the establishment of political institutions among suppressed Peoples. The habit of democracy must be made to encircle the earth. Despite the attempt to prove that its practice is the secret and divine Gift of the Few, no habit is more natural and more widely-spread among primitive peoples or more easily capable of development among wide masses. . . .[4]

In West Africa itself there was no official connection between the Pan-African Congress and the N.C.B.W.A.,[5] although Robert Broadhurst, secretary of the London African Progress Union,

---

[3] Padmore's phrasing of this clause is slightly different; this was the clause that was to frighten Blaise Diagne into calling the Manifesto 'Bolshevist' at the Brussels session.

[4] *African World* Supplement, op. cit., pp. xv–xvi.

[5] Schoell, op. cit., p. 239, however, states: 'D'abord, le contact définitif a été établi avec les trois ou quatre organisations indigènes qui font en Afrique sur une plus petite échelle et avec des moyens moins puissants, ce que fait la N.A.A.C.P. en Amérique: le National Congress of British West Africa, le South African Native Congress, l'African Political Organization, l'Union Congolaise.'

acted as liaison between the two organizations and urged the local executive of the N.C.B.W.A. to authorize the setting up of local fund-raising organizations to support the Pan-African Congress and to send delegates to London to open a West African branch of the Pan-African Congress there.[6]

The Pan-African Congress moved to Brussels for its second session, which lasted from 30 August to 2 September and was held in the Palais Mondial. Blaise Diagne presided, aided by Du Bois, Miss Faussett, General Sorela, the founder of the Spanish Anti-Slavery society, two Belgian liberals Messrs. Henri La Fontaine and Paul Otlet who acted as general secretaries of the Congress, General Gillain of the French colonial service, M. Barthelemy, and Paul Panda Farnana, secretary of the *l'Union Congolaise* in Belgium. Among the delegates were some English-speaking Africans, a few French-speaking Negroes, Afro-Americans, and two Portuguese Africans—José do Magalhaes (Angola) who was a member of the Portuguese Parliament and a professor at the Lisbon School of Tropical Medicine, and Nicola de Santos Pinto, a mulatto planter from San Thomé, also a member of the Portuguese Parliament. There were also several missionaries present. Diagne opened the session with a long speech in elegant French, declaring that the Congress was concerned with securing equal rights, not with communism, and that the Negroes having fought in the Great War were entitled to certain rights and privileges. Du Bois followed, then M. Barthelemy, French deputy for Arras, paid tribute to Diagne and emphasized medical and educational work in the colonies. Dr. Vitalien, former doctor to Menelik II, pointed to the example of Ethiopia, concluding that Negroes were capable of great achievements. Paul Panda, the Congolese delegate, protested against the propaganda of the German press against the black troops used in the occupation of Germany.[7]

[6] Robert Broadhurst to the editor, *The Aurora* (22 Oct. 1921), p. 6. Broadhurst was also the assistant secretary for England to the London session of the Pan-African Congress in 1921.

[7] For a report of the proceedings of the Brussels session, see *La Tribune Congolaise* (8 Sept. 1921), no. 13, p. 3. Paul Panda Farnana, secretary of the *l'Union Congolaise* in Belgium, was educated in Belgium and took a diploma in agricultural science. Among his patrons were the Belgian liberals, senators Lafontaine and Paul Otlet. In interviews with Belgian papers like *Dernière Heure* and *Patrie Belge* (1 Jan. 1921) he demanded that Congolese be trained as doctors and administrators as part of the duty of the Belgian government. He even argued that the Congo had been independent since 1563, before the establishment of Leopold's Free State. These statements led an official journal to state: 'Les idées de M. Panda semblent s'orienter dans le sense du "pan-africanisme".' See

On the morning of 1 September, the speakers included Nicola de Santos Pinto who dealt with the problems in San Thomé. General Sorela gave a short speech on the protection and welfare of Spanish subjects, while Panda Farnana proceeded on a lengthy historical defence of Congolese independence, arguing in the process that the discovery of America and the beginning of the slave trade were responsible for the destruction of Negro civilizations.[8] The Congress then adjourned, appropriately, to admire African culture in the Colonial Museum at Terveuren. This was almost a lull before the storm.

The rupture came in the afternoon session on 2 September when the London Declaration came up for discussion. Diagne, stung by Du Bois's attempt to outmanoeuvre the French-speaking delegates at the Brussels session with a *fait accompli*, charged that Du Bois's Declaration encouraged 'radicalism' and 'separatism'; the Afro-Americans, he said, were 'animés des sentiments plutôt dangereux' whereas French and Belgian Negroes believed in co-operation between whites and blacks. Even though the Afro-Americans and English-speaking Africans formed the majority, Diagne 'refused categorically to submit the motion to the vote of the Congress, on account of its "Communist" theories, adding that the Negro race belongs to no party'.[9] Diagne was backed by the Ethiopian delegate, the two Portuguese delegates, General Sorela, and Major Vervloet (Belgium). The Revd. Hurst, the Afro-American Methodist Bishop of Baltimore, vainly tried to mediate; the suggestion that the controversial Declaration should be submitted to a special Committee which would examine it and report to the Paris session of the Congress, found no support. The Brussels Correspondent of the *African World* described the scene as follows:

After some three hours' fierce struggle concerning the refusal by M. Diagne (Chairman of the Congress) to submit the London declaration to a vote of Congress, this distinguished Senegalese proposed the vote of the Otlet (Belgian) and of the do Magalhaes (Portuguese motions), motions asking the creation in each colonial nation of an institution of scientific researches concerning the development of the negroes, institutes of which the work

---

*Congo* (Jan.–May 1921), p. 274: 'Le Panafricanisme'. Pierre Daye, in a hostile and alarmist article on the Pan-African movement, also suggested a possible connection between the ideas of Panda and Garvey's U.N.I.A., 'Le Mouvement pannègre', *Le Flambeau* (July–Aug. 1921), no. 7, pp. 371–2.

[8] *La Tribune Congolaise*, art. cit.

[9] *African World* Supplement, op. cit., p. xvi; Du Bois, W. E. B., 'A Second Journey to Pan-Africa', *New Republic* (7 Dec. 1921), p. 40.

should be centralised by an international body. These motions voted by
M. Diagne and his supporters were proclaimed by him adopted by the
Congress, whilst, in fact, this was not the case, the American and British
Negroes (the majority of the Congress) not having voted for it. Therefore
they protested vehemently against these deeds but in vain, as M. Diagne
proclaimed it closed. This, justly, provoked further vehement protests
from the American and British negroes, who then broke up with M.
Diagne. Towards the end of the Congress Dr. Du Bois had already left
the bureau of the Congress. This gross lack of fair play from the side of
M. Diagne did much to surprise and pain his friends, both white and
coloured, as his only excuse for acting as he did was his wish to avoid
the London declaration being endorsed by Brussels, as such an endorse-
ment should unquestionably have taken away from the negroes' cause the
sympathy it was enjoying. . . .[10]

Eventually the vague and innocuous Otlet formula was accepted as
a compromise, though the Afro-Americans pressed for a reopening
of the discussion of the London Declaration at Paris. It was becoming apparent, however, that an astute politician like Diagne, who
was as well known as Du Bois and perhaps more famous, was
bound to pit his authority as the spokesman of the blacks against
that of Du Bois. In terms of influence and access to those in power
Diagne's voice carried more weight, at least in Europe, than Du
Bois's. Had he not used his influence and prestige to make the 1919
Paris Congress possible and could he not rightly point out the fact
that he really represented the Senegalese in the French Chamber of
Deputies? Even after the 1919 Congress, probably as a result of
Garvey's challenge, he had written to Du Bois raising doubts as to
the latter's right to represent Afro-Americans abroad. Du Bois
replied, sketching the structure of Negro politics in an attempt to
allay Diagne's fear of divisions in the Afro-American leadership:

I write to assure you that there is no reason whatsoever to think that the
Negroes of the United States are sadly divided in their efforts for advancement and in their determination to co-operate with their fellows of the
Negro race throughout the world. . . .
    The leading figures among the American Negroes and those upon whom
the Negro world may depend for co-operation are well known men and
there is between them today no essential differences of opinion. Moreover,
such differences as there are will be amicably settled here in the United
States, and I trust you will not allow yourself to be in the slightest degree
disturbed by people who are interested in misleading you.[11]

[10] Quoted in the *African World* Supplement, ibid.
[11] W. E. B. Du Bois to Blaise Diagne, 18 Sept. 1919, File on Pan Africa 1919 at

Du Bois referred to such Afro-American organizations as the N.A.A.C.P., the American Methodist and Baptist Churches, the National Urban League, the National Races Congress, and Monroe Trotter's Equal Rights Association, but deliberately omitted to mention leaders as far apart as Garvey and R. R. Moton. He added, however, 'The fact that I was almost alone, in representing the American Negro at our Pan-African Congress does not mean that I assume for a moment to represent alone all the twelve million Negroes in the United States. I had the opportunity to come when most of the others did not. . . .'[12]

At Brussels, however, Diagne boldly pressed his challenge and, though outnumbered, imposed his will on the Congress. The Otlet Declaration which he declared carried, read:

Whereas it is proven by the experience of the last half-century, as well as by scientific evidence, that negroes and all men of colour are susceptible of progressive development, which would allow their backward race to attain to the level of all other races, that the development of humanity in general is dependent upon that of all its parts, and that universal civilisation cannot be attained whilst over 200 millions of human beings are left in ignorance and economic incapacity; that the sustained collaboration of all races on a basis of equality and unity of intellectual and moral forces is an urgent desideratum of the present day. Be it resolved that the labours of the Pan-Negro Congress be continued and developed in an international association on the principle of absorbing in one federation all those willing to assist, in all countries, in the education, progress, and protection of the coloured race; that the efforts of this association be directed to organise all workers to this end; that these labours co-operate with those institutions classed together in the International Centre at the Palais Mondial at Brussels, and shall there concentrate on the work of the Pan-African section.[13]

---

Fisk University. I owe this information to my colleague Dr. Kenneth King who has completed an Edinburgh doctoral thesis on 'The American Background of the Phelps–Stokes Commissions and their influences on Education in East Africa especially in Kenya'. Dr. Clifton H. Johnson of the Amistad Research Centre and Race Relations Department of Fisk University also sent the author three copies of Du Bois–Diagne correspondence relating to the arrangements for the 1921 Pan-African Congress.

[12] ibid.

[13] *La Tribune Congolaise*, art. cit., col. 2. It is hardly surprising that the Afro-Americans and English-speaking Africans rejected this declaration; it tended to smack of a colonial, 'anthropological' type of research and development plan *for* subject peoples. The English-speaking Pan-Africanists preferred the more rousing, declaratory, and theoretic London Manifesto which was more explicit about 'the manner of treatment by the ruling white races'. They could justly complain that

Misrepresentation of the aims of the Pan-African movement by the European press, and their association of it with Garveyism and of the latter with Kimbangism in the Belgian Congo was also partly responsible for the undue fear of Afro-American radicalism shown at the Brussels session. An official Belgian journal even asserted that the Kimbangist movement of 1921 was a direct result of the 'Ethiopianism' and Garveyism preached in the Congo by American Methodist and Protestant missionaries, who, it alleged, had distributed copies of *Negro World* and seditious literature and hymns in the Congo, especially around Kinshasa and Stanley Pool.[14] Another Belgian journalist even went so far as to blame the mission of the Phelps–Stokes Fund for putting ideas into the African's head and for conniving at the 'propaganda', disguised as evangelization, of black American missionaries.[15] Yet another saw the Pan-African movement as a bad influence in the Congo, and as a clever plot by the American government to rid itself of turbulent blacks by encouraging their anti-colonial activities in Europe.[16] Amid such suspicion backed by Diagne's conservatism and authority, the Pan-African crusade of Du Bois was checked at Brussels. It never recovered its *élan* after Brussels.

The Congress was continued in Paris on 4 and 5 September in the Hall of the Civil Engineers. Diagne again presided and in his speech eulogized France and the bravery of the Negro troops. Gratien Candace,[17] 'a handsome impressive man of colour', who was also a member of the French Chamber of Deputies from Guadeloupe, sang

they had come to Europe to launch a Pan-African movement, not to have it colonized and departmentalized by French and Belgian spokesmen. See Du Bois's comments in the article in *New Republic*, op. cit.

[14] *Congo*: 'Le Garveyisme en action dans notre colonie', June–Dec. 1921, pp. 575–6.

[15] Daye, Pierre, art. cit.

[16] De Warnaffe, Ch. Du Bus, 'Le Mouvement pan-nègre aux États-Unis et ailleurs', *Congo* (May 1922), p. 725. The most imaginative of the European journalists, one R. Eaton, even saw Pan-Africanism as the handmaiden of communism in the Congo: see *Congo*, 'Le Bolshevisme au Congo' (June–Dec. 1924), pp. 752–7. The Belgian newspaper *Neptune* (14 June 1921) openly accused Du Bois of being in the pay of the Soviet Union. For Du Bois's reply to the *Neptune* article, see *Le Flambeau*, op. cit., 'Notes'.

[17] For a brief biography of Candace, see the *Dictionnaire de biographie Française*, vii (1956), 1027. After the Paris session of the 1921 Pan-African Congress, Candace became the president of the Paris-based *Association panafricaine*; another official was Isaac Beton. Both men resigned from the Association in 1923 partly through strained relations with Du Bois and partly through the irregular activities, sometimes financial, of some of the officials of the Association.

the praise of France, especially in her attitude to her black citizens. M. Dantes Bellegarde, Haitian Minister to France and representative at the League of Nations, dwelt a little on Haiti's history and proposed a resolution that the League of Nations establish a research bureau to protect the interests of black labour.[18] The Paris session, however, was not 'official' and Diagne was less autocratic. In fact the session was as frank in its criticisms of colonial rule as the London session, and the French Negro deputies made no attempt to guide it. This was probably due to Diagne's fear of a show-down by the American and British delegates, to the presence of French critics like Felicien Challaye, president of the Ligue de Droits des Hommes, as well as the presence of a few militant and disillusioned French Negroes, some of whom had served in the French army and had come to see French rule somewhat differently from Diagne and Candace.[19] Du Bois cleared the air by stating that the Afro-Americans had no intention of solving France's colonial problems, nor did they subscribe to Marcus Garvey's extreme nationalism. But, as usual, he repeated his view that 'no Negro in any part of the world can be safe as long as a man can be exploited in Africa, disfranchised in the West Indies, or lynched in the United States because he is a coloured man'. Political power, he argued, would give strength and recognition to black people; this power could only be gained when all blacks united in a common-sense platform of thought and action.[20]

On 5 September discussion centred on plans for the permanent functioning of the Pan-African Congress, the drafting of a constitution, and of bye-laws and other procedural questions. There was little dissension when it came to the resolutions, as those adopted were 'somewhat on the line of the London Manifesto'.[21] Du Bois's

[18] It was largely through the efforts of M. Bellegarde that the League of Nations Labour Bureau finally incorporated a section on Negro labour problems.

[19] For details, see chapter VII.

[20] 'The Congress in Paris', *African World* Supplement, op. cit., p. xvii.

[21] The first five points of the resolutions were identical to those of the London Manifesto; cf. p. 65 n. 71. Point 6 in the Paris version read 'The return to Negroes of the land and its natural fruits . . .' instead of the London version 'The ancient common ownership of the Land and its natural fruits . . .' which Diagne labelled 'Bolshevist'. It is interesting to note that Gratien Candace, who had special interest in the French merchant marine and in commerce in the colonies, worded Resolution 6 differently: 'La restitution progressive *aux noirs évolués* de la terre et des ses fruits naturels.' Candace, Gratien, 'Le Deuxième Congrès de la race noire', *Colonies et Marine*, V[e] Année, no. 39 (Nov. 1921), 729. My italics. The attitude of Candace perhaps supports Du Bois's statement that '. . . what she

attempt between 1921 and 1922 to give the movement some organizational basis in Paris failed[22] and the next two Pan-African congresses of 1923 and 1927 were largely Afro-American manifestations, for Du Bois himself stated later 'The Pan-African Movement had been losing ground since 1921'.[23]

In November 1923, 'without proper notice of preparation', the third Congress met in London and Lisbon, sponsored by the Circle of Peace and Foreign Relations of the National Association of Colored Women (U.S.A.). The London session was held in the Council Chamber of Denison House on 7 and 8 November. Chief speakers included Professor Harold Laski of the London School of Economics, H. G. Wells, Mrs. Ida Gibbs Hunt wife of the U.S. Consul at St. Etienne (France), Du Bois, Dr. John Alcindor, Kamba Simango an American-educated African from Portuguese East Africa, Chief Amoah III of the Gold Coast, Rayford Logan, and a few others. The Executive Committee of the Third Pan-African Congress passed the following resolutions:[24]

1. A voice in their own Government.
2. The right of access to the land and its resources.
3. Trial by juries of their peers under established forms of law.
4. Free elementary education for all; broad training in modern industrial technique; and higher training of selected talent.
5. The development of Africa for the benefit of Africans, and not merely for the profit of Europeans.
6. The abolition of the slave trade and of the liquor traffic.[25]
7. World disarmament and the abolition of war; but failing this, and as long as white folk bear arms against black folk, the right of blacks to bear arms in their own defence.

---

[i.e. France] recognizes is the equal right of her citizens, black and white, to exploit by modern industrial methods her laboring classes, black and white; and the crying danger to black France is that its educated and voting leaders will join in the industrial robbery of Africa rather than lead its masses to education and culture . . . men like Diagne and Candace, while unwavering defenders of racial opportunity, education for the blacks, and the franchise for the civilized, are curiously timid when the industrial problems of Africa are approached'. *New Republic*, art. cit., p. 41: 'A Second Journey to Pan-Africa'.

[22] See p. 82 n. 17 and Du Bois, W. E. B., 'The Pan-African Movement', in *History of the Pan-African Congress*, ed. G. Padmore, pp. 21–2.
[23] ibid., p. 24.
[24] ibid., p. 22.
[25] The influence of the Aborigines Rights Protection Society is evident here; the Revd. John Harris, its secretary, gave a lifetime of service to the abolition of forced labour and the liquor traffic in the colonies.

8. The organisation of commerce and industry so as to make the main objects of capital and labour the welfare of the many, rather than the enriching of the few.

Responsible government was also demanded for the West Indies and British West Africa. For French Africa and West Indies they demanded the extension of the citizenship rights of voting and parliamentary representation. For Kenya, Rhodesia, and the Union of South Africa they demanded restoration of land rights, the right to vote, and 'the abolition of the pretension of a white minority to dominate a black majority, and even to prevent their appeal to the civilised world'. Imperialist exploitation of the Belgian Congo was condemned and a system of state education and recognition of Native law recommended.[26] For the 'independent' states of Abyssinia, Haiti, and Liberia, the Congress demanded 'not merely political integrity but their emancipation from the grip of economic monopoly and usury at the hands of the moneymasters of the world'. Lynching and mob law in America were roundly condemned and racial equality advocated. They also demanded the restoration of the Egyptian Sudan to an independent Egypt and condemned the 'slave trading industrial monopolies' operating in Portuguese Africa. They even reminded the Brazilian and Central American Negro of his 'manhood and right to be'.[27]

The Congress also asked for black representation on the Mandates Commission and the I.L.O. The ambivalent attitude of the French-speaking members of the Pan-African Movement was commented upon and actually described as a 'defection'.[28] In view of this and certain financial irregularities in the Paris branch, the Executive Committee decided

1. That the Pan-African Association of Paris continue its existence as a Pan-African Committee for France and French Colonies. That a Committee be appointed by the Pan-African Association of Paris to audit carefully the accounts and authorise expenses of the Paris Office and to communicate the amount of the deficit to the Pan-African Committees hereinafter provided for.

[26] *Crisis* (Jan. 1924), p. 120.
[27] ibid.
[28] ibid. Candace, the president of the French *Association Panafricaine*, and Isaac Beton, who had always been associated with African political groups in Paris, tendered their resignations at this Congress. For Beton's obituary, see *Voix des Nègres* (monthly publication of the Pan-African-orientated Ligue de la Défense de la Race Nègre in Paris), May 1927.

2. That Pan-African Committees be established at the earliest opportunity in London, Portugal, British West Africa, the British West Indies, the United States of America, in the Union of South Africa, Brazil, Haiti and Liberia.

3. That these Committees through correspondence arrange

(a) For holding and financing the fourth Pan-African Congress in 1925.

(b) For contributing towards paying the past indebtedness of the Pan-African Association in Paris up to November 1923.

(c) For disseminating information concerning the Black World.[29]

On 6 November Du Bois was invited to speak at the annual meeting of the African Progress Union at Denison House. He gave a résumé of the proposed plans of the Congress and spoke on lynching in America. Dr. John Alcindor, who had attended the 1900 Pan-African Conference and was now president of the Union, condemned the registration of African labour in East Africa, describing the system as 'a form of slavery', and the Revd. John Harris expressed the hope that the League of Nations might do something on behalf of coloured peoples. The meeting was attended mainly by coloured students and African visitors like Chief Amoah III of the Gold Coast.[30] Thereafter Du Bois and the American delegates went to attend the Lisbon session organized by the *Liga Africana*,[31] the president of which was the Portuguese mulatto deputy and professor José do Magalhaes of San Thomé. The session was attended by delegates from eleven countries which included Angola, San Thomé, Mozambique, Guinea, Nigeria, Ajuda, Cape Verde, as well as Goa and the U.S.A., and lasted from 1 to 2 December. Anti-imperialist speeches were noticeably eschewed, the Congress being concerned for the most part with an explanation of the Pan-African Movement and the Negro question in America. Du Bois seems to have enjoyed visiting the cultural centres of Lisbon and the cultured company of

[29] *Crisis* (Jan. 1924), p. 120.

[30] *The Times* (7 Nov. 1923), p. 11.

[31] For a brief account of this important but obscure body, see *History of the Pan-African Congress*, op. cit., p. 22, and *Crisis* (Feb. 1924), p. 170; Du Bois, W. E. B., 'Pan-Africa in Portugal'. Only a liberal Portuguese regime could have sponsored such a body; it seems more likely that it was a humanitarian type of organization guided by 'safe' men like the deputies Pinto and Magalhaes, both of whom were members of the colonial élite, Pinto being a planter. The author wrote to several libraries and archives in Lisbon on the subject of the *Liga Africana*. There was no reply. Information about the *Liga Africana* and similar bodies is still very scanty, but see Chilcote, R. H., *Portuguese Africa* (Prentice-Hall, Inc., New Jersey, 1967), pp. 49–50. See also Mondlane, Eduardo, *The Struggle for Mozambique* (Harmondsworth, 1969), p. 104.

Magalhaes. In his view the Lisbon demonstration was 'more success-ful' than the London one. *West Africa*, however, observed that, like the previous Congresses, the 1923 Congress did not possess a comprehensive programme and that its objects were not outlined beforehand. It argued that this looseness of structure in the Pan-African movement was due to the fact that its objects could not be clarified principally because it was a heterogeneous monolith, i.e. that 'Negro' was an abstraction that referred to colour rather than common traditions and objectives. The only problem, said the editorial, which Negroes had in common was that of the colour line, and even this varied: 'the manifestations of prejudice vary tre-mendously in Paris and Johannesburg, in Rio de Janeiro, Kingston and New York'. (Nevertheless, racial prejudice *is* racial prejudice, irrespective of degree). It advised that since there had been little support between the N.A.A.C.P., the *Union Congolaise*, the *Liga Africana*, and other bodies, the primary task of the Congress should be to bring together 'widely sundered' men into consultation with the object of fostering better understanding of their problems.[32]

The last of the Du Boisian Congresses was held in 1927 in New York, a notable feature of that Congress being the active participation of race-conscious American Negro women's church organizations. Thirteen countries were represented, but most of the delegates were Afro-Americans, Africa being represented by the Gold Coast (Chief Amoah III who was at the time connected with the American–West African cocoa trade), Sierra Leone, Liberia, and Nigeria. The late Melville Herskovits, an American anthropologist and author of *Myth of the Negro Past*, was one of the guest speakers at that Congress. The resolutions passed were almost identical to those passed at the Lisbon session of the 1923 Congress,[33] but one interest-ing feature was the presence of a few 'radicals' and the tribute paid by Du Bois to the Soviet Union's fair treatment of her various nationalities.[34] In spite of this 'Left orientation', the Comintern, however, was hostile to such pan-movements which it considered 'Manifestations of *petit-bourgeois nationalism*, to be fought and destroyed before Communism could ever hope to make inroads in Africa to win the allegiance of the Negro masses in America to the

[32] *West Africa* (29 Sept. 1923), p. 1137.
[33] *History of the Pan-African Congress*, ed. Padmore, pp. 23–4; *Crisis*, xxxiv (Oct. 1927), 'The Pan-African Congresses'.
[34] Broderick, op. cit., p. 139. Du Bois had visited the Soviet Union in 1926 and returned full of admiration for the Russians.

cause of the "Proletarian Revolution" . . . .'.[35] Ironically, while the Belgian press and certain French writers were denouncing Communist attempts to infiltrate the Pan-African movement,[36] the Communists, particularly the Profintern, with which Padmore was closely connected in the late 1920s and early 1930s, denounced the movement as petty-bourgeois and reformist, putting more emphasis on class leadership.[37] For the historian, however, one of the most interesting paradoxes of Pan-Africanism is that Malcolm Ivan Nurse (alias George Padmore), who in his Profintern days condemned Pan-Negro nationalism as backward and reactionary with such fervour, was to be expelled from the Comintern for the very heresy he had preached against. Profintern's loss became Pan-Africa's gain,[38] and Padmore was to become the leading theoretician of the new dialectics of colonial liberation—a dialectic that omitted the stage of a colonial proletarian revolution by availing itself of Trotsky's 'privilege of backwardness', and by seeking to transcend both Communism and capitalism.

[35] Padmore, *History of the Pan-African Congress*, p. 133. See also id., *The Life and Struggles of Negro Toilers* (London, 1931), pp. 124–6.

[36] See Padmore, *History of the Pan-African Congress*; also Gautherot, Gustave, *Le Bolchevisme aux colonies et l'imperialisme rouge* (Paris, 1930). Gautherot set up as expert on anti-Communism and tended to see 'l'araignée Bolcheviste' (Bolshevist spider) spreading its revolutionary webs throughout the world. To him, the agitation of the Pan-African movement was an example of 'les ténèbreuses machinations de l'Araignée Soviétique'. Of the 1927 Pan-African Congress he wrote: 'Le bolchevisme avait essayé de s'annexer le mouvement en le noyant. Au Congrès Panafricain de New-York (1927), un "groupe de gauche" avait préconisé la "solidarité avec la classe ouvrière", et "un rapport de son enthousiasme sur la Conférence antiimpérialiste de Bruxelles avait été à la première séance". La manoeuvre échoua et Moscou, considérant désormais les *Congrès Panafricains* et *l'Association pour l'avancement des peuples de couleur* comme des "entreprises aventureuses" et des organisations "réformistes (socialistes) et fascistes", attaqua d'autres groupements et surtout fonda ses propres organisations pan-nègres', p. 272. Allegations of Communist infiltration were, in fact, partly true, though not to the extent alarmist reports indicated. See *The Communist International Between the Fifth and the Sixth World Congresses* (London, 1928), p. 348. For a Communist account of Communist attempts to infiltrate U.N.I.A. and the 1927 Pan-African Congress, see ibid., pp. 348, 450–92.

[37] See the articles by J. W. Ford, Negro theoretician of the Communist party and chief editor of the *Negro Worker* in 1928: 'l'Influence de l'I.C. parmi les nègres au moment du X$^e$ anniversaire de l'I.C.' in *Correspondance Internationale* (27 Mar. 1929); 'Le IV$^e$ Congrès pan-africain au service de l'impérialisme', ibid. (18 Dec. 1929).

[38] For details, see Hooker, James R., *Black Revolutionary: George Padmore's Path From Communism to Pan-Africanism* (London, 1967).

## 3. *West African Attitudes to the Pan-African Movement*[39]

WE have already given a brief account of West African press commentary on the Du Boisian Congresses. In general, opinion in nationalist circles in British West Africa was a mixture of enthusiasm, mild criticism, and an attitude which implied that there was no direct *rapport* between Du Bois's Pan-Africanism and the new Pan-West African nationalism. It was a grand movement to be admired and held up as an indication of a new and vigorous race-consciousness determined to assert itself in the post-war world, but was at the same time not directly related to peculiar economic and political problems of British West Africa. As far as Garvey's Pan-Negro movement was concerned, however, the position, contrary to the opinion of certain European contemporary writers, was different. As Thomas Hodgkin has suggested, the Garvey movement may have had a more significant and widespread effect on African nationalist thought than is commonly supposed.[40] Professor Shepperson has already argued the thesis of Negro American influences on African nationalism, particularly East and Central African nationalism, although the extent and significance of this influence varied somewhat, as we shall show in the West African case. Some of the radical Negro newspapers found their way into Africa; for example, the *Crusader*, frequently quoted by West African papers, wrote: 'The *Crusader* serves . . . the colored people of the world. It circulates in nearly every big town in the U.S. . . . It has circulation in the West Indies and Panama, in South America, and in the coastal districts of West, East and South Africa, penetrating as far as Kano on the Nigerian railway, as far as Coquithatville on the Congo river, and in South Africa as far as Pretoria.'[41] And an American writer describing the network of influences linking Negroes throughout the world wrote as follows: 'Indeed, a reader in Sierra Leone writes to the *Negro World* (26 March 1921): "We have been reading the *Negro World* for about two years. We have been reading other Negro papers, such

[39] For a more general discussion of the impact of one of the Pan-African movements on African nationalism, see Langley, J. Ayodele, 'Garveyism and African Nationalism', *Race*, xi, no. 2 (Oct. 1969), 157–72.

[40] Hodgkin, T., *Nationalism in Colonial Africa* (London, 1956), pp. 101–2. See also Shepperson, G., 'Pan-Africanism and "Pan-Africanism": Some Historical Notes', p. 356. This article is most suggestive in its indications of possible fields of research in Pan-African studies.

[41] Quoted in Detweiler, Frederick German, *The Negro Press in the United States* (Chicago, Ill., 1922), p. 16.

as the *New York Age*, the *Washington Bee*, the *Crisis*, the *Colored American*, the *Liberian West Africa*, the *Liberian Register*. . . ." [42]

Even as late as 1933 there were African nationalists in South Africa who, in spite of police surveillance, were receiving copies of Garvey's *Negro World*. One James Stehazu, for example, (signing himself 'Yours Africanly') wrote to the *Negro World* editor 'to express the feeling of our African brothers towards the American or West Indian brothers'. His observations were frank and sharp:

The Africans are now wide-awake in affairs affecting the black races of the world, and yet the so-called civilized Negroes of the Western hemisphere are still permitting the white men to deceive them as the Negroes of the old regime, Uncle Tom stool-pigeons. If the 'motherland' Africa is to be redeemed, the Africans are to play an important part in the ranks and file of the U.N.I.A. and A.C.L. I have studied comments and opinions of 29 leading American newspapers (all colored) and to my horror it is only one problem that is still harassing. The 250-year-old policy, 'Please and Thank You' (Sir Kick Me and Thank You). But the lion-hearted M. Garvey has cut it adrift from the new Negro. He is now admitted as a great African leader. . . . The intellectuals like Dr. Du Bois, Pickens, Hancock and others are obviously put to shame, hopelessly moving like handicapped professors who are drunk with knowledge, who cannot help themselves. . . . The red, the black and the green are the colors talked about by the young men and women of Africa. It shall bury many and redeem millions. Today in Africa, the only hope of our race is gospel of U.N.I.A.—is sung and said as during the period of the French Revolution.[43]

Yet another South African (E. T. Mofutsanyana) wrote criticizing the anti-Communist craze in South Africa: '. . . These pretenders, these destroyers of happiness, these exploiters, profiteers and parasites . . . under cover of justice, and religion are busy formulating a law that they believe will lock up communism in an iron box never to peep out again. . . . Communism is like grass. They cannot cut it; they can burn it to ashes, but when the time comes for revolution, it will positively get up like fire. . . .'[44]

[42] Detweiler, Frederick German, *The Negro Press in the United States*.
[43] *Negro World* (16 July 1932), p. 6.
[44] *Negro World* (3 June 1933), p. 2. See also *Negro World* (7 Aug. 1926), p. 10: 'An Appreciation of Garvey's "Africa for the Africans"' by the Johannesburg newspaper *Abantu-Batho*; Joseph Masogha, Kimberley, South Africa, to the editor of *Negro World* (14 Aug. 1926), p. 10. Ibid. (30 Apr. 1927), p. 2. Benjamin Majafi, Liddesdaale, Evaton, South Africa, to S. A. Hayes, president of the Pittsburgh Division of U.N.I.A. in *Negro World* (30 Apr. 1927), p. 5. 'Voice from Africa', ibid., 'Organization Work in Africa Growing' (21 May 1927), p. 4. Also,

While Garveyism did not have any permanent influence, the available evidence suggests that it excited more interest and controversy and was a more powerful utopia among African nationalist groups than the Du Boisian movement. In both French and British West Africa between 1920 and 1923 there were a few individuals and organizations associated with Garveyism. It was in Lagos, however, that the movement was strongest where a small but vigorous branch of U.N.I.A. was actually established in mid-1920, almost at the same time as the National Congress of British West Africa came into being. In March 1920 the Revd. Patriarch Campbell, to whom we shall refer in the next few chapters, was approached by some Lagosians on the subject of the Garvey movement and with a proposal for forming a committee of the U.N.I.A. in Lagos.[45] Campbell advised them to postpone discussion until the meeting of the West African Congress where he would take the matter up. He thought there was something to be said for the commercial aspects of Garvey's Pan-Negroism, especially the project of the Black Star Line, but advised British subjects against participation in U.N.I.A. politics 'as conditions in both hemispheres differ altogether from each other'.[46] Campbell then discussed the idea with delegates at the Accra meeting of the N.C.B.W.A. and the conclusion reached was that Garvey's politics should be ignored and the Black Star Line patronized, 'it being a Negro undertaking and its object being solely for the purpose of facilitating and giving us more and brighter prospects as Africans in our commercial transactions'.[47] The *Times of Nigeria* editorial endorsed the view of the N.C.B.W.A., dwelling almost exclusively on the economic aspects of Garveyism:

The idea of establishing a line of steamers owned and controlled by Africans is a great and even sublime conception for which everybody of African origin will bless the name of Marcus Garvey. . . . The inclusion,

---

Mrs. Singer-Baldridge, American journalist and writer as quoted in *Negro World* (18 Aug. 1928): 'What They Think of Garvey'. On the West African side, see some of the newspapers quoted in *West Africa* (27 Nov. 1920): 'The Universal Negro Improvement Association and African Communities League is making progress in Lagos', pp. 1513, 1496, and *West Africa* (11 Dec. 1920), p. 1553.

[45] For another account of the Garvey movement in Lagos, see the article by Olusanya, G. O., 'The Lagos Branch of the Universal Negro Improvement Association', *Journal of Business and Social Studies* (Lagos), i, no. 2 (1970). Also Langley, J. Ayodele, 'Garveyism and African Nationalism'.

[46] J. G. Campbell to the editor, *Times of Nigeria* (24 May 1920), pp. 4–5.

[47] ibid.; see also resolution 5 in *Conference of Africans of British West Africa, Held at Accra, 1920*, p. 3.

however, of such a tremendous political plan, as the founding of a pan-African Empire, is too obviously ridiculous to do aught else than alienate sympathy from the whole movement. We do not suggest that our brethren in America ought not to aim at political autonomy. Liberty is man's highest right . . . particularly in the case of our American brethren, for whom the hardships and disadvantages under which they exist in the land of their exile make it desirable to have some portion of their ancestral land, where they could unmolested shape their own destiny and spread culture amongst their less enlightened brethren—'De 'ole folks at home'.[48]

The *Times* went on to argue in a manner reminiscent of present Pan-African disagreements, that the N.C.B.W.A. concept of independence was incompatible with the U.N.I.A. concept of a Pan-Negro Republic: 'If at all the day should come, and come it must in the process of evolution—when Africa shall be controlled by Africans, each distinct nation, while having the most cordial relations with every other sister nation, will infinitely prefer remaining as a separate political entity to being drawn into one huge melting pot of a Universal Negro Empire.' The N.C.B.W.A. was cited as an example of a movement working towards the gradual independence of British West Africa within the British Empire, and Garvey was told that what Africa needed was banks, schools, industries, modern universities, and the Black Star Line, not 'wild-cat schemes' like a Pan-African Republic.[49]

Towards the end of 1920, with the Government taking a serious view of the unrest the Garvey movement could cause in the colonies, the majority of the Lagos élite dissociated themselves from the U.N.I.A. branch which was being run by Ernest S. Ikoli. The conservative *Nigerian Pioneer* wrote on 26 November: 'We advise the Police to keep an eye on the Garveyites in Nigeria.' Some of the leading members of the U.N.I.A. Lagos branch included the Revd. W. B. Euba and the Revd. S. M. Abiodun. At the unveiling of the U.N.I.A. branch charter on 26 November at Lagos, the Revd. W. B. Euba, while insisting on their loyalty to Britain, made it clear that 'co-operation among Negroes is the first necessity without which it will be futile to try to co-operate with other peoples'. The *Lagos Weekly Record* condemned Garveyism because of 'its aggressive and militaristic tendencies' but said of the Lagos branch: 'To us they

---

[48] *Times of Nigeria*, art. cit., p. 5.
[49] ibid.

are neither traitorous nor revolutionary, neither fantastic nor visionary.'[50] The objects of the Lagos U.N.I.A. branch were:

(1) To establish a universal Confraternity among the race and reclaim the fallen; to administer to and assist the needy, and to assist in civilizing the backward tribes of Nigeria.

(2) To establish technical and industrial institutions for boys and girls. To conduct local commercial and industrial enterprises on co-operative lines, and to work for the moral and social uplift and betterment of Negro Communities (in compliance with our loyalty to the Crown under the protection of the laws of the country).

(3) The Universal Negro Improvement Association and African Communities League is undenominational. Meetings were to be held on Saturday evenings at St. Peter's Schoolroom, Ajele Street, Lagos.

If the middle-class nationalists were opposed to U.N.I.A. politics, there were a few Lagos radicals like J. Babington Adebayo who mercilessly criticized the Lagos branch of the N.C.B.W.A. and the conservative Lagos press. He criticized the Revd. J. G. Campbell for accusing Garveyites of sedition and disloyalty and for concerning himself with conservative bodies like the Peoples Union, the Lagos Anti-Slavery Society, and with such institutions as the inter-colonial cricket match. Adebayo went on to attack the criticisms the *Nigerian Pioneer* made of the Garvey movement—criticisms like: 'The thousands of tribes in any section of Africa never at any time regarded themselves as one people or one nation'—the standard argument of the conservatives who were also opposed to the N.C.B.W.A. According to Adebayo, his fear was that the trouble with most Africans, especially those with the mentality of the *Nigerian Pioneer*, was that they clung too closely to 'the best traditions of British rule', forgetting that sometimes these 'best traditions' were not always in their own interests: 'It is this we consider and believe the greatest obstacle and one that can scarcely be annihilated. We need not be reminded that the best traditions had not always been upheld among us without a break', and drove home his point by quoting Paul Lawrence Dunbar's poem about the oppressed yet eternally forgiving African. It was this attitude, he said, that constituted 'the greatest obstacle to the materialization of this glowing Utopia' (i.e. Garvey's utopia).[51] As for the Lagos branch of the

[50] *Lagos Weekly Record* (27 Nov. 1920), p. 5.
[51] Adebayo, J. Babington, 'The British West African Congress: Marcus Garvey's Pan-Negroism and the Universal Negro Improvement Association', *Lagos Weekly Record* (27 Nov. 1920), p. 7.

N.C.B.W.A., Adebayo thought that though its leaders were sincere, their methods were dictatorial, publicity poor, and internal struggles disastrous; office-holders were far too numerous, 'chairman came over chairman, officers galore as lieutenants in the Haitian Army . . .'.[52]

The Colonial Office, aware of the unrest Afro-American activity had created in other parts of the continent, took the Garvey movement seriously, for in 1922 it sent a secret dispatch to Sir Hugh Clifford, inquiring about U.N.I.A. activities in Nigeria, especially the operations of the Black Star Line. Sir Hugh in turn furnished the reports of two Lieutenant-Governors on the subject, indicating that the Lagos Garveyites were harmless. According to him, the movement appeared to be 'inspired mainly by a not unnatural desire on the part of Marcus Garvey and his associates to obtain money from natives of Africa for which it is not proposed to make any very adequate return'.[53] According to his source of information, financial contributions and subscriptions had in fact been made in some cases and sent to America by 'mal-content Africans living in Nigeria and in the employment of the Government'. Sir Hugh, however, had little to fear from Garveyism because, he said, from what he knew of the West African, he felt certain that his 'notorious ability to take care of himself where money is concerned' would provide a powerful check on any commercial exploitation by Garvey or others. H. C. Moorhouse, Lieutenant-Governor of Southern Provinces, added that a Negro American called Cockburn, formerly employed by the Nigerian Marine, was rumoured to have been given command of one of the Black Star ships, and that Garveyism 'has made very little headway here and if as appears probable, the association becomes discredited in America, it will . . . gradually die out here'.[54] According to W. F. Gowers, Lieutenant-Governor of the Northern Provinces, investigations in early 1921 in the north had shown that copies of the *Negro World* were being circulated among Africans and West Indians 'to a very small extent in some Provinces,

---

[52] Adebayo, op. cit.; for the reference to the Haitian army, see Korngold, Ralph, *Citizen Toussaint* (Left Book Club ed., 1945), p. 67: '. . . To compensate for the paucity of equipment and training there was a superabundance of general officers. There were few who confessed to any rank lower than captain, and the number of generals was bewildering. . . .'

[53] Sir Hugh Clifford, Report on U.N.I.A. activities in Nigeria, C.I. 583/109/28194, 27 Feb. 1922, para. 2. The intelligence reports, on which Sir Hugh's report was based, seem to be fairly reliable, particularly when checked against newspaper material relating to the activities of the Garvey movement in Lagos.

[54] ibid.

among them Kano, Munshi, and Illorin', but that there was no
evidence of U.N.I.A. propaganda. He added: 'There is no likelihood
at all of the principles of the Marcus Garvey movement finding any
encouragement outside a very limited class of native, not indigenous
to the Northern Provinces . . . there is even less interest taken in
Marcus Garvey and his movement than there was last year.' So far
as he knew, there could be no question of Pan-Africanist activity in
the North.[55]

The Nigerian Deputy Inspector-General of Police then outlined
the aims of the U.N.I.A. and dwelt a little on the Black Star Line,
stating that a number of West Africans had bought shares. Branches
of the U.N.I.A. had been formed in Africa, America, and the West
Indies, and in Nigeria its headquarters was at 72 Tinubu Square,
Lagos, the president of which was Winter Schakleford, a clerk of
S. Thomas & Co. The Secretary was Ernest S. Ikoli, editor and
manager of the *African Messenger*, but he had been succeeded by
the Revd. Ajayi of the C.M.S. in 1922. Membership was around the
300 mark, but paying members amounted to a mere 28—heavy
subscriptions and levies ensured a rather lukewarm support. There
was also a brass band which the movement owned; official instructions from headquarters in New York stated that the African
National Anthem ('Ethiopia, Land of My Fathers') was to be
played on all public occasions. It was also stated that the Nigerian
agent for the industrial wing of the U.N.I.A. was a Mr. Agbebi,
but no shares had been sold in Lagos though there was some interest
in the matter. According to the police, Mr. Ikoli had resigned as
secretary of the local branch 'on the grounds he was opposed to its
political aims, though he approved of the Industrial scheme'.[56] He
(the Deputy Inspector-General) had also seen a private letter from
Herbert Macaulay when the latter was in England, to a friend of
his in Lagos, 'warning him to be very careful in having anything
to do with this Association as it is perilously near the border line of
treason and sedition'.[57] In conclusion, the report noted: 'The movement is not meeting with much local success and with the exception
of the leaders, the members are lukewarm and the public generally
are not in favour of it. They recognise they are much better off under
British Rule and have no desire to change . . . for American Negro
rule. . . .'

Apart from Lagos, Garveyism attracted considerable attention in

[55] ibid.                    [56] ibid.                    [57] ibid.

Liberia, where its activities inevitably involved Liberian–American and British relations, and the interests of the Firestone Rubber company.[58] Apart from Liberia and Lagos, the U.N.I.A. does not seem to have had much impact on other parts of West Africa. Between 1920 and 1923 copies of the *Negro World* entered Dahomey via one of Quenum's sons in Paris, probably Kojo Tovalou Quenum who was associated with radical African groups in Paris.[59] In the Senegal, Gambia, and Sierra Leone, governments introduced immigration restriction bills against 'undesirables'. Agents of U.N.I.A. appeared in Dakar (Senegal) but were expelled, as well as those in Liberia. In the latter territory, U.N.I.A. made serious but abortive efforts at a colonization and trading scheme; their representatives arrived in Monrovia in January 1924, amply provided with funds to put before President King a scheme for the settlement of 3,000 Afro-Americans from the United States. It was planned to establish six settlements of 500 families each, four on the French border and two on the British border. The Liberian President offered them an initial trial concession of 500 acres, but not on the border. The mission, however, failed principally because of Garvey's intemperate attacks on the Liberian government and his tactless criticism of the colonial powers. In the Senegal a small group of Sierra Leoneans led by Francis Webber, Farmer, Dougherty, H. W. Wilson, and John Camara were preaching Garveyism. The British Consulate General in Dakar reported that the French authorities were 'engaged in watching with some uneasiness the activities of a small group of men, natives of Sierra Leone, who were believed to be local representatives of the Universal Negro Improvement Association of the United States . . .'. The homes of these men were raided and documents seized; it was alleged that they had established at Rufisque 'an active branch of the Association, provided with the usual elected officers, which branch was engaged in spreading the objects of the

[58] See Padmore, G., *Pan-Africanism or Communism?*, pp. 91–101; also the dispatches of the British Legation in Monrovia contained in Gambia Confidential M.P. No. 727, 3/59, 21 June 1922; 'Universal Negro Improvement Association: Activities of representatives of': Francis O'Meara to H.M. Principal Secretary of State for Foreign Affairs, 22 Feb. 1924; ibid., 7 July 1924; ibid., 23 Aug. 1924. G. Grindle to H.M. Chargé d'Affaires, Monrovia, 15 Oct. 1924, and Edwin Barclay, Secretary of State, Liberia, to The Agent, Elder Dempster and Co. Ltd., Monrovia, 30 June 1924; and *African World* (1925), pp. 124–5: 'Marcus Garvey and Liberia—An Epitome of the Liberian Government's Attitude'.

[59] Ballard, John, 'The Porto Novo Incidents of 1923: Politics in the Colonial Era', p. 66.

parent body and in collecting subscriptions for the furtherance of its schemes'. John Camara was mentioned in the documents as the U.N.I.A.'s 'Travelling Commissioner' who visited most of the U.N.I.A. branches in West Africa in 1922, and in Dakar, 'meetings were held which were addressed by him in most violent language exhorting his hearers to spread the revolutionary movement which would, in the end, cast the white man out of Africa . . .'.[60] In 1923, shortly before Garvey was imprisoned in the United States, an application by him to the British authorities for a passport to visit West Africa as part of his 'speaking tour' of the world (to correct misrepresentations of the aims of U.N.I.A.) was refused by the Colonial Office on the ground that his visit might lead to more unrest. A Colonial Office dispatch observed that 'Marcus Garvey probably has a larger following in West Indies than he has in West Africa, but it is in Africa that he wants to institute his Negro State: consequently his object must be to stir up trouble and to incite sedition in Africa. What he wants from the West Indies is money. Probably that is his chief want so far as Africa is concerned as well; but if his movement is over to achieve anything he must also create a spirit of unrest in Africa.'[61] Members of the Nigerian Executive Council unanimously advised against his visit, the importation of the *Negro World* was prohibited 'as coming within the category of seditious, defamatory, scandalous or demoralising literature'; besides, his visit would be used 'to collect further sums of money on false pretences from the most ignorant and gullible sections of the semi-educated Africans of the West Coast'.[62]

The admirers of Garvey, however, were not all 'semi-educated', 'ignorant and gullible'. As M. Labouret argued in the 1930s, there were a few of the nationalist intelligentsia in British Africa who had studied Garveyism closely and had related it to nationalist politics.[63] And it certainly comes as a surprise that the most outspoken and eloquent commentator on the Garvey movement among this intel-

[60] R. C. Maugham, British Consulate General, Dakar, to H.E. the Governor, Gambia, 15 June 1922, Confidential No. 384/255/22, Gambia 3/59, Confidential M.P. No. 727: 'Universal Negro Improvement Association: Activities of representatives of', also R. Maunier, op. cit. i. 50.
[61] Nigeria Confidential 'C', C.O. 583/118/34197, 9 July 1923.
[62] ibid.
[63] Labouret, H., 'Le Mouvement pan-nègre aux États-Unis et ses répercussions en Afrique', *Politique Étrangère* (1937), p. 320; Kohn, Hans, and Sokolsky, W., *African Nationalism in the Twentieth Century* (Princeton, N.J., 1965), p. 34.

ligentsia was 'that remarkable Cape Coast lawyer' (as Thomas Hodgkin rightly describes him), William Essuman Gwira Sekyi (or Kobina Sekyi), Gold Coast philosopher, nationalist, lawyer, and traditionalist. A controversialist and prolific writer, Sekyi was one of the most interesting personalities in Gold Coast public affairs, and an example *par excellence* of the African intellectual in nationalist politics.[64] Sekyi devoted two interesting chapters to the Negro question in America in his violently anti-colonial book which recommended as little contact as possible between Africans and European colonials.[65] Writing in defence of the Garvey movement he argued that any manifestation of solidarity between Africans and other Negroes was generally regarded with great suspicion by the white man who had 'got so hopelessly alarmed by the *necessary spade-work* that Marcus Garvey is doing towards the erection, in the not very remote future of [an] abiding edifice of racial collaboration, that he has further overlooked the truth of the well-known remark: "Abuse is no argument." ' He went straight to the main point in his Pan-African thesis when he asserted:

The present attitude of a section of the white writing public, coupled with certain somewhat questionable, though legally authorised, acts of interference with the freedom of the press ... has made it essential that we in Africa should dispassionately ... register our own opinion on this Garvey scare and therewith set down our considered views on the subject of our brethren in America. The recent official outburst against the Congress movement may have been very closely connected with the white eruption against Garveyism ... we should do well to guard against any future white propaganda against the Congress, now that it is well known that the Congress stands for the unification of British West Africa, and therefore is bound ultimately to consider seriously the question of co-operation with our brethren in French West Africa, for example, then with those in other parts of Africa, and finally with those abroad. .... It is therefore necessary, in fact, vital, to our future development as a race, that we should *now* inaugurate a period of systematic observation of our brethren not only in America but also elsewhere abroad.[66]

Unlike the majority of the Pan-African utopians, however, Sekyi was able to perceive that the African Diaspora, for various historical

[64] Sampson, Magnus, 'Kobina Sekyi as I Knew Him', *Sekyi Papers*, Cape Coast Regional Archives, 716/64.

[65] Sekyi, K., *The Parting of the Ways* (n.d.). Internal evidence (e.g. his reference to 'the recent opening of Achimota') suggests that the work was published in 1925; the author came across it while studying the Sekyi papers at Cape Coast, Ghana, in 1966.     [66] ibid., p. 23.

and sociological reasons, had ceased to have any of the attributes of a nation and that West Indians and Afro-Americans, in spite of the new race-consciousness and Pan-Melanism, had inherited Anglo-Saxon prejudices against the African and were *ipso facto* disqualified from assuming any political leadership in the African continent:

From Marcus Garvey's announcements regarding Africa, it is clear that he does not know even the level of acquaintance with Western ideals and of capacity to assimilate and adapt whatever comes from or is traceable to the modern world. What is much more important is that he does not understand how we Africans in Africa feel about such matters as the Colonial Government; neither can he and his set . . . realise that republican ideals in the crude form in which they are maintained, in theory, at least, in America go directly against the spirit of Africa, which is the only continent in the whole world peopled by human beings who have in their souls the secret of constitutional monarchy. . . . What Marcus Garvey and any other leader of Afro-American thought has first to appreciate before he can present a case sufficiently sound for Africa to support in the matter of combination or co-operation among all Africans at home and abroad, is the peculiar nature of the African standpoint in social and political institutions. *The salvation of the Africans in the world cannot but be most materially assisted by the Africans in America but must be controlled and directed from African Africa and thoroughly African Africans.*[67]

Sekyi's other strictures against the Pan-Africanism of Afro-Americans and West Indians merit quotation not only because they indicate a different concept of Pan-Africanism on the part of the West African nationalist intellectuals but also because they illustrate the dilemma posed by the Afro-American 'double consciousness'. To the Afro-American, Africa in the abstract was both a romantic illusion and a sharp reminder that he was an American first, and this dichotomy, in Sekyi's view, meant that political leadership of Africa must come from within Africa:

If there is anything now that militates or is likely to militate against any American Negro movement towards Africa, it is the Americanisation of the American Negro. So long as he remains an American in ideal, his sphere of usefulness in Africa, if and when he gets there, will be very much circumscribed, in fact so restricted as to become a hindrance to his own happy existence. . . .

Even now in the West Indies and in America will be found people who think we are in such a condition that the only part we can play in the prevailing endeavour on the part of the darker races to attain a better place since the Great War than they had before it, is to be led by them.

[67] ibid., pp. 23–4.

That is a very serious mistake which ought to be corrected as early as possible. We in Africa can, and so, claim to be the only persons qualified to keep the tone of the present spirit of unrest at the proper pitch, because we are in possession and charge of the great and glorious traditions of our ancestors and the peerless social and political institutions which our ancestors perfected long ago, and which it is our sacred duty to preserve from the inroads of European irresponsibility as regards things non-European. We claim that we should be the architects, and that our brethren in America and those in the West Indies should be among the builders of the structure of racial oneness. . . . We admit that we are behind in steady acquaintance with the mechanical devices of the Western world . . . but we contend that we have the controlling forces in our hands, and we in Africa alone understand these forces and can direct them aright for the good of the whole Negro race.[68]

Chapter 3 of Sekyi's manuscript, entitled 'Our Brethren Abroad' dealt with Liberia and Haiti and was a vigorous defence of these symbols of Negro emancipation. Like Alexander Crummell[69] (Blyden's contemporary), he argued that the failure of these states was not due to any inherent inability of Negroes to rule themselves as European critics maintained, but to a wrong concept of the state on the part of the Negro. He anticipated modern Pan-Africanists by arguing that these states had failed in the task of nation-building precisely because they were 'artificial' states created by 'artificial means and maintained by methods equally artificial'. Here for the first time perhaps one finds the germ of the 'Balkanization' idea[70] in Pan-African theory and a rejection of the European concept of the state:

The South American and the Balkan states, particularly the new state of Albania as it was before the Great War, might as well be taken as proof positive that the Southern Europeans are not capable of self-rule in a state. The white thinker on the theory of the state has hitherto based himself on the ground that the state can be created only by force, so that in the last resort force or war . . . is the only means to the end of creating and maintaining a state. On the other hand, when there are enough

[68] ibid., pp. 24–7.

[69] Crummell, Alexander, *The Relation and Duties of the Free Colored Men in America to Africa* (Hartford, Conn., 1861); *The Duty of a Rising Christian State* . . . (London, 1856); *Africa and America* (London, 1891).

[70] Cf. Shepperson, G., 'Pan-Africanism and "Pan-Africanism": Some Historical Notes', p. 357: '5. Balkanization: How far is the fear of this in Africa which plays an important part in contemporary all-African movements . . . of relatively recent introduction? . . .' W. E. G. Sekyi's arguments are particularly relevant in the attempt to answer this question.

African thinkers to impress the world with their essentially African theory of the state, it will be found that they are seeking to get the world to accept the view that there is another kind of state, so called patriarchial, which is not based on or kept by force in the artificial shape of war; and such states can be found to be the units in confederations such as the group of small states in the Gold Coast. . . . In other words, the sort of force that is applicable in the national African state differs from the sort of force applicable in the artificial state, whether African or non-African which is based on force in the sense of war . . . the latter is such that every subordinated or subdued state feels it its most sacred duty to itself to overthrow it as soon as it is able so to do without danger to itself (i.e. people under alien rule based on force must do all in their power to regain their freedom).[71]

The influence from Sekyi's argument was that 'artificial' states like Haiti and Liberia lacked the 'impulse' to remain truly sovereign in a world dominated by Europe; even the Balkan and South American states, he said, were weak and unstable in that environment. Had Haitian and Liberian leaders learnt the secret of African democracy, he argued, they 'would have learnt a great deal to make them unique among the present day states, for . . . the African who, in addition to his being African, has attained to the knowledge of things European, is at any time more than a match for any European who thinks himself of outstanding ability. . . . Therefore Liberia and Haiti being primarily African and only secondary [sic] Americans, should have sought to africanise America instead of americanising Africa.'[72]

Sekyi then reiterated the argument frequently made by West African nationalists in relation to the Garvey movement; he supported the industrial and economic aspects of Garveyism while rejecting its political pretensions: 'We have little or nothing to learn from West Indian or American political institutions; but we have very much to learn from their industrial or economic organisations.'[73]

[71] Sekyi, op. cit., pp. 28–9. The author saw drafts of manuscripts on African political theory by Sekyi in the Sekyi papers—entitled 'An African Political Hierarchy' (Sekyi Papers, Cape Coast); there was also the draft of a thesis for the London M.A. entitled 'The Relation Between the State and the Individual Considered In the Light of Its Bearing on the Conception of Duty', the first chapter being on 'The Social System of the people of the Gold Coast' (ibid.). For details, see Langley, J. Ayo, 'Modernization and its Malcontents: Kobina Sekyi (1892–1956) and the Re-statement of African Political Theory', Centre of African Studies Conference on 'Ideology and Political Theory in African Society', Edinburgh, Feb. 1970.

[72] ibid., p. 32.                              [73] ibid., p. 34.

He also commented on the cultural differences between Afro-American and Africans, and recommended student exchanges as a step
towards better understanding and as a means of freeing African
students from the 'incarceration' of Achimota where they were
'under the absolute rule of white tutors without experience or
inside knowledge of the complexities of the African mind and
temperaments'. His Pan-Africanism thus amounted to cultural and
technical co-operation with Afro-Americans and West Indians in
order to prepare West Africa 'to face England, when she shall
become too arrogant to be considered our guardian, to remonstrate
with her to abandon her dog-in-the-manger policy which has reduced us to our present condition of ineptitude in many respects',[74]
and to a very critical assessment of Afro-American and West Indian
visions of liberating a benighted Africa. He commented on black
nationalism in America, especially on the Du Bois–Garvey controversy adding:

In my opinion the gap between the two camps is inevitable and will itself
produce the element that will bridge it. We in non-Mohammedan Africa
where classes of the very low order observable in so-called civilised
countries are unknown, cannot very well understand the situation in
America. It should however be noted that Dubois was opposed to certain
aspects of the late Booker Washington's policy and propaganda, and
rightly opposed. Tuskegee can no more solve the racial problem in
America than lynching and political and social oppression can. . . . I
think Garveyism is the only possible step in the United States towards the
harmonious blending of the ideas of Booker Washington, the apparent
materialist, with those of Dubois the apparent idealist, into a real solution
of, or a solidly progressive effort to solve, the question, if not of race,
at any rate that of colour, in its operation against social and political
enfranchisement in America.[75]

Turning specifically to Garvey's Pan-Negroism he commented:

Garvey may make blunders in policy, and perhaps either does not take
sufficient time to study conditions before he issues out his orders or begins
to formulate his conclusions, or is not aided by a sufficiently competent
and painstaking staff in his efforts to deal with facts relating to Africa
and Africans. . . . If the only objection to Garvey is that he sometimes
makes blunders, that objection is weak if urged by Englishmen or anglicised
Britishers who have nothing else to say against him. At any rate, we, who
are after all those whose opinions matter as regards the American situation . . . believe that Marcus Garvey is doing necessary work, and would

[74] Sekyi, op. cit., p. 37.          [75] ibid.

very much regret if Liberia is being led by braised [*sic*] propaganda to interpose obstacles which will only make the force of the Garvey movement fiercer when it overcomes its obstacles and sweeps on.[76]

Finally, Sekyi examined the idea of Negro emigration to Africa but, though sympathetic, he ruled it out on the ground that it would 'create new sources of trouble'. He repeated the West African bourgeois nationalist view that 'The question of a return to Africa from America of our brethren there is not to be encouraged by us. . . . The most we can allow is to open a way for the influx of the money of capitalists of our own race in America and the West Indies in order that we may ourselves compete with the gigantic combinations that are being formed in England for the undisguisable purpose of establishing a sort of legal or legalised monopoly of trade.'[77]

We have already outlined the history of the Pan-African movement from 1914 to the close of the 1920s and examined the attitudes of West African nationalists towards it. On the basis of the evidence, it is reasonable to conclude that in spite of their objections to Garvey's concept of a Pan-African state, the majority of the petty-bourgeois nationalist leaders of the N.C.B.W.A., on the whole, tended to be more sympathetic to Garvey's Pan-Negro nationalism and its economic goals, than to the more majestic, more intellectual but ineffective movement of W. E. B. Du Bois. As the subsequent chapters on the N.C.B.W.A. will show, they attempted between 1920 and 1930 to blend Pan-African idealism with a realistic consideration of their social and economic interests.

[76] ibid., pp. 37-8.
[77] ibid., p. 40.

# PART TWO

... As a Congress, we must be in advance of the current racial thought of the day. We must, to a certain extent, be able to guide and control it. There is intense activity in racial progress both in the United States and in the Islands of the Sea. But, admittedly, in the last analysis, the right inspiration must come from the mother continent; and in no part of Africa can such inspiration be so well supplied as in the West. ... As there is an international feeling among all white men, among all brown men, among all yellow men, so must there be an international feeling among all black folk. ...

As a Congress, we have nothing to do with the local politics of the component sections of Congress. We stand upon an open platform in the interest of all British West Africa. Ours is an open fold to which all British West Africans are welcome. ... Men of Congress ... through you I appeal to all Africans everywhere to smoke the peace pipe together whatever sacrifice that may involve, for the African God is weary of your wranglings, weary of your vain disputations, weary of your everlasting quarrels which are a drag upon progress and which keep from you, as a people, the good that is intended for you.

> J. E. CASELY HAYFORD, Presidential
> Addresses to the Third and Fourth
> Sessions of the National Congress of
> British West Africa, quoted in Magnus
> J. Sampson: *The West African Leader-*
> *ship* (Ilfracombe, 1951).

CHAPTER III

# The National Congress of British
# West Africa: 1920–1930

## 1. *Background and Origins*

IF movement on the political stage after the Great War was mainly concerned with the post-war readjustment of European interests in the continent and with the redistribution of the German colonial empire, it was not entirely limited to this. There was also apparent a stirring of African desire for a larger share in their own affairs, even if voiced by a self-appointed leadership of the intelligentsia through various congresses and deputations convened in the post-war years. Encouraged by Woodrow Wilson's new edition of nineteenth-century liberal democracy, by the general optimism of the post-war years, and by the prospect of a new world-wide reconstruction,[1] the press of the Pan-African movement in the United States and of the nationalist groups in West and South Africa, seriously came to believe in their ability to influence the decisions of the peacemakers at Versailles. As one correspondent to the *Gold Coast Leader* observed:

What the average Gold Coast man should be made to know very thoroughly is that this war is but the presage of an unprecedented revolution in the social, economical and political life of all the nations of the earth, and that behind the great forces of destruction that have ranged themselves one against the other are yet more potent forces having for their object the reconstruction of the world.[2]

Yet another lengthy editorial entitled 'Racial Unity' spoke in glowing terms about the millennium; in particular about the dawn

---

[1] Carr, E. H., *The Twenty Years' Crisis: 1919–1939* (London, 1942), pp. 36–7; Charles Adrian in *Phylon*, xxiii (1962), 11, argues that 'A third source of the Pan-African ideology is the Wilsonian idealism in international affairs'. 'The Pan-African Movement: The Search for Organization and Community.'
[2] *Gold Coast Leader* (5 Jan. 1918), p. 5.

of Pan-Africanism, and the contribution the newly awakened Africans would make to post-war civilization.[3]

It was this 'new utopia',[4] created by the transplantation of the theories of liberal democracy to non-Western countries, that was to lead to the disillusionment of the late twenties and thirties.[5] What follows in the *Leader* is to a large extent typical of the utopian thought-style of pan-movements, and of that mixture of idealism, nationalism, and moral imperialism:

Now we are a scattered race even as are the Jews. In some respects we have been the burden bearers as they are. But those very facts make it necessary that our race consciousness should be as pronounced as theirs. It is but asserting the commonplace when we say that the expatriation of some of our people to America and to the West Indies in times past was, in the order of Providence, to hasten a national consciousness; and today our brethren there are turning with longing eyes to the fatherland. Moreover, he is but a poor observer who does not realise that it is but a matter of time when Africa North, West, South and East will come together. . . .

Unity, the editorial stated, was not necessarily based on force; neither was power based on force alone. On the contrary, it resided 'in that calm moral law in the consciences of men'. 'African racial unity, therefore', reasoned the editorial, 'does not necessarily predicate force. . . .' Moreover, Africa, 'intelligently combined and cooperative', could assist a materialistic Europe in the pursuit of peace. Africans, the *Leader* concluded, no longer wanted to shed their blood for European imperialism. Economically Africa could 'starve Europe in no time' in spite of Europe's military power. The solution to the world's problems, therefore, was for mankind to 'adopt a new moral perspective'.[6]

While America was showing Europe how to be better Europeans after the war, the black citizens of that republic were doing pioneering work for a world-wide movement of coloured peoples and at the same time sharpening an already incipient racial consciousness in many parts of Africa. As the *Gold Coast Leader* put it in an editorial:

. . . what about the signs of encouragement we opened with? They come to-day from America, from the promoters of a movement full of hope for the future of our beloved fatherland. It seems that Africans all the world

[3] *Gold Coast Leader* (24–31 July 1920), pp. 4–5.
[4] Carr, op. cit., p. 36.
[5] ibid., p. 37.
[6] *Gold Coast Leader* (24–31 July 1920), pp. 4–5.

over are thinking, thinking of a day which shall see great things for the race. This is the outcome of a racial consciousness which takes in the members of our group variety in all parts of our Continent and whereever else their habitat may be in other parts of the world.[7]

An editorial of the same paper acknowledged the extent of Afro-American influence when it declared: '. . . our intelligent brethren on the other side of the Atlantic are to-day in close touch with all our local movements, as we with theirs.'[8] Franck Schoell, writing in 1923, was worried about what he called 'l'epanouisement soudain de solidarité raciale qui fixe de plus en plus l'attention des Noirs des États-Unis sur leur frères de couleur dans l'Ancien comme dans le Nouveau Monde',[9] and drew attention to the inability of Afro-Americans to see that different problems existed within 'la grande famille intercontinentale des Noirs'.[10]

It is against this political and psychological background that the pan-movements in Asia, Africa, and the Middle East after 1918 should be studied.[11] Pan-Islamism, Pan-Turanism, Pan-Asianism, and Pan Negroism were not the same; what was common to them was their appeal either to religion or to race, and their refusal to be influenced by what they considered alien ideologies.[12] Similar to these movements, but with more concrete demands and operating within a more institutionalized political framework was the incipient inter-territorial organization[13]—the National Congress of British West Africa.

Thus it was that the South African Native National Congress (later African National Congress), formed in January 1912 at Bloemfontein,[14] in December 1918 drew up a memorial to the King

[7] ibid. (28 Oct. 1920), pp. 4–5.
[8] ibid. (14 Aug. 1920), p. 4.
[9] Schoell, Franck L., *La Question des noirs aux États-Unis*, chapter IX, p. 221.
[10] ibid., p. 223.
[11] Shepperson, G., 'Pan-Africanism and "Pan-Africanism": Some Historical Notes', p. 353. Also Michels, Roberto, 'Patriotism', in *First Lectures in Political Sociology*, tr. A. de Grazia (New York, 1965), p. 159.
[12] See Eudin, Xenia, and North, R. C., *Russia and the Far East: 1920–1927: A Documentary Survey* (Stanford, Cal., 1957); Record, Wilson, *The Negro and the Communist Party* (Chapel Hill, N.C., 1951).
[13] *The Political Awakening of Africa*, ed. Rupert Emerson and Martin Kilson, (New York, 1965), p. 43; Rothchild, D. S., *Toward Unity in Africa* (Washington, 1960), p. 179.
[14] A forerunner of the National Congress (South Africa) was the Native Convention which met in Bloemfontein in 1909 to discuss the projected union of the four South African provinces. That meeting was attended by African nationalists like Dr. Walter Rubusana an opponent of the co-operationist Tengo Jabavu,

in which they drew attention to existing grievances. This delegation was composed of Solomon Plaatje, J. T. Gumede, L. T. Mvabaza, R. V. Selope Thema, and the Revd. H. R. Ngcayiya. After an interview with Lloyd George they went on to lobby in Versailles where they met other deputations—including that of the South African Dutch-Afrikaner nationalists led by General Hertzog who were lobbying for the creation of a republic in South Africa. The delegation, like its contemporary the National Congress of British West Africa, achieved very little; in fact, it achieved nothing. Almost about the same time, the Pan-African Congress of W. E. B. Du Bois was holding its first session in Paris (1919). The West African National Congress had also been formed in March 1920 at Accra, and had already collected funds to send a delegation to London the same year to petition the King. Little, it seems, was it realized that the Wilsonian principle of self-determination of small nations would cause so much restlessness in the Colonies.[15] Granted that these were self-appointed leaders of a politically conscious minority and in no way representative of the masses, they were nevertheless the proverbial straw that showed how the wind was blowing.

The idea of a 'West African nationality' did not find sudden expression in the 1920s. West African nationalist literature is full of references to this vague, artificial, and imaginary entity. At least one historian, in dealing with its wider circle of antecedents, has contended that attempts at West African unification date as far back as the Negro 'empires' of the Old Sudan and the Islamic revolutions of the early nineteenth century.[16] Dr. James Africanus Beale Horton of

John Dube, and M. Masisi, see Roux, Edward, *Time Longer Than Rope* (London, 1948), pp. 116–18; also Plaatje, Sol, *Native Life in South Africa* (London, 1916).

[15] In an interview M. Allegret from Cameroons who was director of the Paris Evangelical Missionary Society, replied to the question 'What is the principle movement among your people?': 'Oh, the cry "Africa for the Africans"; the desire to guide their own destiny. This is true both of their political life and in the church, too. They want self-determination.' *Outward Bound*, iii, no. 31 (London, Apr. 1923), 482. Also Lugard, Sir Frederick, 'The Colour Problem', *Edinburgh Review*, ccxxiii (Jan.–Apr. 1921), 275–6.

[16] Aderibigbe, A. B., 'West African Integration: An Historical Perspective', *Nigerian Journal of Economic and Social Studies*, v, no. 1 (Mar. 1963), 9–13. For a discussion of a similar phenomenon in Europe, see Joseph, Bernard, *Nationality: Its Nature and Problems* (London, 1929), pp. 162–3. It is interesting to note that L. Sedar Senghor, President of the Republic of Senegal, returned to this theme argued by Dr. Aderibigbe of reconstructing the old empires of the Sudan into a West African federation. See Senghor, Leopold Sedar, *Constituent Congress of the P.F.A.: Report on the Principles and Programme of the Party* (Paris, 1959), pp. 14–19.

Sierra Leone had, as early as 1867, advocated 'the Self-government of Western Africa'[17] in a book which was a combination of West African history and anti-racist polemics against the 'false theories of modern anthropologists'. It was Horton who asserted in 1867: '. . . it will be my province to prove the capability of the African for possessing a real political Government and national independence; and that a more stable and efficient Government might yet be formed in Western Africa under the supervision of a civilised nation. . . .'[18] Horton, like the West African middle class of the mid-nineteenth century, saw his nationalism in the context of the whole of West Africa; thus he referred in one breath to 'Iboes, Yorubas, Mandingoes, Soosoos, Joloofs . . . Timnehs, Krew, and Dahomians . . .'. He talked about 'the African Race', preferring to use 'nationality' to 'tribe'. The reason for this may be that while conceding that 'nationality' was a European concept, he was also interested in telling the 'anthropologists' that there were political kingdoms in Africa before the advent of the Europeans.[19] 'Examining Western Africa in its entirety,' he said, 'we find it to be composed of a number of political communities, each ruled by a national Government, formed in many cases of distinct nationalities occupying determined territory; but some national communities are broken up into innumerable fractional sections, governed by rebel chiefs, or satraps; others depend upon a political body whose sovereign chief rules over life and property; and others, again, are under well-regulated civilised government.' One of Horton's aims was 'to develop among these different nationalities a true political science'.[20] To him, the self-government recommended for the West African Settlements by the 1865 Select Committee of the House of Commons[21] was 'a glorious idea', 'a grand conception'[22] to be put into practice within a Christian framework and the imperial connection.[23]

[17] Horton, James Africanus, *West African Countries and Peoples: A Vindication of the African Race* (London, 1868), p. vii. Also Shepperson, G., 'An Early African Graduate', *University of Edinburgh Gazette*, xxxii (Jan. 1962), 24; July, Robert, 'Africanus Horton and the Idea of Independence in West Africa'.
[18] Horton, *West African Countries and Peoples*, p. 2.
[19] ibid., chapter IV.
[20] ibid., p. 2.
[21] See *Report From the Select Committee on Africa (Western Coast)*, 26 June 1865, vol. v.
[22] Horton, *West African Countries and Peoples*, part II, 'African Nationality', p. 68.
[23] ibid., p. 273.

By far the most important and most influential theoretician and prophet of *Négritude* and Pan-Africanism in the mid-nineteenth and early twentieth century was Edward Wilmot Blyden.[24] History, as E. H. Carr has reminded us, is not only concerned with the success of great men; it is also concerned with the impact of other great men, whose thought was in advance of their generation.[25] Though he was neither a charismatic leader nor the type of nationalist dreaded by the colonial administration, Blyden, in spite of occasional criticisms as to the impracticability of some of his ideas, commanded the respect and serious attention of a significant section of the colonial intelligentsia in British West Africa.[26]

Blyden was not only the 'ideological father of the idea of West African unity';[27] he also spearheaded (alongside Bishop James Johnson) the cultural nationalism that accompanied it. As a matter of fact, James Johnson did publicly acknowledge: 'I need not say with what pleasure I have read your contributions on the subject of Christianity and the Negro Race. Your writings have always enlightened and edified me; and I have no doubt, very many Africans abroad, as well as many Europeans. . . . What will you recommend me to help me in the study of the Koran in Arabic and English?'[28] Contrary to popular notions, *Négritude* did not begin in Paris or Harlem in the 1920s and 1930s; most of the seeds of this intellectual revolt of colonized men against European civilization can be traced to the equally important 'Back to Africanism' movement of the late nineteenth and early twentieth centuries. And this revolt, it may be added, owed little to outside ethical or philosophical influences. It

[24] Lynch, Hollis R., *Edward Wilmot Blyden, 1832–1912: Pan-Negro Patriot*; Holden, Edith, *Blyden of Liberia*; July, Robert W., 'Nineteenth Century Négritude: Edward W. Blyden'.

[25] Carr, E. H., *What Is History?* (Harmondsworth, 1961), p. 55. Znaniecki, F., *The Social Role of the Man of Knowledge* (New York, 1940), p. 72.

[26] Lynch, op. cit., p. 249.

[27] ibid., p. 250; Lynch, Hollis R., 'Edward W. Blyden: Pioneer West African Nationalist', *Journal of African History*, vi, no. 3 (1965), 373–88.

[28] The Revd. James Johnson to Edward Blyden, quoted in the *Sierra Leone Weekly News* (3 Sept. 1887). For the Dress Reform Society in Freetown sponsored by James Johnson, Blyden, the Revd. J. C. May, Faduma, and J. Langley Grant, see the *Sierra Leone Weekly News* (24 Sept. and 7 Dec. 1887). One is not, of course, arguing that Blyden 'influenced' Johnson; as Ayandele has shown recently in *Holy Johnson* (London, 1970), Johnson had his own independent views on cultural and ecclesiastical nationalism. In any case, there are serious limitations to the usefulness of the concept of 'influence' in the history of ideas: most attributions tend to be largely mythological. See Skinner, Q., 'Meaning and Understanding in the History of Ideas', *History and Theory*, viii, no. 1 (1969).

was very largely the work of Blyden, Bishop James Johnson, Mojola Agbebi, J. E. Casely Hayford, and the Revd. Orishatukè Faduma of Sierra Leone. No doubt, the new interest in African historiography pioneered by W. E. B. Du Bois, Carter Woodson, J. E. Bruce, and Arthur Schomburg in the United States created some interest in West African intellectual circles,[29] but this must not blind us to the movement from the inside and to its reciprocal aspects. For example, the Revd. Orishatukè Faduma, alias James Davies of Sierra Leone, of whom more later, had studied divinity at Yale University where he also had the opportunity to study Islamic history. His cultural and ecclesiastical nationalism was intensified in America. In 1896 we find him attending the conference on Africa at the Gammon Theological Seminary and criticizing missionary work and Christianity in Africa on lines well developed by Blyden and Bishop James Johnson.[30] After teaching in North Carolina from 1898 to 1913, in 1913–14 we find Faduma acting as the ideologue of Chief Alfred Sam's unsuccessful African Movement, which was a colonization scheme to settle Negro American families on the Gold Coast. Bishop James Johnson, as we have noted in chapter II, gave his blessing to this movement. The movement towards 'Africanity' and the name changing which took place in Freetown in the first decade of the twentieth century were largely the work of nationalists like Orishatukè Faduma.[31] This movement continued throughout English-speaking West Africa up to the 1930s and beyond. In his study of the West African press between 1918 and 1939, W. D. Edmonds observes:

The claim that West Africans formed a distinct, racial entity was one of the main reasons for the very existence of a newspaper press in British

---

[29] Shepperson, G. A., 'The African Abroad or the African Diaspora'. Paper read at the International African History Conference, Tanzania, 1965, pp. 9–10; also published in *African Forum*, ii, no. 1 (Summer 1966), 76–91. 'The African Diaspora—or The African Abroad.'

[30] Bowen, J. W., ed., *Africa and the American Negro: Congress on Africa*, 'Religious Beliefs of the Yoruba People in West Africa', pp. 31–6; 'Success and Drawbacks of Missionary Work in Africa by an Eye-Witness', pp. 125–36; Ayandele, E. A., *The Missionary Impact on Modern Nigeria, 1842–1914*, p. 246, especially chapter 8.

[31] Fyfe, Christopher H., *A History of Sierra Leone* (London, 1962), p. 468. I am grateful to Mr. Fyfe who has drawn my attention to the life and work of the Revd. O. Faduma and his contribution to cultural nationalism in Sierra Leone. The contribution of Faduma to Sierra Leone and West African nationalism will be discussed in the section on the Sierra Leone branch of the National Congress Movement.

West Africa . . . in the midst of its passionate and prolonged campaign to convince Africans that contact with Europe was crushing African originality and that, to save themselves, they should revert to African ways of life, and thereby build a truly native culture and civilization, the newspaper press found time to point out that if European civilization had defects it had, equally obviously, some advantages. Therefore press attacks on 'Europeanization' were modified by the suggestion that there should be an eclectic approach to the 'back to African culture' problem. . . . In short, there should be 'Africanisation' and adaptation of Western civilization rather than slavish imitation or wholesale rejection.[32]

Most of the nationalists associated with these newspapers had either known Blyden personally or were acquainted with his Pan-Negro and Africanist writings.[33]

After Blyden's death in 1912, J. E. Casely Hayford, his ideological heir, revived the West African dream, this time giving it some organizational form. It was between 1913 and 1915 that the idea of a Pan-West African meeting was first conceived.[34] In early 1914 Casely Hayford and Dr. Akiwande Savage of Nigeria, who was then practising in the Gold Coast, sent circulars from Sekondi to influential people in Lagos, Freetown, and other parts of the Gold Coast, inviting their opinions on the subject of a West African conference and suggesting that such a meeting was overdue.[35] In

[32] Edmonds, W. D., 'The Newspaper Press in British West Africa 1918 To 1939' (Bristol University M.A. thesis, 1951), p. 113.

[33] Lynch, op. cit., p. 250.

[34] Ruth Perry argued that as far back as 1904 the *Lagos Standard* called for such a conference: Perry, R., *A Preliminary Bibliography of the Literature of Nationalism in Nigeria* (London, 1966), p. 5. Dr. Akiwande Savage, who originated the idea with J. E. Casely Hayford, puts the date between 1912 and early 1917, *Times of Nigeria* (28 Mar. 1920). He was certain, however, that it was in 1912 and early 1913 that the *Gold Coast Leader*, on whose editorial staff he was, started a propaganda campaign for a West African conference. The campaign was joined by Lagos and Freetown newspapers in a concerted bid to sell the idea, the *Lagos Weekly Record* (26 June 1920), p. 6. See also the *Gold Coast Leader* (7 Sept. 1912 and 11 Jan. 1913). David Kimble in *A Political History of Ghana: The Rise of Gold Coast Nationalism, 1850–1928* (London, 1963) does not seem to be certain about the origins of the Congress. As early as 1911, Casely Hayford had referred to the 1905 Gold Coast Pan-African Conference held under the auspices of the G.C.A.R.P.S. as the 'prototype of the kind of African National Assemblies which must be called into being in the near future for the solution of African questions', *Ethiopia Unbound: Studies in Race Emancipation*, pp. 182–3. Sir Leslie M'Carthy, one of the participants in the movement, puts the date at late 1913—Denzer, La Ray, 'The National Congress of British West Africa: Gold Coast Section' (M.A. Thesis, University of Ghana, Legon, 1965), chapter 3, p. 26.

[35] *Lagos Weekly Record* (26 June 1920), p. 6.

early 1915 Casely Hayford and Dr. Savage wrote to the Gold Coast
Aborigines Rights Protection Society concerning 'the question of the
proposed West African Conference which appears to be engaging
the attention of several public men throughout West Africa', adding:
'So far the consensus of individual opinion would seem to indicate
the great desirability of such a Conference being held with as little
delay as possible. We shall be glad of your co-operation and of all
assistance you can give in making the scheme a success.'[36]

## 2. 'Dream of Unity'[37]

. . . This great pioneer of the forward African movement has something
to say on an African League of Nations. You know after the war there
is going to be an European and American League of Nations. . . . Why
should there not also be an African League of Nations . . . with the
same object i.e. to safeguard against all hooligans, whatever their pretensions, those sacred rights mankind has been at such sacrifice and
palms to secure, pledged to boycott as to raw materials any so-called
civilized nation, which attempted to resort to the rule of force and to
disturb the peace of the world?[38]

For Casely Hayford, as for most of the early West African
nationalists, 'British West Africa' existed before 'Gold Coast',
'Sierra Leone', or 'Nigeria'.[39] This identification of the part with the
whole was to continue up to the depression of 1929 and the 1930s
when a narrower conception of nationality became dominant.[40] The
educated West African urban 'middle class', from the Sierra Leonean
diaspora of the nineteenth century to the late 1930s, had more in

[36] File no. 92, 197/65. Casely Hayford and Akiwande Savage to the Secretary,
Gold Coast A.R.P.S., Hamilton Hall, Cape Coast (26 May 1915). A.R.P.S.
files, Ghana National Archives.
[37] The sub-title is taken from Claude Welch's *Dream of Unity: Pan-Africanism
and Political Unification in West Africa* (New York 1966).
[38] *Gold Coast Leader* (19 Oct. 1918), p. 3.
[39] Kimble, op. cit., pp. 374–5.
[40] e.g. *Gold Coast Leader* (26 Sept. 1928) asserted: 'This idea of a Gold Coast
Nation is a fundamental one.' *Sierra Leone Weekly News* (27 Oct. 1928) also
declared: 'Whatever may be said to the contrary Sierra Leone is our country, and
our requirements and advancement should obtain full consideration.' It is
interesting to learn, however, that between 1918 and 1939 'no really considerable
body of evidence is to be discovered in the newspapers to suggest that the press
did not consistently view matters from a wider, West African point of view rather
than from the point of view of individual colonies'. Edmonds, op. cit., p. 128.

common, and communicated more easily with their counterparts along the coastal towns than with their brethren in their own hinterland.[41]

Having been told that they had no history worth taking seriously, and conscious of the fact that their own socio-economic group had limited opportunities in the colonial system, it is perhaps not surprising that the nationalist intelligentsia came to prefer a visionary 'West African nationality'[42] to a political system in which they had no voice and which, in any case, was alien and therefore, in their view, oppressive.[43] In fact, Gold Coast newspapers never tired of denouncing alien rule. As John Plamenatz has observed, 'The greatest misfortune that can befall a nation is when it is ruled by an alien Power not chosen by the people themselves. . . . Alien Governments never prove successful. . . . Unfortunately for Africa the self-determination applied to the Little States of Europe or its modified form as applied to the peoples who had lately been under Turkish misrule was not applicable.'[44] Indeed one of the editorials observed 'The introduction of the British system of Government in place of

[41] Kimble, op. cit., pp. 374–5. There were, of course, a few outstanding exceptions, including Casely Hayford, to this attitude. The earliest of these was Edward Blyden; see Blyden, E. W., *Africa and the Africans: Proceedings on the Occasion of a Banquet . . . August 15th, 1903 to Edward Blyden by West Africans in London* (London, 1903), p. 43. For a discussion of Blyden's ideas on nation-building in a developing society, see the article by Wilson, H. S., 'The Changing Image of the Sierra Leone Colony in the Works of E. W. Blyden', *Sierra Leone Studies*, xi (1958), 136–48.

In the Gold Coast the Revd. S. R. B. Attoh-Ahuma protested that the Gold Coast was a nation because it had a history and an indigenous system of government: *The Gold Coast Nation and National Consciousness* (Liverpool, 1911), quoted in Kimble, op. cit., p. 524.

[42] The report on the federation of the British West African Colonies (1939) dismissed the idea of a West African Nationality as a 'theoretical abstraction', and a unitary state of British West Africa as 'an artificial creation', adding that 'It is only recently that the Africans, e.g. Nigeria have begun to acquire a consciousness of political unity as "Nigerians": to superimpose the idea of unity as "British West Africans" would set back the present healthy growth of Colony-pride'. GAMBIA 3/360. Conf. M.P. No. 2535, 14/12/39: 'Committee appointed to consider closer union between the West African Colonies', *Gambia Records Office*.

[43] Joseph, op. cit., pp. 133, 324. See also Arendt, Hannah, *The Origins of Totalitarianism* (London, 1958), pp. 231–2, 237; Shils, Edward, 'The Intellectuals in the Political Development of the New States', in Kautsky, John H., ed., *Political Change in Underdeveloped Countries: Nationalism and Communism* (John Wiley, New York, 1962); and Michels, op. cit., pp. 160–2.

[44] *Gold Coast Leader* (3 May 1919).

the one existing before was an encroachment which no self-respecting nation would allow.'[45]

In spite of all this objection to 'alien rule', there was never any mention of severing relations with the colonial power; alien rule was bad but there were good reasons for consenting to it: it was better to demand more opportunities for a particular social group and make moderate demands than to do away with alien rule completely; and one could still be 'free', 'under the Union Jack'. Even Herbert Macaulay, regarded by the administration as the gadfly of Lagos politics, could speak sincerely about the 'manifold blessings of Pax Britannica'. The National Congress of British West Africa, for example, declared

That the policy of the Congress shall be to maintain strictly and inviolate the connection of the British West African Dependencies with the British Empire, and to maintain unreservedly all and every right of free citizenship of the Empire and the fundamental principle that taxation goes with effective representation . . . to aid in the development of the political institutions of British West Africa under the Union Jack . . . and, in time, to ensure within her borders the Government of the people by the people for the people; to secure equal opportunity for all, to preserve the lands of the people for the people. . . .[46]

To take two more examples of this attitude to the Empire from the local press. In May 1920 the *Colonial and Provincial Reporter* (Sierra Leone) was of the opinion that, 'The great ideal before us is the distant one of West Africa as a self-governing state in the British Commonwealth of Nations.'[47] While the *Gambia Outlook and Senegambian Reporter* asserted, 'We hold that the British Constitution is sufficient to meet our needs as a people destined to grow and develop. We therefore resolve to maintain our attachment to the British Empire. . . . We advocate autonomy within the British Empire.'[48]

Within such a framework, it is not surprising to find Casely Hayford vigorously advocating the Pan-Africanism and *négritude* he

[45] ibid. (3 May 1919); also Plamenatz, John, *On Alien Rule and Self-Government* (London, 1960), pp. 1–2 and 84 below.
[46] Paras. 17–19 of *The Constitution of the National Congress of British West Africa: Passed by the Second Session of the National Congress . . . Held at Freetown, Sierra Leone, January–February, 1923*. Also, p. 9 of the *Resolutions of the Conference of Africans of British West Africa Held at Accra, Gold Coast from 11th to 29th March, 1920*.
[47] *Colonial and Provincial Reporter* (1 May 1920).
[48] *Gambia Outlook and Senegambian Reporter* (29 Aug. 1931).

inherited from Blyden and at the same time couching his political demands in legalistic and constitutional language. It is this mentality which leads Padmore to conclude, à la Mannheim, 'Judged in terms of his social background and the period in which he lived and worked, Casely Hayford was undoubtedly the greatest national political leader and social reformer West Africa had yet produced. His political faults were the common failings of his class. Born in 1866 and educated under Nonconformist middle-class influences, he reflected all the virtues and political limitations of mid-Victorian liberalism. . . .'[49]

What did Casely Hayford mean by 'West African Nationhood' or 'United West Africa'? The concept, as has been pointed out, is an artificial one.[50] He himself never clearly defined it; it was the sentiment behind it, rather than any clear-cut programme of national unification, that gave the idea wide currency. The appeal to race and to collective disabilities found ready acceptance along the coast.[51] According to Magnus Sampson

. . . Casely Hayford always thought in terms of Nationhood of British West Africa as distinct from Self-Government. That was the dominating political philosophy of his. It is significant that this remarkable man of vision drew a line of demarcation between 'Nationhood' his favourite term and 'Self-Government' which may mean just political power without the prerequisites that go to make a self-sufficient and self-reliant Nation. Thus Casely Hayford did not believe in the new doctrine 'Seek ye first the political kingdom and all else shall be added unto you', because he knew as a wise man that mere power constitutes a strong temptation to selfishness. . . . As a great leader of men he saw that one touch of nature

[49] Padmore, G., *The Gold Coast Revolution* (London, 1953), p. 52; also Sampson, Magnus J., 'Casely-Hayford And The Idea Of A United British West Africa', Cape Coast Regional Archives, *W. E. G. Sekyi Papers*, 715/64, lecture delivered at the New Year School at Adisadel, Cape Coast, 4 Jan. 1952. The theme of the colloquium was 'The Changing Gold Coast'.

[50] Kimble, op. cit., p. 374. For a general discussion of similar concepts, see the perceptive essay by Mazrui, Ali A., 'On The Concept "We Are All Africans"', *American Political Science Review*, lvii (1963), 88–97.

[51] Hayford, J. E. Casely, *The Truth About the West African Land Question*, pp. 101–3; *United West Africa* (London, 1919), *passim*. For the reception of the latter book, which was launched to coincide with the Accra Conference, see the *Times of Nigeria* (17 May 1920), p. 4, which, in a review of *United West Africa*, exhorted its readers: 'It is time that we should rise above that mean spirit which thinks that because we have different political opinions therefore we must become sworn enemies to each other and seek each other's ruin. . . . Unity must be the watchword and patriotism the principle. . . . We must strive for a United West Africa. . . .'

had made British West Africa kin. The common threat to our ancestral lands had made British West Africa one—one in danger, one in safety. It was the view of Casely Hayford that Africa would always be Africa both in Church and State. . . . He thought also that the methods of the pioneers of civilisation among us were peculiar. They were even dangerous because they tended to destroy African nationality.[52]

Like the political ideas of most visionaries in politics, Casely Hayford's Pan-West African dream contained an element of unreality. Yet he was regarded by contemporaries as 'the greatest man of action to whom the Gold Coast has given birth'.[53] It is arguable that it was precisely because his ideal sought to 'transcend history' that it commanded the attention of the West African intelligentsia, and that it was mainly because it was so 'unreal' that it became a necessary complement to action.

His Pan-Negro philosophy had been stated as early as 1911 in his *Ethiopia Unbound: Studies in Race Emancipation. United Empire* (Oct. 1911), in a review of the book, described it as 'a study in the self-realisation of the negro'. But like Sir Hugh Clifford, it went on to say that Hayford was applying his ideas to 'a continent where races are innumerable, and nations, as we understand the term, do not exist'. The review added, however, that West Africans were thinking 'upon lines that are at present foreign to European methods of thought . . . retaining all that is good in native institutions, and preserving fundamental laws and customs that are part and parcel of the national consciousness'. As is well known, John Edward Bruce attributed much of Hayford's Pan-Negro views expressed in this book to the intellectual influence of Edward Blyden; Blyden himself referred to the work as 'an inspiration'.

After Blyden's death we find Casely Hayford actively propagating the idea of West African unity. He described his widely read *The Truth About the West African Land Question* as a work 'hopefully inscribed to United West Africa', and preached unity and nationalism in its pages.[54] As Dr. Blyden III has argued, Casely Hayford was a co-operationist and a constitutional nationalist.[55] When he spoke of 'united West Africa', he meant not only unification of most of

[52] Sampson, op. cit., pp. 4–7. See also Casely Hayford's article, 'Nationalism As A West African Ideal', *WASU*, ii (1926), 23–8.

[53] Sampson, op. cit., p. 2; *Aurora* (Sierra Leone) (30 Apr. 1921), p. 8.

[54] *The Truth About the West African Land Question*, pp. 101–3.

[55] *New Nations in a Divided World*, ed. Kurt London (New York, 1965), contribution by Dr. Blyden III, pp. 149–50.

the administration of British West Africa, but also recognition of the principle of elective representation and of 'African nationality' or 'individuality' within this imperial framework. As he himself put it in 1913,

In 1903 United Nigeria had not been thought of. What is there to prevent United West Africa of the near future? It may seem presumptuous for an African to have any views upon the matter. It may appear more so to advance them. . . . We in West Africa are ardent imperialists. But our imperialism is tempered with common sense. . . . What, then, of united West Africa? . . . will British policy in West Africa be one of repression, or one that will give free scope to the individuality of the people? . . . We believe in British Imperial Africa. . . .[56]

In spite of its shortcomings,[57] the West African nationalist press provides a useful guide to 'public opinion' on the idea of a West African inter-territorial movement. In his useful study of the West African press between 1918 and 1939 Edmonds concludes:

. . . the press seems to have been devoted to the cause of fostering and promoting a spirit of nationalism and supporting the political, economic and social aspirations which were the inevitable corrollaries of such growth . . . the general attitude remained unchanged and strongly in favour of those who were claiming for their people racial peculiarities and distinctions making for political separateness, and the right for an immediate and substantial increase in native participation in public service leading to an ever increasing degree of political autonomy. . . . The sentiment most often appealed to, the creed most systematically taught, the reason for publication most boldly advanced, the cause most constantly defended, and, perhaps one of the words most frequently used, was nationalist [sic]. . . . Nationalism formed the very raison d'être of the press in British West Africa. This was, naturally a somewhat vague, indefinite impression, an amalgam of all those sentiments and ideas expressed in so many ways by different newspapers.[58]

According to Edmonds, 'a kind of vague Pan-African movement' was discernible in the press, and 'there was about the idea a kind of hazy nationalist-intellectual appeal'. Most of the influential nationalists of this period were closely connected with some of these newspapers. Casely Hayford, for example, had been a journalist from the 1890s; he took over the Western Echo which was owned by his

[56] Hayford, The Truth About the West African Land Question, pp. 9–12.
[57] Edmonds, op. cit., pp. 6–27, 43, 259–66.
[58] ibid., pp. 76–7. For the role of the press in the development of nationalist sentiment, see Joseph, op. cit., chapter IX, p. 146.

uncle James Brew of Dunquah during the latter's absence in Europe between 1888 and 1915, and rechristened it the *Gold Coast Echo* in which he advocated municipal government.[59] He was also associated with the nationalistic *Gold Coast Leader*. J. Claudius May of Freetown, another influential figure in Freetown politics and in the Congress movement, owned the moderate but well-produced and widely circulated *Sierra Leone Weekly News*; Beoku-Betts owned the *Aurora* which flourished briefly after a fiery start in 1919; Kobina Sekyi wrote extensively in various Gold Coast papers; Dr. Akiwande Savage who originated the Congress idea with Casely Hayford, later owned the *Nigerian Spectator* in Lagos. 'Professor' Adeoye Deniga and the Revd. Patriarch J. G. Campbell, both active members of the Lagos Committee of the N.C.B.W.A., frequently contributed to various Lagos newspapers, Deniga became the editor of the 'radical' *Lagos Weekly Record* in August 1918; E. F. Small of the Gambia founded and edited the *Gambia Outlook and Senegambian Reporter* in 1930.

As we have already noted, the newspapers of the period under review frequently spoke about a vague geo-political entity which was usually referred to as 'United West Africa'. This term in fact formed the title of some of the nationalist tracts written by well-known West Africans. For example, Casely Hayford's widely read *United West Africa*; Ladipo Solanke's *United West Africa (or Africa) at the Bar of the Family of Nations* (London, 1927); Dr. J. A. B. Horton had written *West African Countries and Peoples* and *Political Economy of Western Africa* in the 1860s. Then too there was J. W. de Graft Johnson's *Towards Nationhood in West Africa* (London, 1928). There were other variations: J. C. Zizer, an ardent supporter of the Congress movement, called his Lagos newspaper *West African Nationhood* which, he stated, supported the programme of the N.C.B.W.A. and was not interested in 'party politics'. After the Accra Conference in 1920, the Congress planned to publish a newspaper to be called the *West African National Review*, although this was never published. The idea persisted in the depression of the

[59] Sampson, Magnus, *A Brief History of Gold Coast Journalism* (Winneba, July 1934), p. 13. For an account of the Brew family (with which Casely Hayford was connected) and its participation in nationalist politics, see Priestly, Margaret, 'The Emergence of an Élite: A Case Study of a West Coast Family', in *The New Élites of Tropical Africa*, ed. P. C. Lloyd (London, 1966), pp. 87–100. Also Priestly, Margaret, *West African Coast Settlements: A Family Study* (London, 1969).

1930s even though its practicability was being questioned;[60] for example, Dr. Nnamdi Azikiwe, one of the modern exponents of Pan-Africanism, named his popular paper the *West African Pilot* in 1934 and stated in full his Pan-Negro philosophy in *Renascent Africa* (London, 1968). Even as late as the 1950s there were brief references to this idea: the late Alhadji Adegoke Adelabu, that irrepressible political exhibitionist, wrote a tract called *Africa in Ebullition* in which he declared, 'Nigeria is too small for my vision. My ideal is a West African States Union, stretching from the banks of the Gambia to the shores of the Congo in panoramic beauty and unparalleled grandeur.'[61] In 1955 Dr. Chike Obi, an able mathematician but somewhat peripatetic politician, advocated what he called Kemalism and 'regimental government', in the course of which he referred to a 'Greater West Africa' as 'ideal from overwhelming considerations'.[62] Ex-President Nkrumah, with whom Pan-Africanism will always be associated, stated in 1953 that West African unification was his 'basic personal philosophy'.[63] Some of Nkrumah's writings constantly return to this subject. The West African National Secretariat he set up with Wallace Johnson, Ashie Nikoi, and others in London in 1946, and Nkrumah's little-known Kumasi Congress of 1953 were, as we shall show, conscious attempts to revive and extend the ideals of the N.C.B.W.A.

The persistence of the Pan-West African idea is illustrated by the fact that as late as 1945, long after the N.C.B.W.A. had been relegated to the scrap heap of history, a section of the Gold Coast nationalist intelligentsia, which included W. E. G. Sekyi, Dr. Nanka Bruce, Dr. J. B. Danquah, the Hon. G. E. Moore, the Hon. Akilagpa Sawyerr, A. M. Akiwumi, and K. B. Ateko, sought to revive the same movement.[64] The Hon. I. M. Garba-Jahumpa of the Gambia, who was a delegate to the 1945 Manchester Pan-African Congress, and was associated with George Padmore and Dr. Nkrumah, states

[60] Hopkins, A. G., 'Economic Aspects of Political Movements in Nigeria and in the Gold Coast 1918–1939', *Journal of African History*, vii, no. 1 (1966), 150–1.

[61] Adelabu, Alhadji Adegoke, *Africa In Ebullition* (Ibadan, 1952), p. 76.

[62] Obi, Chike, *Our Struggle: A Political Analysis of the Problems of the Negro Peoples Struggling for True Freedom* (Ibadan, 1955), p. 23.

[63] Quoted in Rothchild, D. S., *Toward Unity in Africa* (Washington, 1960), chapter X, p. 184; see also pp. 182–8. Timothy, Bankole, *Kwame Nkrumah: His Rise to Power* (London, 1955), pp. 32, 51, 59–60, 172. Nkrumah, Kwame, *The Autobiography* (Edinburgh, 1957), pp. 43–4.

[64] See chapter IX.

that 'For West Africa it [i.e. the year 1945] marked the revival of the idea of the West African National Congress of the early 1920s.'[65] As E. F. Small was, in a sense, the political mentor of Mr. Jahumpa, it is not surprising that the latter has inherited the pan-African tradition.

Following the call to action by Casely Hayford and Dr. Akiwande Savage, the West African newspapers began to campaign for a West African Conference in earnest as early as 1916,[66] but very little was done by way of organization up to the end of 1917. By 1919, however, press support for the projected conference had reached a new peak. In March 1919 the *Sierra Leone Weekly News* was of the opinion that 'the proposed British West African Conference, if materialised, would be of great advantage to the West African colonies'.[67] The same paper declared in 1921, 'The description given by Europe to the word Nation may not apply to us. But if the name is inapplicable the thing is there. From Nigeria to Sierra Leone we are one people and what applied to one portion applies to the other.'[68] The *Gold Coast Leader*, which led the campaign to popularize the conference movement, summed up, 'So accustomed has the public mind become to the idea of a united British West Africa that it is quite the fashion now politically, economically and educationally to speak of British West Africa as a whole.'[69] The rhetorical columns of the outspoken *Aurora* called with its usual fervour, 'Let the soul of the people vibrate to the tune of relief . . . we pray for this body politic, this central political body from whose winged borders we look for the bursting forth of a dazzling light emitting the potential sparks of freedom and freedom only.'[70] And another paper observed, 'One lesson above all others which the results of the late world upheaval have taught the African races is the need for organising an African Brotherhood.'[71] The *Gold Coast Leader* put the matter very simply, 'We like the phrase "United West Africa".'[72] But the radical *Lagos Weekly Record*, under the editorship of Thomas H. Jackson,

[65] Personal communication from the Hon. I. M. Garba-Jahumpa, Member of the Gambia House of Representatives, 17 Nov. 1966.
[66] See *Gold Coast Leader* (3 Aug. 1916).
[67] *Sierra Leone Weekly News* (8 Mar. 1919); also *Sierra Leone Weekly News* (6 Mar., 29 May, 26 June 1920).
[68] ibid. (12 Mar. 1921).
[69] *Gold Coast Leader* (28 June 1924).
[70] *Aurora* (1 Oct. 1921; also 31 Dec. 1921).
[71] *Times of Nigeria* (1 Mar. 1920).
[72] *Gold Coast Leader* (28 June 1924).

one of the local congress officials, was not to be outdone; in verse equal to its prose it exhorted:

> Come join ye blacks with unity
> 'Tis up to you to show
> The sons of white community
> Thy manhood not laid low.
> With unison your might will come,
> Let all thy racial pride
> Burst forth, as doth the morning sun
> On life's great seething tide. . . .[73]

### 3

BY the middle of 1919, only the Sierra Leone and Gold Coast territorial committees of the N.C.B.W.A. had been fully organized for the projected conference at Accra. Meanwhile, after corresponding with the various committees, the Gold Coast Section had assumed a co-ordinating and directing role of the whole movement. In early 1919, with its focus on Versailles, it drew up a declaration, which was sent to the other committees and British West African governors. The declaration, which was unmistakably the work of the lawyers, was substantially the same as the resolutions passed at the Accra Conference of the N.C.B.W.A. a year later.[74] The resolution was prompted by a telegram on 24 December 1918 from Robert Broadhurst, secretary of the newly formed African Progress Union in London, advising the Congress to approach the Colonial Office through the various governors.

By the first week in January 1919 the Gold Coast section had already consulted the other West African committees[75] and had submitted a resolution to the Governor, Sir Hugh Clifford who, as usual, replied that he wanted to know how the Gold Coast section

---

[73] *Lagos Weekly Record* (28 Sept. 1920).

[74] For the copy of the resolution, see F. V. Nanka Bruce, Secretary of the Eastern Province Section of the British West African Conference to the Private Secretary, Christianborg Castle, Accra, 14 Feb. 1919, p. 3. Correspondence Relating to the National Congress of British West Africa, A.D.M. 5 Apr. 1919. G.N.A.; also undated draft resolution in Herbert Macaulay Papers, iv. 11, 4 Jan. 1919—Letters of the National Congress of British West Africa, Ibadan University Library.

[75] T. Hutton-Mills, President Accra Committee, F. V. Nanka Bruce, and C. H. Fird (President of the Secondee Committee) to Dr. Akiwande Savage, Secretary of the Nigerian (Lagos) Committee, 4 Jan. 1919; Herbert Macaulay Papers, iv. 11: Letters of the N.C.B.W.A., 1920. Ibadan University Library.

came into being, by what authority it claimed to speak on behalf
of the chiefs and people of the Gold Coast, and why the resolutions
of a 'projected' conference were already public knowledge.[76] Hutton-
Mills replied that the N.C.B.W.A. was 'composed of several of the
most enlightened and educated people of the Gold Coast' and that
some of the Principal Chiefs served on its Committee. In a sentence
as nebulous as Hobbes's covenant, he argued that these committees
were 'appointed by Resolutions at public meetings at which both
the literate and illiterate classes of the Communities were duly
represented'. Noting the growing social and economic status of the
educated and professional class in traditional society and in relation
to the Chiefs whose authority the administration was increasing,
Mills also argued that 'the educated and enlightened community of
the Gold Coast in presenting any prayer for the redress of grievances,
for needed reforms, as subjects and citizens of the British Empire,
do not require the mandate of all the Chiefs . . . they, the educated
classes themselves, form a substantial and influential and integral
part of the people of the Gold Coast . . .'. He also explained that the
resolution Sir Hugh was worried about was the result of the co-
operation of the various West African committees.[77] The petition of
the Freetown Creoles to Lord Milner in connection with the rice
and anti-Syrian riots of 1919 was also included in the correspondence with Sir Hugh.[78]

In March 1920, mainly through the efforts of the Gold Coast
Section, the Conference of Africans of British West Africa, composed
of forty-five delegates,[79] met at the Accra Native Club. The Conference lasted from 11 March to 29 March. At the Conference the
financing of a deputation to England was discussed; £25,000 was
considered necessary for the purpose. On the very first day of the
Conference about £10,000 was subscribed; T. Hutton-Mills, the

[76] C. M. Holme, Private Secretary, to the Secretary, Eastern Province Section
of the Committee of the Projected West African Conference, Jamestown, Accra,
17 Feb. 1919, p. 4: Correspondence Relating to the N.C.B.W.A.
[77] *Nigerian Pioneer*, vi, no. 264 (31 Jan. 1919); draft resolution in Macaulay
MSS. iv. 11, 4 Jan. 1919; Correspondence Relating to the N.C.B.W.A. G.N.A.
ADM, 5 Apr. 1919. pp. 8–9.
[78] Correspondence Relating to the N.C.B.W.A., pp. 53–60. G.N.A.
[79] Macmillan, Allister, *The Red Book of West Africa* (London, 1920), p. 140.
E. J. P. Brown, Nana Ofori Atta, and Dr. Akiwande Savage were noticeably
absent; apart from the Ga Manche (Paramount Chief of Accra) and Manche
Kojo Ababio, only W. E. G. Sekyi turned up in traditional dress. D. Westermann
puts the number of delegates around fifty: 'Ein Kongress Der Westafrikaner',
*Koloniale Rundschau* (Berlin, 1920), p. 164.

President, subscribed £1,050 and the Gold Coast Section £10,345. It was then decided to increase the Congress inaugural fund to £100,000.[80]

This important conference in the history of Pan-Africanism attracted wide attention in Africa, London, and as far afield as the West Indies (Trinidad).[81] Diedrich Westermann, a sympathetic observer, remarked that this unique gathering was more than a flash in the pan:

The territorial separation of the four colonies and their partly differing conditions and interests will always be a serious impediment to an impressive people's movement. . . . In any case the relevance of this first congress of the West Africans should not be underestimated; doubtless it is a milestone in the development of the negro race. Who would have thought it possible twenty years ago that negroes from distant parts of West Africa would come together to discuss seriously and with dignity the problem of their political future; that they would be able to raise millions of Marks for purely idealistic purposes! The general opinion was, that a feeling of national cohesion has either never been present among negroes or has been destroyed a long time ago by the influence of colonial powers.

To-day we realise, that in the coloured race a new feeling of community is awakening, a feeling which has been made possible only by the influence of the colonial powers; it is the same education, the same language, the same views which they learned from the nation of their masters; the

[80] Westermann, op. cit., p. 166; Dennett, R. E., *The West African Congress and Government on Native Lines* (*African World* publication, London, 1920), p. 5. S. O. Akiwumi, T. Hutton-Mills, H. Van Hien, the Ga Mantse, Prince Ata Amonu, and J. E. Casely Hayford would have been the principal donors. The correlation of wealth and social status with office-holding in the Congress has already been commented on in the sections dealing with the territorial committees of the N.C.B.W.A.

[81] *Gold Coast Times* (15 Sept. 1931), p. 11, correspondence between S. R. Wood, General Secretary of the N.C.B.W.A. and Charles Taylor of Port of Spain, Trinidad, and the *Negro Progress Convention* of Georgetown, Demerara, British Guiana. Charles Taylor, editor of the Trinidad *Nationalist* even suggested establishing a branch of the N.C.B.W.A. 'in the western world' to 'work in co-ordination with Congresses on your side, and at certain times meet either here or on your side for round-table conferences'. In fact, a branch of the N.C.B.W.A. was established in Trinidad in October 1930 for 'the larger advancement of the African race . . . [and] a more intimate knowledge of, and contact with, our Fatherland— Africa—. . .'. See also *West African Nationhood* (9 Apr. 1931): 'The Negro Voice and Activities the World Over: The West Indies and the Congress of British West Africa.' It is interesting to note that C. Fredericks, the president of the Georgetown *Negro Progress Convention*, had also attended the London session of the 1919 Pan-African Congress and may have met some of the African participants.

hard, externally benevolent, but in reality suppressing treatment, intended
to exploit them, which asked for protest and made them form a bond of
unity. . . . The negro knows that among European values too not all
that glitters is not gold. That means not at all a rejection of all things the
white man has to bring him. He wants to make use of European values
in order to reach his own ideals. He wants to employ the things he can
learn from the Europeans so as to become a true, self-assured African.[82]

Dusé Mohammed Ali's pan-coloured *Africa and Orient Review*
waxed eloquent on that occasion:

. . . We have all along said . . . that unity among West Africans is an
essential to commercial and political prosperity . . . it is unthinkable
that a Native of Sierra Leone should be accounted a foreigner on the Gold
Coast or in Nigeria, and *vice versa*.
  This being an age of combinations of one kind or another, it behoves
the coloured people of the world to show a solid front. There must no
longer be the question of a coloured foreigner in the country of other
coloured men. All non-Europeans are labelled 'niggers' by Europeans;
coloured peoples being therefore in the same political and economic ship,
It is extremely ludicrous for men of the same ethnographic stock to regard
each other as foreigners.

Whether or not there were semantic difficulties inherent in the
concept of 'we are all Africans', the *Africa and Orient Review* did not
care to know; as far as it was concerned, the simple act of bringing
'leaders of West African thought' together was more important
than scholarly disputations about the elements of nationality.[83]
  In West Africa itself, the convening of the Accra Conference gave
a wonderful opportunity to the budding poets of the nationalist
press to try out their Edwardian metres. One such poet entitled his
work *An Epoch* and saw fit to begin it with a Pan-African preamble:

Be it noted that Africa is the only continent the interests of whose peoples
are identical in that they are geographically united, while from an ethno-
logical point of view they are of one race. The rise or fall of one of her
many peoples, therefore, affects all the others. It goes without saying
that her inward greatness and consequently her outward recognition is
locked up in one word: UNITY. Individualism, selfishness, and such like
monopolistic tendencies may thrive elsewhere, but to Africa they have
been known to be her bitterest enemies. . . . The writer sees in a vision a
day, be it to-morrow or some centuries to come, when persons representing all the different peoples of Africa and every interest that is in that

[82] Westermann, op. cit., pp. 167–8.
[83] *Africa and Orient Review* (May 1920).

continent . . . will meet on a common platform, and plan to work out their own salvation which can only be done by themselves.

On the first day (11 March) the Congress delegates discussed elective representation, equality of opportunity based on merit and regardless of colour, and the establishment of a West African University along the lines proposed earlier by E. W. Blyden and Pope Hennesy in the 1880s. On the constitutional side, the most important resolutions were:

2. That this Conference recommends a Constitution on the following lines: (1) An Executive Council as at present composed. (2) A Legislative Council composed of representatives, of whom one-half shall be nominated by the Crown and the other half elected by the people, to deal with Legislation generally. (3) A House of Assembly, composed of the members of the Legislative Council together with other financial representatives elected by the people, who shall have the power of imposing all taxes and of discussing freely and without reserve the items on the Annual Estimates of Revenue and Expenditure prepared by the Governor of the Executive Council and approving of them.

3. That each British West African Community shall have the power of electing members to both the Legislative Council and the House of Assembly through such local groups as may be found most convenient and expedient, and that where indigenous institutions do not provide a ready means of ascertaining the will of the people, other qualifying method of voting, such as property or an Educational standard, shall be resorted to. . . .

5. That this Conference desires to place on record its disapprobation of the invidious distinctions made in the present West African Civil Service by reason of colour, and is of the opinion that all future entries should be based on merit by competitive examinations, and pledges itself to submit proposals thereanent [sic] at the proper quarter.

6. That Municipal Corporations with full powers of local self-government be established in each principal town of the British West African Colonies, and that of the members of such Municipal Corporations four-fifths shall be elected by the rate-payers and one-fifth nominated by the Crown, and that such elected and nominated members have the power of electing the Mayor of the Corporation, who however must be an elected member.[84]

On educational reforms, the Conference advocated a British West African University 'on such lines as would preserve in the students a sense of African Nationality', the appointment of African and other

[84] *National Congress of British West Africa: Resolutions of the Conference of Africans of British West Africa. Held at Accra, Gold Coast, from 11th to 29th March, 1920*, p. 1.

educationists by the various Boards of Education, to give advice on reforms, 'guided by the experience of such communities as Japan which have encountered similar problems to that of West African Communities', and that each section of the N.C.B.W.A. should start a National Educational Fund, 'so as to ensure the development of a National Educational Scheme', and also promote schemes for secondary education 'on national lines supported by the people'. They also recommended, 'That compulsory Education throughout the British West African Colonies be introduced by law, and that the standard of both the Primary and the Secondary Schools be uniformly raised to meet the Standard of the University.'[85]

On the second day they discussed 'Alien Problems with Particular Reference to the Syrian Question', the much disliked Empire Resources Development Committee, and important problems of banking and shipping which directly affected the interests of the African merchant class, the produce merchant, and the middleman who were experiencing great difficulties because of post-war fiscal and economic controls and the growing power of extra-territorial firms. It is interesting to note that In their desperation the Conference, influenced by the merchants, and by approaches of Marcus Garvey's U.N.I.A. through the Revd. Patriarch J. G. Campbell, resolved:

That this Conference, being of the opinion that Trade competition in the British West African Dependencies should be free from restriction, views with great dissatisfaction the passing of the Palm Kernels Export Duty Ordinance. . . . That, in view of the difficulties hereto experienced in the matter of space on British bottoms by legitimate African Traders and Shippers, this Conference welcomes competition in the shipping line with particular reference to the 'Black Star Line'.[86]

On the third day the Conference dealt with legal reforms affecting all the four territories, especially the establishment of a West African Court of Appeal. They also resolved to set up a West African Press Union in recognition of 'the important part the Press plays in National Development'; a committee of experienced journalists was to look into the problem of better co-ordination of the press policy of the English-speaking West African press. It was also proposed to start an official organ of the N.C.B.W.A., under the editorship of

[85] ibid., p. 2. Resolutions 2–7.
[86] ibid., p. 3. Resolutions 2 and 5. For details of the economic aspects of the Congress, see chapter V.

J. E. Casely Hayford, and financed by the Congress Inaugural Fund, to be called the *British West African National Review*.[87]

At the fourth sitting of the Conference, sanitary and medical reforms were thoroughly dealt with, and highly technical papers read by Dr. H. C. Bankole-Bright of Sierra Leone; they also dealt with residential segregation of races and the position of African doctors in government service. The eternal and important land question was also discussed, with the Conference tartly declaring: 'That in the opinion of this Conference the principle of Trusteeship with respect to the lands of the people of British West Africa has been overdone, and that it is proper to declare that the average British West African is quite capable of controlling and looking after his own interests in the land.'[88]

The fifth sitting dealt with 'The Right of the People to Self Determination', after hearing a paper read by E. F. Small of the Gambia. After the usual declaration of its 'unfeigned loyalty and devotion to the throne and person of His Majesty the King-Emperor', the Conference went on to state:

That the Conference views with alarm the right assumed by the European powers of exchanging or partitioning Countries between them, without reference to, or regard for, the wishes of the people, and records the opinion that such a course is tantamount to a species of slavery.

That this Conference condemns specifically the partitioning of Togoland between the English and the French Governments and the handing over of the Cameroons to the French Government without consulting or regarding the wishes of the peoples in the matter.

That it respectfully desires an assurance from His Majesty's Government that under no circumstances whatsoever will it be a consenting part to the integrity of any of the four British West African Colonies, being disturbed.

It was also at this sitting that the Conference resolved itself into the N.C.B.W.A.[89] Finally, the Conference discussed the representation

[87] *National Congress of British West Africa: Resolutions of the Conference of Africans of British West Africa. Held at Accra, Gold Coast, from 11th to 29th March, 1920*, pp. 4–5.
[88] ibid., p. 7. Resolution 1.
[89] ibid., p. 8. Resolutions 1–3. Resolution 3 was mainly prompted by Gambian fears of cession to France: see Richards, J. D., 'Gambia and France', *West Africa* (8 Dec. 1917), p. 762. In 1923 France again approached Britain for exchange of the Gambia for French Somaliland, but the offer was rejected principally because of the recovery of Gambia's trade and because 'public opinion' in the Gambia was opposed to any cession.

of West African views in London by the N.C.B.W.A. delegation which was to proceed to London late in 1920. The delegation was empowered to seek the aid of solicitors in London on the question of elective representation and on other reforms, and 'to take such preliminary steps and undertake such propaganda work, and to do all acts necessary and expedient' to achieve their various goals.[90]

At this point, it will be in order to remark on the political attitude of the N.C.B.W.A. delegates. As we shall show in our analysis of their social and occupational background in chapter IV, the leadership had inherited the possessive individualism of Western liberal democracy, particularly some of its Victorian tenets—*laissez-faire*, the idea that knowledge meant power, belief in progress and the natural harmony of interests, as well as the belief that 'ordered liberty' and property went hand in hand. They were Pan-Africans but not revolutionaries; to them Marxism was 'Bolshevism' and Bolshevism was bad. It was precisely that political theory which Sir Hugh Clifford claimed was the monopoly of Anglo-Saxons that these men were now using to reinforce their demands. As the *Lagos Weekly Record* tells us, the leaders of the N.C.B.W.A. '. . . were quite conversant with the history of political or philosophical thought from Aristotle to Bergson . . . [and] were already deducing disquieting doctrines from the political philosophies of Herbert Spence [sic] and J. S. Mill and the popular tenets of Modern Socialism . . . which they were applying most vigorously to the solution of the manifold problems of colonial administration in West Africa'.[91]

[90] ibid., p. 9. Resolutions 1–2.

[91] *Lagos Weekly Record* (19 Feb. 1921). Sir Hugh Clifford, however, was of the opinion that 'good government' was much better than 'self-government', and was particularly impatient with English 'liberal-minded philosophers . . . and enlightened academic theory'. According to Sir Hugh, 'Democratic self-government, as we understand it, is a conception of Greek origin . . . and it must be regarded as the distinctive fruit of European and, in a special degree, of British political genius. Recently, with the world-wide spread of European ideas and influence, the minds of certain classes of men in many parts of the non-European world have become infected by this alien bacillus, very much as the bodies of thousands throughout the tropics have received from white men the phthisis germs . . . the inspiration from which these political movements derive their force is of an origin as distinctively exotic as are the phthisis bacilli to which I have likened it . . . it is as contagious in the realm of ideas as are the latter in the physiological sphere, and . . . it is no less incapable of control. . . .' Sir Hugh continued, 'When, however, we get back to the more primitive peoples, we find ourselves still among non-Europeans who, taken in bulk, have never entertained the exotic conception of self-government; who find it an idea impossible to grasp; and who indeed are wholly incapable of governing themselves. . . . In the Southern

The *Lagos Weekly Record* may have exaggerated, but it is probable that half the lawyers connected with the movement had read either the Greek and Roman classics or J. S. Mill; at least one of them (W. E. G. Sekyi), nicknamed during his student days in London as the 'G. B. Shaw of West Africa', could be assumed to have been conversant with the literature of English socialism. Yet Sekyi was no blind admirer of English democracy: his London master's thesis was concerned with political obligation in Akan-Fanti society; he was as much concerned with elective representation as with the protection of Ghanaian political institutions against the corrosive influences of alien systems.[92]

It is also worth noting that the N.C.B.W.A. leaders saw themselves as the only class of people who, by virtue of their social and occupational status, were qualified to control by constitutional means what hysterical racists like Lothrop Stoddard and Madison Grant called 'the rising tide of colour against white supremacy'. Dr. H. C. Bankole-Bright informed the League of Nations Union on 8 October 1920:

It should be observed that the organisers of this movement are neither fanatics nor recalcitrants to the British throne. . . . They are of that particular class of peaceful citizens who apprehensive of the culminating danger resulting from the present political unrest in West Africa—an unrest which is silently moving throughout the length and breadth of that Continent, and who also appreciating the fact that the present system of administration will inevitably lead to a serious deadlock between the

Provinces [Nigeria], "self-government" would mean a recrudescence of savage superstition, accompanied by universal lawlessness . . .': Clifford, Sir Hugh, 'The Story of Nigeria', paper read at the West African Section of the British Empire Exhibition (Lagos, 1924), pp. 31–3. I am grateful to Christopher Fyfe for drawing my attention to this pamphlet. The speech gives some insight into Sir Hugh's attitude towards the 'educated Native' and to representative institutions within the non-white Empire. For Clifford's contradictory attitudes to the Congress nationalists, see chapter VI.

[92] See the plan of Sekyi's thesis in the *Sekyi Papers* and his unpublished manuscript 'The Parting of the Ways' (n.d., probably 1927). Also Langley, J. Ayo, 'Modernization and its Malcontents: Kobina Sekyi of Ghana (1892–1956) and the Re-statement of African Political Theory', paper presented at Centre of African Studies Seminar (Edinburgh) on 'Political Theory and Ideology in African Society', 27–28 Feb. 1970. Note also the remarks by Wolfgang H. Kraus in 'Authority, Progress and Colonialism', *AUTHORITY*, NOMOS I, ed. C. J. Friedrich (Harvard University Press, Harvard, 1958), pp. 155–6; Johnson, K. E. De Graft, 'The Evolution of Élites in Ghana', in Lloyd, P. C., ed., *The New Élites of Tropical Africa*, pp. 182–4; Rohdie, S., 'The Gold Coast Aborigines Abroad', *Journal of African History*, vi, no. 3 (1965), 389–98. For another view, see Wight, Martin, *The Gold Coast Legislative Council* (London, 1946), pp. 182–4.

'Government and the Governed' decided to set themselves to the task of ameliorating this pending disaster by putting forward constitutionally a programme, the carrying of which into operation will alleviate all pains and misgivings . . . since the inauguration of these Committees [the N.C.B.W.A. Committees] there has been some calm amongst the extremists and a decision to await the result of this movement. . . . We have not come over here with the intention of making any noise; we do not believe in unconstitutional principles or the principles of Bolshevism. We have been under British environment for over two hundred years and we desire to work on constitutional lines. Although we have frequently been described as Black Englishmen, yet we have no intention of losing our race individuality. . . . You have difficulties at present in India. You have tried to give satisfaction to Egypt and Ceylon . . . you have at present troubles in Ireland, but believe me, when I tell you with all seriousness that if this political unrest does not come to a standstill, in West Africa, you will have greater difficulties with West Africa . . . and it is because we do not want to encourage such unrest, it is because we want to live under a peaceful government that we who represent the intelligentsia and the heterogeneous mass of the populace, have come to this Country with the object of educating public opinion to our condition by placing our grievances before you and at the same time seeking for the necessary reforms. . . .[93]

It is important to clarify the attitudes of the leaders of this movement in order to emphasize the fact that in spite of all the race rhetoric they were essentially co-operationists with exceedingly limited political objectives, a sub-élite whose interests generally coincided with, and were in fact protected by, the foreign rulers they were agitating against. Although they claimed to speak in the name of 'the people', the interests of the nationalist petty-bourgeoisie were not identical with those of the people; in fact, it was the contradictions within the colonial system itself that they sought to harmonize in order to protect and expand their own interests without upsetting the system; hence their constitutionalism and their recognition of the benefits of the *Pax Britannica*. Their Pan-Africanism apart, their main objective was the acquisition of representative institutions to protect their socio-economic interests and to enhance their opportunities in colonial society.[94]

[93] *The National Congress of British West Africa: Report of the Proceedings held in London between the League of Nations Union and the Delegates of the National Congress of British West Africa*, pp. 6–10.
[94] See also Hobsbawm, E. J., *The Age of Revolution* (New York, 1964), pp. 176–7; Kraus, op. cit., pp. 154–5; and the useful essay by Kilson, Martin, 'Nationalism and Social Classes in British West Africa', *Journal of Politics*, xx (May 1958), 368–87.

CHAPTER IV

# The Territorial Committees of the N.C.B.W.A.

MOST pan-movements have collapsed either through the interminable feuds and doctrinal disputations of the intellectuals, or have simply ceased to exist with the passing of rousing resolutions—'la parole est créatrice'. As the foregoing account of the debate on the Congress has shown, the Congress leadership was reasonably coherent in its statement of objectives and had some general idea as to the kind of institution through which to articulate and realize those objectives. As Europe was only just beginning to experiment with international political institutions, the least that could be said in criticism of the N.C.B.W.A. organization is that it too was a beginner in the difficult art of co-ordinating and reconciling differing goals and interests. How widely the territorial units differed from each other in their internal politics and in their interaction with the local administration will be seen in the analysis of the politics of the individual committees which follows. Indeed, one of these committees has already formed the subject of a thesis;[1] accordingly, what is done here is to review the local committees in their wider context and at the same time to highlight the peculiar characteristics of the units of this interterritorial movement.

## 1. *The Gambia Section*

THE Gambia was the last of the four English-speaking West African colonies to organize a local branch of the National Congress movement. As in Sierra Leone the local committee was dominated by 'middle-class' Creoles, although active Muslim members included Sheikh Omar Fye, who played a leading role in local politics up to the early 1950s and was a leading spokesman of the Muslim community in Bathurst. Other Muslim members were Njagga Saar, a

[1] Denzer, op. cit.

local carpenter; Omar Jallow, described as a 'prominent agricultur-ist'; Mamady Ceesay, a carpenter; Momodou Sowe, a trader; Amar Gaye Cham, vice-president of the 1923-4 local executive committee and a dealer; and Samba ⁿ'Dow, a trader. Creoles active in the local committee came largely from the mercantile and legal professions. Isaac J. Roberts, who was president of the 1925-6 committee, was a prominent solicitor of Sierra Leone descent. He was a merchant before going to England to read law; he practised in Bathurst and Lagos despite the loss of his eyesight which occurred during his student days in England. He represented the Gambia at the Lagos Session of the N.C.B.W.A. in 1930. He died in Freetown in April 1933 at the age of eighty-two.[2] M. S. J. Richards, one of the vice-presidents of the 1923-4 local executive committee was a local trader; J. A. Mahoney (later Sir John Mahoney and Speaker of the Gambia House of Representatives) was formerly a government employee who later worked for the French firm C.F.A.O. as a mercantile clerk; the Hon. S. J. Forster, first president of the local committee, came from a distinguished Creole family and served for several years on the Legislative Council; J. F. Mahoney was the nephew of S. J. Forster and was also a trader. B. J. George, local secretary of the committee from 1921 to 1923, and delegate to the Freetown Session in 1923, was a commission agent; Henry M. Jones was a wealthy trader and was one of the Gambian delegates to the N.C.B.W.A. London committee in 1920-1; until the 1921 slump and the depression of the 1930s, 'Pa' Jones was influential both in business circles and in local politics.[3] Other prominent Creole traders associated with the local committee were E. F. Small, delegate to the Accra Conference and the London committee; E. A. T. Nicol, E. J. C. Rendall, E. N. Jones, Joseph ⁿ'Dong,[4] and Sultan M. Davies, both traders.

The Gambia committee came into being through the efforts of Mr. I. J. Roberts, to whom J. E. Casely Hayford and Professor Orishatukè Faduma of Sierra Leone had written towards the end of 1918. According to Roberts, the two gentlemen wrote 'asking whether any movement has been made in Bathurst towards further-

[2] *West African Nationhood* (Apr. 1933); Macmillan, Allister, *The Red Book of West Africa*, p. 294. He was born in 1851 in Freetown, studied at the Collegiate School of the Rt. Revd. Dr. James Johnson, and came to Bathurst in 1877.

[3] There is a profile of him in Macmillan, op. cit., p. 292.

[4] J. A. Mahoney, Secretary of N.C.B.W.A. (Gambia) to the Acting Colonial Secretary, 31 Oct. 1923, GAMBIA 3/46, File No. 498. Gambia Records Office.

ing the aims of this project, and assuring me that the West African Conference was to secure for West Africa a recognition of those social, political, and national rights which the representatives of Great Britain in the Colonies have not infrequently denied us'.[5] Roberts replied, promising 'to stimulate local interest in the matter'.[6] It was not, however, until early March 1920, just before the Accra Conference had resolved itself into the N.C.B.W.A., that a nucleus of the movement was established in Bathurst.[7] The vision of the Accra Central Committee of the projected West African Conference[8] has it that it was the *Gambia Native Defensive Union* which resolved itself into a local committee of the Congress 'for the purpose of negotiating on Gambian affairs', adding that it was the aim of the Accra Conference 'to centralize native thought and native interests: in fact, to unite together peoples of the same race and country into one compact nation'.[9] The Gambia Native Defensive Union, which was a rather ineffective pressure group, had no known political aims. It was a society of government clerks, both Gambians and Sierra Leoneans, which was formed during the war to negotiate for higher wages at a time when the rise in food prices was causing hardship among several sections of the population. On the whole its aims and objects were to look after the welfare of 'native' civil servants in the Colony. Officialdom saw it, not as 'a political concern', but as 'the local native counterpart of the West African Civil Servants Association, which started about the same time'.[10]

Unlike the difficulties the Gold Coast Section had in capturing the leadership of the Gold Coast A.R.P.S., it was relatively easier for the Congress organizers to take over the existing organization of the Gambia Native Defensive Union, although E. F. Small, one of the most active organizers of the local movement, refers to the

[5] *Welcome Address to the Overseas Delegates by I. J. Roberts, Esquire, President Gambia Section, December 1925.* G.R.O.

[6] ibid.

[7] ibid.

[8] *Sierra Leone Weekly News* (11 Oct. 1919), p. 9.

[9] ibid.; also *Gold Coast Leader* (6–13 Dec. 1919) quoted in Denzer, La Ray, 'The National Congress of British West Africa: Gold Coast Section' (University of Legon M.A. thesis, 1965), p. 40.

[10] GAMBIA, 4/11, Secret Minute Paper No. 63, 26 Apr. 1922. The Hon. Colonial Secretary to The Travelling Commissioner, Karantaba, MacCarthy Island Province. According to B. J. George, a Committee of Gentlemen, with the Hon. S. J. Forster as president, formed the nucleus of the Bathurst local branch of the Congress: B. J. George, Secretary Bathurst Section to B. P. E. Bulstrode, 30 Aug. 1923, GAMBIA 583/23, File No. 2/575.

difficulties encountered in mobilizing local support for the Gambia Congress committee: '. . . the delay in getting the Mass Meeting has put back my plans. I am glad to say that, after some unnecessary rowing, it came off successfully. By a most practical demonstration, the people have, in a gathering of upwards of 300 inhabitants, endorsed the acts and resolutions of the Conference.'[11]

Like most educated Africans who agitated for constitutional reforms, Small was, in the eyes of the colonial administration, worse than an agitator. An official described him in 1937 as 'this self-appointed champion of non-existing grievances felt by an imaginary body of citizens . . .; he seems to find agitation irresistible'.[12] An account of Small's local political and trade-union career, as well as his Pan-African activities, would require a separate article. Small was born in Bathurst on 29 January 1890. He was educated in Sierra Leone, where he obtained a government scholarship and was sent to the Wesleyan High School for two years. He entered the General Post Office, Freetown, on 31 March 1910 as a probationer and was later appointed Assistant Stamp Seller. He was later transferred to the Gambia as Cost Clerk, public works department, on a daily wage. He arrived at Bathurst on 25 January 1912 after his application for promotion had been refused. Small then worked with the French firm Maurel and Prom, from which he subsequently resigned. Then he went to the Wesleyan High School as a teacher, and was afterwards employed as Wesleyan Missionary Agent at Ballanghar in MacCarthy Island Province, but he soon clashed with the local commissioner and some European residents in Ballanghar over the use of the local church station. The commissioner made a great issue out of an apparent misunderstanding, and the Revd. J. C. Lane, who regarded Small as a promising young man, was compelled by the administration to dismiss him. Small severed his connection with the Wesleyan Mission and was re-employed as a clerk by Maurel and Prom, from which he resigned again.[13]

A discontented man, Small became connected with the projected

[11] Letter intercepted by the Gambia police, enclosed in Gambia Confidential Minute Paper, no. 663/21, File no. 3/53, E. F. Small to Ebenezer MacCarthy, 20 June 1920. For E. F. Small's part in N.C.B.W.A. activities, see GAMBIA Confidential Minute Papers 498/20, 633/20, 766/20. G.R.O. *West Africa*, 3 Sept. 1921, p. 1009: 'The Congress Movement in the Gambia Colony'.
[12] Minute to GAMBIA 3/291 by the Hon. Colonial Secretary, 18 May 1937. G.R.O.
[13] C.O. 554/51, Governor Armitage to the Secretary of State for the Colonies C.O. 26537, 7 May 1921.

West African Conference after 1919, and was appointed secretary of the local committee, which sent him as its delegate to the Accra Conference in March 1920 and to London in 1920–1 with the N.C.B.W.A. delegation.[14] It must be emphasized, however, that like all the other West African 'agitators', Small was in outlook a black Edwardian, though slightly more radical in his politics.

Between 1928 and 1934, when Comintern involvement in the colonial question was at its zenith and came to be identified with political and labour unrest in the colonies, Small was branded as one of the 'link-subversives' recruited to spread Bolshevik propaganda in the colonies and foment unrest.[15] Small had attended a conference in Moscow in 1930 organized by the Crestinstern (Peasants International—a branch of the Comintern); he had also attended conferences in Hamburg and Paris between 1931 and 1933, and had been in touch with Padmore, who was at that time connected with the African section of the Comintern. Through Padmore, Small was put in touch with the International Trade Union Committee of Negro Workers and the League Against Imperialism. In fact his newspaper, the *Gambia Outlook and Senegambian Reporter*, carried reprints from Padmore's *The Negro Worker*, and a Marxian analysis of Small's moderately successful Bathurst Trade Union strike of 1929 by Padmore. Small was also a member of the local Committee of Citizens, a group which constantly lobbied the administration about various complaints.[16]

In a confidential dispatch to the Secretary of State for the Colonies concerning an application from the Liberian Minister at the Court of St. James for the issue of an Exequatur to Mr. Small to act as honorary Liberian Consul at Bathurst, C. R. M. Workman stated: 'I am not aware whether Mr. Small has definitely joined the Communist Party, but his attendance at meetings of the European Congress of Working Peasants in Berlin, and his correspondence with the League Against Imperialism, sufficiently indicate his attitude. . . .'[17] In the same dispatch it was added, however, that

---

[14] ibid.; also GAMBIA 3/140 and 3/212. G.R.O.

[15] GAMBIA 4/42, Secret M.P. No. 140, vol. i, 29 Mar. 1934. H. R. Oke to the Rt. Hon. Sir Philip Cunliffe-Lister, Secretary of State for the Colonies, 29 Mar. 1934.

[16] For Small's alleged affiliations with Comintern and with Malcolm Nurse, see GAMBIA Confidential M.P. No. 1308/30, File No. 3/165. G.R.O.

[17] ibid., C. R. M. Workman, Acting Governor of the Gambia, to Lord Passfield, Secretary of State for the Colonies, 2 June 1930.

'though his [Mr. Small's] activities on the National Congress, as organiser of the B.T.U. [Bathurst Trade Union], and even as a member of the Communist party, if he has joined it, are all objectionable, none of them are criminal'.[18]

Another less-known aspect of E. F. Small's career is his attempt to put into practice a part of the economic programme of the N.C.B.W.A. by founding the co-operative movement in the Gambia between 1929 and 1940. The present Gambia Co-operative Union is largely the result of E. F. Small's pioneering effort, a work he carried out in spite of the tremendous opposition of the administration. The history of this movement cannot be dealt with here, because of lack of space, but its significance must not be overlooked in any discussion of the economic aspects of nationalism in West Africa.[19]

In 1920 the Bathurst section of the N.C.B.W.A. was constituted as follows: the Hon. S. J. Forster, chairman of the General Committee; S. J. Auber, treasurer; E. F. Small, secretary; C. J. Goddard, E. Thomas, Dr. T. Bishop,[20] J. R. Clarke, T. B. Jones, E. de Kola Richards, B. O'Brien Coker, M. S. J. Richards, J. T. Oldfield, Amar Gaye Cham, Ousman N'jai, B. J. George, J. M. Roberts, Cyril Richards, Cecil Richards, J. Bass, J. S. Thomas.[21] The Gambia delegation to the March 1920 Accra Conference was selected at a mass meeting in early March 1920 (the usual procedure of all the N.C.B.W.A. committees) called by the working committee of the Gambia section of the N.C.B.W.A., of which the Hon. S. J. Forster was the chairman. Small (who was the only delegate selected), described the N.C.B.W.A. as 'an inter-colonial council and an entirely democratic institution of Africans of British West Africa,

[18] ibid., Minute to, 22 May 1930.

[19] Valuable information about the origins and growth of the Gambia co-operative movement can be found in: GAMBIA 4/42: 'Activities of E. F. Small, 1918–1931' and File No. RCS/EDU/12 (Gambia Co-operative Department) especially the papers prepared by students on co-operative course, 1961: 'A Historical Research: Co-operation in the Gambia'. The irony of the career of this 'agitator' is that his services were finally recognized in 1953 when he was awarded the then much coveted O.B.E.

[20] The Hon. Dr. Thomas Bishop was born in Freetown in 1868; educated at the Wesleyan High School and at Birmingham, Durham, and Edinburgh universities; he set up medical practice in Bathurst in 1904 after serving in Freetown and was appointed member of the Bathurst Legislative Council in 1916: Macmillan, op. cit., p. 294.

[21] E. F. Small to the Colonial Secretary, 11 June 1920, GAMBIA 3/62, Colonial Secretary's Office, File No. 766. G.R.O.

though by no means anti-government or anti-racial in its nature and objects'.[22] The most active members of the local committee since its early beginnings were John A. Mahoney, M. S. Oldfield, half-brother of E. F. Small; J. J. Oldfield, a former assistant clerk of the Legislative Council and a member of the Anglican church body; Jatta Joof, a Mohammedan member of the Legislative Council and a carpenter by trade; Benjamin J. George, M. S. J. Richards, S. J. Forster, Isaac J. Roberts, and L. J. Roberts, president of the local committee.[23]

What is clear from the membership list of the local committee is that the leadership was mainly in the hands of the propertied and conservative 'middle-class' Creoles who were usually of Sierra Leone extraction; some of these were retired civil servants, mercantile clerks, traders, lawyers, or local contractors and artisans. Like their counterparts in Sierra Leone, they held 'the British Constitution' in high esteem, and prided themselves on the fact that the Gambia was an 'ancient and loyal Colony', and were very much attached to property and legality.[24] As in most areas along the west coast, the Western-educated and propertied Creoles generally assumed the leadership of protest and political movements in the late nineteenth and early twentieth centuries.[25] The Muslims involved in the politics of the local committee were few in relation to the population of the Muslim community, and in most cases participants were either leaders of Muslim opinion who had their own political and social ambitions, like the Hon. Sheikh Omar Fye who was also a trader, or were Muslims who had social or business contacts with their Creole counterparts, or were merchants and traders with grievances against foreign firms.

[22] ibid., E. F. Small to the Colonial Secretary, 7 June 1920.
[23] ibid., Minute to, 7 June 1920.
[24] See Gray, J. M., *A History of the Gambia* (Cambridge, 1940), pp. 440–1.
[25] Garigue, P., 'An Anthropological Interpretation of Changing Political Leadership in West Africa' (London University Ph.D. thesis, 1953), pp. 183–6, 204–6, 225–6, 312–14; Porter, A., *Creoledom* (London, 1963), pp. 119–28; Fyfe, C., *A History of Sierra Leone, passim*; Kopytoff, Jean Herskovits, *A Preface to Modern Nigeria: The 'Sierra Leonians' in Yoruba, 1830–1890* (Madison, Wis., 1965), chapters 9–10. For a critical review of this book, see *Journal of African History*, vii (1966).

## Politics and Pressure-Group Activity of the Gambia Section of the N.C.B.W.A.

The Bathurst section of the N.C.B.W.A., contrary to David Kimble who asserts that there was 'hardly any scope for politics at all in the Gambia',[26] was not the most inactive of the Congress branches in West Africa. Presumably, much would depend on how 'politics' in a colonial context is defined. Although interest in the N.C.B.W.A. was not sustained, the Gambia Congress committee was more active in its early years (1920–5) than the Lagos branch, which was not only divided internally, but was opposed by an influential section of the Lagos social élite. Perhaps the most interesting aspects of the Gambia Congress committee were its attempts to win the support of the conservative Mohammedan community in order to 'prove' its representative character, and the interest the colonial administration showed in the Congress's activities—an interest out of proportion to the strength and popularity of the local movement.

In Bathurst colonial and municipal politics revolved around the Mohammedan community which had its internal differentiation and cleavages, the Chamber of Commerce, and the local congress movement, which was smaller in numbers, but more articulate in its demand for a limited form of elective representation. The paradox was that while it was government strategy to neutralize or isolate the Mohammedan community from the Congress,[27] the Almami of Bathurst and Sheikh Omar Fye, a leading member of the Mohammedan community, were favourably disposed towards the Congress. When asked why he had endorsed the resolutions passed by a meeting of the Gambia Congress committee on 18 April 1925,[28] the Almami replied that he had endorsed the resolutions as he was particularly opposed to the 'black-listing' of local merchants by foreign firms, and that all religious leaders had endorsed the resolutions. He also added, 'I am quite ready to participate in any movement from the inhabitants of Bathurst for the welfare of my country on things that I am satisfied are worth writing, but not imposed by any one.'[29]

[26] Kimble, D., *A Political History of Ghana: the Rise of Gold Coast Nationalism 1850–1928*, p. 399.
[27] B. A. Finn, Minute to Confidential 776/20, 4 July 1921. G.R.O.
[28] The Colonial Secretary to the Almami, GAMBIA 160/1925, File no. 2/671, 2 May 1925. G.R.O.
[29] ibid., the Almami of Bathurst to The Colonial Secretary, 4 May 1925. G.R.O.

Earlier in 1922, when the Congress movement was at its zenith, Government had considered the attempts by the Congress committee to enlist the support of the Almami of Bathurst, a 'serious political question', as

the position of the Almami in Bathurst is . . . analogous to that of a Roman Catholic priest in Ireland, and though primarily religious, his political influence depends on his personality. The argument that his investiture with a Chief's Badge makes him the head of the Mohammedan community here for all purposes is ingenious, and is no doubt the chief reason why the Congress people want him on their platform. The propaganda of the Congress has altered the situation since H. E. wrote . . . that the Mohammedans had agreed that they would have nothing further to do with the Congress. It is significant that among the supporters of the Congress Sheiku [*sic*] Fye is now numbered. He was said to have been unacceptable to the Bathurst Moslems formerly because he declined to join the Congress to which the late Almami subscribed £10. . . .[30]

The Government, however, had a useful ally in the person of Alhadji Ousman Jeng, a member of the Legislative Council and a former Secretary of the Bathurst Congress committee. On 19 October 1922 Ousman Jeng, in correspondence with the Colonial Secretary, referred to 'the existence of a party amongst the younger members of the muslim community, who are victims of the Congress propaganda'. The Congress militants, he said, had tried very hard to persuade the Almami to attend their meetings to symbolize the active support of the Mohammedan community, but he (Ousman Jeng) had been able, 'with the Almami's advisory committee's assistance, to keep away my people as also the Almami from identifying themselves with the movement. . . . I am engaged in very active propaganda to keep my people out. . . .' Jeng also described Congress activity as 'poisonous propaganda' which might very well 'raise the question of intercommunication with the Government, and political representation'. He advised the Colonial Secretary: 'To settle this, and put the question of representation on a safe hand. I will ask you, Sir, to pass every communication intended for the Almami and the muslim community through me, and to ask the Almami to make me the medium of whatever communication he wishes to make to His Excellency and the Government. This will make him above the ramifications [*sic*] of the Congress propaganda

[30] Minute to Confidential 776/20, File no. 3/62 by C. R. M. Workman, 19 Nov. 1922. G.R.O.

and . . . will eventually safe [*sic*] my people from its poison.'[31] The secretary of the Almami's advisory council had also been in correspondence with Alhadji Ousman Jeng, informing him that 'The National Congress is once again on the move, and a good deal of incitement is going on through the agency of our most ignorant co-religionists, who interviewed the Almami with the intention of forcibly making him a supporter of the Chairman [i.e. of the Congress branch]. . . .' The delegation that waited upon the Almami were Saloum N'Jie, Ousman N'Jie, Sheikh Omar, and Mustapha Jallow. The Almami was asked to attend as representative of the Community, whose identification with the Congress was to be the pledge of Muslim support. He also observed that the Almami could either support the Congress, in which case he would have to resign the Almamiship, or eschew the Congress and all its works. Jeng, the letter added, was the 'trustee of the Political interests of the Community' (i.e. the Mohammedan community) and should 'take the requisite action for safeguarding the true interests of the Community . . . in concert with the government', and should warn the Mohammedan community against the involvement in the Congress movement.[32]

The rivalry between Alhadji Ousman Jeng and the Hon. Sheikh Fye was not simply a question of the former posing as the recognized spokesman of the Mohammedan community against a fellow-Mohammedan who had joined the ranks of the Congress 'agitators'. It was essentially the personalization of the cleavage in the Mohammedan community over the question of elective representation.[33] In Bathurst the majority of the Mohammedans followed the conservative 'no change' line of Alhadji Ousman Jeng, but the 'influential minority'[34] among them desired a modest form of elective representa-

[31] Alhadji the Hon. Ousman Jeng to the Hon. Colonial Secretary, 423/20, File no. 3/62, 19 Oct. 1922. G.R.O.

[32] ibid., Omar B. Jallow to the Hon. Ousman Jeng, 18 Oct. 1922. Omar B. Jallow to the Colonial Secretary, G. R. M. Workman, 18 Oct. 1922. Omar B. Jallow to C. R. M. Workman, GAMBIA 221/1922, File no. 2/507, 6 Mar. 1922.

[33] 'Among the muslim community there is a distinct difficulty in the way of elective representation since as they themselves admit, "we are divided into castes and classes", and the election of any one man to represent their interests would lead to further dissentions.' GAMBIA 3/433, Confidential M.P. No. S. 2831, 17 Dec. 1942: 'Historical Notes on Executive and Legislative Councils'. G.R.O. There could have been other differences of opinion, probably of a religious nature among the leaders of the Mohammedan community. I owe this suggestion to my colleague Dr. Lamin M'Bye, formerly of Birmingham University.

[34] ibid.

tion. The Bathurst Chamber of Commerce, which embraced 'practically all the trading interests', had little to worry about, franchise or no franchise. As for the Protectorate peoples, it was the Government's view that they exhibited 'no desire to become involved in the affairs of the colony', and were 'happy and content to accept the generally benevolent rule of their chiefs and headmen under the watchful eye of the commissioner'.[35] The third group was the local committee of the N.C.B.W.A., which advocated a limited franchise and claimed to be the barometer of 'public opinion'. The very nature of its membership, however, disqualified it from the beginning from making such a claim. Although it was numerically inferior, its agitation for elective representation was not entirely ignored.[36] Its advocacy of a limited form of elective representation was thought to be a corrective to the system under the old constitution whereby the Governor could nominate unofficial African members of the Legislative Council after formal consultation with the Urban District Council, or Bathurst Advisory Council as it was called in the 1920s.[37]

Although limited forms of elective representation were introduced in Nigeria (1923), Sierra Leone (1924), and the Gold Coast (1925), similar reforms were not introduced in the Gambia. The intense agitation mounted by the local Congress committee in 1922–5 led to no changes. The Secretary of State for the Colonies, J. H. Thomas, reiterated Lord Milner's earlier policy of 1921 when he stated in a dispatch to the Governor in 1924, '. . . while I sympathise with their desire for elective institutions, I do not consider that education and political thought in the colony, and still less in the protectorate (which could not well be separated from the colony in any constitutional arrangement which might be made) have yet reached a level which could render elective institutions valuable.'[38] It was not until 12 September 1947, twenty-seven years after the demand for elective representation, that the Legislative Council was reconstituted, with provision for one elected member to represent the Colony and Kombo St. Mary.[39]

The economic slump of 1921 created a temporary lull in the activities of the local Congress movement, as the merchants, traders, and artisans who provided the leadership of the movement were hard hit; it had the effect of increasing the bitterness of the African

[35] ibid.      [36] ibid.      [37] ibid.
[38] ibid.      [39] ibid.

middleman who complained that he was being 'squeezed in'.[40] Agitation was continued in 1922–4, with the usual petitions, protestations of loyalty, and 'mass meetings' at which funds were collected. In 1923 the local congressmen renewed their demand for limited elective representation only to be told that, apart from the fact that their views were unrepresentative of Colony opinion, they were generally people of Sierra Leone origin.[41] The Colonial Secretary also told them that with three unofficial members on the Council further representation was unnecessary, and that they were 'becoming a nuisance'.[42] Yet another petition in early 1924[43] was rejected, with Workman replying laconically that His Excellency had 'nothing to add' to his previous correspondence with them on the subject.[44] When *West Africa* took up the case of the local committee, Armitage charged its editor, Cartwright, with ignorance of local conditions, noting that Mr. J. A. Mahoney, secretary to the Gambia Branch, and his lieutenants were so busy during the trade season that they had little time to indulge in political agitation, but that from June to the end of November

they appear to find time hang heavy on their hands and employ it in bombarding the Secretariat with letters and in holding what they are pleased to term 'Mass [*sic*] Meetings', at which they attempt to collect contributions to the Gambia Branch. So far as I can ascertain, no accounts of such contributions have been kept, nor has any sort of benefit accrued to the contributors, most of whom have given up throwing good money after bad. . . . I am justified in taking steps to insure that the Gambia

[40] Herbert Macaulay Papers (Ibadan University Library), v. 35, pp. 14–15, Henry M. Jones to Herbert Macaulay, 11 Aug. 1931; GAMBIA No. 249, C. H. Armitage to the Colonial Secretary, 31 Dec. 1926; GAMBIA Confidential M.P. No. 3/46: 'Conference of Africans of British West Africa', especially the 'Report on the Bathurst Branch by Commissioner of Police, Captain C. Greig', Confidential No. 28, 26 Mar. 1926; *Gold Coast Leader* (6 Feb. 1926); Finden Dailey, 'The Trade System of the Gambia is Ruining the African Middleman', *West African Review* (Oct. 1936), pp. 46–7.
[41] GAMBIA 2/575, 581/1923: 'Legislative Council: Request for Elective Representation', Minute to 2/575 by C. R. M. Workman, 11 Aug. 1923, para. 2.
[42] ibid., Minute by C. R. M. Workman, 27 Mar. 1924. G.R.O.
[43] ibid., 'Petition of the Gambia Branch of N.C.B.W.A. to Rt. Hon. Secretary of State for the Colonies', 6 May 1924.
[44] GAMBIA 581/1923, File no. 2/575, Workman to the Secretary, Gambia Section, N.C.B.W.A., 28 Mar. 1924. Ibid., B. A. Finn, Acting Colonial Secretary to Secretary Gambia Section of N.C.B.W.A., 30 July 1924; J. H. Thomas, Secretary of State for the Colonies to Captain C. H. Armitage, 18 June 1924. *West Africa*: 'The Gambia and Electoral Representation', p. 866, 23 Aug. 1924, and 'The Gambia Government and Municipal Politics', pp. 1252–3, 8 Nov. 1924.

Section of the National Congress of British West Africa may not come to be regarded as the medium of communication between the Governor of this Colony and the inhabitants of Bathurst and the Protectorate.[45]

To the charges made by the administration, J. A. Mahoney, secretary of the local committee in 1924, replied that the Bathurst Committee of the Congress felt that its petition for elective representation 'was obviously not one of numbers, but of principle', and that the constitutional reforms granted to Nigeria and Sierra Leone should be extended to The Gambia.[46] He observed that the suggestion that the Hon. S. J. Forster (former chairman of the Bathurst Committee of the N.C.B.W.A.) was qualified to represent the African community in the Legislative Council was 'diverting and misleading', adding that nomination was not the same as election.[47] As for the election of the Hon. Alhadji Ousman Jeng to represent the Mohammedan community, Mahoney was of the opinion that his selection 'did not carry the essentials of electioneering', and even if it did, 'it is further submitted that it would be un-British and unfair to allow of one Section electing its own representative while another (and indisputably a more competent) should be compelled to content itself with a Government nominee to guard its interests'. Finally, Mahoney asserted that the fact that prominent Congress members were Sierra Leoneans was 'very extraneous' to any argument about their right to make political demands or participate in local 'politics'. In fact, he said, 'the result of the recent Election in Nigeria . . . will serve to correct such an erroneous and pernicious idea'.[48] B. J. George also described the Government's disapproval of Sierra Leoneans participating in Bathurst politics as an argument 'shrouded in an enigma', and asserted that it was one of the aims of the Congress 'to foster and establish the spirit of Unity and Co-operation among the peoples of the four British West African Colonies wherever their lot may be cast; and any policy or measure which tends to divide and rule is viewed with much alarm and grave concern'.[49]

[45] *West Africa* (8 Dec. 1924), pp. 1226, 1252–3.
[46] J. A. Mahoney to the Colonial Secretary, GAMBIA 581/1923, File no. 2/575, 26 Mar. 1924. G.R.O.  [47] ibid.
[48] ibid.; the elections referred to were those of 1923 when the Nigerian National Democratic Party of Herbert Macaulay, among whose candidates was Dr. C. C. Adeniyi-Jones, who was of Sierra Leone extraction, won all the seats in Lagos. T. N. Tamuno, *Nigeria and Elective Representation, 1923–1947* (London, 1966), 79–82.
[49] B. J. George, Secretary Gambia Section to B. P. E. Bulstrode, Officer-in-Charge, Secretariat, 30 Aug. 1923. GAMBIA 581/23, 2/575. G.R.O.

The third session of the N.C.B.W.A. was held in Bathurst in December 1925–January 1926 after some organizational difficulties. Nigeria sent no delegates. But even by 1926 the local Congress movement, partly because of persistent rejection of its petitions and partly because of a prospering economy, had begun to lose its earlier *élan*. The following resolutions were passed:

1. That the Congress, having taken into careful consideration the several Constitutions of British West Africa, records the view that that Constitution is best, that makes provision for the effective and efficient expression of public opinion.
2. That in the opinion of the Congress, the time has arrived for the elective system of representation to be fully applied to the Colony of the Gambia. . . .
3. That the Congress, having seriously considered the question of British West African Federation with a Governor-General, is of the opinion that the matter should be kept in view, and in due course representations made to His Majesty's Government to take it into deep and sympathetic consideration, and records the view that the time has now arrived for the various Sections of the Congress to consider the question seriously with a view to representation.[50]

The 1926 Bathurst Session also advocated the setting up of 'National Schools' in West Africa, alongside those of missionary schools.[51] These were to be modelled on Booker T. Washington's Tuskegee Institute.[52] They also advocated compulsory education in all towns in British West Africa; industrial and agricultural training 'combined with sound elementary education' was specially recommended for the Gambia Protectorate, and a Secondary Boarding School for Bathurst, 'so as to fit the youths to cope, in due course, with modern conditions'.[53] The establishment of an Education Department with a Director and an Inspector of Schools was also recommended for the Gambia. More importantly, the Bathurst Session contended that 'the system of Education is best for the

[50] Africana Pamphlets, Ibadan University Library, S. R. Wood to editor of the *Lagos Daily News* (6 Oct. 1931), no. 186/1931/F11: 'Resolutions of the Third Session of Congress Held at Bathurst, Gambia, Dec. 1925 to Jan. 1926 and of the Fourth Session Held at Lagos, Nigeria, Jan. 1930. Drawn up in parallel form, with footnotes and appendices containing previous resolutions therein referred to. General Secretary's Office, Axim. Gold Coast, West Africa.'
[51] Resolution 3–4 of the Lagos Session, 1930.
[52] ibid.; GAMBIA, M.P. 160/1925; Résumé of the Proceedings of the Third Session of the N.C. of B.W.A., held at Bathurst, River Gambia, from 24 Dec. 1925 to 10 Jan. 1926.
[53] Resolution 8, Bathurst Session, 1925–6.

African, as for any other nationality, which aims at the highest efficiency while preserving the national traits of the African not repugnant to good conscience'.[54]

Economic questions were also discussed; the aim of the Congress was to secure 'commercial and economic independence' for West Africa, which meant the creation of more elbow-room for the African middleman. As usual, the land question was raised; the proposed introduction of the plantation system roundly condemned, as well as the blacklisting of African merchants and commercial clerks by the Chambers of Commerce. Agricultural banks and co-operative marketing of produce were also recommended to help the producer to command reasonably high prices, and as a 'means of countering combinations which control the market'.[55] The branches of the Congress were exhorted to carry out 'more extensive propaganda work . . . to promote the commercial and economic independence of the people'. The 'imperative necessity and urgency' of a West African Appelate Court was also stressed, and the appointment of Africans to higher posts in the judiciary recommended. On self-determination the Bathurst Session, no doubt fearing a possible British exchange of the Gambia for French territory, resolved: 'That it [the Congress] respectfully desires an assurance from His Majesty's Government that under no circumstances whatever will it be a consenting party to the integrity of any of the four British West African Colonies being disturbed . . ., regrets that no pronouncement has yet been made and begs that the matter may receive the attention of His Majesty's Government and with particular reference to the Colony of the Gambia.'

The Bathurst Session, like the 1923 Freetown Session, was almost turned into a public holiday. It began with an impressive church service in which the social élite of Bathurst praised the Lord

> For the Christian parentage,
> And sweet days of tutelage.

They prayed for all 'enlightened and Christian Governments', 'particularly that of the British Empire under His Gracious Majesty, George V'. Nor were they indifferent to economics, for they asked the Almighty to 'Remove the world-wide depression in Trade and bid stagnation and all unrest cease'. They also prayed that the

[54] ibid., Resolution 2.
[55] ibid.

Congress would become 'an effective instrument for the Redemption and uplift of Africa'.[56]

The proceedings of the session read almost like a seminar; there were visits to interesting projects, and there was a good deal of entertainment. One interesting feature was the participation of ladies. There was, in fact, a Women's Auxiliary Committee of the Gambia Section of the Congress, whose secretary was Mrs. Hannah Forster.[57]

Like its contemporary, the Pan-African movement of W. E. B. Du Bois, the National Congress movement was weak in organization and co-ordination; it had become a biennial seminar of the West African nationalist intelligentsia after 1923, with the various local committees using their organizations to lobby their respective governments for specific reforms. The 1921 slump had dampened its enthusiasm, while the 1923 Cliffordian reforms, followed by similar reforms in Sierra Leone and the Gold Coast, politically anaesthetized the movement. But as long as Casely Hayford was its president, the Pan-West African idea lived on, especially in the Gold Coast and in Sierra Leone. In the Gambia, however, disappointment with the failure to achieve even a limited form of elective representation led to conservatism and then apathy. As the report of the Commissioner of Police stated, from 1924 onwards, 'the views expressed by members of the Gambia Branch of the West African National Congress and the tone of their meetings has been much more moderate'.[58] The report continued: '. . . they appear to better realise today, that reforms with regard to representation must come more gradually than they advocated some years ago. I am glad to say that there is now an entire absence of "Africa for Africans only and as early as possible", which was at one time the suggested undercurrent of the speeches of the younger and more extreme members.'[59] Captain Greig thought that the Congress had failed to appeal to the majority of Mohammedans in Bathurst and to the Protectorate as a whole. He also observed that it had lost its *élan* because of 'a return to more normal conditions of life after the boom years of trade, the fictitious prosperity of which misled many into the belief that continued prosperity was easy of achievement and that it would continue to give them the leisure and means that originally

[56] GAMBIA Confidential M.P. no. 3/46, Colonial Secretary's Office: 'Conference of Africans of British West Africa. Report on the Bathurst Branch by Commissioner of Police, Captain C. Greig', Confidential no. 28, 26 Mar. 1926. G.R.O.
[57] ibid.                    [58] ibid.                    [59] ibid.

made them abnormally ambitious'.[60] Another factor, according to Greig, was that 'the Extremists found that their methods lost them the support of the more influential and responsible Africans' like J. T. Roberts and Dr. Thomas Bishop.[61]

After 1924 the meetings of the local Congress branch became 'less influentially and numerically attended'. Their 'mass' meetings were no more than gatherings of thirty to forty people in a school-room. The Mohammedans became less interested the more they were called upon to contribute to Congress funds.[62] The intense agitation of 1920–4 had given place to a more conservative and constitutionally minded leadership; the 1921 slump had already severely affected the small merchant class which was most influential in the movement, while the failure of the 1920–1 London Congress Delegation to obtain some measure of elective representation from the Colonial Office and the Cliffordian reforms of 1923 further disillusioned an already poorly organized Pan-West African national-ist movement. In the Gambia the 'gradual' evolution of elective institutions was so gradual that it was only achieved in 1947.

Even after the demise of the Congress movement in the early 1930s, Gambian newspapers like the *Gambia Echo* and E. F. Small's *Gambia Outlook and Senegambian Reporter* continued agitating for 'the Franchise'; with this also went their policy of constitutional agitation, but from the beginning all they had asked for was a limited measure of elective representation. As one newspaper put it:

No one has ever sought to defeat the official majority on the Legislative Council. It is well that this fact be clearly understood by advocates of the franchise. It is well that they should suffer no disillusionment hereafter; and they should be quite certain about it, that a limited franchise will only have a moral influence on the representation of the people, but would make no real difference to the official strength of the Legislature. . . .

[60] ibid.
[61] ibid.; also Appendix A, Confidential no. 11, 3/46, the Commissioner of Police to the Hon. Colonial Secretary, 19 May 1924: 'Report on Congress Meeting held on 17/5/1924'. G.R.O.
[62] ibid., para. 6; paras. 8–9 of Appendix B, Confidential no. 17, 12 Nov. 1925, 3/46; ibid., no. 84, the Hon. Ousman Jeng to the Hon. the Acting Colonial Secretary, 2 July 1924. Ibid., no. 87, 9 July 1924, B. A. Finn to Ousman Jeng; also the Hon. Ousman Jeng to the Colonial Secretary, 3/46, no. 58, 30 Oct. 1922 in which after reporting that he had already communicated the Government's attitude to the Congress to the Almami of Bathurst, Jeng assured the Colonial Secretary that 'it will take a very long time to awaken real interest in this move-ment, amongst the rank and file of the Muslims'.

Representative Government for the Gambia is out of the question for the present. A fair measure of direct representation of the people is all we mean by the demand for the franchise.[63]

M. S. J. Richards, vice-president of the local Congress branch, gave a more realistic summary of constitutional progress in the Colony when he stated: '. . . it would appear that the Government has been keeping the wheels of progress backward and contenting itself with remaining *in statu quo* for over a hundred years with the same old constitution.'[64]

But if the realists accepted the *status quo*, the Pan-African idealists still clung to their vision of a united West Africa. J. W. Quye (one of the few surviving members of the movement, known locally as Pa Quye), who seems never to have tired of theorizing about the right of the people to self-determination, and was a great admirer of Edward Blyden, Sir Samuel Lewis, and W. E. B. Du Bois, asserted in 1926:

This sentiment of African race and African nationality has become more important in this century than ever before; it is interesting to note its wonderful development among West Africans, for to-day, it is the classic of society. . . . Although we have become British by alliance, yet not un-African in aspiration. We have secured the great benefits of the Pax Britannica, we want also to preserve our race individuality. . . . In visions of the future of West Africa, I behold her people everywhere inspired with the consciousness of one common brotherhood from the hinterland of mighty Nigeria, through the diamondiferous districts of wealthy Gold Coast, past the salubrious hills of progressive Sierra Leone, on to the peaceful banks of secluded Gambia; from the humble hut in the hinterland of 'primeval innocence and glory' to the stately edifice of twentieth century civilisation. I see too chiefs and people, Christians and Mohammedans and pagans, the intellectual celebrities and the unsophisticated artisans, the leaders of African thought and the confiding mass of the country all daring and doing something for the progress of the race.[65]

Such is the tenacity of ideology, even in the face of harsh colonial realities.

This study of the Bathurst section of the N.C.B.W.A. has attempted to show that, like the other committees of the Congress in

[63] *Gambia Outlook and Senegambian Reporter* (18 Jan. 1936), p. 2.

[64] ibid. (28 Nov. 1936), p. 4.

[65] *Gambia Outlook and Senegambian Reporter* (21 Nov. 1936), p. 7, reproduction of speech by J. W. Quye at Third Session of the N.C.B.W.A., Bathurst, 1925–6. Mr. Quye is one of the few surviving members of the Bathurst Committee of the N.C.B.W.A.

the Gold Coast, Sierra Leone, and Nigeria, the social basis of its leadership was extremely limited, although a little more broadly based in relation to the other territorial committees. Its membership was generally characterized by a high level of education, social status, and commercial success. Indeed, a few of its members either came from old families whose social advantages were based on mercantile success, or had already established successful businesses of their own. As in the other branches of the N.C.B.W.A., a few lawyers, merchants, mercantile clerks, and artisans, who regarded themselves as gentlemen rather than career politicians, tended to dominate both the internal and agitational politics of the movement. As David Apter has pointed out, their type of nationalism was based on the political theory of the market society, i.e. it 'served to enhance economic rather than political entrepreneurship'.[66] As the permissible area of political activity was severely limited, and as only a few individuals tended to perform functionally important roles in Congress politics in Bathurst, the incidence of political and status competition was generally high and political rivalry was easily translated into personal antagonism and factional politics. This was the characteristic pattern in the other committees of the N.C.B.W.A.[67] One important difference between the politics of the Bathurst section and that of the other West African sections, however, was that religion was exploited by some of the leaders, thereby further weakening an already ineffective movement and leaving it completely to the tender mercies of the colonial bureaucrats to whom this proto-nationalism was quite clearly an aberration from the traditional political quiescence of the Colony. Unlike the other British West African territories, Downing Street did not even find it necessary to kill the Bathurst Congress movement by constitutional kindness—internal disunity and clashes of personality had obviated that necessity. Like the nationalist élites of the inter-war years in West Africa, the leadership of the Bathurst section of the N.C.B.W.A. laboured under two major disabilities. Having been moulded by bourgeois colonial society, and by the Christian missions, they were

[66] Apter, David E., 'Political Organization and Ideology', in Moore, Wilbert E., and Feldman, Arnold S., eds., *Labor Commitment and Social Change in Developing Areas* (New York, 1960), p. 336.

[67] For details relating to the politics, ideology, and economic aspects of the N.C.B.W.A., see the author's thesis 'West African Aspects of the Pan-African Movement: 1900–1945' (University of Edinburgh Ph.D. thesis, 1968), chapters iv–v.

naturally flattered by their special status in colonial society and therefore became victims of what in Marxist terminology is called 'false consciousness', and this false consciousness rendered them incapable of objectively perceiving their political potential in dictating or influencing the direction and pattern of political change. Their inability to rid themselves of the notion that they constituted a self-selected leadership of a colonial bourgeois movement meant that it was impossible for them to identify their movement with the majority of the people—peasant farmers, urban workers, petty traders, etc.—by exploiting the economic grievances of the 1920s and 1930s. Then, as now, there was neither ideological coherence nor any significant political mobilization. Their politics was essentially the politics of survival and the politics of the *status quo*.

## 2. *The Sierra Leone Section*

APART from the Gold Coast, the most enthusiastic support for the N.C.B.W.A. was given by the Freetown élite which experienced a relatively smaller degree of disagreement on the objects and methods of the movement than the Gold Coast and Lagos branches. In fact, it was in Freetown that concrete organizational proposals were first made towards the realization of the N.C.B.W.A. Early in 1917, Dr. Akiwande Savage and Casely Hayford had already been in touch with the Hon. J. H. Thomas and Claudius May (editor of the *Sierra Leone Weekly News*) about the feasibility of a West African Conference and the extent of local support for the idea in Freetown. In early 1918 J. H. Thomas and Claudius May sent a circular inviting members of the Freetown community to attend a public meeting at the Wilberforce Memorial Hall on 29 April, 'to discuss the proposal of a West African Conference'.[68] Earlier in January 1918 E. S. Beoku-Betts [69] had written to the editor of the

[68] *Sierra Leone Weekly News* (27 Apr. 1918), pp. 8–9; the earliest editorial on the Conference project appeared in *S.L.W.N.* (13 Mar. 1915), pp. 8–9.

[69] E. S. Beoku-Betts was born in Freetown in 1895; educated at the Leopold Educational Institute and Fourah Bay College; called to the Bar (Middle Temple) in 1917; gained the B.C.L. and M.A. degrees at Durham (1915) and the LL.B. (London) in 1917. He was the younger son of C. W. Betts, a general hardware and wholesale merchant of Kissy Street. His father specialized in a wide range of hardware supplies, importing from Europe and America, and owned five stores in Freetown. He was 'one of the most noteworthy and successful of the local native traders'. Macmillan, op. cit., pp. 264, 271. Betts founded and edited the fiery *Aurora* in 1919 and championed the N.C.B.W.A.; he was also one of the Sierra

*Gold Coast Leader*, describing the projected West African Conference as 'a necessity which nothing can disguise'. Betts thought that the British West African Colonies were 'under guardianship of a race that cares little for sentiment. Action is what they respect, by action they have proceeded all their days.'[70] The West African press, he said, should have a common policy on representative government, as it was 'the mouthpiece of the people' and did not serve the interests of any one party.[71]

Already organizational proposals were being suggested in the Freetown newspapers; one correspondent suggested that although there were some problems peculiar to the various colonies, in general (1) local newspapers should call for opinions on the subject of the projected Conference for a period of six weeks; (2) a 'committee of learned, thoughtful, and experienced gentlemen' should then be formed to consider these suggestions, the same procedure being adopted in the other colonies, each colony preparing a rough programme which would then be co-ordinated by a Gold Coast general committee; (3) editors of local newspapers should serve on the local congress committees, one of them being selected as a delegate to the Accra Conference; (4) the cost of propaganda and the expenses of delegates should be met by public subscriptions collected by the local committees.[72]

At the public meeting called by J. H. Thomas and Claudius May in April 1918 at the Wilberforce Memorial Hall, J. H. Thomas declared that the idea of a West African Conference was neither visionary nor impracticable; on the contrary, he said, there were precedents from which to learn, such as the little-known Pan-African Conference called by Booker T. Washington in Tuskegee, Alabama, in 1912 ('inspired possibly by the Universal Races Conference which it immediately followed'). That Conference, he said, was attended by Afro-American delegates, delegates from the West Indies, South Africa, and a few from West Africa, but was organizationally unsound as 'the great diversity of interests, not to speak of the distance, robbed the Conference of interest and importance

---

Leone delegates to the 1920 Accra Conference; he later became a magistrate after participating in Freetown politics with H. C. Bankole-Bright, the Hon. J. H. Thomas, and the Hon. Shorunkeh Sawyer.

[70] *Gold Coast Leader* (19 Jan. 1918), p. 7.

[71] ibid.; also the issues for 9–23 Feb. 1918, p. 4, and 2 Feb. 1918, pp. 3–4.

[72] *Sierra Leone Weekly News* (5 Jan. 1918): 'Proposed West African Conference —Organisational Proposals by S. T. Jones.'

as far as Africa was concerned'.[73] The South African Native Congress and the Indian National Congress, said J. H. Thomas, were more relevant examples to the immediate objectives of the projected West African Conference, especially as the Indian National Congress formed in 1885 'has been the means of securing many privileges for the people, including an open door in the Civil Service for their talented sons; it has given India a policy and shape to its national ideals and aspirations . . .'. Although the British West African colonies were not territorially contiguous, sea and postal communications had made intercommunications easier; in any case, their common grievances under colonial rule would always afford an area of agreement.[74]

A. S. Hebron, a local barrister, presided at the Wilberforce Hall meeting; a lively interest was shown in the Conference idea, and the attendance was 'large and unusually representative'.[75] The Hon. J. H. Thomas[76] opened the meeting, explaining how he and Claudius

[73] ibid. (27 Apr. 1918), pp. 8–9. For an account of the Tuskegee Conference of 1912, see Harlan, Louis R., 'Booker T. Washington and the White Man's Burden', *American Historical Review*, lxxi, no. 2 (Jan. 1966), 464–7. According to Harlan, Washington 'ignored the important but controversial issues of race and nationalism'; a letter from J. E. Casely Hayford to Washington declared that 'There is an African Nationality, and when the Aborigines of the Gold Coast and other parts of West Africa have joined forces with our brethren in America arriving at a national aim, purpose, and inspiration, then indeed, will it be possible for our brethren over the sea to bring home metaphorically to their nation and people a great spoil', quoted in Harlan, op. cit., pp. 465–6. It is interesting to note that although leading West African nationalist intellectuals generally approved of racial movements among Afro-Americans and were enthusiastic about their educational institutions, they always insisted that their political and ideological interests were different. Content analysis of the West African press on West African reactions to Pan-Negro movements from the Tuskegee Conference to the Garvey and Pan-African movement of Du Bois bears out this observation. Of particular interest are the writings of E. W. Blyden, Hayford, Casely, *Ethiopia Unbound*, and the unpublished manuscript of W. E. G. Sekyi, 'The Parting of the Ways' (1925), which the author found in the Sekyi Papers at Cape Coast. Three chapters of this last-named work are devoted to a critical examination of Afro-American claims to political leadership of Africa; here Marcus Garvey comes out in a favourable light, although his political pretensions and American republicanism are rejected.

[74] *Sierra Leone Weekly News*, art. cit.

[75] ibid. (4 May 1918), p. 5.

[76] The Hon. J. H. Thomas was born in 1846 at Hastings village near Freetown and was 'probably the oldest merchant in Freetown'. At 14 he went to Rionunez, a neighbouring French territory with his uncle, a trader, and remained for seven years. He became a book-keeper in Freetown with the Company of African Merchants Ltd.; he resigned in 1872 and started his own business as a general merchant at Malamah. He later moved to Freetown as his business expanded in

May were approached by Casely Hayford and Dr. Savage respectively in 1917 about the possibility of a Conference. After a few speeches, J. A. Fitzjohn moved the first resolution which referred to West African unity and pledged support for the idea.

Mr. Fitzjohn made an eloquent plea for the Conference movement, in the course of which he observed that Sierra Leone, being the oldest of the British West African colonies, should have spearheaded the movement; there were those who said that there was neither public opinion nor public spirit in Freetown: this was so, he said, in the 'portals of the rich and highly placed, but not in the street corners and market places'. The Revd. Orishatuké Faduma, cultural nationalist and ideologue to Chief Sam's abortive Back to Africa Movement of 1914, who seconded the resolution, said that the idea of co-operation between different Negro communities had long commended itself to him. Before the war, arrangements were being made for a visit of Afro-American teachers and agriculturalists to West Africa. He believed a British West African Conference would do a lot of good. 'Politics apart,' he continued, 'it would be excellent if doctors, lawyers, educationalists, agriculturists and merchants could meet with their *confrères* from other Colonies, and exchange ideas with a view to mutual improvement. Many unfair criticisms levelled at the Native were due to ignorance. If the Conference could publish a comprehensive statement of the achievements of the native, it would go far towards disarming criticism of that sort.'[77] Faduma's speech seems to have created some confusion, for as the editorial commented, 'As soon as the discussion began the atmosphere became warm. Professor Faduma had unwittingly created the impression that he held that politics would be beyond the scope of the Conference. This, however, he corrected.'[78]

A few speakers were critical of the Conference idea and criticized its promoters for not previously issuing programmes and for not explaining its strategy: 'the project of a Conference was very alluring, but what about the *modus operandi*?' The opposition, however, was

---

1882. He was a member of the Legislative Council from 1907 to 1912 and was reappointed in 1915; he became Mayor of Freetown eight times—1905–7, 1910, 1912–13, 1914–15. He was known locally as Malamah Thomas; he died in 1925—Macmillan, op. cit., p. 269. The *Sierra Leone Weekly News* wrote his obituary in verse, calling him 'Sa Leone's Grand Old Man' and 'our late J. H. T.', *Sierra Leone Weekly News* (25 Feb. 1925).
[77] *Sierra Leone Weekly News* (27 Apr. 1918), pp. 8–9.
[78] ibid.

pacified when the Revd. J. T. Roberts, seconded by Mr. J. S. T. Davies, moved a second resolution providing for the appointment of a committee of twelve to settle the composition of the Sierra Leone delegation to the Accra Conference.[79]

A Committee of twelve was appointed, the names being suggested by Claudius May, but others present at the meeting felt that the new committee had been packed or prearranged, and there were protests. The meeting was adjourned until 6 May in the same Hall. Mr. Hebron again presided. After some disagreement on the procedure for electing the twelve-man committee, they finally got down to electing them by acclamation and by a show of hands. Thirty people were nominated and, by elimination, the required number was secured. These were: the Hon. J. H. Thomas, A. S. Hebron, C. May, S. Barlatt (the Mayor of Freetown),[80] L. E. V. M'Carthy, Professor O. Faduma, S. J. Coker, R. C. P. Barlatt, Dr. G. N. Metzger, J. A. Songo Davies, A. E. Tuboku Metzger, and J. A. Fitzjohn. Professor Faduma was elected *in absentia*, but had sent a draft for the organization of the West African Congress grand committee, in which he suggested the creation of a General Committee, Financial Committee, Programme Committee, and Executive Committee of the Sierra Leone branch of the Congress, to draw up realistic plans in the social, educational, and economic fields.[81]

Faduma's draft scheme was certainly both functional and idealistic, and had the N.C.B.W.A. adopted such a scheme, perhaps with a few modifications, the movement would have been far more coherent, effective, and better able to refute the criticisms of the Colonial Office and of Sir Hugh Clifford. As a member of the American Academy of Social and Political Science, and as one who had observed American machine politics, perhaps Faduma was in a

[79] ibid.

[80] S. J. S. Barlatt was born in 1867; educated at the C.M.S. Grammar School and Fourah Bay College. Acted as chief clerk to the Royal Garrison Artillery before going to study law in England in 1906. Called to the Bar (Gray's Inn) in 1909; M.A. (Dunelm) 1909. Practised in Freetown from 1910; elected Mayor on 11 Nov. 1918. He was part owner with his brother, R. C. P. Barlatt, in their father's general merchandise business which had been established in 1876—Macmillan, op. cit., p. 271. Barlatt was influential in local politics, and, with Dr. H. C. Bankole-Bright, was instrumental in restoring order after the rice and anti-Syrian riots of 1919. He was also an active supporter of the Congress movement, recommending the London Congress delegation of 1920-1 as the bona fide representatives of their various territories; re-elected Mayor in 1921, in spite of his nationalist activities.

[81] *Sierra Leone Weekly News* (11 May 1918), p. 8.

better position to appreciate the advantages of sound organization and political realism.

By May it was decided that the main functions of the newly established local congress committee (which had the power to add to its number) were: to prepare the various topics to be brought before the projected West African Conference, to disseminate information as to the aims of the movement and to campaign for support, to establish contact with other Congress committees in the colonies 'to settle all the business preliminaries', and if possible to establish a Women's Auxiliary of the Committee.[82] Meanwhile, Faduma's scheme was taken up enthusiastically by the *Gold Coast Independent*:

We are in entire agreement with the Professor's [Faduma's] suggestions, and the sooner they are acted upon throughout British West Africa, the better. The economic situation brought about by the world war now . . . ought to stimulate the best thought. After all, thoughts and conferences will be useless unless backed by sacrifices of time and money. . . . Let Committees—practical, and not talking committees—be formed as early as possible in all the various towns . . . on the Sierra Leone model, and let us get to business at once.[83]

The Freetown local committee co-opted Mayor Barlatt in December 1918, and invited twenty others to join the committee. These included 'clergymen, doctors, lawyers, businessmen, artisans, and, last but not least, a prominent member of the Mohammedan community'.[84] E. S. Beoku-Betts advised that subjects like the colour bar, the position of Africans in the British Empire, medical appointment of Africans in the Civil Service, finance, representative government, and trade monopolies should be included in the programme of the forthcoming Conference which, he thought, ought to be published beforehand, as the Conference was not a subversive body. The Conference, in his view, should be 'not so much of an enlarged or enhanced debating Society, as a practical assembly of practical men'.[85]

Apparently the local committee met at irregular intervals between the latter part of 1918 and early 1919, primarily because they feared that progress in Lagos and the Gold Coast was too uncertain for the

[82] ibid.
[83] *Gold Coast Independent* (22 June 1918).
[84] *Sierra Leone Weekly News* (14 Dec. 1918), p. 5.
[85] ibid.

Freetown committee to go ahead with its plans. Within that period additional members to the Freetown local committee included Archdeacon Wilson, the Revd. F. H. Johnson, the Revd. J. B. Nicol, the Revd. H. M. Steady, the Revd. A. T. Sumner, Councillors E. A. C. Davies, E. A. C. Noah, D. C. Parker, J. Jenkins Johnson, Dr. Abayomi Cole, E. S. Beoku-Betts, M. S. Brown, H. Deen, W. P. Golley, S. T. Jones, J. F. Knox, J. S. Labour, J. B. Luke, T. G. Reffel, J. T. Richards, H. C. Solomon, and S. D. Turner. Press, clerical, and lay sub-committees were formed to educate the populace about the Conference; the clergy were particularly useful in public meetings.[86] Also influential in providing membership and funds for the Sierra Leone committee were the following voluntary organizations, some of whose members, it must be noted, constituted the core of the local movement: the Sierra Leone Bar Association, of which A. S. Hebron was the president and L. E. V. M'Carthy the joint secretary; the Freetown Ratepayers' Association, the Free-town branch of the African Progress Union which was based in London; the Freetown branch of Marcus Garvey's Universal Negro Improvement Association and African Communities League; and above all, the Anti-Slavery and Aborigines Protection Society, to which Beoku-Betts and nearly all the clergymen belonged. The Muslim community of Freetown was also represented, but there was no attempt by the Creole-dominated leadership, with its ex-cessive legalism, to represent the mass of the peasantry in the Protectorate through its chiefs.

It will be seen from the list of members of the Sierra Leone Congress committee that the leadership was overwhelmingly middle-class Creole, with the exception of a few 'Creolized' Muslims—who were included for the purpose of demonstrating a non-existent Colony/Protectorate unity of purpose. What strikes the observer is the preponderance of clergymen, lawyers, doctors, and journalists, together with a fair sprinkling of traders. Numerically, the Creole colonial élite was inferior; politically, though they no longer occu-pied top jobs in the administration (as a result of the changed tempo of imperial rule towards the end of the nineteenth century), they still dominated the all-important legislative and municipal councils, education, and the legal profession. Creole middlemen, although suffering from the economic effects of the war and from Syrian and foreign competition, were still relatively prosperous,

[86] *Sierra Leone Weekly News* quoted in *Gold Coast Leader* (15 Mar. 1919), p. 3.

though quite a number had lost their business in the Protectorate to the astute Syrian traders. These factors, together with unemployment after the Great War and the rise in food prices, created an atmosphere in which they could easily assert their leadership. History, and the socio-economic values they had inherited, justly led them to claim the position of 'natural rulers'. Here, then, was a situation characteristic of most colonial nationalist movements where an educated minority came to see itself as the natural leader of 'the people', even if in reality their social position, and the nature of colonial rule, disqualified them from claiming such a role. As further analysis will show, when we discuss the economic aspects of the nationalism of the period under review, it was this socially dominant group in Freetown whose interests were most affected in the rice and anti-Syrian riots of 1919 and the deteriorating economic conditions of the immediate post-war years. To this intelligentsia of 'displaced and blocked persons', nationalism meant glorification of the Negro race, *laissez-faire*, constitutionalism, and 'ordered liberty'. They employed the language of democracy, yet representative government to them meant the representation of the propertied few—or 'the better class of people', as they described themselves.

The politics of the Sierra Leone Congress committee generally followed the pattern of the Gambia committee; lobbying the administration through deputations, memorials, and telegrams had become a standard technique. Like the Gambia committee, the Sierra Leone committee also tried to secure the support of non-Creole community leaders in Freetown. For example, in March 1921, led by their local secretary Mr. E. S. Beoku-Betts, the local committee dispatched a telegram directly to the Colonial Office, without the knowledge of the Governor. The telegram was signed by only one of the unofficial Creole members of the Legislative Council; among the community leaders, only Almami Fofana, head of the Mandingo community, appended his signature to the telegram; but even he had lost much of his political importance.[87] This was followed by a 'mass' meeting on 4 April, at which Bankole-Bright reported on the results of the Congress London delegation. On 18 April 1921, at a public meeting which was attended by leading citizens, church dignitaries, Muslim Almamis, and chiefs, the local committee, in response to Lord Milner's rejection of the N.C.B.W.A.

[87] C.O. 551/2290, 23 Apr. 1921, Governor Wilkinson to Winston S. Churchill, Secretary of State for the Colonies.

petition, condemned Milner's views as 'erroneous' and contended that the reforms demanded by the Congress were 'in accordance with the British Constitution' and had the support of the whole population. Cornelius May, a member of the Legislative Council, J. H. Thomas (president of the local congress committee), Archdeacon Wilson, Chief Fofana, and Alimami Usman (representing the Muslim community) were present at that meeting.[88]

Perhaps the granting of limited elective representation to Sierra Leone in 1924 owed much to Governor Wilkinson who, in general, was milder in his criticisms of the N.C.B.W.A. Unlike the other British West African territories, Sierra Leone was fortunate in having a Governor who had 'every sympathy with progress towards self-Government', though he disapproved of the methods of agitation adopted by the local committee.[89]

Throughout 1921 and 1922 the agitation of the local committee was mainly directed against the decision of the Colonial Office in 1921; on the whole, enthusiastic support was still given to the Congress movement in spite of the failure of the 1920–1 London delegation. In January–February 1923 the second session of the N.C.B.W.A. met in Freetown. This important meeting gained the full support of the social élite of Freetown; it was preceded by an impressive church service which was extensively reported in the press. It was at this session also that the Constitution of the N.C.B.W.A. was ratified, in which the functions of President, General Secretary, Executive Council, Financial Secretary, and Central Executive Committee were laid down, and rules of debate formulated. It was also proposed to start a journal of the Congress, to be called the *British West African National Review*, in which 'all elections, charges, notices, news or reports of Sections and Local Committees shall be published'. The Secretary of each local committee was to make quarterly reports to the General Secretary, whose office was to be at Sekondi. It was also agreed that the various local committees should be allowed to 'enact bye-laws for their government, provided the said bye-laws do not conflict with the Constitution and general laws and rules of the National Congress of British West Africa'.[90] One clause in the Constitution, significantly

---

[88] ibid., copy of telegram from Governor Wilkinson to Winston Churchill, 23 Apr. 1921.
[89] ibid.
[90] *The Constitution of the National Congress of British West Africa*, pp. 3–6.

enough, dealt with economic co-operation in West Africa: 'That the Congress shall, in order to promote the co-operation of the peoples of the British West African Dependencies and their economic development, educate public opinion as to the African Financiers and others promoting business combinations in such wise as shall inspire and maintain a British West African economical development.'[91]

The Sierra Leone Section was to make effective use of the organizational structure of the local branch, for so successfully did the local leaders, particularly Beoku-Betts, utilize the local branch with its auxiliary associations in Freetown during the Legislative Council elections of September–November 1924, when the new constitution providing for three elected Africans was introduced, that Governor Sir Alexander Ransford Slater was compelled to acknowledge that the voting figures[92] 'are striking and encouraging facts, testifying to the fact that the franchise is highly prized, and that the class of persons placed on the register appreciated the system of secret ballot and were fully competent to use it'. Indeed, with the exception of the municipal elections in 1938, which were won by candidates fielded by Wallace-Johnson's West African Youth League, all the elections held in Freetown up to the outbreak of World War II were won by N.C.B.W.A. candidates. It is true that the Sierra Leone section, emboldened by its electoral success in 1924 and by its growing political prestige in the Colony, nearly succeeded in upsetting the colonial political system by giving organizational and financial aid to the strikers during the serious strike of the Railway Workers' Union in February 1926. This was the first serious occasion since 1919 when the colonial petty bourgeoisie openly allied itself with the wage labourers. In 1919 they were accused of 'disloyalty' against the British Empire and of making common cause with the lumpenproletariat in the colony; in 1926 Governor Slater made a similar accusation, referring to 'the disorderly and undisciplined elements always unhappily present in the Colony of Sierra Leone' and of 'the danger arising from such elements', condemned the 'political perversity' of the Sierra Leone Congress leaders and

[91] ibid., p. 5.
[92] Approximately 1,350 people were eligible to vote under the 1924 constitution; 89 per cent of the registered voters cast their votes—see paper by Kilson, Martin, 'National Congress of British West Africa 1918 to 1930's' in Rothberg, R. I., and Mazrui, Ali A., eds., *Protest and Power in Black Africa* (Cambridge, Mass., and New York, 1970).

referred to the 'widespread defiance of discipline and revolt against authority'.[93] The fact remains, however, that like their counterparts in the Gambia, the Gold Coast, and Nigeria, the local Congress leadership exhibited a deplorable lack of strategic thinking and a singular incapacity to form political alliances with, or manipulate, the new élites in the Protectorate, particularly at a time when the latter were being brought into the centre of the colonial political system through their chiefs.

## 3. The Gold Coast Section

THE interesting and complicated story of the Gold Coast Section, which was the nucleus of the Congress movement, has already been told in great detail.[94] All that will be done here is to give a brief account of the movement in the Gold Coast as we have done in the case of the other territorial committees; in this case, material not available to either Denzer[95] or Kimble will be used to clarify a few points.

The origins and politics of the Gold Coast Section cannot be understood in isolation from the all-important Gold Coast Aborigines Rights Protection Society, the pivot of all nationalist politics in the Gold Coast from 1897 to the second decade of the twentieth century.[96] In fact, by 1914 the Gold Coast A.R.P.S. was in decline, still clinging to the old methods of agitation since the successful Lands deputation of 1898; thereafter it remained largely a Cape Coast affair, a shadow of its former glory. By 1912, '. . . the Society had lost, and was never to recapture, the political initiative in the Gold Coast. Their main trouble arose not so much from lack of government recognition . . . nor from any lack of interest in constitutional development . . . but largely from their inability to adapt the leisurely, parochial techniques of nineteenth-century Cape Coast politics to the more militant outlook and wider horizons of the twentieth century.'[97] The development of race-consciousness

[93] Dispatch of Sir Alexander Ransford Slater to Rt. Hon. L. S. Amery, 20 Apr. 1926, quoted in Kilson, op. cit.
[94] Denzer, op. cit.; Kimble, David, *A Political History of Ghana: 1850–1928*, pp. 374–403.
[95] Miss Denzer's sources are mostly from Gold Coast newspapers; the Archives at Cape Coast contain some correspondence she seems to have overlooked.
[96] For an account of the Gold Coast A.R.P.S., see Kimble, op. cit., pp. 330–74.
[97] ibid., p. 374.

after the Great War, reinforced by Wilsonian idealism, together with the economic effects of the war, led to the emergence of a younger, idealistic group within the basically conservative A.R.P.S., seeking to use that body as the vehicle of its idealism. This, in turn, implied a redefinition of the political objectives of the A.R.P.S., and a sharing of traditional authority with the younger element. Although it would be inaccurate to describe what happened within the A.R.P.S. between 1914 and 1921 as a power struggle, the dispute over objectives between the traditional leadership and Casely Hayford's Pan-African group was not resolved until 1921 when the old guard of the Executive Committee of the A.R.P.S. were swept out of their positions.

It would appear that the antagonism between Casely Hayford and the older, more conservative leadership of the A.R.P.S. had existed even before 1914.[98] According to W. E. G. Sekyi:

. . . the trouble that arose in the Society, which the prompted imagination of Mr. Wight[99] dates 'from the time of the West African National Congress', started very many years before Mr. Casely Hayford first mooted the idea of the Congress. The rift started as a result of rivalry between Mr. Casely Hayford and Mr. E. J. P. Brown, said to have a very unedifying origin in London, when both these gentlemen, with Dr. B. J. Quartey-Papafio, and Mr. T. F. E. Jones, many times President of the Society, were on the Forest Bill Delegation (1912). At any rate, when the rivalry became most noteworthy, the cause appeared to be the M.B.E. which had been conferred on Mr. Casely Hayford for work done in connection with the collection of money for the Red Cross Fund during the War. At that time, Mr. Casely Hayford, who no less than Mr. E. J. P. Brown, always wanted to head some movement or other apart from what the Society was organising, set up a separate organisation for the collection of Red Cross contributions from chiefs in the Western Province who were all members of the Society. . . .[1]

The chiefs who were asked to contribute to Casely Hayford's collection were puzzled as the A.R.P.S. had already started a fund of its own, with the Axim Branch collecting for the Western Province.

[98] Kimble dates it from 1914, op. cit., p. 376.
[99] Martin Wight is author of *The Development of the Gold Coast Legislative Council*; the Sekyi Papers contain several review articles written by Sekyi himself, attacking much of Wight's account of the Gold Coast Legislative Council. It is only fair to mention here that Sekyi resented Wight's criticisms of his attitude to the 1925 Constitution and of his political outlook in general.
[1] Kobina Sekyi Papers, Cape Coast Regional Archives, 461/64, paper on 'Our Political Education'.

Casely Hayford's conduct was then reported to the Axim Branch to which he belonged, 'and Mr. Hayford, who was noted for his agility whenever he tried to get out of an awkward situation, began to skip'.[2] The angry A.R.P.S. accused Hayford of seeing things from an 'imperial' point of view and roundly told him that charity began at home,[3] but in reality they were jealous of his initiative and ambition:

The members of the Executive Committee at Cape Coast, who knew all about Mr. Casely Hayford's tendency to evade the provisions of the Constitution as often as he could, several of whom regarded him with suspicion, eventually became definitely antagonistic to him. Mr. E. J. P. Brown, a much younger and less eminent man who nevertheless would brook no rival, was one of the members of the Executive Committee. He was a Fanti (Abura) whilst Mr. Casely Hayford was an Asebu (Moree) man. The mutual dislike of these two politicians became more and more intensified. Mr. Brown was strongly supported by the Fanti clique in the Executive—Abura, Anamaboe, Nkusukum. . . .[4]

When E. J. P. Brown was nominated a member of the Legislative Council in 1916 (the same year Casely Hayford entered the Legislative Council) he made the acquaintance of a rising young chief of the Nsonna clan, Nana Ofori Atta, Omanhene of Akyem Abuakwa, a favourite of Sir Hugh Clifford and his Colonial Secretary Mr. (later Sir) Alexander Ransford Slater. 'Mr. Brown being himself of the Nsonna clan, and being fond of "high company", soon formed an alliance with this rising young Chief.'[5]

It was against this background of jealousy and personal rivalry that Casely Hayford and his supporters along the west coast were campaigning for a West African Conference. The Conference idea itself was originally suggested by *West Africa*, from an imperial point of view,[6] and was taken up by the West African press in 1917. Already in the Gold Coast Nana Ofori Atta and T. Hutton Mills, a member of the Casely Hayford school of thought, had disagreed on the scope and objectives of such a West African movement.[7] In early 1918 the *Gold Coast Leader* reminded its readers that West Africa was 'entitled to a representation at the Imperial reconstruc-

[2] ibid.
[3] Kimble, op. cit., p. 376.
[4] Kobina Sekyi Papers, op. cit. See also Kimble, op. cit., p. 378 n. 5.
[5] Kobina Sekyi Papers, op. cit.
[6] Kimble, op. cit., p. 377.
[7] ibid., p. 377.

tion after the war. On no account must we go to sleep over that all-important desideratum.'[8] Division of opinion on the scope of West African representation in London after the war, however, became crystallized when in May 1918 Casely Hayford and E. J. P. Brown, the legal advisers of the A.R.P.S., disagreed over the procedure to be adopted in the petition for elective representation: was the petition to embrace 'united West Africa' or was it to follow the well-tried methods of the A.R.P.S. which the Pan-African group considered obsolete?

Several meetings between the Casely Hayford group (which had already started to form local committees of the projected West African Conference at Sekondi in the Western Province with Casely Hayford, Awoonor Williams, and R. J. Hayfron as officials; T. Hutton Mills was president of the Eastern Province section and H. Van Hien led the Western Province section) and the members of the A.R.P.S. Executive Committee were held between August 1918 and January 1920 in order to secure the support of the A.R.P.S. Prominent among the advocates of a wider Pan-West African movement were Awoonor Williams, the Revd. O. Pinanko, Mr. D. M. Abadoo, K. Ata Amonu, T. Hutton Mills, H. Van Hien, W. W. Brew, the Revd. Mark Hayford, W. E. G. Sekyi, and most important, the Ga Mantse. Of these, Sekyi, Pinanko, the two Hayfords, Prince Ata Amonu, and Van Hien were on the Executive Committee of the A.R.P.S. Another meeting of the Amanhin and Ahinfu (Kings and Chiefs) of the Central and Western Provinces with the A.R.P.S. Executive was held at Cape Coast in September 1918 (19 September to 21 September). At that meeting the Conference idea was brought up again, but this merely served to confirm the differing points of view within the A.R.P.S. After the meeting the *Gold Coast Leader* commented: 'The day is past forever in Gold Coast history when in public movements the people's representatives can meekly bow to what emanates from self-elected authorities. . . . We have among our Amanhin trained minds . . . and the new blood that has entered into Gold Coast politics can also give a good account of itself.'[9] Another editorial dealt more extensively with the meeting, and considered the proposed West African Conference 'by far the most important question discussed' at the Cape Coast Conference, in particular as the discussion had brought to

[8] *Gold Coast Leader* (2 Feb. 1918), pp. 3–4.
[9] ibid. (28 Sept. 1918), p. 3.

the open the divergence of opinion on the desirability of a West African Conference. The majority of the chiefs were reported to be in favour of a West African Conference and a joint petition to H.M.'s Government for the granting of elective councils. But 'a few of the members of the Executive Committee of the Gold Coast Aborigines Rights Protection Society also spoke, but so pessimistically that the Natural Rulers finding their "Doctors disagree", expressed themselves in full sympathy with the scheme', but decided to wait before committing themselves.[10] E. J. P. Brown, supporting the anti-Hayford group of the Executive Committee, criticized the Conference idea as unnecessary, pointing out that Canada, New Zealand, Australia, and Jamaica had only attained elective Legislative Councils gradually; he thought that the West African colonies should send petitions separately but simultaneously to the Colonial Office. Brown was supported by J. E. Biney, president of the A.R.P.S., T. F. E. Jones, an ex-president, and William Coleman, vice-president. On the second day of the conference, it appeared that some of the chiefs had come round to supporting the Hayford group, and were urging provincial co-operation to achieve the formation of the Gold Coast branch of the Conference; on that day, T. F. E. Jones and E. J. P. Brown 'were conspicuous by their absence'.[11] On the third day of the conference, however, they reappeared and again criticized the proposed West African Conference 'as much as their breath could allow them'. Casely Hayford and Van Hien had already addressed the A.R.P.S. Committee on behalf of the Gold Coast local committee of the projected Conference, but already it was becoming clear that they could not carry the A.R.P.S. with them, and the *Gold Coast Leader* openly blamed the conservatives on the A.R.P.S. Executive Committee for the deadlock caused by 'certain persons who have cliqued together that anything not introduced by them should be considered useless. . . . Is it not true that the two Deputations sent to Downing Street *re* the Lands and Forestry Bills, our people asked to be allowed to elect their own men to the legislative Council? If so, has the time not yet arrived?'[12]

A stronger article appeared in the form of an open letter to E. J. P. Brown, accusing the latter of occupying 'a false position in

[10] ibid. (5–12 Oct. 1918), p. 2: 'The Conference of the Amanhin and Ahinfu of the Central and Western Provinces and the Proposed West African Conference'.
[11] ibid.
[12] ibid.

the confidence of the people'; it also went on to challenge him to declare his position on the Conference project 'in the public interest', since those who posed as guides of the people should be unambiguous. The letter then went on to compare Brown very unfavourably with John Mensah Sarbah. If the latter were alive, the *Leader* did not doubt that he would have been the first 'to reshape the Aborigines Society so as to meet the exigencies of the times', that is, use a relatively conservative body to articulate Congress views; but Brown, it went on, was not receptive to new ideas; and though he could still mesmerize 'the old fogies' who monopolized the presidential offices of the A.R.P.S., it was the considered opinion of the *Leader* that Brown was 'a hopeless case'. Brown was curtly told that there was a 'new world-a-comin'' after the war, and that it was 'evident that old fossilized ideas must give place to new'.[13] By the end of 1918, however, *ad hoc* committees of the projected Conference were being formed in the territories concerned, but the *Leader* had still not settled accounts with the opposition which it described as 'cantankerous persons who would oppose the advent of the millennium itself if the Almighty did not first take them into His confidence'.

In 1919 W. F. Hutchison, a Gold Coast journalist working for Dusé Mohammed Ali's *African Times and Orient Review* in London, visited the Gold Coast. Hutchison, who was later to take a prominent part in the affairs of the London-based African Progress Union and in giving publicity to the Pan-African Congresses in West African newspapers, belonged to 'one of the most ancient and illustrious families'[14] in the Gold Coast, and had been an extraordinary member of the Gold Coast Legislative Council in 1887, after which he went to England, staying there for twenty years, returning for a visit in 1919.[15] During his visit, Hutchison met members of the A.R.P.S. and addressed them on 13 and 16 May on various post-war questions, including the Empire Resources Development Committee; he also urged them to 'take advantage of the reconstruction of the British Empire, which would follow on the return to peace, by sending Representatives to England during the sittings of the Imperial Conference . . .'. He pointed out that any action taken by the British West African Colonies should be jointly

[13] ibid., p. 3.
[14] ibid. (31 May–7 June 1919), p. 3; Kimble, op. cit., p. 456.
[15] Kimble, op. cit., p. 546.

carried out by the four colonies acting in concert, and that the influence exercised by a joint delegation would be vastly greater than that of four separate delegations. Hutchison also advised concentration on elective representation and co-operation with the Chambers of Commerce in London and Liverpool to secure this objective.[16] This was ammunition enough for Casely Hayford and his group. The *Leader* again castigated the conservatives of the A.R.P.S. Executive Committee who might refuse to publish Hutchison's address in their organ the *Gold Coast Nation*, and 'whose delight is to assume a *non possumus* attitude with respect to any new ideas that don't fit in with their brain capacity'. In the eyes of the A.R.P.S. conservatives, Hutchison had 'committed the unpardonable sin of referring to the supreme necessity' of a West African Conference.

From mid-1919 to early 1920 the Conference group toured various areas campaigning for the Conference project. Already local committees had been formed in Western and Eastern Provinces; in early 1920, after a delegation led by Casely Hayford, Van Hien, the Revd. O. Pinanko, and Prince Ata Amonu to Elmina, a branch was opened there; a local committee was also started at Tarkwa, with H. Vroom as secretary.[17] But the 'Anti-Progressive Party', led by E. J. P. Brown, J. E. Biney, T. F. E. Jones, W. Coleman, W. S. Johnstone, George Amissah, and the Revd. Ebenezer A. Sackey, were also opposing the movement in the columns of the *Gold Coast Nation*, declaring that it was the business of the natural rulers, not the educated young men, to initiate such movements.

In the end the Casely Hayford group won the tactical battle of convening a West African Conference in Accra in March 1920; psychologically, they had good reasons for congratulating themselves on this momentous occasion, but they still had to win the more important war within the executive of the A.R.P.S. if the new Pan-West African movement was to be run smoothly from Axim. The second phase of the struggle between the two groups in the A.R.P.S. assumed greater scope and importance when the 1920–1 London Congress Delegation, having failed to convince Lord Milner that West Africa was ready for elective representation and that they the N.C.B.W.A. were the true representatives of 'the people', returned empty-handed, angry at what it thought was a stab in the

[16] *Gold Coast Leader* (31 May–7 June 1919), p. 3.
[17] ibid. (3–10 Jan. 1920).

back by their opponents at home, particularly Nana Ofori Atta, Nana Amonoo V Omanhene of Anomabu, E. J. P. Brown, and Dr. B. W. Quartey-Papafio of the Gold Coast. Even before the return of the Delegation, a flood of telegrams from several Gold Coast chiefs denouncing Nana Ofori Atta's Legislative Council speech had reached the Colonial Office; even in Freetown (Sierra Leone) marked hostility towards Ofori Atta was evident in the press. Further propaganda by the various Congress committees in the Gold Coast resulted in the adherence of a few more chiefs to the Congress movement.[18]

Politically, Nana Ofori Atta and his group had blundered in their back-door attack on the Congress; technically, however, there was very little Casely Hayford and his group could complain about: their joint petition was a combination of the relevant and the irrelevant, and their tactics in London were not as sustained or professional as they ought to have been. Moreover, although the majority of the Amanhene were in favour of the Congress, it must be remembered that Nana Ofori Atta, an intelligent and enlightened traditional ruler, had secured the authority of a majority of the Amanhene of the Eastern Province to speak on their behalf; he had also received 'on behalf of the Central and Western Provinces a mandate from the Executive Council of the Aborigines Society to oppose the Congress movement'.[19]

Casely Hayford carried the attack on Nana Ofori Atta into the Legislative Council in April 1921; in a series of verbal battles he rebutted the latter's claim that the educated class had no claims to political leadership and accused his group of treachery to the Congress movement.[20] With the support of the Ga Mantse, all that remained now was to capture the leadership of the A.R.P.S., and this was achieved at its meeting in July 1921. There can be no doubt that the manoeuvres of the Gold Coast Section of the N.C.B.W.A. had sufficiently impressed the administration to acknowledge Nana Ofori Atta's mistake and even to concede that reforms were truly necessary. As one minute paper put it in late 1921: 'We can only wait now . . . for the various electoral schemes to be put forward

[18] Kimble, op. cit., p. 393.
[19] Taylor, Kobina, 'Our Political Destiny—a paper in commemoration of the 43rd Year of the Gold Coast Aborigines Rights Protection Society, August 1941', pp. 7–8.
[20] Kimble, op. cit., pp. 393–6.

. . . no further action is necessary at present.'[21] Another official commented: '. . . the vast majority of the Chiefs have come round to support the Congress movement. The Omanhin of Fanti Nyankumassi . . . informed me that before the Congress went to England, they explained the nature of these proposals to the Chiefs, and that had they waited a little longer, formal approval would have been given and money found for them for their expenses', although this policy of the Chiefs was at variance with an earlier resolution passed by the Chiefs in September 1918 and confirmed in May 1919, which had not been rescinded when the Chiefs gave approval to the Congress in 1920. After observing that there was very little difference between the contending groups in the A.R.P.S. about the desirability of reforms, the dispatch concluded: 'There is also no doubt that the bulk of the Chiefs represented at the recent Conference [Cape Coast Conference of July 1921] are now whole heartedly in favour of the Congress movement, and I think that their lead will followed [sic] by the majority of those who were not present. . . .'[22]

In the complicated history of the politics of the Gold Coast Section, sometimes the politics of chieftaincy got entangled in Congress affairs. In the course of the struggle between the Congress supporters and the conservative group of the A.R.P.S., relations between Nana Ofori Atta, Omanhene of Akim Abuakwa, a leading critic of the Congress, and Tackie Yaoboi, the Gã Mantse, a leading supporter of the Congress among the traditional rulers, became strained, particularly after the former was booed after a heated Legislative Council meeting on 24 April 1921, during which Casely Hayford made his major attack on Nana Ofori Atta. The administration, which had prompted Nana Ofori Atta to ask the supporters of the Gã Mantse for an apology, wrote to the Gã Mantse complaining of his treatment, but so seriously did the latter espouse the cause of the intelligentsia that he merely sent in a rather non-committal reply, avoiding any apology.[23]

The Gã Mantse's support of the Congress also provided his

[21] Ghana National Archives, ADM 11/1427, Case no. 1/1921: Colonial Secretary's Minute Papers. 15884/21, 26 Aug. 1921.
[22] H. E. G. Bartlett, Acting Provincial Commissioner, Central Province, to the Acting Colonial Secretary, Accra, no. 456/C.P.151/1921, 22 Aug. 1921. G.N.A.; also *Gold Coast Independent* (25 June 1921), p. 171.
[23] G.N.A. no. 622/69/21, 1 June 1921, and no. 521/21, 27 Apr. 1921. The Gã Mantse to Hon. Nana Ofori Atta, C.B.E., no. 36/318/21, 6 May 1921. Minutes to S.N.A. Case no. 1/12, para. 6, ADM 11/1427.

opponents in the Gã Division with a convenient weapon they could use to destool him or undermine his authority. For example, when the 1925 Constitution provided for the creation of a Provincial Council of Head Chiefs, the Gã Mantse, along with the Congress officials, refused to attend its meetings. The Mantsemei of Gbese, Asere, Sempe, and Akumaji (four of the seven subdivisions of Accra) protested against the boycott of the Provincial Council, charging that the Gã Mantse had not consulted the Gã people, and that he had boycotted the Provincial Council 'as the result of a meeting between him and the *intelligentsia*'.[24] The purpose of this attack on the Gã Mantse, however, was not to demonstrate support for the new Constitution, but to attempt to undermine the authority of the Gã Mantse. The sub-chiefs who made the protest had grievances against him in the past, when he supported Government policies inimical to the interests of the sub-chiefs; at that time they had tried unsuccessfully to get the administration to recognize them if they destooled the Gã Mantse. Now that the Gã Mantse was supporting the Congress, his opponents seized the opportunity to embarrass him; but as one official put it: '. . . this time he [i.e. the Gã Mantse] has not supported the Government in a matter in which they are really very little interested one way or the other. Any stick is good enough to beat him with . . . their attitude must be considerably discounted as being rather anti-Gã Mantse than pro-Constitution.'[25]

From 1920 the Gold Coast Section had steadily campaigned to secure the adherence of the Chiefs to the aims of the Congress. There were some members who thought that the chiefs could give their support to the Congress while not becoming actual members; others thought that the Congress would speak with greater authority if the natural rulers became members. The Revd. Mark C. Hayford of the Accra Section, who supported the latter view, regretted 'the misunderstanding of the position with reference to the suggestion that the Amanhin and Natural Rulers . . . should formally be or be invited to become members of the Congress'. It was one thing being a supporter of the Congress (as most of the natural rulers were) he said, and quite another to become a member. The Cliffordian argument that the Congress did not represent 'the people' would still

---

[24] G.N.A. M.P. 1344/26, para. 48, SNA 925. Case no. 28/1925: 'Reconstituted Legislative Council'.
[25] ibid.

be used against the Congress if the natural rulers remained mere sympathizers. The Revd. M. C. Hayford thought that 'the matter would stand upon a different basis and would have the weight it was held out to have on the last occasion', if the natural rulers, who were also influential in the A.R.P.S., were asked to become members of the Congress.[26] He then went on to compare the Congress, rather inaccurately, with the Indian National Congress, asserting that, in the latter case, the Indian princes had given active support to the Indian National Congress. He concluded by advising that unless his suggestion was put into effect, they might as well cancel the 1923 Freetown session of Congress. Whether his proposal was put into practice is not known; what is known is that by 1922 the majority of chiefs had declared for the Congress and that the Congress had succeeded in installing itself within the traditional apparatus of the A.R.P.S. So strong had the Gold Coast Section become in 1922 that at the A.R.P.S. meeting of June–July 1922 the remnant of the old guard were unceremoniously removed from their executive positions. The declaration of the Natural Rulers after the conference read: '. . . We the undersigned Natural Rulers , . . do hereby in writing confirm . . . the removal by us of the said Joseph Edward Biney and those holding office under him from their offices in our said Society . . . and the appointment in their stead of Henry Van Hien Esquire as President, Joseph William de Graft Johnson Esquire and William Ward Brew Esquire . . . as Vice Presidents. . . .' J. E. Biney, E. J. P. Brown, and others were accused of betraying 'the confidence reposed in them by their election and installation as officers of our said Society by entering . . . into a secret correspondence with Nana Ofori Atta, Omanhin of Akyem Abuakwa directed against the National Congress of British West Africa for which action they were publicly blamed by the Conference of Natural Rulers which sat at Cape Coast in July and August One Thousand Nine Hundred and Twenty-Two . . .'.[27] They were accused of submitting a scheme for elective representation to the Government without the knowledge of the Natural Rulers and of 'grossly insubordinate and disrespectful' behaviour towards the

[26] Mark C. Hayford to Henry Van Hien, 22 June 1922. A.R.P.S. Papers, Cape Coast, 109/65, File no. 22. Van Hien was both President of the A.R.P.S. and a leading official of the Gold Coast Section of the N.C.B.W.A.

[27] *Deed of Confirmation and Ratification by the Natural Rulers In Conference Assembled at Cape Coast this 30th Day of June, 1922* by W. Esuman-Gwira Sekyi, p. 4.

Natural Rulers because they had failed to appear before them when commanded to do so.

Earlier in 1921, the group of J. E. Biney and E. J. P. Brown had been fined 'the sum of one Benda and a quantity of drinkables to pacify the party of the said contending members which had been wronged to wit the party belonging to the said National Congress of British West Africa'. Because they disagreed with the ruling of the Natural Rulers they were fined one ox, 'which said penalty, as a result of a prayer for pardon made by Nana Mbra the Third himself at the protracted suit of the said Joseph Edward Biney and those holding office under him, supported by certain of our elderly ladies whose hearts were touched by the pathetic plight in which the said Joseph Edward Biney and his party had placed themselves, was subsequently transmitted into a fine of the sum of Two Bendas and One Sua . . .'.[28]

By the middle of 1922, then, the strategic decision-making centre of the Gold Coast A.R.P.S. had been captured by the Gold Coast Section; from then on, few voices were raised in criticism of the Congress: the administration had no choice but to accept its *de facto* assumption of power within the A.R.P.S.; the powerful critics within the A.R.P.S. had been discredited. It is doubtful, however, whether the Gold Coast Section fully succeeded in converting the A.R.P.S. into an effective base from which the whole Congress movement could be directed. There is evidence that the relationship between the Gold Coast Section and the A.R.P.S. was still one in which the former continued to accept the traditional authority of the latter, even though some of its leading members were now officials of the A.R.P.S. W. E. G. Sekyi, for example, was both a nationalist intellectual and a traditionalist. The Gold Coast Section still had to obtain the sanction of the A.R.P.S. on several matters, notably financial, relating to the Congress.[29] This relative lack of serious friction may have been due, as Miss Denzer rightly argues, to the fact that the social basis of the Congress leadership was extremely limited. Members possessed 'similar education, status, success, and

[28] ibid., pp. 1–2.
[29] A.R.P.S. Papers, Cape Coast Regional Archives, Secretary of the A.R.P.S. to Ohene Kwesie Agyiman, 4 Jan. 1923. This correspondence relates to authorization by the A.R.P.S. for the Gold Coast Section to collect funds and approach the Natural Rulers for the expenses and passage of the Gold Coast delegates to the 1923 Freetown session. Also T. Hutton-Mills, President of the N.C.B.W.A., to S. R. Wood, Secretary of the N.C.B.W.A., 10 Jan. 1923, ibid.

in one way or another, were related to each other. Thus, it appears that there was a tendency for the National Congress meeting to disrupt if there were any personal quarrels among the delegates as well as the possibility that views on reforms and nationalism would largely be the same.'[30] In general, Congress members showed a high level of education, occupational success, high status both in traditional society and in their occupational group, a high occurrence of family, educational, and occupational interrelationships, and personal histories of nationalist activities. In the majority of cases, they received their higher education either in Freetown or in London.[31] As we have observed in the other territorial Congress committees, lawyers and merchants who were usually wealthy in nearly all cases formed the leadership of the movement. Wealth and position were prime determinants in participating actively in the movement and holding office.[32] For example, S. O. Akiwumi, who donated a large sum to the inaugural Congress fund in 1920, is said to have been a wealthy merchant who had sent his twelve children to England, and is described by Macmillan as a successful cocoa trader 'whose extensive knowledge and experience of the cocoa trade of the Gold Coast goes back to the inception of the industry there in 1891'. His cocoa business was concentrated mainly in the Mangoase and Parko districts, and he was 'exceedingly fastidious in obtaining only the best quality, which, under the designation of "S.O.A." quality—the letters being his own initials—he exports to Europe'.[33] We are also told that Akiwumi 'occupies a leading position amongst the native merchants of the Gold Coast, and is connected, on his mother's side, with the Royal Family of Lagos, at which town he was born in 1858'. His father also belonged to the Lagos nobility and was a chief of Abeokuta.[34] Educated at the Wesleyan High School in Lagos, he started business at Accra in 1887 as a general merchant; in 1912 he turned from import trade to produce trade. He was chairman of the Accra Native Club (where the 1920 Accra Conference met) in 1917 and 1918 in succession to Sir Hugh Clifford the Governor. The Club's tennis-courts were constructed at Akiwumi's expense as a gift to the Club. In 1918 he was one of the Vice-Presidents of Lady Clifford's Red Cross League and donated £150 to it. Two of his four sons studied law and civil engineering in England; four of his daughters were at the Girls' High School at

[30] Denzer, op. cit., p. 18.    [31] ibid., p. 13.    [32] ibid., pp. 14–15.
[33] MacMillan, op. cit., p. 208.    [34] ibid.

Taunton, Somerset. At the Accra Conference in March 1920 the Gold Coast Section alone contributed £10,345 to the Inaugural Fund, while T. Hutton-Mills, another merchant and barrister who later became the President of the N.C.B.W.A., contributed 1,000 guineas to the fund.[35] There is also evidence to show that T. Hutton-Mills financed the London Congress Delegation of 1920–1 throughout its stay in England, and even paid the passages of some of the delegates, being reimbursed (only partially) by collections from the territorial committees. He had spent £1,500 on that occasion. In 1923 he flatly refused to finance the passage and accommodation of the Gold Coast delegates to the Freetown session of the N.C.B.W.A., telling S. R. Wood that

If the Congress aims would result in beneficial reforms and changes in the Crown Colony system in West Africa and the Gold Coast in particular, our Chiefs and peoples should contribute towards the inevitable expenses which have been thrown on me by my appointment as President of the Congress. . . .

Further, may I ask what committee will provide funds for the expenses of the Gold Coast Delegates to and from Sierra Leone and their stay there because I am up to date out-of-pocket of over one thousand five hundred pounds for my detention and works in London during the period of nearly six months detention there in 1920.[36]

Finally, H. Van Hien, Treasurer to the London Committee in 1920, also heavily financed the delegation during its stay, particularly when funds were not forthcoming from the territorial committees in West Africa. When Van Hien died at Cape Coast in July 1928, he left property to the amount of £19,628 6s. 6d.; this included a stock of £6,774 18s. 8d.[37]

[35] Westermann, Von Diedrich, 'Ein Kongress Der Westafrikaner', p. 166. Dennett, R. E., *The West African Congress and Government on Native Lines*, p. 5. T. Hutton-Mills was born at Jamestown, Accra, in 1865; his father was connected with the Stool of Jamestown, and his mother was the second daughter of the Hon. James Bannerman, Lieutenant-General of the Gold Coast Settlement in 1850. Hutton-Mills was educated in the Gold Coast, then at the Wesleyan High School in Freetown. In 1891 he went to England and was called to the Bar (Inner Temple) in June 1894. He practised in Accra and Calabar and was an Unofficial Member of the Legislative Council until 1918. For biographical details, see Macmillan, op. cit., pp. 224–5.

[36] T. Hutton-Mills, President of the National Congress of British West Africa, co S. R. Wood, Secretary of the National Congress of British West Africa, 10 Jan. 1923. A.R.P.S. Papers, Cape Coast Regional Archives.

[37] Cape Coast Regional Archives, Acc. no. 585/64; *Documents Belonging to Henry Van Hien Esq.* The financial aspects of the N.C.B.W.A. are discussed neither by D. Kimble nor by Miss Denzer.

Ironically, the Gold Coast, which was the spearhead of the Congress movement, and which was most articulate in its demand for elective representation, was the last (excluding the Gambia) to be granted limited elective representation. It is to the credit of the Gold Coast leadership of the Congress movement that it continued to stimulate interest in the movement even when its political goals were not immediately realized. The inter-war years will certainly go down in history not only as a brilliant chapter in the history of modern Ghana but also in the political history of English-speaking West Africa as a whole and in the history of the early Pan-African movement. The Accra Conference of 1920 can rightly be seen as a worthy forerunner of the momentous 1958 Accra All-Africa People's Conference.

## 4. *The Nigerian Section*

SEVENTEEN years ago Ruth Perry drew attention to the importance of studying the contents of Nigerian newspapers and political pamphlets as a source of information on colonial politics and nationalist movements in the inter-war period. She observed that 'the newspapers which comprised this African press have in very few cases been studied or quoted by historians'.[38] She also observed that

The history of Nigerian participation in the National Congress of British West Africa, which has briefly been touched upon and dismissed as unimportant by most writers on the period, takes on a new colour when the newspaper files of 1921 are studied, and it is an interesting speculation as to how much influence they exerted on Governor Clifford's reversal of his opinion between December 1920, when he condemned severely the request for an elected Legislative Council, and November 1922, when Nigeria became the first territory in British Africa to have such a Legislative Council.[39]

While it is agreed that the Nigerian section of the N.C.B.W.A. was the weakest of the local branches, scholars have not paid sufficient attention to the causes of this weakness nor, with a few exceptions,[40]

---

[38] Perry, Ruth, 'New Sources for Research in Nigerian History', *Africa*, xxv (1955), 430–2. An analysis of the contents of Nigerian newspapers, however, was made in 1951 by Edmonds, op. cit.

[39] Perry, op. cit., pp. 430–1.

[40] Tamuno, T. N., *Nigeria and Elective Representation, 1923–1947*; Coleman, J. S., *Nigeria: Background to Nationalism* (Berkeley, Cal., 1958).

have they given any account of the political activities of some of the personalities involved in the politics of the local committee, and the relation of the local committee with other sections of opinion in Lagos politics in the 1920s. Names which immediately come to mind are Dr. Akiwande Savage who, with J. E. Casely Hayford of the Gold Coast conceived the idea of a Pan-West African movement in 1913; 'Professor' Adeoye Deniga, the Revd. Patriarch J. G. Campbell, E. M. E. Agbebi, J. Egerton Shyngle, and J. C. Zizer, lawyer, nationalist, and proprietor of the *West African Nationhood.*

The origins of the Congress idea in Nigeria, according to Ruth Perry, date as far back as 1904, when the *Lagos Standard* 'suggested a conference of West African natives to bring forth native opinions on questions affecting the social, political and religious conditions in West Africa, and a wider and more accurate study of native customs and institutions'.[41] Other accounts, however, put the date between 1915 and 1917. When asked by the president of Lagos Colony, Henry Carr, to give the Governor a brief account of the 'origin and functions of the organisations at work in Nigeria in connexion with the National Congress of British West Africa', and to describe its membership and its methods of election,[42] Savage in reply stated that in early 1917 or towards the end of 1916, a number of gentlemen met at the house of a Mr. David Taylor at Breadfruit Street, Lagos, 'to discuss the advisability of reviving the idea of founding a British West African Conference', an idea which had been discussed for some years in the West African newspapers and had been suggested by J. E. Casely Hayford of the Gold Coast and Dr. Savage some time in 1914 in a circular letter addressed to local leaders in the Gold Coast, Sierra Leone, and Lagos.[43] Savage himself was not certain about the exact year in which the Congress (or Conference) idea was conceived. In another context, in which he was refuting the argument of the *Nigerian Pioneer* of 11 June 1920 that Dr. Randle first broached the subject of a West African Conference, he outlined its origins thus:

[41] Perry, Ruth, *A Preliminary Bibliography of the Literature of Nationalism in Nigeria*, p. 5.

[42] Henry Carr to Akiwande Savage, *Times of Nigeria* (28 Mar. 1920).

[43] Savage to Carr, *Times of Nigeria* (24 Sept. 1920 and 28 Mar. 1921); also A.R.P.S. File no. 92, 179/65, Casely Hayford and Akiwande Savage to the Secretary, Gold Coast A.R.P.S., Hamilton Hall, Cape Coast, 26 May 1915. Cape Coast Regional Archives.

In 1912 or the early part of 1913, the *Gold Coast Leader* (with the Editorial Staff of which I was then connected) began to publish articles on the necessity of a West African conference being constituted.[44] The idea was warmly taken up by the Lagos Press and the Sierra Leone Press; and the entire West African Press agitated the question for many months. In the early part of 1914 Mr. Casely Hayford and myself sent from Seccondee circular letters to leading men in Lagos, Sierra Leone and other parts of the Gold Coast inviting opinions on the subject and suggesting that the time had come for leading men to meet in conference and have a West African Congress instituted. Dr. Randle was among those in Lagos we wrote to and was one of those who replied to our letter. . . . And it is astonishing that Dr. Randle should now be attempting to use this curteous acknowledgement of his views and suggestions as a basis for advancing his claims to the paternity of the West African Conference movement.[45]

Casely Hayford and Dr. Savage postponed the scheme at the outbreak of the Great War, and the latter returned to Nigeria in 1915; a few months later he called a meeting in Lagos to discuss the project.[46] Those present at the meeting were Dr. Randle, Dr. Lumpkin, Dr. O. Obassa of Ikeja, J. Egerton Shyngle, J. H. Doherty, B. C. Vaughan, David Taylor, and T. H. Jackson.[47] The meeting then decided to appoint a committee to sort out the matter and appointed Dr. Randle as its chairman, with Thomas H. Jackson of the *Lagos Weekly Record* and Dr. Savage as joint secretaries.[48] They then corresponded with similar *ad hoc* committees in Sierra Leone and the Gold Coast on the organization of the projected conference. Meanwhile there had been some disagreement between Dr. Randle and Dr. Savage on the organization of the Lagos Conference Committee, but there were no resignations. On 24 January 1919 the committee met at the Glover Memorial Hall, and with some additional members, formed itself into a Provisional Committee of the West African Conference, Lagos branch. Again, Dr. Randle was appointed chairman of the new committee, Dr. Savage its secretary, and the Revd. Patriarch J. G. Campbell and 'Professor' Deniga as propagandists to popularize the Conference

[44] See the *Gold Coast Leader* (7 Sept. 1912 and 11 Jan. 1913); Dr. Savage was then practising in the Gold Coast; Casely Hayford took over the *Leader* after the former left for Lagos in 1915.
[45] Dr. Akiwande Savage to the Editor of the *Lagos Weekly Record* (26 June 1920).
[46] *Lagos Weekly Record* (26 June 1920), p. 6.
[47] *Times of Nigeria* (28 Mar. 1921), p. 6.
[48] ibid.; *Lagos Weekly Record* (26 June 1920), p. 6.

movement.[49] They issued leaflets in English and Yoruba explaining the objects of the Conference and urging the necessity of forming a Lagos branch; public meetings were also advertised in Lagos. On 28 March 1919 another meeting was held at Ilupesi Hall in which the Provisional Committee resolved itself into the Lagos Committee of the West African Conference. Officers of the new committee were: Dr. Randle (chairman), the Hon. S. H. Pearce (vice-chairman), Dr. Savage (honorary secretary), Patriarch J. G. Campbell and Karimu Kotun (honorary assistant secretaries), and Dr. O. Obasa (treasurer). Further disagreement between Dr. Savage and Dr. Randle, however, led to the resignation of the latter, who started a small opposition group among the 'conservatives' of Lagos.[50] The committee canvassed in various towns in the Provinces, and local committees were formed in Calabar, Ibadan, and Ebute-Metta in the usual procedure—at public meetings.

On the instruction of the Lagos Committee, Deniga delivered a public lecture early in 1919 in Lagos. The lecture was later published and distributed and was on the *Necessity for a British West African Conference*. Deniga lightheartedly began the lecture with a parody of John Milton:

> What in me is dark, illumine;
> What is low, raise and support;
> That in the course of this great subject,
> I may invoke the aid of Eternal Providence.
> And justify the necessity there is
> For the existence of a West African Conference
> (With Apology to Milton).

Deniga added that the Conference idea could be traced 'as far back as the year 1913 or thereabouts', and that the newspapers which advocated the idea were the *Sierra Leone Weekly News*, the *Gold Coast Leader*, the *Nigerian Chronicle*, and the *Lagos Standard*.[51]

As in the other territorial committees of the N.C.B.W.A., the small, articulate Lagos committee found itself flanked by an influential, conservative anti-Congress group largely composed of persons whose social status was high, and the vast army of 'don't

---

[49] *Times of Nigeria*, loc. cit.

[50] *Lagos Weekly Record*, loc. cit.

[51] Deniga, A., *The Necessity for a British West African Conference* (Lagos, 1919), pp. 1–2. Copy sent by Deniga to K. Sekyi—Sekyi Papers 313/1964, Cape Coast Regional Archives.

knows'. The *Nigerian Pioneer*, whose interests were generally more closely identified with those of the administration, accused Dr. Savage of undemocratic practices and of bringing personal disputes into Congress affairs. It charged that no minutes of branch meetings were kept, that the organization of the Lagos branch was deplorable, that order during meetings was 'better asserted than observed', and that 'the assumption of autocratic imperiousness made the meetings a perfect nuisance'.[52] The *Nigerian Pioneer*, however, was, if not a pro-Government paper, generally hostile to the new 'politics'; hence it claimed on another occasion that 'as far as Nigeria is concerned only a few hundred people have heard of the Conference, of its self-elected delegates or of its intention to send super-delegates to London with a list of grievances they have never submitted or heard anything about'.[53] The *Times of Nigeria* scarcely paid attention to the proposals to hold a West African Conference, though in March 1920, when the Conference met at Accra, it devoted an editorial to it, for the most part a criticism of the Lagos Conference Committee, describing the only meeting held in Lagos by the Committee as 'this solitary meeting of physicians and a few members of the community', and criticizing it for failing to publicize the objects of the Conference. The rest of the editorial was the usual attack on the Europeanized African and his shortcomings.

The Accra Conference, however, seems to have rekindled interest in the affairs of the Lagos committee, which was now renamed the Nigerian Central Committee of the Congress of Africans of British West Africa. The timely publication of Casely Hayford's *United West Africa* moved the *Times of Nigeria* to declare: 'It is time that we should rise above that mean spirit which thinks that because we have different political opinions therefore we must become sworn enemies to each other and seek each other's ruin. . . . Unity must be the watchword and patriotism the principle. . . . We must strive for a United West Africa. . . .'[54] Disunity, however, continued to plague the efforts of the Lagos branch, so that it found it difficult to collect sufficient funds to maintain its delegates, Chief Oluwa and J. Egerton Shyngle, in London.[55] Unlike Sierra Leone, where there

[52] *Nigerian Pioneer* (20 Aug. 1920), p. 6.
[53] ibid. (27 Aug. 1920).
[54] *Times of Nigeria* (17 May 1920), p. 4.
[55] Macaulay Papers iv. 11, pp. 74–5: A. Savage to H. C. Bankole-Bright, 30 Oct. 1920; Bright to Savage, 23 Nov. 1920, ibid.

was greater consensus among the social élite on the object and organization of the local Congress branch, and the Gold Coast where under the leadership of Casely Hayford, Hutton-Mills, the Revd. O. Finanko, W. E. G. Sekyi, the Gä Mantse, and a part of the A.R.P.S., the Congressmen were able to muster sufficient financial support and the support of other influential traditional rulers to overcome the opposition of 'conservatives' on the A.R.P.S. executive committee, the Lagos branch was rendered less effective partly because of the overwhelming public opposition of Sir Hugh Clifford, partly because the chiefs (with the exception of Chief Oluwa and Chief Essien Offiong Essien) had little or no opinion on the movement (as their interests were not threatened by its existence), and partly because of preoccupation with the affairs of the House of Docemo. Although the long-term interests of the influential groups in Lagos were compatible with colonial rule to the extent that such a relationship meant the consolidation and possible extension of their privileges and social status, the opposition of influential conservatives led by Sir Kitoyi Ajasa's *Nigerian Pioneer* must not be overlooked. The *Nigerian Pioneer* not only opposed the Congress movement on procedural and technical points but firmly identified itself with current government opinion on the subject of elective representation. Its views were largely shared by the professional or 'learned' classes.[56] It was, according to Ernest S. Ikoli, 'the first really Nigerian national', owned and edited by Sir Kitoyi Ajasa, a prominent lawyer, a 'conservative and a man of very strong character . . . who in his day exercised considerable influence on the public life of the country'. It was generally believed that the *Pioneer* was inspired by Sir Frederick Lugard, a friend of Ajasa, and even subsidized by the Government. The paper, however, was widely read, though circulation does not seem to have exceeded 1,500.[57] In 1921 the *Pioneer* went so far as to declare that 'Nigeria must

[56] Coker, Increase, *Seventy Years of the Nigerian Press* (*Daily Times* Publication, Lagos, 1952), pp. 14–17.

[57] Ikoli, Ernest, 'The Nigerian Press', *West African Review* (June 1950), pp. 625–7. 'The *Nigerian Pioneer* was not so much pro-Government as conservative which term, in the eyes of its enemies, was synonymous with treachery . . . it was almost the only newspaper which might be called pro-Government. Of all the newspapers studied, the *Nigerian Pioneer* was, by far, the most conservative. At times it actually criticised the Government for adopting a too progressive and advanced policy.' Sometimes its opponents called it 'pro-Government', 'Lugardian', 'anti-progressive', 'Uncle Tom', 'lick spittle', etc. Edmonds, op. cit., pp. 11–12 and 85.

reject the invitation and cannot profitably associate with the movement of the National Congress of West Africa for obvious reasons. We have a Yoruba Nation and a Hausa Nation but so far we have no Nigerian nation.'[58]

In addition to this opposition, the Cliffordian reforms of late 1922 largely removed the *raison d'être* of the Lagos committee. Also, the victory of Herbert Macaulay's Nigerian National Democratic Party in the 1923 elections meant concentration on local politics as a result of the scope provided by elective councils, rather than concentration on the aims and objects of a not too well organized interterritorial political association. Point XVI of the constitution of the N.N.D.P. merely pledged 'To recognise the status of the National Congress of British West Africa and work hand in hand in co-operation with that body to support the entire schemes and proposals of the National Congress of British West Africa as expressed in its Memoranda and to endorse the various Resolutions passed and confirmed in the First and Second Sessions of that Congress'.[59]

But the N.C.B.W.A., as J. C. Zizer argued, was not interested in party politics: '. . . the National Congress of British West Africa transcends the narrow limits of Party Politics. It aspires to the greater and more envious pretention of Nationhood.'[60] Herbert Macaulay, however, in spite of Coleman's assertion that he played a 'prominent role behind the scenes in the National Congress of British West Africa',[61] was more concerned with Lagos, the Eleko, and the Legislative Council, now that the Cliffordian reforms had given him further opportunity.[62]

Perhaps the most important factor that contributed to the organizational chaos and, one might say, virtual non-existence of the Lagos branch of the Congress, was the personality clash between Drs. Savage and Randle. The former, in spite of his record as a nationalist agitator and journalist and his earlier co-operation with Casely

[58] *Nigerian Pioneer* (15 Apr. 1921); see also the *Pioneer* for 26 Apr. 1929.

[59] *Constitution, Rules and Regulations of the Nigerian National Democratic Party* (Lagos, n.d.). Macaulay MSS. no. 1. iv. 15.

[60] *West African Nationhood* (10 July 1931), p. 4; (10 Dec. 1930) p. 3.

[61] Coleman, J. S., *Nigeria: Background to Nationalism*, p. 456 n. 48. There is no evidence to show that Coleman's assertion is correct; it is highly unlikely that Macaulay influenced decisions taken at Axim; what the Macaulay Papers show is that he was kept well informed about the movement between 1919 and 1921.

[62] Tamuno, op. cit., pp. 41, 45–6. On the relation of electoral politics to the extension of popular suffrage, see Duverger, M., *Political Parties: Their Organisation and Activity in the Modern State* (London, 1954), pp. xxvii–xxviii.

Hayford, seemed authoritarian in his methods, while the latter tended to personalize differences relating to the local branch, and even went so far as to form the Reform Club, which was supported by the *Nigerian Pioneer*, as a counter-organization. This was a purely negative reaction, the result of which was to discourage recruitment into an organization already weakened by personal rivalry and acrimony. In fact, so seriously did these factions and rivalries weaken the Lagos branch that the West African Conference, according to Dr. Olusanya, originally scheduled for October 1919[63] was postponed, as the local branch could not agree on the delegates to represent Nigeria. Besides, the Eleko crisis of early 1920, inevitably involving Herbert Macaulay, further intensified factional politics in Lagos.

Attempts to revive the Nigerian section of the N.C.B.W.A. led to the co-operation of the Lagos and Ebute-Metta branches in 1925 to plan the reorganization of their branches, and at a meeting on 15 December 1925 it was agreed that there was need for a revivifying visit to be paid to Nigeria by delegates from the Gold Coast or Sierra Leone. New officers were elected—E. M. E. Agbebi (chairman), S. H. A. Baptist (treasurer), A. Latunde Johnson and E. A. Franklin (joint secretaries)—most of them lawyers.[64] An earlier editorial in *West Africa* thought that lack of interest in Nigeria was due to the fact that

Nigeria understands the ideals of the movement, but her educated men appear to find the 'applied' science of government more interesting than the 'pure' variety, and prefer to recognise that the term 'African racial aspirations' is a portmanteau phrase, including a range of ideals extending from representative self-government on the one hand to a simple desire to be freed from European domination to carry out more primitive customs on the other. When Nigeria has attained to a more homogeneous structure . . . it will be time for her to consider interesting herself in ideals which the experience of Lagos has proved are not yet practicable.[65]

The *Sierra Leone Weekly News* was more severe in its criticism of the Nigerian Section of the Congress movement; after commenting

[63] I owe the information in this paragraph to Olusanya, G. O., 'The Lagos Branch of the National Congress of British West Africa', *Journal of the Historical Society of Nigeria*, iv, no. 2 (June 1968), 324–33. Dr. Olusanya's article also contains a list of names associated with the Lagos branch not mentioned in this chapter.

[64] *West Africa* (31 Jan. 1925), p. 55.

[65] ibid. (11 Oct. 1924), p. 1083: 'Nigeria and the National Congress'.

on the lack of tact displayed by the Gambia Section during the 1925–6 Session held in Bathurst, the editorial observed that it was 'distressingly humiliating' for the Lagos Branch to be unable to send delegates to the Bathurst Session. It continued:

To think of the number of worthy citizens of Nigeria who could answer most satisfactorily to the call of the Congress for service . . ., and yet to appreciate that up to the present it has not been possible for such distinguished and worthy representatives of the race to answer the roll call in connection with the Congress Movement . . ., is to come face to face with one of the stern realities, however our pretentions may be, that mark us Africans still at a frightful discount towards those essentials that make for true nationhood. . . . Our co-patriots in Nigeria have allowed themselves to be the victims of the force of disintegration. . . .[66]

The N.N.D.P., however, came to the rescue of the Nigerian committee when in 1930 it helped to organize the Fourth Session of the N.C.B.W.A. in Lagos. In 1931 the Lagos Committee made a feeble attempt to secure extension of the limited franchise granted in 1923. Between 1930 and 1932 the Lagos Committee was fortunate to have J. C. Zizer as its secretary, the Revd. W. B. Euba (president), and Magnus Macaulay and E. M. E. Agbebi as vice-presidents. Zizer's *West African Nationhood* was certainly a great asset to the struggling Lagos N.C.B.W.A. Committee. His paper pledged itself to 'support the British Constitution' and 'render some little service in shaping the destiny of the Negro on the West Coast of Africa'.[67] It carried articles on the Negro question in America and Britain, as well as on 'The Negro Voice And Activities The World Over', including extracts from J. A. Roger's *The Negro in European History*. The paper generally complained of the worsening economic situation in West Africa, particularly unemployment and bad trade. As the demand for cocoa sharply decreased, Zizer lectured from the editorial pulpit: 'We mention these facts for the consideration of our African producers; for it seems, being out of touch with the theory of Demand and Supply, they keep on producing commodities for which the world does not now make as much demand as in previous years. . . .'[68] On 29 November 1930, the *West African Nationhood* carried a lengthy article by its proprietor, Zizer, on 'The National Congress of British West Africa: The Greatest Political Organisation on the

[66] *Sierra Leone Weekly News* (20 Mar. 1926).
[67] *West African Nationhood* (18 Oct. 1930), p. 2.
[68] ibid.

West Coast—The West African Negro Must Rally Round its Banner'. After a rambling introduction in which Zizer tried to show that the African had 'a definite and exclusive history of his own', he finally managed to define the N.C.B.W.A. as 'the only powerful organisation on the West Coast of Africa which aims at unification and consolidation of Negro ideas, aspirations and demands . . . a burning flame in the political history of the West Coast of Africa'. His views, however, were not as radical as they sounded, as is seen from his condemnation of 'party politics', his references to 'the hampering tactics of Bolshevism', his fondness for constitutionalism (he was a lawyer), and his view that the Congress was concerned with securing jobs occupied by Europeans for Africans.[69] Writing at a time when the N.C.B.W.A. itself had reached its nadir, it is not surprising that Zizer's attack was directed mainly against 'that band of Negro calumniators within and without the borders of Congress who . . . would wreck the Congress; first because they do not man the reins of its destiny, and just because they would not follow leadership'. In 1933, however, he stopped activity, and with his departure the Lagos Section ceased functioning. As in the Gold Coast unsuccessful efforts were made to revive it after 1945.[70]

The social, occupational, and economic status of the majority of members of the Lagos Committee of the N.C.B.W.A., as well as some of their personal histories, was almost identical to that of the other territorial committees. To take a random sample of Nigerians connected with the Lagos Committee: Prince Bassey Duke Ephraim of Calabar, who accompanied the Nigerian delegation to the Accra Conference in 1920, was born in 1878, the son of King Duke of Calabar; he continued his education in England in 1887 at Seaforth High School and at Waterloo College, near Liverpool. He returned to Calabar in 1892 and worked with the Niger Coast Protectorate under the Consul-Generalship of Sir Claude Macdonald. He resigned in 1894 and started business as a trader. From 1903 he was a member of the Native Court of Calabar, being elected its President in October 1914. It is interesting to note that in 1913 Prince Bassey Duke Ephraim was elected by the Calabar community as its representative in the dispute over the Calabar land tenure question; he went to England in 1913 and presented Mr. Harcourt, the Colonial Secretary, a petition on behalf of the Calabar community.[71]

---

[69] ibid. (29 Nov. 1930), pp. 1–3.  [70] Coleman, op. cit., p. 195.
[71] Macmillan, op. cit., p. 122.

Unlike the majority of Nigerian chiefs and traditional rulers, his education and early activity in protest movements were important factors in his association with the N.C.B.W.A.

Karimu Kotun, whom Dr. Savage refers to as one of his early collaborators in the creation of the Lagos Committee, is described by Allister Macmillan as 'a resident commercial traveller', specializing in cotton goods, and as a self-confident and able businessman. Born in Lagos in 1881, he started business activity after leaving school in 1896, becoming sole agent for E. H. Stein and Co. of Liverpool in 1910. But as the firm closed its business at the opening of the War, Kotun was recommended to S. L. Behrens (Manchester) Ltd., whom he represented in Lagos until the end of 1919 when, because of shipping difficulties, he started business on his own. Socially, too, Karimu Kotun was successful. In 1907 he was appointed President of the first Mohammedan Cricket Club in Lagos, and became Managing Director of the Alowolagba Society in 1913. In 1919 he was appointed by the Lagos community, in succession to Adolphus B. Martins, as Private Secretary to Prince Eshugbayi Eleko,[72] and no doubt became involved in the politics of the Eleko case.

One of the leading Lagos merchants associated with the Lagos branch of the Congress was the Hon. Samuel Herbert Pearce, F.R.G.S. After leaving the C.M.S. Grammar School, Lagos, Pearce became apprenticed to W. B. MacIver and Co. Ltd. and 'had the good fortune to be under the direct supervision of a Mr. Carr, a strict disciplinarian, a fastidious and punctilious exponent of the best way of doing things, and withal a Scotsman of great business ability, under whose able training the young Nigerian lad acquired in course of time a knowledge of general merchandise and commercial law and practice probably equal in every respect to that of his discerning teacher . . .'.[73] Pearce worked with this firm for five years before forming his own, Pearce and Thompson Ltd. This business, however, was wound up in 1894 as a result of the local wars in Nigeria. Between 1894 and 1906, Pearce did advisory work on the Soto Rubber Plantations and was local agent for the African and Gold Coast Trade Corporation.

He went to Calabar in 1907 and started an ivory trade business there 'with such phenomenal success that six years later he had amassed a large fortune and returned in affluence to Lagos' where

[72] ibid., p. 113.
[73] ibid., p. 97.

he continued as a produce merchant.[74] Again, it is worth noting that Pearce too had a history of nationalistic activity. In 1913 he led the Nigerian Land Deputation to London under the auspices of the Anti-Slavery and Aborigines Society; 'he has long been a prominent and capable leader in political, religious, and social circles of the colony, and is a member of the Legislative Council, Town Council . . .'. Pearce also became a Fellow of the Royal Geographical Society in 1915, as well as a Fellow of the Royal Colonial Institute; and, of course, he was a member of the Lagos Racecourse Board of Management.

Another member of the Lagos Committee, J. H. Doherty, is described as 'one of the most successful of the native merchants' in Lagos; he started import business in 1899 in Alakoro, gradually extending his stores to Oshogbo, Zaria, Lokoja, and Kano. One of his sons studied law in England, the other studied at Fourah Bay College, Sierra Leone.[75]

David Taylor, at whose house Dr. Akiwande Savage discussed the formation of the Lagos committee with other leading Lagosians in 1915, like S. H. Pearce had his commercial experience with W. B. MacIver and Co. Ltd., starting his own business in 1891 at Balogun Street, 'where he did so well that in 1894 he opened an excellent general merchandise store on the Marina. By 1916 he had succeeded to such an extent that he leased the last-mentioned building to the Colonial Bank. . . .'[76]

Then we have the typical black Edwardian T. H. Jackson, outspoken editor of the radical *Lagos Weekly Record* with its humorous Latinisms and lengthy sentences. Jackson, whose father started the paper in 1890, was one of the early officials of the Lagos committee, and his newspaper fully and continuously supported the Congress movement, always lambasting Sir Kitoyi Ajasa's reactionary *Nigerian Pioneer*. He was educated in Liberia and Freetown, and took to journalism at an early age; by 1905 he had become 'an able and versatile writer and a bold and influential champion of the Negro race'.[77] Here again, a man like Jackson could not fail to take

[74] ibid., p. 98. Pearce represented the Egba division in the Legislative Council as a nominated member from 1923 to 1933, and is described as 'one of the most moderate members of the Council'; Wheare, J., *The Nigerian Council* (London, 1949), p. 199, Appendix III, and p. 123.

[75] ibid., p. 99.                       [76] ibid., p. 108.

[77] ibid., p. 109; also the recent study by July, Robert W., *The Origins of Modern African Thought*, pp. 358–65.

part in nationalist and Pan-Negro activities. He went to England in 1907, not only as a visitor, but as the leader of the deputation to Lord Elgin in connection with the Ijebu timber concessions—'so well did he accomplish his purpose that the House of Commons decided in favour of the aggrieved natives . . .'. Again in 1918 Jackson visited England 'and was largely instrumental in the formation of the African Progress Union, which is rapidly extending in every direction, and of which he is organising Secretary for the world'. And, of course, the black Edwardian could not fail to become a member of the London Chamber of Commerce and the Essex County Cricket Club.[78] Perusal of the *Lagos Weekly Record* between 1919 and 1925 makes it quite clear that Jackson was no narrow-minded nationalist.

Dr. Richard Akiwande Savage, founder of the Nigerian Congress Committee, had participated in 'politics' since his student days. While at Edinburgh University (1897–1905) he was a member of the Students' Representative Council, and a member of the Executive Committee of the same Council from 1898 to 1900. In that period he also served as sub-editor of *The Student* and as joint editor of the *Edinburgh University Handbook* and attended the 1900 Pan-African Conference as one of the delegates of the Afro-West Indian Literary Society of Edinburgh. He served as Medical Officer of Health, Cape Coast Castle, from 1907 to 1911, and was also on the editorial staff of the *Gold Coast Leader*. He returned to Lagos in 1915 and began work on the formation of the Lagos branch of the N.C.B.W.A.; his insistence on personal leadership and his personality were disliked by the conservative section of Lagos opinion, with the result that the Nigerian committee never became as effective as it might have been; he is described as 'an accomplished litterateur, and makes a hobby of journalism'.[79]

J. Egerton Shyngle, like most of the Africans who contributed to the growth of early nationalism in Nigeria, was a non-Nigerian. He was born in Bathurst, Gambia, in 1862 and attended the Wesleyan Boys' High School there, transferring to the C.M.S. Grammar School in Freetown. He studied at Fourah Bay College and at

[78] ibid.
[79] ibid., p. 136. For Savage in student politics at Edinburgh, see *Student*, xiii, no. 1 (20 Oct. 1898), 8; xiii, no. 3 (3 Nov. 1898), 65, 207; xiii, no. 10 (5 Jan. 1899); no. 18 (2 Mar. 1899), 405; no. 18 (1 Mar. 1900), etc. Dr. Savage was appointed Assistant Colonial Surgeon in 1901 and was the last African to hold this post in the British West African Medical Service.

Christ Church, Oxford, but never graduated. In 1888 he was called to the Bar as a member of the Inner Temple, and settled in Lagos in 1892, rising 'rapidly into fame by virtue of his wonderful forensic abilities and legal acumen'.[80] He and Chief Oluwa represented Nigeria in the N.C.B.W.A. delegation to London in 1920–1 and was also the first elected member for Lagos in the new 1923 Legislative Council, as well as a Town Councillor and a patron of the N.N.D.P. He took great interest in the latter body and in local politics and was a close friend of Herbert Macaulay. He died in 1926 at the age of sixty-four.[81]

Miss Denzer states in her study of the Gold Coast Section that 'several of the Nigerian delegates to the Congress were leaders of the radical nationalist religious splinter groups'.[82] With the exception of the Revd. Patriarch J. G. Campbell (who attended) and the Revd. Euba (who did not), this statement is incorrect. Only the Revd. J. G. Campbell and the Revd. Euba were such leaders; Deniga was more of a journalist and cultural nationalist, although he did in fact write pamphlets on subjects like polygamy and on questions relating to African religious sects.

'Professor' Adeoye Deniga was the author of *African Leaders Past and Present*[83] as well as the editor of *Herald-Alore* and author of articles on topics such as 'Monogamy and the Church', 'What is Religion?', and 'A Defence of Native Customs'. *African Leaders Past and Present* was intended as an account of the lives of some of 'Africa's greatest sons who . . . have played and are still playing their parts towards the rise of the race to which we belong'. The African patriots dealt with included Bishop Crowther, Sir Samuel Lewis, John Mensah Sarbah, G. W. Johnson ('Reversible Johnson'), J. A. O. Payne, Mohammed Shitta Bey of Lagos, Bishop James Johnson ('Holy Johnson'), the Hon. J. J. Thomas of Sierra Leone, the Hon. C. A. Sapara-Williams, O. Johnson the historian of the Yorubas, and E. W. Blyden.

The object of Deniga's *African Leaders* was partly to tell his readers 'that we as Africans, have been making efforts to up-lift the standard of our race . . . an encouragement to us all, further, to

---

[80] *Lagos Weekly Record* (27 Mar. 1926), p. 5, obituary on J. Egerton Shyngle.

[81] *West Africa* (24 Apr. 1926), x (1926–7), 497. See also L. C. Gwam's article on the Hon. C. A. Sapara-Williams in *Ibadan*, xxi (1965), 36–8, and Tamuno, op. cit., pp. 45, 80.

[82] Denzer, op. cit., p. 66 n. 32.

[83] *African Leaders Past and Present*, 2 vols. (Lagos, 1915).

rally round the cause and advancement of our dear fatherland . . .',[84] and partly as an attempt at some form of mental decolonization.

Deniga was born in Lagos in April 1881, the son of Sergeant Olukotun Thomas of the Lagos Police Force, and Lydia Famoluke 'a Lady-Ivory and General Merchant of the Lagos of yesterday'.[85] He was first educated at the Anglican school of St. Peter's (Lagos) and later at the C.M.S. Grammar School. He entered the civil service as an Express Delivery mail-man in the local Post Office in 1901. He returned to his old school, St. Peter's, in 1902 as a certified teacher, and became assistant master of St. Paul's (Breadfruit) School between 1903 and 1908. He was also headmaster of Wesleyan Tinubu School from 1910 to 1911. In 1908 he changed his name from Gabriel Adeoye Thomas to Adeoye Deniga 'mainly because I desire to be known and addressed by my native name'.[86] Between 1913 and 1914 he founded and edited a monthly bilingual magazine called the *Herald-Alore*; a letter writer by profession, he was appointed sub-editor of the fiery *Lagos Weekly Record* in 1918.

The Revd. Patriarch James George Campbell was perhaps the greatest publicist in Nigeria of the N.C.B.W.A., and one of the most fearless nationalists of the time. He was born in Lagos on 4 May 1876, the son of Edward Henry Macaulay Campbell and Elizabeth Campbell, both Sierra Leoneans; he claimed, however, that 'my paternal Grandfather is of the Ijesha tribe in the Yoruba Country'.[87] He had been an outspoken critic ever since his early missionary days.[88] Campbell was then posted to Opobo where he was assaulted and injured for clearing human skulls from the Delta Pastorate Church Mission at Opobo; but the Juju chiefs lost and the Church was established at Opobo, Iboro, Akwete, Ohambele, and Asuniri.

He resigned from the Delta Pastorate Church in 1899 and was admitted into the Ministry of the United Native African Church in Lagos where he worked for four years, after which he founded the West African Episcopal Church in 1893, of which he became the Patriarch. His church had branches at Ikorodu, Shagamu, Ogere, Ode Akaka, Ilaje, and Ikale districts, as well as in the Gold Coast. In 1919 he became the honorary Presiding Patriarch of the Christ Army Church (Garrick Braid Connection) at Bonny.

---

[84] ibid., i. 10.  
[85] *Times of Nigeria* (7 Mar. 1921), p. 6.  
[86] ibid.  
[87] ibid.  
[88] ibid.

The Revd. Patriarch Campbell was also the author of *Observation on Some Topics, 1913–1917, During the Administration of Sir Frederick Lugard*, a work generally relegated to the footnotes. Here he states quite clearly his belief in what he called 'the British Tradition' and in political evolution as opposed to revolution; yet the book is an anti-colonial tract as well as a criticism of Lagos politics. It begins with a condemnation of the atrocities of the Great War, and then goes on to describe the adverse economic and political effects of the war on Nigeria.[89] Although Nigerian trade had prospered under Lugard's administration, he said, the war had dislocated shipping and 'the blacks are losing their position as Merchants and they are becoming simply middlemen; despite all that the late Bishop Johnson has said . . . no heed is taken by us the natives and we refuse to form a combine or limited company. . . . The Syrians who only but yesterday were hawkers in the streets of Lagos have now through combination become masters of the trade and prominent big Merchants. . . . At present there are no blacks in the Lagos Chamber of Commerce. . . .'[90]

The Revd. Patriarch Campbell also dealt with the land question, taxation, the criminal code, education, the Eleko case, and the need for Africanization of certain government posts. He complained that the Lagos Auxiliary of the Anti-Slavery and Aborigines Protection Society was no longer airing the grievances of the country, but praised the Society's work under the 'radicals', Bishop James Johnson and Mojola Agbebi, over the land question; the People's Union, led by Dr. Randle and Dr. O. Obasa, also came under fire for its failure in the water rate agitation. As for the *Nigerian Pioneer* which had attacked Campbell and the Lagos 'radicals', as well as the Lagos Committee of the N.C.B.W.A., Campbell thought that 'It has gained popularity in some quarters more as anti-native than native. . . . It opens its pages with an unwarrantable criticism against Bishop Johnson which has hurt the feelings of all those who love their country.' 'In my opinion,' he concluded, 'the paper has done good. It gives the opinion of the minority.'[91]

The inadequacies of the Legislative Council did not escape the observation of the reverend gentleman either; there should be more

---

[89] Campbell, J. G., *Observation on Some Topics, 1913–1917, During the Administration of Sir Frederick Lugard* (Lagos, 1918), p. 3.

[90] ibid., p. 24.

[91] ibid., p. 56.

educated Nigerians in the Council.[92] On the Nigerian Council, Campbell noted that there was nothing democratic about it, as there was no African opposition.[93] He then listed twenty-two proposals (including a West African university and an agricultural bank) most of which were later to be advocated by the N.C.B.W.A. in 1920.

Of the Marcus Garvey movement he said: 'Although I am against Marcus Garvey in his political programme, yet I am for his Industrial scheme.'[94] As for Sir Hugh Clifford's famous attack on the Congress, Campbell protested:

> May I respectfully ask who selected and appointed those European Nations who met in Berlin in 1884 and divided the blackman's country amongst themselves? Who appointed and entrusted the white man to appoint himself Trustee of the African peoples? No one than the white man's own common sense. . . . My respectful reply to His Excellency is that the Black man's reason and common sense has now reached the stage when he thinks that he should have a National Congress to demand his rights . . . according to his own point of view. . . .[95]

In spite of its defects and the narrow basis of its leadership, strong claims can perhaps be made for the N.C.B.W.A. as the first attempt in Africa at Pan-Africanism on a regional basis; the Constitution of the N.C.B.W.A. has all the features of an interterritorial assembly. A major criticism that can be levelled against it is that it was not coherent or fully institutionalized. For example, paragraph 22 of the Constitution which dealt with the important offices of President and Executive Council reads:

> The business and affairs of the National Congress of British West Africa shall be directed, managed, and controlled by the President and an Executive Council composed of himself, the Vice President, the Treasurer, where and when practicable, and other persons not exceeding seven in number easily accessible to him, who shall be nominated by him, and who shall execute the will of the National Congress . . . in the light of resolutions passed when last assembled and shall be competent to act on behalf of the Congress in all cases of emergency until the Congress shall next assemble.

Such an unworkable scheme was typically the creation of gentlemen politicians. What is important, however, is not its failure as a Pan-

[92] ibid., pp. 10–11.
[93] ibid., p. 11.
[94] *Times of Nigeria* (7 Feb. 1921).
[95] ibid. (14 Feb. 1921), p. 4.

West African organization, but the very fact of its inception. One very careful student of this organization of the West African intelligentsia was Kwame Nkrumah, and it comes as no surprise when, with his passion for organization, he revived the idea in 1946 in the form of the West African National Secretariat, putting great emphasis on the office and the co-ordinating role of Secretary-General. Up to his deposition in February 1966, Nkrumah's African policy was to oscillate between the regional and continental approaches to African unity.

# CHAPTER V

# Nationalism, Pan-Africanism, and Colonial Economics: 1918–1939

ONE of the least understood aspects of African protest and nationalist movements is the significance and effect of the colonial economy on nationalist thought and politics. Discussion relating to the connection between the two has either been too general or has tended to concentrate exclusively on the period after 1945.[1] As Dr. Hopkins has rightly argued, the monotonous shibboleth about the impact of 'western economic forces' on African nationalism has done little to shed light on the question.[2] While a mechanistic interpretation is avoided here, we believe there is sufficient evidence to warrant the conclusion that the reaction of certain sections of the West African populace, whether in the form of riots, protests, nationalist movements, or economic Pan-Negroism, was influenced by commercial crises and changes in that economy and by factors inherent in its operation under the colonial system.

Aspects of the development of the colonial economy in British West Africa up to the outbreak of the Second World War have already been examined in detail by economic historians;[3] what concerns us here is not an economic history of the inter-war period but an examination of West African responses to the impact of economic forces during that period, and the significance of those responses

---

[1] Studies of this aspect of West African nationalism are few; the most useful are: Hopkins, A. G., 'Economic Aspects of Political Movements in Nigeria and in the Gold Coast 1918–1939'; Ballard, John, 'The Porto Novo Incidents of 1923: Politics in the Colonial Era'; Suret-Canale, Jean, *Afrique noire: l'ère coloniale: 1900–1945* (Paris, 1964). The excellent article by Hopkins, however, contains a few gaps and does not give the 'feel' of the nationalist politics of the period.

[2] Hopkins, op. cit., p. 133.

[3] McPhee, Allan, *The Economic Revolution in British West Africa* (London, 1926); Edokpayi, S. I., 'The External Trade of the Gold Coast (Ghana) and Nigeria 1885–1945' (University of London M.Sc.(Econ.) thesis, 1958); Cox-George, N. A., *Finance and Development in West Africa: The Sierra Leone Experience* (London, 1957); Hopkins, A. G., 'An Economic History of Lagos, 1880–1914' (University of London Ph.D. thesis, 1964).

for the study of nationalist activity during the period under review. But before considering the nature of those responses, it is necessary to give a brief outline of the post-war economic situation in British West Africa.

With the exception of the temporary break in 1914–16, the British West African colonies experienced a gradual expansion in export and import trade. A price boom in 1917 continued the upward trend which reached its peak in the first half of 1920. With the exception of palm produce in the Gold Coast and Sierra Leone and of rubber in both the Gold Coast and Nigeria, the value of all export staples expanded during the war period; vegetable products also commanded high prices after the 1914–16 contraction, especially during the boom of 1919–20. In the war years, the value of imports contracted, leading to an unprecedented import boom in 1919–20. The exclusion of the German firms and markets from West Africa during the war also meant that the African merchants had better commercial opportunities; it also meant that the colonies increased their imports from imperial and American sources. Up to the 1919–20 boom, the major stimulus to exports came from increasing world demand for primary products which was reflected in rising prices. The demand for vegetable oils, for example, coincided with technological changes in their use, particularly in the food industry; the demand for rubber also coincided with the growth of the pneumatic tyre industry. In the case of cocoa, consumer demand, particularly during the war, was the main factor. On the whole the war years through 1920 were a period of prosperity for West African merchants, producers, and middlemen. With the growth of cash crops went the growth of individual and communal 'plantations', especially in palm oil. At the same time, trade fluctuations influenced the level of prosperity in the domestic sectors of each colony; for example, price changes in world markets influenced local market prices and the economic interdependence between wage labour, export, and food croppers. The incomes of these classes of producers and of middlemen, therefore, fluctuated with external trade, and in times of crisis this led to hardship on the producers and to indebtedness, as well as to the ruin of many a middleman.[4] Higher income from cocoa and rubber farms also led to less concentration on food crops, a development which was to have serious consequences particularly in the towns during the 1921–2 slump and the depression of the 1930s.

[4] See Edokpayi, op. cit., pp. 196–7.

While war inflated prices and benefited the producers, external demand also had the effect of generating instability into the production, as is seen in the 1920–1 slump. World market conditions changed as a result of the war and of post-war reconstruction. In the 1920s most of the industrialized economies of Europe stagnated and in the 1930s they became depressed as international trade disintegrated and economic nationalism became the creed of the day. The depression had adverse effects on primary producers in general as world demand for such products lost its rising trend in terms of real value after 1929. In reaction to the changed world conditions after 1918, Europe and America adopted measures which directly constrained world trade. France, Britain, and Holland resorted to tariffs, financial controls, preferences, and quotas to secure the trade and resources of their colonies for their own markets. Great Britain even set up an Empire Resources Development Committee—an institution which was vigorously opposed by bewildered West African merchants and nationalist groups, and in fact played an important part in the decision of the West African intelligentsia to form an interterritorial nationalist organization and to demand representative institutions.

With this new protectionism, the traditional *laissez-faire* commercial policy in West Africa was severely modified. The new policy began with the imposition of discriminatory export duties on palm kernels in 1919–22 and on tin between 1919 and 1938. Although some of these impositions were made for revenue purposes only, they were viewed as discriminatory duties in the interests of the Empire and at the expense of the producers whose markets were curtailed and whose shipping facilities were very limited.[5]

The 1919–20 boom, however, did not last,[6] and the period 1921–39 was characterized by violent fluctuations in which depressions followed booms at regular intervals. Although the export volume for the British West African colonies rose between 1919 and 1929, prices remained low; however, the value of trade in general was slightly above that of 1916–20.[7] Output of palm produce, cocoa, groundnuts, and cotton rose substantially, but export trade con-

[5] Meyer, F. V., *Britain's Colonies in World Trade* (London, 1948), pp. 88–9.
[6] Lewis, W. A., *An Economic Survey: 1919–1939* (London, 1949), *passim*; Arndt, H. W., *The Economic Lessons of the Nineteen Thirties* (London, 1944), pp. 9–33; Rowe, J. W. F., *Primary Commodities in International Trade* (London, 1965), pp. 78–9.
[7] Edokpayi, op. cit., p. 58.

tracted until 1924, and the fairly stable price level gradually fell. Average price index dropped from the 1916–20 level to a point below that of 1918, though there was a slight improvement for cocoa in the late 1920s.[8] From 1930 to 1937 there was a market depression, with the severe depression of 1930–4 followed by a slight recovery after 1935. Volume continued its upward trend to the peak of 1937 but prices and value fell from the level of the 1920s. Except for cocoa, rubber, and certain minerals, general recovery after 1935 was very slow and, unlike the 1920s, prices fluctuated violently in the 1930s.[9] The general price trend was downward throughout the 1930s. For example, average commodity prices for Nigerian palm kernels declined from £17·30 per ton in the period 1921–5 to £7·40 in 1931–5, while groundnut prices declined from £19·40 per ton to £9·70 per ton in the same period. Gold Coast cocoa showed a similar trend, declining from an average of £35·20 per ton in 1921–5 to around £20·80 per ton in 1931–5. Total value of Nigerian trade declined from the record peak of £37·72 million in the boom year 1920 to £27·65 million in 1930 and £14·24 million in 1934.[10]

The 'economic revolution' in West Africa not only introduced a monetary economy and expanded commerce, it also introduced certain social and economic values among African entrepreneurs and social classes, notably the lawyer–merchant class. These groups had evolved in the atmosphere of economic liberalism and had imbibed the values of what Delavignette calls 'bourgeois colonial society': their nationalist politics was, therefore, greatly influenced by these values. Although the position of these classes, particularly the small traders, had begun to change with the development of the colonial economy in the 1890s,[11] it was in reality the Great War and its attendant economic crisis which had a more immediate and significant impact on their status. It had been already apparent during the stagnation of the 1880s and in the 1890s that the growing sophistication of commerce, expansion of markets, and competition from extra-territorial firms meant that the African businessman would either have to be more efficient or play a secondary role in the colonial economy. Economic survival demanded efficiency; but as in

[8] ibid., p. 59.
[9] For a detailed commentary on the economic situation in the inter-war period, see Dobb, Maurice, *Studies in the Development of Capitalism* (London, 1946), chapter 8, esp. p. 331.
[10] Edokpayi, op. cit., p. 55 and Appendix I.
[11] McPhee, op. cit., pp. 72–4.

most cases, this warning was partly unheeded as trade gradually expanded between 1900 and 1920.[12] During the war, however, with economic controls, discriminatory export duties, currency shortage, and loss of shipping, there was a growing realization among educated Africans both in business and in the professions that the cosmopolitan days of harmony and less aggressive competition were over and that the era of the combine and of monopoly capitalism had arrived. It was also towards the end of the war that the old type of protest was succeeded by a more articulate liberal nationalism directed by the very groups whose interests were at stake in the post-war colonial period. And one of the fascinating aspects of this nationalism is the way in which passionately felt economic grievances were accompanied by moderate constitutional demands by a leadership which created a Pan-African organization (the N.C.B.W.A.) as a political pressure group and as a means of finding a solution to the economic plight of the African merchant, producer, and businessman. What strikes the student is the persistent manner in which this middle-class nationalist leadership analysed the legacy of the war and the constitutional consequences of the economic revolution in British West Africa. It was clear to these gentlemen that the solution to their problem, as well as the protection of their socio-economic privileges and the creation of more openings for their social class in the colonial administration, lay in their acquisition of some measure of political responsibility in the colonial legislatures which were still the rubber stamps of a 'veiled oligarchy'. It is true that Pan-African idealism and the appeal to racial solidarity did play an important part in their agitation but, fundamentally, their very constitutionalism was a defence of their own interests. Their implied assumption was that they 'represented substantially' the people by virtue of education, commerce, and civilization; that they constituted 'the advanced thought' of British West Africa, and were capable of enough cohesion and responsibility to support elective political institutions in their various colonies. This claim was at first rejected by Whitehall and the colonial administration, and the history of the Congress movement is largely the story of how this clash was resolved in a constitutional compromise between 1922 and 1926.

In Sierra Leone, where the Congress movement was to have its strongest support, the frustration of the educated classes and the African traders, and the unemployed in the big towns was given

---

[12] ibid., pp. 42 ff.

open expression in the rice and anti-Syrian riots of 1919 and in the workers' strike that same year. Though directed against the Lebanese traders, these riots were in fact a violent and uncoordinated protest against what were believed to be injustices arising from the management of the colonial economy. It was in Freetown, Sierra Leone, that post-war discontent in West Africa first found expression.

One French commentator writing on the economic and financial aspects of the nationalist movement in British West Africa observed that in Sierra Leone:

L'année 1919 fut pour cette colonie une année calamiteuse. Une épidemie d'influenza fit périr 10.000 personnes. L'insuffisance des vivres, surtout du riz, causa la famine. Le mécontentement des habitants de Freetown se tourna contre les Syriens, impopulaires, accusés d'accaparement. Ceux-ci furent attaqués, pillés; trois d'entre eux moururent, massacrés. D'autres causes de troubles furent le chomage de nombreux travaileurs, devenus san emploi depuis que Freetown avait cessé d'être une base navale, le cours forcé du papier monnaie, les spéculations de profiteurs de guerre et l'élévation du prix des marchandises européennes. . . . Les employés du chemin de fer se mirent en grève. . . .[13]

In the following pages we shall examine in detail the economic situation which led to the strike and the rice riots in Freetown in 1919, and which stimulated a new style of nationalist politics. We shall also examine in detail the economic grievances and arguments of the Congress movement which met in Accra eight months after the Freetown incidents, and we shall show how a smaller group of 'radicals', especially the youth movements, became dissatisfied with the leadership of the Congress nationalists and with their method of solving the economic crisis in British West Africa. Finally, we shall examine briefly some early attempts by West Africans at economic self-help and Pan-African commercial co-operation.

The war immediately affected the external trade of Sierra Leone; both export and import trade declined throughout the war, slowly recovering after the war. The depression which had begun since early 1913 was also accentuated.[14] This decline in the volume of trade was partly due to the loss of the German palm-kernel market which, in 1913, accounted for 87 per cent of the total value and volume of all palm-kernel exports from Sierra Leone, but had declined to 53·29 per

[13] Martin, Camille, 'Afrique Occidentale anglaise: le mouvement nationaliste', *Bulletin du Comité de l'Afrique Française*, xxxii (1922), 47–55.
[14] Cox-George, N. A., op. cit., pp. 171–2.

cent by mid-1914. By 1916 trade with Germany had ceased completely. The decline in output was also partly affected by crop failure. The first rice harvest of 1914 failed and the majority of farmers diverted their attention from kernel collection to the cultivation of a second rice crop to ward off a possible hunger season. Decline in prices also affected the decline in the export sector. With the exception of piassava, there was a recorded drop in prices in 1914 for all the main articles of export. Palm-kernel prices steadily declined, only recovering slowly after 1916; in 1915 they reached a low of £12·10 per ton. Although commodity prices recovered after 1916, the profitability of the export trade was reduced by increased freight, insurance, and handling costs; also, labour wages had gone up as prices of foodstuffs had risen after the war. The loss of German shipping, the commandeering of British shipping for military and naval purposes, and the U.K. dockers' strike in 1915 created a shipping bottle-neck which greatly inconvenienced West African merchants and businessmen. Moreover, Elder Dempster Lines, the West African shipping monopoly, had increased its freight charges by 15 per cent above pre-war charges. Tonnage declined from 2,931,085 in 1913 to 1,736,247 in 1918.[15] This holding up of export goods affected the profits of producers and middlemen not only in Sierra Leone but all along the West Coast.

Increased demand, the price boom, as well as more effective protection of British shipping from German submarines improved the economic situation in 1917. Moreover, the kernel-crushing industry in Britain was being given a boost. Increased demand for imported foodstuffs in 1917 was due to war conditions, particularly the diversion of agricultural labour into combat and carrier services, and the inflation in the economy.[16] The use of Freetown as an imperial coaling station also increased the demand for local foodstuffs. This not only swelled the income stream but also relieved the depression in the colony's external trade, while creating a boom in the internal economy. Unemployment was also partly relieved by the awarding of army contracts for building barracks and other works and by the drafting of men (about 8,000) into the army. These tended to stimulate the internal economy by strengthening demand for merchandise, but they also created a wage-induced inflation.[17] Long before the

[15] ibid., p. 173.
[16] ibid., pp. 177, 183.
[17] ibid.

wage-induced inflation, however, the price inflation, of which Free-town newspapers complained so loudly, had also had its effect. The outbreak of war and the attendant security measures taken created a panic, with the result that there was a rush to buy and hoard food supplies; business houses correspondingly charged high prices for their goods.[18] The Government set up a committee to regulate food supplies and to fix prices, but the control was not comprehensive; while the price of all controlled imported foodstuffs rose, the terms of trade of the Native rice producer deteriorated,[19] and this not only added to the rice shortage but most probably encouraged black-marketing of rice, especially among the Lebanese, which became an important factor in the riots and agitation of mid-1919. Wholesale firms which profited more from the price increases were at an advantage over petty or retail traders who were to form the bulk of the petitioners during the riots. As Cox-George has observed, 'the control of prices was a factor leading to the transfer of wealth from the small man, the petty trader, to the wholesaler or the larger firms. Competition became more favourable to the larger commercial houses, and this, together with such devices as the hiring of "selling girls" to retail their goods, helped them to undersell effectively the old class of African "merchants" or middlemen and so hasten the decline of the latter.'[20] Indeed, the more articulate members of the lawyer–merchant class had concluded, as early as 1916–17, that in order to do something about the economic situation, they would have to have some voice in their own legislatures and that the obsolete Crown Colony system of government would have to be replaced by representative institutions. The Lebanese question was widely discussed, although it was in Sierra Leone that it became the peculiar problem of the Creole middle class. Throughout British West Africa, the most important topics in nationalist circles were the much hated export duty on palm kernels, the Empire Resources Development Committee, and the growing threat of foreign firms. One of the leading Sierra Leone merchants who was later to play a prominent role in the Congress movement thought that the imposition of the export duty would put the Native exporter

---

[18] *Sierra Leone Weekly News* of 8 Aug. 1914 reported: 'Owing to the scare of the failure of foodstuff in the city, prices rose nearly 100 per cent within twenty-four hours. Paterfamilias moved from store to store to secure the necessaries of life for their households and many were glad to pay fancy prices for whatever they could get.'

[19] Cox-George, op. cit., p. 185 n. 35.    [20] ibid., p. 185.

absolutely at the mercy of all the Agents both here and in England as the brokers in England . . . the majority of those who pose themselves as African Merchants aided by Capitalists and a few Brokers in England have hitherto fattened on the exploitation of the Native Shippers, Middlemen and Producers, . . . any Government support would be disastrous in that it foreshadows the elimination of the intelligent Native absolutely from earning a livelihood from the products of his own country, a condition emphasised by the rigging of the Market already.[21]

C. D. Hotobah During, another leading Creole and local politician, mounted a similar attack on the export duty and on the activities of the combines; in conclusion he asked his readers 'why are Colonies like Sierra Leone, Lagos and the Gold Coast still denied representative governments? Or, on the other hand, why is it impossible for the establishment of a United West Africa with a House of Representatives?'[22] Significantly enough, reviews of free-trade literature like J. A. Hobson's *The New Protectionism* began to appear in some of the Freetown newspapers.[23] Beoku-Betts even reviewed one book on free trade, *Essays on Duty and Discipline*, while the editor of the *Sierra Leone Weekly News* advised his readers to read *The New Protectionism* 'in conjunction with the evidence and report on the Palm Kernel question. . . . Each country should adopt free trade or protection or both in accordance with its needs.' This was followed by a sharp attack on both European merchants and Lebanese who were accused of hoarding rice in a time of scarcity. Another editorial urged that the solution to the high cost of living and to the division between Creoles and Protectorate people lay in organized leadership: 'The people have got to be convinced that leadership or no leadership this matter of the shortage of local foodstuffs is the offspring of a new time in our history—a time of transition . . . it has got to be tackled by them. . . .'[24]

Mid-1918 did not improve the situation; food prices continued to rise and early heavy rains threatened to affect the rice harvest: the 'up country' farmers had little time to burn the bushes for the sowing season. Influenza was on the way. The outlook for 1919 was indeed gloomy.[25] By the end of 1918, when the idea of a West African

[21] F. W. Dove to the Editor, *Sierra Leone Weekly News* (17 Feb. 1917), p. 5.
[22] ibid. (3 Feb. 1917), p. 13.
[23] See the *Colonial and Provincial Reporter* (14 Oct. 1916), p. 6.
[24] *Sierra Leone Weekly News* (24 Feb. 1917), p. 8.
[25] ibid. (11 May 1918), p. 9.

Conference was being widely discussed in the press, the *Weekly News* lost no time in going straight into the economics of the agitation:

... the main planks in the programme for discussion are taxation and representation, equality of opportunity, and a West African University. Although suggestions for the programme have not yet been exchanged by the different Committees, it is highly probable that these subjects will be prominent features of the discussions. *Nevertheless, the protection of the economic interests of the native is a subject that will be second to none in importance.* Nothing has done more to stimulate the Conference movement than the menacing campaign of the Empire Resources Development Committee. No more effective instrument than the Conference could be found by which to meet the astounding proposal that the Imperial Government should establish a monopoly of the palm oil and other vegetable products of British West Africa as a means of helping to pay for the war. Then again the Palm Kernel Export Duty Ordinance, which will depress the price paid to the native producers and correspondingly favour British consumers, will certainly call for close examination.[26]

---

[26] ibid. (7 Dec. 1918), p. 9, 'The Programme For the British West African Conference' (my emphasis). Allan McPhee wrote of the export duties, 'The duties were spread over the staple articles of export, such as palm oil, cocoa, groundnuts, palm kernels, palm kernel oil, and hides and skins in the Colony of Nigeria. The duties have been universally condemned in theory. Even the officials do not defend them as being good measures ... much of what the merchants allege against export duties could be truthfully urged against every species of taxation, that it hinders trade. ... There remains, however, the valid objection that a tax on raw material is more hampering to trade than a tax on a finished product. ...' The duties were passed in the British West African legislatures 'without the assistance of the Government majority in Nigeria, while in the Gold Coast all the unofficial members unanimously voted against it'. McPhee further observed, 'Whether it is wise to institute Preference in a Crown Colony which does not have responsible government and therefore has it imposed on it from Downing Street, is another matter. At any rate, the British West African experiment was on an altogether different plane from the Preferences given by, say, Canada to England, which was noted in an assembly representing the people of the country, whose vote was a voluntary gesture. In the case of British West Africa, where the legislature is virtually a "packed" house, the imposition savoured a little of the "Old Colonial System", which is out of date in an age of Mandates ...' (McPhee, op. cit., pp. 224–6). Sir Sydney Oliver, author of *White Capital and Coloured Labour* and several other books, was more outspoken in his criticism of the export duties imposed on the British West African colonies: see his article, 'The Repartition of Africa', in *Contemporary Review*, cxv (Jan.–June 1919), 15–22. If the agitation of the nationalists is seen in the light of what they saw as the constitutional consequences or implications of post-war economic policies pursued by the imperial government, then their demand for constitutional changes, 'so as to give the people an effective voice in their affairs both in the Legislative and Municipal Governments', and their contention that 'taxation goes with effective representation' becomes understandable. In fact, agitation for representative government for Sierra Leone can be traced to the 1850s.

Socially, the wage inflation from 1917 tended to increase the income gap between the relatively privileged professional classes and the wage earners. Government and commercial employees, especially the large army of clerks, were hard hit, though the hardship of the former was relieved by the grant of war bonuses after 1918. It is significant, however, that many who described themselves as clerks, traders, or artisans actively participated in the disturbances of 1919.

The first of these occurred on 14 July when the technical staff and labourers in the railway and public works department went on strike demanding that they too must benefit from the war bonus given to clerical staff. They were mostly daily-wage men who had hitherto not been included in the bonus scheme—their wages ran from 1s. to 5s. a day.[27] They argued that while their wages were calculated on a daily rate ranging among technical staff from 3s. to 5s., and among labourers from 1s. to 3s. per day, they were in fact paid monthly, were in permanent government employment, and that their aggregate salary was equal to that of some of the clerical grades who had received a war bonus while they (the workers) were excluded. They also claimed that they belonged 'for the most part to the same social class as that from which the clerical staff is recruited, and that their exclusion from the war bonus scheme brings them into contempt with their more fortunate brothers in the clerical branch'.[28] Apart from their exclusion from the war bonus and their sensitivity to their socio-economic status in Creole society, the workers had other economic grievances like rising food prices at a time when wage levels remained low. On 15 July technical staff and labourers employed by the Public Works followed the example of the railwaymen and went on strike. They too wanted a war bonus and had been hard hit by rising prices.[29]

The rice and anti-Syrian riots broke out in Freetown on the night of 18 July 1919 during the celebrations to mark the conclusion of the Peace Treaty. Troops were called out and a public inquiry was held.[30] In spite of bitter opposition from leading persons in Freetown dis-

[27] The Sierra Leone Executive Council recommended that the men other than labourers be paid war bonus on the scale approved for clerks in Jan. 1917, i.e. 20 per cent on salaries not exceeding £90 p.a., and that labourers should get an increase of 3d. per day. C.O. 267/582/45278.
[28] ibid.; also Sierra Leone Weekly News (19 July 1919), p. 8.
[29] C.O. 267/582/45278.
[30] See correspondence enclosed in C.O. 267/558.

claiming responsibility for the disturbances, the Governor decided that the city revenues should be debited with the cost (£36,510) of the Lebanese losses since, in his view, 'the Protectorate natives . . . were in no sense anti-Syrian'.[31] The Freetown petition to Viscount Milner was organized by leading Creoles among whom were Sam Barlatt the Mayor of Freetown, J. H. Thomas a merchant of Little East Street, R. N. Hebron a barrister, C. Hotobah During, also a barrister, as well as Claudius May, editor of the *Sierra Leone Weekly* —all these gentlemen were to play prominent parts in the formation and in the politics of the Sierra Leone branch of the N.C.B.W.A. The petition itself was signed by a representative cross-section of Freetown, mostly produce merchants, traders, clerks, artisans, labourers. Out of 657 petitioners, 146 described themselves as traders or merchants, 189 were artisans, 119 were clerks; 24 described themselves as teachers, clergymen, or lawyers; the rest included labourers, pensioners, and a great number of unemployed. The original petitioners were mainly the Creole élite together with six chiefs and headmen. Out of the original 102 petitioners, 24 were merchants and produce dealers, 24 were lawyers, doctors, and councillors, 10 were teachers and clergymen, the rest were artisans and clerks.[32]

The riots began when attacks were made on the shops and houses of Syrian traders and merchants in Freetown: these attacks began simultaneously in the Eastern, Central, and Western Wards and resulted in considerable damage to property and extensive looting of merchandise.[33] Why the riots coincided with the torchlight procession held that night in Freetown by 'a band of young men, mostly mercantile clerks, who had formed themselves into a Society called *The Native Commercial Employees' League* to celebrate the armistice' was not clearly explained by the petitioners, except that it might have been a coincidence. Those who took part in this procession which later developed into extensive looting and damage to property were described by the petitioners as 'the bulk of the population of the better classes'.[34] Nor was it explained who actually started the rioting that night; the petition merely stated that the riots were

[31] Para. 6. of dispatch no. 58875, by Governor Wilkinson (13 Nov. 1920), C.O. 267/588.

[32] See petitions in C.O. 267/582, vol. iii.

[33] See 'Petition of the Ratepayers of Freetown, Sierra Leone, Against the Passing of a Bill Entitled "The Colony and Protectorate Riot (Damages) Compensation Ordinance, 1920" ', para. 1.

[34] ibid., para. 3.

'commenced simultaneously' and that those arrested after the riots were neither merchants, nor shopkeepers, nor clerks who, it is reasonable to assume, would have had a direct interest in the matter; on the contrary, said the petitioners

The class of people who would have engineered the disturbances, if that view were correct; viz: the Sierra Leone Merchants and shopkeepers, were as much taken aback at the riots as any one else. Not a single one of the hundred and fifty or so persons who were arrested and tried in connection with the rioting belongs to this class. Moreover, Sierra Leone Merchants of high standing who were believed to have been profiteering in rice were the objects of attacks as violent and as persistent as that against any of the Syrians.[35]

It was also vigorously denied that the disturbances, which lasted over a month and were widespread in the Protectorate, were 'engineered in the interests of some Sierra Leone traders'. According to the petitioners, 'the rioters belonged to the hooligan and irresponsible section of the people of whom a large number are immigrants from the Protectorate who, under normal conditions, supply the casual and unskilled labour of the City'.[36]

Whether the incidents of 1919 amounted to a 'conspiracy' of the Creoles, as most of the officials believed, is difficult, if not impossible to answer. Like most conspiracy theories, the explanation would be easy and simple. The fact, however, remains that the disturbances, whether organized or not, were the culmination of two important factors—the economic effects of the war and the failure of the rice crop in 1919 largely because of heavy rains and an outbreak of influenza.[37] The government's failure to distribute stocks of rice in time to prevent unrest also contributed to the desperation of the

[35] ibid., para. 14 (a), p. 4.
[36] ibid., para. 14 (e).
[37] See the *Aurora* (26 July 1919) and the *Sierra Leone Weekly News* (2 Aug. 1919). The former newspaper was virulently hostile to the Lebanese, describing them as the mythical 'hobgoblin' and as the Iagos of West African commerce. The *Weekly News*, a moderate weekly, merely argued that to go to 'the heart of the matter', one had to recognize that the raid on the Lebanese was 'not an *offensive* but a *defensive* act. . . . If Creoles . . . were connected with the business this is their justification—namely, that the act was one of defence by people whose very life was being rudely shaken almost to extinction by heartless traders who are aliens.' See also the minute to C.O. 48071, C.O. 267/582 (19 Aug. 1919): 'As regards the cause of the riot, it is undoubtedly largely economic. For some years there have been complaints that the Syrians outmatch the Creoles and their unpopularity is increased by the accusation, which seems to have a good foundation, that they have been profiteering in rice, which is the staple food of the people

unemployed and low-paid workers.[38] The labourer who earned 1s.
a day found that rice had risen from 1d. a cup to 5d. a cup. Native
merchants resented the economic dominance of the Syrians who had
not only by their business ability taken over most of the retail trade
but had also virtually monopolized the kola trade in the Protectorate.[39]
The petitioners also accused the Syrians of forming 'rings and combines by which prices of produce and merchandise were being artificially forced up', and of employing local women to capture the
petty trade from Freetown women.[40] Other allegations of a more
emotional and racial nature referred to the sexual proclivities of
Syrians and their alleged corruption of the 'young girls attending
the higher seminaries' and 'girls of reputed respectability'. The
'arrogance' of Syrians who called Sierra Leoneans 'niggers' and
'slaves' was also complained of alongside grievances arising from
economic competition.[41] Race was further mixed with economics
when at the beginning of the petition it was stated that during the
few weeks preceding the riots, 'there was considerable indignation
in some parts of the City at the report of the racial disturbances in
Liverpool, Cardiff, and a few other places in England and Wales
which gave rise to considerable apprehension that the "Sea-boys"
repatriated from those places with a deep sense of injury would
instigate reprisals in Sierra Leone against the white residents . . .'.
The Freetown City Council, however, was 'convinced that the
disturbances were due wholly and solely to the excessively high
prices demanded for food, which goaded the classes most severely
affected past endurance; and that the plot was sedulously concealed
because those who conceived it would not obtain general appro-
bation'.[42]

---

and is almost at famine prices. . . .' See also the report of Acting Governor Evelyn
in C.O. 267/582/48071 (31 July 1919), paras. 17–18.

A poem entitled 'The Syrians' which appeared in the *Sierra Leone Weekly
News* of 13 Sept. 1919 read:

> Grass he tells us we will eat,
> When with vengeance on rice did sit;
> Leaves and brooms and all he cornered,
> Farina, palm oil and kola;
> On the blood of the land.

[38] Section D, enclosure to dispatch no. 580, C.O. 267/588 (13 Nov. 1920).
[39] Appendix 'B', 'Notes respecting illegal practices by Dealers in Rice', C.O.
267/582/58875.
[40] Para. 4 of Petition.
[41] ibid., para. 12, p. 3.                    [42] ibid., para. 15, p. 4.

From Freetown, the riots spread into the Protectorate—Moyamba (25 July) and Kangahun (26 July).[43] Sporadic anti-Syrian riots and lootings also occurred in Mano, Boia, Makump, Bo, and Bonthe. At Mange and Port Lokko, where Syrian stores were also threatened, the rice situation was so desperate that the rumour was quickly spread around that 'the Government no agree for the Syrians to be here'.[44] In Freetown itself, raids on Syrian shops continued and about three people were killed; the police and the military were so stretched that little could be done to stem the violence: a few of the troops even joined in the looting.[45] Although some order was restored, the atmosphere was so tense that between July and October, Gold Coast troops had to be sent to Freetown.[46] Viscount Milner took a serious view of the situation when he stated: 'The existing position appears to be a very serious one. The riots, which began a month ago, have not been put down. . . . It seems to me that it is a case for strong measures to restore the authority of the law and to mark the distinction between the civilization of the British and the Ottoman Empire.'[47]

It is noteworthy, however, that the riots and lootings in the Protectorate involved very few Creoles: the vast majority of rioters were Protectorate peoples, and the attacks were made on Lebanese traders only. European merchants and Creole traders were not attacked, though Creole traders suspected of storing Lebanese goods were threatened.[48] Official opinion was agreed that the riots were a direct consequence of post-war economic hardships, especially unemployment, food shortage, and commodity control schemes imposed by the imperial government. Governor Wilkinson described the socio-economic situation accurately when he observed in his address to the Legislative Council in 1919,

The year 1919 has been one of much distress. The early rains of last year had hindered the clearing of the farms: the Influenza epidemic had inter-

[43] See telegram enclosed in C.O. 44115, C.O. 267/582 (29 July 1919).
[44] Telegrams in C.O. 48071, ibid. (31 July 1919).
[45] Minute to C.O. 267/582/49632 (27 Aug. 1919); also enclosure to C.O. 55464 (24 Sept. 1919). Acting Governor to Viscount Milner. In the Protectorate, soldiers joined the looters at Makene in the Karene district on the Boia–Makump line, C.O. 267/582/48226 (7 Aug. 1919), paras. 6, 9–11.
[46] C.O. 267/583/64385 (20 Oct. 1919); the troops left Freetown on 27 Oct. 1919 —C.O. 267/583/6659 (6 Nov. 1919).
[47] Minute to C.O. 48071 (19 Aug. 1919).
[48] C.O. 267/582/51292, Confi. (21 Aug. 1919), Officer Commanding the Troops, West Africa, to the Secretary, War Office.

fered with the harvesting of the crop. The shortage of rice has been the main feature of the current year. There was a famine; and there were riots. . . . Our taxation . . . weighs more heavily on the poor. Export duties and railway-freights fall ultimately on the producer. The tax-payer in this case is the inhabitant of the Protectorate who collects and prepares palm-produce for the market; he represents, in fact, the very poorest section of the community. And it is unfortunate that while the price of all imported commodities had risen enormously during the war, the price of palm oil and palm kernels had been kept at the pre-war level: and this—to some extent at least—by direct state control. The peasantry of the Protectorate have suffered severely. I do not wish to minimise the claims of others to some compensation for the increased cost of living: but unless economy is observed we shall only be lessening the troubles of the wealthier classes by throwing increased burdens on the poorer. . . .

In the Colony the war has seen great changes. The use of Freetown as a naval base led to a great demand for casual labour. . . . That special demand has now ceased. Many men who were attracted to the port by the prospect of high pay have been thrown out of employment. It is to this element of the population—now become a dangerous element—that we owe the prevailing unrest. . . .[49]

The strikes by the workers, together with the processions during the night of the celebrations, had created an atmosphere for the disturbances that erupted on 18 July,[50] but there was uncertainty as to whether the riots and strikes were organized, and if so, by whom. Concerning the rice riots, Colonel Faunce, officer commanding the W.A.F.F., thought that 'the affair was planned by the educated natives, with the intention of seizing and selling cheaply hoarded stocks of rice by the agency of the aboriginal residents in Freetown, and that the mobs at once increased so rapidly that those responsible lost all control'.[51] The Acting Governor, Mr. Evelyn, was of the opinion that there was 'little doubt' that the riots were 'planned and organized beforehand'.[52] G. W. James, District Commissioner of

[49] Address to the Legislative Council, 1919; C.O. 267/582/71851.

[50] C.O. 267/582/51292 (6 Aug. 1919), Colonel B. Faunce to the Secretary, War Office. If official accounts are accepted, the Protectorate Natives showed no real hostility towards the Lebanese traders—see the letter to the District Commissioner, Moyamba, from Chief Alimamy Coroma (24 Aug. 1919), enclosed in dispatch no. 456, C.O. 267/583/60683 (9 Oct. 1919). According to the Revd. Max Gorvie, a Mende writer, during the riots, 'the Creole traders appealed to African solidarity, persuading the Natives that they were all one people and popularising the ditty "We all nar wan konko" '; quoted in Banton, M. P., *Urbanization in Sierra Leone* (Social Sciences Research Centre, University of Edinburgh, 1954), p. 122.

[51] C.O. 267/582/48071 (31 July 1919), para. 20.

[52] C.O. 267/582/51291 (19 Aug. 1919).

896

8

Sherbro, thought that those caught looting Lebanese shops in the
Protectorate were merely those who could be found in any mob;
according to him, 'The real culprits, the prime movers in the whole
movement, have yet to be traced . . . the Syrians who know the most,
are at present not a little nervous about coming forward, and the
Creoles, being sympathisers with the movement, do not wish to
give anything away.'[53] Mr. R. A. Maude the Attorney-General was
more certain than the others. In his view, 'The riot was organized by
Creoles and started by them; once it had been started the crowd
got out of hand . . . that surprised the Creoles. . . . The people had
the idea that the loot was their bonus.'[54] The Governor, however,
thought it 'most unlikely' that leading Creoles would have organized
the riots: instead, he attributed the riots to unemployment and the
high cost of living. In the general confusion, however, the strike was
confused with the rice riots, and the bonus question conveniently
used to explain away the anti-Syrian riots. Consequently, 'bonus'
became the battle-cry of the hungry lumpenproletariat, assisted by a
depressed urban petty bourgeoisie (and an unemployed clerkly class
which was at last applying its useless Latin to colonial politics) and
the refrain of a rather cleverly constructed song:

Strike don cam for Bonus
We unite for bonus;
Creole Boy ner danger Boy,
Bonus, Bo-Bonus!

Kaiser[55] make Bonus,
When we take Bonum;
Peace Terms wan Bonam up,
Bonus, Bo-Bonus!

Milner[56] say pay Bonus,
Barker[57] say bite first,
Maud[58] say make Red-belleh shoot,
Bonus, Bo-Bonus!

[53] Enclosure to S. Leone Confi. 7505 (29 Jan. 1920), p. 10 ibid. It may be useful
to recall that the Creoles were made scapegoats in the 1898 Hut Tax War.
[54] ibid.
[55] Refers to Kaiser Wilhelm of Imperial Germany.
[56] Refers to Viscount Milner, Secretary of State for the Colonies.
[57] Barker was the Acting General Manager of Sierra Leone Railway whose
workers went on strike over the bonus question.
[58] R. A. Maude, Attorney-General of the Sierra Leone Government.

Bonus Bona Bonum
Boni Bone Bona
We want small Bonus
Bonus, Bo-Bonus! etc.

Last year we say ner Flu,
This year we call am Strike;
When all dem Coral[59] go,
Then Bonus, Sweet Bonus![60]

The strikes, which lasted over a week, were so well organized, and the riots so serious and prolonged, that the administration came to attribute this unprecedented wave of disturbances, since the Hut Tax War, to outside subversive influences.[61] Even Governor Wilkinson believed that those alleged outside influences (which he could not identify) were at the back of the riots: 'There is no doubt in my mind that there is a focus of disloyalty in this Colony. This disloyalty, I have some reason to believe, is inspired from outside the Empire and has money and organisation behind it.'[62] As far as the Freetown press was concerned, however, the strikes and riots, together with the agitation against the proposed Criminal Code, were purely internal matters which partly reflected the growing race-consciousness of Negroes everywhere. Indeed, an editorial on the Lebanese was of the opinion that some kind of political party or pressure group was needed to sustain the anti-Syrian and Criminal Code agitation and that the agitation would not be allowed to peter out but must be used to create the foundations of some kind of political movement:

The disappointing after-effect, as a result of any great movement in the direction of an agitation by the native community against measures or attitudes initiated or adopted by the Government may be due, whatever other causes, to the absence of a recognized Public Institution, not in any

[59] The Lebanese traders were also called 'corals' because of the coral beads and other cheap articles they used to hawk around the streets and markets when they first appeared as petty traders.

[60] This was known as 'The Bonus Song' and was 'sung during the Great Strike and Peace Celebration, July 18th to 22nd 1919'; see enclosure to Sierra Leone Confi. 7505 (29 Jan. 1920), C.O. 267/582.

[61] See the official reports in Sierra Leone Confi. 7305 (29 Jan. 1920), ibid.

[62] ibid.; the alleged outside influence was probably Marcus Garvey's U.N.I.A. which was then at the height of its activities; it could also have been a reference to the Comintern, although it is most unlikely that the latter organization, founded the same year, had anything to do with the disturbances; see Gambia Secret M.P. no. 57, 4/9, 'Reports on Bolshevik political and labour agitation', especially the secret circular by Winston S. Churchill (10 June 1921). G.R.O.

way under obligation to the Government; and it is time that this be recognized. It is curious how this opportunity was allowed to slide away. . . . Government diplomacy or not, the Syrians will go. Africa for the Africans; it is their God assigned heritage. . . .[63]

Immediately after the railwaymen's strike another editorial with a Pan-African bias put the disturbances in the context of the new nationalism:

There is already a great and serious awakening among the backward race. This has been called by those who know best and are following the profound movements of the times, the birth of a new race consciousness. . . . If the great worldwide war has occasioned many valuable developments it has done this one great thing for the backward peoples of the world. It has opened their eyes to their own grand possibilities. It has moved them to see visions and dream dreams. . . . America has wonderfully taken the lead. Indeed, it is the race manhood that has gained consciousness of its own existence. . . . No man henceforth ought to be a puppet in the hands of another. . . . Is it not time we call together a big mass meeting of all our best men to consult as to our future salvation? Why has not Sierra Leone taken a part in the Pan-African Congress held in Paris. . . . Is she not ripe and strong?[64]

Before concluding our remarks on the economics of the new bourgeois nationalism in Freetown, we must consider another interpretation of the grievances of the African middleman against the Lebanese traders. Dr. Marwan I. Hanna,[65] taking a Lebanese point of view, argues that resentment against Lebanese immigrants and traders in West Africa was not confined to the African middleman who is generally depicted as a victim of the aggressive competition of the Lebanese. In his view, as early as 1910 the Government of French West Africa, 'under pressure from the French Chamber of Commerce',[66] had already introduced legislation restricting Lebanese immigration to the whole of French West Africa, and in British West Africa similar legislation was passed between 1914 and 1926. He contends that in British West Africa, hostility against the Lebanese retail traders was

due mainly to pressure of Foreign commercial interests which feared increasing competition of the Lebanese. . . . In British West Africa the big

[63] *Sierra Leone Weekly News* (30 Aug. 1919), p. 5.
[64] ibid. (19 July 1919), p. 4.
[65] Hanna, Marwan I., 'Lebanese Emigrants in West Africa: Their Effect on Lebanon and West Africa' (D.Phil. thesis, Oxford University, 1959).
[66] ibid., p. 92.

European firms did not come out openly against the Lebanese as was the case in French African territories, but chose to press the issue under the guise of protecting the interests of the native African population. They did in fact do much to incite the natives against the Lebanese traders by accusing these latter of hoarding essential food stuffs and displacing the small African traders.[67]

Dr. Hanna proceeds to argue that even if the Lebanese had displaced the African merchant from his trade, 'it is very doubtful whether in those early years, 1924–1926, the natives were so much aware of this fact and so articulate as to be able to start an agitation in the papers'.[68] The history of post-war nationalism in British West Africa shows that Dr. Hanna's contention is groundless. It may well be that the European firms feared competition from the Lebanese retailers and that they did 'incite the natives against the Lebanese traders', but as we have tried to show earlier, there is no evidence for this assertion. All the available evidence shows that the 'articulate vocal minority'[69] of which Dr. Hanna speaks was perfectly capable of seeing the implications of economic competition and commercial crises for its role and status in the colonial system without external guidance. One may argue that the position of the Lebanese as 'strangers' and the relative absence of social distance between them and the Sierra Leoneans made them easy targets and convenient scapegoats in any disturbance stemming from economic causes;[70] but to argue that those who were hostile to them and viewed them as exploiters were 'incited' by other foreigners who were equally suspect,[71] amounts to a misunderstanding of petty-bourgeois nationalism. As Stalin observed, 'the chief problem of the young bourgeoisie is the problem of the market. Its aim is to sell its goods and to emerge victorious from the competition with the bourgeoisie

[67] ibid., pp. 94–5.
[68] ibid., pp. 96–7.                    [69] ibid., p. 97.
[70] Winder, R. Bayly, 'The Lebanese in West Africa', Comparative Studies in Society and History, iv, no. 3 (Apr. 1962), 296–333; see also comments on 'the stranger' by Lloyd A. Fallers in the same journal. It may be noted that economic hardship also led to similar country-wide boycott of European and Lebanese merchants in the Gold Coast in 1943 and 1948: see Apter, D., The Gold Coast in Transition (Princeton, N.J., 1955), pp. 169 ff.; Nkrumah, K., Ghana: The Autobiography of Kwame Nkrumah (Edinburgh, 1957), p. 75.
[71] See Resolutions of the Conference of Africans of British West Africa . . . (Electric Law Press Ltd., London, 1920), pp. 2–3: 'Alien Problems with Particular Reference to the Syrian Question'; also the Report of Proceedings of a Meeting held in London between the League of Nations Union and the Delegates of the National Congress of British West Africa (London, 1920), pp. 19–20.

of another nationality. Hence its desire to secure its "own", its "home" market. The market is the first school in which the bourgeoisie learns its nationalism.'[72] Dr. Hanna's 'articulate vocal minority' were, as we have seen, very much concerned about the market, and they did say so.

In Nigeria too, prices rose, especially in Lagos; prices of meat and 'gari' went up. One editorial referred to 'the abnormal rise in the price of Gari' and concluded that it was the 'working class' who were hardest hit.[73] In the Eastern Provinces and Calabar yams also rocketed in price; this, according to the *Pioneer*, was due to the fact that dislike of paper currency had led many of the yam growers in the interior districts around Port Harcourt and Calabar to refuse to part with their stocks to the middlemen who bought up their produce for resale in a better market. The high prices offered for palm produce also tended to cause farmers in the Eastern Provinces to plant only enough for their own needs. In the Western Provinces, however, it was the cocoa farms, mostly owned by Lagosians, and the profitability of labour that caused rising food prices, for the labourer could now make a few shillings a week by carrying cocoa bags and then retiring to his village and cassava plot.[74]

Although 1919 and the first half of 1920 witnessed a boom in trade in West Africa, the price inflation of 1919 also had its social and political effects. In the Gambia, 1919 was a good year commercially,[75] but rising prices caused some sporadic outbursts of looting and petty theft and led to a seamen's strike for better wages and to the formation of unions, notably the Gambia Native Defensive Union.[76] In Lagos, too, the high cost of living led to the formation, in September 1919, of the Nigerian Mechanics Union which by early 1920 claimed a membership of about 800. Its vice patron was Herbert Macaulay whom the *Pioneer* accused of using the railwaymen's strike of 7 January 1920 to support the Eleko's case and to enhance his political stature in Lagos.[77]

[72] Stalin, Joseph, *Marxism and the National Question* (New York, 1942), p. 38, quoted in Minogue, K. R., *Nationalism* (London, 1967), p. 141; cf. *Nationalism* (London, 1939), pp. 239–42.
[73] *Nigerian Pioneer* (24 Oct. 1919), p. 8.
[74] ibid. (21 May 1920), p. 8.
[75] *West Africa* (23 Oct. 1920), p. 1335.
[76] Martin, op. cit., p. 53. Also Appendix I of the *Address of His Excellency The Acting Governor to the Legislative Council* (17 Dec. 1920): Gambia Legislative Council Minutes, 1914–23, p. 6, C.O. 89/14.
[77] See the *Lagos Weekly Record* (31 Jan. 1920).

1920–1, the years of boom and slump,[78] had profound effects on West Africa. 1919 and part of 1920 were periods of unprecedented boom in West Africa. Europe's rush to replenish drove prices up, especially primary commodities. Gold Coast cocoa prices had risen gradually from 45s. per cwt. in 1910 to 130s. in the peak year 1919. The local producer did very well out of Accra cocoa as the periods of depression had been more than set off by his huge profits in boom periods. In the Gambia, 1920 was described as 'commercially, one of unprecedented prosperity locally'; groundnut prices rose from £10 per ton in 1914 to £50 per ton in 1920. In Sierra Leone and Nigeria the trend was similar. The boom collapsed when raw materials and foodstuffs which the lack of shipping had accumulated abroad during the war, began to arrive in Europe. In March 1920 prices began to fall and by 1922 were halved, the worst year being 1921. In West Africa, the small African trader and merchant, usually not very efficient and competing with the combines, was the first to succumb to the economic blizzard. Merchants went short of money for trading purposes because during the boom years most of them had committed themselves to the purchase of great quantities of manufactured goods at high prices; in 1921 their deliveries entered the markets in many cases surfeited with goods. They were unable to receive more goods because a large part of their profits had been paid to the Government in excess profits duty and income tax. Had business been wisely conducted, these profits would have been sufficient to compensate for the largely increased capital required in the early part of 1920 when they were replacing their cheaper stocks on which these profits had been made by goods at much increased values; also, a wise decision by the banks not unduly to increase overdrafts or advances would probably have helped to cushion off some of the effects of the slump. The African customers of these merchants were also short of cash. First, in the early part of 1920 the African traders knew that the goods being offered them were lower in price than later deliveries; secondly, as they did not know how safely to dispose of their paper currency, which had caused so much trouble since its introduction to West Africa in 1916, they bought much more largely than was necessary for their immediate trade requirements, so that the slump met them with considerable stock on their hands. The customers of these merchants in turn were unable to purchase even their average quantity of goods, as prices had fallen sharply between

[78] Lewis, op. cit., pp. 18–20.

February 1920 and December 1920. Then the African producer got less for his produce, as railway freights and labour costs had risen; purchasing power was low, and the margin of expenses between buying prices in West Africa and selling prices in Liverpool was greatly increased.

The agitation for constitutional change and the appeal to nationalism increased in proportion to the scale of economic difficulties.[79] One correspondent, complaining about the problems raised by the issue of paper currency and about the shortage of silver, believed that European merchants were hoarding the notes and charging high prices while 'the wealth of the classes is oozing away. . . . The kings, chiefs, and all classes will soon be paupers.' The people, he said, should wake up and protect themselves 'from the wily manouvrings [sic] of combined magnates'.[80] Throughout British West Africa there was agitation against the issue of non-silver alloy in 1920–1, and against the issue of Treasury Notes, particularly the notes whose introduction in 1916 (because of the silver shortage in England) resulted in great loss to the West African trading community—European and African merchants alike. In 1920, however, the 1913 silver currency was changed; abnormally high price of silver, due to post-war conditions, made the cost of minting silver coinage for West Africa prohibitive. The West African Currency Board therefore decided to adopt, with the approval of the Secretary of State (and the protests of West African merchants) a coin of similar design to the West African silver coins but made of an alloy of brass, copper, and other metals. It was the introduction of these coins which the N.C.B.W.A. and the nationalist press were protesting against.

[79] For a valuable discussion of the connection between economic interests and nationalism, see Hayes, Carleton J. H., *The Historical Evolution of Modern Nationalism* (New York, 1948), chapter VII: 'Economic Factors in Nationalism', especially pp. 244–8 where he discusses how neo-mercantilism usually disturbs the balance between economic liberalism and liberal nationalism and leads to a more articulate form of nationalism which he calls 'integral nationalism'. Also Dobb, Maurice, ' "Super-Profit" and West Africa', *The Plebs*, xix (Aug. 1927), 256–60; Dobb's article sought to explain colonial nationalism from the Marxist viewpoint. Commenting on 'The real historic significance of colonial nationalism' he wrote: 'Colonial nationalism has so far usually begun with the rise of a native bourgeoisie and native *intelligentsia*, who rely for support upon the peasants, urban petty bourgeoisie and workers, on whom the chief burden of exploitation rests. The colonial bourgeoisie, however, only want freedom to develop their own colonial capitalism, and are soon likely to break off from the general movement and accept a few concessions from the Imperialists, particularly if the masses behind them push forward too strongly so as to frighten them . . .' (p. 259).
[80] *Gold Coast Leader* (31 Jan. 1920), p. 4.

The issue of new currency notes was not popular either. The merchants found it difficult to issue currency notes to producers who preferred coins, which they could hoard.[81] Currency notes came to be referred to as 'filthy lucre' and as unhygienic: not that these were the real reasons for the opposition. The fact was that most of the smaller African merchants and traders in competition with the European firms were not doing good business with their own people. Even the *Nigerian Pioneer* had to protest: 'Though it is economically unsound to put in circulation coins so debased as the proposed non-silver alloy coins, nevertheless, the people have shown an anxiety to accept them, proportional to their detestation of the flimsy, easily destructible currency notes. . . .'[82] A more radical newspaper observed 'We learn that the British West African Conference went further . . . and required an assurance that whatever the medium of exchange introduced, the face value should be pound for pound in Britain as in the Dependencies. It is obvious that British West Africa will not stand for long the wrongs of a depreciated medium of exchange in addition to differential duties and inflated prices. . . .'[83]

On the whole, the agitation in the press covered a very wide range of economic grievances. The interesting point is that throughout the discussion in the press between 1916 and 1920 about the formation of the N.C.B.W.A., economic issues were constantly juxtaposed with constitutional ones. For example, the *Gold Coast Leader*, which was foremost in its advocacy of the Congress movement, sermonized in 1920, apropos the cocoa market:

We have had trouble already with the preferential Export Duty on Palm Kernels, and the complaint has been long and bitter throughout British West Africa; and on top of this comes the apparent manipulation of the cocoa market as well. If this is not a species of economic servitude, we do not know what is. The people of West Africa in our opinion should be free to trade in any market they please throughout the world. . . . The contrary attitude would mean in the long run our being reduced to conditions in which we shall lose every vestige of economic freedom, the prelude to loss of free political development and progress. We trust this matter will seriously engage the attention of the National Congress of British West Africa. . . .

[81] See Report of the West African Currency Board: Cd. 8372, Dec. 1916; Cd. 8883, Dec. 1917; Cmd. 15, Feb. 1919; Cmd. 475, Dec. 1919; Cmd. 1189, Mar. 1921.
[82] *Nigerian Pioneer* (7 May 1920), p. 8.
[83] *Gold Coast Leader* (21 Aug. 1920), p. 4.

To this radical newspaper, it was 'politics' that would lead West Africa from the kingdom of economic unfreedom into the kingdom of economic opportunity and well-being. Economics was indeed the crux of the matter, but it was 'the Constitution' that must first be secured: 'All this,' the editorial concluded, 'leads up to one consideration and that a very important one, the great urgency for British West Africa to possess a Constitution capable of giving effect to the will of the people. That is the only remedy to the various ills that the West African political situation is exposed.'[84] In order to have some control over their economic affairs, they believed they ought to have some voice in a representative assembly to which half of them would be elected by the people—or by those among the people who mattered—and not nominated by a benevolent autocrat administering a system of indefinite tutelage. And to achieve this goal, they believed it was necessary to change the Crown Colony system—constitutionally. There was never at any time any question of radically altering the balance of economic forces wholly in favour of the African. That would have been unthinkable for a leadership brought up on Adam Smith, Locke, and Mill. Like all good liberals, all they wanted was mutual accommodation of interests, equal opportunity, and 'an effective voice in their affairs'.[85]

When the Conference finally met at Accra in March 1920, therefore, its economic programme, or rather a statement of its economic grievances and aspirations, had already been agreed upon by the four territories concerned. Under the heading 'Commercial Enterprise with Particular Reference to (a) The Scheme of the Empire Resources Development Committee; (b) Banking; (c) Shipping', the Conference which later resolved itself into the N.C.B.W.A. resolved:

1. That this Conference views with great disfavour the propaganda of the Empire Resources Development Committee with respect to the British West African Colonies, and is strongly of the opinion that the natural resources of the British West African Dependencies are not for the exploitation of the Concessionaires under State control.

---

[84] ibid. (14 Aug. 1920), p. 4.
[85] See the remarks by J. E. Casely Hayford in *Report of the Proceedings of a Meeting held in London between the League of Nations Union and the Delegates of the National Congress of British West Africa* (London, 1920), pp. 13–16. For the role of the 'depressed bourgeoisie' in the evolution of nationalism, and the attitudes of the various social classes towards the nation, see *Nationalism* (London, 1949), chapter XV, pp. 270 ff.

Further, that it condemns any policy which would make such resources available for the liquidation of the Imperial War Debt or any part of it, and pledges itself by constitutional means to oppose strenuously any such policy. . . .

2. That this Conference, being of the opinion That Trade competition in the British West African Dependencies should be free from restriction, views with great dissatisfaction the passing of the Palm Kernels Export Duty Ordinance in the various British West African Dependencies. . . .

3. That this Conference, being strongly convinced that the time has come for the co-operation of the peoples of the British West African Dependencies in promoting their economical development, recommends the consideration by the various Committees of the formation of a Corporation, to be known as the British West African Co-operative Association, under the Companies Acts, with powers, *inter-alia*, to found Banks, promote shipping facilities, establish Co-operative Stores, and produce buying centres, in such wise as to inspire and maintain a British West African Economical development.

Further, to ensure the object in view, this Conference pledges itself to educate the public opinion of the different communities, through their local Committees as to the raising of a substantial capital in the British West African Co-operative Association and subject to the rules, regulations and conditions of the Companies Acts.

Further, that the collection and banking of such sums shall be under the direction and control of such Committee provided that the aggregate sum collected is to be treated as one fund and directs that this suggestion be referred to the different Committees for their consideration and report at the first sitting of the proposed Congress of Africans of British West Africa.

4. That this Conference disapproves of the issue by the Currency Board of coins and notes of a different face value from coins and notes outside British West Africa, and desires to place on record its opinion of the unfairness of such discrimination. . . .

7. That this Conference desires to record its deep sense of the importance of British West African Farmers retaining their interest in the land and in the crops thereof, and would welcome legislation on the same lines as the Sierra Leone 'Sama Law'. . . .

8. That this Conference condemns profiteering and the cornering of foodstuffs in any shape or form, and recommends Legislation in the several British West African Colonies to meet the evil.[86]

---

[86] An obvious reference to the activities of foreign firms and Lebanese traders. Resolution 3 on the 'Syrian Question' referred to Lebanese traders as 'undesirables and a menace to the good Government of the land', and demanded their repatriation from West Africa. It is interesting to note that Herbert Macaulay's Nigerian National Democratic Party which was founded in 1923, endorsed the policies of the N.C.B.W.A. in Point xvi of its constitution and also paid some attention to economic matters. Point xiii of its constitution called for the intro-

By the time the Accra Conference ended, it was apparent to most contemporary observers that the Westernized intelligentsia of lawyers, merchants, and journalists which inaugurated the Congress movement was not merely an idealistic group with visions of West African unity and representative institutions, but also a group which saw its interests and mobility in colonial society threatened and even obstructed by a system of rule which, they thought, did not sufficiently accommodate their interests and therefore had to be reformed. One widely read journal with pan-coloured interests explained the 'economic basis' of the movement with rather uncharacteristic Marxian dialectic; after pointing out the exploitation and frustration inherent in Crown Colony rule it went on to argue as follows

... a moment arrives when Crown Colony government is no longer possible. Economic conditions become acute. The small Native trader is pushed out: his class disappears. The big combine, the 'billion-dollar trust', on the one hand is opposed to the millions of propertyless wage slaves on the other. A class of intelligentsia is thrown up from below by the struggle, and they lead a revolt against conditions which are growingly intolerable. They confer and petition; they agitate and threaten. Under economic stress the political education of the masses makes great leaps. At a certain point a crisis is reached, not before many apparent crises have been averted and overcome. Then one of two things happens. Evolution makes a violent move forward (and is called revolution for its pains), or Government concedes an inch ... and remarks how easily fools are pacified.[87]

Sir William Geary, who gave much assistance to the London Congress delegation, believed that 'The Congress was not an arena for seditious speeches against the Government. ... There was no snarl of non-co-operators', and that 'the Africans of the Congress are shrewd business men who recognise that Africans and Europeans have worked together in West Africa for mutual benefit and profit'. The Africans, he said, needed European capital but were also entitled to an effective representation in the affairs of their country.[88]

duction of 'every reasonable scheme for the economic development of the natural resources of Nigeria by Government or Private enterprise so long as such development does not imply the exploitation of the Natives or their lands or their economic servitude'. Point xiv pledged the party 'to the policy of Free and Fair Trade in Nigeria ... [and] ... for the recognition of the principle of "live and let live" on the part of the European and all other Foreign Merchants and Traders in all commercial dealings with the Native Traders and Producers of Nigeria'.

[87] *Africa and Orient Review* (Dec. 1920), pp. 39–42: 'The West African Problem'.

[88] Sir William Geary to the Editor, 'Political Reform in West Africa', *West Africa* (8 Jan. 1921), p. 1661.

Even the most conservative observers did not fail to notice that economic hardship was partly responsible for the political unrest in West Africa. The *African World Annual* (another commercial journal) observed that 1920 was a memorable year in West Africa

*It [i.e. 1920] has seen the birth of much that is destined to effect permanent change; it has also witnessed the passing-away of an old order of things . . .* in the West African Colonies generally . . . discontent was rife throughout the country in 1920's early months owing to the currency problem, the shortage of native foodstuffs, the high price of imported provisions and labour unrest . . . from August 1921, and continuing with increasing strength through 1922, very important movements—political, educational and ethical—gradually came to birth under the cessation of ordinary interests. During the whole of last year [1922] this has been very marked indeed. *Politically it has expressed itself on the part of the natives of West Africa in a very close and critical attention to all Government proposals; demands to have a share in electing the Legislative Councils; and the increasingly strong support being given to the National Congress of British West Africa by both chiefs and people.*[89]

*West Africa*, another organ of various commercial interests in West Africa, was quick to see the economics of the West African movement for political reform changing its attitude to the N.C.B.W.A. from lukewarm support in 1920 to a recognition of the necessity of political change after the slump; its editorial ran:

It would be foolish to deny that 1921 opens with conditions in West African countries, commercial, financial, and to a certain extent, political, very far from what could be wished for. . . . At the same time as disappointment in trade we have deep disappointment in politics (in the wider sense of that word, there must be few business men who do not realise that politics in this sense and commerce are inextricably connected) . . . the British people must realise that the war has affected Africa as it has all other countries, and that political advance must be made. It may be that the system being applied to India—the central principle of which we take to be the setting apart of certain imperial and international matters and the dealing with these by one set of machinery, while other, more local, matters are dealt with in another way—will provide a model. We do not doubt that if this issue were threshed out fully and candidly with the West African National Congress delegation now here, lines of practicable progress would soon indicate themselves. This is why we have urged the necessity for a frank exchange of views between the delegation and our British West African commercial leaders. . . .[90]

[89] See the *African World Annual* (1920-1), p. 69, and (1922-3), p. 65. Emphasis mine.        [90] *West Africa* (1 Jan. 1921).

In British West Africa, nationalist circles saw the question in very much the same light as *West Africa*, the only difference being that for them the N.C.B.W.A. had been chosen by 'the people' as the instrument of their economic salvation. To take only a few examples: one editorial, after lamenting the destruction the slump had brought on many a West African trader and merchant, some of whom had jumped on the bandwagon of prosperity in early 1920, recommended that

. . . the time has come when Africans should call a conference of prominent West Africans from the Gambia to Nigeria to consider the question of the depression in trade and the way out: but there need be no separate Conference. This is one of the duties for which the National Congress of British West Africa came into existence and this is a fitting opportunity to start work at once. We believe that one of the special subjects to be discussed in the Congress meeting to take place in Sierra Leone is the depression in trade as it affects the Africans and the way out. . . . It is evident that if we in Nigeria depend only on cocoa, palm oil, and kernel as our export produce, we shall be disappointed. . . . There is plenty of work for the National Congress to do which, if we turn our attention to it, will hasten our entranchisement even quicker than the calculation of the most enthusiastic optimist . . . no time should be wasted in calling together a meeting to consider this most vital and important subject, namely the depression in trade . . . Africans Rise up! Awake from sleep! The hour is come. . . .[91]

The indefatigable Revd. Patriarch J. G. Campbell urged his audience to buy shares in Garvey's Black Star Line so as to avoid the shipping bottle-neck and get goods at a cheaper freight rate from Canada and the United States. He concluded his political sermon

It should not surprise our reader if we speak of the Dulness of trade. For trade affects both the Government, the Clergy and the Farmer; in fact all and every one: there ought to be some substantial trade combinations amongst us the Educated Africans. Individual efforts can do but very little in the face of combined efforts of the Europeans. The National Congress of British West Africa stands for trade combination amongst Africans; the work of Congress is not only politics, but it concerns different branches of life in Africa. . . .[92]

Although they realized that political action was necessary as a means of expressing and redressing their economic grievances, the leaders of the N.C.B.W.A. did not, however, produce a coherent

[91] *Times of Nigeria* (18 Apr. 1921), p. 5: 'The Recent Depression in Trade'.
[92] ibid. (25 Apr. 1921), p. 4.

and realistic policy of economic reconstruction and co-operation in British West Africa. Their economic utopias never left the conference resolution stage. The lawyer–merchant class which formed the core of the leadership, and could have provided the capital for an embryo West African Co-operative Association and similar schemes, does not seem to have pursued the idea whole-heartedly. There was hardly anything 'national' about the 'economical development' this social class wanted; like most liberal democrats and bourgeois nationalists, they believed there was no inherent conflict between their interests and the interests of the people in whose name they claimed to speak—'sons of the soil', as they called themselves. As long as their interests could be accommodated in a colonial structure within which they could exert some influence, the more idealistic aspects of their nationalism could safely be left to the Pan-African visionaries. Liberty might well be one of the glories of the *Pax Britannica*, and none of these men would have denied its importance in the post-war world; the fact that impressed them most was that liberty contributed directly to economic activity and they defended it partly because it was a commercial asset of undoubted value. Yet, they do not seem to have realized the fundamental difficulty of reconciling their claim to this liberty with the system of indirect rule which had now become an imperial dogma. There was little room for them in that system. In the end, however, it was a characteristic British compromise that resolved the difficulty. It is not surprising, then, that with the introduction of elective institutions in 1922–5, the N.C.B.W.A. reached its nadir, sustained only by the enthusiasm of a few idealists like Casely Hayford, Bankole-Bright, S. R. Wood, and Kobina Sekyi. In Nigeria, the movement was almost non-existent after 1923.

Economic conditions improved very slowly from 1923 to 1929, the Gold Coast and Nigeria recovering more rapidly than the other colonies; but the effects of the 1920–1 slump were still visible. One newspaper complained in 1927 that there was no sign that the cloud of stagnation and depression had cleared; export prices were fluctuating and were showing a downward tendency; import trade did not improve, and merchants were worried.[93] Yet another paper complained of rising unemployment and hard times.[94] As in 1920, export duties caused a considerable furore in the press in the late 1920s.

[93] *West African Mail and Trade Gazette* (27 Apr. 1927).
[94] *Sierra Leone Weekly News* (30 June 1928).

A Gold Coast paper protested: 'The taxation of exports is bad in principle and a serious violation of the laws of economics; it is practically a tax on capital, and the trouble is that this system of taxation handicaps the producer when he comes to sell his wares in the open market in competition with producers of other countries who have no export taxes to pay.'[95] The necessity of agricultural banks and co-operative methods of production and marketing was widely discussed in the press during the twenties and thirties. One paper expressed universal opinion on the subject when it declared that 'combination and co-operation by and between West African traders and middlemen seem to us the only panacea for stemming the rapid current of declension and threatened extinction of West African traders'.[96] Dusé Mohammed Ali, however, who was by then an expert on the West African economy and on the methods of modern business, would have none of the wailing and heated debate about the monopoly of European firms and about the depression; self-help and organization, he said, must be the watchwords of the African.

The lack of unity among Nigerians is absolutely appalling. Here is a rich country hungering for collective effort to make its people independent and those who have the capacity to help in the needful organisation stand around whining about depression as though they possessed a monopoly in that objectionable adjunct to post-war civilization. . . . Obviously co-operative marketing is the real solution of the cocoa problem in Nigeria as well as in the Gold Coast.[97]

With the exception of the fairly good years 1934–5, there was no relief from the depression which began in 1929 and lasted until the outbreak of World War II. Surprisingly enough, there was no serious social or political unrest, although hundreds were unemployed in the towns, particularly the clerkly class who were always the first victims of retrenchment. It was during this period that the various Youth Movements made a determined bid to 'democratize' colonial politics by wresting political control from the petty-bourgeois nationalists of the early 1920s. It is important to emphasize that the vast majority of these impatient young men, most of them in their middle and late thirties, were neither revolutionaries nor trade unionists. Some, like Azikiwe, were merely rebelling against the

[95] *Gold Coast Independent* (29 Sept. 1923).
[96] *West African Mail and Trade Gazette* (28 Mar. 1925).
[97] *Comet* (21 Oct. 1933).

limited political concerns of the 'fathers' but had no attachment to the 'isms' they were bandying about, while others like Wallace-Johnson, a trade unionist who had studied in Moscow in 1931–2, attempted to take advantage of the depression by creating a new political force based on wage labourers and the increasing concentration of unemployed in the urban areas. There were radical protest groups like I. T. A. Wallace-Johnson's West African Youth League[98] and the Nigerian Youth Movement, as well as demonstrations and strikes in Freetown, Sierra Leone (1926 and 1931), and in Bathurst, Gambia (1929), but as long as these movements, particularly the youth movements, were not supported by the middle-class moderate leadership,[99] they merely flourished briefly, and even wrested political control of some urban councils from the old guard of City Fathers, as happened in Lagos, Accra, and Freetown in the 1930s, but never became national movements with a comprehensive programme. These movements encountered the open hostility of the old nationalist group; in Freetown, Creole nationalists of the Congress stamp like Bankole-Bright and Beoku-Betts made it clear that they would have none of Wallace-Johnson's new radicalism; in Accra, where Wallace-Johnson founded the Youth League before retiring to Freetown, the Youth Movement (led by Kojo Thomson and Azikiwe) supported the Mambii Party against older and more conservative nationalists like Dr. F. V. Nanka-Bruce; in Lagos, the pattern was similar; Azikiwe's *West African Pilot* backed the Nigerian Youth Movement, formed in 1938 and led by Dr. Akinola Maja, H. O. Davies, Ernest Ikoli, and Dr. Abayomi, against Herbert

[98] Wallace-Johnson's membership of so many political organizations and his constant movement across West Africa and between London and West Africa in the period 1935–8 make neat classification of his activities difficult. Sometimes the organizations overlap. In this chapter his attempt, in concert with other youth movements in West Africa to replace the Congress nationalists by capitalizing on the depression is briefly dealt with. Chapter VIII deals with a separate theme—Wallace-Johnson's role in the Ethiopian protest movement and in the anti-colonial politics of the International African Service Bureau. In both latter cases Wallace-Johnson's West African Youth League tended to operate as a 'front' to create or absorb other protest groups as occasion demanded.

[99] According to George Padmore, unemployment, taxation, and retrenchment had driven the unemployed in the towns into the hands of 'the petty-bourgeois, especially the "Left" leaders of the West African National Congress. . . . In this way the thousands of unemployed workers and agricultural labourers are being brought under the influence of petty-bourgeois nationalism. Every move on the part of the petty-bourgeoisie to-day is made in order to subordinate the growing proletarian mass movement to their own class interests' (*Communist International*, viii, no. 13 (1 July 1931): 'The Agrarian Crisis in British West Africa').

Macaulay's N.N.D.P. which had dominated Lagos politics since its foundation in 1923.[1]

The rivalry between the N.Y.M. and the N.N.D.P. is illustrated in a lengthy thirty-page electioneering speech by Dr. C. C. Adeniyi-Jones, President of the N.N.D.P., attacking the leadership of the N.Y.M. By 1938 the N.N.D.P. was on the defensive, having lost three seats to the new movement which had rudely challenged its supremacy in Lagos politics. It was further weakened when another dissatisfied splinter-group, the Young Democrats, led by Ayo Williams, detached themselves from it. Dr. Adeniyi-Jones, himself a Nigerian of Sierra Leone extraction, complained of the walk-outs staged by N.Y.M. members of the Lagos Town Council and of their 'policy of unwarrantable aggressiveness' during elections. To him, the method of agitation of the N.Y.M. resembled those of the Hitler Youth Movement, not the constitutional nationalism of the old days:

... Youth we are told is impetuous. . . . Bear constantly in mind that evolution is a gradual process, and that when people are too much in a hurry, chaos is more often the result than progress. . . . What do we see to-day? A hot-headed political party, with a tendency amongst the Executive of this new Organisation towards aggressive measures crying themselves hoarse in their frenzied parochialism of 'Nigeria for the Nigerians'.

The N.Y.M., he said, was opposing individuals who, like him, 'for years have been carrying the lamp of political progress as brightly as can be expected under conditions such as obtain in a dependency with Crown Colony Administration'.[2] Herbert Macaulay also fulminated, in typical style, against 'This mixed pickle group of Nigerian Youth and middle-aged men composed as it is of a medley of irresponsible political Tyros who have suddenly been stricken by the introsusception [sic] of crinkum-crankum ideas of modern European revolutionary politics', whose 'pretentious "endeavour to break down tribal prejudices" may be nothing short of a camouflage of the sinister object of mobilizing a united mass of the unsophisticated natives of the hinterland provinces, with whose support they might be able to achieve the goal of their political activities, namely:— "a complete taking-over of the Government of Nigeria into the hands of the indigenous people of our country" . . .'.[3] Mass politics

[1] See Tamuno, T. N., *Nigeria and Elective Representation*, pp. 51 ff.

[2] Election Speech by Dr. C. C. Adeniyi-Jones (n.d.), Macaulay MSS. iv. 15, pp. 15–19.

[3] *West African Pilot* (14 June 1938), p. 6.

with self-government as its goal was, in Macaulay's view, incompatible with politics as the leadership 'carrying the lamp of political progress' saw it.

In the Gold Coast, the Government's sedition laws and the opposition of the conservative nationalists compelled Wallace-Johnson to retreat to Freetown where he founded branches of the League in Freetown and Bo. In Accra, the League was regarded by the conservatives as a body of dangerous agitators and its organizing secretary Wallace-Johnson was singled out as an agitator who had no business in Gold Coast affairs. Azikiwe, however, thought differently, warning the conservative critics that 'unless there is an organisation which would create a feeling of oneness, professions of patriotism or nationalism are figments of the imagination. The conference idea . . . should be a dynamic process to the activities of the various delegates who should stand fast and support the ideals of this worthwhile organisation in the history of African nationalism.'[4]

Back in Sierra Leone, Wallace-Johnson's Youth League, with the *Sentinel* as its organ, agitated against labour conditions and the Education Ordinance and, like its counterpart in Nigeria, got involved in local politics, contesting and winning the November municipal elections in Freetown in 1938.[5] Azikiwe, who had followed the elections, echoed the growing dissatisfaction with the petty-bourgeois nationalists in the 1920s:

Most of those who are the self-professed leaders of the various sections of West Africa are, in reality, and with all due deference to them, worthy of one piece of job, that is, to commit *felo-de se*. In Sierra Leone one finds intelligent looking leaders pussy-footing with their hats in hands, presenting their petition to His Most Excellent Governor reminding His Most Excellent Majesty that Her Most Excellent Majesty regarded Sierra Leone as the Most Ancient and Loyal Colony of Uncle Toms. Is there any wonder that the youth of Sierra Leone are stifled and are made to be subservient to persons who have no pretentions whatsoever to leadership? . . . Renascent Africans . . . the era of ciphers and Uncle Toms is in transition. The days of hat-in-hand-me-too-boss political scavengers are numbered.[6]

    [4] *African Morning Post* (21 Mar. 1936), p. 4.
    [5] For details of this election, see the *West African Pilot*, 'Freetown Politics' (15 Nov. 1938).
    [6] ibid. (15 Nov. 1936), p. 4.

Colonial politics in West Africa, according to Azikiwe, was already in transition, and the old colonial, missionary-educated lawyer class was being challenged by the angry young men of the 1930s. It was, therefore, 'with the most excellent delight' that Wallace-Johnson in 1938 announced the 'welcomed and timely demise of the Society of City Fathers and Uncle Toms as represented in the fall of Brah-ism and the triumph of Youth at the Polling Stations of the City Council . . .'.[7] The electoral successes of the youth movements, however, as we have argued, failed to dislodge the conservative leadership and, in spite of chronic economic conditions, these movements never commanded a wide following. It is wrong to argue, therefore, as some writers have tended to do,[8] that a new and radical leadership emerged after the 1930s as a result of the failure of the moderates and conservatives of the 1920s. That they were dissatisfied with the old leadership is clear enough; but the notion that their approach to nationalist politics constituted a radical departure is not substantiated by the evidence. A closer look at the social and professional composition of the political leadership during this alleged change shows that from the 1920s of the Congress movement to the foundation of the United Gold Coast Convention in 1947, the leadership was still predominantly middle class and conservative.[9] And J. B. Danquah's views in *Self Help*, far from being revolutionary or socialistic, are characteristic of liberal nationalism of the period. They opposed liberal capitalism only in so far as it failed to accommodate the interests of their social class; analysis of its contradictions and the political capacity to resolve them were either beyond them or incompatible with their interests. They only wanted 'a share of the benefits' of monopoly capital.

In general, the discontent of the depression years found expression principally in a widely shared desire for greater economic co-operation among West Africans.[10] It became fashionable for every newspaper to deal with 'the economic problem' and to pontificate on the virtues of economic self-help and co-operation, and pieces of advice like: 'economic and industrial independence is a necessary step to our

[7] ibid. (22 Nov. 1938), p. 7.
[8] e.g. Hopkins, op. cit., p. 152.
[9] Garigue, op. cit., pp. 295-303; for Azikiwe's comments on the Congress leadership, see the *West African Pilot* (4 July 1938), p. 3.
[10] See Casely Hayford's speeches at the Second, Third, and Fourth Sessions of the N.C.B.W.A., reproduced in Magnus Sampson's *The West African Leadership* (Ilfracombe, 1949), pp. 75, 79-80, 89.

political freedom'[11] were commonplace. With this went the tendency among nationalists to lament the ruin or disappearance of the African merchant and trader. Very often this was ascribed to the monopolistic practices of the European firms. For example, one Gold Coast newspaper covering the Third Session of the N.C.B.W.A. in Bathurst alleged that the three British firms in Bathurst had 'squeezed out' nearly all the Gambian merchants. The same paper made this observation on nationalist politics and economic competition at the beginning of the Third Session of Congress

. . . it is possible to secure that balance between local conservations and modern economic aggression typified by restless governmental policy. If it is true that the policy of the Colonial Office with respect to British West Africa as a whole is one and the same; if business men are directing their energies into the same channels guided by the same considerations throughout West Africa, then it stands to reason that the peoples of British West Africa must also think together. And that this is the essential principle upon which the Congress movement is founded cannot be too often emphasised. . . . The economic development of British West Africa and the means by which the indigenes may come in for their proper substantial share of the benefits is one of the problems of West Africa to which practical minds must address themselves. Not all our political propaganda is going to help us much unless we can command a fair share of the wealth of our own country. That is a practical conclusion as clear as daylight . . . and we trust Congress will not fail to give attention to the matter.[12]

J. M. Stuart-Young, an 'old Coaster' and an Englishman who had witnessed the peaceful days before the arrival of the combine, made a similar observation in a circular addressed to political and commercial groups in Lagos when he complained in 1930 about 'the strangle-hold the Merger and BIG CONCERNS have on the River', and invited the West African Co-operative Producers Ltd. (formed by Winifried Tete-Ansa in Accra between 1925 and 1928)[13] to establish a branch at Onitsha:

I am *positive* that the moment an Agency was established here, and powers were offered for shipments by the Natives (instead of local sales at ruled prices of the Merger) there would be such a rallying to your standard as you would find more than gratifying. Today in the whole of

[11] *Vox Populi* (23 Apr. 1932).

[12] *Gold Coast Leader* (7 Nov. 1925): 'The Third Session of Congress'.

[13] For the significance of Tete-Ansa's West African Co-operative Producers Ltd. and other commercial organizations in West African nationalist politics in the inter-war period, see Hopkins, op. cit., pp. 133–52.

this Province [i.e. Onitsha] there is not ONE African shipper; whereas, in pre-war years, and war years, there were at least a dozen from Initsha, . . . I myself always averaged some 1,000 casks of oil and 13,000 bags (roughly a thousand tons) of kernels a year. Today I am nobody. Today all the Natives are held under the vice-like grip of the Merger, and other BIG firms, who are willing (in their own interests) to play the Merger Game.[14]

Stuart-Young also observed that between 1910 and 1919 'there were only FIVE European Concerns' and 'around a dozen HEALTHY and SOUND Native Traders, mainly Sierra Leoneans and Lagosians', but that 'since the Armistice (reaping what they have now sown) other "Merger Associated" firms have come here (Walkdens, Trading Assoc. of Nigeria, African and Eastern, Welsh's etc.)'. 'As to the African Community,' he concluded, 'not a SINGLE ONE HAS SHIPPED for years! They are all bound to sell locally—and it is from *THEM* that the firms buy the cask (wholesale). . . . I have tried to tell you the facts—now weigh them up, and save the River from becoming the Cemetery of the Native Trader, and the Garden of the Merger and the Merger's Fellow-Conspirators.'[15] A similar view was expressed by a leading Gambian merchant of considerable business ability and experience. This merchant, Henry M. Jones, had inherited his father's business and continued it until the sudden slump in 1920–1. Now he too was in the Congress movement, was 'in touch with all leading European political ideas', was closely following Macaulay's association with Tete-Ansa's Nigerian Mercantile Bank (which had succeeded the Industrial and Commercial Bank) and was interested in 'Finance, Commerce, and Politics'.[16]

In the cocoa industry too, discontent was expressed in the form of hold-ups and attempts to create African owned combines and co-operatives.[17] A. J. Ocansey, an Accra cocoa merchant who was

[14] Circular by J. M. Stuart-Young, Onitsha, to the West African Co-operative Producers Ltd., Lagos, 11 Mar. 1930: Macaulay Papers, iii. 9: 1930, General Correspondence.

[15] ibid.

[16] Henry M. Jones to Herbert Macaulay, 11 Aug. 1931: Macaulay Papers, iv. 35, pp. 14–15. It is regretted that the business papers of the late 'Pa' Jones (he died in 1965) were not available to the author when he was in Bathurst on research in 1966. Access to such papers may well reveal a complex network of relations between various West African merchants and political bodies in West Africa during the inter-war period. Until such papers are available, however, we shall have to depend on what can be gleaned from secondary sources.

[17] George Padmore, who was at the time closely following the 'revolutionary movement' in the colonies, wrote in 1931: 'This system of indirect business rela-

associated with Tete-Ansa's West African Co-operative Producers Ltd., had discussed the idea of a Cocoa Federation for the Gold Coast and Ashanti with Herbert Macaulay during the depression years. He had also discussed it with various Paramount chiefs, sub-chiefs, and cocoa farmers at Nsawam and had sent a copy of the resolutions passed at that meeting to Macaulay, urging him to show them 'to all whom the matter of unity in respect of the cocoa industry may concern', and to 'establish a similar movement in Nigeria, suggesting the name "The Nigerian Cocoa Federation" '. Ocansey added: 'I must again emphasise the fact that the movement has secured the approval of all, and at present, not a single bean of cocoa is being sold to any firm. The European firms are feeling the effect of resistance so much so [sic], that from the 21st instant to the time of my writing, the price of cocoa has risen from 10/6 to 15/- at Nsawam. . . . I feel that unless we stand up and fight for our rights, the end will find us in economic slavery.'[18] Ocansey's and John Ayew's Gold Coast and Ashanti Cocoa Federation was formed 'for the protection of the cocoa industry generally having reference particularly to control of the output of the crop and improvement of quality and price', but the hold-up, designed to force prices up, failed, and the cocoa farmers sought the assistance of a more realistic and imaginative businessman, Tete-Ansa, who advised them to form their own co-operative backed by their own banks.[19]

Winifried Tete-Ansa himself was one of the very few West African businessmen who was realistic enough to grasp the importance of co-operatives and banking in the struggle for economic reconstruction and in the struggle against the combines, within the imperial framework. To this end, he founded the West African Co-operative Producers (1925–8) to which we referred earlier, the Industrial and Commercial Bank Ltd. (1924), and the West African

---

tionship between the imperialists and the peasants of the interior has contributed to the creation of a class of West African petty-bourgeois traders, who have recently begun to organise co-operative market agencies, as well as a bank (the Industrial and Commercial Bank of West Africa) in order to compete with the foreign wholesale merchants who, they realise, are ruthlessly exploiting the peasantry through monopoly and pool purchasing. This represents the first open economic struggle on an organised scale, between the Native trading capitalists and the foreign imperialists : 'The Agrarian Crisis in British West Africa', p. 370.
   [18] A. J. Ocansey to Herbert Macaulay, 27 Oct. 1930; Macaulay Papers, iii. 9: 1930; General Correspondence.
   [19] Hopkins, op. cit., pp. 148–9.

American Corporation (1930).[20] The last-named body was incorporated in the State of Delaware, U.S.A., with an authorized capital of $1,000,000 composed of ten 7 per cent cumulative preference shares of $100 each (par value) and 100,000 ordinary shares of no par value. Among its officers were H. D. Van Sindern (President and Chairman of the Board of Directors), H. M. Daugherty (Vice-President), W. Tete-Ansa (Deputy Vice-President), J. B. Beaty (Secretary and Treasurer), and G. E. Biscaye. Like its predecessor, the Akim Trading Company (also incorporated in the U.S.A. by another Gold Coast businessman, Chief Alfred Sam in 1912), the West African American Corporation was conceived as a Pan-Negro commercial venture which would benefit the exploited groups on both sides of the Atlantic. Its office was at 19, West 44th Street, New York City, and it was 'understood that business in its shares is conducted among the Negro population in the Harlem Quarter of New York'.[21] It dealt mostly in cocoa, and its American representatives in Accra and Lagos, Mr. Daugherty and Mr. Macpherson, bought cocoa on a commission basis, i.e. on an instalment basis to the grower. It was estimated that the Corporation, which was affiliated to West African Producers Ltd., had a capital of $1,000,000 of which $70,000 had been sunk in West African interests, and that it was backed by the firm of Messrs. C. Tennant and Sons of London.[22] The Corporation was also inextricably connected with Tete-Ansa's other concerns and with banks in Britain. It was also connected with E. F. Small's Gambia Co-operative Marketing Association, with which we shall deal later. Small's co-operative in turn was connected with Messrs. C. Tennant & Co. Ltd., headed by Lord Glenconner, which the West African American Corporation described as 'our affiliate in Farmers Co-operative foreign offices'.[23] The Corporation, however, like all the enterprises Tete-Ansa had founded, came to grief: in fact, it did very little business and Tete-Ansa, despite his efforts, never became what the *African World* called him—'the commercial wizard of West Africa'.

[20] ibid., pp. 138 ff.

[21] Gambia Confidential, no. D.C.S. 15/31/24, 3/194, File no. 1466: G. A. S. Northcot, Colonial Secretary Accra, to the Hon. Colonial Secretary, Bathurst, 28 July 1931. Gambia Records Office.

[22] ibid., paras. 2 and 8, no. 1866/11, C. W. Duncan, Inspector-General of Police to the Chief Secretary to the Government, Lagos, 27 June 1931.

[23] H. M. Danquah and H. M. Daugherty to H. E. the Governor of the Gambia, 27 Apr. 1931, ibid. For an official account of Tete-Ansa's career and the West African American Corporation, see Gambia 3/194, File no. 1466. G.R.O.

Unlike Tete-Ansa, E. F. Small of the Gambia was one of the leading figures in the N.C.B.W.A., and throughout his political career remained a trade unionist and Pan-Africanist. He was the founder of the co-operative movement in the Gambia and was a prominent political figure in the 1930s and 1940s. He entered commercial politics and trade unionism via agitation and nationalist politics and, in spite of the administration's suspicion that he was a subversive and an agitator, by the time he died had laid the foundations of a trade union and co-operative movement in the Gambia. Significantly, it was during the depression years that he tried to start a local co-operative movement. He saw the co-operative marketing of groundnuts in Europe as an alternative to the ordinary method of selling groundnuts to the established local firms. The attitude of the administration, however, was not encouraging; for while it recognized the importance of the groundnut industry to the country, it felt (confusing Small's enterprise with 'politics') that it was 'not possible . . . to regulate in time of peace, such matters as the prices of products and the freight rate charged on ocean-going steamers', and that it would 'be impracticable . . . to assist any one section of the community at the expense of the others . . .'.[24]

With the European firms virtually monopolizing the market, and the administration negatively acting as economic umpire, any self-help movement '. . . to get the people of the Gambia mutually associated for the economical improvement of the Gambia'[25] was bound to be a frustrating business. Small was certain that if he succeeded in getting commercial firms in England to back him and put their buying agents in four or five buying stations in the Protectorate, he would successfully oppose the dominance of the Chamber of Commerce. For, as a contemporary of his reminds us, 'The Chamber of Commerce then was the mortal enemy of any other commercial branch in Gambia, whether by private persons or the organisation of the citizens.'[26] Small's co-operative movement, however, only began to bear fruit in the early 1950s, after a chequered career in the 1930s and 1940s: 'Mr. Small failed mainly because the Government was not prepared to give the necessary aid, and the Co-operative project had no finance, material, and adequate staff

[24] B. A. Finn, Acting Colonial Secretary, to E. F. Small, 18 June 1930, Gambia Co-operative Department, File no. R.C.S./EDU/12.
[25] ibid., Mr. Babou B. Kebbeh interviewed by students on co-operative course project 'Historical Research: Co-operation in Gambia', 1960.
[26] ibid.

to stand a strong opposition against the Chamber of Commerce.'[27] Yet, if there were any 'practical minds' (as the nationalist press used to describe those concerned about economic questions) among the Congress nationalists, E. F. Small was assuredly one of them.

The strategy of the petty-bourgeois nationalists did not change significantly, even during the depression of the mid- and late 1930s. Samuel Rohdie has carefully documented the political economy of the cocoa hold-ups of 1930–1 and 1937 and has analysed the gradual loosening of the alliance between the 'traditional merchant and farming interests, which were all essentially concerned with opportunity and advance within the political and economic framework of colonialism'[28] from the early 1930s to the cocoa hold-up of 1937 and during the war. By the late 1930s the alliance between the lawyer–merchant class, chiefs, and cocoa farmers was beginning to disintegrate, as chiefs began to support government cocoa control schemes exploiting them in their own interests. The depression of the mid-1930s, as we have noted, had already taken its toll of African businesses; urban unemployment soared as a result of retrenchment; there were strikes in most West African urban centres, as well as growing resentment of chiefly authority in the rural areas.[29] The important thing about the cocoa hold-ups in the Gold Coast is that although the issue was basically economic, like the economic issues of the Congress movement, it was often combined with agitation of a political nature, such as the agitation against the Provincial Councils, and the Waterworks and Sedition Bills.[30] The Congress agitation in the 1920s for fuller African representation on the legislative councils, liberalization of economic controls, and greater African participation in the colonial trading economy, was paralleled in the 1930s by nationalist agitation in the Gold Coast for similar reforms. In both cases, the nationalist petty-bourgeoisie viewed the combination of economic and political power as the most effective means to secure their interests in the colonial system.

Kofi S. Obu, a typical representative of this class, was both a businessman and a nationalist. A close friend and business associate of Kobina Sekyi, Obu, who died in September 1969 in Kumasi, was also a leading member of the Gold Coast Aborigines Rights

[27] ibid.
[28] Rohdie, op. cit., p. 396.
[29] ibid., p. 398.
[30] For details, see ibid., pp. 397–409.

Protection Society. Obu was in London negotiating various cocoa and mining deals during the mid- and late 1930s, and his correspondence with Sekyi illustrates quite clearly not only the political thinking of the West African petty bourgeoisie but also its weaknesses as a social class—its lack of capital and entrepreneurial skills, its disunity, the tendency of the lawyer class to dabble in business speculation, and the rapidly declining economic position of the African merchant and middleman. In March 1936 Obu wrote from London: 'If only I could get aid from *Africa* in the shape of cocoa [as a] starting point, I would bring finance home personally and conduct mass meetings on Economics, but purely for [a] Political end.'[31] Later in March he addressed yet another letter to Sekyi, stating more clearly the dilemma of the African merchant:

I am so anxious to start the *great* or big *business* for our people ... I hear native Companies are on the move again ... you see, Kobina, each year that Africans who do not know well European methods of carrying business this end start a good thing and they do not combine with the few Africans that know, ends in getting us back to where we were and possibly with debts! ... It is no use our doing small business. Its just debts and troubles! We must organise before we can get *help* here. It is so difficult *now* to obtain sufficient Capital for Cocoa this end. ... My idea is to combine all the African Companies. Take that which are good and others ignore. Their farmers can be absorbed. But we must start this year. ...[32]

Obu himself was ruined financially in the process of negotiating a 'New Deal' relating to mining concessions in the Gold Coast; he complained bitterly of his treatment by such financiers and share pushers as Paul Maurice Darwin, John Long, and Robert Ward Daw of Ward Daw and Company, London. 'Behold they were a bad lot,' he cried. This economic *cri de cœur* from one of the most energetic members of the West African merchant class merely serves to underline the entrepreneurial weakness of that class.

In his analysis of the West African nationalist leadership, Obu noted that the professional men who led it were dissipating their efforts by dabbling in cocoa and concessions, and generally diverting potential businessmen into politics. 'I still maintain,' he wrote, 'that it would be a good thing to divide things out there. One Political

[31] Kofi Sunkersette Obu to Kobina Sekyi, 3 Mar. 1936, Kobina Sekyi Papers, Acc. no. 385/64, Ghana National Archives, Cape Coast.
[32] Obu to Sekyi, 31 Mar. 1936, ibid.

section and the other pure commerce. We must also use diplomacy until we can acquire some money because we cannot do anything these days without it.'[33] Like a good businessman he was desperately trying to get the politicians to be 'realistic'; his argument was that politicians like Sekyi should encourage their business friends 'to start business on sound lines out there *first* and then when they have or can show *their own capital*, come here for more'. Otherwise, he said, in 'a few years more . . . the African trader will be totally eliminated in overseas business, except, perhaps, buying locally from the big white firms at home'. 'Every year,' he concluded, 'the net encircling Africans to that extent draws closer and unless some friends at home start something, there is no doubt that the lot of African businessmen will be more hard than now [or] in the days ahead.' Obu strongly advised the businessmen politicians to 'drop Politics entirely (for the present at least) and take to Commerce'; besides, he warned, his business friends in London were not prepared to 'entertain political machinations which is sapping the life of Gold Coast business' and destroying valuable contacts in the City.[34]

In common with the West African petty bourgeoisie, Obu saw no contradiction between a politico-economic combination of African against international monopoly capital and partnership with foreign capital. To quote him once more:

. . . unless we at home organized properly to take up this question of cocoa which is now the only chief product we have which assures our daily bread, believe me in less than 5 years from now, not a single African at home can be able to sell cocoa to any other firm but one HUGE GROUP composed of all the main Chocolate Manufacturers in the world!! It will be like the Oil and Palm kernel trade, which is now absolutely in the hands of the Lever Group and its powerful associated firms all over the Continent. . . . We must lay down the fundamentals and that being accomplished moral strength and success will result in attaining the power and influence which wealth will bring. We must have money to be able to combine first amongst ourselves in the Gold Coast and then our brethren in other parts of West Africa which will enable us to have our own commercial undertakings and Banking institutions.

It is time we become partners with Foreign Capitalists for the development of our country and not sellers only. And unless something effective is done by Africans themselves, the financial stricture on ambitious

[33] Obu to Sekyi, Acc. no. 383/64, 4 Aug. 1937, Sekyi Papers.
[34] Obu to Sekyi, Acc. no. 385/64, 2 Apr. 1937, Sekyi Papers.

Africans will be so tight (through the two Banks' actions at home) that they will continue to be poor miserable hard-working middle-men or clerks in their own country deriving no benefit from it, to which they are fully entitled, so as to qualify for the prominent part they will be called upon to play in the near future . . . but we have the Big Commercial Houses who will do their best to crush by opposition any worthy organisation that we start. . . . But we got to save Gold Coast Farmers and the hosts of clerks against themselves! [35]

Bourgeois nationalism, however, never succeeded in penetrating the core of the problem: it was the generation of West African nationalists, which, after 1945, was to make more explicit the fundamental opposition between alien rule and the political and economic interests of the colonized. The paradox is that they too, like the moderates before them, had to 'seek the political kingdom' first before settling the less glamorous but more important question of economic freedom. The 'dialectics of backwardness'[36] was such that the nationalist leaders had to start from the superstructure, not the economic basis, in order to lead the people from the kingdom of necessity into that of freedom. And the argument between younger nationalists like Danquah and Azikiwe and the Congress moderates was not so much a question as to whether economic development and co-operation were important in the struggle for political freedom. It was rather whether the nationalization of economic development (nationalism in one country, or 'Nigeria for the Nigerians' as the Nigerian Youth Movement put it) was preferable to Pan-African co-operation at that stage. The debate is still of seminal importance in the politics of the Third World.

We have attempted in this chapter to outline chronologically and as far as our material allows, a wide range of economic grievances which commercial and nationalist groups in British West Africa were convinced lay at the back of their discontent and their dissatisfaction with the old Crown Colony system of rule which, they felt, needed to be brought into line with representative institutions so as to take account of their interests. We have also endeavoured to give the 'feel' of nationalist thought and politics so far as this concerned post-war economic conditions, for no account of the

---

[35] Obu to Sekyi, 4 Aug. 1937, Acc. no. 383/64, Sekyi Papers; see also Obu's pamphlet, *Commerce in West Africa* (Cape Coast, 1938).

[36] For the significance of this phenomenon in the Leninist theory of modern nationalism in colonial countries, see chapter 12 of A. G. Meyer's brilliant *Leninism* (Cambridge, Mass., 1957), pp. 271–2.

economics of nationalism is complete without reference to the opinions of those who, rightly or wrongly, saw themselves as the representatives of the people. Historians are coming more and more to recognize the importance of the inter-war period in the economic and political history of British West Africa. For not only did this period witness the beginning of the 'economic revolution'; it also witnessed the emergence of a more articulate and coherent, albeit moderate and liberal nationalism, as well as the formative stages of the constitutional evolution that was to take place in Anglophone West Africa after 1945. The close of the period under review also saw the dissatisfaction of the younger generation of nationalists, notably I. T. A. Wallace-Johnson, Nnamdi Azikiwe, and the leaders of the Nigerian Youth Movement, with the old style of nationalist politics of the 1920s and with the failure of the moderates of the 1920s to involve themselves in grass-roots politics and realistic economic reconstruction.[37] Yet, the first clash with the Crown Colony system after 1919 could be seen as a turning-point in the evolution of representative institutions in British West Africa; in the process, the argument between the colonial administration and the West African petty-bourgeois nationalists became inextricably bound with racial, constitutional, and economic questions.[38] The clash resulted neither in a fundamental alteration of the colonial political system nor in any limitation of the economic dominance of the European interests, but in a constitutional compromise, the first of its kind in Britain's African colonies, which conceded some responsibility to this political leadership and, to a limited extent, accommodated their interests and allowed them some mobility within the existing system.

[37] Hopkins, op. cit., pp. 150–2.

[38] 'Economic nationalism is a wide term of somewhat vague meaning but, in this instance, it should be taken to denote an approach to economic problems influenced by racial and political sentiments. That is to say, the press rarely, if ever viewed economic affairs with the coldly dispassionate disinterest of the pure economist but frequently allowed nationalist feeling to mingle with and influence, not to say distort, economic judgement. This fact is, perhaps, best illustrated by reference to the attitude of the press to monopolistic enterprises such as combines, rings, cartels, mergers and pools. . . . To such commercial formations the entire press in British West Africa . . . was most violently opposed during the years of slump reaching a furious climax during the Gold Coast cocoa holdup of 1937. Rings and combines were frequently attacked as being economically unfair and dangerous but there was also the nationalist aspect of the attack which sought to represent such commercial constructions as the special instrument of white men expressly designed to crush and subdue the negro . . .' (Edmonds, W. D., 'The Newspaper Press in British West Africa 1918 to 1939').

The Pan-West African movement of the 1920s was indeed influenced partly by Wilsonian idealism and partly by the growth of Pan-Negro consciousness after the war, especially those of W. E. B. Du Bois and Marcus Garvey, and West African nationalism during this period can be interpreted in this Pan-African context.[39] Nevertheless, there is much truth in Professor Gellner's argument that 'Men do not in general become nationalists from sentiment or sentimentality, atavistic or not, well-based or myth-founded: they become nationalists through genuine, objective, practical necessity, however obscurely recognised.'[40] It is these 'obscurely recognised' social and economic factors in the nationalism of this period that we have attempted to outline and explain, and to show how Pan-African ideology and nationalist rhetoric were brought to bear on questions of the day.

[39] T. Kerstriens, for example, sees the N.C.B.W.A. as 'a kind of regional branch in Africa itself of the Pan-African movement . . .'. *The New Elite in Asia and Africa* (New York, 1966), p. 124.

[40] Gellner, Ernest, *Thought and Change* (London, 1964), p. 160, quoted in Minogue, K. R., *Nationalism*, p. 152.

# PART THREE

The salvation of the Africans in the world cannot but be most materially assisted by the Africans in America but must be controlled and directed from African Africa and [by] thoroughly African Africans.

KOBINA SEKYI: *The Parting of the Ways*


... it was this Fifth Pan-African Congress that provided the outlet for African nationalism and brought about the awakening of African political consciousness. It became in fact, a mass movement of Africa for the Africans.

KWAME NKRUMAH: *The Autobiography*

CHAPTER VI

# A Pan-African Pressure-Group in London:
## 1920—1921

BY October 1920 all the N.C.B.W.A. delegates had assembled in London for their important campaign in the metropolis; some of the delegates, like T. Hutton-Mills and H. M. Jones, who were business-men as well, had arrived earlier and were transacting various busi-nesses before the lobbying started. Perhaps it is because the dele-gation failed that historians have tended to pay little attention to the details of its elaborate and fascinating pressure-group campaign in London. In retrospect, however, the methods employed in 1920–1 did not differ substantially from those of the N.C.N.C. delegation in 1947,[1] though the objectives and the leadership of the latter delegation were different.

In December 1920 the London *Times* announced the existence of the London Committee of the N.C.B.W.A. with the caption: 'Home Rule for West Africa: Natives Appeal to the Colonial Office';[2] while the African Society favourably commented on its aims and problems, it could not help commenting on the black Edwardians of West Africa:

The inauguration of the British West African Congress tends to show that West Africa should no longer be regarded as composed of separate colonies . . . but as one self-conscious and articulate community. There are some respects in which the West African might with advantage, express his new sense of racial consciousness. At present, the educated West African is too ready to Europeanise himself. . . . It is a pity that West Africans have so freely adopted European names. If the Aga Khan writes to the *Times* on behalf of his fellow Muhammedans, the most ignorant Englishman who reads the letter realises from the signature that the Aga Khan pre-sumably knows what he is talking about. But those who read in the news-papers to-day that Mr. Casely Hayford and Mr. Hutton-Mills advocate

[1] *Pan Africa*, i, nos. 10–12 (Oct.–Dec. 1947), 1–14: 'We Glance Back—The N.C.N.C. in Perspective'.
[2] *The Times* (16 Dec. 1920), p. 11.

changes in the West African constitution . . . Englishmen show their
bad taste in their costume, and many West Africans show that they too,
have bad taste in copying it. . . . Now that West Africa is demanding a
voice in its own affairs, might it not with advantage devise a culture of its
own, a culture in which everything European eminently suited to West
Africa should be adopted, but in which top-hats, Paris frocks and English
patronymics should have no place?[3]

The gentlemen of the Congress, however, apparently unaware that
the legacy they inherited had now disqualified them, in the eyes of
the colonial administration, from assuming leadership of the masses,
resolutely went on with their campaign for elective representation.

As early as September 1920, H. M. Jones, one of the Gambian
delegates who was already in London, had submitted a rough plan
of action to an *ad hoc* committee of the London delegation—which
was awaiting the arrival of Casely Hayford. In it he optimistically
observed: 'In so far as I could judge the political atmosphere of
England at the present time, it does not appear to me that we shall
meet with any great opposition or difficulty in our demands; they
are moderate, and the atmosphere is full of concessions.'[4] Jones
thought that the propaganda of the London Committee was to be
confined to

a. Interviews with Editors of Responsible journals like *The Times,
Manchester Guardian, Daily Telegraph, Morning Post, West Africa,
African World.*

b. Insertion of articles in the above journals; such articles to be moderate
in tone and truthful in expression.

c. Interviews with members of the House of Lords and House of
Commons.

[3] *Journal of the African Society,* xx (1920–1), 142 ff. Oba Samuel Akinsanya,
the Odemo of Ishara, who was born in 1898 and was active in the Nigerian Youth
Movement of the 1930s, tells us they 'dressed like Edwardian dandies': 'How did
high society live then? Oh, it was a really posh society. It was the tail end of the
Victoria era and the sophisticated people were very smooth and elegant. Women
went out in long skirts; they wore big corsets and their busts were padded high
up; they wore elegant hats with feathers and they had gloves in their hands with
chic umbrellas. The men wore high collars and top coats. . . . Those were the
days. Then came the age of King Edward and people wore beard because King
Edward had a beard and a big moustache. . . . In those days there was no nation.
We were subject races; we were living under the influence of British Colonial
people and we adopted their forms and their fashions . . .' (*Spear* (Aug. 1966),
p. 9).

[4] Henry M. Jones to H. C. Bankole-Bright, Macaulay Papers, iv. 11 (2 Sept.
1920), 2–3.

d. Interviews with directors of leading Mercantile Houses and Banks, especially those operating along the Coast.

e. For the purposes of the Cause, all intercourse with the Press of the Labour Party should be eschewed as any intercourse or connection with them would prejudice our cases in the eyes of the moderate element among politicians of all parties.

f. . . . to interest the Editor of *John Bull* and get him to write a leader on the movement.[5]

The London Committee of the N.C.B.W.A., he said, should confine its lobbying to the plan he had outlined, and should attempt no more until their return home, and then prepare the ground for the next meeting of the N.C.B.W.A. Meanwhile, he had met Max Thompson, chairman of the African Progress Union in London, and had been told that the Union would co-operate with the London Committee. This was a moderate plan, and as we shall see, most of it was adopted by the London Committee, although their involvement with the Parliamentary Labour Party went beyond what they had intended.

Even before the delegation arrived in London, the African Progress Union[6] had been in touch with the Congress leaders. An amalgamation of the Union of African Peoples and the Society of Peoples of African Origin, the A.P.U., was founded in London in 1918. Its original membership included the Pan-Negro Dr. John Alcindor (a West Indian and a graduate of Edinburgh University) who became its president in 1921, T. J. Jackson of the *Lagos Weekly Record*, Dusé Mohammed Ali, Robert Broadhurst of the Gold Coast, Max Thompson, and E. F. Fredericks of British Guiana who also attended the 1919 and 1921 Pan-African Congresses and later became a member of the Georgetown Legislative Council and chairman of the Negro Progress Convention in Georgetown. The Anti-Slavery papers at Rhodes House Library contain the constitution of the A.P.U. It was largely a student body of peoples of African descent and saw itself as a Pan-Negro club linking Afro-Americans with other African peoples. It established some *rapport* with the Pan-African Congresses and, throughout, Broadhurst and Hutchinson helped to propagate the aims of the Pan-African Congress in West Africa. It also established contact with the N.C.B.W.A., both in its formative stages between 1918 and in 1919, and introduced its London delegation

[5] ibid.
[6] *Gold Coast Leader* (11–18 Jan. 1919), p. 3.

to members of the South African Native Congress delegation which included Sol Plaatje and Josiah Gumede. In January 1919 the *Gold Coast Leader* reported that the A.P.U. was in 'direct communication' with West African opinion, and that 'it is more than likely that the Union will be a medium of intercommunication too between American black folk and their brethren on the West Coast . . . it is desirable that our people should keep abreast of current political movements'. Robert Broadhurst, secretary of the A.P.U., wrote to Hutton-Mills in September 1920, asking him whether a meeting of the N.C.B.W.A. delegation due in London with the A.P.U. Committee could be arranged, as the A.P.U. Committee 'exists here for the sole purpose of advancing the welfare of Africans in every possible way'.[7] Bankole-Bright, now secretary of the Congress London Committee, replied that the delegates would be in London in September and would meet the A.P.U.[8] On the same date (9 September), the Anti-Slavery and Aborigines Protection Society wrote that they had seen Mr. E. F. Small, one of the Gambian delegates, who had told them that the Congress deputation had arrived in London. Meanwhile, the President of the Anti-Slavery Society would be informed of the delegation's wishes, as they the Congress had not yet decided to approach the Colonial Office directly.[9]

Between 9 and 16 September 1920 the London Committee of the N.C.B.W.A. had prepared the ground for their lobbying in London by approaching various influential newspapers and public figures. They wrote to the editor of the *African World* (Leo Weinthal) seeking an interview, which was fixed for the morning of 13 September;[10] it was also arranged to give the N.C.B.W.A. and its constitutional demands a write up in the following issue of the *African World*.[11] At the same time, the London Committee had approached *West Africa* for an interview and for publicity.[12]

Hutton-Mills proposed that a good method of proceeding would be to refrain from sending the Congress Resolutions to the Secretary of State for the Colonies, until the result of the interview with the Anti-Slavery Society had been reported to the full London Com-

---

[7] R. Broadhurst to T. Hutton-Mills, 23 Aug. 1920, Macaulay Papers, iv. 11.
[8] ibid., Broadhurst to Bankole-Bright, 9 Sept. 1920.
[9] ibid., Travers-Buxton to Bankole-Bright, 9 Sept. 1920.
[10] ibid., Leo Weinthal (editor) to Bankole-Bright, 10 Sept. 1920; Bankole-Bright 'to the various Delegates', 11 Oct. 1920.
[11] ibid., M. A. Thomas (assistant editor) to Bankole-Bright, 16 Sept. 1920.
[12] ibid., Albert Cartwright (editor) to Bankole-Bright, 10 Sept. 1920.

mittee, including Chief Oluwa.[13] Hutton-Mills, however, did not continue long in his organizing role; as he had to return to West Africa.[14]

Apart from reporting to the various territorial committees in West Africa, and replying to its critics in West Africa, the London Committee was also engaged in establishing contacts with influential people in England, and distributing nationalist literature to them. For example, they were invited to tea by Lady Scott, mother of McCallum Scott, parliamentary secretary for war, on 27 September. That meeting seems to have been arranged by J. H. Harris of the Anti-Slavery Society.[15] They also approached the League of Nations Union after they had been invited by its chairman Lord Robert Cecil, to meet the Executive Committee of the League 'with a view to discussing the bearing of the League of Nations on West African problems'.[16] Interviews were also sought with Elder Dempster, no doubt with a view to discussing racial discrimination on ships sailing to and from West Africa.[17] But its main points of contact were with the League of Nations Union, various M.P.s, including the Parliamentary Labour Party, and with journals like West Africa and the African World. Taking advantage of the rapport established with Liberal radicals like Professor Gilbert Murray through the League of Nations Union, the London Committee sent the Executive Committee of the latter body copies of the N.C.B.W.A. resolutions together with the introduction by the Mayor of Freetown, Samuel Barlatt. Bankole-Bright requested 'that the enclosed resolutions and copies of the Mayor's letter be distributed amongst the members of the Executive Committee of the League of Nations Union' prior to the interview arranged for 8 October.[18] The London Committee even applied for membership of the League of Nations Union, subscribing to its journal Headway. This was done 'on behalf of the

[13] ibid., Hutton-Mills to Bankole-Bright, 16 Sept. 1920.

[14] ibid., Hutton-Mills to Bankole-Bright, 28 Sept. 1920.

[15] ibid., Bankole-Bright to Lady Scott, 23 Sept. 1920.

[16] ibid., J. C. Garnett to Hon. Hutton-Mills, 30 Oct. 1920; Bankole-Bright to Dr. Maxwell Garnett, General Secretary of the League of Nations Union, 4 Oct. 1920.

[17] ibid., Liverpool Managing Director to Bankole-Bright, 2 Oct. 1920; Bright to Managing Director, 1 Oct. 1920; Bright 'to the various Delegates of the London Committee', 4 Oct. 1920.

[18] ibid., Bankole-Bright to Dr. Maxwell Garnett, 6 Oct. 1920; Bright to 'editors of various West African journals', 1 Nov. 1920; J. C. Garnett to Bright, 2 Nov. 1920; Bright to the editor of West Africa, 3 Nov. 1920.

National Congress of British West Africa', and as 'a practical demonstration of the feelings of British West Africa towards the aims and aspirations of the League'.[19] On 9 December the Executive Committee replied that they had 'unanimously resolved' to ask Major the Hon. Ormsby-Gore and Mr. J. H. Harris to accompany the N.C.B.W.A. delegation to Lord Milner of the Colonial Office, as representatives of the League of Nations Union, and asked to be informed as to when the London Committee proposed to see Lord Milner.[20]

Bankole-Bright then reported to the Congress Committee secretaries in West Africa that 'the propaganda work is now in full swing. Our committee is meeting everywhere with favourable reception.'[21] Summarizing their meetings with the Anti-Slavery Society, the League of Nations Union, and Elder Dempster lines, Bright cautioned that the pressure campaign was becoming expensive and called for more funds to defray 'the enormous propaganda expenses'.[22] He also referred to the inactivity of the Gold Coast Section, saying that one of its delegates, Van Hien, who was the treasurer of the London Committee, had attempted a walk-out as a protest against the inactivity of the Gold Coast Section. In conclusion he stated that trips to various parts of Britain and a meeting with the Labour Party were being arranged, and that 'It has now become imperative that the spaces in the various influential journals of Great Britain should be procured for the publication of our "Case" . . . in addition to other propaganda work, it is expected that this Delegation would have as its last action to proceed to the Colonial Office accompanied probably by influential elements from the League of Nations Union and other influential personages to have their final word.'[23]

The finances of the London Committee show the extensive scale of their lobbying. By October 1920 they had spent over £90 in printing 1,000 copies of the N.C.B.W.A. resolutions, 2,000 copies of the Petition, and 2,000 copies of the Memorandum; other expenses included the allowances of the delegates and the now famous group

[19] ibid., Bankole-Bright to Garnett, 9 Dec. 1920, p. 159a; Garnett to Bankole-Bright, 11 Dec. 1920.
[20] ibid., Garnett to Bankole-Bright, 9 Dec. 1920, p. 159c.
[21] ibid., Bankole-Bright 'To the Secretary of the various Colonies', 5 Oct. 1920.
[22] ibid.
[23] ibid., Bankole-Bright to Hutton-Mills, 23 Nov. 1920, p. 1920.

photographs of the delegation.[24] At one time the Nigerian delegates, who were actually in London on the Eleko case and only joined the N.C.B.W.A. delegation to save face, had to ask the Lagos Committee for £2,000, but apathy and dissension within the latter body made that impossible. In fact, Nigeria had no 'official' delegates in London. As Dr. R. A. Savage, secretary of the Lagos Committee explained:

My Committee desires to inform the London Committee that our local fund is not yet sufficiently strong to bear the expense of £2,000 you asked us to send to you; . . . we would prefer to make our own arrangements with Chief Oluwa and Mr. Shyngle who left Lagos for England for other purposes than the Congress and who, by kindly acting as our delegate in London, saved Nigeria and the National Congress of British West Africa from an awkward situation.[25]

Savage also referred to the problems of the Lagos Committee, particularly the opposition of Dr. Randle and Dr. Orisadipe Obasa of Ikeja: 'We in Lagos had a very uphill work in pushing in Nigeria the cause of the National Congress. Local political differences among different sections of our Community have hampered our work. . . .'[26] Savage, however, claimed that the Lagos Committee had held a 'mass meeting' at which 3,000 people were present, and was planning to send a deputation, consisting of three members of the Committee, to important towns outside Lagos 'for propaganda work . . . to make the aims and objects of the Congress matters of life and moment throughout the vast extent of Nigeria'.[27]

The London Committee replied, insisting on the financial obligations of the Lagos Committee, observing that Nigeria had so far not contributed to the Congress fund, and that its decision to pay Chief Oluwa and Shyngle separately violated the idea of 'one united fund'; in any case, they reasoned, the job of 'educating the British public' involved heavy expense. Bankole-Bright noted with approval that the Nigerian Committee was now better organized and that it was making serious efforts in the hinterland 'with the object of educating the masses', and expressed the hope that if the next session of the

[24] ibid., Electric Law Press Ltd. to Bankole-Bright, 26 Oct. 1920.
[25] ibid., Dr. R. A. Savage to Bankole-Bright, 26 Oct. 1920.
[26] ibid., Savage to Bankole-Bright, 30 Oct. 1920.
[27] ibid., the figure of 3,000 was probably exaggerated. Three hundred would be a more credible figure.

N.C.B.W.A. was held in Lagos instead of Freetown, as planned, they would be afforded the 'opportunity of sounding the tocsin of alarm to the recalcitrants at Lagos' (i.e. would put the fear of Congress into Dr. Randle and company). Bright also observed that the London Committee had been 'following with interest the political blunder of a section of the Lagos Community', and that it 'viewed with regret that at this particular time when the soul of a people should vibrate in accordance with the universal tune for the amelioration of the conditions of humanity, certain sections of your Community should demonstrate the spirit of political blindness to its own interest. The London Committee is, however, encouraged by the recent political upheaval at Lagos and is further encouraged to carry on its work regardless of what may be considered as an outside abused privilege [sic].'[28] In addition to these criticisms, the London Committee attempted to get individual Nigerians to form branches of the Congress throughout Northern Nigeria, and to distribute at least two hundred copies of Congress propaganda.[29]

Meanwhile H. Van Hien, one of the Gold Coast delegates, had been gallantly lending money to defray the expenses of the London Committee, but by November 1920 the bill had mounted to £666 4s. 7d.[30] Van Hien's balance had sunk to £8 13s. 10d., hardly enough to keep the West African lobby going; in November Bright was compelled to write to T. Hutton-Mills, the President, about 'the seriousness of the Committee's financial position'.[31]

Through J. H. Harris of the Anti-Slavery Society, the London Committee was introduced to such well-known public figures as

[28] ibid., Bankole-Bright to Dr. R. A. Savage, 23 Nov. 1920, p. 121.
[29] Macaulay Papers, iv. 12, p. 29, Casely Hayford and Bankole-Bright to W. Wallace-Lowell, Passenger 'S.S. Appam', 8 Jan. 1921.
[30] Macaulay Papers, iv. 11, H. Van Hien to Bankole-Bright, 5 Nov. 1920; Bank of Liverpool and Martins Ltd. to Van Hien, 5 Nov. 1920.
[31] ibid., Bankole-Bright to Hutton-Mills, 23 Nov. 1920. The pressure-group campaign cost the N.C.B.W.A. delegation £3,566 9s. 2d., £1,000 of which was a loan from the Colonial Bank; another £1,296 4s. 2d. was loaned by its treasurer H. Van Hien. 'Propaganda' (which included dinners, lunches, travel expenses, printing and distribution of literature, and the insertion of articles in various newspapers) accounted for over £860. Documents Belonging to Henry Van Hien Esq. Kobina Sekyi Papers. Acc. no. 585/64. The Colonial Office seems to have been concerned about the seriousness of the Committee's lobbying. G. M. L. Calder commented in the minutes: 'I should very much like to know where all the money for this expensive printing comes from!' (C.O. 554/63188, 28 Dec. 1920). Cape Coast Regional Archives, Ghana: Statement of Account in Connection with the London Delegation, National Congress of British West Africa.

Sir Harry Johnston[32] and Lord Henry Bentinck; it was arranged to
meet the latter at the House of Commons at the end of October;
but as some members of the delegation tended to indulge in elaborate
speeches, they were advised by Harris that such interviews should be
limited to conversation and not speeches as parliamentarians had
very little time for such speeches.[33] Lord Bentinck was sent the usual
propaganda stuff 'with the object of enlightening your Lordship on
the Petition'; and in view of 'the interest your Lordship has manifested in West African affairs', it was hoped that his Lordship would
identify himself with the demands of the Congress.[34]

Other distinguished public figures were also approached by the
delegation, including Premier David Lloyd George and Asquith.[35]
F. W. Dove, one of the Sierra Leone delegates, claimed that the
Parliamentary Under-Secretary for War, Mr. McCallum Scott, was
'a friend of mine' and that he had arranged with him to meet the
London Committee at the House of Commons on 19 November;
Dove believed that 'through this Minister we could almost at once
[get] in direct touch with Lord Milner', and that such an opportunity
should not be lost.[36] The interview never took place.[37]

At the same time the London Committee was also working through
the Parliamentary Labour Party in their attempt to lobby the Colonial
Office. H. M. Jones, one of the Gambian delegates, had advised
against any connection with the press of the Labour Party, as this, he
thought, would prejudice the case of the N.C.B.W.A. delegation; he
preferred a multilateral approach to 'the moderate element among
politicians of all parties'.[38] On 10 November they introduced them-

[32] ibid. J. H. Harris to Bright, 13 Oct. 1920; Harris to Bright, 28 Oct. 1920;
Harris to Sir Harry Johnston, 28 Oct. 1920.
[33] J. H. Harris to Bankole-Bright, 13 Oct. 1920; Bankole-Bright to Lord Henry
Cavendish Bentinck, M.P., 3 Nov. 1920.
[34] ibid., Bankole-Bright to Bentinck, 3 Nov. 1920, p. 90.
[35] ibid., Vivian Phillipps, secretary to Asquith, to Bankole-Bright, 2 Dec. 1920,
p. 142; Bankole-Bright to Phillipps, 4 Dec. 1920, p. 147; Lloyd George to
N.C.B.W.A., p. 101; F. L. Stevenson to Bankole-Bright, 11 Nov. 1920.
[36] ibid., F. W. Dove to Bankole-Bright, 19 Nov. 1920, p. 110; Dove to Casely
Hayford, 17 Nov. 1920, p. 107.
[37] ibid., Dove to Bankole-Bright, 19 Nov. 1920, p. 111.
[38] Macaulay Papers, iv. 11, p. 2; H. M. Jones to Bankole-Bright, 2 Sept. 1920.
W. R. Crocker also commented on the *rapport* between Labour and anti-colonial
groups in his *Self-Government for the Colonies* (London, 1949), p. 71. West African
newspapers, however, were generally inclined to view the Labour Party as the
party of the underdog, and as early as 1918 we find the *Gold Coast Leader* commenting on the Manifesto of the Labour Party: 'We notice the British Labour
Party in its latest manifesto includes in its planks self-determination for British

selves to the Parliamentary Labour Party and sent the usual copies of the N.C.B.W.A. resolutions and Memorandum. They also requested whether 'the party would find it convenient to receive them with the object of enlightening the "Labour Party" on the petition and "Case" '.[39] The Parliamentary Labour Party replied that its Policy Committee would be pleased to receive a small deputation from the London Congress Committee on 24 November in the Lobby of the House of Commons.[40] At the interview, the N.C.B.W.A. demands were discussed in full, and another interview was arranged for December to discuss the Petition and Memorandum in detail before approaching the Colonial Office.[41] The London Committee's meetings with the Labour Party did have some effect, as questions relating to some of their grievances were asked in the Commons,[42] and as the Secretary of State for the Colonies, Mr. Winston Churchill, was approached, though unsuccessfully, by Labour M.P.s.

Wider Pan-African affairs were considered when the A.P.U. organized a *conversazione* and invited the London Committee to meet all Africans resident in London.[43] Earlier in October Broadhurst had written to the London Committee drawing attention to the financial and other difficulties of the South African Bantu nationalist and Pan-Africanist, Mr. Sol Plaatje,[44] soliciting a donation for

subjects and peoples' (*Gold Coast Leader* (28 Dec. 1918)). The same newspaper declared in 1924: 'The phenomenon that is at present arresting attention throughout Christendom is the ascent into power in the British Constitution of the LABOUR PARTY . . . What are the prospects of British West Africa under a Labour Government? . . . More discriminating than either Conservatives or Liberals. And for that reason we may fairly expect a certain degree of sympathy with British West African aspirations in their march to nationhood in the British Commonwealth of Nations' (ibid. (2 Feb. 1924)). It is significant that Casely Hayford, a year before his death, addressed a nationalist tract as an appeal to the Labour Party entitled *The Disabilities of Black Folk and their Treatment with an Appeal to the Labour Party* (London, 1929) Colonial (now Commonwealth) Office Library. *West African Pamphlets No. 160.*

[39] Macaulay Papers, iv. 11, p. 98, Bankole-Bright to The Rt. Hon. William Adamson, M.P., 10 Nov. 1920.

[40] ibid., p. 106, H. S. Lindsay, Secretary to the Parliamentary Labour Party Policy Committee, to Bankole-Bright, 16 Nov. 1920; Bankole-Bright to Lindsay, 22 Nov. 1920; Lindsay to Bankole-Bright, 23 Nov. 1920, p. 123.

[41] ibid., p. 177, Bankole-Bright to Lindsay, 23 Dec. 1920.

[42] H.C. Debates, 143 (30 June 1921), 2333–4, para. 57.

[43] ibid., R. Broadhurst to Bankole-Bright, 2 Dec. 1920, p. 139. Bankole-Bright to Broadhurst, 1 Dec. 1920; Broadhurst to Bankole-Bright, 13 Dec. 1920, p. 161. Broadhurst to Bankole-Bright, 29 Dec. 1920, p. 182.

[44] Solomon Tshedkiso Plaatje was a member of the unsuccessful South African Native Congress delegation which came to London in 1920 to protest against the

Plaatje's efforts to make the voice of the black South Africans heard in the imperial metropolis. He felt that 'if the Delegates would grant an interview to Mr. Plaatje he would willingly give an exposé of the case and what opposition he has experienced both in South Africa and recently in London in advancing the Cause of Africans'.[45] The all-Africa *conversazione* was held on New Year's Day 1920, attended by members of the South African National Native Congress delegation in London. One of them, Josiah Gumede, who later attended the Brussels Conference of the League Against Imperialism in 1927, later wrote to the London Committee, seeking an interview with them before leaving for South Africa.[46] Gumede had also established contact with Herbert Macaulay, who was then Chief Oluwa's secretary, and had sent him literature on the Bantu question in South Africa and Southern Rhodesia, together with various newspaper cuttings on race relations in South Africa.[47] That Macaulay was highly thought of in nationalist circles outside Nigeria is illustrated by a letter written to him from Kroonstad, South Africa, marked 'Very Urgent', in which the author offered to subscribe to Macaulay's *Lagos Daily News* and concluded, 'Today the Negro man has got to be in touch with his Negro brother man from distant countries, that's why today we are doubly anxious to get your papers, so as to exchange views with our brothers in far countries.'[48]

The London Committee opened the new year with a determined effort to carry the campaign for elective representation into the Colonial Office itself. They got in touch with the League of Nations Union and requested that Lord Robert Cecil accompany them to the Colonial Office. Several (about 100) copies of the proceedings of their meeting with the Union were distributed to speakers and members of the Union; another 25 copies were sent to the Anti-Slavery

---

1913 South African Lands Bill. He was known for his opposition to Tengo Jabavu's conciliatory and co-operationist policy towards South African liberals, and participated in various Pan-African gatherings in Europe and America between 1921 and 1927. He was also the author of *Native Life in South Africa* (1916), *Some of the Legal disabilities suffered by the native population of the Union of South Africa, and imperial responsibility* (1913?), and *Sechuana proverbs with literal translations and their European equivalents.*

[45] ibid., R. Broadhurst to Bankole-Bright, 6 Oct. 1920, p. 42.
[46] Macaulay Papers, iv. 12, 18, J. T. Gumede to Bankole-Bright, 6 Jan. 1921.
[47] Macaulay Papers, iii. 2, 23: General Correspondence: 1918–23, J. T. Gumede to Herbert Macaulay, 16 Nov. 1920.
[48] Macaulay Papers, iii. 9: General Correspondence: 1930, R. A. M. Dumah to Macaulay, 2 Dec. 1930.

Society.[49] Literature and circulars were sent to Sir Thomas Hitching-Brooke, Sir Harry Johnston, Sir Sydney Olivier, the Rt. Hon. David Lloyd George, the Rt. Hon. H. H. Asquith, Albert Cartwright (the editor of *West Africa*), the editor of the *African World*, the editor of the *Africa and Orient Review*, the Earl of Mayo, Lord Henry Cavendish Bentinck, M.P., Lord Emmott, and Lady Scott. Hitching-Brooke replied that he was interested in the affairs of the N.C.B.W.A. and expressed the hope that the Congress proposals would be 'sympathetically received'.[50] The Parliamentary Labour Party also replied, promising to 'use its influence' if the Congress London Committee found it difficult to secure an interview with the Colonial Office.[51] Bright then informed them that the London Committee had now decided to interview the Colonial Office and that influential representatives from the League of Nations Union would be accompanying them; the Committee, however, had tried 'to have representatives from the different sections of the House of Commons to accompany it', and had suggested Mr. W. M. Adamson of the Parliamentary Labour Party and another Labour M.P.[52] McCallum Scott, Under-Secretary for War, and Leo Weinthall, editor of the *African World*, all of whom were asked to give their 'moral support' to the Congress movement and to accompany the Congress delegation to the Colonial Office, but were unable to do so because of other public engagements.[53]

The London Committee then wrote to the Rt. Hon. H. H. Asquith, and regretted that an interview with him had not been possible, reminding him that he had taken some interest in West African politics as early as 1898:

... Our Committee hopes you have not lost interest in the 'Case' of West Africa, an interest which was manifested by you in the fact that you prepared the 'Case' for the Gold Coast in its demand for the franchise in the year 1898 ... the request for an interview with you is a mandate from united West Africa. ... It is the wish of this Delegation to interview

[49] Macaulay Papers, iv. 12, p. 5: Bankole-Bright to Garnett, 3 Jan. 1921; iv. 12, p. 4: Bankole-Bright to Harris, 3 Jan. 1921.

[50] ibid., Hitching-Brooke to Bankole-Bright, 4 Jan. 1921, p. 12.

[51] ibid., Lindsay to Bankole-Bright, 3 Jan. 1921, p. 8.

[52] ibid., Bankole-Bright to the Secretary to the Labour Party, House of Commons, 6 Jan. 1921, p. 19.

[53] ibid., Bankole-Bright to McCallum Scott, Leo Weinthal, and Leslie Scott, 6 Jan. 1920, p. 20. M. A. Thomson, *African World*, to Bankole-Bright, 7 Jan. 1921, p. 25. McCallum Scott to Bankole-Bright, 8 Jan. 1921. Leslie Scott was the author of *Struggle for Native Rights in Rhodesia* (1918?).

the Colonial Office shortly but . . . its propaganda work will not be complete without seeing you prior to our interview with the Colonial Office.[54]

Congress literature was also sent to the Foreign Secretary Lord Curzon, the Rt. Hon. Winston Churchill who had succeeded Lord Milner at the Colonial Office, the Hon. E. S. Montagu, the Rt. Hon. Austen Chamberlain, Dr. Addison the Minister of Health, and the Rt. Hon. Edward Short the Home Secretary, soliciting their 'careful and serious attention'.[55]

As far as publicity was concerned, the Committee had useful allies in *West Africa*, the *Morning Post*, the *Africa and Orient Review*, and the *African World*. *West Africa*, however, was particularly useful to them as its editor, Albert Cartwright, was sympathetic to the political programme of the N.C.B.W.A.[56] Cartwright's journal, however, took a rather moderate line in its interpretation of the elective principle, particularly after Sir Hugh Clifford's devastating attack on the Congress's pretensions to leadership of the West African masses.[57] Because of its ambivalence, *West Africa* soon fell foul of the London Committee which also accused it of publishing what was understood to have been a private conversation between Bankole-Bright, the secretary to the London Committee, and Albert Cartwright, and of publishing the contents of a letter written by Casely Hayford to Sir William Geary.[58]

In spite of this misunderstanding, relations between *West Africa* and the West African nationalists remained cordial and Cartwright continued to take interest in the affairs of the Congress movement. In 1922, in response to a letter from S. R. Wood, Secretary-General of the N.C.B.W.A., Cartwright counselled:

[54] ibid., Bankole-Bright to the Rt. Hon. H. H. Asquith, M.P., 8 Jan. 1921.
[55] ibid., Bankole-Bright to Earl Curzon, Winston Churchill, E. S. Montagu, Austen Chamberlain, Dr. Addison, Edward Short, 8 Jan. 1921.
[56] *West Africa* was established in London in 1917, mainly as an organ of West African commercial interests: 'In those days the journal was directed at Europeans. Because of its attitudes, however, it soon became popular with members of the African élite . . .'; Chief Awolowo wrote of the first editor, Mr. Albert Cartwright, that he was a 'genuine believer in and fighter for accelerated political advancement for the Africans. Mr. Cartwright commended the aims of the first West African National Congress to British firms in the early twenties' (*West Africa*, no. 2570 (3 Sept. 1966)). See also the Fiftieth Anniversary issue of *West Africa* which touches briefly on Cartwright's relations with Lord Milner (*West Africa*, no. 2592 (Feb. 1967), p. 153).
[57] Kimble, David, *A Political History of Ghana*, p. 388.
[58] Macaulay Papers, iv. 12, Casely Hayford to Cartwright, 17 Jan. 1921.

. . . in my humble judgment, the greatest *immediate* work with which the Congress can occupy itself is the work of securing the principle of the elective franchise in the four colonies, my strong feeling being that if this is brought about, all other reforms will, little by little, and as the countries develop, be advocated and gradually brought into being . . . if the Congress concentrated upon broad principles such as that of the elective franchise, it would do a good day's work for British West Africa and the British-African connection.[59]

It was this 'principle of the elective franchise' that was already in 1921 engaging the attention of Sir Hugh Clifford, one of the shrewdest and most enigmatic Governors in the colonial empire—and one of the most disliked by nationalists in Ceylon and West Africa. It now remains to be seen whether it was the N.C.B.W.A. or its arch-opponent, Sir Hugh, who did 'a good day's work' in bringing elective representation to West Africa.

1. *'Good Government'* v. *'Liberty of the Subject'*

*The N.C.B.W.A.* v. *The Colonial Office: 1920–1*

ACTIVE official opposition to the N.C.B.W.A. did not begin until its delegation was in London. There can be no doubt that the Congress, by bypassing the Governors and appealing to His Majesty in Council, irritated the progressive-conservative (or conservative-progressive?) Guggisberg of the Gold Coast and Wilkinson of Sierra Leone, and enraged the aristocratic Sir Hugh Clifford of Nigeria, who, since his Malay days, had claimed that he really 'understood the native'. There is much truth, however, in W. E. G. Sekyi's contention that the neutralization of the N.C.B.W.A. delegation was 'an act of official diplomacy'.[60] In fairness, however, it must be stated that the delega-

---

[59] Albert Cartwright, editor of *West Africa*, to S. R. Wood, Secretary of the N.C.B.W.A., Gambia 221/1922, File no. 2/507, 17 Oct. 1922. G.R.O. Cartwright had also given some journalistic assistance to Herbert Macaulay's prosecution of the Eleko case; see Thomas, I.B., *A Life History of Herbert Macaulay* (3rd ed., Lagos, 1947), pp. ii–iii.

[60] 'The defeat of the Congress Petition was an act of official diplomacy. This act of official diplomacy was rendered successful or effective by the weight which the rivalry between the two legal advisers of the Gold Coast Aborigines Rights Protection Society made it possible for the Executive of the latter Society to lend to the claim of the Omanhene of Akyem Abuaka to oppose the Congress aims in the name of the principal national authorities on the Gold Coast . . .' (Sekyi, W. E. G., 'On Some Recent Movements in West Africa: A Study of White Methods of Repression', *Gold Coast Times* (23 May 1931), pp. 7–8).

tion erred tactically in appealing direct to Caesar and in the drawing up of its Petition which became an uneasy combination of idealism and practical politics, of the trivial and the important. These weaknesses made it an easy target both to the mandarins at the Colonial Office and to the gubernatorial thunderbolts from West Africa.

On 23 October Governor Guggisberg cabled the Colonial Office, repudiating the claims of the N.C.B.W.A.; in particular, he deprecated the 'Government of Gold Coast Colony being short circuited by delegates going direct Colonial Office' and recommended to Lord Milner that:

. . . if your Lordship receives [these] delegates, utmost caution desirable and that H.M.G. should not commit itself in any way beyond promising to forward any memorial to me for considered recommendations after consulting with representatives of the various communities of the Gold Coast. . . . This telegram is intended to forearm S. of S. and Under S. of S. for the Colonies with reference to my conversation with them in case interview is asked for.[61]

Guggisberg was assured that Milner would 'certainly not promise any constitutional changes without consulting . . .' him.[62]

On 25 November 1920 Sir Hugh Clifford followed Guggisberg with an almost identical telegram against the N.C.B.W.A.; the only difference was that Sir Hugh's prose was more elegant:

With reference to petition to His Majesty the King in Council from so-called 'National Congress of British West Africa' copies of which have been forwarded to me. . . . I regard it as important that it should be known that their self-appointed body is in no way representative of Nigeria, that is, and all its ways and works, have been formally repudiated by a number of Lagosians who stand for the best educated elements of African opinion in the more Europeanised areas near the coast; that neither of the *Soi-Disant* Nigerian Delegates at present in London has any personal knowledge of more than insignificant portions of Nigeria, or of more than a mere numerical fraction of the various native states and tribal divisions of which Nigeria is composed; that the published programme of the Conference, if it were possible of realisation, which it

[61] C.O. 554/46/52395, 23 Oct. 1920: 'Paraphrase of a telegram from Governor, Gold Coast, received at the Colonial Office on the 23rd October at 4.30 p.m.' The full text of the telegram is contained in this dispatch. See also C.O. 555/IND:1924, dispatch no. 52395, 25 Oct. 1920. Contrary to Martin Wight (*The Gold Coast Legislative Council*, p. 27) 'several Gold Coast chiefs and members of the Aborigines Society' did *not* cable to the Colonial Office denouncing the N.C.B.W.A. That was done by Guggisberg, Nana Sir Ofori Atta, and a few chiefs from Nana Ofori Atta's region, Western Province.
[62] Lord Milner, minute to dispatch no. 52395, C.O. 554/46, 26 Oct. 1920.

today is not, would be subversive of all the native Governments and of the indigenous political and social institutions by the agency of which Nigerian kingdoms and tribal areas are ruled, would cause anarchy, wholesale discontent and probably sporadic insurrections in many parts of Nigeria, and would deal a death blow to genuine local national native self Government. My Government therefore regards the doings of these 'Nigerian Delegates' as diametrically opposed to the interests of the African population of Nigeria, and the delegates themselves totally unrepresentative of them.[63]

Sir Herbert Read at the Colonial Office agreed with Sir Hugh; he thought J. Egerton Shyngle was a non-Nigerian, and was very harsh with 'this precious pair of rascals', i.e. 'that ridiculous petty chief Oluwa who is masquerading as a Nigerian potentate with his ex-convict Secretary Mr. Macaulay . . .'. It was decided to send the Congress a modified version of Sir Hugh's telegram.[64]

At the end of October, just before Clifford dispatched his telegram, the London Committee of the N.C.B.W.A. submitted the Petition to the Colonial Office, requesting that it be laid before His Majesty the King Emperor in Council. From that moment the Colonial Office assumed an attitude which can only be described as hostile and contemptuous—and in some cases petty. They referred to them as 'Herbert Macaulay and his gang', and when in November the Committee applied for permission to lay a wreath on behalf of West Africa at the foot of the Cenotaph on Armistice Day, certain officials at the Colonial Office saw their request as a move to score more publicity, and accordingly suggested that it would 'not be a bad thing to take the wind out of their sails by telegraphing to Gold Coast and Nigeria suggesting they should instruct Crown Agents to lay a wreath on their behalf'. Eventually it was decided to allow them to lay wreaths—'after the ceremony'.[65]

How did the Colonial Office view the N.C.B.W.A. Petition? In the first place, it was wrongly assumed that the Congress delegation was asking for self-government.[66] They rightly criticized the

[63] Dispatch no. 5890; C.O. 553/46, 25 Nov. 1920. At least one commentator has attributed Sir Hugh's 'urge to express himself in words' to the literary influence of his grandfather, Joseph Anstice, a professor of classical literature at King's College, London, and to the literary interests of his mother, Josephine, who contributed regularly to periodicals edited by Charles Dickens. Roff, William R., ed., *Stories by Sir Hugh Clifford* (London, 1966), p. viii.
[64] Dispatch no. 5890; C.O. 553/46, 25 Nov. 1920.
[65] Minute to C.O. 554/46/54091, 3 Nov. 1920.
[66] Minute to C.O. 554/46/53561, 16 Nov. 1920 by Clarsson, Calder, and Ellis.

petitioners for mixing up the affairs of all the West African colonies in 'rather a haphazard manner' and for failing to differentiate between the circumstances in one colony and another.[67] In their view, the very names of the petitioners showed that the Congress represented no one 'except the "intellectual" natives of the barrister and trader class'. As for the London Committee, which claimed it represented West African opinion, its position was rather anomalous, and the Colonial Office was advised not to 'go any distance towards recognising the existence of the London Committee'.[68] More specifically, the Colonial Office rejected the Congress's view (Para. 14 of the Petition) that nominated members of the Legislative Council did not represent the people: 'There can be little doubt that a nominated man will provide better representation of the views of the people than any kind of election can produce. The people in West Africa are, as General Guggisberg says, not ripe for representative institutions, and it would be a very cruel kindness to any West African colony to grant any such constitution.'[69]

The demand for the reconstruction of the Legislative Councils, it was thought, stemmed mainly from objections to the Palm Kernels Export Duty Ordinance, criticism of which was mainly confined to the Gold Coast. In any case, they reasoned, any reconstruction of the Legislative Councils, by which half the members were elected and the Council was vested with the power of imposing taxes, 'would

[67] ibid.
[68] ibid.; Calder also agreed that 'The London Committee has no "locus standi" at all, especially considering its totally unrepresentative nature', and added with a Machiavellian touch, 'but we can hardly turn it down entirely on that ground. We can leave it to the Governors to demolish, the absolute omission of any mention of the native courts in Nigeria is the sort of point we can count on Sir H. Clifford to point out.' Ibid., minute to, 12 Nov. 1920. J. A. Calder counselled: 'As regards recognising the London Committee I think it is purely a matter of policy, and that our line should be that we do not wish to give these people any needless cause for offence. The London Committee is probably just as capable of representing the views of these people as the Committee appointed with Headquarters at Sekondi to continue the work of the Accra National Conference.' Ibid., minute to, 19 Nov. 1920. Yet another official (probably Colonel Amery) rudely commented on 19 Nov. 1920: 'This is emphatically a case of the Ten Tutors of Tooley Point—who, it will be recollected, sent in a petition beginning: "We the people of England" etc.—. . . . In Sierra Leone at any rate the last native . . . is the Creole, and if our protection were withdrawn the chief question would be with what particular sauce Messers Barlatt, Dove etc. should be eaten. . . .' It is not surprising that this view was not entertained by the Secretary of State for Colonies.
[69] ibid., minute to, 16 Nov. 1920.

mean the abandonment of financial control in the British West African colonies' and would be 'disastrous'. The Congress's criticism of the Empire Resources Development Committee was dismissed as a 'very dead horse'; as for a West African Appeal Court, the Colonial Office thought that in spite of the Congress's proposal, and the recent proposal for such reforms by Chief Justice Sir G. Purcell to the Governor of Sierra Leone, no useful purpose could be served by its creation.[70] The demand for municipal councils was not favourably received either; it was pointed out that they had not been a success in Freetown, Accra, and Sekondi.[71]

J. A. Calder made perhaps the most succinct and balanced assessment of the Government's attitude towards the N.C.B.W.A. He recommended:

It is only by referring to the Governors for observations that we can decide on what points, if any, it is possible to meet their views. Even if one were in sympathy with their aims, it is impossible to deny that none of our West African Colonies are ripe for an elective franchise or an unofficial majority in the Legislative Council while the legal reforms suggested are designed almost solely to benefit the native barrister, not to further the cause of justice or to protect the aboriginal native. . . .

The petition does not lie to the King in Council and we might refer it back on that ground, but on the whole I think it should be referred to H.M. and that it is sufficiently important to merit a formal submission by the S. of S. The submission should be generally to the effect that the S. of S. is unable to advise H.M. that the time is yet come for the introduction into any of the British West African Colonies and Protectorates of the principles of election to the Legislative Councils or of unofficial majorities on these Councils; that as regards the legal changes, such as a new constitution for the West African Appeal Court, the repeal of certain ordinances and the admission of Counsel in all cases, he is unable to advise that the changes suggested would improve the administration of justice or be in the interests of the great bulk of the population; and that as regards the many other points raised in the petition . . . the S. of S. advises that he be authorized to consult the Governors and determine regarding each particular point what action, if any, is possible and desirable.[72]

[70] ibid.
[71] Sir H. J. Read commented: 'The question of extending the functions of town councils in the Gold Coast is engaging General Guggisberg's attention, but I do not think that Municipal Government by natives of West Africa can ever be anything of a success for some time to come' (ibid.).
[72] ibid., minute to, by J. A. Calder, 19 Nov. 1920.

Calder's minute was to form, almost verbatim, Lord Milner's reply to the N.C.B.W.A. respecting elective representation.[73] It is worth noting, however, that whereas Calder, Ellis, and Clarkson generally took the no-change line, Sir H. J. Read was usually open to alternative arguments, as the correspondence with Sir Hugh Clifford regarding elective representation was to show.

While the Colonial Office was settling the fate of the N.C.B.W.A. delegation, the West African Governors, particularly Guggisberg, were doing their utmost to discredit the N.C.B.W.A. Only Governor Wilkinson of Sierra Leone could be said to have been sympathetic to the Congress movement, although he too disapproved of the way its leaders selected themselves. On 2 January 1921 Guggisberg cabled the Colonial Office explaining that Nana Ofori Atta, paramount Chief of Akyem Abuakwa, had vigorously criticized the N.C.B.W.A. at a meeting of the Legislative Council on 30 December. Guggisberg also reported that Amonu, paramount Chief of Anomabu, Dr. Quartey Papafio, and E. J. P. Brown had made similar criticisms and had denounced the Congress for bypassing the Governors in spite of the promises of Clifford and Guggisberg, as early as 1918 and 1919, to look further into the matter of legislative reforms.[74] On the basis of Ofori Atta's speech, Guggisberg concluded, with some exaggeration: 'My personal conclusion is that whole tone, considering carefully speeches of four African members, shows that vast majority of Gold Coast people, probably 99% bitterly resent claims of few self-selected individuals to represent a country in which the elective system is so strong a feature of the constitution of tribal rule, which is certainly one of the finest types of democratic Government extant.'[75] Guggisberg requested that the telegram be laid before the King, to show His Majesty the true feeling of the people of the Gold Coast. He also strongly urged that a copy should be sent to the League of Nations Union 'whose personal interview with Delegates not accredited by Gold Coast on subject which does not form part of League's duties has produced mischievous effect',[76] and that a summary of the telegram be published in the press.

As a result of Guggisberg's telegram, Calder thought that His Majesty should be advised to authorize the Secretary of State for the

[73] ibid., minute to, 23 Dec. 1920: 'The S. of S. agrees to action proposed—i.e. by Mr. Calder. . . .'
[74] Guggisberg, telegram of 2 Jan. 1921, C.O. 554/50/233.
[75] ibid.
[76] ibid.

Colonies to inform the London Committee of the N.C.B.W.A. that he would not consider their petition unless it was submitted through the governments concerned.[77] Calder's new procedure, influenced by Guggisberg's reporting of Ofori Atta's speech, however, was later modified and his minute of 19 November 1920 (C.O. 53561/20) preferred. To insist on sending the Congress petition through the Governor because the delegates were unrepresentative seemed rather illogical. The most they could do was to send the London Committee a 'fitting reply' to their petition.

On 8 January, Lord Milner advised His Majesty along the lines suggested by J. A. Calder:

... Your Majesty will observe that the claim of this Congress to represent native opinion in West Africa is expressly repudiated by those best qualified to speak on their behalf, and that the policy advocated by the Congress is regarded by them as inimical to native interests.

Lord Milner is unable to advise Your Majesty that the time has yet come for the introduction into any of the West African Colonies and Protectorates of the principles of election to the Legislative Councils and of unofficial majorities on those Councils; nor does he consider that the legal changes suggested would improve the administration of justice and be in the interest of the great bulk of the native populations. He advises that he be authorised to reply to the petitioners accordingly.[78]

Three days after this dispatch was sent, the London Committee asked for an interview with Lord Milner; their delegation was to be accompanied by Professor Gilbert Murray of the League of Nations Union, the Hon. Major Ormsby-Gore, M.P. (also of the League of Nations Union), Charles Roberts former Under-Secretary of State for India, the President of the Anti-Slavery Society, and two other committee members of the Society, McCallum Scott (Liberal Coalition M.P.), two Labour M.P.s, and Mr. J. H. Batty and Major-General Grey, who were connected with West African commerce.[79] The request for an interview was turned down.[80] The London Com-

[77] ibid., minute to, 2 Jan. 1921.

[78] ibid., draft of dispatch from Viscount Milner, Secretary of State for the Colonies, to H.M. the King, 8 Jan. 1921. It is interesting to note that Milner was also undecided at that time about Southern Rhodesia's claim for responsible government. H.C. vol. cxxxi, 30 June 1920, p. 444, para. 70.

[79] Casely Hayford and Bankole-Bright to the Secretary of State for the Colonies, C.O. 554/50/53561, 11 Jan. 1921.

[80] '... Lord Milner does not consider that any useful purpose would be served by his granting an interview to the Delegates now in London with the object of discussing with them the salient points in the petition.' C.O. 554/50/233, 26 Jan. 1921: Sir H. J. Read to Dr. H. C. Bankole-Bright.

mittee was also sent the full text of Lord Milner's dispatch to the King.[81]

Having settled, for the time being, the question of elective representation, Milner sought the opinion of the West African Governors as to what should be done regarding the other points raised in the Congress petition. Guggisberg again sent a telegram, requesting that Nana Ofori Atta's speech should be published in *West Africa* and the *African World*. Sir Herbert Read was 'doubtful' about the tactical soundness of this move, as he was 'afraid that, by appearing to attach so much importance to these people, we may give them an advantage which they would not otherwise get'. Lord Milner, however, thought otherwise: in his view, the National Congress men were 'pretty busy just now making converts', and would continue as long as no attempt was made to discredit them. The only way to do this, he thought, was by publishing General Guggisberg's telegram as widely as possible, as that 'would throw doubt on their representative character. It is not wise to ignore them.'[82]

Though refused an interview with Lord Milner, the London Committee wrote a lengthy letter to him on 1 February, in a fruitless attempt to prove their representative character.[83] Calder thought that as the Colonial Office had refused to discuss the petition with the London Committee, it would 'be very unwise to allow ourselves to be drawn into further controversy with them regarding their preposterous claims to represent the British West African Colonies', and that the decision not to grant them an interview could not be reconsidered. Harding added that any talk of the elective principle and of unofficial majorities, as well as legal reforms, was out of the question, as Lord Milner had decided. Colonel Amery advised that to prevent further nuisance, Lord Milner's dispatch should be published extensively.[84]

The London Committee, however, decided to fight on, and got a Labour M.P., Mr. J. R. Clynes, to write to Mr. Winston Churchill, Lord Milner's successor, on their behalf. Churchill replied on 17 February that he had already sent the delegation a copy of Milner's dispatch, that reports from West Africa said the London Committee was not representative of West African opinion, and that 'it would

[81] ibid.
[82] ibid., minute to dispatch, in C.O. 554/50/4547, 27 Jan. 1921.
[83] ibid., C.O. 554/50/5352, 2 Feb. 1921.
[84] ibid., minutes to, 2 Feb. 1921.

not be in the best interests of those Colonies if I were to depart from my predecessor's decision'. A letter to the same effect was sent to the London Committee.[85]

On 19 February the London Committee conceded the first round to the Colonial Office; they noted with regret that in spite of all their efforts at persuasion, Winston Churchill was unable to revise the decision of Lord Milner on elective representation. Under the circumstances, all they could do was to return to West Africa to report to the N.C.B.W.A. and to plan another campaign. The Committee added, partly as a veiled threat and partly as a parting shot:

We are, also, to welcome your assumption of the office of Colonial Minister at this eventful period of West African National aspiration, and to hope that your administration would mark the beginning of a healthy mutual understanding and co-operation with the people of British West Africa in the management of their own internal affairs, thereby establishing in the Colonial Office a policy for the recognition of healthy West African opinion.[86]

Harding interpreted the Committee's letter as 'more or less complete capitulation at any rate for the present'. He advised that the Secretary of State should reply that he noted the Committee was returning to West Africa, and that any further developments, based on the reports of the Governors, relating to constitutional changes would be made public in the colonies concerned.

On their return to West Africa the delegates set to work to demonstrate local support for the N.C.B.W.A. and to deal with the opposition groups. In March an avalanche of telegrams, letters, and summaries of Congress resolutions reached the Colonial Office from the four colonies, one of them addressed to the Prime Minister. Most of the Gold Coast telegrams came from chiefs who attacked Nana Ofori Atta's views on the Congress, and reaffirmed their support for the movement.[87] The telegrams and the denunciations seem to have

[85] ibid., Winston Churchill to Bankole-Bright; M.1/5352/W. Africa, 17 Feb. 1921.
[86] ibid., Bankole-Bright and Casely Hayford to Winston Churchill, Secretary of State for the Colonies, C.O. 8440, 19 Feb. 1921, C.O. 554/50.
[87] Letters enclosed in C.S.O. no. 13863, 22 July 1921; C.O. 554/51. Nana Atta Fuah, Omanhene of Akim-Kotoku, in a letter dated 7 Apr. 1921 to S. R. Wood stated: 'If the Honourable Nana Ofori Atta when speaking said he spoke with the knowledge, consent and authority of the Chiefs of the Gold Coast, he spoke a lie as far as I am concerned. I am one of the Amanhene in the Gold Coast, and I know absolutely nothing of what the said Honourable Omanhene intended to say or said before the Legislative Council on the 30/12/1920. . . . I am in sympathy

made no impression on the Colonial Office. J. E. W. Flood, posing as the Machiavelli of the piece, commented rather mischievously, 'I rather thought this would turn up—or something like it. We can leave them to squabble.'[88] Nana Ofori Atta seemed left in the lurch; Guggisberg maintained a dignified silence befitting an emperor disrobed, no doubt consoled with the knowledge that in the last analysis what was important was that the Congress did not get what it wanted, at the time it wanted it, and in the way it wanted it.[89]

### 2. The 'Clifford Constitution': Politics, Pressure, and Personality

BUT was that really the case? What was the reality behind all those gubernatorial manoeuvres? Why the hasty condemnation of the Congress and all its works and then the sudden political concessions less than two months after the Congress leaders had been 'sent empty away'?

It is argued here that all the studies that have been made so far on the origins of the Nigerian constitution of 1923 have not answered the question as to whether the agitation of the National Congress of British West Africa had any direct bearing on the granting of elective representation. The orthodox interpretation, in spite of the partial relaxation of the fifty-year rule, seems to be that Sir Hugh Clifford, like that supreme political archer Henry VIII, single-handed brought about the reforms. The tendency is to see him as a powerful colonial official benignly interpreting the African mind and graciously handing them a constitution, as if their political demands were either inarticulate or irrelevant. It is my contention that this view of constitution making is too simplistic in that it regards Sir Hugh Clifford

---

with the movement and the aspirations of the Congress. . . . I agree with you in the topics discussed by you at the grand meeting at Accra.' Also C.O. 554/51/ 42284, 27 June 1921.

[88] ibid., minute to, 26 Mar. 1921.

[89] *African World* (1912–22) noted that 1921 was a year of much activity and controversy in the Gold Coast: 'The first series of incidents pertained to the National Congress movement, when the Government, acting on the strength of a speech made by a well-known Paramount Chief—who stated he, on behalf of practically all the chiefs in the country, opposed the demands made by the London deputation, cabled a summary to the United Kingdom. This proved premature for in a series of activities that culminated in a meeting of Chiefs the Hon. Nana Ofori Atta's statement was repudiated by all but three Chiefs, and resolutions cabled to this side showed that the Chiefs under Nana Mbra III, Omanhene of Cape Coast, were practically *en masse* in favour of the National Congress movement' (p. 89; Kimble, op. cit., pp. 396–7).

as the sole political actor and takes his public and private utterances on the question of elective representation at face value. This view of Clifford as a reforming colonial governor also fails to note his opposition to similar demands from the Sinhalese nationalists between 1907 and 1911. Indeed, Sir Hugh's dispatches on the question of elective representation for Ceylon during his Colonial Secretaryship in that country are remarkably similar in tone and wording to his denunciation of the National Congress of British West Africa in 1920. There is also another problem: we know little of Sir Hugh's personality and of his conception of his role in the government of subject peoples. In my view, Sir Hugh's apparent volte-face can be partially attributed to his complex and unstable personality. The only study we have had so far is H. J. Hulugalle's brief portrait of Sir Hugh in his *British Governors of Ceylon*.[90] Historians who write about Sir Hugh as if he was some kind of colonial demi-god would be interested to learn that he was not only an ardent disciple of Kipling (whose works he read to his guests at parties) with a definite view as to the relevance of Western political institutions and ideas to colonial peoples, but an 'incorrigible romantic' of the British Raj who wrote colonial novelettes, was in correspondence with Joseph Conrad, his friend and mentor, and shared the latter's fascination with that strange, twilight, and sometimes frightening encounter—the human drama enacted in 'the heart of darkness', that 'frightening fascination of living completely immersed within a culture alien to his own . . .'.[91] Sir Hugh always insisted that he 'understood' his subjects, was authoritarian in personality, aristocratic in style, extremely energetic and hard-working, very particular about the ceremonial side of the governor's duties, and sometimes prone to illusions of grandeur. Ever since his Malay days in the early 1880s Clifford, 'a thorough Anglo-Saxon, clean-bred and a good specimen of his race, strapped from childhood into the conventions of the English upper-class and the Roman Catholic Church',[92] had been profoundly disturbed by two conflicting ideals: the ideology of imperialism which he was begin-

---

[90] But see the remarks in the recently published volume by Nicolson, I. F., *The Administration of Nigeria, 1900 to 1960* (London, 1969), p. 217, which bear out some points I have raised about Sir Hugh Clifford's personality in the first section here. The Introduction by William R. Roff to *Stories by Sir Hugh Clifford* (London, 1966), pp. vii–xviii, is particularly useful on Sir Hugh's family background and political attitude. See also Allen, J. de V., *Journal of the Malaysian Branch of the Royal Asiatic Society*, xxxvii (1964), pt. 1, 41–73.

[91] Roff, op. cit., p. xiii.

[92] ibid., p. xvi.

ning to question but which he had thoroughly imbibed, and the intrinsic value of the civilization of the colonized people. This 'nagging doubt', the result of the conflict he saw between the peace and progress of imperialism and the freedom of the colonized, created in Clifford 'a considerable crisis of the Spirit'[93] which he never succeeded in solving. It was a crisis, a biographer tells us, that was to lead to 'cyclical insanity' and to Sir Hugh's 'eccentricities of behaviour'.[94] As a matter of fact he worked himself to a pitch of nervous frenzy during the Prince of Wales's visit to Nigeria in 1925 and suffered a nervous breakdown shortly before taking up the much coveted Governorship of Malaya. He had a complete mental breakdown just after his arrival in Malaya, and was discharged from the Colonial Service in 1929.[95] I would like to suggest that our inability to assess the influences and pressures that led to the granting of elective representation to British West Africa in 1923–6 and our tendency to attribute the origins of these constitutional reforms *solely* to Sir Hugh Clifford are partly due to our failure to understand a simple fact, namely that a colonial autocrat of Sir Hugh's rather complex personality was hardly likely to admit openly and directly that he was acting in response to the opinion and agitation of politically articulate Africans. Indeed he could not have reacted otherwise, particularly when those nationalists committed the unforgivable offence of bypassing him, appealing directly to the Colonial Office, and lobbying M.P.s in the metropolitan parliament. After all, the colonial 'man on the spot' was supposed to know all the problems and needs of the subject peoples. The opinion of educated Africans could only matter when it received His Excellency's benediction. Sir Hugh's immediate reaction was to denounce and ridicule the N.C.B.W.A. and its leadership as that 'self-selected, self-appointed congregation of African gentlemen, calling themselves the National Congress of British West Africa . . .', etc. Some historians write as if 'relevant documents' in official archives are conclusive evidence, or as if the writers of official dispatches are incapable of distorting the real nature of a political situation. E. H. Carr complained about this 'fetishism of documents' some time ago.[96] We must therefore bear the foregoing remarks in mind if we do not wish our understanding of the origins of the Nigerian constitution of 1923 to be

[93] ibid.                                    [94] ibid., p. xviii.
[95] See Allen, op. cit., p. 70.
[96] Carr, E. H., *What is History?*, pp. 14–19.

clouded by the myth of Governor Clifford or by the fetishism of documents.

Between March 1920 when the National Congress of British West Africa was inaugurated and March 1921, when Sir Hugh Clifford, Governor of Nigeria, began to modify his rigid opposition to the question of elective representation, Sir Hugh's attitude to elective representation remained negative. In fact he hardly referred to the question in public between these dates. He seems to have been more concerned with resurrecting and refurbishing the moribund Nigerian Council to accommodate 'representative members of the unofficial communities'[97] than with implementing the elective principle in the Legislative Council. In his address he referred to the 'inutility of the Nigerian Council as at present constituted', and made it clear that he was looking at the question 'purely from the standpoint of the Administration . . .' and on 'the lines upon which the Nigerian Council might profitably be reconstructed' in order to make it 'a serious factor in the government of the colony and Protectorate', and also 'as truly and practically representative of all Nigerian interests . . .'[98] as far as that was possible. With respect to the Legislative Council, Sir Hugh did not have anything new or radical to say either during the period March 1920 to early 1921. Although he always claimed that he planned to reform the Legislative Council even before the N.C.B.W.A. drew attention to its inadequacies, Sir Hugh was really flying a kite already constructed by his predecessor in Nigeria—a policy which aimed at the reconstitution of the Nigerian Legislative Council, but made no mention of elective representation.[99] Such reconstruction meant the retention of an official majority, four unofficial (nominated) members, and the inclusion of the Colony Commissioner.[1]

It appears, then, that up to March 1921 when Sir Hugh abandoned his plan to reconstitute the Nigerian Council and opted for its abolition, he had been toying with the idea of galvanizing that body

[97] Nigerian Council: Address by the Governor, 29 Dec. 1920, p. 17.
[98] ibid., p. 117.
[99] C.170/1918, Acting Governor of Nigeria to Rt. Hon. Walter H. Long, Secretary of State for the Colonies, 7 Dec. 1918, Nigerian National Archives, Ibadan.
[1] ibid., minute to dispatch C/17/18, sec. 8, 14 Nov. 1918. This reform proposal was not drawn up by Clifford, as he became Governor of Nigeria on 23 July 1919: see C.S.O. no. N3280, 1920; Lord Milner to Clifford, 1 Dec. 1920, Nigerian National Archives, Ibadan.

in an attempt to solve the dilemma of how to reconcile the claims for representative institutions with the system of indirect rule. There are indications that even by the end of 1919 he had not envisaged any changes before 1921:[2] instead he elected to treat the Nigerian Council which he called a 'debating society', to his celebrated gubernatorial lectures on the impossibility of a 'West African Nationality' and of a Nigerian nation.[3] In the early part of 1921 he informed the Colonial Office of his scheme for the reconstruction of the Nigerian Council and the Legislative Council. There was no mention of elected members, but the Colonial Office did not view his proposals favourably, and decided to shelve them, 'as if they led to the abolition or modification of the Nigerian Council . . .'.[4] The Secretary of State for the Colonies (Winston Churchill) would not take any action on Sir Hugh's proposals, as he was already considering certain 'changes which may render it unnecessary to consider these proposals . . .'.[5]

The London Committee of the N.C.B.W.A. must have made some impression on Sir Hugh, or he must have felt that his proposal to reconstitute the Nigerian Council and the Legislative Council did not sufficiently impress the Colonial Office. For in March 1921 one month after Lord Milner, aided by Clifford himself, rejected the petition of the London Committee, Sir Hugh dispatched a lengthy and impressive memorandum to the Secretary of State for the Colonies, in which he recommended the abolition of both the Nigerian Council and the Legislative Council, and the creation of a new Legislative Council for Southern Nigeria with provision for four elected members.[6]

Before 1906 the Colony and Protectorate of Lagos had a Legislative Council which legislated for Lagos Colony and, as far as British jurisdiction extended, for the Lagos Protectorate. The Protectorate of Southern Nigeria was legislated for by the High Commissioner who also legislated for Northern Nigeria where there was no Legislative Council. When the Colony and Protectorate of Lagos

[2] Wheare, J., *The Nigerian Council*, p. 30.

[3] Ezera, K., *Constitutional Developments in Nigeria* (2nd ed., Cambridge, 1964), p. 27. See *Nigerian Council: Addresses by the Governor*, 1920.

[4] Minute to dispatch in C.O. 17150/Nigeria; C.O. 538/100, 29 Apr. 1921.

[5] ibid.; the nature of these changes was not disclosed, but it is certain, judging from Churchill's attitude (*a*) to the question of Indian reforms and (*b*) to Clifford's scheme for limited elective representation in mid-1921, that such 'changes' would not have been as liberal as they sound.

[6] Dispatch in Gov. 1959/21 (Confidential): 'Legislative Council: Reconstruction', C.O. 583/100.

was amalgamated with the Protectorate of Southern Nigeria, and became the Colony and Protectorate of Southern Nigeria in 1906, the Legislative Council of Lagos was slightly expanded to become the legislative body for the whole Colony and Protectorate of Southern Nigeria. Northern Nigeria remained as before. In his proposals for the amalgamation of Northern and Southern Nigeria,[7] Sir Frederick Lugard considered the difficulties involved in unofficial representation on the Legislative Council 'insuperable'. It was difficult, if not impossible, he said, to create one Legislative Council for Nigeria, in which the North would be effectively represented. To protect the interests of various groups, therefore, the Governor had to legislate for 'scheduled' or backward areas without reference to his Council. In the words of Sir Charles Dilke, his Council became 'not a liberal institution, but a veiled oligarchy of the worst description'. Lugard also proposed the establishment of a Nigerian Council, similar to the General Council of the French West African colonies, consisting of two lieutenant-governors, the Administrator of Lagos, together with the three Secretaries, the Political Secretary, and other officials under the presidency of the Governor-General. There were also unofficial Members nominated by the Lagos Chamber of Commerce, the Calabar Chamber, and the Chamber of Mines, in addition to eight others, no fewer than four of whom were to be Africans nominated by the Governor. The Lagos Legislative Council passed laws for the Colony, but these were first approved by the Governor. The Nigerian Council possessed neither executive nor legislative powers: it became an 'unpaid anthropological department' of the government.[8]

On 26 March 1921 Sir Hugh Clifford, in a confidential dispatch, drew the attention of the Secretary of State for the Colonies to the inadequacy of the machinery at present in existence in the Colony and Protectorate of Nigeria for the passing and criticism of legislation, for the scrutiny, by those whose interests are affected, of the financial affairs of the country, for authoritatively announcing and explaining the actions of the Government to the local public, and for enabling the latter to follow and understand them.[9] He subjected the Lugard constitution of 1913 to detailed criticism,[10] noting that

[7] See C.O. 16460/1913.
[8] Tamuno, T. N., *Nigeria and Elective Representation, 1923–1947*, p. 29.
[9] Confidential dispatch in C.O. 19595, C.O. 583/100, para. 1.
[10] ibid., paras. 3–15.

... the impotency and insignificance of the Council are so generally recognised that it is not now possible to restore to it such prestige as the Legislative Council of the Colony of Southern Nigeria formerly possessed, to galvanise it into any sort of activity or reality, or to awaken any public interest in its proceedings and deliberations. After attending a large number of its meetings, I have no hesitation in expressing the opinion that this Legislative Council fails completely to fulfil the purpose for which such Bodies ordinarily established and maintained.[11]

The Legislative Council, he argued, whose competence was severely limited by clauses viii–xiii of the letters Patent of the 1913 constitution, had come to be regarded by the politically significant section of Southern Nigeria as 'little more than a debating society' whose resolutions were 'deprived of any save the merest academical interest'.[12]

As early as 29 December 1919 Mr. McNeill, one of the commercial Members, had put on the agenda of the Nigerian Council the resolution: 'That this Council be either reconstituted so as to make it a serious factor in the government of this Colony and Protectorate, or else be abolished.' But at Sir Hugh's request Mr. McNeill refrained from pressing that resolution to a division, though both official and unofficial Members shared the latter's view of the Council.[13]

While admitting the inadequacy of the Government Gazette and of the local press for examining and discussing legislation, Sir Hugh was certain that '. . . there is growing up among the more educated classes a feeling that the machinery in existence for the discussion of local affairs is wholly inadequate and that the Government occupies a position of untramelled autocracy which is without a counterpart in other West African Colonies. That this is, in fact, the case cannot be gainsaid. . . .'[14] More significantly he added: 'I am convinced that this state of things is opposed alike to the interest of the public and of the Government, and *I think that an attempt should be made to find a remedy. Sooner or later the position must be recognised as intolerable by the more advanced sections of the indigenous population, and I suggest that it is preferable that the initiative in the matter of reform should be taken by the Government.'*[15] His new

[11] ibid., paras. 3–4; at least, he seems to have accepted the N.C.B.W.A contention that the Crown Colony system was an anachronism.
[12] ibid., para. 9.
[13] ibid., p. 6, paras. 10–11.      [14] ibid., p. 8, para. 15.
[15] ibid., p. 8, para. 15; my emphasis.

scheme, he said, would be 'inevitably imperfect', and might not be very effective initially; nevertheless, it was 'a substantial advance on the existing system'. As more capable representatives became available, the new Legislative Council would become an important factor in the administration. It was with this end in view, said Sir Hugh, that he was putting forward his scheme to give fuller representation of local interests and to give a larger share in the discussion and management of public affairs 'to articulate members of the various Nigerian communities' than were provided by existing institutions.

The new Legislative Council for the Southern Provinces would hold its sessions in Lagos, the principal commercial centre of Nigeria. To the extent that Sir Hugh did not find it practicable to include the Northern Provinces in the new scheme, his proposal, as he put it, was 'a compromise and a half measure'; in any case, he said, the backwardness of the Northern Provinces should not 'prevent the development of representative institutions in those parts of the Dependency where they already existed prior to the amalgamation' and where, if amalgamation had never taken place, those institutions would have been gradually extended as a matter of course. Objections to his new scheme, which involved the abolition of the old Legislative Council, he continued, would merely be in the nature of 'sentimental considerations', but these could be reconciled 'if special privileges were to be awarded to the Colony in the matter of its representation on the new Council', i.e. 'that on the new Council the Colony be represented by three elected and one nominated member'.[16]

The new Legislative Council was to be called The Legislative Council of the Colony and Protectorate of Nigeria and was to be constituted as follows: 27 official members, 14 nominated members, and 4 elected members, 3 for the Colony and 1 for Calabar. The franchise was to be granted to residents of the municipal area of Lagos who had a gross income of not less than £100. Sir Hugh was not sure whether the electors would be enthusiastic about the new scheme, but he was hopeful that the granting of the franchise to Lagos would not create much difficulty as the municipal area of Lagos was at once 'compact and populous, and the proportion of educated persons among its inhabitants . . . unusually large'.[17]

[16] ibid., pp. 12–13, paras. 25–6.
[17] ibid., p. 14, para. 29.

Having surveyed his scheme, Sir Hugh recommended it with a slight Machiavellian touch:

The privilege of electing their own representatives is much sought after by politically minded persons in West Africa . . . but the occupation of seats on a Legislative Council by local demagogues would tend to imbue them with a sense of responsibility which they do not feel so long as they are able to spread all manner of mischievous rumours among an ignorant population without incurring the risk of being publicly brought to account therefor. I consider that the experiment is one that should be tried.[18]

Meanwhile in London, the Colonial Office was studying Sir Hugh's scheme before discussing it with him during his leave in England in June. A. Harding, an Assistant Secretary at the Colonial Office, disagreed with nearly all of Sir Hugh's points. He believed that though the Nigerian Council could be criticized as little more than a debating society, it could fulfil its functions as well as a Legislative Council, if only it met oftener. Harding would dispense with un-official members as 'experience has shown', he said, 'that little useful advice is obtainable in Nigeria by the Government except from officials . . .'.[19] He also criticized Sir Hugh's argument that to explain government policy it was necessary to enlarge the Legislative Council and publish its proceedings in a government Hansard. He recalled that when Sir Hugh was Governor of the Gold Coast he 'induced the Secretary of State to alter and considerably enlarge the Legislative Council in order to provide a larger audience for his speeches and deliveries . . .' and that Guggisberg was now finding it difficult to communicate with local opinion. Sir Hugh's difficulty, he said, was that he was 'looking at the Gold Coast through magnifying spectacles, and thinking that the result is the same as Nigeria, and that the Northern Provinces are merely a larger edition of Ashanti and the Northern Territories of the Gold Coast'.[20] Lagos, in his view, should not be represented by three elected members, as the electors were not even taking interest in the Municipal Council. He concluded his minute:

It is not all clear to me what good would really be served by making the proposed changes in present circumstances. When a popular demand comes for further representative institutions, then would be the time to give them. At present representative institutions cannot possibly in

[18] ibid., pp. 14–15, para. 29.
[19] ibid., minute by A. Harding, 2 June 1921.
[20] ibid.

Nigeria be in the very least representative: the material is not there, and if it were, communications are so imperfect, and the country so large, that meetings of representatives from all over Nigeria cannot be held except once in a blue moon. . . . It seems to me that all the advantages lie in the direction of carrying on for the present time under the existing Constitution. In a few years' time it may be possible to do something in the direction of enlarging the scope and membership of the Legislative Council, but till then, its impotence, which so grieves the Governor, is in practice, a considerable asset to the Government of the country. . . .[21]

Sir Herbert Read (Assistant Under-Secretary of State at the Colonial Office) thought that the 'most expeditious' method of settling the problems posed by Sir Hugh's reform proposal would be for Harding, Wood (Parliamentary Under-Secretary of State), and himself to 'discuss the matter personally with Sir Hugh Clifford when the latter would be on leave in England'. On the afternoon of 10 June Wood, Harding, and Sir H. Read reported to Sir George Fiddes and Winston Churchill that the reform proposals had been discussed with Sir Hugh Clifford that afternoon,[22] and that the latter had '*pressed for his proposals being adopted so that they could come into force towards the end of this year or early next and that they should not be postponed for a few years or until a popular demand for such a change arose*'.[23] On the question of nominating unofficial members for the Provinces of Oyo, Abeokuta, Ijebu, Ondo and Benin, the Niger Delta, and the Ibo country, Sir Hugh thought nomination with regard to possible persons available would be a convenient method but insisted that Oyo and Abeokuta should have representatives, as he could find suitable English-speaking African merchants acceptable as representatives to the Alafin and the Alake respectively. He also insisted on the preparation of the draft instruments to implement his proposals, the details of which could be discussed later.[24] On 16 June 1921 Sir H. Read instructed that the Instruments be prepared, and on 18 June Wood informed Churchill about the discussions with Sir Hugh Clifford, adding that the Colonial Office had 'agreed in substance to his proposals', and had also proposed

[21] ibid. Harding's advocacy of the policy of muddling through can perhaps be explained by the fact that he was absent from the Colonial Office when the London Committee of the N.C.B.W.A. unsuccessfully tried to educate English public opinion on elective representation.
[22] Minute to C.O. 19595; C.O. 583/100.
[23] ibid.; my emphasis.
[24] ibid.

the preparation of the draft instruments for further discussion with Sir Hugh. Between July and September 1921 draft Orders in Council and Letters Patent for the new Constitution were made by the Colonial Office and a copy sent to Sir Hugh on 24 October for his observations and criticisms.

By December 1921 the revised drafts of the new Nigerian Constitution were completed, under the scrutiny of Risely and Harding, the latter retaining his scepticism throughout.[25] Harding commented that the minutes to C.O. 19595/21, in which Sir Hugh Clifford's proposals were discussed, did 'not contain any definite decision of the Secretary of State to approve Sir H. Clifford's proposed reorganization of Nigeria's legislative arrangements', that the adoption of the elective principle in the new Legislative Council of Nigeria, though confined to Lagos and Calabar, might lead to demands for similar institutions in the Gold Coast and Sierra Leone, and that it was 'not quite easy' to reconcile the present policy of limited change with Lord Milner's reply to the N.C.B.W.A. delegation on 26 January 1921.[26] Clearly Harding was sticking to Milner's policy earlier that year; after all, Churchill too was known to be opposed to constitutional reform for West Africa. Yet, in the same minutes, Sir Herbert Read dismissed Harding's objections and opted for the Cliffordian reforms,[27] saying that as far as the minutes to C.O. 19595/21 were concerned, the decision rested with the Secretary of State for the Colonies. As for Harding's fear that the Gold Coast and Sierra Leone would demand reforms similar to Nigeria's, Sir Herbert Read thought that it had been proposed '*to apply the elective principle on a very restricted scale in Nigeria, and if Sierra Leone and Gold Coast desire similar treatment, there seems to be no reason why it should not be given*'.[28] As to the view that the new policy contradicted that of Lord Milner, Sir Herbert Read thought that Harding need not worry about that, 'in view of the limited extent to which election is being introduced'.

It appears, however, that although by January 1922 Clifford's constitutional proposals had been approved by the Colonial Office, a few of the senior officials who were against reforms, led by Harding, had succeeded in putting their views to Churchill. For in the dispatch

[25] Minute to C.O. 63185, 21 Dec. 1921; C.O. 583/100.
[26] ibid.
[27] ibid.; 'I would suggest that the scheme should be proceeded with.'
[28] ibid.; my emphasis.

to Clifford on the new constitution, Churchill reluctantly accepted Clifford's proposals, as is seen from paragraph 2 of his dispatch:

I do not think it is possible, in the present circumstances of Nigeria as regards educational, political and commercial development and means of communication, to set up a Legislative Council which could be regarded as in any sense really representative of the inhabitants of even the Colony and Southern Provinces of the Protectorate. Nor do I think that such a Legislative Council could be secured for many years to come. . . . The question has however been discussed with you during your recent leave in England; and you are, I understand, satisfied that the advantages which the Nigerian Government will gain by the arrangements which you propose will on the whole outweigh the disadvantages. I am not therefore prepared to reject your proposals and I have caused to be prepared drafts of Instruments for carrying them into effect.[29]

Eventually Sir Hugh got his Constitution, but took exception to paragraph 2 of Churchill's dispatch and to the reluctance of the Colonial Office to accept the grand title (Council of Government) which, characteristically, he had given to his new Council.[30] He also drew Churchill's attention to the 'considerable measure of reluctance' with which the former had viewed his reform proposals, in spite of his experience of local conditions in Nigeria, adding that his scheme, given the conditions in Nigeria, was 'the best that can at present time be devised'. He went on to argue that the creation of a new Legislative Council was 'at least as desirable, if judged exclusively from the standpoint of the advantages which will accrue therefrom to the Government, as it is if gauged solely from the point of view of the more advanced sections of the indigenous communities of the Southern Provinces of Nigeria'. Not only would his scheme make officials more accountable, it would also be useful in 'exposing and dispelling mischievous rumours and reports' spread by 'astute and unscrupulous folk who are dealing with very ignorant and incredibly credulous people, among whom they desire only to stir up discontent and disaffection'.[31] As for the nationalists in the Southern Provinces,

---

[29] ibid., dispatch in C.O. 63185/21Nig.; the Rt. Hon. Winston Churchill, Secretary of State for the Colonies to Sir Hugh Clifford, Governor of Nigeria.

[30] Dispatch contained in Confidential C.O. 36669; C.O. 983/111.

[31] ibid., p. 3, para. 3. Tamuno notes that 'Lagos was considerably quieter after 1923; and at the conclusion of the fourth session of the N.C.B.W.A. at Lagos in 1930, the Congress as far as Lagos was concerned, became a fast dying body . . .' (op. cit., p. 31). In fact by 1926 only a few dedicated individuals in Lagos took interest in the affairs of the N.C.B.W.A. Clifford's political anaesthetic largely succeeded in centring 'politics' on the Legislative and Town Councils.

said Sir Hugh, his new scheme would be hailed by many of them as a 'removal of the menace to all chance or prospect of their natural political growth. . . . The privilege of electing their own representatives to occupy seats on the Council will, in theory at any rate, be very highly prized by them . . .', though he was certain that the nationalists would have to find some means of making the 'bulk of the unpolitically minded among the electors' interested in local elections. In any case, a Legislative Council would sober up the demagogues who would now have less exciting tasks. He had tried that policy in the Gold Coast, he said, and it had been a 'complete success', but the problem in Nigeria was how to 'devise a scheme which, while allowing the natural political development of the more Europeanised communities of the South to proceed without undue restraint, would protect the autonomy enjoyed by the Native Administrations . . .'.[32]

Although Sir Hugh was uncertain as to whether his scheme would succeed in harmonizing the contradictions of the Lugardian system, he felt strongly that the authorization of his new scheme was 'right in principle', adding that 'the creation of the new Council will tend to satisfy legitimate aspirations and ambitions; that it will fulfil useful and practical purposes; that it will eventually prove to be susceptible to progressive reforms and improvements, and that it will help to produce a healthier political atmosphere throughout the principal centres in the Southern Provinces'.[33] He made it clear, however, that he was certain that Churchill was 'only partially convinced' of the expediency (note Clifford's constant juxtaposition of 'expediency', 'necessity', and 'principle') of his proposals,[34] to which Harding replied that there was nothing in Churchill's dispatch of 63185/21 to justify the view that he approved Clifford's scheme 'with a considerable measure of reluctance'; all Churchill did, he said, was to express doubts about its feasibility. Sir Hugh, said Harding, was implying publicly that the Secretary of State for the Colonies was 'opposed to representative institutions in West Africa', whereas what the Secretary of State really meant was that such institutions could only serve the interests of the educated Africans.[35] On balance,

[32] Paras. 4–5 of dispatch in C.O. 36669; C.O. 583/111.
[33] ibid., pp. 6–7.
[34] ibid., p. 7, para. 6.
[35] ibid., memorandum by Harding; Lugard's remarks on the 'educated African' (*The Dual Mandate* (London, 1925), pp. 79–90) were quoted by Harding to illustrate his point. See also Lugard's view on the question in *Representative Forms*

however, it seems that Sir Hugh had come to realize, equally reluctantly, that things had changed since 1914 and that the Lugardian
edifice needed slight, albeit reverential, readjustment to post-war
conditions. Clifford had not forgotten that he had opposed the
nationalists in Ceylon on the same issue between 1907 and 1911,
using almost exactly the same arguments he used in 1920,[36] and had
lost: why should he now oppose reforms he himself considered both
'necessary' and 'right in principle'?

The question will be asked: was the granting of the elective principle due to pressure exerted by the N.C.B.W.A.: that is, was Clifford
compelled or 'encouraged' to concede some of the constitutional
demands of the N.C.B.W.A.? The answer is yes. Did Clifford,
acting on his own initiative, outmanoeuvre the N.C.B.W.A. by
secretly recommending a limited franchise? The answer is still yes:
at any rate, he thought he was doing so. The problem is one that has
not been satisfactorily answered by historians so far. Martin Wight
concluded that 'It [the Congress] has no direct effect, but it crystallized demands which received partial fulfilment in the Constitution
of 1925. . . .'[37] Padmore dismissed the Congress from an *a priori*
Marxian viewpoint: its failure was 'inevitable', because it lacked 'the
active support of the plebeian masses, especially the peasantry . . .'.[38]
David Kimble's detailed study, understandably, is too much pre-
occupied with the Gold Coast aspects of the Congress to shed more
light on the question.[39] K. A. B. Jones-Quartey raises the problem

---

*of Government and 'Indirect Rule' in British Africa* (London, 1928). Lugard seems
to have envisaged an indefinite continuation of the system allowing only for
elected councils in the coastal towns; of the Cliffordian reforms he said: 'The
action of the Colonial Office in first consenting to the creation of this Council and
the restriction of the powers of the Legislative Council to the colony, and then
revising the policy without any local demand or evidence of the need of such a
course, and the introduction of the elective principle which Lord Milner had
declared to be premature, was not in accord with its role of maintaining continuity'
(p. 16 n. 2). For further discussion of the problem of representative government
and indirect rule, see Hailey, Lord, *An African Survey* (1st ed., 1938), pp. 134–5;
also Lucas, Bryan Keith, 'The Dilemma of Local Government in Africa', pp.
194–5 in *Essays in Imperial Government Presented to Margery Perham by Kenneth
Robinson and F. Madden* (Oxford, 1963); especially Austin, Dennis, *West Africa
and the Commonwealth* (Harmondsworth, 1957), pp. 77–82.

[36] Hulugalle, H. J., *British Governors of Ceylon*, chapter XXIV.

[37] Wight, Martin, *The Gold Coast Legislative Council*, p. 27.

[38] Padmore, G., *The Gold Coast Revolution*, pp. 52–3.

[39] It must be added, however, that the volumes containing Clifford's dispatches
were not available to researchers when Kimble completed his work on the Gold
Coast.

when he states: 'Three years later elective representation did come to West Africa for the first time, though on a strictly limited franchise, as it was bound to do. . . . Was this reform due in large part to the Congress movement and the efforts of Casely Hayford and his tenacious fighters for freedom?'[40] Dr. T. N. Tamuno makes some interesting guesses as to the genesis of the 1923 Constitution; unfortunately his book appeared before the partial relaxation of the fifty-year rule.[41] Miss La Ray Denzer's thesis correctly assesses the weaknesses of the N.C.B.W.A., but does not attempt an explanation of its role in the introduction of the elective principle.[42]

W. E. G. Sekyi, a contemporary and a participant who made it his special duty to study the psychology of colonial bureaucrats, assessed the Congress's influence thus: '. . . there can be no doubt that the terror which this movement inspired in the hearts of Sir Hugh Clifford and his supporters led him to recommend a form of elective representation for West Africa, which the various Governors have each stamped with his own individuality and capacity to understand African aspirations aright'.[43] The West African press, almost without exception, claimed that Clifford's volte face was the direct result of Congress agitation. The *Lagos Weekly Record* interpreted the 1923 Constitution as a *pis aller* hastily construed to outmanoeuvre the agitators and steal a march on the progressive Guggisberg of the Gold Coast:

. . . But stranger things were yet to happen; for Sir Hugh Clifford who had antagonised the National Congress of British West Africa at its birth and had ridiculed its advocacy of the introduction of the franchise as 'loose and gaseous talk' suddenly underwent a political metamorphosis and became a great protagonist of the scheme of elective representation, despite the parrot cries of a certain section of the community which had

[40] Jones-Quartey, K. A. B., 'Thought and Expression in the Gold Coast Press: 1874–1930, Part II', *Universitas* (University of Ghana), iii, no. 4 (Dec. 1958), 116.

[41] Tamuno, op. cit., pp. 25–31. But see Tamuno's recent article, 'Governor Clifford and Representative Government', *Journal of the Historical Society of Nigeria*, iv, no. 1 (1967), 117–24. The article, however, does not answer the question in spite of the remarks at p. 122, which are inconclusive.

[42] Denzer, La Ray, 'The National Congress of British West Africa: Gold Coast Section' (M.A. thesis, University of Ghana, Legon, 1965). Her thesis is mainly concerned with emphasizing 'the African influences of both traditional culture and status which produced the nationalistic thought expounded by the delegates . . .' (Preface).

[43] Sekyi, W. E. G., 'On Some Recent Movements in West Africa: a Study of White Methods of Repression', *Gold Coast Times* (23 May 1931), pp. 7–8.

taken up Sir Hugh's jeremiad that Nigeria was still unripe for representative Government . . . and reviewing the situation at this distance of time,
one is almost tempted to surmise that Sir Hugh rushed through the
Nigerian scheme, presumably as a necessary expedient for taking the wind
out of Sir Gordon's sails and forestalling the Gold Coast in the grant of
the franchise, for up to his departure from Nigeria Sir Hugh had not been
able to explain satisfactorily to his critics his sudden conversion . . .; the
result inevitably was that the Nigerian constitution—hastily improvised
by Sir Hugh without any previous consultation with the progressive
elements of the community or acknowledged leaders of the people—
stands today as the least liberal in outlook by its overwhelming official
majority which has practically nullified the benefits intended to be conferred by the franchise. . . .[44]

The *Weekly Record*, though generally a radical paper in Lagos politics, was not always noted for the accuracy of its political judgements;
but, as our account of the making of the 1923 Constitution has
shown, its view that Clifford took the wind out of the Congress sails
by initiating the reforms is correct. Also, its view that Clifford 'rushed
through the Nigerian scheme . . . as a necessary expedient', without
consulting any 'public opinion', is substantially correct. Why Sir
Hugh found it necessary to rush through the scheme is not clear, for
that same year the Congress delegation had suffered a severe tactical
defeat in London; on the other hand, Clifford could have rushed
through the scheme with an eye to the possible unrest which might
result from the slump in 1921. Whatever the factors involved, he *had*
to take action in a time of crisis.

Perhaps the most realistic assessment of the relative influence
exercised by the N.C.B.W.A. in the introduction of the elective
principle is that by Dr. T. O. Elias: '. . . But having thus effectively
thwarted their cherished ambition in Britain, Clifford was quick
to sense the gathering storm on the political horizon. He accordingly
proceeded to dismantle Lugard's edifice of the Nigerian Council
which, together with the old Legislative Council, he finally abolished
in 1922, replacing both by a single Legislative and a new Executive
Council.'[45]

Most of these interpretations, however, suffer from too much

---

[44] *Lagos Weekly Record* (16 Nov. 1926): 'Elective Representation in British
West Africa: a comparison between the Gold Coast and Nigerian constitutions',
pp. 5–9.

[45] Elias, T. O., *Makers of Nigerian Law*, quoted in Ezera, op. cit., p. 26; also
Odumosu, O. I., *The Nigerian Constitution: History and Development* (London,
1963), pp. 15–16.

emphasis on the institutional aspects of the decision-making process which resulted in the creation of the 1923 Constitution. Sir Hugh's public speeches do not give an accurate indication of his motives; and, as I have indicated, scholars have not taken into account the influence which such a powerful personality as Sir Hugh's could have on policy making at the Colonial Office. He was aristocratic, very able, hard-working, shrewd, paternalistic, and flamboyant with a touch of the dramatic. Sir Hugh believed in progress and in the 'regeneration' of subject races, yet was profoundly pessimistic about its effects; he genuinely respected the cultures of subject peoples, and believed that it was the duty of the European official to 'become conscious of native Public Opinion, which is often diametrically opposed to the opinion of his race-mates on one and the same subject',[46] yet he was constantly at loggerheads with the educated 'middle-class' nationalists who presumed to initiate change on behalf of their fellow subjects.[47] Any study of the 1923 Nigerian Constitution must take account of Sir Hugh's personality.

But decision making is never a final act or a one-man process. To picture Sir Hugh as an omniscient and liberal-minded Governor benignly handing down a constitution to vociferous nationalists, as Ezera does,[48] or to portray the Congress forcing a colonial autocrat to yield to its demands, is perhaps to ignore the complex reality of political processes. We have shown that the whole issue was made complex by the active participation of people and interests (both economic and humanitarian interest groups) whose influence cannot easily be measured.[49] That the London Committee of the N.C.B.W.A. exerted some influence on the Colonial Office and, in spite of his hostility, on Sir Hugh himself, cannot be gainsaid. That commercial interests also exerted some influence is also clear from the interest

[46] Roff, op. cit., p. 207; see also p. x for family influences on Sir Hugh's 'strong bent for benevolent paternalism'.
[47] The most useful accounts I have seen of Sir Hugh's philosophy of colonial rule and of his personality are Hulugalle, op. cit., chapter XXIV; Roff, op. cit.; and Allen, op. cit. See also the comments on Sir Hugh in the *Times Literary Supplement* (Feb. 1967). So far there is no biography of Sir Hugh. Lady Holmes (his sister) informs me that Sir Hugh's papers were destroyed or lost in 1942. Hulugalle strongly suggests that largely as a result of overwork, Sir Hugh suffered from periodic bouts of depression and mental instability shortly before he left Nigeria for Malaya and that this illness eventually terminated what would have been one of the most successful colonial governorships. Roff, op. cit., even suggests that this mental instability had its roots in Clifford's early Malay days.
[48] Ezera, op. cit., p. 27.
[49] For details, see my thesis, op. cit.

shown in the matter by the Liverpool Association of African Merchants,[50] commercial papers like *West Africa* and the *African World*, as well as Sir Hugh's long argument with Lord Leverhulme on economic questions which were in fact political ones.[51] It was also an unofficial Member representing commercial interests who first tabled a motion in the Nigerian Council for the reconstitution or abolition of that body.[52] The Association of West African Merchants did in fact seek, and were granted, an interview with the Colonial Office in early 1921 on questions directly connected with the proposed constitutional reforms.

It is clear from the dispatches that Sir Hugh actually persuaded, almost compelled, the Colonial Office, which did not believe in the introduction of the elective principle to West Africa at that time, to accept his draft constitution with provision for four elected members. And it is also clear that Churchill reluctantly accepted Sir Hugh's Constitution in deference to the latter's authority and experience. Sir Hugh in turn makes it plain in his dispatches that his constitutional changes were partly intended to keep the 'local demagogues' quiet; there are indications also that the 'feeling' of 'the more educated classes' and of 'the more advanced sections of the indigenous popu-

---

[50] Sir Hugh Clifford himself admitted the influence commercial bodies (extra-territorial) could exert on colonial governments: 'As matters stand today, almost the only criticism of the actions of the Government, which is able in any degree to make itself felt, emanates from the Chambers of Commerce in London, Liverpool or Manchester or from the Association of African Merchants in Liverpool, and these bodies concentrate their scrutiny almost exclusively upon matters that affect or are believed likely to affect commercial interests.' Para. 14 of dispatch in Nig. Confi. C.O. 19595; C.O. 583/100. See also Wheare, op. cit., pp. 81–3, 108. The extra-territorial interests would not be concerned with politics *per se* but would certainly be with the financial arrangements of the Constitution, how far unofficial members could discuss economic and financial questions, fiscal and economic controls, etc. See *Mining, Commerce and Finance in Nigeria* (London, 1948), ed. M. Perham, p. 46; also Fiddes, Sir George V., *The Dominions and Colonial Offices* (London, 1926), p. 153. Fiddes was Permanent Under-Secretary of State for the Colonies from 1916 to 1921.

[51] Sir Hugh Clifford's speech in the African Trade Section at the Liverpool Chambers of Commerce in which he denied Lord Leverhulme's view that government in West Africa was autocratic and bureaucratic; he also argued that self-government for British West Africa 'would not add to the security of English capital or to the expansion of their commerce' (*The Times* (28 Aug. 1923), p. 7). See also Hancock, W. R., *Survey of British Commonwealth Affairs*, vol. ii: *Problems of Economic Policy, 1918–1939* (London, 1942), pp. 190–4.

[52] Dispatch in C.O. 19595; C.O. 583/100, p. 6. Wheare, op. cit., p. 30. The financial arrangements of the Lugard constitution were most unsatisfactory, see dispatch by Clifford, 583/19595/100.

lation' was an important factor which affected his decision—a fact he tries to suppress in his dispatch but which he is compelled to acknowledge. Those who tend to see constitutional 'development' as a series of decisions, may perhaps note, as Dr. S. C. Ghosh reminds us, that 'Decision is a choice between two alternatives that cause a conflict; it is the solution of a clash; it is the deliberate end of a conflict. Such conflicts are rare, and they are episodes in the process of growing and maturing rather than in the process of ruling and of policy determinations.'[53] From the moment the elective principle was conceded, its application to the other territories (except the Gambia) was almost automatic—Sierra Leone (1924) and the Gold Coast (1925): *bis dat qui cito dat*. For Sir Hugh and the leaders of the N.C.B.W.A., elective representation had become not a 'principle' but a 'necessity' and an 'expedient' in 1920-1, as Sir Hugh himself admitted less than a year after he had publicly pronounced their unfitness for such institutions. For liberalism, according to Hobhouse, is concerned with civil, fiscal, personal, social, economic, domestic, racial, national, and international liberties and creates demands for political liberty and popular sovereignty:[54] and it was this liberalism of 'bourgeois colonial society' that the Congress leaders had imbibed. To deny its application to them merely because they were unrepresentative of the whole population did not make sense, either to Sir Hugh or to the Colonial Office.

As for the Congress movement, it is easy to dismiss it as an itinerant seminar of the West African nationalist bourgeoisie and its Sessions as ineffective congregations of a frustrated and outmoded intelligentsia; or to picture its leaders as outmoded nationalists preaching doctrines inherited from mid-Victorian anti-imperialism and advocating a liberal democracy of which a chastened Europe was becoming sceptical.[55] The view of some historians that the N.C.B.W.A.

[53] Ghosh, S. C., 'Decision-making and Power in the British Conservative Party: a case study of the Indian problem, 1929-1934', *Political Studies*, xiii (1965), 198–212.

[54] Hobhouse, L. T., *Liberalism* (London, 1911), pp. 21–49.

[55] Denzer, op. cit., sees them as old-fashioned black Victorians vainly trying to have their load of the white man's burden, pp. 2–3. She does indeed mention the change of policy towards the beginning of the twentieth century which made increasing use of chiefs in the system of indirect rule (which meant that the 'educated African' would have the worst of both worlds), but does not relate this to the important socio-economic and technological changes which took place in Europe and which directly affected imperial attitudes. See Delavignette, R., *Christianity and Colonialism* (London, 1964), pp. 43–6. For an account of the ways in which

had no influence on the 1923 Constitution *merely* because Sir Hugh did not mention that organization in his dispatch does not only do violence to the facts but betrays a *naïveté* about the conclusiveness of official documents which is incompatible with responsible and objective scholarship. Lest we forget, official documents are written by human beings. And colonial Governors are human. As far as African opinion on the question of constitutional change was concerned, Sir Hugh's strategy was to

> damn with faint praise, assent with civil leer;
> And, without sneering, teach the rest to sneer.

It seems the trick has worked, for we are still sneering at the nationalists. But how many of us have bothered to study the letters and papers of these nationalists to see what *they* thought about the Cliffordian paradox? Is it not just possible that the emperor suddenly discovered that he had no clothes at all and was desperately trying to conceal the fact from his subjects? Of course, it is extremely difficult, by merely studying Clifford's dispatch, to argue that the National Congress of British West Africa had any influence on the constitutional reforms. One may argue either way, depending on what sources are available, and who wrote them. For example, my study of the Kobina Sekyi papers in Ghana revealed the persistence with which Sekyi, who was one of the 'radical' nationalists at Cape Coast during the 1920s and 1940s, charged Clifford with dishonesty and official pride. What emerged from Sekyi's letters and unpublished manuscripts, as well as his poems, is that although an uncompromising conservative nationalist, he was genuinely hurt that Clifford and the colonial government in West Africa in general should contemptuously dismiss the nationalists' reasonable demands in public and then set about conceding them privately, as if 'official prestige' was more important than the views of moderates seeking 'reasonable accommodation'. Within the Gold Coast itself, Sekyi and the Congress nationalists experienced a similar difficulty in establishing meaningful dialogue with Governor Guggisberg who by all accounts had the interests of the country at heart but failed to communicate with the Congress nationalists principally because his techno-

---

European concepts like authority and liberty were transplanted to the colonies and subsequently distorted or adopted, see Kraus, Wolfgang, 'Authority, Progress and Colonialism', in *Authority*, NOMOS I, ed. C. J. Friedrich (Harvard University Press, 1958), pp. 151–6: Maunier, Réné, *The Sociology of Colonies*, especially vol. i.

bureaucratic paternalism made him insensitive to changed political conditions and to the ambitions of the colonial sub-élite.[56] In 1925, for example, Sekyi wrote in an unpublished MS.:

> By now we are well aware that the white man does not like at any time to admit before the black man that he is in the wrong in anything he does or proposes to do. We know that although no notice appears to be taken of the more serious side of our activities in the interest of the fatherland, the white man's way in all things affecting the black man is to refuse all applications by the black man for solid improvements in his condition, and dole out such improvements some time afterwards as if they were being granted as a result of the white man's own superior judgment of the fitness of the African for such improvements. Certain suggestions ridiculed so assiduously by Sir Hugh Clifford and his supporters have now been adopted as though they were suggested by Sir Hugh Clifford and we have seen a good deal of praise showered on him and other Governors for policies of improvement which have been forced out of them by the sustained endeavours of the despised leaders of African political thought in the crown colonies. . . .[57]

If the papers of African nationalists are accepted as 'relevant documents' by historians, then one can safely conclude that there are at least two interpretations of the coming of elective representation to West Africa. Or are documents 'relevant' only when they are contained in official correspondence? As one of the nationalists of the time put it, 'From official despatches, good Lord deliver us.'

[56] On this point, see Wraith, R., *Guggisberg* (London, 1967), chapter VII.
[57] Sekyi, Kobina, *The Parting of the Ways*, pp. 84–5.

CHAPTER VII

# The Movement and Thought of Francophone Pan-Negroism: 1924–1936

The story, the spirit of Pan-Africanism, although originating in America and France, was brought to our country by a man whose name and memory I should like to recall here. I am speaking of Marc Kodio Tovallo Queno, who—as an authentic African forerunner of the movement—claimed his négritude even before the word was coined. He brought us to know Marcus Garvey, Dr. Du Bois, and so many others; when I was a child I heard my parents speak of these names and evoke these problems. That is to say, if the first sketch of this movement was begun in America and Paris, it had, before it was publicly evident, repercussions and an extension in Africa.[1]

Histories of the Pan-African movement have usually depended so heavily on the partisan accounts of Du Bois and Padmore, and have put so much emphasis on the ritual of the Du Boisian Congresses between 1919 and 1927, that the view has been accepted that prior to 1945 French Negroes had never taken an active interest in political Pan-Africanism. Nearly all histories of Pan-Africanism have confined their attention (as far as French Negroes are concerned) to the theory of *négritude* evolved by Leopold Senghor, Jean Price-Mars, and Aimé Césaire in Paris in the 1930s.[2] In this chapter, an attempt will

[1] Dr. Emile Zinsou, Secretary of the African Federation Party, Dahomey, in *Pan-Africanism Reconsidered*, ed. American Society of African Culture (Stanford, Cal., 1962), p. 74. Dr. Zinsou served as Foreign Minister of Dahomey, and was President of that country from 1968 to November 1969.

[2] Even the two standard works on the subject suffer from this defect—Decraene, P., *Le Panafricanisme* (Paris, 1959). Legum, Colin, *Pan-Africanism: A Short Political Guide*. Padmore's *Pan-Africanism or Communism* devotes only a few lines to it, while Du Bois is completely silent on the subject.
As far as the author is aware, only Professor George Shepperson, the leading authority on the historical study of Pan-Africanism, has drawn attention to the possibility of studying French Pan-Negro groups as part of the Pan-African movement of the 1920s and 1930s—see Shepperson, G., 'Pan-Africanism and "Pan-Africanism": Some Historical Notes'. Professor Shepperson, however, confines his attention to the roles of Blaise Diagne and Gratien Candace in the period

be made to show that (1) French African participation in the Pan-African movement after 1921 was not negligible but was very active, was political, and was closely following not only the activities of Pan-Negro groups in America but also the nationalist politics of organizations, based in Paris, of North Africa and Indo-China. (2) There were several Negro political organizations in Paris between 1924 and 1936[3] with varying degrees of political orientation, among which, in the author's view, the most important was the *Ligue Universelle pour la défense de la Race Noire* of Tovalou Houénou, and the two other organizations—the *Comité de la défense de la Race Nègre* (C.D.R.N.) led by the Senegalese Lamine Senghor and the *Ligue de la défense de la Race Nègre* (L.D.R.N.) led by Tiemoho Garan-Kouyaté (Soudan) and Abdou Koite (Soudan) respectively—which succeeded it from 1925 to 1936. (3) There was a radical group of French Negro West Indian and African intellectuals and ex-servicemen in Paris in the 1920s and 1930s, from whose ranks the leadership of the *Ligue* was recruited, which had serious doubt about the desirability of assimilation and who attempted to replace Negro deputies like Diagne and Candace by Negro deputies more in line with their Pan-Negro sympathies. (4) Finally, that this group subscribed to the current Pan-African dream of establishing a Negro state in Africa as a solution to the racial and colonial problem, although it acknowledged differences in the social and political condition of American and French Negroes. The origins of the theory of *négritude* are not dealt with in this study, as the subject has already been adequately dealt with recently.[4]

In the French Empire, as in the British Empire, the end of the Great

1919–21, and states that 'If French-speaking African participation in the Pan-African movement seems to have been negligible from 1921 until after the 1945 Manchester Congress, the emergence of négritude in the 1930's indicated that they were making a distinct contribution to cultural pan-Africanism . . .' (p. 356).

[3] James Spiegler, has completed a doctoral dissertation on French African political organizations in Paris in the inter-war period. My concentration on the *Ligue* and its successors by no means implies that other Negro groups were unimportant.

[4] See Hymans, Jacques Louis, 'French Influences on Leopold Senghor's Theory of Négritude: 1928–48', *Race*, vii, no. 4 (Apr. 1966), 365–70. Kesteloot, Lilyane, *Les Écrivains noirs de langue française: naissance d'une littérature* (2nd ed., Université Libre de Bruxelles, 1965); Irele, Abiola, 'Négritude or Black Cultural Nationalism', *Journal of Modern African Studies*, iii, no. 3 (1965), 321–48. Also of some interest is the article in *Ethics*, lxxvi, no. 4 (July 1966), 267–75 by Baron, Bentley Le, 'Negritude: A Pan-African Ideal?'

War witnessed many new problems, among which one of the most important, to French Negro intellectuals in Paris at any rate, was a re-examination of the rather delicate policy of assimilation, and of political representation of the colonies in the Metropolitan parliament. Prior to the outbreak of the war and during the war, these questions had not been brought to the level of serious debate. At that time the representation of the colonies by such Negro deputies as Blaise Diagne and Gratien Candace was deemed satisfactory and Diagne, by virtue of the high offices he held in the French Government, had come to symbolize for the Negroes how far their aspirations could be satisfied in the French empire, and for the Europeans, that incredible phenomenon of an ambitious, able, and responsible African politician playing the game as any Machiavellian would have done. The end of the war and demobilization of French Negro troops led to a strong feeling of disillusionment and dissatisfaction among the Negroes. Whether, or how far, Afro-American troops or the bad treatment of Afro-American troops by white American soldiers had affected the attitude of French Negro soldiers is not known. What is known is that during the war some of them had mutinied and that after the war they condemned some of the methods of recruitment into the army. Diagne was specially singled out for attack; he was even accused of accepting a commission for Negro soldiers he had recruited. Evidently recruitment had not proceeded as smoothly as the French Government had made it appear to the world. It was also evident, as has often been said, that Europe emerged from her civil war less civilized in the eyes of her subject races. Had not black troops fought in Europe and had they not helped France to occupy an already humiliated Germany? Surely, they argued, blacks deserved a better place in the French empire after the war than a half-hearted policy of assimilation and an unreal representation of black interests by black deputies who, they alleged, had betrayed the interests of French Negroes? How could they, so the argument ran, reconcile a Colonial France with the 'democracy' and 'civilization' they had just fought to preserve? Was there not a contradiction between a Colonial, and therefore oppressive, France and the France of 1789?

These were some of the questions being asked by disillusioned French Negroes in Paris after the war, and although Diagne was still unpopular in the empire after the war, he had become in the 1920s and 1930s the most unpopular black man among radical and nationalistic black intellectual circles in Paris, and among a few African politicians and intellectuals like Lamine Gueye and N. S. Galandou Diouf who were now challenging his political power in the Senegal.[5] These black critics of Diagne were joined by other black intellectuals who had migrated to Paris in the 1920s.[6] Even with the formation of the *Association Panafricaine* led by Diagne, Candace, and Du Bois in Paris after the 1921 Pan-African Congress session, Diagne and Candace had already earned the contempt of this radical black group when they publicly dissociated themselves from Garveyism and proclaimed that they were Frenchmen first and black men afterwards.[7] That such a group of French Negroes existed which was opposed to the French-flavoured and dubious Pan-Africanism of Candace and Diagne is confirmed by M. Lamine Gueye, veteran politician and Senegal's eldest statesman, who was in Paris in 1921 to present his thesis for the doctorate in law at the University of Paris:

Some Afro-Americans, under the leadership of Dr. Burghardt Du Bois, but including a minority of elements who seemed to share the views of Marcus Garvey, met Haitians such as Mᵉ Vilcus Gervais, a member of the bar of Port-au-Prince, Drs. Clement Lanier, Couba, Sajous, West Indians among whom were Gratien Candace, a member of parliament for Guadeloupe; Isaac Beton, a teacher at the Lycée Saint-Louis of Paris; Jules Alcandre, a barrister to the Paris Court of Appeal; young academics and

[5] For a general background to the interaction of French and Senegalese politics (the 'metropolitan axis of reference') in the period before 1940, see the informative article by Johnson, G. Wesley, 'The Ascendancy of Blaise Diagne and the Beginning of African Politics in Senegal', *Africa*, xxxvi, no. 3 (July 1966), 235–53. Dr. Johnson's forthcoming book will be on Senegalese politics to 1940. Also Hodgkin, Thomas, 'Background to A.O.F.:2—The Metropolitan Axis' and 'Background to A.O.F.:3—African Reactions to French Rule' in *West Africa* (9 and 16 Jan. 1954), pp. 5–6, 31–2. For some of Diagne's views on colonial and political questions, see Cros, C., *La Parole est à M. Blaise Diagne, premier homme d'état africain* (privately printed, 1961). For French assimilation theory and policy, see Lewis, M. D., 'The Assimilation Theory in French Colonial Policy', *Comparative Studies in Society and History*, iv (1962), 129–53, and Crowder, Michael, *Senegal: A Study in French Assimilation Policy* (Institute of Race Relations, London, 1962). For the scale of the opposition to Diagne, as reflected in the Senegalese press, see the useful bibliographical article by Boulegue, Mme Marguerite, 'La Presse au Sénégal avant 1939. Bibliographie', *Bulletin de l'I.F.A.N.* xxvii, Ser. B, nos. 3–4 (1965), 715–50.
[6] Johnson, G. Wesley, 'Blaise Diagne: Master Politician of Senegal', *Tarikh*, i, no. 2 (1966), 54–6.
[7] Johnson, G. Wesley, 'The Ascendancy of Blaise Diagne and the Beginning of African Politics in Senegal', p. 252.

old soldiers wearing medals which told a lot about the quality of their services in the army. . . .[8]

Dr. Leo Sajous (Haiti), André Beton (son of the Isaac Beton mentioned by M. Gueye), and some of the young university students and ex-servicemen (Houénou, Kouyaté, and Lamine Senghor among them) were to play leading roles in the affairs of the *Ligue* and its successors from 1924 to 1936.

Concerning the early life of Marc Kojo Tovalou Houénou, there is little information. Usually he is glibly described as the playboy son of a wealthy Dahomean merchant who spent half his life in the Bohemian society of Paris and who later turned into a racialist and irresponsible political agitator with left-wing sympathies after being publicly humiliated by white Americans.[9] Houénou was born in Cotonou in April 1877, the son of a well-educated and wealthy Dahomean merchant. Joseph-Tovalou-Padonou Quenum (or Houénou),[10] Tovalou's father, died in 1925 at the age of 70; in his lifetime he became a 'chevalier de la Légion d'Honneur', 'officier de l'étoile noire du Benin', and 'chevalier de l'ordre du Cambodge'. Tovalou's great-grandfather Azanmado Quenum (a Roman Catholic) hailed from Zado (Dahomey) and settled in Ouidah in April 1810; in 1827 he was nominated president of the Chamber of Commerce by His Majesty Ghezo of Abomey. He died at Ouidah on 6 August 1866. The real founder of the Houénou family and the architect of its fortune was Azanmado's son Possy Berry Houénou, said to have

---

[8] Gueye, Lamine, *Itinéraire africain* (Paris, 1966), p. 52.

[9] See, e.g., Ottley, Roi, *No Green Pastures* (London, 1952), pp. 107–8; Ottley wrongly spells his name 'Kogo'.

[10] Interview with Mme Rose Elisha (*neé* T. Quenum), Cotonou, 2 Oct. 1966. Mme Elisha, who is Houénou's sister, informed the author that Houénou was sent to Paris for his education at an early age (he lived in France and elsewhere in Europe between 1890 and 1925, becoming politically active in 1921–36), was very clever, but was 'stubborn' and was a persistent critic of the French colonial administration. Nearly all the surviving members of the Houénou family living in Cotonou and Ouidah whom the author interviewed spoke of Tovalou's 'stubbornness' and fondness for politics. One of his critics, M. Alidji (local historian of Ouidah and formerly *chef de canton*), flatly refused to talk about him but merely called him a 'rascal'. This reluctance to talk about Houénou may partly be due to family feuds and partly to the fact that Houénou's agitation against the colonial administration adversely affected the fortunes and the status of the Houénou family. The author was informed by Madame Houénou, however, that Houénou's correspondence, books, etc., which she collected from Dakar, Senegal, after Houénou's death there in 1936, were stolen from her after she returned from the Senegal. I am satisfied that Madame Houénou's account of her brother's early life is, in general, reliable.

died at the age of 100. Tovalou's grandfather, Padanou Quenum, who died in 1887, was also president of the Dahomey Chamber of Commerce.[11] Tovalou Houénou is described by the Afro-American journalist, Roi Ottley, as 'tall, smooth and shiny as ebony ... educated in Europe, and was fluent in French, German and English'.[12] He read law at the University of Bordeaux, where he received his *licence* and set up legal practice in Paris. At the outbreak of the Great War he, like his fellow-French Negroes, enlisted with the French Army and fought bravely at Douomont and Verdun where several black soldiers lost their lives.[13] After the war he still remained popular with high Parisian society which fêted and lionized him, but it was not easy for him to forget that he was a member of the family of Behanzin, the King of Dahomey who was deposed and exiled by the French. Moreover, the war had had a tremendous effect on his attitude to European civilization and on his views as to the future of the black race, especially the French Negro. Up to the time of his espousal of Pan-Negroism in 1924, however, Tovalou 'had the good taste not to mix politics and racialism with smart bohemianism'.[14] His race-consciousness was also influenced by the Pan-African movements which gained prominence between 1919 and 1925, for in 1921 he wrote a short book in Paris, which can perhaps be described as a forerunner of the more literary theory of *négritude* of the 1930s. The book bore the harmless title of *L'Involution des métamorphoses et des métempsychoses de l'univers*.[15] The book is a combination of

[11] The information on the history of the Houénou family was gleaned from the inscriptions in the family vault of the Houénous at Ouidah. The author would like to express his thanks to M. Felix François Quenum and to M. Etienne F. Quenum, *chef de Collectivité*, Quartier Brésil, Ouidah, for their assistance in tracing the history of the Quenum family.

[12] Ottley, op. cit., p. 107.

[13] Garvey's *Negro World* (24 Aug. 1929) states that Houénou trained both as a doctor and as a lawyer and that he served in the war as a doctor. See Gautherot, Gustave, 'Le Bolchevisme en Afrique', *Bulletin du Comité de l'Afrique Française* (1930), p. 423; also Houénou's speech, 'Le Problème de la race noire' on 20 Feb. 1924 at a conference held at the École Interalliée des Hautes Études Sociales: 'My sympathy, my affection, my love for France cannot be questioned, since during the critical period of 1914, without any compulsion, spontaneously, I assumed every citizen's duty and I risked my life like any other Frenchman. . . .'

[14] Ottley, op. cit., pp. 107–8.

[15] I am grateful to a relative of Houénou, M. Clétus Quenum, who is principal of a school in Cotonou, for allowing me access to this book and to other newspaper material relating to Tovalou. Dr. Emil Zinsou stated at a symposium on Pan-Africanism that Houénou 'as an authentic African forerunner of the movement, claimed his négritude even before that word was coined', *Pan-Africanism Reconsidered*, p. 74.

linguistics, theology, and philosophy, and was intended to demonstrate the unity of language and of cultures; by implication, it was an attack on Eurocentricism and a questioning of the right of Europeans to dominate other races on the assumption of cultural superiority. It was also a plea for racial equality. Like his distinguished successor, Léopold Senghor, Tovalou in a less artistic manner argued that each people and culture was part of a whole and had its own distinctive contribution to that universal civilization. A few examples will suffice: 'Just as rivers have a common source in the bosom of the earth, mingling their waters in the ocean, and in the air by evaporation, in the same way languages, which appear distinct, intermingle and melt together within the basic rules of phonetics.' Houénou quoted Renan's *Origins du christianisme* with approval: 'In the very beginning lies chaos, but a chaos rich in life; it is the fertile primeval slime, where a being is coming into existence, still monstrous, but endowed with a principle of unity, and strong enough to dispel impossibilities, to acquire the essential organs.'[16] He continued, explaining that his purpose in writing the book was 'to bring the complex, irreducible individualities of the universal evolutionary system back to their primitive homogeneous identity'.[17] The war, as we have said, had opened his eyes; towards the end of the same book he observed that, 'on coming to Europe, I understand that civilization is an enormous practical joke, achieved through mud and blood, as in 1914'.

Like most 'clerks' who desire to enter the lists on the side of 'the people', Tovalou not only saw a connection between the thought he was expounding and action he anticipated, but also saw himself in a messianic role: 'The wise man is he who has the wisdom to admit right away that his value is no greater than that of his brothers. The worth of the man gives value to the principle. . . . My work will be as everlasting as the thought which has brought it forth.'[18] And in an outburst of nationalist fervour he asserted: 'Africa has not yet made her contribution to city life, to civilization, but her turn will come. Beware of these men of bronze, whose strength and light will startle your misty lands; the sun comes from their country. . . . Tradition is the conscience of those, the majority, who have none themselves;

---

[16] Houénou, K. Tovalou, *L'Involution des métamorphoses et des métempsychoses de l'univers* (Paris, 1921), p. 5. These extracts are translated, as are all lengthy quotations, from the original French in the pages which follow.

[17] ibid., p. 6.

[18] ibid., p. 77.

guard it devoutly. . . . A foreign guide disappears and dies: conscience does not die, and it can even outlive us.'[19]

Between 1921 and 1923 Tovalou seems to have become more actively engaged in political activity and appears to have been associated with the French Communist Party. He was certainly in touch with Marcus Garvey's U.N.I.A. between 1921 and 1923, for we are told that copies of the *Negro World* reached educated circles in Dahomey through one of Quenum's sons at Paris.[20] At the same time in Paris, radical anti-colonial newspapers, sometimes Communist in sympathy, made their appearance and usually filtered through the docks to French West Africa. These left-wing newspapers and the *Negro World* (which had already been banned in the British African colonies as 'seditious and demoralizing literature') almost created a revolutionary scare among French officials in West Africa. In the official correspondence for 1923–5 one of these newspapers is referred to, and control of its circulation in West Africa, particularly Dahomey (which had witnessed a series of disturbances in 1923), recommended. *Le Paria*, a French Communist publication, was one of the newspapers classified by the French colonial authorities as 'newspapers of subversive tendency published both abroad and in France' and which had found its way into Porto Novo. As for the circulation of the other Paris-produced papers, Governor Fourn was of the opinion that 'their circulation and distribution in native circles represent a danger, with which it is the duty of the local Government to be concerned'.[21] Among the anti-colonial newspapers produced

[19] ibid., pp. 71–2. In Cotonou I interviewed four contemporaries of Tovalou, three of whom could still recite this passage verbatim.

[20] Ballard, John, 'The Porto Novo Incidents of 1923: Politics in the Colonial Era', p. 66. This was not the first time that French Negroes had taken an interest in Negro American race leaders and movements; some of them, resident in Paris, had had contacts with the Tuskegeean Booker T. Washington: see Harlan, L., 'Booker T. Washington and the White Man's Burden', *American Historical Review*, lxxi, no. 2 (Jan. 1966), 464; extracts from the *Negro World* were also published in French, and Tovalou is described in the *Negro World* (17 Aug. 1929) as 'U.N.I.A. Representative in France'.

[21] Départ Confidentiel, 3 janvier 1921 au 20 avril 1925; 182 C, 29 juin 1923, l'administrateur commandant cercle de Cotonou. Archives Nationals du Dahomey, Porto Novo. *Le Paria* was in fact published in Paris between Apr. 1922 and Apr. 1926 by Hô Chi Minh who also founded the Pro-Communist *Union intercoloniale* whose official organ was *Le Paria*. Both Hô's *Le Paria* and his violent pamphlet *Le Procès de la colonisation française* condemned French rule in general, including colonial abuses in Dahomey, Madagascar, and the French West Indies. Hô Chi Minh is also said to have written articles for *La Race Noire* during his stay in Russia in 1924. See Lacouture, Jean, *Hô Chi Minh* (Paris, 1967), pp. 22, 29–36.

in Paris, M. Fourn thought 'one of the most dangerous ... is
*Le Paria* the organ of the Communist Party', a paper which had found
its way into the hands of influential Dahomeans in Cotonou like
J. J. Garcia a Cotonou merchant, and local teachers like M. Emile
Zinsou Bode of Ouidah, and François Quenum of Dasso; it had even
found its way into Lome. It was also believed that recipients of this
journal were 'genuine agents of Communist propaganda'.[22] Then,
after the Porto Novo disturbances, which the administration believed were influenced by revolutionary propaganda from Paris,[23]
Fourn in a dispatch to the chief administrator (cercle Allada) advised him to keep an eye on two other suspected Communist agents
—A. Tolo and Almeida L. Vincent of Abomey-Calavi, adding: 'You
are not unaware of all the difficulties with which the so-called intellectual circles sought to harass us at the time of the events of 1923;
therefore you cannot and you must not fail to take an interest.'[24] Yet
another dispatch observed that *Le Paria* contained genuine calls to
revolution, addressed to all the natives of our colonies.[25] In July
1924 Kojo Tovalou Houénou's *Les Continents*, organ of his newly
founded Pan-Negro *Ligue Universelle pour la défense de la Race
Noire*, and another radical and anti-colonial paper, *L'Action Coloniale*,
made their appearance in West Africa and were widely circulated
around Ouidah and Porto Novo; these two journals were also
described as subversive.[26]

In the same year (1924) in Paris, Houénou (whom the anti-

[22] ibid.
[23] Ballard, John, 'The Porto Novo Incidents of 1923: Politics in the Colonial
Era'; Garigue, P., 'An Anthropological Interpretation of the Changing Political
Leadership in West Africa', pp. 343–5. *Le Journal*, a Paris newspaper, stated in
Mar. 1923 that the cause of the disturbances was the intrigues between rival
chiefs, but Kojo Tovalou Houénou, no doubt closely following developments in
Porto Novo from Paris, told a reporter of this newspaper that, on the contrary, all
the disturbances had been caused by increases in taxation: ibid. Buell, R. L., *The
Native Problem in Africa* (London, 1928), i. 1019 and ii. 16, adds recruitment in
the French army and resentment against the discrimination in status between
citizens and subjects to the causes of the incidents of 1923. It must be remembered,
however, that bad economic conditions in the 1920s and the virtual stopping of
the palm-oil trade must have greatly contributed to the political unrest—see
Garigue, op. cit., pp. 344–5, 349, 366; also *Les Continents* (1 Sept. 1924):
'Quelques Revendications Dahomeens'.
[24] Départ Confidentiel, 3 janvier 1921 au 20 avril 1925; 141 C, 4 avril 1924, M.
l'administrateur en chef, commandant cercle Allada. Archives Nationals du
Dahomey, Porto Novo.
[25] ibid., 142 C, 4 avril 1924.
[26] ibid., 304c, 1 juillet 1927, M. le Gouverneur General a Dakar.

Communist writer M. Gustav Gautherot believes was for some time after the war aligned with the Comintern and with Marcus Garvey)[27] founded the *Ligue Universelle de la Défense de la Race Noire* and a monthly journal with the Pan-Negro title of *Les Continents*, after he had suffered humiliation and racial discrimination at the hands of white Americans at a Montmartre café: 'Having been expelled from a cabaret in Montmartre by American tourists who were shocked by contact with negro in evening dress, Kodjo-Tovalou, infuriated by this really odious effrontery, became susceptible to communist overtures and took up the cudgels on behalf of his race against "European capitalism". He created the paper *Les Continents* which carried communist diatribes . . .'[28] Houénou, however, was already an anti-colonist before 1924; it only required the shock of American racism to turn him into a Pan-Africanist. Such humiliation was too much for a sophisticated Frenchman and a 'prince' of Dahomey.

Houénou became President of the *Ligue* as well as proprietor of *Les Continents*· the chief editor was Jean Fangeat. Associated with the editorial staff was Prince Ouanillo Behanzin of Dahomey and the celebrated French Negro West Indian novelist René Maran (vice-president), whose book *Batouala*, which was a bitter indictment of Europe's senseless '*mission civilisatrice*' in Africa, won the French Academy's Goncourt Prize in 1921.[29] Maran contributed several articles, notably on Negro literature and culture. Among his most interesting articles is an open letter to the Afro-American Professor Alain Locke, author of *The New Negro* and one of the leading spirits in the Negro renaissance in the 1930s, criticizing an article Locke wrote in the Negro journal *Opportunity* for his uncritical admiration of France: Locke, he said, had failed to distinguish between 'official'

[27] Gautherot, Gustav, *Le Bolchevisme aux colonies et l'imperialisme rouge*, p. 272; 'Le Bolchevisme en Afrique', p. 423. It is unlikely that Houénou had any direct liaison with the Comintern, although his anti-colonial agitation was supported by the French Party; he was, however, a supporter of Marcus Garvey and visited the United States in 1924 as guest of the U.N.I.A.; his sister, Mme Rose Elisha, informed the writer that Houénou was a 'friend of Marcus Garvey' and that Garvey's activities were well known in Cotonou and Porto Novo in the 1920s. Houénou married Roberta Dodds, an Afro-American, in 1925. In 1927, however, he was involved in a scandal in Chicago with a Mrs. Zulme Knowlton, French-born wife of a white American: see the *Negro World* (4 June 1927), p. 2.

[28] Gautherot, Gustav, 'Le Bolchevisme en Afrique', pp. 423–4.

[29] For the influence and significance of Maran's *Batouala*, see Kesteloot, op. cit., pp. 83–7, and *Hommage a René Maran* (Paris, 1965), especially Léopold Senghor's tribute 'Réne Maran, Precurseur de la Négritude', pp. 9–13.

or imperialist France and the France of culture and humanity.[30] Houénou wrote the editorials as well as several articles on colonial oppression. Events in both British and French colonies were reported, as well as extracts on Haitian history, politics in Madagascar, and Gandhiism. In particular, there was a wide coverage of Afro-American affairs, especially Marcus Garvey's U.N.I.A. by J. J. Adam, described as the paper's U.N.I.A. delegate; in fact, several issues of *Les Continents* carried reprints of Garvey's speeches and accounts of U.N.I.A. meetings in America.[31] Some poems of Langston Hughes and Countee Cullen were reprinted occasionally and a regular column under the title 'La Race noire d'Amérique' summarized news from Negro newspapers.

Article II of the constitution of the *Ligue* pledged it to:

develop the bonds of solidarity and of universal brotherhood between all members of the black race; to bring them together for the restoration of their country of origin—Africa, the oldest of all the continents; to defend them against all violence . . . or extortion; to fight the calumnies of those interested in exploitation who propagate the idea of racial inferiority, in order to justify their servitude and perpetuate their tutelage; to ensure that the black races should be treated, all over the world, as free men enjoying the inalienable rights of citizens; to come to the aid of the needy, the poor, and the sick, to bring the benefits of instruction and education even to the most remote tribes of Central Africa; to co-operate in the development and evolution of the Race, in setting up institutions of science and the arts, including primary, secondary, industrial, and agricultural schools—which should be compulsory—colleges, academies, universities, . . . centres, meeting rooms, libraries, journals, and newspapers; to watch over and maintain the territorial integrity and independence of those states governed by Africans or African states which at present have their own autonomy: Abyssinia, Liberia, Haiti, San Domingo, etc. . . . and to oppose, by all material and moral means, the new form of treaty which involves the cession of sale of a country or a colony to a foreign power.

It is interesting to note, however, that the *Ligue*, like most radical Negro groups in Paris, was anti-Blaise Diagne whom it persistently and violently reviled as a 'traitor' to the black race and as a reactionary. Apart from voicing the grievances of ex-servicemen and condemning the abuses of French colonial rule, the *Ligue* also campaigned for the naturalization of French subjects and the aboli-

[30] *Les Continents*, Première Année, no. 13, 15 juin 1924.
[31] e.g. ibid., no. 4, 1 juillet 1924: 'Un Appel de M. Marcus Garvey'.

tion of the *Indigénat*, whereas Diagne came to the defence of forced labour in the colonies, supported a conservative colonial policy in general, and vaguely envisaged the eventual independence of French African colonies.[32] Houénou, on the other hand, argued that the duties rendered by French Negroes entitled them to the rights enjoyed by Frenchmen, and that any modification of these rights amounted to a system of tutelage:

We have shed our blood for France as our mother country; now at peace, voluntarily or involuntarily, we continue to fulfil the citizen's supreme duty of military service. Why do we not enjoy the rights of citizenship? We demand to be citizens, whatever the country, and that is why, if France rejects us, we call for autonomy; or, if she welcomes us, then for total assimilation and integration. Enough of lies and hypocrisy! 'Association' under present circumstances is but thinly disguised slavery.[33]

On 16 August 1924 Houénou was in New York, and on 19 August was presented to the Congress of Garvey's U.N.I.A. by Garvey himself and by T. Stephens, described as 'directeur de la Section française du "Negro World" '. *Les Continents* described the U.N.I.A. meeting at Liberty Hall where Houénou spoke to a crowd of about 5,000, as 'cette imposante manifestation'.[34] At the U.N.I.A. meeting, however, Tovalou was not as anti-French as was expected. On French attitudes to the Negro he said on 20 August at Liberty Hall in New York: 'Metropolitan France refuses to tolerate and will never tolerate colour prejudice. She regards her black and yellow children as the equals of her white children.' He added, with a Garveyite touch: 'We insist on our place in the sun, we insist on working for the redemption of Africa.'[35] His speech was preceded by the usual Garveyite pomp and display of all the symbols of the new Ethiopianism, after which 'the prince of Dahomey' was lionized by the Garveyites. Harlem, of course, was visited, as well as Buffalo. Houénou then went on to Philadelphia where he was welcomed by the local branch of the U.N.I.A. and by the mayor. He also addressed meetings in Chicago, Detroit, and Cleveland.[36] At the Harlem

---

[32] Cros, *La Parole*, 'Le Testament politique de Blaise Diagne', p. 137; but see chapter VI, pp. 25–9.

[33] *Les Continents*, Première Année, no. 4, 1 juillet 1924: 'L'Esclavagisme colonial: nous ne sommes pas des enfants . . .' by Prince Kojo Tovalou-Houénou.

[34] ibid., no. 8, 1 septembre 1924: 'Notre Directeur en Amérique'.

[35] ibid., no. 9, 15 septembre 1924: 'Notre Directeur en Amérique: Du *Liberty Hall* au *Carnegie Hall* et à Philadelphie'.

[36] ibid., no. 15, 15 décembre 1924.

U.N.I.A. meeting, Houénou touched on the problems of blacks in America, and accused white America of deliberately encouraging its black men to despise their African origin. The U.N.I.A., he said, was 'the Zionism of the Black Race. It has the advantage in its radicalism of clarifying the exact problem, and of indicating the broad, metalled road which must lead us to salvation.'[37]

It is significant that although Houénou approved of Garvey's radicalism and equated it with true Pan-Africanism, he was careful to distinguish between Pan-African radicalism and utopianism: 'I understand the emptiness of oratorical formulae, and of even the most considered and best thought-out writings . . . Africa, the oldest of all the continents, may well make her own arrangements more legitimately than these phantom nations created by Wilsonian hallucinations.' Diversity, not a monolithic Pan-Negro movement with the same programme and method for all black groups, was his preference: 'The black race provides important groups throughout the whole world; they must be allowed to contribute to the work of redemption according to *their own methods, disciplines, and activities.* Towards this end of diversity in action, we have founded in Paris *La Ligue Universelle pour la défense de la Race Noire.*' Paris had been chosen as the seat of the new Pan-Negro movement, he said, because from many considerations it was 'the heart of the Black Race'.[38]

Back in Paris, the hostility of the *Ligue* to Diagne soon developed into a head-on collision sparked off by an article in *Les Continents* on 15 October 1924 entitled 'Le Bon Apôtre' ('The Good Apostle') which described Diagne as an agent of French colonialism and accused him of receiving a commission for the black troops he had recruited during the war. Diagne, an astute politician and a man of explosive wrath, interpreted this attack as an attempt to discredit him in Africa, and sued Jean Fangeat, the editor-in-chief, and René Maran for libel in the Cour d'Assises, the second highest tribunal in France. The *Ligue* and other radical race groups in Paris rightly saw Diagne's action not only as a civil proceeding but as a political litigation to discredit parties supporting the anti-colonial and anti-Diagne politics of the *Ligue*; they also seized the opportunity to crystallize all their grievances and make Diagne appear to all Frenchmen as the symbol of everything radical black intellectuals disliked. Points of difference between Diagne and his critics—colonial policy,

----

[37] ibid., no. 10, 1 octobre 1924.
[38] ibid.

recruitment of black troops, Communism, and nationalism—
inevitably came to be bound up with the case. According to Fangeat,
M. Diagne had accused the *Ligue* and its supporters of Bolshevist
tendencies and of being anti-patriotic (i.e. for criticizing French
colonial policy).[39] It was during this trial that Lamine Senghor (not
to be confused with Léopold Senghor, President of the Republic of
Senegal) made his first appearance in the politics of black groups in
Paris. Before 1924 he had joined the French Communist Party on his
return from Senegal in 1923 and was becoming increasingly critical
of the French administration (which had refused to allow him to settle
in Senegal because they feared he might spread communist doctrines
there), and, in spite of his attachment to France, was also becoming
a racialist. At the trial, he volunteered as a witness and revealed some
of the irregular methods of recruitment of black troops during the
war, and complained of the low wages they were paid; Senghor
ended his accusation by warning Diagne 'not to condemn a white
man who defends us, we negroes'. Diagne, however, had his revenge,
and at the end of the trial, Fangeat was given a suspended sentence
of six months' imprisonment, plus a fine of 2,000 francs.

Diagne's encounter with the *Ligue* was widely interpreted as a
logical outcome of the clash between two schools of thought on
French colonial policy—the progressive critics led by René Maran
and Tovalou Houénou and the reactionary group of which Diagne
was an influential member. As one editorial explained: 'It was the
point of explosion where the two opposing tendencies met; in short,
between Maranism and Diagnism.' The same editorial continued:
'By all who know him, Mr. Diagne is admitted to be a brilliant
parliamentarian, a subtle politician and a truly clever man. . . . But
they differ with vehemence as to the wisdom of his racial outlook and
disagree on the amount of interest he displays in the welfare of his
own people.'[40] Why, it was asked, did Diagne see fit to turn his
anger on the struggling newspaper of a Pan-Negro group and batter
it with the heavy artillery of the State Criminal Department, rather
than reply to European newspapers which had steadily ridiculed and
criticized him? It was certain that the Garveyism of the *Ligue* was
relatively harmless, and that the *Ligue*, as an organization, could not
effectively function in the colonies where its activities would be

[39] ibid., nos. 13–14, 15 novembre–1 décembre 1924; also *West Africa* (20 Dec·
1924), p. 1441: 'M. Diagne's Action for Defamation'.
[40] ibid., 'M. Diagne prosecutes "Les Continents": Maranism versus Diagnism.'

banned; but it was clear, however, that dissident intellectuals like Houénou, Maran, Kouyaté, and Senghor could effectively erode Diagne's standing in metropolitan politics. In 1926, however, Houénou's *Ligue* was driven underground, partly as a result of Diagne's opposition to it, and partly because the riots and strikes in Dahomey between 1923 and 1926 (which the administration attributed to outside revolutionary propaganda and to a few Dahomean agitators) led to stricter surveillance of nationalistic groups. Added to this was Houénou's rash attempt in 1925 to 'liberate' Dahomey with some black Americans. According to Roi Ottley, Houénou

made a long visit to Harlem, where he was fêted and somehow became involved with fiercely race-conscious blacks, who urged him to strike a blow for his black countrymen. He returned to Paris with notions of liberating Dahomey. His racial awakening unfortunately dovetailed with country-wide strikes among the natives of French West Africa, which caused hardships to coupon-clipping Parisians. Before long he was publicly humiliated. Paris newspapers attacked his personal affairs . . . He was 'exposed' as a bogus prince. . . . He became persona non grata, and was quickly driven into obscurity. The Negro had committed the unpardonable sin of talking about freedom for colonial blacks in Parisian circles dependent upon income from Africa.[41]

Houénou was in fact arrested in Togo by order of the Parquet of Cotonou; in Paris his case was taken up by the *Ligue* and by Henry Torres and Jacques Doriot, representing the 'Commission coloniale' of the Communist Party.[42] Houénou himself turned his attention to Senegalese politics, supporting Diouf against Diagne in the elections of 1928 and 1932. He died in Dakar in 1936 as a result, it is believed, of injuries sustained when opponents attacked a meeting he was addressing during the 1936 election of the communes.[43]

Houénou's *Ligue Universelle de Défense de la Race Noire* was succeeded in 1926 by a more radical group, among whom we first encounter the phrase 'Negro personality' among the Francophone Africans. The successor to Houénou's *Ligue*, the *Comité de Défense*

---

[41] Ottley, op. cit., p. 108; also Gautherot, Gustav, 'Le Bolchevisme en Afrique', *Bulletin du Comité de l'Afrique Française* (1930), p. 424. It seems, however, that small sections of the population in parts of Togoland and Dahomey still looked to Garvey for deliverance from French rule, see Batson, J. Milton, 'Negroes of Togoland Want Garvey to Lead', *Negro World* (30 May 1931).

[42] Gautherot, op. cit.

[43] Information supplied by Mme Rose Elisha, Cotonou, 3 Oct. 1966.

*de la Race Nègre* (hereafter referred to as the C.D.R.N.) was led by the Senegalese Lamine Senghor, who after his discharge from the French army in 1919 studied at the Sorbonne, and joined the Communist Party in 1924. The *Comité* declared its radicalism from the outset: 'we shall introduce a new formula of realism and sincerity into so-called colonial politics, and a vigorous, positive element into the Negro question—the affirmation of the Negro personality. The interests of each will be safeguarded in the defence of the general interest.'[44] In March 1926 the *Comité* was founded by a small group (about a dozen) of politically inexperienced but sensitive young blacks all opposed to Diagne and the colonial policy he supported. On 4 July, at another meeting held at the École des Hautes Études Sociales, the title of Houénou's *Ligue* was formally changed into the C.D.R.N. with Lenin as honorary president, and a telegram sent to the Executive Committee of the Comintern: 'Bring to your knowledge election of Lenin, perpetual honorary president of Committee. Fraternally welcome meeting opening, examination of world situation. Direct your generous attention to Negro workers of the world. Pledged to work in common to realize sincere universal fraternity For le Comité de la Race Nègre: the general secretary, J. Gothon Luniou.'[45] The monthly organ of the C.D.R.N. was *La Voix des Nègres*, subsequently changed, in 1927 to *La Race Nègre*. By the end of 1926 the C.D.R.N. numbered over 300 members. In Senghor's eyes, however, the enemies of the C.D.R.N. were still the Government, especially the black deputies; he even spoke of 'the complicity of the Negro deputies in parliament who see in our movement only the end of their reign' and who saw the C.D.R.N. as a Communist and anarchist organization. These Negroes, he alleged, had allowed themselves to play an 'ignoble' and 'criminal' role against the C.D.R.N. which genuinely represented the interests and views of French Negroes. Senghor also asserted, for the benefit of both black and white critics, that the C.D.R.N. was not a minstrel show managed by some humanitarian white politician, but a universal race move-

---

[44] *La Race Nègre*, no. 1 (juin 1927): 'La Nécessité de nous organiser'.

[45] Text of telegram quoted in Gautherot, op. cit., p. 424. It is curious that Lenin, who had died since 1924, should have been made president—or did the C.D.R.N. leadership simply prefer him to a J. V. Stalin who was more interested in 'socialism in one country'? I suspect Lamine Senghor must have been fascinated by Lenin's personality and style; besides, was he not like Lenin trying to create the kind of disciplined revolutionary party Lenin struggled to create between 1903 and 1917?

ment for the protection of the rights, interests, and prestige of the
Negro race:

> To those who do not demand that our movement for the defence of the
> Negro race should be universal: to those who would like to make of us
> a group dancing the 'Charleston' and other alien steps, presided over
> by the benevolent eye of some white politician: to all these I say . . .
> Negro brothers of the whole world (and especially you African Negroes,
> who have so much cause for complaint!), remember that the supreme
> duty of a Negro is to aid and support the *Ligue*, both materially and
> morally. . . . To aid and support this organization is to contribute to
> the defence of the rights, the interests, and the prestige of the race itself.[46]

Lamine Senghor, the president of the C.D.R.N., was born in 1889
in Kaolack, Senegal, and was of the Serere tribe. At the outbreak
of the war he was recruited into the army and saw service in France
in 1915–19. Contemporary accounts state that Senghor was noted
for his courage and loyalty, that he refused to participate in a mutiny
of Senegalese infantrymen at Fréjus, and that he was awarded the
'croix de guerre'. The use of gas during the war severely affected his
health. He was discharged from the army in 1919 with the rank of
sergeant, and returned to the Senegal;[47] in 1922 he returned to
Paris and attended classes at the Sorbonne, taking some interest in
metropolitan politics. He joined the French Communist Party in
1923 after failing to convince the Government that his deteriorating
health demanded his return to Senegal. The Government, however,
feared that he might spread Communist and anti-colonial propaganda
if he was allowed to return: Senghor had already become a nationalist:

> At that time, he was concerned only little with politics, naïvely confessing
> his ignorance in this field. But the irritating question of his race pre-
> occupied him most and this led him to agitate within the Union Inter-
> coloniale and then within the Communist Party. However, the unfortunate
> trial Diagne v. *Les Continents*, in 1924, played a decisive part in his
> hitherto diffident political life. Ever since then, he was seen displaying a
> feverish energy wherever he could be useful to his race.[48]

In 1924 he stood as Communist Party candidate in the Paris (thir-
teenth *arrondisement*) cantonal elections, obtaining 965 votes; he
lost the election, although he had a good run. A few weeks later an
unsuccessful attempt was made on his life by a fellow black.[49]

[46] *La Race Nègre*, no. 1 (juin 1927).
[47] ibid., no. 5 (mai 1928), obituary.
[48] ibid.                          [49] ibid.

Senghor then joined Houénou's Pan-Negro *Ligue* in 1924–6, and together with radicals like Kouyaté and Dr. Sajous opposed Diagne's policies. After the arrest of Houénou in 1925 he continued the *Ligue*, renaming it the C.D.R.N., the core of whose leadership had left-wing sympathies. The office of the C.D.R.N. was at 43, rue du Simplon in Paris; its treasurer was Stephane Rosso, a West Indian, and its secretary-general, Gothon Luniou. Another official of the C.D.R.N. was the Soudanese Tiémoho Garan-Kouyaté, a Communist, who was then a student of literature at the university of Paris, but was active in political circles like the *Club International des Marins* (through which revolutionary literature reached black sailors) and the Marseilles section of the *Association des Indochinois*; Kouyaté was also section leader of the L.D.R.N. at Var and *des Bouches-du-Rhône* in 1928. In 1929 he became president of the L.D.R.N.

No sooner was the *Comité* established than Senghor, who had Leninist ideas about organization, clashed with the secretary-general Gothon Luniou; there seems to have been some disagreement on the political orientation of the C.D.R.N. between Gothon Luniou (who was supported by other officials—Satino, Mouthia, Capitaine, and William) and the majority of the Bureau of the C.D.R.N. Senghor held that in all matters of policy, the secretary-general had to accept and carry out the decision of the majority of the Bureau; Gothon Luniou was accused of repeatedly refusing to call meetings of the Bureau at the request of the president, of dispatching correspondence on behalf of the C.D.R.N. without reference to the policy-forming Bureau, and of confusing his functions with those of the treasurer. It transpired, however, that the real reason for the dispute lay in the ideological differences between Senghor and Gothon Luniou: 'the decision taken in Luniou's case by the majority of the Bureau originates from the political opposition between his ideas and those of Lamine Senghor'.[50] As the dispute ended in a stalemate (the voting on the issue was confused), the Bureau of the *Comité* was replaced by a provisional one of three members—Amadou Diaze (a Senegalese), Satino, and Bloncourt (West Indians). Senghor, who still remained president, explained in an article that the former secretary-general had misinterpreted the aims and political sympathies of the C.D.R.N.

[50] *La Voix Des Nègres*, Première Année (mars 1927): 'Au Comité de Défense de la Race Nègre: assemblée générale extraordinaire du dimanche, 16 janvier 1927'.

to a French public which had been led to think that the C.D.R.N.
was a non-political club; he also confirmed that the policy of the
C.D.R.N. was 'permanent collaboration with those organizations
which are genuinely struggling for the liberation of oppressed peoples
and for world revolution'.[51]

In 1926 Senghor's tuberculosis worsened and he had to move away
from Paris to Roquebrune-sur-Argens (Var), though he regularly
returned to Paris to report on his activities. In February 1927 he
accepted, on behalf of the C.D.R.N., an invitation from Willi
Muenzenberg's *League Against Imperialism and for National Independence*[52] to attend its inaugural and anti-imperialist conference in
Brussels.

Senghor was accompanied to that conference by Narcisse Danae
and Max Bloncourt (Antilles),[53] also members of the C.D.R.N.
The first meeting of the conference was presided over by Edo
Fimmen, secretary-general of the International Transport Workers
Union. Apart from Lamine Senghor and Max Bloncourt, there were
delegates from Africa and the West Indies: Hadjali Abd el Kader
(North African Star), Chadli Ben Mustapha, and A. H. Mattar;
I. A. La Guma (South Africa); Josiah Tshangana Gumede (South
African National Congress);[54] Ibrahim Yousseff (Egypt); Elie
Bloncourt (Antilles) and Camille Saint Jacques (Inter-Colonial
Union, Negro Peoples Section). Syria, Korea, Cuba, Indonesia,
India, U.S.A. (R. B. Moore representing U.N.I.A.);[55] Venezuela,

[51] ibid., no. 1 (janvier 1927): 'Ce qu'est notre Comité de Défense de la Race
Nègre' by Senghor, Lamine. Senghor was, of course, referring to the Comintern
and metropolitan Communist parties as well as radical trade unions.

[52] See Muenzenberg, W., 'The Colonial Conference in Brussels', *Pravda*,
xxviii (4 Feb. 1927), 1.

[53] Max Bloncourt, a West Indian Negro, practised law in Paris and defended
the Dahomean nationalist Louis Hunkarin in the 1920s: see John Ballard's article
on the Porto Novo Incidents of 1923 in *Odu*, ii, no. 1 (July 1965), 66, 68. Bloncourt and Senghor were associated with left-wing circles in Paris; both Narcisse
Danae and Max Bloncourt were leading members of the *Union Intercoloniale*
(*Section des vieilles Colonies et Peuples noirs*).

[54] La Guma had been the leader of Sydney Bunting's League of African Rights
in South Africa; according to Padmore (*Pan-Africanism or Communism?*, p. 351),
he and Gumede visited Moscow where they were fêted after the Brussels Conference of the League Against Imperialism. Curiously enough, Harry Thuku, who
had led a riot against the British administration in Kenya in 1922, is included
among the delegates to the Brussels Conference: see Gautherot, Gustav, *Le
Bolchevisme aux colonies et l'imperialisme rouge*, pp. 85–6.

[55] R. B. Moore was denounced by Garvey's U.N.I.A. in 1927 as a 'communist'
and 'impostor' for speaking on behalf of the U.N.I.A. '. . . the Association sent
no delegate to the Brussels conference, and Mr. Richard Moore, the New York

Argentina, Mexico, Haiti, Peru, and Indo-China were also represented. At the conference, Senghor came into prominence by his
violent and nationalistic diatribes against French colonialism;[56] it
was at that conference also that he made the prophetic remark:
'The Negroes have slept too long. But beware, Europe! Those who
have slept long will not go back to sleep when they wake up. Today,
the blacks are waking up!'[57] Before the close of the Conference, he
was elected a member of the executive committee of the *League* and
of the Bureau of the *League*.[58] He returned to Paris, but his anti-
colonial attacks had made him a marked man; in March 1927 he was
arrested at Cannes and imprisoned at Draguignan prison on an
obscure charge. Partly because of his bad health and partly because
of representations to M. Poincaré, president of the Conseil, by the
League, by deputies of the French National Assembly, and by some
members of the Reichstag and of the Belgian parliament, Senghor
was released in late 1927, although a strict watch was still kept on
his activities; but he remained an unrepentant Communist and Pan-
Negroist: 'The officials have overlooked the fact that Senghor was
sincerely African, of a fierce nationalism, full of hatred even. To the
work of the emancipation of his race he brought the mystical stubbornness of Polyeucte.'[59] In July 1927 he had another serious attack
and was confined to his bed for several months, during which time

representative of the American Negro Congress, an organization preaching the
doctrine of Lenin and Trotsky, was never empowered to appear as its representative. . . . There is a great gulf fixed between communism and Garveyism' (*Negro
World* (19 Feb. 1927), p. 2). For Moore's recollections of the Brussels Conference,
see his contribution entitled 'Africa Conscious Harlem' in Clarke, John Hendrik,
ed., *Harlem, U.S.A.* (Berlin, 1964), p. 68.

[56] The late Mr. Bridgeman who attended that conference, told me that Senghor's
speech was noted for its vehemence. For Senghor's speech and that of Bloncourt
at the Brussels Conference, see *La Voix des Nègres*, Première Année, no. 1 (mars
1927): 'Au Congrès de Bruxelles du 10 au 15 fevrier 1927: condamnation de l'impérialisme et de la colonisation'; also the official record of the conference in the
League's publication *Das Flammenzeichen vom Palais Egmont: Offizielles
Protokoll des Kongresses gegen koloniale Unterdrückung und Imperialismus,
Brüssel, 10.–15. Februar 1927. Herausgegeben von der Liga gegen Imperialismus
und für nationale Unabhangigkeit* (Berlin, 1927), pp. 113–19.

[57] Senghor, Lamine, quoted in Padmore, *Pan-Africanism or Communism?*, p.
324. Senghor had also written an anti-colonial pamphlet called *La Violation d'un
pays*, in which he envisaged a colonial revolution aided by the working classes of
the capitalist Colonial Powers.

[58] For a list of the committee members of the League Against Imperialism
and of the League's various organs, see Gautherot, op. cit., chapter V, especially
p. 84.

[59] Obituary, *La Race Nègre*, Première Année, no. 5 (mai 1928).

his father and then his son Diene (22 August 1927) died. His tuberculosis was followed by paralysis and loss of speech. He died at
Fréjus at 11 p.m. on 25 November 1927—'un bon nègre, un sincère
africain . . . soldat de sa race'.[60]

La Race Nègre reflected the opinions of nearly all political groups
in Paris—from the Indo-China nationalists to the Étoile Nord Africaine; even the proceedings of the West African Students Union based
in London were sometimes reported.[61] The C.D.R.N. was also anti-
Diagne, and apart from criticizing his views on colonial policy, it also
gave its anti-Diagne campaign a nationalistic slant. For example, a
call by the Ligue to all Senegalese in France who qualified to vote in
the elections to the Chamber of Deputies urged them not to vote for
any deputy who did not have the interests of Senegal at heart; Diagne,
the C.D.R.N. charged, 'considers himself a white Frenchman and
not a colonial subject'.[62]

Like its predecessor Les Continents, Senghor's paper commented
extensively on Afro-American organizations, particularly the Garvey
movement. There were reprints of Garvey's poem 'Africa for the
Africans' taken from his The Tragedy of White Injustice; colonialism
was condemned as the negation of the principle of self-determination;
the equality of all races was asserted, and there were sympathetic
accounts of Garvey's activities after his imprisonment in 1925.[63] The
activities of the N.A.A.C.P., the Equal Rights League of Boston, and
the John Brown Memorial Association of Philadelphia were also
reported in La Race Nègre, but in the opinion of the C.D.R.N.,
Marcus Garvey's U.N.I.A. was 'the best known in Africa'. The
C.D.R.N. also took pride in the growth of banks owned by Afro-
Americans and in black schools and colleges, but it made it clear
that while these self-help schemes of the Afro-Americans were of the
greatest importance to all black men and ought to be emulated, the

[60] ibid.
[61] See, e.g., the summary of J. B. Danquah's presidential address to W.A.S.U.,
La Race Nègre, Première Année, no. 4 (nov.–déc. 1927).
[62] ibid.
[63] In fact, Garvey visited France in July 1928 and met French Negro groups in
Paris, and claimed that U.N.I.A. had 'already cemented a working plan with the
French Negro by which we hope to carry out the great ideals of the U.N.I.A. My
visit to France is, indeed, profitable, and I do hope for great results' (Negro
World (4 Aug. 1928), p. 2 and (11 Aug. 1928)). There are indications that Garvey
paid another visit to France around Nov.–Dec. 1931. Information supplied by
Robert A. Hill, Jamaica, who is currently researching on West Indian influences
on African nationalism.

social and political problems of French Negroes were of a different order from those of Afro-Americans:

*We do not have to suffer in France such acute hostility as in America,* but it is nevertheless true that we must draw inspiration from their example in order to introduce some improvement of our social and political position in French civilization. We cannot endure being used—and abused—in circumstances where most frequently we meet indifference rather than a just approach to our legitimate aspirations for betterment. *Our American brothers offer us a living example of the way in which we should struggle. It is in their school that we shall learn how to emancipate ourselves, while contributing some original expression of our own personality, in harmony with the environment that precipitates the reaction.*[64]

Afro-Americans in turn were sympathetic towards the C.D.R.N. and were quick to point out that in spite of the French policy of assimilation and in spite of France's cosmopolitanism, there was a group of French Negro intellectuals who were dissatisfied with the methods of French rule and were agitating for more autonomy within the French empire. One Afro-American newspaper, noting the interest which the C.D.R.N. was taking in Afro-American affairs, commented in 1927:

In common with the most enlightened African Negroes, this group is inspired by American Negroes. . . . It is encouraging to learn that an intellectual element exists among French Negroes, and that revolt is rumbling in the colonies. Discontent is half-way to progress. The Africans who are awakened must themselves liberate Africa; but in triumphing over the many obstacles which surround us, we can encourage them to achieve that ideal.[65]

Active members of the C.D.R.N. included Dr. Leo Sajus from Haiti, Sabia Sangaré, Samba Dia, André Béton or Bérthon a lawyer at the Cour d'Appel in Paris (not to be confused with the Marxist and surrealist poet and philosopher André Bréton), Adolphe Mathurin, Emile Faure a Senegalese, Jean Toulouse, Garan-Kouyaté (Soudan), Kodo-Kossoul, Jean Bareau (Haiti), as well as a large number of Senegalese, a few Dahomeans and Soudanese, and several West Indians. It was a militant body and was outspoken in its criticism of French colonial policy and tended to align itself with the

[64] ibid., no. 3 (Sept. 1927): 'Aux États-Unis d'Amérique: l'activité des Nègres'.

[65] Extract from the *Pittsburg Courrier* quoted in *La Race Nègre*, Deuxième Année, no. 1 (mars 1929): 'Ce que les Nègres des États-Unis pensent de *La Race Nègre*'. See also Garvey's articles in the *Negro World* (4 Aug. 1928), p. 2 and (11 Aug. 1928).

Communists and trade unions. In particular, the trade union section of the C.D.R.N. had as its object the radicalization of black sailors, ex-servicemen and labourers through various clubs, cultural groups, and all-Negro restaurants, etc. On the political front, it opposed Diagne and vigorously supported his more radical opponents N'Galandou Diouf, Lamine Gueye, and Tovalou Houénou; when Diagne defeated Diouf at the election of the communes in Senegal in 1928, the C.D.R.N. roundly condemned the electors for renewing their confidence in a 'traitor' and, perhaps with some justification, spoke of 'l'election frauduleuse de M. Diagne'. The militancy of the C.D.R.N. and its preoccupation with nationalism and colonialism was something new to the French administration in whose view anti-colonialism was synonymous with anti-France and therefore with Communism. It did not take them long to identify Senghor (who was now bed-ridden with tuberculosis), Dr. Sajous, and Kouyaté as Communist link men. Under Senghor's leadership, the C.D.R.N. went so far as to declare itself, rather naïvely, in favour of the Comintern and to condemn the European socialist parties and the Second International as betrayers of the liberation movement in the colonies:

The Second International has betrayed the cause of the colonial peoples. . . . The socialists in Brussels have proved that they have no intention of interfering with any of the prerogatives of the governing bourgeoisie. They accept colonization as a *fait accompli*. . . . On the other hand, the Communist International claims and demands the complete and absolute independence of the colonial peoples. It rejects the theory of the superiority of white over black, and works for universal brotherhood. It supports all the national liberation movements, and thus brings out into the open the clear realities of the true Wilsonian formula of the peoples' right of self-determination. In such conditions, it is not difficult for Negroes to judge and to make their choice . . . they recognize unanimously that the Communist International is the only true defender of the oppressed peoples.[66]

The editorial then quoted the theses of the Sixth Congress of the Comintern to the effect that black workers should be aligned to the Red International of Labour Unions and other radical metro-politan unions.

It is true that in relation to nationalist and revolutionary move-

[66] *La Race Nègre*, Première Année, no. 6 (oct. 1928): 'Bruxelles et Moscou'. For a more detailed account of the attitudes of both the Socialist International and Comintern towards the colonies and semi-colonies, see Padmore, *Pan-Africanism or Communism?*, pp. 320 ff.

ments in the 1920s and 1930s, the Comintern pursued an 'Asia First' policy, and that its 'theses' on the colonial question, especially the Negro question, were superficial.[67] It is also true that it was only in South Africa that a Communist Party was established in Africa between 1920 and 1925; but to argue that Communist interest in colonial Africa suddenly began in the 1950s is to miss the brief but interesting courtship of Negro nationalist groups by the Comintern in the 1920s. The German Communist deputy and publisher Willi Muenzenberg, whom Padmore knew well and described as 'the Barnum of the Comintern',[68] played a key role in the infiltration of such groups and turning them into Comintern satellites. The *League Against Imperialism* was created in Moscow and Berlin and was the brain child of Comintern organization man, Muenzenberg. It was one of the many fronts or 'Muenzenberg Shows', or 'Innocents' Club' for the creation of 'sympathising mass organisations' and organizing the intellectuals of the bourgeoisie. This theory of infiltration is credited to the C.P.S.U.'s chief theoretician Otto Kuuisinen who counselled that the Comintern 'must create a whole solar system of organisations and smaller committees around the Communist Party, so to speak, smaller organisations actually under the influence of our Party (not under mechanical leadership) . . .'.[69]

The League Against Imperialism had its headquarters in Berlin, with branches in France and Britain, as well as in Mexico and China. Mr. Reginald Bridgeman, who was at the time expelled from the Labour Party, became the secretary of the British section of the League. A Bulletin of the League was published in Berlin for the

[67] See Cattell, David T., 'Communism and the African Negro', *Problems of Communism*, viii (1959), 35–41.

[68] *Pan-Africanism or Communism?*, p. 324.

[69] Quoted on p. 3 of Labour Party Pamphlet: *The Communist Solar System* (1933). For a detailed list of these 'fronts' and their publications, see Sworakowski, W. S., *The Communist International and its Front Organizations* (Stanford, Cal., 1965), and the Labour Party Pamphlet referred to earlier. Padmore gives a general account, based on his personal experiences, of Comintern tactics and attitudes to revolutionary and nationalist groups, but he said little about Muenzenberg except that he was a master organizer and a friend of oppressed peoples. Fortunately, Arthur Koestler, who was at one time associated with Muenzenberg, has given us an account of him in his *The Invisible Writing* (London, 1954), pp. 194–212, and the late R. N. Carew Hunt has dealt fully with many controversial points in Muenzenberg's career, including the mysterious circumstances surrounding his death in 1940: see Hunt, R. N. Carew, 'Willi Muenzenberg', in *St. Anthony's Papers. Number 9: International Communism*, ed. David Footman (London, 1960), pp. 72–87.

members of the Executive, the International Council of the League, and for the secretaries of the national sections of the League. The *International Bureau*, run by L. Gibarti, another Communist, was located in Paris. The General Council met periodically and its resolutions were published in English, French, German, and Spanish. In 1928 the membership of the Executive Committee was as follows: President (James Maxton, M.P., Britain, I.L.P.—later expelled because he could not 'keep straight'); Vice-President, Edo Fimmen (Holland), secretary of the International Federation of Transport Workers; Secretaries—Liau Hansin (China) and L. Gibarti (Germany). Committee Members were Jawaharlal Nehru (I.N.C.); Mastapha Chedli (North Africa), *North African Star*; Mohammed Hatta (Indonesia); S. Saklatvala, M.P. (Britain). After Hitler came to power in 1933, the headquarters of the League were transferred to London, where Mr. Bridgeman became its International Secretary.[70] The French section published a monthly called *Journal des Peuples Opprimés* in the 1930s, and another broadsheet called *Chaînes* in Paris.

After Senghor's death in late 1927, the C.D.R.N. was reconstituted into the *Ligue de Défense de la Race Nègre* (hereafter referred to as the L.D.R.N.) and a more militant leadership, with Tiémoho Garan-Kouyaté as secretary-general and director of the Central Bureau, took over. During Kouyaté's tenure of office (1928–31) the L.D.R.N. became closely associated with the R.I.L.U. (Profintern), with the French Communist Party (which included self-determination and independence from French colonies in its programme), and with radical unions like the C.G.T.U. (la Confédération Générale du Travail Unitaire)—a Communist-controlled trade union affiliated to W.F.T.U. As usual, the opposition to Diagne was vociferous; in fact, the L.D.R.N. was opposed to all 'les nègres europeanisés' who disagreed with its aims and politics. Diagne was accused of 'betraying the interests of Senegal' and of 'infidelity to his

---

[70] I owe much of the information on the League to the late Mr. Reginald Bridgeman who lived in Middlesex. In the course of the interview (20 Apr. 1967) he made it clear that the League was not a Communist front organization (as Lord Brockway thinks in *Inside the Left* (London, 1942), pp. 167–9), although it approved of the Comintern's anti-colonial policy. Mr. Bridgeman was also connected with the Negro Welfare Association and with West African nationalists like Wallace-Johnson and E. F. Small; unfortunately, space does not permit detailed treatment of these. There is no doubt, however, the League Against Imperialism was the product of Muenzenberg: see the latter's article in *Pravda*, xxviii (4 Feb. 1927), 1.

native land'; as for the other black deputy from Guadeloupe, M. Gratien Candace, who styled himself 'le fils spirituel de la République', Kouyaté advised members of the L.D.R.N. to ignore the patriotic effusions of this deluded black man. The choice before French Negroes in France, argued Kouyaté, lay between the L.D.R.N. and the 'fourriers [sergeant-majors] de l'impérialisme' represented by Diagne and Candace.[71]

The L.D.R.N. also took up the cause of the North African nationalists, notably the *L'Étoile Nord-Africaine* of Messali Hadj (which was in fact being infiltrated by the French party at the time), as well as the Indo-Chinese nationalists. On the Negro question, it divided areas of Negro discontent (following the Comintern's classification) as follows: (*a*) Colonized Negroes in Africa (British, French, Belgian, Spanish, Portuguese, Italian; Dutch, French, and British Indies. (*b*) Negroes in the semi-colonies—Haiti. (*c*) Negroes in the U.S.A. (*d*) Ethiopia and Liberia. As for the strategy of liberation for these areas, the L.D.R.N. had no clear answer except the utopian programme characteristic of Pan-Negroism during that period: 'The payment for race prejudice will be made in full on the day when a great Negro state is established on a modern basis: African Zionism. The peoples will love one another because they will live in the framework of national liberty and international equality.'[72] The L.D.R.N., however, had a more clear-cut programme for the Negro in the French empire, and one of the key issues in its agitation was the question of the representation of French subjects in the metropolitan Chamber of Deputies. Although the matter was delicate and somewhat complex, the L.D.R.N. was generally violent in its criticism of the Diagne–Candace thinking on colonial policy. In fact, it came very near to demanding political autonomy and more decentralization of authority in the French colonies. The L.D.R.N. argued that in Algeria, for example, the deputies represented exclusively the interests of the 'colons'. Assimilation, it said, was merely a clever formula to protect the interests and privileges of French Europeans in the colonies. Against Diagne's case for 'symbolic' representation, the L.D.R.N. argued for proportional representation: 'Proportional representation, for lack of something better, would be, for us, a guarantee against the treason of the colonial

---

[71] *La Race Nègre*, Deuxième Annèe, no. 1 (mars 1929): Tiémoho Garan-Kouyaté, 'Vox Africae'.
[72] ibid., 'Vers l'élaboration d'un programme'.

deputies who could be tempted to sell their race-brothers. . . .
Assimilation, without the political consequences it involves, is
nothing but a farce, a chimera, a lie used to cover a policy of out and
out exploitation which people fear to expose in full daylight.'[73]

Though preoccupied with anti-colonial activity, nationalism, and
trade-union politics in France, Kouyaté was also associated with the
*League Against Imperialism* whose second conference he attended,
on behalf of the L.D.R.N., at the Zoological Gardens, Frankfurt,
in July 1929. He was also on the editorial staff of Padmore's *Negro
Worker* which was published in Hamburg and later in Copenhagen.
Through Afro-American contacts in the *League Against Imperialism*,[74] he was also able to get in touch with black American
race organizations and to solicit assistance from them. Below is a
letter from him (intercepted by the French police) to W. E. B. Du
Bois whom the French Ministre de Colonies wrongly described as a
'professeur à l'Université Tuskegee'.[75] The letter goes a long way
towards dispelling the myth of non-participation of French-speaking
Negroes in political Pan-Africanism, and therefore merits full
quotation:

Dear Sir,
   Our friend Roger Baldwin has just written to us, informing us of the
results of his approaches to you, and to other Negro leaders in the United
States, in our cause. We had in fact asked him, in December 1923, to
appeal to your organizations, with their moral and financial solidarity,
to assist us in our struggle. . . .
   The aim of our Ligue is the political, economic, moral and intellectual
emancipation of the whole of the Negro race. It is a matter of winning
back, by all honourable means, the national independence of the Negro
peoples in the colonial territories of France, England, Belgium, Italy,
Spain, Portugal, etc. . . . and of setting up in Black Africa a great Negro
State. The Negro peoples of the Caribbean will retain the right to form
their own confederation, or to rejoin black Africa, once this has been
regained. On the other hand, we desire to co-ordinate our actions with
your efforts to obtain, for our racial brothers of the United States, the

[73] ibid., no. 2 (avril 1929): 'La Représentation parlementaire coloniale ou la
panacée chimérique'.
[74] e.g. Roger Baldwin who represented the N.A.A.C.P. in the League Against
Imperialism; Baldwin incurred the wrath of the Communist-dominated League
which duly dubbed him a traitor and 'liberal bourgeois American' at the Frankfurt conference of the League in 1929.
[75] W. E. B. Du Bois's theory of the 'talented tenth' was the very antithesis of
Booker T. Washington's view which Tuskegee Institute symbolized.

repeal of the 13th and 14th laws of the American Constitution,[76] equality of political and civil rights, etc. . . . or else it is for the American Negroes to tell us what they wish, and how they intend to fulfil their aspirations. *The cardinal point lies in the unification of the world Negro movement and the building up of a common movement without ever losing sight of differences of detail.*[77] We think that the reason why our race suffers so much is that it is dominated, above all politically, by the other races. Its internal divisions, its lack of any spirit of solidarity, have always made it an easy prey, ceaselessly enlisted in the service of others. Yet we are very devoted to the high human ideal of understanding and brotherly co-operation between the races. But we consider that this ideal, if it is to carry weight in future, remains conditioned by our national liberty and by international equality. We should be wrong to content ourselves with self-pity and to entrust other races with the task of liberating our own. It is indeed most just to praise the admirable efforts of the whites who wish to help us, and to show them our profound gratitude. Nevertheless, experience demonstrates that the action of a part of our race remains sterilised, if it is not first sustained by the solidarity of all.

Thus Haiti fell under domination in 1915 while the Negroes, hundreds of thousands of them, were hastening to their deaths in Europe. Let us sadly admit this neglect of our own cause. Tomorrow, Abyssinia and Liberia might submit to the same fate. This would then be a total servitude for the whole race. Such a vision of our general situation angers every Negro truly convinced of his own equality with the other ethnic elements in the world. . . .

. . . Moreover, the financial help which we are asking from your organisations will be temporary. It will enable us to extend our action, and to face up to certain current difficulties in strengthening our contacts with the Negro masses in Africa and the Caribbean. We hope to reach an understanding with you, before the forthcoming Negro congress.

While awaiting a fraternal response, we beg to assure you of our cordial greetings.

On behalf of the Central Bureau,<br>signed Kouyaté, Secretary General.[78]

In May 1930 Kouyaté was re-elected Secretary-General but was at the same time associated with the *Comité Syndical International des*

[76] An error on Kouyaté's part; probably refers to the second part of Section 4, Art. 14, of the U.S. Constitution.

[77] My emphasis; Tovalou Houénou stressed the same point when he visited the U.S.A. in 1924.

[78] Copy of letter from Tiémoho Garan-Kouyaté, secretary-general of the L.D.R.N., to Dr. W. E. B. Du Bois, 29 Apr. 1929. This letter was found in a dossier on Kouyaté and the L.D.R.N., *Archives Nationales du Dahomey* (*Porto Novo*), *1929-1931*: Lettre, C.A.I. (cabinet des affaires indigènes), 25 May 1929, Ministre de Colonies à M. le Gouverneur Général de l'A.O.F., Dakar, no. 567/A.P./2.

*Ouvriers Nègres* based in Hamburg and later at Copenhagen, and with Padmore's journal the *Negro Worker*. Through him there was some *rapport* between the L.D.R.N. and the *International Committee of Negro Workers*.[79] In the period 1930–2 Communist influence was very much in evidence in the affairs of the L.D.R.N. and in the pages of *La Race Nègre*. To this tendency was added an articulate Pan-Negroism which viewed events in Haiti, America, South Africa, and Indo-China as part of a world-wide struggle of coloured peoples. In 1930 also the Senegalese engineer Emile Faure became editor of *La Race Nègre* and president of the Central Bureau of the L.D.R.N. Other officers of the Central Bureau were: François Tarpeau (vice-president), Pierre Kodo-Kossoul (vice-president), Abdou Koité (joint secretary), Stephane Rosso (general treasurer), Amady Diara (joint treasurer). Members of the *Commission de Controle* were André Béton (or Bérthon) president; Dr. Leo Sajous (financial member); Ramanjato and Ibrahim Sylla. Earlier in January Kouyaté had toured the provincial branches of the L.D.R.N. in the Bouches-du Rhône and the Gironde, as well as Marseilles and Bordeaux to organize the Negro workers.[80] At Bordeaux he was assisted by M. Durant, secretary of the *Syndicat des Inscrits Maritimes* (C.G.T.U.), and at Marseilles the C.G.T.U. put some of its facilities, including the *Club International des Marins*, at Kouyaté's disposal. At a meeting at Marseilles on 19 January 380 Negroes reorganized their section into the Bouches-du-Rhône section of the L.D.R.N. and elected an ethnically balanced bureau which was constituted as follows: M. Alfred Afene, a merchant (president); M. Pierre Baye, a merchant (secretary); M. Cyprien Sodonou, merchant (treasurer), Benoit-Michel Diagne (Wollof), Bakary Samba Traoré (Sarancolé), Lucien Chicaya (Congolese), Navé Diakité (Bambara), Sy (Toucouleur), Ambruse Mendy (Mandingo), Germain Hodorou (Dahomean), Alexandre Modes (Antilles), and Louis Daouda (Soussou).[81] In the Seine section Amadou N'Diaye, a Senegalese, was elected president,

[79] See *La Race Nègre*, Quartième Année, no. 3 (nov.–déc. 1930).

[80] A detailed account of Kouyate's movements in France in 1930 is contained in the dossier on him (1929–31) which can be found at the Archives Nationales du Dahomey at Porto Novo, no. 567/A.P./2.

[81] *La Race Nègre*, Troisième Année, no. 2 (fév.–mars 1930); also A.N.D. dossier: *Ligue de Défense de la Race Nègre: Institut Nègre de Paris*, confidential letter no. 865, C.A.I. 9 May 1930: 'A.S. de la Ligue de Défense de la Race Nègre et du Syndicat Nègre' and enclosure, letter no. 459, 14 Apr. 1930, Le Délégué du Service de Controle et d'Assistance en France des Indigènes to Monsieur le Directeur des Affaires Politiques, Ministère des Colonies, Paris.

Mme Jeanne Kodo-Kossoul secretary, and M. Ludovic M. Lacombe treasurer. In the Gironde section Charles Carvalho a shipwright (secretary), Victor Derica a student of literature (secretary), and Calixte Dolsure Clairisse a hotel proprietor (treasurer).

Throughout the period 1929–31, Kouyaté denied any connection either with the French party or with Profintern organizations, although it was known that some L.D.R.N. members were officials of the *Syndicat Nègre* which spoke in the name of the L.D.R.N. but published a Communist-inspired journal *Le Cri des Nègres* which was smuggled into the colonies. Kouyaté vigorously denied M. François Coty's allegation that Pan-Negro organizations, including the L.D.R.N., were either being infiltrated by the Communists or were already being managed and financed by them.[82] Coty, he said, was one of those journalists who saw a Communist plot everywhere: 'He sees red, he sees Communism everywhere. . . . He accuses us of having received gold from Moscow. Let him substantiate that without delay. . . . According to him, it is the Communists who have given us the idea of Africa as a country, of Negro national independence. It is obvious that he is ignorant of the history of the Negro race and of the ancient Negro-African civilisations.'[83]

The French Government, however, was hostile to the L.D.R.N., and viewed even its cultural activities as subversive. When, for example, in February 1930, the *Comité Universel de l'Institut Nègre de Paris* (similar to its contemporary, the West African Students Union in London) was founded at the inspiration of Dr. Leo Sajous and Kouyaté, both men were described by the administration as active members of the L.D.R.N., 'whose attitudes are revolutionary and clearly anti-French'.[84] The president of the new *Comité* was Dr. Leo Sajous of Haiti, with Kouyaté, described as 'étudiant en lettres', as Secretary-General. The secretary was Mlle Hélène Jodfard, a dentist; the treasurer was Emile Faure the Senegalese engineer we have already referred to in connection with the L.D.R.N., and advisers included M. Guerrier and M. Samuel Stefany, both lawyers. M. Du Coudret observed in his dispatch that although the *Comité* was not

[82] *La Race Nègre*, Troisième Année, no. 2 (fév.–mars 1930): 'François Coty, Directeur de "L'Ami du Peuple" a Colomnie'. The article by M. Coty was entitled 'l'Organisation de la révolte noire' and appeared in *L'Ami du Peuple* (6 Dec. 1929). Cf. Gautherot, op. cit., p. 271 n. 1.
[83] ibid.
[84] A.N.D. dossier on Kouyaté and the L.D.R.N., M. Du Coudret to M. le Gouverneur General de l'A.O.F., Dakar; Paris, 2 May 1930, lettre no. 804.

actually receiving funds on behalf of the L.D.R.N., and although its constitution stated that it eschewed 'toute action politique ou religieuse' and was merely interested in receiving national and international subscriptions to serve its purpose as a cultural, intellectual, and art centre for all Negroes,[85] it was the opinion of the French Government that the *Comité* was merely another cleverly disguised Communist front organization:

The president, the secretary general, and the treasurer are members of the L.D.R.N. and their political sympathies are drawn from the Communist party. . . . Dr. Sajous believes that this administration has to accuse the leaders of wishing to make use of the organization for Communist political ends, when there is not a single Communist actually attached to the party. . . . He accuses this administration and the Colonial Minister of having given false information to a journalist, Coty, who used it against the L.D.R.N. He adds that the colonial peoples are in revolt against the so-called protecting powers, who exploit and even murder them through forced labour.

He adds that he personally is Communist, but he does not belong to the party; he struggles for the peoples' liberation. . . .[86]

Dr. Leo Sajous was also among those black intellectuals in Paris who in the late 1920s and 1930s led the intellectual revolt against French civilization and published the short-lived literary journal *La Revue du Monde Noir* which appeared in French and English. Associated with Sajous were René Maran of *Batouala* fame, Dr. Jean Price-Mars (who was later in the 1930s to formulate the theory of *négritude* with Léopold Senghor, Césaire, and Leon Damas), Claude Mackay, Mlle Andree Nardal, and the Achille brothers. Another more radical and politically minded group, which at one time included Sajous, published *Le Cri des Nègres* which was Communist in orientation, and was shortly banned.[87] In the early 1930s also, another younger group of West Indian mulatto middle-class students led by Etienne Lero, René Menil, and Jules Monnerot, started a cultural journal called *Légitime Défense* whose ideas directly influenced the thinking of Senghor, Césaire, and Price-Mars. This new student group embraced Communist ideology and surrealism, following Marx, Freud, Rimbaud, and André Bréton

[85] ibid., see statutes of the *Comité Universel de l'Institut Nègre de Paris* in letter no. 668, C.A.I., 7 Apr. 1930.
[86] ibid., 'Rapport de desere', 19 Mar. 1930, in letter no. 668, C.A.I. 7 Apr. 1930.
[87] Kesteloot, op. cit., pp. 19–20.

in their criticism of European civilization.[88] Dr. Sajous's group also contributed to the contact between black American writers and West Indian and African students in Paris. The Negro question in America, the Harlem Renaissance, and the works of Claude Mackay, Jean Toomer, Langston Hughes, Sterling Brown, and Counttee Cullen were seriously being discussed in these student circles at the time. Miss Nardal, who founded the *Revue du Monde Noir*, also opened a literary salon where Africans, Afro-Americans, and West Indians met, Professor Alain Locke, Felix Eboue, Price-Mars, and Claude Mackay among them.[89]

Meanwhile on the political front, Kouyaté continued his militant agitation and frequently lambasted the Negro deputies. Diagne's acceptance of a post at Geneva in 1930, where he defended forced labour in the French colonies, did not escape Kouyaté's anger. In a violent and sarcastic editorial he ridiculed Diagne's latest promotion as political and moral suicide, and as the zenith of Diagne's 'treason' against the black race. Diagne and Candace ('these two villains . . . these Siamese twins') said Kouyaté, had betrayed the Negro and therefore did not deserve to be re-elected.[90] These attacks, together with Kouyaté's open flirtation with the Communist Party, soon led to a dispute between him and the *Commission de Controle* of the L.D.R.N. In 1931, after an internal dispute lasting about five months, he was not re-elected to the Central Bureau, whose officers were now: Emile Faure (president), F. Tarpeau (vice-president), Abdou Koité, a student (secretary-general), and Amady Diarra (treasurer). André Béton, Dr. Leo Sajous (who was now Liberia's chargé d'affaires in Paris and Consul General of Haiti in Poland), and M. Ibrahim Sylla remained members of the *Commission de Controle*. At the time no clear reason was given for Kouyaté's dismissal, though it appears that misappropriation of funds, extremism, and too close an association with the French Party and international Communist organizations were the main reasons.[91] Oddly enough, André Béton and Emile Faure, two leading L.D.R.N. officials, were also condemned in the course of the 'purge' and were labelled 'provocateurs'. Béton was

[88] ibid., pp. 29–62.
[89] ibid., pp. 63–4.
[90] *La Race Nègre*, Quartième Année (juillet 1930): 'M. Diagne s'est suicidé'.
[91] ibid., no. 4 (avril 1931). One of the important figures in the later Pan-African movement from 1945, T. Ras Makonnen, informs the author that Kouyaté at the time had close personal connections with leading Soviet party officials (purged by Stalin in the late 1930s) like Radek and Bukharin.

condemned for using the L.D.R.N. for his personal political propaganda, but was not expelled. Faure was accused of 'treason' against the L.D.R.N. It was alleged that as a result of a disagreement on objectives between Faure and the L.D.R.N., Faure had set the police on to the L.D.R.N. and certain documents were confiscated, as a result of which Kouyaté, Mme Kossoul, and Stephane Rosso were arrested, and the L.D.R.N. compromised; it was also alleged that a document purporting to be the plan for an insurrection in the Cameroons had also been planted on the L.D.R.N.[92] Mme Raymonde Danaè was elected president of the *Commission de Controle* of the L.D.R.N. in place of Faure. Perhaps a more plausible explanation of the in-fighting in the L.D.R.N., apart from Kouyaté's embezzlement, is that government hostility to the L.D.R.N. and the latter's radicalism and nationalism tended to frighten away potential Negro members. Moreover, Kouyaté had widened the activities of the L.D.R.N. by representing it on radical trade-union platforms and international organizations of the Comintern. In public, however, the L.D.R.N. attributed its troubles to the hostility of the Paris press and the opposition of white organizations. It also claimed that its line was neutral and Pan-Negro:

The white imperialists have a fundamental quality which seems to be missing in our race, and which is a natural aptitude for their immediate collective interest. Faced with the *Ligue* which, despite all the attractive propositions, refuses to deviate from the direction of its Negro policy either on the right or on the left, this aptitude has led imperialism to attempt to submerge us. In this attempt to divide us, to cause confusion and contradiction, it pushes from all sides for the formation of political or non-political Negro groups all dependent upon some white groups.[93]

The L.D.R.N. also argued that, surrounded and infiltrated by white-controlled Negro organizations with anti-radical views, it was incapable of functioning effectively. It also asserted that although it had accepted the resolutions relating to the alliance of Negro workers with the international trade-union movement passed at the Fifth Congress of R.I.L.U. held in Moscow in 1930, it was by no means a Communist front: 'Our aim is clear: independence, pure and simple.' It was not pro-Communist and it was opposed to those like Kouyaté, whom it called 'sham Communists'. Finally, the L.D.R.N. alleged that Kouyaté had been paid by the Communists to infiltrate and

[92] *La Race Nègre*, no. 4 (avril 1931).
[93] ibid., Cinquième Année, no. 1 (fév. 1932): 'To Be or Not To Be'.

disorganize the L.D.R.N. which was mainly concerned with independence of Negro peoples:

The former general secretary Tiémoho Garan-Kouyaté . . . had the best part of the Bolshevik cake. This shirker now has a fixed salary, his travels to France and abroad paid for (and we know how it establishes his expense bills). A few undisciplined members made common cause with him to begin with, mistaking him for a victim, as the central bureau refused any explanation. . . . In order to allure the people he had to deal with, Kouyaté displays a would-be programme which expands month after month and which is nothing but the same long list of the main claims of the blacks. By means of a hackneyed fallacy he creates the impression that anyone who is not with him is against this would-be programme.[94]

Kouyaté went over to the more militant *l'Union des Travailleurs Nègres*, taking a part of the L.D.R.N. with him. Whatever his weaknesses may have been, it is clear that his departure greatly weakened the L.D.R.N., which ceased to function between 1932 and 1933. His splinter group, confused by the Government with the L.D.R.N., published the *Cri des Nègres*, and in November 1930 participated in the Sixth National Congress of the C.G.T.U., accepted its programme, and called upon all Negro workers in France and in the colonies to do the same.[95] In its declaration to the Negroes of the world, it stated that the Negro was oppressed and discriminated against both in America and in Africa, and that its aim was the political and economic liberation of oppressed peoples. It also rejected the idea that it was a 'Moscow creation', admitting that its members belonged to socialist or radical parties. The Communist Party, however, was its ally:

But our programme was and still remains essentially revolutionary, since its aim is to liberate the Negro millions from the chains of imperialist servitude. Neither the Radicals, nor even the Socialist party recognize the

[94] ibid.
[95] A.N.D. dossier: 'Affaires Politiques, 254/32: Ligue de Défense de la Race Nègre: Institut Nègre de Paris', enclosure to no. 1438, C.A.I., Dec. 1931; Le Ministre des Colonies à Monsieur le Gouverneur Général de l'Afrique Occidentale Française à Dakar, 7 Dec. 1931; the enclosed resolutions, which are too lengthy to be quoted here, included equal legal rights for Negro workers in France, social benefits, freedom to travel between France and the colonies, access to all workers' unions in France, freedom of Negroes to form political and labour organizations in France, an eight-hour day, more opportunities for Negro soldiers. In the colonies, they demanded the right to form trade unions and to strike; primary and elementary education as well as adult education for workers, and freedom of the press, etc. See L.D.R.N. resolution: 'Aux Travailleurs Nègres de France et des Colonies'.

Negroes' rights to total liberation; only the Communist party has written
into its programme Negro rights and aspirations to their political liberty
and national independence. This common ground between our programme
and that of the Communist party has been enough for us to be accused
of Communism . . . for our part, it would be unjust not to grant our
sympathy to the only political party which is disposed to assist Negroes
in their struggle for justice, liberty, and liberation.[96]

While the L.D.R.N. was temporarily disorganized, Kouyaté
assumed leadership of the militant *Union des Travailleurs Nègres*,
and seems to have made a great impression on George Padmore
who was then head of the African section of the Profintern.[97]
Possibly, through Padmore's influence, Kouyaté succeeded in interesting African students in Paris in Afro-American and Pan-
African affairs. In a letter to W. E. B. Du Bois in 1934, Padmore
stated that the Negro problem was discussed at a conference of young
Negroes in Paris organized by Kouyaté: 'It was the most serious
political discussion which I have ever listened to among Negroes.
The Conference decided to take the initiative to convene a Negro
World Unity Congress, for the purpose of hammering out a common
program of action around which world unity among the blacks can
be achieved. . . . I took the opportunity of informing the French
Negroes about the work of the NACP [*sic*] and your work in connection with the Pan-African movement. . . .'[98] This phase in the

[96] ibid., enclosure to no. 329, C.A.I., 7 Mar. 1932: 'Aux nègres du monde
entier'.
[97] Hooker, James R., *Black Revolutionary: George Padmore's Path From Communism to Pan-Africanism*, pp. 33, 37–8. Although Hooker has only briefly discussed the French African contribution to the development of Pan-Africanism in
the 1920s and 1930s, his study of Padmore's interesting career has established beyond doubt the very complex relationships between various Pan-Negro organizations during that period.
[98] Padmore to Du Bois, 17 Feb. 1934, quoted in Hooker, op. cit., pp. 39–40. It
will be recalled that Kouyaté himself had written a similar letter to Du Bois as
early as 1929. Unfortunately, the letter was intercepted by the French police; see
p. 313 n. 78. Padmore erred in telling Du Bois that Kouyaté was the editor of *La
Race Nègre* in 1934: Kouyaté was expelled from the L.D.R.N. in 1931 for embezzlement, among other things; he joined the *l'Union des Travailleurs Nègres*,
to which Hooker refers on p. 41, in 1931. Like Padmore, Kouyaté's association
with the Comintern ended in 1934, but in his case embezzlement, again, was one
of the reasons for his expulsion. He was executed by the Nazis during the occupation of France (see Hooker, pp. 37–8). Judging by the conversations the author
has had with T. Ras Makonnen, one of the ex-Marxists and black radicals of the
1930s, Kouyaté's activities and political contacts from the time of his expulsion
from the L.D.R.N. to his liquidation by the Nazis are yet to be thoroughly

history of Pan-Africanism was certainly a major turning-point, for it was at this stage, after Padmore had dropped his Comintern shackles, that close co-operation between him and Du Bois began, when the 'father of Pan-Africanism' was brought into 'contact with the wider world of the new-style Pan-Africanists'.[99]

In 1934 the L.D.R.N. re-emerged in time to celebrate Diagne's death and Galandou Diouf's electoral victory that year. It admitted that its agitation for black emancipation and its claim to reflect Negro opinion in the French empire had been largely nullified by Diagne's re-election in 1932: 'Les élections de 1932, au Senegal, nous avaient placés dans une position internationale intenable. De quel front pouvions nous prétendre refléter l'opinion nègre, puisque le corps électoral, prèsque exclusivement nègre, du Sénégal, avait réélu, ou en tout cas laissé revenir en France *Blaise Diagne*, le défenseur, à Genève, du travail forcé?'[1] Diouf, the L.D.R.N. argued, was the real victor in the rigged Senegalese election of 1928, and his victory (which, according to the *Ligue*, was the work of Providence) meant that the dignity of the black race had been re-established.[2]

It is interesting to note that having removed the Communists from its ranks in 1931, the L.D.R.N. renewed its attack against them in 1934, once again claiming to be neutral in French politics and Pan-African in sympathy. It stated that it had no connection whatever with the *Union des Travailleurs Nègres* ('notre adversaire'), and warned all Negroes to steer clear of the other Negro newspaper *Le Cri des Nègres* ('financée par le Parti Communiste . . .').[3] It went on to explain that in African political movements there were usually three blocs: '. . . there will always be three kinds of ligues: one of exclusively radical essence and two others in which the Negro interests and those of the white classes of the right and the left will be hopelessly mixed. This state of things partakes of the principle: "divide

---

researched. Interviews with contemporaries still in Paris may well yield further information.

[99] Hooker, op. cit., p. 41.

[1] *La Race Nègre*, Septième Année, no. 1 (nov.–déc. 1934): 'Notre Ligne politique'.

[2] In fact, the L.D.R.N. did intervene in the elections of the Senegalese communes in 1934 by sending several copies of a document by Emile Faure, Abdou Diara, and André Béton, which listed Diagne's 'crimes' and urged the Senegalese electors to vote for any candidate, white or black, except Diagne: *La Race Nègre*, Septième Année, no. 1 (nov.–déc. 1934): 'Sénégal: les trois communes et le mouvement nègre'.

[3] ibid.

and rule", coupled with the scheming of Moscow in order to appro-
priate, by much noise, the moral capital of our efforts and of our
results.'[4] The L.D.R.N. anticipated the current doctrine of non-
alignment when it urged that all Negroes who were genuinely concerned with Negro emancipation ought to be indifferent to both
Capitalism and Communism, as well as to metropolitan politics in
general:

> Negroes, especially those of Africa, could not stop short at these social
> doctrines, which are of limited interest to those who recall their ancestral
> ways and customs and wish to remain faithful to them. It is vain to speak
> to them of capitalism and the proletariat when, in their homeland, they
> see only the masters and the slaves. The indifference of Negroes from all
> parts of the world towards the recent political convulsions in France
> proves beyond doubt that the fate of this country does not affect them.
> That is why our *Ligue* is exclusively concerned to express itself only on
> matters which affect them, and why we do not wish to be confused with
> those who, in exchange for financial and various other means of support,
> have traded away part of their independence.[5]

The growth of fascism in Europe and Italian aggression against
Abyssinia merely served to sharpen the Pan-Negroism of the
L.D.R.N. and to make it more disillusioned with European civilization. For example, André Béton, examining the Negro question in
the light of the fascist movement in Europe concluded: 'As a
nationalist, I accept all nationalisms; I am with those who cry,
"Germany for the Germans, France for the French." But I do not
stop there; I add, "India for the Indians, Africa for the Africans." '[6]
In 1935 the L.D.R.N., like most Negro political groups, adopted a
'back to Africanity' and 'down with the Europeans' outlook in
response to the Italo-Ethiopian crisis.[7] In a very long editorial, only
parts of which can be quoted here, the L.D.R.N. condemned European education and the 'intellectualisme stérile ou l'individu' of
European civilization as the enemy of the black man. Negro African
civilizations, it asserted, symbolized humanity, diversity, and fraternity as opposed to European individualism, uniformity, and what it
called the 'fetishism of European science' which, it said, must not
be confused with progress, as Europe was already preparing for its
own civil war. The L.D.R.N. repeated the utopian argument that

---

[4] ibid.      [5] ibid.
[6] ibid., 'Chacun chez soi'.
[7] Cf. Kesteloot, op. cit., p. 20.

the only way to prevent the humiliation and exploitation inherent in colonialism was to create a Pan-African state in which all Africans (including West Indians and even North Africans) could live in harmony:

We wish to regain our political independence and to revive, by that means, our ancient Negro civilization. The return to the customs, philosophy, and social organization of our ancestors is a vital necessity. We have only to ape the whites, who in any case have no clear system of belief. Our race is the champion of a human system, for which soon a great need will be felt.

We are a brotherhood, standing against the fierce individualism of the westerners.

We represent variety, as against white uniformity, which generates boredom.

We have created artistic, peasant civilizations. . . . Furthermore, we cannot admit in any way that the fate of the Negro race should depend upon the good will of another race. . . .

We demand a single Negro State, encompassing the whole of black Africa and the Caribbean, and within this State we shall make of the racial question what it used to be: a matter of diversity, mutual approval, and enjoyable competition, and not an excuse for bitter antipathies. The North Africans, too, if they wish, may accede to this State. . . .[8]

And in a savage attack on the budding Negro surrealists and the new *négritude* school of thought the editorial added:

Those who, debased by centuries of oppression, dare not take the slightest interest in whatever emanates from their race, and who seek, in submission to white culture, a possible basis for our evolution, are unaware that civilizations are not made for a few intellectuals but for the people. They are not an artificial creation, but their roots lie within the nation. . . . It is legitimate to wish to continue these contributions to humanity, while remaining ourselves.[9]

The L.D.R.N. viewed Italian aggression in Abyssinia as a conflict between white and black, but unlike most Negro groups, it praised Great Britain for her efforts to preserve the independence of Abyssinia. It also recognized the useful work the Communist party had done for Afro-Americans in the Scottsboro case, but insisted that this was one of those very rare occasions when the Communists did

[8] *La Race Nègre*, Huitième Année, no. 1 (juillet 1935): 'Nous voulons'.

[9] ibid. This attack on cultural synthesis by a group of French Negro intellectuals against the Senghor–Césaire group may perhaps come as a surprise to those scholars who have tended to concentrate on the intellectual origins of *négritude* to the exclusion of other groups and strands of thought.

not act strictly in the interests of their party. Various resolutions on the Abyssinian crisis were passed at several protest meetings of the L.D.R.N., and Negroes in France were even invited to volunteer for service in Abyssinia. France was condemned for conniving at Italy's aggression, and the opportunity was seized to pillory the Negro deputies for their failure to follow race-conscious blacks in America, the West Indies, and Africa in condemning Italian aggression. But what, the L.D.R.N. said, could one expect from 'impudent clowns' and 'renegades'?[10]

In the mid-1930s the L.D.R.N. began to show some interest in Negro protest organizations in Great Britain, just as it had shown similar interest in Garveyism in the 1920s. *La Race Nègre* occasionally reported on the activities of The League of Coloured Peoples led by Dr. Harold A. Moody of Jamaica, and whose journal was *The Keys*; The Negro Welfare Association which was connected with the *League Against Imperialism* through its secretary Mr. Reginald Bridgeman; and the International African Friends of Ethiopia whose secretary was C. L. R. James and whose members included Kenyatta, Padmore, Mrs. Amy Ashwood Garvey, Arnold Ward, and Sam Manning of Trinidad. The L.D.R.N. paid special attention to the protests of the International Friends of Ethiopia against Italian aggression. In return the L.D.R.N. held joint meetings with the *L'Étoile Nord-Africaine* in Paris on behalf of Ethiopia and as a demonstration of racial solidarity.[11] Nationalist hopes of a more liberal colonial policy under the Popular Front Government, however, were soon disappointed; for although laws relating to trade unionism and political parties in the colonies were partly relaxed during the Popular Front régime, the administration was determined not to tolerate nationalist and liberation movements either in France or in the colonies. Moreover, Moscow's support of the Popular Front policy also meant that militant anti-colonial and nationalist groups would be deprived of the support of left-wing metropolitan parties.[12] In 1937 both the *Étoile Nord-Africaine* and the L.D.R.N.

[10] ibid., Neuvième Année, no. 1 (jan–fév. 1936): 'Épurons notre race'.

[11] ibid., Choubelle, Gaston, 'Les Organisations nègres d'Angleterre'. For further details of the Negro protest movement in France on the Italo-Ethiopian question, see ibid., 'En France: hommage aux bonnes volontés'.

[12] For criticism of the French Communist and Socialist parties for their failure to support the anti-colonial politics of black groups in France and in the colonies during the Popular Front period, see Guerin, Daniel, *Front populaire révolution manquée* (Paris, 1962).

were suppressed and Emile Faure, president of the L.D.R.N. as well as secretary of the pan-nationalist *Rassemblement Coloniale*, was arrested and banished to the Sahara for the rest of the war.[13] The L.D.R.N., like its American counterpart the U.N.I.A., did not achieve much by way of influencing government; like the U.N.I.A. also, its influence on Negro thinking and on the development of Pan-Africanism has either been minimized or has not been investigated. As Daniel Guerin rightly complained in his interesting criticism of Padmore's *Pan-Africanism or Communism?*, French Negroes like Emile Faure (Lamine Senghor, Tovalou Houénou, Kouyaté, and Dr. Leo Sajous) have not been given sufficient credit for their equally important contribution to the development of Pan-Africanism.[14] It is hoped that this chapter will help to correct this bias and to illustrate some of the less-known influences in the complex history of Pan-Africanism.

[13] Padmore, George, *Pan-Africanism or Communism?*, p. 335.
[14] Daniel Guerin to Padmore, 18 Sept. 1956, quoted in Hooker, op. cit., p. 128.

# CHAPTER VIII

# Prelude to Manchester: Pan-African Radicalism and Protest, 1935–1939

IN chapter VII we examined in detail the anti-colonial activities of a Marxist-oriented Pan-African organization in Paris during the inter-war period; in this chapter we shall examine the activities of a similar group on the English-speaking side which, like the *Ligue de la Défense de la Race Nègre*, also claimed to be neutral as far as other ideological systems were concerned. By 1936, with the demise of the Pan-African movements in the United States, in West Africa, and in Paris, together with Negro disenchantment with the performance of the Comintern in the colonial sphere, and the rise of the fascist movement in Europe, Pan-African ideas and activity had come to be centred around a small group of West Indian and African intellectuals and agitators in Britain. Pan-African thought and activity during these years can therefore be seen both as the reaction of politically disillusioned young Negroes and as a radical protest movement against fascism and colonialism. In 1936 this group began to formulate a new ideology of colonial liberation designed to challenge existing ideological systems, including Communism. The key figures in this new movement were 'renegades' like Padmore and C. L. R. James, Jomo Kenyatta, T. Ras Makonnen (alias Thomas Griffiths) of British Guiana, I. T. A. Wallace-Johnson (Sierra Leone), and Sam Manning (Trinidad). In 1934 they formed The International African Friends of Abyssinia 'to arouse the sympathy and support of the British public for the victim of fascist aggression and "to assist by all means in their power in the maintenance of the territorial integrity and political independence of Abyssinia" '.[1] In 1937 they set up the International African Service Bureau, which was merged into the Pan-African Federation in 1944. These new institutional Carriers of Pan-African ideas held political views independent of both the liberal-humanitarians, the Communists, and such organiza-

[1] Padmore, G., *Pan-Africanism or Communism?*, p. 145.

tions as Dr. Harold Moody's League of Coloured Peoples and the Negro Welfare Association. Their aim was to organize a united front among the scattered segments of the Pan-African aggregate, and this solidarity was to be used to strengthen nationalist movements in Africa and the West Indies with a view to creating socialist states in those areas, aiding all minority coloured groups in Britain and the United States, and engaging in constant propaganda both in Britain and abroad, on behalf of Negro peoples.[2] The new Negro revolt, in which one could detect the origins of a later ideology, has been described by one of its leading architects:

This period was one of the most stimulating and constructive in the history of Pan-Africanism. It was then that Congress had to meet the ideological challenge from the Communist opportunists on the one hand and the racist doctrines of the Fascists on the other, and to defend the programme of Pan-Africanism—namely, the fundamental right of black men to be free and independent and not to be humbugged by those who preached acceptance of the *status quo* in the interest of power politics. It was also at this period that many of the Negro intellectuals who were later to emerge as prominent personalities in the colonial nationalist movements began to make a detailed and systematic study of European political theories and systems (Liberalism, Socialism, Communism, Anarchism, Imperialism, Fascism), and to evaluate these doctrines objectively—accepting what might be useful to the cause of Pan-Africanism and rejecting the harmful. In this way the younger leaders of the Congress were able to build upon the pioneering work of Dr. Du Bois and formulate a programme of dynamic nationalism, which combined African traditional forms of organisation with Western political party methods. . . .[3]

## 1. *Impact of the Italo-Ethiopian Crisis on Pan-African Thought*

THE main impetus to the new utopian thought-style in the mid-1930s was provided by Mussolini's aggression in Ethiopia. Technically, the issue was an international one involving the sovereignty of a small state and the question of collective security in the peaceful settlement of disputes, but in the eyes of the new Pan-Africanists it represented fascist aggression against a 'black' state (and therefore, in their view and in the view of most articulate Negroes, against all coloured peoples) and Europe's cynical connivance at such flagrant

[2] Drake, St. Clair, 'Value Systems, Social Structure and Race Relations in the British Isles' (Ph.D. thesis, University of Chicago, 1954), pp. 110–12.
[3] Padmore, op. cit., p. 151.

breach of international law.[4] This unity of race feeling against the white oppressor had already been stressed by Du Bois who warned an indifferent Negro public that when it came to the question of survival the Negro

. . . must calmly face the fact that however much he is an American there are interests which draw him nearer to the dark peoples outside of America than to his white fellow citizens. . . . And those interests are the same matters of color caste, of discrimination, of exploitation for the sake of profit, of public insult and oppression, against which the colored peoples . . . and every country in Asia, complain and have long been complaining . . . these people should draw together in spiritual sympathy and intellectual co-operation, to see what can be done for the freedom of the human spirit which happens to be incased in dark skin. . . . This was the idea that was back of the Pan-African Congresses.

He defined Pan-Africanism as 'intellectual understanding and co-operation among all groups of Negro descent in order to bring about at the earliest possible time the industrial and spiritual emancipation of the Negro peoples'.[5]

This 'spiritual sympathy and intellectual co-operation' among Negroes was intensified by the rise of fascism in Europe and the apparent readiness of certain European powers to appease the dictators with African territory. Padmore argued in 1935 that Italian imperialism in Africa was a greater threat to world peace than Nazism. After tracing the complicated diplomatic background to the Ethiopian crisis, he went on to give his interpretation of Pierre Laval's agreement with Mussolini in Rome (whereby he said, France agreed to give Italy a piece of French Sahara, French Somaliland, and part of her shares in the Abyssinian railway) as the most glaring example of the united front of white Europe against black Africa. 'It should serve to open the eyes of Negroes the world over, that white nations,

[4] Commenting on the reactions of the newspaper press in West Africa to the Ethiopian crisis, one writer observed '. . . the war was portrayed as an important aspect of the nationalist cause in West Africa. In the eyes of the press the struggle was essentially a racial war; Italy stood for the worst aspects of European greed and immorality and Abyssinia represented the Negro cause. No doubt could possibly be entertained that, on grounds of nationalist solidarity, the press was violently hostile to Italy. . . . Moreover, the press was at pains to point out that what occurred in Abyssinia concerned directly other parts of Africa. West Africa was taught that Italy's attack upon Abyssinia was but another aspect of white aggression upon black.' Edmonds, 'The Newspaper Press', pp. 118–19.

[5] Du Bois, W. E. B., 'Pan-Africa and New Racial Philosophy', *Crisis*, xl, no. 11 (Nov. 1933), 247.

regardless of their political systems, have no scruples in joining hands in assigning parts of Africa to whichever one stands most in need of colonies. . . . In other words, Africa is not worth while for whites to fight over. . . .'[6] Padmore also attributed Europe's equivocal attitude to Italian aggression in Ethiopia to a secret desire on the white man's part for revenge against the only coloured nation apart from Japan, to have defeated white troops. He also attributed Europe's indecisiveness to a general feeling among Europeans that 'abstract justice' could not be applied in the case of Ethiopia because she was 'not a civilized nation'; moreover, Ethiopia was the only independent African state determined to thwart European penetration.[7]

In West Africa, the whole English-speaking press protested against and condemned Italian aggression. From the very outset the *Sierra Leone Weekly News* warned its readers 'We in West Africa are not disinterested in this Italo-Abyssinian situation, for our past experience has taught us that though out of the "heats", we cannot escape the "finals".'[8] *Vox Populi* (Gold Coast) declared with equal conviction: 'The Italo-Abyssinian crisis is teaching the world a new

[6] Padmore, G., 'Ethiopia in World Politics', *Crisis*, lxii, no. 5 (May 1935), 139. For reinterpretations of the diplomatic background to the controversial, Laval–Mussolini agreement, see Robertson, Esmond, 'Mussolini and Ethiopia: The Prehistory of the Rome Agreements of January 1935', chapter 18 in a forthcoming volume of essays in honour of Professor D. B. Horn, University of Edinburgh. See also Watt, D. C., 'The Secret Laval–Mussolini Agreement of 1935 on Ethiopia', *Middle East Journal*, xv (1961), 69–78. Robertson and Watt have used the *Documents diplomatiques français* which cover the crucial period July 1932–March 1933, the recently published diaries of Baron Pompeo Aloisi, and files of the Committee on Foreign Affairs of the French Senate relating to the Laval–Mussolini meeting. Watt's comment that 'The Franco-Italian agreements concluded on January 7, 1935, are best understood as an illustration of the interplay, visible even in the classic period of European imperialism, between European and "colonial" considerations. In this barter of interest for interest without even any pretence of a relation to the views of the local inhabitants, they mark perhaps the last major example of classical imperialism in action in the Middle East. . . .' would seem to confirm the suspicions of the West African nationalist press. For details of the West African reaction to the crisis, see Asante, S. K. B., 'The West African Reactions to the Italo-Ethiopian Crisis', thesis in preparation for the University of London.
[7] Padmore, op. cit., p. 157. In this connection, i.e. the equation of European aggression against an African state with racism and as an attack on *African* racial sovereignty, the article by Ali Mazrui is most illuminating: Mazrui, Ali A., 'Consent, Colonialism, and Sovereignty', *Political Studies*, xi (1963), 36–55; also Mazrui, *Towards A Pax Africana* (London, 1967), chapter 2, 'On the principle of Racial Sovereignty'.
[8] *Sierra Leone Weekly News* (3 Aug. 1935).

and useful lesson, especially the members of the African race. It is revealing to us what is at the back of the mind of the European powers against the weaker peoples of the world and impresses it upon us that no reliance should be placed in the most solemn promise or in the most sacred treaty made by a European power with a subject race.'[9] In Lagos, the *Nigerian Daily Times* asserted in late 1935: 'The feelings of the Africans have been more hotly aroused because Italian aggressiveness towards Abyssinia is a return to the old European game of making African lands theirs, to be seized at will upon any pretext however grotesque. . . . Italy's decision to gratify her economic wants at the expense of Abyssinia is, therefore, League or no League, a crime of the first order.'[10] And *Vox Populi*, as authoritative as ever, again advised its readers: 'What we should like to impress on the inhabitants of this country is that war with Abyssinia is our war.'[11]

I. T. A. Wallace-Johnson, whose other political activities we briefly examined in chapter V, argued in the *Gold Coast Spectator* that, while in Europe in 1933, he had studied the policy of the League of Nations towards smaller states and had come to the conclusion that before peace and inter-racial harmony could be established, 'every nation and every race upon the face of the earth must first of all have a sort of economic, political, social and religious emancipation'.[12] He argued that independent African States such as Liberia and Ethiopia, i.e. 'those independent African States holding a sort of National Independence Charter and have been inveigled into the diplomatic net of the League . . .', had very little chance of survival in a world of power politics. He also argued that both Germany and Japan had left the League for good reasons—Germany because she felt cheated by the Versailles Treaty, and Japan because the

[9] *Vox Populi* (11 Sept. 1935). Such comment was typical of the reaction of many West African newspapers to the Italo-Ethiopian crisis; see Edmonds, op. cit., p. 95 n. 3. Edmonds, however, does not sufficiently assess the impact of the crisis on West African attitudes to Europeans in general, nor does he deal with press reactions to the Scottsboro case in the United States. The 1930s not only witnessed extensive commentary in the West African press on the economic depression but also a growing preoccupation with racial discrimination and economic exploitation by Europeans, and increasing criticism of 'Europeanism' and its dangers to African society.

[10] *Nigerian Daily Times* (5 Oct. 1935).

[11] *Vox Populi* (9 Oct. 1935).

[12] Wallace-Johnson, I. T. A., 'The League and the Africans As One Sees It: Ethiopian War should be eye-opener to Africans', *Gold Coast Spectator* (11 Jan. 1936), p. 46.

Allies refused to concede racial equality—and that Japan's aggression in Manchuria was 'different' from Italy's aggression against Ethiopia.[13] Wallace-Johnson was surprised that Russia, which had condemned the League as a 'Capitalist Clique', should join it in the 1930s.

Her changed front was a surprise to me and it set my brain a-working in an effort to find out what the result of such co-operation would be in the near future, and also whether the injunction of Lenin that Russia should always defend the world's proletarians and assist the coloured races especially the colonial peoples toward the achievement of national independence, is now to be cast into the dustbin as a political refuse.

What Wallace-Johnson probably did not know was that Russia's Popular Front tactics and her abandonment of ideology to suit short-term interests were also worrying the conscience of many other Negro Marxists who were tentatively searching for a pro-Negro doctrine—an ideological alternative to both Communism and Capitalism. On the other hand, Wallace-Johnson was so disillusioned with Europe that he came to advise Africans to formulate their own religion and turn away from what he called 'capitalistic Christianity', particularly Roman Catholicism.[14] He asserted that Africans must develop their own civilization and must not allow themselves to be deceived by European civilization; nor must they let their national aspirations be suppressed by the 'propaganda' of European Christianity, and concluded with the Pan-African battle cry 'Princes are come out of Egypt and Ethiopia has stretched forth her hands unto God through the great Emperor Haile Selassie. Africa must be free.'[15]

The *Gold Coast Spectator* and the *West African Pilot* carried several other articles commenting on the Ethiopian crisis: one issue of the *Gold Coast Spectator*[16] reprinted an article from *WASU* magazine by William Ofori Atta,[17] son of Nana Sir Ofori Atta, on 'Clogs in Our Social Machines', an article which also dealt with the Ethiopian crisis and emphasized the need for unity of action among Africans. The *West African Youth League*, in association with the

[13] ibid.
[14] ibid. Wallace-Johnson may have been referring to the Roman Catholic Church in Italy.
[15] ibid., p. 78.
[16] *Gold Coast Spectator* (18 Jan. 1936), p. 90.
[17] Minister of Education, Ghana, 1969 to Feb. 1972.

Ex-Servicemen's Union, established in 1936 by Wallace-Johnson, set up a series of Ethiopian Defence Committees in the Gold Coast to give financial and moral support to the Ethiopians. In 1936, the Gold Coast section of W.A.Y.L. was composed as follows: J. J. Ocquaye (president), J. W. M. Cudjoe (vice-president), E. D. Impraim (secretary), R. P. Nunoo (assistant secretary), Martin Sowah (treasurer), C. E. O. Williams (financial secretary), C. J. Myers (auditor). Committee members included J. A. Addison, E. W. N. Dowuona, C. S. Adjei, B. E. Tamakloe, and the Revd. J. E. Bart-Blange; Wallace-Johnson remained its organizing secretary; executive members included K. Bankole Awooner-Renner, R. B. Wuta-Ofei, Ellis Brown, and the indomitable Miss Mary Lokko.[18] At its first annual conference from 21 to 27 March 1936, Nnamdi Azikiwe, who was then a journalist in Accra, delivered a lecture on 24 March on 'Haiti—A Study of African Nationalism', while Wallace-Johnson spoke on 'The West African—His economic advantages and disadvantages'.[19] At the end of the conference, W.A.Y.L. passed the following resolutions on the Italo-Ethiopian question

1. . . . Having carefully and seriously considered the after effect of the 1914–1918 World War, [W.A.Y.L.] hereby registers its protest against the attitude of the fomentors of war and calls upon the League of Nations to use all the influence at its disposal against the plunging of Europe into another World War that would cause the unnecessary sacrificing of the lives of Youths and particularly those of West Africa, in another carnage.

2. That this Conference also registers its serious protest against Italian aggression in Ethiopia and the murderous slaughtering of innocent Ethiopian women and children by Italian invaders and calls upon the League of Nations to denounce the aggressor in a more practical form by the application of Oil Sanctions—the only effective means of putting an end to Italian hostilities in Abyssinia.

3. That this conference calls upon all Youth Organisations, all associated and affiliated bodies of the West African Youth League to register their protest against War and against Italian aggression in Abyssinia by effective resolutions. . . .[20]

Psychologically, as Lord Hailey argued in an important article, just as Japan's defeat of imperial Russia in 1905 served to rekindle

[18] *Gold Coast Spectator* (25 Jan. 1936), p. 157.
[19] ibid. (21 Mar. 1936), pp. 490, 503.
[20] 'Resolutions Against War and Italian Aggression on Abyssinia', in collection of Wallace-Johnson Papers, Institute of African Studies, University of Legon (Ghana).

Asian, particularly Indian nationalism, so did the Italo-Ethiopian conflict serve as a rallying-point for race-conscious Africans in South and West Africa:

At the outset there was no striking evidence of general interest; a few meetings were held in the Union and the West Coast, and a few subscriptions collected. But as the campaign proceeded ... the interest quickened. There was a phenomenal sale of the Native papers in the Union which contained articles on the struggle ... I cannot quote evidence that the effect went really deep or is likely to be enduring; and it may well be that to thinking Africans the fact that its three most prominent colonising nations were not competent to check the militaristic aggressiveness of a new arrival was more striking than the evidence that Europeans could still desire to possess themselves of African lands. But I feel that the Abyssinian campaign may yet be destined to have its effect on African thought, for it breaks harshly into the era of altered attitude towards the African Native which the Mandate policy had seemed to signalise.[21]

To the West African press, the crisis could only be interpreted in terms of racial strife, cynicism, and power politics; though the weaknesses of the League of Nations as a peace-making body and the delays occasioned by lengthy negotiations were admitted, it was a general feeling of helplessness, humiliation, and betrayal that underlay all the protest. As one paper put it, the question whether sanctions were effective was immaterial, for

it cannot be disputed that had Ethiopia been a European country, or a country inhabited exclusively by the Caucasoid races, the League of Nations would have been much more energetic in its policy. . . . We make bold to say that had Ethiopia been a white country like Belgium, Holland or Greece, not only would the League have imposed economic and financial sanctions, but military and diplomatic sanctions would have been in order. . . . But a country which is populated by the black race has no rights which Italy, a white race, must respect, and it has no influence to challenge the League of Nations, an organisation whose membership preponderatingly belongs to the white race, to live up to the terms of its Covenant. . . . Now is the time for Africans to think of race and not grace. . . .[22]

---

[21] Hailey, Lord, 'Nationalism in Africa', *Journal of the Royal African Society*, xxxvi, no. 143 (Apr. 1936), 143. Sir Sydney Barton, former British representative in Addis Ababa, spoke after Lord Hailey, observing that the rising power of Japan and the resistance of the Ethiopians had contributed not a little to African nationalism; see *West Africa* (23 Jan. 1937), p. 51.

[22] *African Morning Post* (27 Apr. 1936), p. 4.

As far as the *African Morning Post* was concerned, Italy's aggression symbolized not only the powerlessness of the League but also the triumph of Machiavellism and 'the betrayal of the black race':

... the fall of Addis Ababa signifies the fall of the metropolis of the only African Kingdom existing 'over here'. Should Ethiopian autonomy be dismembered, it means Africans are doomed for many, many years to come, for that will shake badly all the hopes of Africans and the coloured races all over the world. .... Africans, your last hope is passing. Even if you cannot fight you can at least make noise.[23]

The *Gold Coast Spectator*'s editorial furiously attacked Britain, France, and above all, the League of Nations, which was portrayed as a white man's club:

Force, the white man's god, is again supreme. Addis Ababa is occupied. ... Poison gas, British oil, and the white man's duplicity all combined to make the Italian advance victorious. .... After the Great War the League lent money to some of the small Central Powers to rehabilitate them. But these are whites. The League refused funds to Ethiopia, even though Article XVI stipulates it. Ethiopia, being black, could not be supported, even in affliction, and her financial solicitations were treated with derision. This is the Christian nations at work![24]

The *Spectator* in a defiant note, concluded

A people so jealous of their independence cannot easily submit to the Fascist tutelage. It must be rightly understood that it was due only to the treachery of the League of Nations that the present situation has come about. .... The League will collapse notwithstanding all the smooth assurances of Anthony Eden. .... And when the next war comes, Europe will realise that the African has not forgotten the white man's treachery to him nor will he ever forget it.[25]

Wallace-Johnson, who always tended to equate European Christianity with colonial subjection,[26] reiterated the view he had always

[23] ibid. (6 May 1936), p. 5.
[24] *Gold Coast Spectator* (9 May 1936), p. 814.
[25] ibid.
[26] Wallace-Johnson was secretary of the Koppeng African Universal Church Society in Lagos between 1928 and 1932. In June 1936 he and Azikiwe were arrested for sedition as a result of an article he wrote in the *African Morning Post* on the subject 'Has the African a God?' Perhaps there is a connection here between Wallace-Johnson's Ethiopianism and his anti-colonialism. For a detailed discussion of the various meanings of 'Ethiopianism' and its significance in early proto-nationalist movements in Africa, see Shepperson, G. A., 'Ethiopianism: Past and Present' in Baëta, C., ed., *Christianity in Tropical Africa* (London, 1968), pp. 249–68.

held about the crisis. In an interesting mixture of moral indignation, protest, and exhortation, he dismissed the Italo-Ethiopian conflict as merely another instance of European 'macht-politik' which might well serve as a spur to reawaken African national consciousness:

> The white man—yea the European in this instance—has proved that Christianity and barbarism are identical. He has proved that European Christian ethics are nothing but a farce and that after all, the sum total of the Christian faith and doctrine is Blessed are the strong for they shall weaken the weak. . . . The whole Ethiopian Empire may be annexed by Italy. But it is just the beginning of a new struggle. It is just the opening of a new page in the history of African nationalism for which every African should be justly proud. The name of Hailie Selassie should be the slogan of Africans throughout the length and breadth of this great continent . . . Africa's children should take a lesson from this Italo-Ethiopian war and be awake to national consciousness. . . .[27]

Outside Africa, other more articulate Pan-Africanists, particularly George Padmore and C. L. R. James who were leading members of the London based Pan-African Federation, viewed the crisis in the context of world imperialism and the reopening of the Colonial Question. In an essay on international politics[28] published on behalf of the Pan-African Federation, Padmore sought 'to show the circumstances through which Africa came to be drawn into the orbit of Power Politics, and how this process of colonial expansion led from one crisis to another', how Italian aggression in Ethiopia became the signal for the dissatisfied 'Have-Not' Powers to undermine the *status quo* by demanding a redistribution of raw materials and markets, and why the League of Nations was incapable of functioning as an effective instrument of Collective Security.[29] Although he condemned the Soviet Union for its 'indifference' in the enforcement of sanctions against Italy and for supplying the aggressor with coal and petroleum, his main conclusion was that 'Every great European Power has at some time or another entertained designs upon Abyssinia. Italy's onslaught is merely the culmination of half a century of

---

[27] Wallace-Johnson, I. T. A., 'Lessons of Italo-Ethiopian War Clearly Tabled . . .', *Gold Coast Spectator* (16 May 1936), pp. 838, 864. As Edmonds has observed, the crisis provided West African journalists and nationalists with 'a great rallying point and the press did not neglect the many opportunities it afforded to whip up nationalist feeling' (Edmonds, op. cit., p. 119).

[28] Padmore, George, *Africa and World Peace* (London, 1937).

[29] ibid., pp. 1-7.

such plotting, and represents the blackest chapter in the history of European colonial expansion in Africa.'[30] In the same year (1937), James wrote his classic *The Black Jacobins*, and a lesser known work, *World Revolution 1917–1936*, which was pro-Trotsky and was dedicated 'to the Marxist Group'.[31] It is interesting to note how James used Russian opportunism over the Italo-Ethiopian conflict to attack Stalinism and denounce Stalin's 'murder' of the colonial revolution:

Only thoughtful revolutionaries, however, realise how the International, following Stalin, missed the greatest opportunity in years of at best striking a powerful blow against the colonial policy of imperialism, and at worst rallying round itself the vanguard of the working-class movement. . . . Nothing was more certain than that the capitalists would ultimately do a deal at the expense, large or small, of Abyssinia. . . . The International from the first moment could have pointed out that nothing but working-class action could have saved Abyssinia. . . . Abyssinia might have been saved—Abyssinia is not saved to-day—but the International would have had a chance to build up around itself a mass-resistance to wars for collective security and international law and all the shibboleths. Instead they followed the new line, driven by the Russian bureaucracy's hope that a successful sanctions policy might be a useful precedent against Germany for Russia in the future. . . . The whole adventure ended in ignominious failure. . . . If the Soviet Union, the Worker's State, had come out clearly for a boycott against all war-material to Italy or any other country which interfered in Abyssinian affairs, the hand of those working at Brussels would have been strengthened. . . . The mass feeling that had been aroused all over the world would have been directed into a single channel under the direction of the Third International. . . . It would have been an urgent matter for British and French imperialism to press for a solution, in order to quiet the unrest at home. Abyssinia might have escaped with a certain loss of territory. . . . But a workers' bureaucracy cannot think in this way.[32]

Jomo Kenyatta, who was then honorary secretary of the International African Friends of Abyssinia, also contributed to the debate on the crisis with an article in the *Labour Monthly*,[33] while to a future theoretician and leader of the Pan-African and colonial

---

[30] ibid., p. 123.

[31] James, C. I. R., *World Revolution 1917–1936: The Rise and Fall of the Communist International* (London, 1937), Preface, p. xi.

[32] ibid., pp. 386–8; cf. Koestler, Arthur, *Darkness at Noon* (Harmondsworth, 1969), pp. 61–2.

[33] Kenyatta, Jomo, 'Hands Off Abyssinia!', *Labour Monthly*, xvii, no. 9 (Sept. 1935), 532–6.

liberation movement, the news of Italy's invasion of Ethiopia 'was all I needed. At that moment it was almost as if the whole of London had suddenly declared war on me personally. For the next few minutes I could do nothing but glare at each impassive face wondering if those people could possibly realise the wickedness of colonialism, and praying that the day might come when I could play my part in bringing about the downfall of such a system. My nationalism surged to the fore. . . .'[34]

## 2. The Protest Movement in Britain and West Africa

ALTHOUGH the International African Service Bureau and the Pan-African Federation never became important institutions within the framework of race-relations in Britain,[35] they became active instruments of protest and propaganda against colonial abuses, for the fostering of Afro-Asian solidarity and for the mobilization of coloured protest against Italian aggression in Ethiopia. By the end of the war, and with the decline of the League of Coloured Peoples, they had become the rallying points of radical coloured groups in Britain; some of their newspapers and ideas reached parts of West Africa, where a similar protest movement was launched between 1937 and 1939.

In March 1937 the International African Friends of Abyssinia Society was replaced by the I.A.S.B. Apart from Padmore, Chris Braithwaite (alias Chris Jones), and C. L. R. James, the most influential new-comers to the new Pan-African organization were Wallace-Johnson and Thomas Griffiths, better known as T. Ras Makonnen.[36] Wallace-Johnson, who was now in London after fleeing the Gold Coast to avoid charges of sedition, became its general

[34] Nkrumah, K., *Ghana: the Autobiography of Kwame Nkrumah*, p. 27.

[35] Drake, op. cit., p. 114.

[36] Griffiths came from British Guiana and had assisted Padmore in Denmark in 1934 after the latter had been sacked from the Comintern and deported by the Germans to Denmark. Both were later deported from Denmark and sent to London. Griffiths became an 'honorary' Ethiopian after Emperor Haile Selassie's arrival in England in 1935, and has been known as Makonnen ever since. He had a flair for business, and owned restaurants and bakers' shops in Manchester in the 1940s, and his business connections may have been of some value to the organizations which planned the Pan-African Congress there in 1945. With Nkrumah's rise to power, Makonnen went to Ghana where he managed the Star Brewry; was later put in charge of other corporations under the Nkrumah regime.

secretary, Padmore became chairman, and James editorial director, with Makonnen as treasurer and fund raiser. The executive committee included Chris Jones, J. J. Ocquaye (Gold Coast), L. Mbanefo (Nigeria), K. Sallie Tamba (Sierra Leone), Garan Kouyaté (Soudan), N. Azikiwe (Nigeria), Gilbert Coka (South Africa). Among its patrons were Nancy Cunard, Dorothy Woodman, D. N. Pritt, Noel Baker, A. Creech Jones, Victor Gollancz, F. A. Ridley, Sylvia Pankhurst, and Max Yergan.[37] Two short-lived papers, *Africa and the World* and *African Sentinel*,[38] were also published in late 1937 by Wallace-Johnson.

The I.A.S.B. claimed that it 'owed no affiliation or allegiance to any political party, organization or group in Europe'; it eschewed the Communist 'hypocrites' and the 'pettifogging reforms' of Fabians and Liberals, but was well disposed towards the declining Independent Labour Party. It did not exclude whites, yet it was a race organization; it eschewed Communism but most of its Negro intellectuals were left-oriented: or, as its chief ideologist bluntly put it, they 'orientated themselves to Pan-Africanism as an independent political expression of Negro aspirations for complete national independence from white domination—Capitalist or Communist'.[39] The I.A.S.B. was formed primarily as a response by coloured peoples in Britain and by disillusioned young Negro Communists, to Italian aggression in Ethiopia and to fascism in general:

[37] O. G. R. Williams to Sir Thomas Southorn, Governor of the Gambia, 27 Jan. 1938: Gambia 4/73, File no. 179, Secret dispatch 7046/3/38: 'Wallace Johnson and the International African Service Bureau'. Professor J. R. Hooker's *Black Revolutionary* quite rightly treats intelligence reports on political groups with suspicion, but it seems that this has been overdone and has tended to minimize somewhat the role of Wallace-Johnson in the protest movement in the 1930s. Wallace-Johnson was 'a forgotten man' in 1965 precisely because unlike several African nationalist leaders, he remained a Pan-Africanist (in fact, an internationalist) even during the agitation for independence. As he himself made clear in some of his reminiscences, he had always remained an internationalist: see *Wallace-Johnson Papers*, Legon University, Ghana. Finally, Wallace-Johnson carried on far more effective agitation in West Africa with his Youth League and West African Civil Liberties League during the period 1935–8 than the I.A.S.B. was able to achieve anywhere in the colonies.

[38] The *African Sentinel*, an early organ of the I.A.S.B., was printed in London and edited by Wallace-Johnson on behalf of the West African Youth League. The first issue came out in mid-1937; the paper was concerned with all Negro problems, and dealt in particular with the Italo-Ethiopian crisis, the West African Youth League, anti-sedition laws in the colonies, and labour problems in the colonies. It was placed on the prohibition list in British West Africa.

[39] Padmore, *Pan-Africanism or Communism?*, p. 148.

. . . never since the emancipation of the slaves have Africans and other subject races been so awake to a realisation of the wrongs and injustices inflicted upon weak and defenceless peoples as since the brutal Italian fascist war against Abyssinia. This cold-blooded organised act of imperialist aggression against a people who had been led to place their security in the League of Nations and the Kellog Peace Pact, demonstrated as never before that the world is still dominated by the philosophy of might over right. It has also opened the eyes of Africans the world over, that they have no rights which the powerfully armed nations are bound to respect. And precisely because of this they have decided to close their ranks and place their hopes for the future, not in imperialist statesmen, but in the organised will of the common people and progressive forces of all lands who are passionately devoted to the cause of peace.[40]

The Bureau's main function was to help enlighten British public opinion by distributing literature and giving talks on the colonial problem to 'the working and middle classes'; Labour Party branches, trade unions, and co-operative guilds were also welcome.

The *International African Opinion* succeeded Wallace-Johnson's short-lived journals as the monthly organ of the I.A.S.B. in July 1938. The motto of the new journal was 'Educate, Co-operate, Emancipate: Neutral in nothing affecting the African Peoples'.[41] The I.A.S.B., more familiar with the problems of Negroes in the British Empire, appealed for support to all Negroes: 'Problems differ from country to country, but there is a common bond of oppression, and as the Ethiopian struggle has shown, all Negroes everywhere are beginning to see the necessity for international organization and the unification of their scattered efforts. The crisis of world civilisation and the fate of Ethiopia have awakened black political consciousness as never before. . . .'[42] The journal was described as no literary paper giving advice from ivory towers but as a journal for political activists. Articles ranged from the American Negro and United States politics to the Ethiopian question, problems of coloured seamen, May Day in the West Indies, and the Australian Aborigines. Like its counterpart the *Ligue de la Défense de la Race Nègre* in Paris, the I.A.S.B. demanded the right of African peoples to form trade unions and co-operatives, a minimum standard of wages in keeping with the

[40] I.A.S.B. broadsheet.
[41] See *International African Opinion*, i, no. 1 (July 1938). The author saw copies of this rare journal in an unmarked file of Padmore's newspaper cuttings in the former Padmore Research Library, Accra, Ghana, as well as in the Gambia Records Office.
[42] ibid.

cost of living; an eight-hour day; equal pay for equal work regardless of colour; removal of discrimination in the Civil Service against Africans and peoples of African descent; abolition of forced labour, hut and poll tax, pass laws, etc.; freedom of the press, of movement, and of assembly. It stated that it did not seek to dominate other Pan-Negro organizations (such as those that existed in Cardiff and London), but sought to co-ordinate and centralize their activities so as 'to bring them into closer fraternal relation'.[43]

The I.A.S.B. does not seem to have been active between 1939 and the end of the war. This period was for Padmore one of journalistic activity on subjects related to imperialism and the war, socialism, racial discrimination in the British armed forces, colonial questions from the West Indies to West Africa, and agitation on the Spanish Civil War.[44] On 13 April 1938 Wallace-Johnson returned to Freetown, Sierra Leone, after an alleged dismissal from the I.A.S.B. over financial matters, according to intelligence reports from London.[45] On arrival, it is reported that two thousand copies of the *African Sentinel* which he had brought with him were declared seditious literature and confiscated.[46]

Wallace-Johnson at once got into action in Freetown, capitalizing on the unemployment and hardship resulting from the depression. Several of his meetings, which were fully attended, were held in the Wilberforce Memorial Hall. Apart from the West African Youth League he also formed the West African Civil Liberties and National Defence League on 29 April 1938. Officials of the latter body included Tregson Roberts, Mrs. Edna Horton, F. A. Miller, D. A. Yaskey, and Mrs. Elsie Cummings-John, a school mistress. According to police reports, the aims and objectives of the West African Civil Liberties League had 'obviously been drawn up by the International African Service Bureau at home', and that Johnson was planning to raise enough money to start a West African press which would counter the reactionary views of the Creole bourgeois press in Freetown. The aims and objects of the League were:

[43] ibid. i, no. 3 (Sept. 1938).
[44] For details of Padmore's activities during the war period, see Hooker, op. cit., chapters 4–5.
[45] O. G. R. Williams to Sir Douglas Jardine, Governor of Sierra Leone, 19 Apr. 1938, dispatch no. 7046/3/38, enclosed in Gambia secret M.P. no. 179, 4/73, 22 Feb. 1938.
[46] ibid., Jardine to the Rt. Hon. Malcolm Macdonald, Secretary of State for the Colonies, 30 June 1938.

(1) To protect and defend the Civil rights and liberties of the inhabitants of West Africa individually and collectively and to agitate for reforms throughout the West [sic] Colonies.

(2) To collect and disseminate informations regarding social, political and economic conditions of affairs in West Africa with a view to arousing public opinions in Europe in regard to conditions of affairs in the Colonies.

(3) The maintenance of a 'West African House' in London whereto all information socially, politically, economically and otherwise regarding affairs in the West African Colonies could be sent for the purpose of dissemination and from where all information that may be of value and interest to the peoples of West Africa could be easily obtained.

(4) To agitate for a responsible representative in the British Parliament.

(5) To establish, support and maintain an official national organ of articulation within the metropolis of the British Empire that would serve as a means of contact between the African peoples and the British public.[47]

*West Africa* (June 1938), reporting the seizure of Wallace-Johnson's *African Sentinel*, was not sure whether Johnson's new League was 'likely to be in co-operation or competition with the existing branch of the National Congress',[48] adding that 'In a Colony where such matters as workmen's compensation and even wages are still matters that call for improvement, it is not surprising that Mr. Johnson awakened an interest which will no doubt be noted, and acted upon, by members of the Legislative Council.'[49]

Total membership of the League was estimated at 800, but Johnson does not seem to have had any definite political goal such as responsible government; he was more concerned with trade union matters and in particular with the Public Works Department and the railway workers, as well as Africans employed by European firms, and with the question of racial discrimination. His West African

[47] ibid., sub-enclosure to Enclosure II in secret M.P. no. 179, 22 Feb. 1938.

[48] It is unlikely that Wallace-Johnson would have co-operated with the middle-class Creoles who controlled this branch of the moribund N.C.B.W.A. Commissioner of Police, R. J. Craig (Sierra Leone) reported on 20 June 1938 that Johnson's meetings were 'well attended by enthusiastic audiences drawn from all classes of the community, though he has received no support from any leading public men. In fact he has attacked this class consistently and he says that the African has been betrayed by his old leaders. His appeal is definitely to the wage-earner. He has made a special appeal to the Mohammedan community and numbers about 300 of them among his followers' (R. J. Craig, Enclosure II in Sierra Leone, secret dispatch, dated 30 June 1938, Gambia secret M.P. no. 179, 4/73). His attitude to this class was usually one of contempt, though he did co-operate with Dr. H. C. Bankole-Bright's National Council of the Colony of Sierra Leone in the 1950s, see Kilson, Martin, *Political Change in a West African State: A Study of the Modernization Process in Sierra Leone* (Cambridge, Mass., 1966), pp. 222-7.

[49] Enclosure, p. 41, secret M.P., no. 179, 22 Feb. 1938, Gambia Record Office.

Civil Liberties League was reported to consist of two branches—
a League of Youth (presumably the local branch of the West African
Youth League) and a Labour Union, though these were ineffective
because of poor organization. On the whole the authorities, as in all
colonies, dismissed him as 'a rascal who has found that the career
of a professional agitator provides an easy living'. They suspected
that he planned to extend the League throughout West Africa so
that he could become 'Grand President of the whole outfit'. Johnson
agitated against the Education Bill, the Rural Areas Bill, and the
Municipal Laws; he advocated the return of the Municipal Council
to African control, and equal African voting power in the Legislative Council; he even proposed altering the British Constitution to
enable African representatives to go direct to the Imperial Parliament at Westminster![50] In fact, Wallace-Johnson's political activities
were far more serious than the police reports indicated: Sir Douglas
Jardine, the Governor, knew better. On 30 June 1938 he admitted to
the Secretary of State for the Colonies:

It may be said at once that Johnson has succeeded far beyond our ex-
pectations and far beyond what his previous experience led us to anticipate.
His achievement in attracting about 800 people to his 'West African Civil
Liberties and National Defence League' is a not inconsiderable one. His
audiences have been drawn from all sections of the community; but it is
noteworthy that both the press and the more prominent public men like
Dr. Bankole Bright have given him the cold shoulder so far. . . .
   Nevertheless, there is no gainsaying the fact that Johnson's presence
in Sierra Leone is an embarrassment; and that at any moment in the
event of a strike at one of the mines he would be a potential danger to the
peace and good order of the country. . . .[51]

In late November 1939 Wallace-Johnson was convicted in the
Sierra Leone Supreme Court of criminal libel and sentenced to a
year's imprisonment. Prior to his imprisonment, the Governor had
already ordered his detention under Regulation 18 of the Model
Colonial Defence Regulations.[52]
   Meanwhile in London, financial squabbles among members of the
I.A.S.B. led to the defection of Johnson's successor, the Nigerian
Edward Sigismund (also known as Babalola Wilkey), who started

[50] Commissioner of Police R. J. Craig, see chapter VIII, p. 341 n. 48.
[51] ibid., paras. 5–6 of secret dispatch, Sir Douglas Jardine to the Rt. Hon.
Malcolm Macdonald, Secretary of State for the Colonies, 30 June 1938.
[52] ibid., Governor, Sierra Leone to Governor, Gambia, 6 Sept. 1939; telegram,
Governor of Sierra Leone to Governor of the Gambia, 23 Nov. 1939.

a small organization of his own called the Negro Cultural Association, affiliated to the National Council for Civil Liberties. Special Branch reports indicated that the latter body was being infiltrated by the British Communist Party to use it to embarrass Britain by convening a conference of colonial leaders in London on its behalf, 'with a view to obtaining publicity for alleged discontent in the Colonial Dependencies . . . and in order to underline the contention that if Britain were fighting Germany to preserve democracy it would extend more democracy to the colonial peoples, and thus show that Britain's declared war aims are hypocritical and untrue'.[53] It was alleged that the Communists planned to 'arrange' an anti-colonial conference, carefully packed so that they could 'damp down the notorious Trotskyite tendencies of many colonials'.[54] Fears of Communist control of Negro organizations, however, were exaggerated, and Padmore remained in charge of the I.A.S.B. in 1939 and throughout the war, assisted by Jomo Kenyatta and Chris Jones; far from collaborating with the Communists, Padmore drew closer to the I.L.P. and was virtually in charge of its colonial section. Even the Special Branch observed that the 'communist' Edward Sigismund (Babalola Wilkey) was 'unlikely to carry much weight as secretary of the Bureau' and that 'the policy of the International African Service Bureau will remain in the hands of the Trotskyist, George Padmore'.[55]

Towards the end of 1944 the I.A.S.B. was merged with another Negro body in Manchester whose founders were Dr. P. Milliard and T. R. Makonnen to form the Pan-African Federation. Associated with this new group were the Kikuyu Central Association, the West African Youth League, and some other Negro student bodies in Britain, though there was some objection from Negro groups in Cardiff to the aims of the Padmore–Makonnen leadership. The new Pan-African Federation attempted to promote both the humanitarian and political interests of Dr. Milliard with the commercial

[53] Malcolm Macdonald, Secretary of State for the Colonies in secret circular, 19 Jan. 1940 to West African Governors, Gambia, 4/73, Gambia Records Office; also Chief Constable E. Canning, Special Branch, Metropolitan Police, to Home Office, 20 Dec. 1939.

[54] This may be the conference of coloured peoples referred to by Hooker, op. cit., pp. 55–6, in which 'the communists tried to control the proceedings' but were resisted by Padmore who spoke on behalf of the I.A.S.B. and the Sierra Leone Youth League.

[55] O. G. R. Williams to Sir Thomas Southorn, Governor of the Gambia, 11 Apr. 1939, 7046/3/39: Gambia 4/73, secret M.P. no. 179, 22 Feb. 1938, Gambia Records Office.

and publishing schemes of Makonnen. It set up a Pan-African Institute to publish and sell its publications relating to various aspects of the colonial question.[56] Nationalist groups in some of the British colonies were encouraged to form local branches of the Pan-African Congress Movement—at least one was formed in Bathurst, Gambia. The Pan-African Federation sought

(1) To promote the well-being and unity of African peoples and peoples of African descent throughout the world.

(2) To demand self-determination and independence of African peoples, and other subject races from the domination of powers claiming sovereignty and trusteeship over them.

(3) To secure equality of civil rights for African peoples and the total abolition of all forms of racial discrimination.

(4) To strive to co-operate between African peoples and others who share our aspirations.[57]

In meetings and in the pages of the *International African Opinion* theoretical and organizational questions on the future anti-colonial movement in the colonies were discussed and, more importantly, the future policy of the historic Manchester Congress and the Pan-African movement in the late 1950s anticipated, when the Pan-African Federation decided that it would 'take an independent ideological position on the colonial question'. Unlike the early Pan-Africanists the young men of the Padmore school were determined, with the support of their allies, to combine thought with effective agitation to assist the colonial Powers to make Africa 'safe for democracy' too. Already in British West Africa, nationalist leaders were advancing the unanswerable argument that the 1941 Atlantic Charter be applied to the colonies in the form of responsible self-government—a demand that became more and more difficult to ignore as the 1940s drew to a close. Besides, the war itself was having a significant impact in an unexpected quarter—in the jungles of Asia where African troops had been taken to fight Japanese imperialism. Although the colonial powers were not fully aware of its significance at the time, the anti-Japanese war was to unleash a decade of nationalism and revolution in South-East Asia and in Africa.[58]

[56] See Padmore, *Pan-Africanism or Communism?*, p. 150.
[57] ibid., p. 149.
[58] A fairly substantial literature on the impact of the Second World War on the development of nationalist movements in Africa already exists. For a cautious and liberal assessment, see Gerald Hanley, *Monsoon Victory* (London, 1969). Cedric Dover's *Hell in the Sunshine* (London, 1943) is both pro-British and anti-

As early as 1944, a Gold Coast soldier was inspired to pen the following lines, parodying Psalm 23:

> The European Merchant is my shepherd,
> And I am in want;
> He maketh me to lie down in cocoa farms;
> He leadeth me beside the waters of great need;
> He restoreth my doubt in the pool parts . . .
>
> .    .    .    .    .    .    .    .
>
> The general managers and profiteers frighten me.
> Thou preparest a reduction in my salary
> In the presence of my creditors.
> Thou anointest my income with taxes;
> My expense runs over my income
> Surely unemployment and poverty will follow me
> All the days of my poor existence,
> And I will dwell in a rented house for ever![59]

Another Gold Coast soldier serving in Burma even wanted to send some of the books and pamphlets he had been reading in Burma to some nationalist leaders in the Gold Coast. For him, the Japanese were defeated, but the real enemy was not Japan. There were still some young Africans sufficiently angry to compel the colonial government not only to reform but to quit.

We have finished the war physically, but morally it is not over. We have to struggle for liberty; at home the suppression is great. We have been spared back to life from the fighting front: but unless God gives us grace we shall fight to death about the suppressive mode of Rule we are encountering out here. In comparisin [sic] we are regarded less human: as to our lowliness in this sphere of the world, it is worse.

We are discovering the truths of Wallace-Johnson's writings: and I would to God that He gives us more Wallace-Johnsons when we come back home.

We have made up our minds to help build the country, free from all

---

imperialist. It is basically a plea for more enlightened policies in Africa and Asia so that revolution in the colonies would be avoided. More recent studies are Schleh, Eugene P. A., 'The Post-War Careers of Ex-Servicemen in Ghana and Uganda', *Journal of Modern African Studies*, vi, no. 2 (1968), 203–20, and Olusanya, G. O., 'The Role of Ex-Servicemen in Nigerian Politics', *Journal of Modern African Studies*, op. cit., pp. 221–32.

[59] 'A Psalm 23' first appeared in *African Morning Post* (Accra) (2 Sept. 1944); reprinted in *WASU Magazine*, 1944.

oppression, and in our oath to the Lord, we shall never miss you in all our plans to build our motherland. . . .[60]

These were some of the men who were determined to resort to bullets if the ballot were denied them. Would the old petty-bourgeois nationalist leadership in West Africa exploit this formidable weapon in the coming political struggle? The next three years in the Gold Coast were to show. One man at least, did not fail to appreciate the political potential of ex-servicemen. His name was Kwame Nkrumah whose remarkable rise to power and whose lasting contribution to African liberation and the search for unity began with the 1945 Pan-African Congress which we shall examine in the next chapter.

[60] N.C.O. Emil K. A. Sackey (CC35286), 835 Coy, W.A.A.S.C. India Command, to Kobina Sekyi, 4 Sept. 1945. See also letter from Trooper Kojo Tawiah, 'B' Squadron, 81 West African Division, Recce. Regt., India Command, to Kobina Sekyi, 12 Dec. 1945. Kobina Sekyi Papers, Acc. no. 571/64.

# CHAPTER IX

# The Manchester Congress and Revival of the Pan-West African Idea

## 1. The Manchester Congress

IT was gradually becoming clear, as the war entered its third year and as colonial peoples were called upon to contribute more in men and materials to the defence of the British Empire, that the result of participation in such global conflict would be the sharpening of African race-consciousness and encouragement of demands for a reassessment of the old doctrine of *Pax Britannica*.[1] Side by side with this self-discovery went a certain ambivalence perhaps 'neutralism' towards Europe and its civilization. The fall of Singapore in 1942, usually compared to the fall of Constantinople, signified the end of European hegemony in Asia and ushered in a new era of nationalism and revolution whose effects have survived to the present day.[2] To Padmore, the fall of Britain's eastern fortress was largely the retribution against an unimaginative imperialism which resolutely denied liberty and equality to its colonial subjects.[3] 1942 also witnessed the 'Quit India' movement in India, as well as growing demands from British West Africa that the Four Freedoms set forth in the Atlantic Charter must also apply to them.[4] Their demands were ignored, and it was made quite clear to them that as far as Africa was concerned the Atlantic Charter did not apply. W.A.S.U. took up the question again in its summer conference in 1942, which,

---

[1] Mazrui, Ali A., *Towards a Pax Africana: A Study of Ideology and Ambition* (London, 1967), pp. 161–2.

[2] Panikkar, K. M., *Asia and Western Dominance: A Survey of the Vasco Da Gama Epoch of Asian History, 1498–1945* (London, 1953).

[3] See his letters to F. A. Ridley and Nancy Cunard, quoted in Hooker, op. cit., pp. 65–6.

[4] See *The Atlantic Charter and British West Africa* (1943), memorandum issued by the N.C.N.C. See also *The Atlantic Charter and Africa From An American Standpoint* by the *Committee on Africa, The War, and Peace Aims* (New York, 1942).

among other things, demanded immediate self-government and independence within five years.[5] In America too, Nkrumah and the African Students Association of North America were assisting between 1942 and 1944 various American Committees on Africa, on the subject of the Atlantic Charter and African self-government.

Late in 1944 the I.A.S.B. was merged into the Pan-African Federation, the body which was responsible for planning the next Pan-African conclave. A few months later the World Trade Union Conference, summoned by the General Council of the Trades Union Congress since 1943 and postponed from June 1944, met in London on 5 February 1945. At that conference the World Federation of Trade Unions (W.F.T.U.) was established in opposition to the older International Federation of Trade Unions (I.F.T.U.).[6] Although the conference was mostly concerned with European trade union politics and with post-war European issues, colonial trade unionists were also invited. Those who attended and raised questions on colonial matters included Wallace-Johnson (Sierra Leone), E. F. Small and I. M. Garba-Jahumpa (Gambia), J. Annan (Gold Coast), Bankole Timothy (Nigeria), S. A. Dange (leader of the All-India Trade Union Congress delegation). The conference resolved 'to bring to an end the system of colonies . . .' and to lay the foundations 'of a world order in which non-self-governing communities and nations can attain the status of free nations . . .'.[7] At the end of the conference, Padmore took the opportunity to invite the colonial delegates to Manchester to discuss the possibility of a Pan-African Congress that September. In April the Pan-African Federation, in co-operation with Dr. Moody's League of Coloured Peoples, W.A.S.U., the I.A.S.B., the Negro Welfare Centre (Liverpool and Manchester), and the colonial trade-union leaders addressed a Manifesto to the United Nations conference at San Francisco. The Manifesto reminded the Great Powers of their adherence to the Atlantic Charter, recommended economic and social development of Africa through the agencies of the United Nations, and African participation in such

[5] For details of this conference, see *W.A.S.U. Magazine* (May 1943): 'Conference on West African Problems'.

[6] Horner, Arthur, 'The World Trade Union Conference', *Labour Monthly*, xxvii (Jan.–Dec. 1945), 41–6.

[7] ibid., report by S. A. Dange, leader of All-India Trade Union Congress delegation, pp. 75–6. For a critical assessment of the political role of trade unions in colonial and post-colonial politics, see Roseberg, Carl G., Jr., and Coleman, James S., ed., *Political Parties and National Integration in Tropical Africa* (Stanford, Cal., 1964), pp. 340–81.

development, 'full self-government within a definite time limit', and the eradication of mass illiteracy. The Manifesto, signed by Padmore, Moody, J. S. Annan, H. N. Critchlow (British Guiana Trade Unions), Garba-Jahumpa, K. A. Korsah, and R. W. Beoku-Betts, included a passage which made it clear that for the Africans self-determination and racial equality were as important as, if not more important than, the preservation of peace:

*United Nations must free themselves of the evils against which they are fighting.*

Africa is a land of varied political forms, economic interests and social and cultural standards. This is complicated by the fact that among the powers with imperial possessions in Africa are fascist Spain and fascist Portugal. It is further complicated by the colour-bar laws and practices obtaining within the territories of some of the United Nations themselves, notably the Union of South Africa. The United Nations are pledged to secure in addition to the military defeat of fascism, the eradication of its moral and political manifestations, chief of which is the theory of the master-race against inferior races. If the principles for which we fight do not apply to Europe, then it is the duty of the United Nations to eliminate the influence of the Spanish and Portuguese fascist regimes and to remove from their own territories those theories and practices for the destruction of which Africans have died on many battlefields. . . .

The present inferior political, economic and social status of the African peoples militates against the achievement of harmonious co-operation among the peoples of the world. International co-operation demands the abolition of every kind of discrimination on account of colour, race and creed wherever such discrimination exists.[8]

Between June and August 1945 various meetings of coloured organizations were organized by the L.C.P. and the Pan-African Federation, and at one of these meetings held on 12 August the groundwork for the projected Pan-African Congress was prepared under the chairmanship of Dr. Milliard. The same period also witnessed the active participation of F. K. Nkrumah, newly arrived from America, in the affairs of the Pan-African Federation and W.A.S.U., and the beginning of Nkrumah's career as a Pan-African radical and revolutionary nationalist. October was agreed upon as the month in which the Congress would be held, invitations were sent to trade unions, nationalist groups, and other organizations in the colonies, and it was expected that the colonial trade-union leaders,

[8] 'Africa in the Post-War World.' 'Manifesto For Presentation to the United Nations Conference, San Francisco, April, 1945', reprinted in *Labour Monthly*, (Jan.–Dec. 1945), 154–6. For full text, see Appendix II.

who were attending the World Federation of Trade Unions (W.F.T.U.) conference in Paris that October, would be able to come to Manchester for the Congress.[9] Du Bois was fully informed about the plans, but it seems that the bulk of the organization was done by Padmore and the inner circle of the Pan-African group which now included Nkrumah.

In the colonies, the trade unions whose formation the imperial government had encouraged during and after the war formed, in addition to local organizations, the nucleus of the local Pan-African committees. In some cases as in the Gold Coast, older organizations like the A.R.P.S. appointed their delegates to the Pan-African Congress. In the Gambia the local committee of the Pan-African Congress was formed in September 1945 'to make the necessary arrangements for the forthcoming Pan-African Congress' and to send a delegation from the Gambia.[10] Councillor Garba-Jahumpa and Mr. Downes-Thomas were the delegates-designate, and application for Government to pay their air passages to London for the Congress was approved.[11] Members of the committee included Mr. R. C. Valantine (chairman), C. Downes-Thomas (secretary), I. M. Garba-Jahumpa (joint-secretary), Mrs. Hannah Mahoney, Mrs. Judith Mensah, Mrs. Hanna Sagnia, Mr. Finden Dailey (journalist), J. Francis Senegal, E. Lloyd-Evans, O. B. Jallow (an N.C.B.W.A. activist in the 1920s), M. D. Faal, Baseru Jagne, Salieu Foon, and Iderisa Samba. Trouble, however, soon developed over the representative character of the delegates appointed to the Manchester Congress. Another faction led by Mr. A. M'Bye an influential trader, calling itself the General Assembly of Loyal Citizens, protested, under the auspices of the Joint Trade Unions Council against 'the unprecedented and undemocratic steps adopted by a Committee of Gentlemen in sponsoring the delegation of Messrs. C. W. Downes-Thomas and I. Garba-Jahumpa. . . . We uphold that they do not represent this ancient colony.'[12] The Government, however, was of

[9] W.A.S.U. proposed that the 1945 Congress be held on Arican soil, preferably Liberia; practical considerations, however, ruled out the idea.

[10] Downes Thomas, Hon. Secretary of the Gambia Pan-African Congress Committee to Miss H. M. Burness, 24 Sept. 1945, Gambia Confidential S. 3008, 25 Sept. 1945: 'Pan-African Congress'.

[11] ibid.; the Gambia Government must have been the only colonial government to pay the passages of delegates to an anti-colonial Pan-African Congress. Its information on the Congress was hardly noticed by the press.

[12] ibid., A. M'Bye, J.P., Chairman, to Public Relations Officer, Gambia, 10 Oct. 1945.

the opinion that as far as they were aware, these delegates were the 'accredited representatives of the local committee', and that having no information about the Pan-African Congress, they advised the General Assembly of Loyal Citizens to address their protest to the Pan-African Federation in London.[13] By this time the chairman of the Pan-African local committee which originally selected the delegates, had gone over to Mr. M'Bye's General Assembly and had asked Mr. E. F. Small, who was representing the Gambia at the W.T.U.C. in Paris, to be Gambia's delegate to the Manchester Congress.[14] On the same day another body calling itself the 'Peoples Party' convened a mass meeting which reaffirmed its confidence in the original delegates[15] who, in fact, did attend the Congress. Mr. Downes-Thomas reported back on the Congress, describing it as 'a new girdle put round the world for closer understanding between all men and nations of goodwill and the peoples of African descent. We are at the beginning of a new era. . . . We have a real identity of interest and a tremendous awakening has brought us all here.'[16]

In the Gold Coast the Pan-African Congress found a supporter in W. E. G. Sekyi who had had contacts with Padmore in the 1930s. Sekyi was then president of the G.C.A.R.P.S., and in September he wrote to G. Ashie-Nikoi, who was then in London with the Gold Coast delegation, asking him to represent the Gold Coast A.R.P.S. at the Manchester Congress. Nikoi accepted the offer after consulting Nkrumah, Regional Secretary of the Pan-African Federation, and Padmore. Forwarding a copy of the Pan-African memo to the Secretary of State for the Colonies, Nikoi shrewdly observed that 'There appears to be little difference between the Conservatives and Labourites in so far as Colonial Policy is concerned. The present position financial position [sic] of this country leaves very much to be desired and it is a miracle that can save the situation. This is the time that we must press for changes.'[17] Sekyi replied that a conference of the G.C.A.R.P.S. had confirmed his appointment of Ashie-Nikoi

[13] ibid., minute to, 13 Oct. 1945.

[14] ibid., R. C. Valantine to E. F. Small, 13 Oct. 1945.

[15] ibid., R. S. Rendall and others to the Colonial Secretary, 13 Oct. 1945.

[16] *Gambia News Bulletin* (16 Oct. 1945); Downes Thomas's other reports on the Congress are contained in the issues for 17 Oct. 1945 and 22 Oct. 1945.

[17] G. Ashie-Nikoi to W. E. G. Sekyi, 27 Sept. 1945: G.C.A.R.P.S. files, Cape Coast Regional Archives, Ghana, File no. 100, 187/65 'Pan-African Congress'. Padmore seems to have held the same view expressed by Ashie-Nikoi: see Hooker, op. cit., p. 88, and Padmore, G., *Pan-Africanism or Communism?*, pp. 156–8.

to represent the Society at the Manchester Congress, and that £100 had been collected for his expenses, to be supplemented when necessary. The G.C.A.R.P.S. Executive Committee had also drafted instructions to Mr. Nikoi:

First, to base your representations on Society's 1934 Petition to King in Council and 1935 Petition to House of Commons. . . . State that since establishment of Provincial Councils Government has passed all opposed legislation with more than usual disregard of public protests. Urge necessity for establishing Pan-African Council with offices in London, New York, Paris, Geneva, Moscow and Delhi with central Press in London. Secondly, with reference to discussion concerning abolition of Crown Colony Rule, to emphasise following important facts: *One* that Africa was self-governing before Europe's intrusion. *Two* that self-government need not take a British shape. *Three* that Democracy is not a British invention. *Four* that Gold Coast forms of Democracy are being forced by legislation in strange and unsuitable moulds designed by Nigerian officials to facilitate ascendancy of white officials and black assistants and to humiliate and thwart respectable patriotic progressive indigenes. Northern Nigeria and Northern Territory political ideas being held out as models for imitation by Gold Coast Chiefs, thus holding out medieval autocracies as substitutes for Democratic Gold Coast Institutions. *Thirdly*, to demand that until legislative power and control of colonial revenue are completely in aboriginal hands there shall be no officially planned or controlled University or University College but that capable students with means or under scholarships be freely permitted as was the practice till recently, to travel and complete their education in European or American Universities. . . . Restriction on admission at European Educational Institutions of non-European students on plea of limited accommodation to be kept within reasonable bounds. *Fourthly*, concerning Trade, to base your representations on programme of Farmer's Committee which Society heartily endorses. Insist on removal of all trade restrictions and restoration of former trade conditions whereunder Africans did establish considerable trading houses. Wherefore better banking facilities required to neutralise sinister influence of local Banks on African commercial and industrial enterprise. Lastly to advocate that Pan-African Council, if established, shall make it part of its policy to expose and prevent evils issuing from persistent attempts officially made to prevent indigenes from enjoying full benefit of British advance in development of civil and criminal Procedure Codes with barbarous innovations designed to render Defence difficult and also to trip up independent-minded indigenes.[18]

Sekyi's instructions nowhere mention the interests of the common people, and the wishes of the Gold Coast middle-class nationalists,

[18] ibid., Sekyi, President of G.C.A.R.P.S. to Ashie-Nikoi, undated.

as expressed in the instructions, are almost identical to the legal, political, and economic demands of the N.C.B.W.A. of the 1920s. One wonders what the revolutionary Nkrumah thought of this type of nationalist politics. Very soon, the question of leadership and the locus of power would have to be resolved and would fundamentally affect the pattern of Gold Coast politics in the ensuing decades.[19]

The Congress[20] was held at Chorlton Town Hall, Manchester, from 15 to 19 October, and opened with an address of welcome by Alderman W. P. Jackson, the Lord Mayor of Manchester. A hundred delegates represented organizations in Africa, the West Indies, and Great Britain. Du Bois representing the N.A.A.C.P. was nominated permanent chairman of the Congress. The two sessions of 16 October dealt with North West Africa and South Africa, the main speakers being Nkrumah, Ashie-Nikoi, Chief Soyemi Coker (Nigeria), F. O. B. Blaize (W.A.S.U.), Marko Hlubi (South Africa), and Peter Abrahams (South Africa). Ashie-Nikoi, who represented the West African Cocoa Farmers' Delegation and the G.C.A.R.P.S., laid all the troubles of West Africa at the door of British imperialism, lamented the creation of the Provincial Councils set up by the 1925 constitution dismissing them as 'nothing short of Government Departments controlled by political officers', and concluded that he had come 'to ask this Congress to see that West Africa gets its political emancipation. It is our right and we must have it. . . . We do not want freedom that is partially controlled—we want nothing but freedom.' C. Downes-Thomas (Gambia) condemned colonial rule as outmoded, undemocratic, and unprogressive, and argued that political independence was the basis of economic independence. French and Belgian Africa found their spokesman in the Togolese poet Dr. Raphael Armattoe, author of *The Golden Age of West African Civilization*. Dr. Armattoe briefly described French colonial philosophy and raised a moot point when he observed that 'It is sometimes questioned whether French West Africans have any feeling of national consciousness, but I can say that French West Africans would be happier if they were governing themselves. They

[19] Looking back on the Congress, Nkrumah observed that it 'shot into the limbo the gradualist aspirations of our African middle classes and intellectuals and expressed the solid-down-to-earth will of our workers, trade unionists, farmers and peasants who were decisively represented at Manchester, for independence', K. Nkrumah quoted in Hooker, op. cit., p. 95.

[20] For details of the proceedings of the Manchester Congress, see *History of the Pan-African Congress*, ed. G. Padmore, pp. 27–74.

sometimes envy the British Africans their intense national feeling—
oppression has bound them together. A French West African should
feel that he is an African first, before he is anything else.' Delegates
representing Kenya, Trinidad, Ethiopia, Jamaica, Grenada, British
Guiana, and Barbados spoke during the sessions of 17 and 18 October, with both Garba-Jahumpa and J. F. Rojas (Trinidad Socialist
Party and T.U.C.) emphasizing the unifying role of the Congress.
Du Bois then reported on the race issue in America, and although he
agreed on the necessity of self-government for Africans, he warned
the militants that such forms of government demanded experience
and practice:

A great many of us want to say that we can govern ourselves now and
govern ourselves well; that may not be true. Government is a matter of
experience and long experience. Any people who have been deprived of
self-government for a long time and then have it returned to them are
liable to make mistakes. That is only human, and we are saying we have
a right to make mistakes as that is how people learn, so we are asserting
that we must have self-government even if we make mistakes.

It was precisely the same argument Nkrumah was to use against the
view that Africans were not prepared for self-government.[21]

The Congress, which tended to be dominated by West African
questions, passed various resolutions on political and economic
questions relating to West Africa, the Congo, and North Africa,
East Africa, South Africa, the High Commission Territories, South-
West Africa, the West Indies, Ethiopia, Liberia, and Haiti, and race
relations in Britain. Most of the constitutional and economic points
listed in Sekyi's instructions to Ashie-Nikoi were included in the
resolutions on West Africa, with Nkrumah adding the Pan-African
argument that 'the artificial divisions and territorial boundaries
created by the imperialist powers are deliberate steps to obstruct the
political unity of the West African peoples'.[22] The Congress's
Declaration to the Colonial Powers, written by Du Bois, affirmed
its belief in peace and in the principles of the Atlantic Charter, but
warned that 'as a last resort' force might be used in the struggle for
independence. It emphasized the importance of organization and the
active participation of the intellectuals in the mass movement for

[21] Mazrui, Ali A., 'Consent, Colonialism and Sovereignty', pp. 50–1.
[22] *History of the Pan-African Congress*, para. e, p. 55.

colonial freedom. Its 'Declaration to the Colonial Peoples of the World', which was written by Nkrumah, also reaffirmed the right of all people to self-determination:

We believe in the rights of all peoples to govern themselves. We affirm the right of all colonial peoples to control their own destiny. All colonies must be free from foreign imperialist control, whether political or economic. The peoples of the colonies must have the right to elect their own government, a government without restrictions from a foreign power. . . .

The object of the imperialist powers is to exploit. By granting the right to the colonial peoples to govern themselves, they are defeating that objective. Therefore, the struggle for political power by colonial and subject peoples is the first step towards, and the necessary pre-requisite to, complete social, economic and political emancipation.

The Fifth Pan-African Congress, therefore, calls on the workers and farmers of the colonies to organize effectively. Colonial workers must be in the front lines of the battle against imperialism.

This fifth Pan-African Congress calls on the intellectuals and professional classes of the colonies to awaken to their responsibilities. The long, long night is over. . . . Today there is only one road to effective action—the organization of the masses.

COLONIAL AND SUBJECT PEOPLES OF THE WORLD—
UNITE![23]

In general the Manchester Congress was seen as the zenith of the Pan-African movement.[24] To Nkrumah, the Congress was particularly important because 'it was quite distinct and different in tone, outlook and ideology from the four that had preceded it'. Former Pan-African congresses were reformist and middle class but the 1945 congress was more broadly based and radical in its nationalism. Above all,

the main reason why it achieved so much was because for the first time the delegates who attended it were practical men and men of action and not, as was the case of the four previous conferences, merely idealists contenting themselves with writing these but quite unwilling to take any active part in dealing with the African problem . . . it was this Fifth Pan-African Congress that provided the outlet for African nationalism

[23] Nkrumah, K., *Towards Colonial Freedom* (London, 1962), Appendix, pp. 44–5.
[24] '1945 must be regarded as an important year as it witnessed the attainment of the greatest height in Pan-Africanism.' Interview with the Hon. I. M. Garba-Jahumpa, Member of the Gambia House of Representatives, 17 Nov. 1966.

and brought about the awakening of African political consciousness. It became in fact, a mass movement of Africa for the Africans.[25]

Indirectly too, and almost as if by chance, the Congress served to revive the N.C.B.W.A. idea[26]—an idea that had been dormant since 1930. It also rekindled Nkrumah's old scheme of West African unity,[27] the first step towards which was the creation on 15 December 1945 of the West African National Secretariat by Nkrumah and radical companions like Bankole-Akpata, Kojo Botsio, Ashie-Nikoi, and Awooner Renner, to act as a co-ordinating centre for nationalist movements in West Africa. The W.A.N.S. idea was radical, populist, and socialistic; in fact one of its officers in a booklet entitled *West African Soviet Union* advocated a Soviet-style approach to the problem of ethnic groups in West Africa.

In West Africa too, a more moderate group of middle-class nationalists had also drawn some inspiration from the 1945 Congress. In the Gold Coast, the Accra intelligentsia led by Dr. F. V. Nanka-Bruce, the Hon. G. E. Moore, the Hon. Akilagpa Sawyerr, K. B. Ateko, W. E. G. Sekyi, J. B. Danquah, and A. M. Akiwumi met at the Rodger Club on 18 December 1945 to revive the N.C.B.W.A.[28] At the meeting it was decided to revive the N.C.B.W.A. in the renewed attack on the Provincial Councils; Sekyi and Awoonor Williams were requested to organize the Central and Western Province branches respectively.[29] The Accra meeting resolved

That WHEREAS the National Congress of British West Africa was formed in 1920 with Branches in the Gambia, Sierra Leone, the Gold Coast and Nigeria, with the object of championing the rights and liberties of the peoples of those territories, and

WHEREAS the Gold Coast Branch of the Congress has ceased to exist for some considerable time and it is now desirable that the Branch be resuscitated.

IT IS HEREBY RESOLVED that the said Gold Coast Branch of the National Congress of British West Africa be resuscitated forthwith. . . .[30]

[25] Nkrumah, K., *Autobiography*, pp. 53–4.
[26] 'For West Africa it [i.e. the 1945 Congress] marked the revival of the idea of East African National Congress of the early 1920.' Interview with the Hon. I. M. Garba-Jahumpa, 17 Nov. 1966.
[27] Nkrumah had preached the idea of West African unity since his student days in America, *Autobiography*, pp. 43–4.
[28] N.C.B.W.A. (Gold Coast Branch) circular by Enoch Mensah and G. J. C. Peregrine Peters, 12 Dec. 1945. *Kobina Sekyi Papers*, Cape Coast, Ghana.
[29] ibid., Joint Secretary to W. E. G. Sekyi, 31 Dec. 1945.
[30] ibid.

The enthusiasm, however, did not last and organization was poor, and by July 1946 this predecessor of the U.G.C.C. sank into oblivion.[31]

The groups which revived the N.C.B.W.A., however, were different in political outlook from Nkrumah's W.A.N.S. group. The former group was reformist, legalistic, and élitist, seeing itself as the natural successor of the black Edwardians of the N.C.B.W.A. days and as potential heir to the colonial regime. Nkrumah on the other hand thought in terms of mass politics, socialism, boycotts, and strikes as the quickest means of seizing power. From the point of view of the colonial élite, then, Nkrumah as we shall see, was regarded as an impostor and as a disruptive force. Nkrumah's tendency therefore, to see himself as a more radical image of West African patriots like Casely Hayford and W.A.N.S. as merely a revolutionary version of the N.C.B.W.A. seems understandable. It was an interesting combination of political messianism and political ambition—in fact, it was the beginning of a powerful myth in the history of Pan-African politics.[32]

## 2. *West African National Secretariat*

THE West African National Secretariat, formed in December 1945, was intended to serve as a co-ordinating body for nationalist movements in West Africa and as a regional organization of the Pan-African Federation. According to Peter Abrahams, however, it was the deliberate creation of Nkrumah and other militants such as Wallace-Johnson who designed to seize power as quickly as possible: 'He [Nkrumah] was one of the members of the inner circle of the Pan-African movement until he broke away to found his own West African National Secretariat. I thought then, and still think, that he was the most practical politician of the lot of us. We were concerned with ideas, with the enunciation of great principles. He was concerned

[31] ibid., Awoonor Williams to W. E. G. Sekyi, 26 July 1946. Ibid., Awoonor Williams to Enoch Mensah, 26 July 1946.

[32] Professor J. R. Hooker seems to underestimate this aspect of political messianism when he criticizes Padmore's coverage of Nkrumah's 1951 electoral victory as 'a review of modern Gold Coast history in the Whig tradition of historiography: all was but a prelude to the advent of Nkrumah and the good times. Nkrumah's West African National Secretariat was linked to the original West African National Congress, despite a seventeen-year hiatus, and Gold Coast progress was made a function of Nkrumah's career . . .' (op. cit., p. 115).

with one thing only, getting power and getting it quickly. . . .'[33]
For Nkrumah and the 'Young Turks', the only road to power lay
in the organization of the masses, and the W.A.N.S. was designed to
facilitate such organization. Its secretary-general was Nkrumah and
Wallace-Johnson was chairman; other officials were Bankole
Awoonor Renner, Mrs. Renner, and Ashie-Nikoi. It aimed

1. To maintain contact with, co-ordinate, educate and supply general
information on current matters to the various political bodies, trade
unions, co-operative societies, farmers organisations, educational, cultural
and other progressive societies in West Africa with a view to realising
an all-West African National Front for a United West African National
Independence.

2. To serve as a clearing house for information on matters affecting
the destiny of West Africa in particular and Africa in general; and to
educate the peoples and the working classes in particular, of the imperialist
countries concerning the problems of West Africa.

3. To foster the spirit of national unity and solidarity among the various
territories of West Africa for the purpose of combating the menace of
artificial territorial divisions now in existence.

4. To work for unity and harmony among all Africans who stand
against imperialism and all forms of exploitation.

5. To engineer the formation of an ALL-WEST AFRICAN NATIONAL
CONGRESS.

Their goal was 'national unity and absolute independence for all
West Africa'. They went on to declare that

Principles alone, when diffused among a people, manifest their right to
freedom and liberty. The test of faith in action, and thought and action
represent an integral concept of man's struggle for freedom. The economic
and political ideas and aspirations scattered among the West African
peoples but lacking in co-ordination need to be reduced to a system for
a united action. . . . WEST AFRICA IS ONE COUNTRY: PEOPLES
OF WEST AFRICA UNITE![34]

This last section is a good example of the use of Marxist–Leninist
concepts employed in the theory of colonial revolution; particularly
interesting is the overwhelming emphasis on mass organization and
the intimate connection between theory or ideology and 'praxis'.
The radicalization and politicization of the masses was obviously a

[33] Abrahams, Peter, 'Last Word on Nkrumah', *West African Review*, xxv (1954),
913.
[34] 'Bye Laws and Aims and Objects of the West African National Secretariat';
copy found in Kobina Sekyi Papers, Cape Coast Regional Archives, Ghana.

novel doctrine whose significance dawned on the bourgeois nationalists when it was too late, for by then the balance of political forces had shifted in favour of the organization men.

Nkrumah probably had no plan in 1946 as to the details of a future nationalist organization in West Africa along the lines laid down at Manchester and he certainly was out of touch with political trends in the Gold Coast.[35] In late January 1946 he wrote to Sekyi informing him that his instructions to Ashie-Nikoi were the inspiration for the formation of W.A.N.S. He explained the purpose of the W.A.N.S. and asked for photographs of Gold Coast public figures like Sekyi and Moore, a copy of the G.C.A.R.P.S. 1934 House of Commons petition, and articles for publication in a projected W.A.N.S. pamphlet series on West African affairs. Sekyi was also asked to become chairman of the governing council of the W.A.N.S. which Nkrumah and his colleagues were planning to establish.[36] Nkrumah wrote again, forwarding W.A.N.S. literature and requesting Sekyi to contribute articles to the *New African*, the proposed organ of the W.A.N.S.[37] Sekyi was later asked to write a special article on the Sedition Bill in the Gold Coast and to advise on the drawing up of bye-laws for W.A.N.S. and on other administrative questions relating to 'the successful working of the Secretariat'.[38] The *New African* was indeed published in March 1946 as promised by Nkrumah, as the official organ of the W.A.N.S. and as a monthly paper dealing with colonial and African affairs, with its motto: 'For Unity and Absolute Independence'. Sekyi, however, replied that apart from pressure of work, ill health had compelled him to do very little by way of agitation and other political activity; moreover, he lamented, 'it is not easy to get things done in this country, and the younger men are not at all helpful; . . . I suggest that for the time being my active assistance be not too much counted upon'. However, he promised to send Nkrumah some suggestions about discussing them with the G.C.A.R.P.S. Executive Committee: he also forwarded a subscription to the new journal.[39]

The first issue of the *New African* lost no time in sounding the

---

[35] Nkrumah, K., *Autobiography*, pp. 61–2.
[36] F. N. Nkrumah to W. E. G. Sekyi, 28 Jan. 1946, G.C.A.R.P.S. files, Cape Coast Regional Archives, Ghana, File no. 24, 111/65, 'West African National Secretariat'.
[37] ibid., F. N. Nkrumah to Sekyi, 12 Feb. 1946.
[38] ibid., F. N. Nkrumah to Sekyi, 21 Feb. 1946.
[39] ibid., Sekyi to Nkrumah, 13 Mar. 1946.

first blast of the Pan-African trumpet against the monstrous colonial regimes

Behind six years of world destruction, and six months of poker playing with the small Powers, and the Colonies as 'the jackpot', it should be plain to the working classes of the world, whatever their colour, that there is only one freedom worth having, and that is, freedom to manage their own affairs. . . . The peoples of the colonies are being taken for a ride, not on a tiger, but on a more dangerous beast, an old, hungry and decrepit lion, suffering from the illusion that the world is still a jungle of which he is King. Power politics suggest that the world is indeed a jungle, but the Lion is no longer the King. In order to save themselves the peoples of the Colonies seem now to be up against a clear-cut proposition. Either they dismount from the lion, and manage their own affairs in their own way, or they will be faced with a future even more catastrophic than their ordeals of the past thirty years. . . .[40]

The *New African* also reiterated the aims of the W.A.N.S.: 'In order for a people to act politically there must be a political concept. Such a concept must be concretized by means of a united national front organization. The mission of the West African National Secretariat, therefore, is to maintain, sustain and push forward the national struggle for West African National Unity and Absolute Independence. . . .' Its 'Credo' read:

We believe

(1) That Imperialism and colonial liberation are two irreconcilable opposites; a compromise between them is impossible. The death of the one is the life of the other.

(2) That without political independence the talk of economic independence is mere waste of time. It stood for the 'complete liquidation of the colonial system', independence for all West Africa and the industrialisation of West Africa. It opposed 'Any form of reactionary nationalism in West Africa; any form of opportunism and reformism in matters affecting the political and economic destiny of West Africa', and it called upon all individuals and organisation in Africa 'to join The West African National Secretariat and to rally the fullest support behind the Secretariat's movement for African unity and freedom', adding: 'The day when West Africa, as one united country, pulls itself from imperialist oppression and exploitation it will pull the rest of Africa with her. . . . The time of politics of words is gone; this is an age of politics of action. Act now!'[41]

By united West Africa the W.A.N.S. meant British, French, Spanish, and Portuguese West Africa, as well as the Belgian Congo

[40] *New African*, i, no. 1 (Mar. 1946).
[41] ibid., p. 5.

and Liberia. Imitating Garvey's U.N.I.A., they took as their slogan 'One Aim! One People! One United West Africa!' The Secretary-General fully stated for the first time his theory of territorial independence and regional unity:

In all matters pertaining to the destiny of West Africa, personal and tribal differences, opinions and shortcomings must not be allowed to hamper our struggle for West African National Unity and Absolute independence. The ideals of West African National Unity and independence must hold supreme and paramount place in our thinking and action. . . . Only in unity and organisation can West Africa find strength, but not in the haphazard unification of dissenting factions. Single factions struggling alone towards the same ends are diverting their energies and may fail. But a unification of these several elements into a concerted effort is a weapon which wields power that cannot be defeated. There is no fortress, however strongly fortified, that a united people cannot overthrow. . . . The West African National Secretariat shall launch the appeal for the formation of an All-West African National Congress. . . . PEOPLES OF WEST AFRICA, UNITE.[42]

Like Casely Hayford and the N.C.B.W.A. leaders in the 1920s, Nkrumah was not very clear about what he meant by West African National Unity, although unlike the former he was quite clear as to what constituted 'the people' and how this united front should be organized. Yet it was not clear whether he wanted an inter-territorial mass party (like the *Rassemblement Démocratique Africaine*) with W.A.N.S. officials as the general staff, or whether he was contemplating a Marxist–Leninist party in alliance with the bourgeois nationalists but acting as the vanguard—and eventually seizing power in the classic Communist pattern. Or was this, like the General Strike and the classless society, merely another myth designed to whip up more positive response in the colonies? At least, some of his friends who nevertheless disagreed with his approach were willing to see the political prophet in him. It was reported that when Nkrumah spoke of unity and absolute independence at a Fabian Colonial Bureau conference on 12–14 February 1946 at Clacton-on-Sea, Dr. Rita Hinden, Secretary of the Fabian Colonial Bureau, referred to his idea as 'representing that of the Italian patriot, Mazzini, who preached Italian unity without planning'.[43]

---

[42] ibid. i, no. 3 (May 1946), p. 2.

[43] ibid., p. 20. Nkrumah later explained, when questioned by the U.G.C.C. that he 'believed in TERRITORIAL BEFORE INTERNATIONAL solidarity', Austin, Dennis, *Politics in Ghana, 1946–60* (London, 1964), p. 54. He abandoned

Evidently there were some, both in the Pan-African movement and in West Africa, who not only disagreed with some of Nkrumah's views and methods, but regarded him as an uncertain ally with dangerous political proclivities. Peter Abrahams had already noted Nkrumah's impatience with armchair nationalist theoreticians and his keen appreciation of political power. Such a man would obviously be an inconvenience to petty-bourgeois nationalists. Thus on 2 August F. Awoonor Williams, a barrister and local politician at Sekondi, writing to Sekyi in connection with the W.A.N.S. and the colonial policy of the Labour Government, observed:

To be quite candid when I saw the name of Wallace Johnson amongst the signatories to the aims and objects i.e. of the W.A.N.S. I recoiled. With my background and antecedents I shrink from associating with anyone who is suspected of associating with the Enemies of his country or being in receipt of pay from doubtful sources, although these imputations may be ill founded. A glance at the aims shows that they are laudable but the names of the sponsors condemn it, and if we wish to secure favourable opinion and support from men of position we ruin our case by such association. I for one have always been suspicious of the majority of Labour Leaders whose avowed aim is wealth and political power and soon as they achieve this, send their sons to Oxford and Cambridge and assume the roll [sic] of the gentry. Out with it and tell ignorant demos that you envy the wealth and position of the gentry and would feign have a share of them and be candid with the matter.

In my view the National Congress of British West Africa should drive their own horse and strive to achieve their destiny without these people.[44]

In a similar vein T. R. Makonnen, one of Nkrumah's close associates, wrote to Sekyi in 1949 after the Accra riots and Nkrumah's dismissal from the U.G.C.C. thanking him for the financial contribution of the G.C.A.R.P.S. to the 1945 Congress. Makonnen also referred to some G.C.A.R.P.S. literature Sekyi had sent him, and to a letter from Sekyi, noting that the letter 'has helped me greatly in putting the whole matter into perspective and in confirming my own tentative judgment of what is wrong'. This was obviously a letter about Gold Coast politics from the point of view of the chiefs and professional classes. Makonnen added:

the West African unification idea in the early 1960s in favour of an even wider and more problematic conception—an all-Africa union government: see *Towards Colonial Freedom*, pp. x–xi.

[44] F. Awoonor Williams to Sekyi, 2 Aug. 1946, G.C.A.R.P.S. files, Cape Coast Regional Archives, Ghana, File no. 24, 111/65.

From what I have gleaned I feel justified in giving my support to the 'traditionalists' among whom you count yourself. . . . Right from the time of the Pan-African Congress, . . . it was obvious to me that Nkrumah was not prepared to play the game, and I am only too aware of the deception on which the Secretariat, and now the Convention, are founded.

I have always felt that if Africa is to adopt Communism as its political philosophy, there is plenty in our own institutions on which to build without giving allegiance to another imperialist group masquerading behind an 'ism'. I have felt all along that the Aborigines Society should have taken the lead in calling a Constitutional Convention as did John Adams, to meet a declaration of the principle that the sovereign status of the people remains what it has always been. Such a Convention should then act as the spear-head of the peoples wishes. . . . I am in fact 100% with you in your criticisms of the Convention, and like you feel that these people who have not had time fully to grasp political doctrine are not the best leaders for the Gold Coast. Merely to leave it to history to judge will not help, and I feel that these men should not be allowed to destroy the good work that others have done and are still trying to do.[45]

It is possible that Makonnen, who had always been a radical Pan-African and a nationalist, was over-reacting to the possibility of the emergence of a Communist-oriented political movement in the Gold Coast; like Padmore, he too had been sufficiently disillusioned with the Comintern, and was now advocating a midway course between Soviet imperialism and Western dominance. Yet only two years prior to the foundation of the Convention Peoples Party ('the Widening of the Gap' as Nkrumah later put it) Nkrumah had written a letter to Sekyi full of enthusiasm and admiration for the initiative he had taken with G. E. Moore, 'Pa Grant', and J. B. Danquah in laying the foundations of the U.G.C.C.[46] How did it come about that the 'traditionalists' had lost power to 'these men' and that one of their leading intellectuals was in 1949 calling upon history to stand in judgement over Nkrumah and the C.P.P.? The story has been well told in Dennis Austin's *Politics in Ghana* and needs no repetition here.

Back in London Nkrumah's W.A.N.S. struggled to keep the short-lived *New African* going, and supported by the W.A.S.U., planned an all-West African conference as early as May 1946. Nkrumah visited Paris to secure the support of Sourou-Migan Apithy, Lamine

---

[45] ibid., T. R. Makonnen to Sekyi; undated letter, probably late 1949.
[46] ibid., F. N. Kwame Nkrumah to Sekyi, 28 May 1947. For the origins of the U.G.C.C., see Austin, op. cit., p. 52.

Gueye, Houphouet-Boigny, Léopold Senghor, who were then deputies in the French National Assembly, for the projected conference. The possibility of a movement for the creation of a Union of West African Socialist Republics along the lines advocated by the W.A.N.S. was also discussed with the French Africans and the conference, attended by Apithy and Senghor, took place later between 30 August and 1 September 1946 in London. The conference rejected the gradualist approach to self-government, 'endorsed the idea of reviving the West African National Congress', and the scheme 'to promote the concept of a West African Federation as an indispensable lever for carrying forward the Pan-African vision of an ultimate United States of Africa'.[47] *W.A.S.U. Magazine* reported that the conference had met 'to discuss the present political, economic and social conditions in West Africa, and to determine in that light a plan for creating a united and independent West Africa'. The reporter, probably Nkrumah, observed that the conference was truly all-West African and that its main theme was unity and independence of all West Africa. He defined the Pan-West African idea thus:

The West African concept of unity has . . . nothing in common with the geopolitician's and imperialists' vision of world conquest and domination of other peoples. It has nothing in common with any imaginary 'African Heartland', so dearly cherished by political marauders and buccaneers. That concept of West African unity is a noble and inspiring idea which asserts that in order to liberate themselves from the shackles of imperialism . . . West Africans must organise and weld together in an all-embracing united national front, which will carry forward the struggle for independence. For in such an organic unity lies the most powerful weapon for effective political action. It further asserts that the unity of the West African people derives not merely from the fact of their natural affinity and oneness, but also from the common danger to their ancestral lands, their common need, suffering and anxiety. It maintains that the possession of political power is the key to economic and social progress. . . . It is axiomatic that a part cannot be greater than the whole; so also with Africa. West Africa cannot be greater than all Africa. The significance and importance, therefore, of the unity and independence of West Africa must be seen in the African context.[48]

[47] Padmore, G., *Pan-Africanism or Communism?*, p. 173; cf. Nkrumah, K., *Autobiography*, p. 57.
[48] 'The West African Conference and After' (Anon.), *W.A.S.U. Magazine*, xii, no. 3 (Summer 1947), 14.

The report concluded with the usual argument that nationalist successes in West Africa would be followed by simultaneous agitation for independence in other parts of Africa. Logically and practically the concept of a Pan-West African Marxist-style movement was fraught with difficulties. W.A.N.S. was not territorially based and had no contact with the English-speaking bourgeois nationalists who, in any case, were suspicious of its aims. Moreover, the constitutional changes in the French colonies after 1946 ruled out any hopes of effective co-operation between the W.A.N.S. and the French West African groups.[49] Whatever the shortcomings of the W.A.N.S. conference it could at least claim to have introduced the Pan-African idea to French-speaking Africa and to have revived a constant theme in West African history.[50]

In 1947 Makonnen's Pan-African Federation started a new journal *Pan-Africa*, described as a monthly journal of African life, history, and thought. Makonnen was publisher and managing director and members of the editorial staff included Dina Stock (executive editor) and Florence Niool (research secretary). The themes were generally concerned with race relations and anti-colonial issues, with contributors from several countries; but articles specifically on West Africa were very few. The P.A.F. also kept a close watch on the affairs of the U.N. Trusteeship Council particularly on matters concerning the British colonies.[51] By 1948 *Pan-Africa* was declared a seditious publication and was banned by some colonial governments; it ceased publication soon after.

In 1946–7 a small revolutionary cell within W.A.S.U. called 'The Circle' was formed by Nkrumah and a few militants dedicated to radical agitation for self-government and West African unity. This group lapsed with the departure of Nkrumah and Kojo Botsio for the Gold Coast the same year, and a projected all-West African conference was never held. Nkrumah's subsequent political career

[49] For French West African politics after 1946, see Hodgkin, Thomas, and Schachter, Ruth, *French-speaking West Africa in Transition* (*International Conciliation*, May 1960, no. 528).

[50] ibid., p. 431; the unification theme in West African history is argued in detail by A. B. Aderibigbe. See chapter III, p. 110 n. 16.

[51] See the P.A.F.'s representation to the United Nations Delegations, 22 Oct. 1948, G.C.A.R.P.S. Files, Cape Coast Regional Archives, Ghana, 187/65, File no. 100; 'Pan-African Congress'. The letter was a rebuttal of a pro-British speech made by Grantley Adams on behalf of the colonies at the Trusteeship Council in 1948; it accused Adams as 'an apologist for imperialism, and an enemy of the cause . . .'.

in the Gold Coast also meant that the Pan-West African idea, a central theme of his nationalist philosophy, had to be soft-pedalled until his accession to power in 1951 when it was again revived. As early as December 1953 he anticipated future African conclaves by calling the Sixth Pan-African Congress at Kumasi. 'Pan-African', in fact, was a misnomer as only a few delegates from West Africa attended this little known Congress—Dr. Azikiwe, Mrs. Ransome-Kuti, and H. O. Davies representing Nigeria, and Mr. Loyd Whisnant, Liberian consul-general in Accra, representing Liberia. Nkrumah's opponents in the Gold Coast did not attend, nor were the Gambia, Sierra Leone, or French West African territories represented.[52] The Congress was intended to be the forerunner of a Pan-African conference to be held in 1954 to discuss Africa as a whole, especially race and politics.[53] It is interesting to note that almost a generation after the N.C.B.W.A. which, among other things, deprecated the 'partitioning of African communities', Nkrumah's Kumasi Congress resolved to create a West African federation and a permanent West African National Congress as the basis of 'a strong and truly federal state that is capable of protecting its territory from outside invasion . . .'.[54] Although Nkrumah described the Congress as 'the nucleus of great potentialities', the fact remained that this form of anti-colonial alliance politics overlooked certain important facts: the absence of any delegate from Northern Nigeria, a country, *West Africa* rightly argued, 'without whose unity a West African federation has no real basis'. Gambia's Consultative Committee report referred to the possibility of 'federation with other West African territories' but federation was opposed, according to *West Africa*, by one of her leading politicians, the Hon. Garba-Jahumpa who had been one of the 1945 Pan-African Congress delegates. Besides, other political groups in the Gambia were cautious of such federal unions. The Gambia Democratic Party, which was based mainly in the capital, argued that self-government must come to the territories individually before federation; and although Point 4 of its policy resolved 'To collaborate and work with other British West African Territories with a view of establishing a Dominion of Federated States of British West Africa in the seeable future', it was

---

[52] Decraene, op. cit., pp. 26–7.
[53] *West Africa* (11 Apr. 1953), p. 325.
[54] ibid. (19 Dec. 1953), pp. 1177–8: 'West African Federation'.

feared that tomorrow if British West Africa is allowed to develop separately into splinter Dominions such as the Federation of Nigeria, The Dominion of the Gold Coast, Sierra Leone Territory and The Gambia Territory, it could be argued that whereas British Central Africa (where the Government is mainly manned by Europeans) federation was effected against the wishes of the main body of Africans—in West Africa where the Government is mainly African, The Mother Country has done hardly anything to bring the individual territories together into a federation.[55]

The Democratic Party also suggested exploratory talks on the possibility of a British West African Federation along the Australian pattern, with the West African Inter-Territorial Council as the nucleus, the ratio of representation being 1:2:4:6. It was also proposed that the federal capital could either be Kumasi or somewhere in Nigeria.

Then too, there was the question of the attitude of the French West Africans: how would they view Nkrumah's idea of a united West Africa within the Commonwealth? There was also the question of Togoland and the British Cameroons. Nkrumah recognized these obstacles to unity and merely spoke of a 'revival' of the ideas of the N.C.B.W.A.[56] To most outside observers and well-wishers Nkrumah was right in seeing the political significance of the Gold Coast in continental terms, but they were equally agreed that a functional approach was more profitable and realistic than an unlikely political federation of West Africa.[57] The problem, however, had not by 1954 assumed continental proportions for Nkrumah's approach to Pan-Africanism up to August 1962 was regional.[58] It may be that tactical considerations dictated advocacy of 'unity as alliance',[59] i.e. regional unity, and that longer-term revolutionary objectives and ambitions in the international sphere led him to believe in 'unity as movement', i.e. continental unity.[60] It may also be that the two approaches to

[55] A. E. Cham-Joof, Assistant General Secretary, Gambia Democratic Party, to the Rt. Hon. A. Creech Jones, M.P., Leader of the Commonwealth Parliamentary Association Delegation to West Africa, 23 Mar. 1956. I am grateful to Mr. Cham-Joof for finding the time to locate this piece of information for me.

[56] *West Africa* (19 Dec. 1953), pp. 1177–8: 'West African Federation'.

[57] ibid., p. 1178.

[58] Nkrumah, K., *Towards Colonial Freedom*, pp. x–xi.

[59] The phrase is Wallerstein's: see Wallerstein, Immanuel, *Africa: The Politics of Unity* (London, 1968), chapter VII.

[60] For a critical assessment of Nkrumah's diplomatic strategy in inter-African relations, see W. Scott Thompson's well-documented *Ghana's Foreign Policy 1957–1966: Diplomacy, Ideology and the New State* (Princeton, N.J., 1969), especially chapters 2–3 and chapter 8.

African unity are not mutually exclusive. What is certain is that after Nkrumah's accession to power Pan-Africanism, which had hitherto been dominated by New-World Negroes, took a new and decisive turn and has had far-reaching effects on the political relations of the African continent and has, to some extent, made its contribution to the conduct and language of international relations. In retrospect, then, the small gathering at Kumasi in 1953 can be seen as a new phase in the evolution of an idea and . . . as the real beginning of the Pan-African movement *in* Africa.

CONCLUSION:

# Past and Present

DETAILED study of the West African aspects of the Pan-African movements to 1945 points to several interesting conclusions. Perhaps the most important point is that contrary to standard accounts, there was not one single Pan-African movement: what emerges is a series of Pan-African movements assuming different characteristics in different areas, under different leadership, but loosely united by an ideology of race and colour and by a sense of injustice and inferiority. Nor was this form of racial solidarity confined to English-speaking Negroes, as is frequently asserted. Although there was no *rapport* between English-speaking and French-speaking West Africans during the 1920s and 1930s, we have already established that such *rapport*, although tenuous, did exist between radical West African Pan-Negro groups in Paris and the Du Bois and Garvey groups in America during the inter-war years. As is generally known, it was only after the 1945 Manchester Congress that some kind of dialogue was established between English- and French-speaking West African nationalists, largely through the efforts of Nkrumah and Padmore.

Another view which has emerged from this study is that the alleged differences between the Du Boisian and Garvey concept of Pan-Africanism seem, on closer examination, to have been minimal. The Du Bois–Garvey controversy was not so much an ideological conflict of personalities and divergence on short-run political tactics: the goal was the same—black political and economic freedom. The controversy was exaggerated out of all proportion by the opposition of both West Indian and Afro-American Communists to Garvey. It is interesting to note in this connection, that Du Bois himself only became a Communist in the 1950s. The Garvey concept, however, was more influential in Africa, and its economic ideology more acceptable to conservative nationalists and Pan-Africanists in Africa, especially the West African petty-bourgeoisie in the 1920s. Harold Cruse's contention that 'it was Du Bois' brand of Pan-Africanism that won out in Africa, *because Garvey was not a socialist but a thoroughgoing capitalist . . .*[1] is, at best, a teleological justification. Du Bois certainly lived longer than Garvey and even died in an independent and 'socialist' Ghana, but this is not the same as saying his brand of Pan-Africanism 'won out eventually'. Interestingly enough, it was the 'capitalist' Garvey who, whatever his ideological aberrations, saw the importance of establishing the economic basis of black liberation by devising a Pan-African economic strategy which would directly confront the power of imperialist monopoly capital in Africa. It is also interesting to note that Stokely Carmichael's revolutionary pilgrimage has led him to a similar conclusion, albeit from a revolutionary socialist standpoint.[2] In any case Du Boisian Pan-Africanism ceased to exist in 1945. If any brand of Pan-Africanism has triumphed in Africa today, it is surely the Pan-Africanism of conservative bourgeois nationalists who have substituted state capitalism for socialism and economic nationalism for planned development—the mere achievement of political independence which, according to Marx, 'leaves the pillars of the house standing'. The West African petty bourgeoisie did not share the political goals of Garveyism, and in fact saw itself as the social class in Africa most suited to lead a Pan-African movement. The view, therefore, that Afro-Americans 'influenced' African nationalism and Pan-African ideology needs considerable modification, particularly when viewed in the light of socio-economic analysis of the West African political leadership in the 1920s and 1930s, and in the light of growing Pan-Negro consciousness among Francophone Africans in the same period.

The Pan-West African movement of the 1920s partly reflected the post-war Pan-African movement of Afro-Americans but to a greater degree reflected the political and economic interests of the West African petty-bourgeois nationalists. We have seen how their agitation for constitutional reform came to be interwoven with Pan-African ideology and practical economic interests—the interests of the colonial élite which were in fact incompatible with any concept of the 'nation' or the 'people' they might have popularized in the course of their political agitation. The political institutions they demanded were precisely those through which their interests and

[1] Cruse, *The Negro Intellectual in Crisis*, p. 559.
[2] See Stokely Carmichael, interviewed by Jonathan Power in 'The Black Man's Burden', the *Guardian*, 9 Feb. 1971, p. 11.

those of the colonial power could be accommodated without any fundamental changes in the colonial political system. Similarly, the educational and legal reforms they demanded, as well as their criticisms of the monopolies and combines, were directly connected with their own class interests. What therefore appeared to the colonial authorities and to European observers in general as a radical movement of newly awakened people was essentially a moderate, constitutionally minded movement led by a conservative and relatively privileged section of the colonial populace incapable of allying itself with, or unwilling to mobilize, colonial sub-élites such as chiefs, urban wage labourers, artisans, and petty traders. Their assumption of the leadership of the Pan-West African movement also points to interesting parallels with the conservative nature of the leadership of other pan-movements such as Pan-Germanism, Pan-Slavism, and Pan-Turanism. This type of leadership dominated West African colonial politics up to the late 1940s in spite of assertions that there was a radical change in the West African political leadership after 1930. We have attempted to show in chapter V that the latter view is not supported by the evidence and is largely one of those academic myths about African nationalism.

We have also briefly dealt with an important and relatively neglected aspect in the development of Pan-Africanism—the impact of the Italo-Ethiopian crisis on Pan-Negro thinking. The reaction of black people, in retrospect, seems to have given impetus to a later organization of Pan-Negro ideas and aspirations. It is arguable that the spontaneous reaction of black people to that crisis is characteristic of African responses to white 'aggression' in Africa to the present day, and has always served as a unifying factor in African opposition to European colonialism. If the delegates who met at Manchester in 1945 had learnt any lesson from the Ethiopian crisis, it was surely that protest and moral indignation alone were useless weapons with which to counter power imperialism.

The extent of Communist interest in Pan-Negro nationalism must also be emphasized:[3] this aspect has hitherto been neglected or minimized by students of the colonial activities of the Comintern. This study has not followed Padmore's biased account of Comintern involvement with or manipulation of Pan-Negro nationalism, but the conclusion reached, though not final, is similar. The reaction of Pan-Negro organizations, except the splinter group in Paris led by

[3] See chapters II and VII for details.

Tiémoho Garan-Kouyaté, was the same as that of several other Negro political organizations: they saw Communism as incompatible with Pan-Negro nationalism: on the other hand, many Pan-African leaders, especially the French-speaking Africans, showed a marked hostility to capitalism. It must be added, however, that among the French African Pan-Negroists, hostility to Communist influence was less evident. In fact, under Lamine Senghor's brief leadership, the L.D.R.N. was definitely Communist-oriented, with Senghor himself advocating the adoption of the manifesto of the French Party and the Comintern theses on the colonies. Evidence from Communist sources also indicates the Comintern's interest in Afro-American and South African nationalist movements in the 1920s.

The concluding chapters of the study have briefly examined the origins of the new movement in Africa beginning with Nkrumah's early ideas about regional unification and the recurrence of this theme in the history of nationalism in West Africa. The evolution of Nkrumah's regional approach to Pan-Africanism in the 1940s has been dealt with in view of his shift to a continental approach from 1962, and in view of the current emphasis on the regional approach in Pan-African politics and economic integration.

This study has not only attempted a new interpretation of the early Pan-African movement; it has also attempted to put in historical perspective the new directions the Pan-African movement has taken over the last thirty-five years. What emerged in the New World as a global ideology of black liberation came to assume a special regional character in West Africa just before the Great War and during the inter-war period. Although the nature of the colonial system in West Africa and the economic interests of the petty-bourgeois nationalist leadership inevitably dictated a more conservative political style and a narrower interpretation of Pan-African unity, the basic ingredients of Pan-African ideology—racial autonomy and unification and economic independence—were never discarded by the constitutional nationalists in West Africa. A similar pattern can be observed in the development of Pan-Africanism both after the Manchester Congress, when the prevailing philosophy was the attainment of independence and regional unification, and after the attainment of independence and the foundation of the Organization of African Unity in the early 1960s when not only was there a clash between the proponents of a radical 'union government' philosophy of Pan-Africanism and the more conservative advocates of limited functional regional co-operation, but also growing evidence of the serious political and economic problems involved, even at the level of regional unification.[4] The current debate on the prospects of regional integration in West Africa no doubt involves complex economic issues, but it is significant that most commentators on economic integration in Africa, while advocating a more pragmatic and realistic approach, do see the need for a wider political consensus as a basis for the creation of a meaningful West African community.[5] Another analyst who has assessed the significance of Pan-African ideology in regional integration in East Africa from 1963, has concluded that 'Probably the most important contribution of Pan-Africanism was its provision of a set of beliefs and values through which leaders perceived their interests.'[6] Like the West African nationalist élite we have been studying, the East African élites, according to Nye, reinterpreted Pan-Africanism to suit their socio-economic and political interests, particularly when ideology and interest clashed. His conclusion, albeit negative, is that the 'primacy of politics' in regional integration is a major factor we cannot afford to ignore. When Casely Hayford, pioneer of West African unification, asserted in the 1920s that 'One touch of Nature has made West Africa kin', he was referring to the consensus of the West African leadership of his generation. In West Africa today, as Welch[7] has shown, that consensus has so far been lacking.

[4] These developments have been fully documented in recent scholarly works, Nye, Jnr., J. S., *Pan-Africanism and East African Integration* (Cambridge, Mass., 1966) and Welch, Jnr., Claude, *Dream of Unity*, to list only two.

[5] Adedeji, Adebayo, 'Prospects of Regional Economic Co-operation in West Africa', *Journal of Modern African Studies*, viii, no. 2 (1970), 226–7, 230.

[6] Nye, Jnr., J. S., op. cit., p. 209.

[7] op. cit., *passim*.

# APPENDIX I

# The London Manifesto (29 August 1921)[1]

THE United States of America, after brutally enslaving millions of black folk suddenly emancipated them and began their education, but it acted without system or forethought, throwing the freed man on the world penniless and landless, educating them without thoroughness and system and subjecting them the while to lynching, lawlessness, discrimination, insult and slander, such as human beings have seldom endured and survived. To save their own government they enfranchised the Negro and then when danger passed, allowed hundreds of thousands of educated and civilised black folk to be lawlessly disfranchised and subjected to a caste system, and at the same time in 1776, 1812, 1861, 1897, and 1917 they asked and allowed thousands of black men to offer up their lives as a sacrifice to the country which despised them.

France alone of the great colonial powers has sought to place her cultured black citizens on a plane of absolute legal and social equality with her white, and given them representation in her highest legislature. In her colonies she has a wide-spread but still imperfect system of state education. This splendid beginning must be completed by widening the political bases of her native government, by restoring to her indigenes the ownership of the soil, by protecting native labour against the aggression of established capital, and by compelling no man, white or black, to be a soldier unless the country gives him a voice in his own government.

The independence of Abyssinia, Liberia, Haiti and San Domingo is absolutely necessary to any sustained belief of the black folk in the sincerity and honesty of the white. These nations have earned the right to be free, they deserve the recognition of the world. Notwithstanding all their faults and mistakes and the fact that they are in many respects behind the most advanced civilization of the day, nevertheless they compare favourably with the past and even recent history of most European nations and it shames civilization that the Treaty of London practically invited Italy to aggression on Abyssinia and that free America has unjustly and cruelly seized Haiti, murdered her citizens and for a time enslaved her workmen, overthrown her free institutions by force and has so far failed in return to give her a single bit of help, aid or sympathy.

What, then, do those demand who see these evils of the colour line and

[1] Source: *African World* Supplement, Sept. 1921, pp. xi–xix, 'West Africa and the Pan-African Congress'

racial discrimination, and who believe in the divine right of Suppressed and Backward Peoples to learn and aspire and be free?

The Suppressed Races through their thinking leaders are demanding:

1. The recognition of civilised men as civilised despite their race and colour.

2. Local self-government for backward groups, deliberately rising as experience and knowledge grow to complete self-government under the limitations of a self-governed world.

3. Education in self-knowledge, in scientific truth and in industrial technique, undivorced from the art of beauty.

4. Freedom in their own religion and customs and with the right to be non-conformist and different.

5. Co-operation with the rest of the world in government, industry and art on the basis of Justice, Freedom and Peace.

6. The ancient common ownership of the Land and its natural fruits and defence against the unrestrained greed of invested capital.

The world must face two eventualities; either the complete assimilation of Africa with two or three of the great world states, with political, civil and social power and privileges absolutely equal for its black and white citizens, or the rise of a great black African State, founded in Peace and Good Will, based on popular education, natural art and industry and freedom of trade, autonomous and sovereign in its internal policy, but from its beginning a part of a great society of peoples in which it takes its place with others as co-rulers of the world.

In some such words and thoughts as these we seek to express our will and ideal and the end of our untiring effort. To our aid we call all men of the earth who love Justice and Mercy. Out of the depths we have cried unto the deaf and dumb masters of the world,—out of the depths we cry to our own sleeping souls. The answer is written in the stars.

The absolute equality of races, physical, political and social, is the founding stone of World Peace and human advancement. No one denies great differences of gift, capacity and attainment among individuals of all races, but the voice of Science, Religion and practical Politics is one in denying the God-appointed existence of super-races or of races naturally and inevitably and eternally inferior.

That in the vast range of time, one group should in its industrial technique or social organisation or spiritual vision lag a few hundred years behind another or forge fitfully ahead or come to differ decidedly in thought, deed and ideal is proof of the essential richness and variety of human nature, rather than proof of the co-existence of demi-gods and apes in human form. The doctrine of racial equality does not interfere with individual liberty,—rather fulfils it.

And of all the various criteria by which masses of men have in the past been judged and classified that of the color of the skin and texture of the hair is surely the most adventitious and idiotic.

It is the duty of the world to assist in every way the advance of the

Backward and Suppressed Groups of mankind. The rise of all men is a menace to no one and is the highest human ideal—it is not an altruistic benevolence, but the one road to world salvation.

For the purpose of raising such peoples to intelligence, self knowledge and self control, their intelligentsia of right ought to be recognised as the natural leaders of their groups.

The insidious and dishonourable propaganda which for selfish ends so distorts and denies facts as to represent the advancement and development of certain races as impossible and undesirable should be met with wide-spread dissemination of the truth; the experiment of making the Negro slave a free citizen in the United States is not a failure; the attempts at autonomous government in Haiti and Liberia are not proofs of the impossibility of self-government among black men; the experience of Spanish America does not prove that mulatto democracy will not eventually succeed there; the aspirations of Egypt and India are not successfully to be met by sneers at the capacity of darker races.

We who resent the attempt to treat civilised men as uncivilised and who bring in our hearts grievance upon grievance against those who lynch the untried, disfranchise the intelligent, deny self-government to educated men, and insult the helpless,—we complain,—but not simply or primarily for ourselves—more especially for the millions of our fellows, blood of our blood and flesh of our flesh who have not even what we have; the power to complain against monstrous wrong, the power to see and know the source of our oppression.

How far the future advance of mankind will depend on the social contact and physical intermixture of the various strains of human blood is unknown. But the demand for the interpenetration of countries and inter-mingling of blood has come in modern days from the white race alone and has been imposed on brown and black folks mainly by brute force and fraud; and on top of that the resulting people of mixed race have had to endure innuendo, persecution and insult; and the penetrated countries have been forced into semi-slavery.

If it be proven that absolute world segregation by group, color or historic affinity is the best thing for the future world, let the white race leave the dark world and the dark races will gladly leave the white. But the proposition is absurd. This is a world of men,—of men whose likenesses far outweigh their differences; who mutually need each other in labour and thought and dream, but who can successfully have each other only on terms of equality, justice and mutual respect. They are the real and only peace-makers who work sincerely and peacefully to this end.

The beginning of Wisdom in inter-racial contact is the establishment of political institutions among suppressed Peoples. The habit of democracy must be made to encircle the earth. Despite the attempt to prove that its practice is the secret and divine Gift of the Few, no habit is more natural and more widely spread among primitive peoples or more easily capable of development among wide masses. Local self-government with a minimum of help and oversight can be established to-morrow in Asia, Africa, America and the Isles of the Sea. It will in many instances need general control and guidance but it will fail only when that guidance seeks ignorantly and consciously its own selfish ends and not the people's liberty and good.

Surely in the 20th century of the Prince of Peace, in the millennium of Buddha and Mahmoud, and in the mightiest age of Human Reason there can be found in the civilised world enough of altruism, learning and benevolence to develop native institutions for the native's good rather than continuing to allow the majority of mankind to be brutalised and enslaved by ignorant and selfish agents of commercial institutions whose one aim is profit and power for the few.

And this brings us to the crux of the matter; it is to the shame of the world that to-day the relations between the main groups of mankind and their mutual estimate and respect is determined chiefly by the degree in which one can subject the other to its service,—enslaving labour, making ignorance compulsory, uprooting ruthlessly religion and custom and destroying government so that the favoured few may luxuriate in the toil of the tortured many. Science, Religion and Philanthropy have thus been made the slaves of world-commerce and industry, and the bodies, minds and souls of Fiji and Congo are judged almost solely by the quotation on the Bourse.

The day of such world organisation is past and whatever excuse may be made for it in other ages, the 20th century must come to judge men as men and not as merely material and labour.

This great industrial problem which has hitherto been regarded as the domestic problem of the culture lands must be viewed far more broadly if it is ever to revive just settlement. Labour and Capital in England can never solve their problem as long as a similar and vastly greater problem of poverty and injustice marks the relations of the whiter and darker peoples.

It is shameful, irreligious, unscientific and undemocratic that the estimate that half the peoples of the earth put on the other half, depends mainly on their ability to squeeze money out of them.

If we are coming to recognise that the great modern problem is to correct maladjustment in the distribution of wealth, it must be remembered that the basic maladjustment is in the outrageously unjust distribution of world income between the dominant and suppressed peoples,—in the rape of land and raw material, the monopoly of technique and culture.

And in this crime, white labour is *particeps criminis* with white capital.

Unconsciously and consciously, carelessly and deliberately the vast power of the white labour vote in modern democracies has been cajoled and flattered into imperialistic schemes to enslave and debauch black, brown and yellow labour and, with fatal retribution, are themselves to-day bound and gagged and rendered impotent by the resulting monopoly of the world's raw material in the hands of a dominant, cruel and irresponsible few.

And too just as curiously, the educated and cultured of the world,—the wellborn and well-bred, and even the deeply pious and philanthropic receive their education and comfort and luxury, the ministrations of delicate beauty and sensibility on condition that they neither inquire into the real sources of their income or the methods of the distribution, or interfere with the legal props which rest on a pitiful human foundation of writhing white, yellow and brown and black bodies.

We claim no perfectness of our own nor do we seek to escape the blame which of right falls on the Backward for failure to advance, but *noblesse oblige*, and we arraign civilisation, and more especially the colonial powers for deliberate transgression of our just demands and their own better conscience.

England with all her *Pax Britannica*, her courts of justice, established commerce and a certain apparent recognition of native law and customs has nevertheless systematically fostered ignorance among the natives, has enslaved them and is still enslaving some of them, has usually declined even to try to train black and brown men in real self-government, to recognise civilised black folk as civilised, or to grant to coloured colonies those rights of self-government which it freely gives to white men.

Belgium as a nation has but recently assumed responsibility for her colonies and has taken steps to lift them from the worse abuses of the autocratic regime; but she has not as yet instituted any adequate system of state education, she has not confirmed to the people the possession of their land and labour, and she shows no disposition to allow the natives any voice in their own government or to provide for their political future. Her colonial policy is still mainly dominated by the banks and great corporations who are determined to exploit Congo rather than civilise it.

Portugal and Spain have never drawn a caste line against persons of culture who happen to be of Negro descent. Portugal has a humane code for the natives and has begun their education in some quarters. But unfortunately the industrial concessions of Portuguese Africa are almost wholly in the hands of foreigners whom Portugal cannot or will not control and who are exploiting Land and Labour and re-establishing the African slave trade.

# Manifesto for Presentation to the United Nations Conference, San Francisco, April 1945[1]

PROMULGATED and supported by The League of Coloured Peoples in co-operation with West African Students' Union (London), International African Service Bureau (London), Negro Association (Manchester), Negro Welfare Centre (Liverpool, and Manchester), Coloured Men's Institute (East London), and endorsed by the following Colonial Trade Union Leaders on behalf of their unions:

J. S. Annan, Gold Coast Trade Unions.
T. A. Bankole, President, Nigerian T.U.C.
H. N. Critchlow, British Guiana Trade Unions.
J. A. Garba-Jahumpa, Secretary, Gambia T.U.C.

The decisions of the historic Crimea Conference represent the consolidation of the alliance of the three great powers, Great Britain, the United States of America and the Union of Soviet Socialist Republics in the final phase of the war of liberation against Hitlerite Germany. They demonstrate the unity and singleness of purpose of the anti-fascist powers to 'destroy German militarism and Nazism and to ensure that Germany will never again be able to disturb the peace of the world'. The decisions aim also at the prevention of any future aggression and at the removal of the political, economic and social causes of war with the close and continuing collaboration of all peace-loving peoples.

By their Declaration the leaders of the three Governments have re-affirmed their faith in the principles of the Atlantic Charter, their pledge in the Declaration by the United Nations and their determination to build in co-operation with other peace-loving nations a world order dedicated to a secure and lasting peace which will 'afford assurance that all men in all the lands may live out their lives in freedom from fear and want'.

The dawn of a new epoch in world relations is thus breaking. Only on the basis of the unity of purpose and of action which has made victory in the war possible for the United Nations can the highest aspiration of humanity—a secure and lasting peace—be realised.

[1] Source: *Labour Monthly*, xxvii (Jan.–Dec. 1945), 154–6.

*Establishment of an International Organisation*

The decision regarding the establishment of an International Organisation confirms and consolidates the decisions of the United Nations already reached at Teheran, Bretton Woods, Dumbarton Oaks and Hot Springs to provide the framework of future world security and prosperity. The problems of mankind are now recognised as the concern of the entire world.

Over large areas of the world millions of people live in poverty, disease, squalor and ignorance. Their continued low standards of life constitute a serious threat to the standards of people everywhere and represent a powerful challenge to the financial and technological resources of the more advanced nations joined together in collaboration to promote world prosperity and the happiness of mankind.

The vast continent of Africa with its 160 million inhabitants and immense though undeveloped resources in mineral, forest and agricultural wealth must command the attention of the international organisation. The rapid economic development, industrialisation and the advancement of the social standards of Africa must form an integral part of any plan to build world prosperity.

*United Nations must free themselves of the evils against which they are fighting*

Africa is a land of varied political forms, economic interests and social and cultural standards. This is complicated by the fact that among the powers with imperial possessions in Africa are fascist Spain and fascist Portugal. It is further complicated by the colour-bar laws and practices obtaining within the territories of some of the United Nations themselves, notably the Union of South Africa. The United Nations are pledged to secure in addition to the military defeat of fascism, the eradication of its moral and political manifestations, chief of which is the theory of the master race against inferior races. If the principles for which we fight do not apply only to Europe, then it is the duty of the United Nations to eliminate the influence of the Spanish and Portuguese fascist regimes and to remove from their own territories those theories and practices for the destruction of which Africans have died on many battlefields. In this way alone can true international collaboration and planning for the future of Africa proceed in conditions free from conflict and favourable to such collaboration.

*Recommendations*

In the belief that it is the eager desire of the United Nations to begin with the least possible delay the solution of these problems, we recommend:

(1) That the International Organisation should immediately adopt policies and set up all necessary machinery to secure the uniform and rapid development of the economic, social and cultural life of the African peoples.

(2) That guided by the principle of equal rights for all men and recognising that the success of any scheme will depend on the measure to which

Africans themselves participate, steps should be taken for the provision of maximum opportunity for such participation at all levels of administration.

The present inferior political, economic and social status of the African peoples militates against the achievement of harmonious co-operation among the peoples of the world. International co-operation demands the abolition of every kind of discrimination on account of colour, race and creed wherever such discrimination exists.

(3) The present system of exploitation by which the bulk of the wealth produced in Africa goes to enrich foreign monopoly firms and individuals must be replaced by systematic planning and development whereby in the first place the Africans themselves shall be the principal beneficiaries of the wealth produced, then an equal opportunity shall be afforded to all nations in the exchange of products. In this regard an international council representative of producer and consumer interests should be established within the framework of the International Organisation for the stabilisation of commodity prices at levels ensuring reasonable returns to producers and maximum satisfaction to consumers.

(4) Simultaneously with economic development progressive steps should be taken to associate Africans with the management of their own affairs with a view toward the achievement of full self-government within a definite time limit, as in the case of the Philippine Commonwealth.

(5) The eradication of mass illiteracy calls for energetic measures no less sustained than those which aim at the ending of poverty, disease and squalor. The greater the spread of education for both children and adults the greater will be the pace of advancement of the peoples as a whole. That it is possible to eradicate mass illiteracy within a short space of time is proved by the experience of Soviet Central Asia, where 20 years ago there was a very small percentage of illiteracy, but where now illiteracy has been practically abolished and universities flourish.

(6) The former Italian colonies now under military rule shall have the same treatment as the rest of the African territories and shall be given every assistance in development along with these other territories on the road to full-self-government.

### African peoples earned right to benefit by new concept

We believe that the African peoples by their contribution in manpower and material resources in the war against fascism; by their service in Ethiopia, East Africa, the Western Desert, Italy and in the Battle of Germany; and by their service in Burma in the eastern war against Japan, have earned the right to expect that they shall benefit as a result of the new concept of international co-operation which has been acquired in the course of the grim ordeal of the war of liberation against fascism.

(Signed by) Harold A. Moody, George Padmore, K. A. Chunchie, J. S. Annan, H. N. Critchlow, Samson Morris, R. W. Beoku-Betts, T. A. Bankole, K. A. Korsah, J. A. Garba-Jahumpa, C. B. Clarke.

# 'To All Oppressed Nations and All Oppressed Classes': The Manifesto of the Brussels Congress on the Struggle with Imperialism[1]

THE representatives of the oppressed nations and the working class of all parts of the world, gathered at the congress, have, in the interest of defending their basic rights and development, concluded a fraternal alliance among themselves.

The position is such that hundreds of millions of people are artificially and forcibly condemned to material and moral vegetation, and are helpless sacrifices to the capitalist exploitation of alien countries, while at the same time the struggle for this exploitation constantly threatens the peace of nations with bloody conflict. This dangerous, fatal, humiliating, and barbarous situation can truly no longer be tolerated. History has pronounced its inexorable judgement on this centuries-old disgrace, which has, in our day, thanks to the policies of imperialism, again increased to an unheard-of degree. For hundreds of years, European capitalism has drawn its main source of nourishment from the ruthless, fierce, stop-at-nothing exploitation of transoceanic, Asiatic, African, and American nations and tribes. Indescribable oppression, inhuman enslavement, and back-breaking labour, the complete extermination of whole nations and tribes, so that even their names have vanished, were necessary for the construction of the proud building of European, later Americo-European capitalism, and its mercenary material and spiritual civilization. But even young state formations which arose on the other side of the ocean, partly on the ruins of other nations and other civilizations, partly as a result of mixing with the natives, had to defend their right to independent national existence by force from the aggressive, self-interested egoism of the capitalist countries. And in most cases it was only the mutual hostility of these capitalist countries that led to the successful outcome of the struggle for national independence.

Each new capitalist state entering the historical arena, as, for example, Germany at the end of the last century, and Italy after her, considered it necessary on their part to enter the road of oppression and enslavement of

[1] Source: *Novy Vostok* (Moscow) xvi–xvii (1927), 401–5, 'Vsem-Ungnetennym Narodam i Vsem Ungnetennym Klassem, etc.'.

colonial nations. No capitalist state considered itself a full capitalist power until it had subdued other, weaker, defenceless nations. This subjugation was manifested in a whole hierarchy, a ladder leading from simple real control, from hidden forms of dependence, to open slavery, to the forms of medieval feudalism and serfdom, which have lately been carried over to the remotest geographical spheres.

In the present age of the highest development of the capitalist nations, in the age of imperialism, this barbarous, cruel system has reached its peak. The surpluses of capitalist accumulation, in the new form of financial capital, categorically demand the subjugation of the whole non-capitalist world. At the end of the nineteenth and the beginning of the twentieth centuries took place the final division of the world between a small group of great imperialist powers. A handful of great powers, and within them a small group of people, relying on the strength of accumulated capital and on the force of bayonets and cannon, on the most up-to-date and refined instruments of death, came to own the whole world. The subjugation and enslavement of one nation led to the subjugation of others. The struggle of the imperialist coalitions of powers for the areas not yet finally divided, and for a redivision of the world led, finally, to the greatest catastrophe and the greatest crime in the history of mankind, to the world war.

But this unprecedented catastrophe, which plunged both hemispheres deep in blood, did not eliminate the monstrous system of which it was a product. The imperialist powers grasped yet more convulsively the booty which threatened to slip from their grasp, and for which they had paid so dearly. The murder of millions of people, including hundreds of thousands of colonial slaves from India and the French African colonies who fell on all the fields of the struggle for the interests of the slave-owners, did not even reduce the number of powers claiming the colonial booty. Fascist Italy hurried to take the place of Germany, and more and more loudly and stubbornly demands the broadening of its colonial possessions, and even in Germany itself, the privileged classes, who have regained their economic and political power, and have already forgotten the bitter taste of foreign dominion, aim at conquering the right to oppress other nations. Such is the merciless logic of this system which exhausts mankind. Now the modern economic system, which wore out the masses of the European nations during the war, can exist (and develop) less than ever without colonial super-profits, without the subjugation of whole nations and whole continents. The less the old capitalism can guarantee the welfare of the masses of the European nations, above all, that of the proletarian masses, the more it has to resort to force to conquer markets for the sale of its goods and capital on other continents. The monopolistic development of capitalism, which accelerated to an extraordinary degree during the war, has turned the insignificant upper layer of the privileged classes of a handful of great powers—mainly Anglo-Saxon powers—into the lords and despots of the world.

However, the world war and its consequences have clearly shown that foreign, imperialist, colonial capitalism, like capitalism in general, is its own grave-digger.

The outbreak of the world war did not only lay bare the unprecedented internal contradictions that rent mankind; millions of people perished in an attempt to remove and smooth out these contradictions. The world war revealed more than this. In the merciless struggle with one another, the imperialist powers were forced to appeal to feelings of national consciousness in the oppressed nations, they were forced to adopt the slogan of self-determination of nations. The oppressed, enslaved nations took, so to speak, the imperialists at their word. These belated and false admissions, followed by a relapse into yet more cruel oppression, all these inhuman and unsystematic ruling methods of post-war imperialism, have disturbed still further the national masses, already agitated by the war and the whole economic development.

The powerful wave of the national-liberation movement has swept across immeasurable, colossal regions of Asia, Africa, and America.

The banner of rebellion against enslavement and oppression was raised in China, India, Egypt, north-west Africa, Indonesia, Mexico, and the Philippines. Hatred for slavery and oppression, the desire for a better, freer, and more cultured life awoke in all corners of the exploited world. After the world war this world-wide national-liberation movement was given a powerful impetus by the Russian Revolution, which affirmed the power of the proletariat and peasantry, and turned the old predatory Russian monarchy, which oppressed hundreds of nations, into a free federation of equal nationalities. The strongest pillar of oppression in the world collapsed irrevocably. An example of universal historical significance, a state of labour, built on the ruins of this pillar of oppression, a state resting on a free alliance of nations and tribes, like a torch, lights the path of the liberation struggle of the oppressed and enslaved nations.

No one will ever be able to put out this powerful will to freedom and independence. Only fools and pitiful Philistines and conservatives can believe that modern civilization and the whole future of the world will be confined to Europe and the U.S.A. The national liberation movements of the Asian, African, and American nations have the scope of world phenomena. And only this movement, organically linked to and growing with the struggle for liberation of the proletariat of the old capitalist world, will turn our planet into a single civilized world, only it, by freeing the whole world, will open a new chapter in the history of mankind, which will become for the first time world history, the history of humanity of the whole world.

The Chinese revolution alone, a liberation movement of 400 million people, is a historical fact of world significance which leaves many 'great', astounding facts of European history completely in the shade. And the national-liberation movement of India, also a whole continent, has the same world significance. Let the rulers of the old, small world renounce their out-of-date illusions which no longer correspond to reality and which, in our day, give a pitiful and ridiculous impression.

The whole world is in ferment, and the slightest impulse in any single part of it finds a response over an immeasurable distance. The example of tiny Nicaragua shows that prolonged resistance is possible even against the most powerful imperialist Hercules, thanks to the echo that resistance found in a number of more powerful nations, which, however, are also pre-occupied with the defence of their own independence.

But the imperialist aggressors will not renounce their booty without fierce resistance. The young Turkish republic had to strain every nerve, for a new war had to move its capital to the interior of the country, in order to defend its independence against marauding attacks. It is since the world war that we have experienced the new colonial wars in Morocco and Syria. Finally, under pressure of the national movement, Great Britain was forced to admit on paper something resembling independence in Egypt, but she continues to violate the Egyptian democracy in the crudest fashion, with the aid of military forces left in that country, and all the more tightly grasps the Sudan, which has not yet forgotten the bloody, 'heroic' deeds of Lord Kitchener. At the same time, in order to maintain their power in the name of so-called 'prestige'—one of the most hypocritical, ugliest, and most shameless imperialist concepts—the contemporary conquerors, who are so proud of their culture and their Christianity, are capable of the most inhuman cruelty, the most barbarous acts of revenge. Who can forget the last act of reprisal of the Dutch Government of plantation-owners against the rebels in the Dutch Indies, where forced labour and serfdom exist to this day? Who can forget the bestial cannon salvo from a distance of six metres at the unarmed Chinese in Vansiang, whose blood turned the Yangtse river red? Who does not remember the triumphant, cannibalistic tone in the descriptions of this unprecedented butchery in the organs of the press of the 'highly-cultured' English nation? Who in India has forgotten the bestial shooting at an unarmed crowd in the square in Amritsar where the exits were blocked? who has forgotten that General O'Dyer received a weapon of honour from the adherents of such bestial actions?

The necessity of restoring the destroyed foundations of their economic life, the fear of revolution, and the weariness of the world war which has not yet been overcome, all this compels the imperialist powers for the time being, somehow to maintain peace in their mutual relationships. Therefore 'pacifism' has become the favourite word of European and American diplomacy, which paved the way for the greatest war in the history of man-kind. However, 'pacifism' is not an export commodity, it is, so to speak, only for the internal consumption of the imperialist powers, it does not apply to those countries which imperialism considers to be colonies or semi-colonies. Here, on the contrary, is the undisguised, unrestrained rule of the iron fist, here the Americo-European soldiery finds space where it can strengthen itself for new battles.

The official Americo-European pseudo-'pacifism' further reveals (apart from what has already been mentioned) that the axis of world antagonism which divides the imperialist powers, the main bridge-head of world war, has moved from the West to the East, to the Pacific Ocean. Here on the banks of the great ocean lie the most important and valuable objects of imperialist greed. And the struggles at both ends of the Ocean, in which are taking part the armed forces of the imperialist powers and their helpers, are only the preliminary advance-guard skirmishes of a great future conflict which threatens mankind with new incalculable sufferings.

British diplomacy attempts uninterruptedly, tirelessly, and stubbornly to draw other imperialist powers into armed conflict with China. After the visit in Rome of the worst adventurist of our time, Churchill, the hero of Gallipoli, to that other unrestrained adventurist, Mussolini, fascist Italy, which has only an insignificant interest in China, hastened to offer Britain its mercenary services and sent an armoured cruiser to Chinese waters, for the exclusive purpose of raising its prestige and receiving gifts in some other part of the world.

Britain herself is to all intents and purposes in a state of open war with the forces of the Chinese national-liberation movement, represented by the Canton government and the Kuomintang. Only the military successes of the South Chinese army, only the fear of full defeat, as well as the failure of the first attempts to create an armed coalition against armed China, prompted the London government to enter negotiations with the Canton government. However, at the same time as these negotiations Britain is supporting the worst enemies of Chinese freedom (in the shape of the completely degraded adventurer Chang-so lin, an ordinary robber and political upstart, who has become a military satrap) and is carrying out a vile campaign against the only sincere friend of young China, the Soviet Union. In addition, these negotiations are accompanied by the sending of large (in Eastern terms) military forces to Shanghai, towards which the victorious Canton army is approaching.

The whole English working class has already made a strong protest against the new danger of war. The national-liberation struggle of the greatest Asiatic nation is in danger of being smothered. A new crusade against the Soviet Union is also threatened: so great is the fault of moral solidarity with the liberation movement of one of the Asiatic peoples in the eyes of the imperialist world.

At the same time on the other side of the ocean, North American imperialism, by means of undisguised force, guarantees its control of all the sea-routes which it needs for united action by its military forces, and threatens the independence of Mexico, where the democratic forces of society have at last found their way to power and are trying for the first time to maintain the sovereignty of the country against the shameless pretensions of the foreigner, in the first place against North American monopolistic capital. Only the protest of democratic circles in the United States, only the growing indignation of the Latin American countries on which North American capital is trying to fix its yoke, and, most important of all, the steadfast position of the Mexican government itself, have forced Kellogg and Coolidge to retreat. But it would be ridiculous not to see the danger of war that is in the air here too. The imperialist powers sell whole nations and whole populated continents like cattle.

Always and everywhere we see the same picture: on the one hand tens and hundreds of millions of people seeking freedom and independence; on the other hand small but powerful groups of exploiters trying to guarantee their super-profits by parasitical forms of privileged trade, by the export of surplus capital and by monopolistic control of the most important raw materials, cotton, copper, iron, etc.

Military action in Europe has ceased. But before war breaks out on the blood-drenched fields of Europe or is transferred to the shores of the Pacific Ocean, where a violent conflict is maturing, it will continue in one form or another in Asia, Africa, and Central America. No pacifist noise can conceal the terrible and shameful fact that the world is always at war, and that the exploitation of colonial and semi-colonial nations remains an inexhaustible source of wars.

Under these circumstances, the 180 delegates who have gathered in February 1927, at the international congress on the struggle with imperialism and colonial oppression have decided to found a league of struggle with imperialism and for national independence. We hereby inform all oppressed nations and all oppressed classes of the ruling nations about the foundation of this league.

Let him who has no interest in oppression, who does not live by the fruits of that oppression, who hates modern slavery and serfdom, and who strives for his own freedom and that of his neighbour join us and support us. The oppressed and enslaved nations count above all on the support of the progressive working class of all countries, since they, like the proletariat, have nothing to lose but their chains. But the broad peasant masses, intermediate groups and the intelligentsia, too, are sacrificed to the oppression of other nations, which, at best, brings them pitiful crumbs, while at the same time the ever-growing weight of militarism brings new torments, creating the violence and terrible sufferings of war.

The liberation of the oppressed, vassals, or merely forcibly subjugated colonial nations, will not lessen the achievements and possibilities of the material and spiritual culture of mankind, but will increase them to an unprecedented degree. And in this sense, the oppressed and enslaved nations, which make up the vast majority of mankind, together with the proletariat of the whole world, will be able to conquer the world of the future.

Oppressed peoples and oppressed classes, unite!

Brussels, 14th February, 1927.

In the name of the Brussels congress the manifesto was signed by the members of honorary praesidium (Professor A. Einstein, A. Barbusse, the widow of Sun-Yat-Sen, general Lu-Chun-Lin); and the members of the executive committee (G. Lansbury, Edo Fimmen, W. Muenzenberg, Jawaharlal Nehru (India), Sen Katayama, and others) and by separate delegations.

# BIBLIOGRAPHY

## I. UNPUBLISHED SOURCES

(i) MANUSCRIPTS IN THE PUBLIC RECORD OFFICE (LONDON)

C.O. 89/14 Legislative Council Minutes, Gambia, 1914–1925.

,,   96/540 ⎫
,,   96/552 ⎬ 'Negro Emigration from U.S.A.'—Chief Sam's 'African
,,   96/554 ⎬ Movement'.
F.O. 388/1154 ⎬
,,   388/1179 ⎭

C.O. 267/582 Governor's Dispatches.
,,   267/583   ,,        ,,
,,   267/588   ,,        ,,
,,   554/46    ,,        ,,
,,   554/50    ,,        ,,
,,   554/51    ,,        ,,
,,   555/IND:19124
,,   583/100 Colonial Office Dispatches.
,,   583/106       ,,        ,,
,,   583/109/28194: Report on U.N.I.A. activities in Nigeria by Sir Hugh
      Clifford, Governor.
,,   583/111
,,   583/118/34197: Nigeria Confidential 'C', 9 July 1923: 'Marcus
      Garvey—Proposed Visit to West Africa'.

(ii) MANUSCRIPTS IN THE GAMBIA

(A) *The Gambia Records Office*

GAMBIA 3/46, File no. 498:
(1) Nos. 58, 30 Oct. 1922; 84, 2 July 1924; 87, 9 July 1924.
(2) Confidential no. 11, 19 May 1924: 'Report on Congress Meeting
    held on 17/5/1924'.
(3) Appendix B. Confidential no. 17, 12 Nov. 1925.
(4) Confidential no. 28, 28 Mar. 1926: 'Conference of Africans of British
    West Africa. Report on the Bathurst Section by Commissioner of
    Police, Captain C. Greig'.
GAMBIA 3/59, Confidential M.P. no. 727, 21 June 1922: 'U.N.I.A.,
          Activities of'.
  ,,     3/140—General Correspondence.
  ,,     3/194, File no. 1466, 'The West African American Corporation'.
  ,,     3/198—'The Hon. S. J. Forster'.
  ,,     3/291—General Correspondence.

GAMBIA 3/212, Confidential M.P. no. 1553, 30 Feb. 1932: 'Small, E. F. Expulsion from French Senegal'.

,, 3/131, Confidential M.P. no. 1206, 26 Jan. 1929: 'Gambia Farmers Co-operative Society'.

,, 3/165, Confidential M.P. no. 1308/30.

,, 3/360, Confidential M.P. no. 2535, 14 Dec. 1939: 'Committee appointed to consider closer union between West African Colonies'.

,, 3/433, Confidential M.P. no. S. 2831, 17 Dec. 1942: 'Historical Notes on Executive and Legislative Councils'.

,, 4/11, Secret M.P. no. 63, 26 Apr. 1922.

,, 4/38 (1930): 'Activities of George Padmore'.

,, 4/42: 'Activities of E. F. Small, 1918–1931'.

,, 4/42, Secret M.P. no. 140, vol. i: 'Small, E .F., Particulars of as a "link Subversive"'.

,, 4/73, File no. 179: 'Wallace Johnson and the International African Service Bureau'.

,, 432/20, File no. 3/62.

,, 766/20, File no. 3/62.

,, 663/21, File no. 2/53.

,, 221/2912, File no. 2/507.

,, 581/1923, File no. 2/575: 'Legislative Council: Request for elective representation'.

,, 583/23, File no. 2/575.

,, 160/1925, File no. 2/67: Résumé of the Proceedings of the Third Session of the N.C. of B.W.A. held at Bathurst, River Gambia, from 24 Dec. 1925–10 Jan. 1926.

Confidential no. 3008, 25 Sept. 1945: 'Pan-African Congress'.


(B) *Gambia Co-operative Department*
(1) File no. R.C.S./EDU/12.


(iii) MANUSCRIPTS IN GHANA

(A) *Ghana National Archives (Accra)*
ADM. 5/4/19: Correspondence Relating to the National Congress of British West Africa.

,, 11/1427

,, 1344/26


(B1) *Cape Coast Regional Archives, Ghana*
A.R.P.S. Papers, 109/65, File no. 22.

,, ,, Acc. no. 187/65, File no. 100: 'Pan-African Congress'.

,, ,, 197/65, File no. 92: 'American Negro Immigrants'.

,, ,, Acc. no. 585/64.

,, ,, 111/65, File no. 24: 'West African National Secretariat'.


(B2) *Kobina Sekyi [W. E. G. Sekyi] Papers*

(C) *Institute of African Studies, University of Ghana, Legon*
Typescript copy of some Wallace-Johnson papers and memoirs.

(iv) MANUSCRIPTS IN DAHOMEY

*Archives Nationales du Dahomey, Porto Novo*
1. 'Départ Confidential', 3 janvier 1921 au 20 Avril 1925; 182 c, 29 juin 1923 [141c–304c].
2. C.A.I. (cabinet des affairs indegènes), 1929–31, no. 567/A.P./2, Ministre de Colonies à M. le Gouverneur Général de l'A.O.F., Dakar.
3. *A.N.D. dossier:* 'League de Défense de la Race Nègre: Institut Nègre de Paris':
   letter no. 668, 7 Apr. 1930
   „      459, 14 Apr. 1930
   „      865, 9 May 1930
   enclosure to letter no. 1438, C.A.I., Dec. 1931.

(v) MANUSCRIPTS IN NIGERIA

(A) *Nigerian National Archives, Ibadan*
1 CS09/1–18/1–C.170 (1918): 'Legislative Council, Nigeria. Proposals for construction of'.
2. CS026/1–6:23610/S480—'A. Deniga, Personal Paper'.

(B) *Ibadan University Library*
1. The Herbert Macaulay Papers.

## II. PUBLISHED WORKS: BOOKS AND PAMPHLETS— SELECTIVE BIBLIOGRAPHY

ADELABU, ADEGOKE: *Africa in Ebullition* (Ibadan, 1952).
AHUMA, ATTOH, S. R. B.: *Memoirs of West African Celebrities* (Liverpool, 1905).
—— *The Gold Coast Nation and National Consciousness* (Liverpool, 1911).
APTER, D.: *The Gold Coast in Transition* (Princeton University Press, N.J., 1955).
ARNDT, W.: *The Economic Lessons of the Nineteen Thirties* (O.U.P., London, 1944).
AUSTIN, D.: *Politics in Ghana, 1946–1960* (O.U.P., London, 1964).
AWOONER-RENNER, BANKOLE: *West African Soviet Union* (W.A.N.S. Press, London, 1946).
AYANDELE, E. A.: *The Missionary Impact on Modern Nigeria, 1842–1914* (Longmans, London, 1966).
AZIKIWE, N.: *Renascent Africa* (Cass, London, 1968).
BARZUN, J.: *Race: A Study in Superstition* (rev. ed., Harper & Row, New York, 1965).
BARRETT, S.: *A Plea for Unity Among American Negroes and the Negroes of the World* (3rd ed., Cedar Falls, Iowa, 1926).
BITTLE, W., and GEIS, G.: *The Longest Way Home: Chief Alfred Sam's Back to Africa Movement* (Wayne State University Press, Detroit, 1964).

BLYDEN, E. W.: *Christianity, Islam and the Negro Race* (Whittingham, London, 1887).

—— *The Return of the Exiles and the West African Church* (Whittingham, London, 1891).

—— *African Life and Customs* (Phillips, London, 1908).

BOWEN, J. W., ed.: *Africa and the American Negro: Congress on Africa* (Atlanta, Ga., 1896).

BROCKWAY, A. FENNER: *Inside the Left* (London, 1942).

BRODERICK, F. L.: *W. E. B. Du Bois: Negro Leader in a time of Crisis* (University of California Press, Stanford, 1959).

BROTZ, H., ed.: *Negro Social and Political Thought 1850–1920* (Basic Books, New York, 1966).

BUTLER, JEFFREY, ed.: *Boston University Papers on Africa, vol. ii, African History* (Boston University Press, Boston, Mass., 1966).

CAMPBELL, J. G.: *Observation on Some Topics 1913–1917, during the Administration of Sir Frederick Lugard* (Bosere Press, Lagos, 1918).

CARMICHAEL, STOKELY, and HAMILTON, CHARLES V.: *Black Power: The Politics of Liberation in America* (Vintage Books, New York, 1967).

CLARKE, JOHN HENRIK: *Harlem, U.S.A.* (Seven Seas Press, Berlin, 1964).

COKER, I.: *Seventy Years of the Nigerian Press* (*Daily Times* Publication, Lagos, 1952).

COLEMAN, J. S.: *Nigeria: Background to Nationalism* (University of California Press, Berkeley, 1958).

COMMITTEE ON AFRICA, THE WAR, AND PEACE AIMS: *The Atlantic Charter and Africa from an American Standpoint* (New York, 1942).

COMMUNIST INTERNATIONAL: *The Communist International Between the Fifth and the Sixth World Congresses* (London, 1928).

—— *The Revolutionary Movement in the Colonies: Thesis on the revolutionary movement in the colonies and semi-colonies, adopted by the Sixth World Congress of the Communist International, 1928* (London, 1929).

—— *Rapport sur la préparation par le Gouvernement Sovietique des révoltes coloniales* (Édition du Bureau Colonial International. La Hague, n.d. *c.* 1930). Copy can be found in the library of Utrecht University.

COX-GEORGE, N. A.: *Finance and Development in West Africa: The Sierra Leone Experience* (Allen & Unwin, London, 1957).

CRONON, E. D.: *Black Moses* (University of Wisconsin Press, Madison, 1955).

CROS, CHARLES: *La Parole est à M. Blaise Diagne, premier homme d'état africain* (privately printed, 1961).

CROWDER, MICHAEL: *Senegal: A Study in French Assimilation Policy* (Institute of Race Relations, London, 1962).

CRUMMELL, ALEXANDER: *Hope for Africa—A Sermon on Behalf of the Ladies' Negro Education Society* (Seeleys, London, 1853).

—— *Africa and America* (Springfield, Mass., 1891).

CURTIN, P.: *The Image of Africa: British Ideas and Action, 1780–1850* (Macmillan, London, 1965).

DAVIS, J. A., ed.: (for the American Society of African Culture) *Pan-Africanism Reconsidered* (University of California Press, 1962).
—— *Africa as seen by American Negroes* (Présence Africaine, Paris, 1958).
DAVIS, J. P., ed.: *The American Negro Reference Book* (Prentice-Hall, New Jersey, 1966).
DAVIS, S. C.: *Reservoirs of Men: A History of the Black Troops of French West Africa* (Chambéry, 1934).
DECRAENE, P.: *Le Panafricanisme* (Presses Universitaires de France, Paris, 1959).
DELAVIGNETTE, R.: *Christianity and Colonialism* (London, 1964).
DENIGA, ADEOYE: *African Leaders Past and Present*, 2 vols. (Lagos, 1915).
—— *The Necessity for a West African Conference* (Lagos, 1919).
DENNETT, R. E.: *The West African Congress and Government on Native Lines* (*African World* publication, London, 1920).
DETWEILER, F. GERMAN: *The Negro Press in the United States* (University of Chicago Press, 1922).
DU BOIS, W. E. B.: *The Souls of Black Folk* (Constable, London, 1905).
—— *The Negro* (London, 1916).
—— *Darkwater: voices from within the veil* (Constable, London, 1920)
—— *Dusk of Dawn* (Harcourt Brace, New York, 1940).
—— *The World and Africa* (Viking Press, New York, 1947).
ESSIEN-UDOM, E. U.: *Black Nationalism: The Search For Identity in America* (University of Chicago Press, 1962).
EUDIN, XENIA, and NORTH, R. C.: *Russia and the Far East: 1920–1927: A Documentary Survey* (Stanford University Press, Stanford, 1957).
EZERA, K.: *Constitutional Developments in Nigeria* (2nd ed., Cambridge, 1964).
FOOTMAN, D., ed.: *St. Anthony's Papers, Number 9: International Communism* (Chatto & Windus, London, 1960).
FYFE, C. H.: *A History of Sierra Leone* (O.U.P., London, 1962).
GARVEY, AMY JACQUES-: *Garvey and Garveyism* (A. Jacques-Garvey, Kingston, Jamaica, 1963).
GARVEY, MARCUS: *Philosophy and Opinions of Marcus Garvey or Africa for the Africans*, ed. Amy Jacques-Garvey (Universal Publishing House, New York, 1923 and 1925).
GAUTHEROT, GUSTAV: *Le Bolshevisme aux colonies et l'impérialisme rouge* (Librarie de la Revue Française, Paris, 1930).
GEISS, IMANUEL: *Panafrikanismus—Zur Geschichte der Dekolonisation* (Frankfurt A/M, 1968).
GRAY, J. M.: *A History of the Gambia* (Cambridge, 1940).
GUEYE, LAMINE: *Itinéraire africain* (Présence Africaine, Paris, 1966).
HAILEY, WILLIAM MALCOLM, LORD: *An African Survey* (rev. ed., O.U.P., London, 1957).
HANCOCK, W. K.: *Survey of British Commonwealth Affairs*, vol. ii: *Problems of Economic Policy, 1918–1939* (O.U.P., London, 1942).

HARRISON, HUBERT: *When Africa Awakes: the 'inside story' of the stirrings and strivings of the new Negro in the western world* (Porro Press, New York, 1920).

HAYES, CARLETON J. H.: *The Historical Evolution of Modern Nationalism* (New York, 1948).

HAYFORD, J. E. CASELY: *Ethiopia Unbound: Studies in Race Emancipation* (Phillips, London, 1911).

—— *The Truth About the West African Land Question* (Phillips, London, 1913).

—— *United West Africa* (Phillips, London, 1919).

—— *The Disabilities of Black Folk and their Treatment with an Appeal to the Labour Party* (London, 1929).

HERSKOVITS, MELVILLE: *The Myth of the Negro Past* (Beacon Press, Boston, Mass., 1958).

HOBSBAWM, E. J.: *The Age of Revolution* (Mentor, New York, 1962).

HODGKIN, T.: *Nationalism in Colonial Africa* (Frederick Muller, London, 1956).

—— *African Political Parties* (Penguin African Series, Harmondsworth, 1961).

HODGKIN, T., and SCHACHTER, RUTH: *French-speaking West Africa in Transition* (International Conciliation, no. 528, May 1960).

HOLDEN, E.: *Blyden of Liberia: An Account of the Life and Labours of Edward Wilmot Blyden, As Recorded in Letters and in Print* (Vintage Press, New York, 1966).

HOOKER, J. R.: *Black Revolutionary: George Padmore's Path From Communism to Pan-Africanism* (Pall Mall Press, London, 1967).

HORTON, AFRICANUS BEALE: *Political Economy of British Western Africa . . . The African view of the Negro's place in nature* (London, 1865).

—— *West African Countries and Peoples: A Vindication of the African Race* (London, 1868).

HOUÉNOU, KOJO TOVALOU: *L'Involution des métamorphoses et des métempsychoses de l'univers* (Paris, 1921).

JAMES, C. L. R.: *World Revolution 1917–1936: The Rise and Fall of the Communist International* (Secker & Warburg, London, 1937).

JOHNSON, J. DE GRAFT: *Toward Nationhood in West Africa* (London, 1928).

JOHNSON, JAMES WELDON: *Black Manhattan* (Alfred A. Knopf, New York, 1930).

JOSEPH, SIR BERNARD: *Nationality: Its Nature and Problems* (Allen & Unwin, London, 1929).

JULY, ROBERT W.: *The Origins of Modern African Thought* (Faber & Faber, London, 1968).

KAUTSKY, J. H., ed.: *Political Change in Underdeveloped Countries: Nationalism and Communism* (John Wiley, New York, 1962).

KESTLELOOT, LILYAN: *Les Écrivains noirs de langue française: naissance d'une litterature* (2nd ed., Université Libre de Bruxelles, 1965).

KILSON, MARTIN: *Political Change in a West African State: A Study of the Modernization Process in Sierra Leone* (Harvard University Press, Cambridge, Mass., 1966).

KIMBLE, D.: *A Political History of Ghana: The Rise of Gold Coast Nationalism, 1850–1928* (O.U.P., London, 1963).

KIRKWOOD, K., ed.: *St. Anthony's Papers No. 10: African Affairs No. 1* (Chatto & Windus, London, 1961).

KOHN, H., and SOKOLSKY, W.: *African Nationalism in the Twentieth Century* (Princeton, N.J., 1965).

KOPYTOFF, J. H.: *A Preface to Modern Nigeria: The 'Sierra Leonians' in Yoruba, 1830–1890* (University of Wisconsin Press, Madison, 1965).

LABOUR PARTY (BRITAIN): *The Communist Solar System* (1933).

LACOUTURE, JEAN: *Ho Chi Minh* (Éditions du Seuil, Paris, 1967).

LEAGUE AGAINST IMPERIALISM: *Das Flammenzeichen Vom Palais Egmont: Offizielles Protokoll Des Kongresses Gegen Koloniale Unterdrückung Und Imperialismus Brüssel, 10–15 Februar 1927. Herausgegeben Von Der Liga Gegen Imperialismus Und Fur Nationale Unabhängigkeit* (Neuer Deutscher Verlag, Berlin, 1927).

—— 'Vsem Ugnetnnym Narodam i Vsem Ugnetnnym Klassem: Manifest Brusselskogo kongressa po borbe s imperializmom' ('To all Oppressed Nations and All Oppressed Classes; The Manifesto of the Brussels Congress on the struggle with Imperialism') *Novyi Vostok* (Moscow), nos. 16–17 (1927), 401–5.

LEGUM, C.: *Pan-Africanism: A Short Political Guide* (rev. ed., Praeger, New York, 1965).

LEENHARDT, M.: *Le Mouvement éthiopien au sud de l'Afrique de 1896 à 1899* (Cahors, 1902).

LEWIS, W. A.: *An Economic Survey: 1919–1939* (Allen & Unwin, London, 1949).

LLOYD, P. G., ed.: *The New Élites of Tropical Africa* (O.U.P., London, 1966).

LOCKE, ALAIN, and BERNHARD, J. STERN, eds.: *When Peoples Meet: A Study in Race and Culture Contacts* (Hinds, Hayden & Eldridge, New York, 1959).

LUGARD, F. LORD: *Representative Forms of Government and 'Indirect Rule' in British Africa* (Blackwood, London, 1928).

LYNCH, H. R.: *Edward Wilmot Blyden 1832–1912. Pan-Negro Patriot* (O.U.P., London, 1967).

MACMILLAN, A.: *The Red Book of West Africa* (Collingridge, London, 1920).

MANNHEIM, K.: *Ideology and Utopia*, tr. Louis Wirth and Edward Shils (Kegan Paul, London, 1940).

—— *Essays on the Sociology of Culture*, ed. E. Mannheim and Paul Kecskemeti (Routledge & Kegan Paul, London, 1956).

MARAN, R.: *Batouala* (Jonathan Cape, London, 1922).

MAUNIER, R.: *The Sociology of Colonies: An Introduction to the Study of Race Contact*, 2 vols., ed. and tr. E. O. Lörimer (Routledge & Kegan Paul, London, 1949).

396 BIBLIOGRAPHY

MCPHEE, A.: *The Economic Revolution in British West Africa* (Routledge, London, 1926).

MEIER, A.: *Negro Thought in America, 1880–1915* (Ann Arbor, Mich., 1963).

MINOGUE, K. R.: *Nationalism* (Batsford, London, 1967).

MYRDAL, G.: *An American Dilemma*, 2 vols. (McGraw-Hill, New York, 1964).

NATIONAL CONGRESS OF BRITISH WEST AFRICA:

    (1) *Resolutions of the Conference of Africans of British West Africa, Held at Accra, Gold Coast, from 11th to 29th March 1920.*

    (2) *Report of the Proceedings of a Meeting held in London between the League of Nations Union and the Delegates of the National Congress of British West Africa.*

    (3) *The Constitution of the National Congress of British West Africa* (Jan.–Feb. 1923).

NKRUMAH, K.: *Ghana: The Autobiography of Kwame Nkrumah* (Nelson, Edinburgh, 1957).

—— *Towards Colonial Freedom* (Heinemann, London, 1962).

—— *Africa Must Unite* (Heinemann, London, 1963).

OBI, C.: *Our Struggle: A Political Analysis of the Problems of the Negro Peoples Struggling for True Freedom* (Ibadan? 1955).

ODUMOSU, O. I.: *The Nigerian Constitution: History and Development* (Sweet & Maxwell, London, 1963).

OMONIYI, BANDELE: *A Defence of the Ethiopian Movement* (Edinburgh, 1908).

OTTLEY, ROI: *No Green Pastures* (John Murray, London, 1952).

PADMORE, G.: *The Life and Struggles of Negro Toilers* (R.I.L.O., London, 1931).

—— *Africa and World Peace* (Secker & Warburg, London, 1937).

—— *The Gold Coast Revolution* (Dennis Dobson, London, 1953).

—— *Pan-Africanism or Communism?* (Dennis Dobson, London, 1956).

—— ed.: *History of the Pan-African Congress* (London, 1963).

PERRY, R.: *A Preliminary Bibliography of the Literature of Nationalism in Nigeria* (London, 1956).

PLAMENATZ, JOHN: *On Alien Rule and Self-Government* (Longmans, London, 1960).

PORTER, A.: *Creoledom* (O.U.P., London, 1963).

*Présence Africaine*, ed.: *Hommage à René Maran* (Paris, 1965).

ROUX, E.: *Time Longer than Rope* (Gollancz, London, 1948).

*Royal Institute of International Affairs: Nationalism* (O.U.P., London, 1939).

RUDWICK, E. M.: *W. E. B. Du Bois: A Study in Minority Group Leadership* (University of Pennsylvania Press, Philadelphia, 1960).

SAMPSON, M.: *The West African Leadership* (Ilfracombe, 1949).

—— *A Brief History of Gold Coast Journalism* (Winneba, July 1934).

SCHOELL, F. L.: *La Question des Noirs aux États-Unis* (Payot, Paris, 1923).

BIBLIOGRAPHY    397

SENGHOR, LAMINE: *La Violation d'un pays* (Bureau d'Éditions, Paris, n.d.).

SENGHOR, LEOPOLD, S.: *Constituent Congress of the P.F.A.: Report on the Principles and Programme of the Party* (Éditions Présence Africaine, Paris, 1959).

SOLANKE, L.: *United West Africa (or Africa) at the Bar of the Family of Nations* (West African Students' Union, London, 1927).

SURET-CANALE, J.: *Afrique noire: l'ère coloniale: 1900–1945* (Éditions Sociales, Paris, 1964).

SWORAKOWSKI, W. S.: *The Communist International and its Front Organizations* (The Hoover Institution on War, Revolution and Peace, Stanford, Cal., 1965).

TAMUNO, T. N.: *Nigeria and Elective Representation, 1923–1947* (Heinemann, London, 1966).

THOMAS, I. B.: *A Life History of Herbert Macaulay* (3rd ed., Lagos, 1947).

TIMOTHY, BANKOLE: *Kwame Nkrumah: His Rise to Power* (Allen & Unwin, London, 1955).

WALLERSTEIN, I.: *Africa: The Politics of Unity* (Pall Mall Press, London, 1968).

WELCH, C.: *Dream of Unity: Pan-Africanism and Political Unification in West Africa* (Cornell University Press, New York, 1966).

WHEARE, J.: *The Nigerian Council* (Faber & Faber, London, 1949).

WIGHT, M.: *The Gold Coast Legislative Council* (Faber & Faber, London, 1946).

WILLIAMS, H. SYLVESTER: *The British Negro: A Factor in the Empire and The Ethiopian Eunuch* (W. T. Moulton, Brighton, 1902). This pamphlet, consisting of two public lectures by Henry Sylvester Williams in 1902, was located in the National Library of Scotland by Mr. Neil Parsons of Edinburgh University.

WRAITH, R. E.: *Guggisberg* (O.U.P., London, 1967).


III. ARTICLES

ABRAHAMS, PETER: 'Last Word on Nkrumah', *West African Review*, xxv (1954), 913.

ADERIBIGBE, A. B.: 'West African Integration: An Historical Perspective', *Nigerian Journal of Economic and Social Studies*, v, no. 1 (Mar. 1963), 9–13.

ADRIAN, CHARLES: 'The Pan-African Movement: The Search for Organization and Community', *Phylon*, xxiii (1962).

*African World* Supplement: 'West Africa and the Pan-African Congress' (Sept. 1921), pp. xi–xix.

ADE, AJAYI J. F.: 'Nineteenth Century Origins of Nigerian Nationalism', *Journal of the Historical Society of Nigeria*, ii, no. 2 (1961), 196–210.

ANON.: 'The West African Conference and After', *W.A.S.U. Magazine*, xii, no. 3 (Summer 1947), 13–15.

AYANDELE, E. A.: 'An Assessment of James Johnson and His Place in

Nigerian History, 1874–1917', part I, *Journal of the Historical Society of Nigeria*, ii, no. 4 (1964), 486–516.

AVEBURY, THE RT. HON. LORD: 'Inter-racial Problems', *Fortnightly Review*, N.S. cx (July–Dec. 1911), 581–9.

BALLARD, JOHN: 'The Porto Novo Incidents of 1923: Politics in the Colonial Era', *Odu*, ii, no. 1 (1965), 52–75.

BARON, BENTLEY LE: 'Negritude: A Pan-African Ideal?', *Ethics*, lxxvi, no. 4 (July 1966), 267–75.

BOIS, W. E. B. DU: 'The Object of the Pan-African Congress', *African World* (1921–2), p. 99.

—— 'Second Journey to Pan-Africa', *New Republic*, xxix (1921–2), 40–2.

—— 'Pan-Africa and New Racial Philosophy', *Crisis*, xl (Nov. 1933).

BOULEGUE, MARGUERITE: 'La Presse au Sénégal avant 1939: Bibliographie', *Bulletin de l'I.F.A.N.* xxvii, Ser. B, nos. 3–4 (1965), 715–50.

BROWN, W. O.: 'The Nature of Race Consciousness', *When Peoples Meet: A Study in Race and Culture Contacts*, ed. Alain Locke and Bernhard J. Stern (Hinds, Hayden & Eldredge, New York, 1949).

CANDACE, GRATIEN: 'Le Deuxième Congrès de la race noire', *Colonies et Marine*, v (1921), 725–41.

CATTELL, DAVID T.: 'Communism and the African Negro', *Problems o Communism*, viii (1959), 35–41.

CRUCHET, J. M.: 'Le Mouvement pannègre et nos colonies d'Afrique', *Annales de l'Institut Colonial de Bordeaux* (1922), pp. 65–73.

DAYE, PIERRE: 'Le Mouvement pan-nègre', *Le Flambeau*, no. 7 (July–Aug. 1921), pp. 359–75.

DELAFOSSE, M.: 'Le Congrès panafricain', *Renseignement Coloniaux*, no. 3 (1919), pp. 53–60.

DEKOBRA, MAURICE: 'La Monde noir Americain: Marcus Garvey, prophète', *l'Illustration* (26 mars 1921), pp. 286–7.

DOBB, MAURICE: ' "Super-Profit" and West Africa', *The Plebs*, xix (Aug. 1927), 256–60.

DRAKE, ST. CLAIR: 'The International Implications of Race and Race Relations', *Journal of Negro Education*, xx (1951), 261–78.

—— 'Rise of the Pan-African Movement', *Africa Special Report*, iii, no. 4 (1958), 5–9.

—— 'Hide My Face? On Pan-Africanism and Negritude', Herbert Hill, ed., *Soon One Morning* (Alfred A. Knopf, New York, 1963), pp. 78–105.

—— 'Negro Americans and "The African Interest" ', ch. 16, in John P. Davis, ed., *The American Negro Reference Book* (Prentice-Hall, New Jersey, 1966), pp. 662–705.

ELLIS, G. W.: 'Liberia in the Political Psychology of West Africa', *Journal of the Royal African Society*, xii (1912–13), 52–70.

FADUMA, ORISHATUKÈ: 'What the African Movement Stands For', *African Mail* (25 Sept. 1914), pp. 521–2 and (2 Oct. 1914), pp. 2–3.

—— 'The African Movement', *African Mail* (20 Nov. 1914), pp. 73–4; (27 Nov. 1914), pp. 82–3; and (4 Dec. 1941), pp. 93–4.

—— 'Christianity and Islam in Africa', *African Mail* (22 May 1914), pp. 343–5.

—— 'Africa's Claims and Needs', *Southern Workman*, liv (May 1925), 221–5.

—— 'Popular Education and the State', *Sierra Leone Weekly News* (17 Aug. 1918), p. 4.

—— 'African Negro Education—Eclectic Education for Negro', *Sierra Leone Weekly News* (31 Aug. 1918), p. 6.

—— 'African Negro Education—Race Mission and Limitation', *Sierra Leone Weekly News* (9 Nov. 1918), pp. 10–11.

FALLERS, LLOYD A.: 'Comments on "The Lebanese in West Africa" ', *Comparative Studies in Society and History*, iv (1961–2), 334–6.

FISHER, HUMPHREY: 'The Ahmadiyya Movement in Nigeria', *St. Anthony's Papers, No. 10, African Affairs, No. 1.*, ed. Kenneth Kirkwood (Chatto & Windus, London, 1961), pp. 60–88.

GAUTHEROT, GUSTAV: 'Le Bolchevisme en Afrique', *Bulletin du Comité de l'Afrique Française* (1930), pp. 418–29.

GLICKSBERG, CHARLES: 'Negro Americans and the African Dream', *Phylon* (1947) pp. 323–30.

GWAM, L. C.: 'The Hon. Christopher Alexander Sapara-Williams, C.M.G. (1855–1915)', *Ibadan*, no. 21 (Oct. 1965), pp. 35–41.

HAILEY, LORD: 'Nationalism in Africa', *Journal of the Royal African Society*, xxxvi, no. 143 (1937), 134–47.

HARLAN, LOUIS: 'Booker T. Washington and the White Man's Burden', *American Historical Review*, lxxi, no. 2 (Jan. 1966), 441–67.

HAYFORD, J. E. CASELY: 'Nationalism as a West African Ideal', *W.A.S.U.* no. 2 (1926), pp. 23–8.

HODGKIN, T.: 'Background to A.O.F.: 2—The Metropolitan Axis'.

—— 'Background to A.O.F.: 3—African Reactions to French Rule', *West Africa* (9 and 16 Jan. 1954), pp. 5–6, 31–2.

HOPKINS, A. G.: 'Economic Aspects of Political Movements in Nigeria and in the Gold Coast 1918–1939', *Journal of African History*, vii, no. 1 (1966), 133–52.

HOUÉNOU, KOJO TOVALOU: 'The Problem of Negroes in French Colonial Africa', *Opportunity*, ii (July 1924), 203–7.

HYMANS, J. L.: 'French Influences on Leopold Senghor's Theory of Négritude, 1928–48', *Race*, vii, no. 4 (Apr. 1966), 365–70.

HUNT, R. N. CAREW-: 'Willi Muenzenberg', *St. Anthony's Papers. Number 9: International Communism*, ed. David Footman (Chatto & Windus, London, 1960), pp. 72–87.

IKOLI, ERNEST S.: 'The Nigerian Press', *West African Review* (June 1950), pp. 625–7.

IRELE, ABIOLA: 'Négritude or Black Cultural Nationalism', *Journal of Modern African Studies*, iii, no. 3 (1965), 321–48.

—— 'Negritude—Literature and Ideology', *Journal of Modern African Studies*, iii, no. 4 (1965), 499–526.

ISAACS, HAROLD: 'The American Negro and Africa: Some Notes', *Phylon*, xx, no. 3 (1959), 219–33.

—— 'Du Bois and Africa', *Race*, i, no. 2 (Nov. 1960), 3–23.

JOHNSON, G. WESLEY: 'Blaise Diagne: Master Politician of Senegal', *Tarikh*, i, no. 2 (1966), 54–6.

—— 'The Ascendancy of Blaise Diagne and the Beginning of African Politics in Senegal', *Africa*, xxxvi, no. 3 (July 1966), 235–53.

JONES, K. A. B. QUARTEY: 'Thought and Expression in the Gold Coast Press: 1874–1930', *UNIVERSITAS* (University of Ghana), iii, no. 3 (June 1958), 72–5.

—— 'Thought and Expression in the Gold Coast Press: 1874–1930, Pt. II', *UNIVERSITAS* (University of Ghana), iii, no. 4 (Dec. 1958), 113–16.

—— 'A Note on J. M. Sarbah and J. E. Casely Hayford: Ghanaian Leaders, Politicians, and Journalists—1864–1930', *Sierra Leone Studies*, N.S. xiv (Dec. 1960), 58–62.

JULY, ROBERT W.: 'Nineteenth Century Negritude: Edward W. Blyden', *Journal of African History*, v, no. 1 (1964), 73–86.

—— 'Africanus Horton and the Idea of Independence in West Africa', *Sierra Leone Studies*, N.S. xviii (Jan. 1966), 2–17.

KENYATTA, JOMO: 'Hands Off Abyssinia!', *Labour Monthly*, xvii, no. 9 (Sept. 1935), 532–6.

KILSON, MARTIN: 'Nationalism and Social Classes in British West Africa', *Journal of Politics*, xx (May 1958), 368–87.

—— 'The Rise of Nationalist Organizations and Parties in British West Africa', John A. Davis, ed., *Africa as Seen by American Negroes* (Présence Africaine, 1958), pp. 35–69.

—— 'Sierra Leone Politics: The Approach to Independence', *West Africa*, xliv (18 June 1960), 688.

LABOURET, HENRI: 'Le Mouvement pan-nègre aux États-Unis et ses répercussions en Afrique', *Politique Étrangère* (1937), pp. 312–21.

LANGLEY, J. AYO: 'The Gambia Section of the National Congress of British West Africa', *Africa*, xxxix, no. 4 (Oct. 1969), 382–95.

—— 'Garveyism and African Nationalism', *Race*, xi, no. 2 (Oct. 1969), 157–72.

LEVINE, J. O.: 'Le Communisme et les Noirs', *Bulletin du Comité de l'Afrique Française*, xlv (1934–5), 87–90.

—— 'Le Communisme et les Noirs', Pt. 2, ibid. xliv (1934–5), 708–13.

LEWIS, M. D.: 'One Hundred Million Frenchmen: The "Assimilation" Theory in French Colonial Policy', *Comparative Studies in Society and History*, iv, no. 3 (1963), 413–33.

LUGARD, F. D.: 'The Colour Problem', *Edinburgh Review*, ccxxiii (Jan.–Apr. 1921).

LYNCH, HOLLIS R.: 'Edward W. Blyden: Pioneer West African Nationalist', *Journal of African History*, vi, no. 3 (1965), 373–88.

—— 'Pan-Negro Nationalism in the New World before 1862', *Boston University Papers on Africa*, ii (1966), 149–79.

MALINOWSKI, B.: 'The Pan-African Problem of Culture Contact', *American Journal of Sociology*, xlviii, no. 6 (1943), 649–66.

MAQUET, JACQUES: ' "Africanity" and "Americanity" ', *Présence Africaine*, xxxi, no. 59 (1966), 8–15.

MARTIN, CAMILLE: 'Afrique Occidentale anglaise: le mouvement nationaliste', *Bulletin du Comité de l'Afrique Française*, xxxii (1922), 47–55.

MAZRUI, ALI A.: 'Consent, Colonialism, and Sovereignty', *Political Studies*, xi (1963), 36–55.

—— 'On the Concept "We Are All Africans" ', *American Political Science Review*, lvii (1963), 88–97.

MOORE, R. B.: 'Africa Conscious Harlem', *Harlem, U.S.A.*, ed. John Hendrik Clarke (Seven Seas Press, Port Arthur, Tex., 1964), pp. 56–75.

MUENZENBERG, WILLI: 'The Colonial Conference in Brussels', *Pravda*, xxviii (4 Feb. 1927), 1.

—— 'The Cologne Meeting of the League Against Imperialism', *International Press Correspondence*, ix, no. 5 (25 Jan. 1929), 77–8.

OLUSANYA, G. O.: 'The Lagos Branch of the National Congress of British West Africa', *Journal of the Historical Society of Nigeria*, iv, no. 2 (June 1968), 324–33.

OMONIYI, BANDELE: 'Is British Government in West Africa a Success?', *Edinburgh Magazine* (19 Jan. 1907), p. 1435; (26 Jan. 1907), p. 1453; and (2 Feb. 1907), p. 1476.

OSOBA, OLUSEGUN: 'Ideological Trends in the Nigerian National Liberation Movement and the Problems of National Identity, Solidarity and Motivation, 1934–1965: A Preliminary Assessment', *IBADAN* (Oct. 1969), 26–38.

PADMORE, G.: 'The Agrarian Crisis in British West Africa', *Communist International*, viii, no. 13 (1 July 1931), 370–6.

—— 'Ethiopia and World Politics', *Crisis* (May 1935).

PARK, ROBERT M.: 'Tuskegee International Conference on the Negro', *Journal of Race Development*, iii (July 1912–Apr. 1913), 117–20.

PATTERSON, O.: 'Slavery, Acculturation and Social Change: The Jamaican Case', *British Journal of Sociology*, xvii, no. 2 (June 1966), 151–63.

PERRY, RUTH: 'New Sources for Research in Nigerian History', *Africa*, xxv (1955), 430–2.

POCOCK, J. G. A.: 'The History of Political Thought: A Methodological Enquiry', *Philosophy, Politics and Society*, ed. Peter Laslett and W. G. Runciman, 2nd Ser. (Oxford, 1962), pp. 183–202.

REDKEY, E. S.: 'Bishop Turner's African Dream', *Journal of American History* (formerly *Mississippi Valley Historical Review*), liv, no. 2 (Sept. 1967), 271–90.

ROHDIE, SAMUEL: 'The Gold Coast Aborigines Abroad', *Journal of African History*, vi, no. 3 (1965), 389–411.

SHEPPERSON, G. A.: 'Notes on Negro American Influences on The Emergence of African Nationalism', *Journal of African History*, i, no. 2 (1960), 299–312.

—— 'External Factors in the Development of African Nationalism, with Particular Reference to British Central Africa', *Phylon*, xxii, no. 3 (1961).

—— 'Pan-Africanism and "Pan-Africanism": Some Historical Notes', *Phylon*, xxiii, no. 4 (1962), 346–58.

—— 'An Early African Graduate', *University of Edinburgh Gazette*, xxxii (Jan. 1962), 24.

—— 'Abolitionism and African Political Thought', *Transition*, iii, no. 12 (1964), 22–6.

—— 'The African Abroad or the African Diaspora', paper read at the International African History Conference, Tanzania, 1965.

VOEGELIN, ERIC: 'The Growth of the Race Idea', *Review of Politics*, xi (July 1940), 283–317.

WARNAFFE, CH. DU BUS DE: 'Le Mouvement pan-nègre aux États-Unis et ailleurs', *Congo* (May 1922), pp. 713–27.

WESLEY, CHARLES H.: 'W. E. B. Du Bois—The Historian', *Journal of Negro History*, l, no. 3 (July 1965), 147–62.

WESTERMANN, D.: 'Ein Kongress der Westafrikaner', *Kolonial Rundschau* (Berlin, 1920), pp. 164–8.

WILSON, H. S.: 'The Changing Image of the Sierra Leone Colony in the Works of E. W. Blyden', *Sierra Leone Studies*, xi (1958), 136–48.

WINDER, R. BAYLY: 'The Lebanese in West Africa', *Comparative Studies in Society and History*, iv, no. 3 (Apr. 1962), 296–333.

## IV. NEWSPAPERS

*African Mail* (1914)
*African Sentinel*
*African Times and Orient Review*
*African Morning Post*
*Aurora* (1921–2)
*Freedom's Journal* (1827)
*Gambia Outlook and Senegambian Reporter* (1935–6)
*Gold Coast Aborigines*
*Gold Coast Chronicle*
*Gold Coast Leader* (1915–26)
*Lagos Weekly Record*
*Liberia Herald* (1830)
*New African*
*Nigerian Pioneer*
*Sierra Leone Weekly News* (1914–22)
*Negro World* (New York) (1925–33)
*Times of Nigeria*
*West African Nationhood* (Lagos)
*West African Pilot*
*Les Continents*
*La Race Nègre*   }(Paris) (1924–36)
*La Voix des Nègres*
*The Times* (London) (1919, 1920–1)
*La Tribune Congolaise* (Brussels) (1921)
To be found: *African Nationalist* (Trinidad weekly; listed in Monroe Work: *Negro Year Book*, 1937–8, p. 346)

## V. JOURNALS

*African World* (London)
*Annales de l'Institut Coloniale de Bordeaux*
*Bulletin du Comité de l'Afrique Française*
*Colonies et Marine*
*Communist International*
*Congo* (Brussels)
*Contemporary Review*
*Crisis* (New York)
*Edinburgh Review*
*Le Flambeau* (Brussels)
*Fortnightly Review*
*International African Opinion*
*International Review of Missions*
*Journal of the African Society*
*Journal of Race Development*
*Kolonial Rundschau* (Berlin)
*Labour Monthly*
*Le Mouvement Géographique: Journal populaire des science géographiques*
*New Republic* (New York)
*Pan-Africa* (Manchester)
*Renseignements Coloniaux*
*Southern Workman* (Hampton, Virginia)
*W.A.S.U.* (London)
*W.A.S.U. Magazine* (London)
*West Africa* (London)

## VI. UNPUBLISHED THESES

DENZER, LA RAY: 'The National Congress of British West Africa: Gold Coast Section' (M.A. thesis, University of Ghana, Legon, 1965).

DRAKE, ST. CLAIR: 'Value Systems, Social Structure and Race Relations in the British Isles' (University of Chicago Ph.D. thesis, 1954).

EDMONDS, W. D.: 'The Newspaper Press in British West Africa 1918–1939' (University of Bristol M.A. thesis, 1951–2).

EDOKPAYI, S. I.: 'The External Trade of the Gold Coast (Ghana) and Nigeria—1885–1945' (University of London M.Sc. thesis, 1957–8).

GARIGUE, P.: 'An Anthropological Interpretation of Changing Political Leadership in West Africa' (University of London Ph.D. thesis, 1953).

HANNA, M. I.: 'Lebanese Migrants in West Africa: Their Effect on Lebanon and West Africa' (University of Oxford D.Phil. thesis, 1958–9).

HOPKINS, A. G.: 'An Economic History of Lagos, 1880–1914' (University of London Ph.D. thesis, 1964).

## VII. BIBLIOGRAPHICAL AIDS

COLLINS, ROBERT, and DUIGNAN, PETER: *A Preliminary Guide to American Missionary Archives and Library Manuscript Collections on Africa* (Hoover Institution Bibliographical Series xii, Stanford University, Cal., 1963).

LEWIN, EVANS: *Select Bibliography of Recent Publications in the Library of the Royal Colonial Institute Illustrating the Relations between Europeans and Coloured Races* (Royal Colonial Institute Bibliographics, no. 3, July 1926).

—— *Annotated Bibliography of Recent Publications on Africa, South of the Sahara, with special reference to Administrative, Political, Economic and Sociological Problems* (Royal Empire Society Bibliographies, no. 9, London, 1943).

PERRY, RUTH: *A Preliminary Bibliography of the Literature of Nationalism in Nigeria* (International African Institute, London, 1956).

WORK, MONROE N.: *A Bibliography of the Negro in Africa and America* (H. W. Wilson, New York, 1928).

# INDEX

# Index

G.C. means Gold Coast, S.L. means Sierra Leone; *p.* means *passim* (here and there), q. means quoted, p.d. means personal details.

A.P.U., *see* African Progress Union
A.R.P.S., *see* Gold Coast Aborigines Rights Protection Society
Abolition (of slavery), and abolitionists, 2, 10 n, 20, 21, 34, 35, 59
Aborigines Protection Society (*see also* Anti-slavery and . . .), 71
Abrahams, Peter, 353, 357, 363; q., 357–8
Abyssinia (Ethiopia, *q.v.*), 85, 326, 335
Accra (G.C.), 91, 110, 124; Central Committee, 136; political demonstrations, 226; Youth Movement, 226, 228; Mambii Party, 226; municipal councils, 260; N.C.B.W.A. revival (Dec. 1945), 356
Accra Conference (of Africans of British West Africa, 1920; *see also* N.C.B.W.A.), 124–33, 134–94, 200, 219–20; resolutions, 219–20; *see also* British West African Conference
*L'Action Coloniale*, 294
Adebayo, J. Babington, 93–4
Adelabu, al-Hajji Adegoke, 122
Adeniyi-Jones, Dr. C. C., 227
Africa: cultural and economic needs of, 92; economic integration in, 373; Europeanized, 26
'Africa for the Africans', 20, 29, 61, 213, 305, 322
*Africa in Ebullition* (Adelabu), 122
African: Association in London, 27; Civilization Society, 21; Communities League, 3, 58; cultural survivals in the New World, 18 n
*African: Leaders Past and Present* (Deniga), 190–1; *Mail*, 46, 50; *Messenger*, 95
African Methodist Episcopal Church, 19
African Movement I (1914–15, Chief Sam's), 24, 41–58, 113, 156

African Movement II (1914–27, Du Bois's and Garvey's), 41, 58–88, 89; West African attitudes to Pan-African movements, 89–103
African: National Anthem, 95; National Congress, 109; nationalism, *see* nationalism; 'nationality', 23, 33; 'personality', 38
*African Pioneer*, 47
African: Progress Union (A.P.U., London), 71, 77, 86–7, 124, 168, 245; responses, 34–40; self-government after World War II, 348
*African Sentinel*, 338, 341
African Students Association of North America, 348
*African: Times and Orient Review*, 46, 127, 168, 254, 255 (q., 127); *World*, 79, 244, 246, 247, 254–5, 263, 282 (q., 79–80); *World Annual*, q. 222
Africanisation of Western civilization, 114
Africans, famous, 23
Afro-American influence on African political thought, 2, 11, 18 23, 70, 307
Afro-Americans, New-World, 1, 19; 'out of touch', 39–40, 98–103
Agbebi, E. Mojola E. (D. B. Vincent), 31, 35, 95, 113, 178, 184, 185
Agusto, L. B., 74–5 & n
Akim Trading Company, 42, 48, 55, 58, 233; objects of, 43
Akiwumi, S. O. (cocoa merchant), 175–6
Alcindor, Dr. John, 71, 73, 84, 86, 245; q., 71–2
alien rule, 'dehumanizing', 8
All-Africa: *Conversazione* (London, 1920), 252, 253; Peoples' Conference (Accra, 1958), 177

Jones-Quartey, K. A. B., 278–9
Jordan, Lewis Garnett, 36

Kansas (U.S.A.): 28; African Emigration Association, 24 n; Exodus (1879), 24
Kenya, 85
Kenyatta, Jomo, 326, 336 & n, 343

Kikuyu Central Association, 343
Kimbangist movement (1921), 82
Kodo-Kossoul, Mme Jeanne, 315, 318
Kotun, Karimu, 180; p.d., 187
Kouyaté, see Garan-Kouyaté
Kumasi Congress (Nkrumah's, 1953), 122

L.C.P., see League of Coloured Peoples
L.D.R.N., see Ligue de la Défense de la Race Nègre
Labour Party, British: Independent, 338, 343; Parliamentary, 71, 245, 247, 248, 251–2, 254
Lagos (colony and protectorate), 49, 51, 54, 91, 92, 95, 96, 114, 135, 158, 183, 230, 250, 269–70, 275; Committee of N.C.B.W.A., 93–4, 141, 153, 178, 180–2 p., 185; Glover Memorial Hall meeting, 179; Ilupesi Hall meeting, 180; Conference Committee, 179–81 p., 186–93 p., Reform Club, 184; rising prices in, 215; political demonstrations, 226; youth movements, 226; Legislative Council, 270–1, 272; and N.C.B.W.A., 276 & n
Lagos Anti-Slavery Society, 93
Lagos: Standard, 29, 178, 180 (q., 29); Weekly Record, 92, 131 & n, 279–80 (q., 92–3, 279–80)
laissez-faire in West Africa, 197
League against Imperialism and for National Independence, 138, 309–10, 312, 324; Brussels Conference (1927), 253, 304–5; International Bureau, 310; Frankfurt Conference (1929), 312
League of Coloured Peoples (L.C.P.), 324, 326, 337, 348
League of Nations, 4, 65, 66, 83, 115, 247, 330–5 p., 339; Mandates Commission and system, 66, 85

League of Nations Union, 132, 247–8, 253, 254, 261, 262
Lebanese in Sierra Leone (and West Africa generally), 200–3 p., 207 n, 209, 212–14 p., 220 n
Légitime Défense, 316
Lenin, Nikolai, 301 & n (45)
Leverhulme, Lord, 282 & n (51)
Liberia, 19–21 p., 25, 31, 34, 37, 42, 57, 63, 75, 85, 87, 96, 100, 101; becomes independent, 20; Government, 69, 96; planned settlement in (1924), 96; President of, 96
Liberia, S.S. (formerly S.S. Curityba, q.v.), 48–56 p., 330
Liberia Herald, 20
Liberty League of Negro Americans, 36
Liga Africana, 87
Ligue de Droits des Hommes, 83
Ligue de la Défense de la Race Nègre (L.D.R.N.), 287, 303, 310–26 p., 319 n, 339, 372; French Government hostile to, 315, 318; officials, 317; Commission de Controle, 317, 318; its troubles, 318; and policy, 318 (q.), 318–19, 322–3; and Italian invasion of Abyssinia, 322–4 p.; and Negro protests in Britain, 324
Ligue Universelle pour la Défense de la Race Noire, 287, 290, 294–303 p.; Article II of Constitution, q., 296; and Diagne, 298–300; succeeded by C.D.R.N., q.v., 300–1
Liverpool Association of African Merchants, 282
Lloyd George, Rt. Hon. David, 76, 110, 251, 254
London: African Progress Union, see African Progress Union; Conference on West Africa (1946), 364; 'Manifesto', 76–7, 77 n, 79, 80, 83 & n (text of, 375–9); Pan-African pressure groups in (1920–1), 243–85
L'Ouverture, Toussaint, 18, 23, 57
Lugard, Sir Frederick, 182, 270; his proposals for Nigeria, 270, 277, 278, 280
Luniou, Gothon, 303
Lynch, Dr. Hollis R., 37 & n

Macaulay: Herbert, 95, 117, 183, 190, 215, 227, 228, 232, 253, 258; Magnus, 185

INDEX 419

Senegal and Senegalese, 79, 80, 96, 289 & n (5), 299, 306, 308, 321
Senghor, Lamine, 287, 299–302 p., 308, 316, 325, 372; p.d., 302–6; and C.D.R.N., 303, 310; and League against Imperialism, 304–5; his death, 310
Senghor, President Léopold Sedar (of Senegal), 2, 286, 292, 316, 364
Shyngle, J. Egerton, 179, 181, 249, 258; p.d., 189–90
Sierra Leone (see also Freetown), 19, 23–6 p., 34, 51, 54, 56, 57, 73, 74, 87, 96, 111, 113, 115, 134, 135, 137, 140, 152, 178, 179, 181, 196, 216, 228, 260, 275, 342; Friendly Society, 19; resettlement in (1811 & 1815), 19; press, 53 & n, 54; section of N.C.B.W.A., 124–5, 153–63; elective representation in (1924), 144, 283; initiation of N.C.B.W.A., 153–9; local Congress committee, 157–62; voluntary organizations helping, 159; politics of, 160–1; limited elective representation (1924), 161; and Legislative Council elections (1924), 162; nearly all elections won by N.C.B.W.A. candidates (1924–39), 162; Railway Workers Union strike (1926), 162; ineptitude of local Congress leadership, 163; Congress movement strong in, 199–200; effects of World War I on, 200–15; rice and anti-Syrian riots (1919), 200, 202, 205–12
Sierra Leone Sentinel, 228
Sierra Leone Weekly News, 184, 203, 206; q., 185, 204 & n, 329
Sigismund, Edward (Babalola Wilkey), 342, 343
silver (alloy) currency in West Africa, 217, 218
Slater, Sir Alexander Ransford (Governor of S.L.), 162, 165
slavery, slaves, and slave trade, 12, 17, 20–5 p., 34, 79, 85
Small, E. F., 135, 136–40, 150, 233–5 p., 246, 348, 351; p.d., 137–8, 234; and Communist Party, 138, 139; on N.C.B.W.A., q., 139–40
Society of Peoples of African Origin, 245–6, 252

Solomon: Job Ben, 23; S. R. B. (Attoh-Ahuma, q.v.), 35
Sorela, General, 78, 79
Sorrell, Judge M. A., 48, 54, 55
Souls of Black Folk (Du Bois), 61 & n
South Africa, Union (now Republic) of, 24, 25, 28, 30–2 p., 62, 71, 76, 85, 89, 90, 253, 309, 314, 349
South African (Native) National Congress (founded 1912, later African National Congress), 31, 109–10, 155, 246, 253
South America, 20, 23, 68
Southern Nigeria, 94, 269–70, 271, 276, 277
Southern Rhodesia, 253
Soviet Union, 87, 335, 336
Spanish: Anti-Slavery Society, 78; Civil War (1936–9), 340; colonies, 63
Spiegler, Dr. James, 2, 3
Spring-Rice, Sir C., 44
Stalin, Joseph V., 214–15, 301 n
Stehazu, James, 90
Stuart-Young, J. M., 230–1
Subenabrabo (G.C.), 44
Sudan, the Egyptian, 62, 85
Sutton, Rev. E. G. Granville, 75, 76
Syrians in Sierra Leone (see also Lebanese and Sierra Leone), 208–9

T.U.C., see Trades Union Congress
Taylor: David, 179, 188; John Eldred, 75, 76
Tete-Ansa, Winifried, 230–4 p., 230 n
Thomas, Rt. Hon. J. H. (Colonial Secretary), 144, 145
Thomas, Hon. J. H. (of Freetown), 153–7 p., 161, 206
Thomas: N. H., 154; Peter, 73, 76
Times, The (London), 243–4
Times of Nigeria, The, 91–2, 181
trade unionism, 14, 348, 349, 350
Trades Union Congress (T.U.C.): General Council, 348
Trotsky, Léon (and Trotskyites), 88, 336, 343
Turner, Bishop Henry McNeal, 24–5, 26, 32
Tuskegee (Alabama) Pan-African Conference and Institute (1912), 31, 32–3, 147, 154, 155 n (73)